2019年四川省重点出版专项资金资助项目
"一带一路"输电线路建设管理专业丛书
OBOR Transmission Line Construction and Management - Book Series

输电线路工程造价
实/训/教/程

Practical Training Course for Project Cost
of Transmission Line

丛书主编／汤晓青
本册主编／汤晓青　卢胜强
副　主　编／汤雨昕
编　者／李　莉　陈　利　熊红星　钟　鑫
译　者／成都优译信息技术股份有限公司

电子科技大学出版社
University of Electronic Science and Technology of China Press

·成都·

图书在版编目(CIP)数据

输电线路工程造价实训教程 / 汤晓青，卢胜强主编 . -- 成都：电子科技大学出版社，2019.12
ISBN 978-7-5647-7547-6

Ⅰ. ①输… Ⅱ. ①汤… ②卢… Ⅲ. ①输电线路 – 电力工程 – 工程造价 – 中国 – 高等职业教育 – 教材 Ⅳ. ①F426.61

中国版本图书馆CIP数据核字（2019）第287053号

输电线路工程造价实训教程
SHUDIAN XIANLU GONGCHENG ZAOJIA SHIXUN JIAOCHENG

汤晓青　卢胜强　主编

策划编辑	陈松明　陈　亮　熊晶晶
责任编辑	辜守义
出版发行	电子科技大学出版社
	成都市一环路东一段159号电子信息产业大厦九楼　邮编　610051
主　　页	www.uestcp.com.cn
服务电话	028-83203399
邮购电话	028-83201495
印　　刷	成都市火炬印务有限公司
成品尺寸	185mm×260mm
印　　张	48.25
字　　数	1262千字
版　　次	2019年12月第一版
印　　次	2019年12月第一次印刷
书　　号	ISBN 978-7-5647-7547-6
定　　价	193.00元

版权所有，侵权必究

前　言

"'一带一路'输电线路建设管理专业丛书"共分十册，该丛书全面系统地介绍了国家电网公司在输电线路上的建设、运行及维护知识。每册图书都由中文版和英译文版组成，可作为"一带一路"上的国家和地区的电力职业教育规划教材，职业教育电力技术类专业培训用书。该丛书的出版对于推动"一带一路"的输电线路管理具有重要的意义。

本书包括背景知识部分及5个学习项目。背景知识部分主要介绍了工程建设预算制度形成、中国电力建设概况、基本建设程序和工程建设预算。全书采用现行的《电网工程建设预算编制与计算标准》《电力建设工程预算定额（第四册　送电线路工程）》、《20kV及以下配电网工程建设预算编制与计算标准》、《20kV及以下配电网工程预算定额》等电力工程有关规范、标准和定额，突出以项目导向、任务驱动特色，选择具有一定代表性的实际输配电线路工程项目作为学习载体，使读者逐步了解并掌握输配电线路工程造价相关理论知识，培养从事输配电线路工程估算、概算、预算、结算和决算等技术、经济工作的能力。

本书依据现行国家、电力行业有关规范、标准、定额以及《国家电网公司生产技能人员职业能力培训规范》，修订了《输电专业人才培养方案》，制定了课程标准，并依据课程标准，按照由简单到复杂、单一到综合的学习规律撰写内容。本书收集、涵盖了10kV、35kV、66kV、110kV、220kV、500kV工程造价案例近30个，选用其中7个工程案例作为学习训练的载体，并参阅了大量工程造价相关科研成果。

由于编者知识、技能水平的不足，加之时间仓促，书中尚有诸多不妥之处，恳请专家读者批评指正。

编　者

2019年9月

Foreword

OBOR Transmission Line Construction and Management - Book Series totally include ten volumes. The books comprehensively and systematically introduce the knowledge of the State Grid in the construction, operation and maintenance of power transmission lines. Each volume of the books consists of Chinese version and English translation version, which can be used as the electric power vocational education planning textbooks for the countries and regions on the "Belt and Road", and the professional training books for vocational education in electric power technologies. The publication of the book series is of great significance for promoting the management of the power transmission lines on the "Belt and Road".

This book consists of the section of background knowledge and 5 Study Programs. The section of background knowledge mainly introduces the formation of project construction budget system, the overview, basic construction procedure and project construction budget of electric power construction in China. The whole book adopts the current Standard for Budget Preparation and Calculation of Grid Project Construction, Detailed Budget Quota in Electric Power Construction Projects (Volume IV Power Transmission Line Engineering), Budget Preparation and Calculation Standard for 20kV and below Distribution Network Engineering Construction, Budget Quota for 20kV and below Distribution Network Engineering Construction and other specifications, standards and quota related to power projects, highlights the project-oriented and task-driven features, selects actual power transmission and distribution line projects with certain representativeness as the learning carriers, so as to make readers gradually understand and grasp the theoretical knowledge related to the cost of power transmission and distribution projects, and cultivate ability to do estimation, budget estimate, budgeting, settlement and final settlement, and other technical and financial works for power transmission and distribution projects.

In accordance with current related national and power industry specifications, standards, quota and Training Specification on Vocational Ability of Production Skilled Personnel of State Grid Corporation of China, the Program for Cultivation of Personnel in Power

Transmission Specialty is revised, and the course standard is formulated, according to which the content of this book is composed based on the learning rule *from simple to difficult, and from single to comprehensive*. In this book, nearly 30 project cost cases are collected, covering 10kV, 35kV, 66kV, 110kV, 220kV and 500kV projects, 7 project cases of which are selected as the carriers of learning and training, and a great number of research achievements related to project cost are taken for reference.

Due to the limited knowledge and skills of the editor, as well as the hurry in time, there are still many places that can be improved in the book, and the criticism and correction from experts and readers are appreciated.

目 录

背景知识 ··· 1

学习项目一　编制10kV配电线路施工图预算 ························ 22

案例工程一　10kV某新建线路工程概况 ··· 22
任务1　熟悉配电线路工程项目划分 ··· 28
任务2　工程量计算 ··· 33
任务3　套用定额填表 ·· 51
任务4　工程费用表 ··· 61
任务5　总预算表 ·· 77
任务6　编写预算说明 ·· 78
小结 ·· 79
实训项目一　某厂配电安装工程 ·· 80

学习项目二　编制220kV架空送电线路工程初步设计概算书 ···85

案例工程二　220kV某送电线路新建工程概况 ····································· 85
任务1　熟悉概算书的组成 ··· 97
任务2　现场搜集资料 ·· 108
任务3　确定工程量 ··· 115
任务4　取费计算 ·· 145
任务5　编写概算编制说明 ·· 208
任务6　送电线路工程概算校审 ··· 213
小结 ·· 218

· 1 ·

  实训项目二 ·· 219

学习项目三 编制500kV送电线路工程估算 ················· 221

  案例工程三 500kV某新建送电线路工程 ····················· 221
  任务1 投资估算资料准备 ··· 223
  任务2 投资估算编制 ·· 226
  小结 ·· 244
  实训项目三 ··· 245

学习项目四 编制220kV送电线路工程结算 ················· 246

  案例工程四 220kV某双回新建线路工程 ······················ 246
  任务1 工程结算资料准备 ··· 248
  任务2 工程结算的编制 ·· 251
  小结 ·· 259
  实训项目四 ··· 260

学习项目五 编制工程决算 ······································· 261

  任务1 竣工决算准备工作 ··· 261
  任务2 编制竣工决算 ·· 266
  小结 ·· 276
  实训项目五 ··· 277

附录1 10kV某新建线路工程预算书 ··························· 279

附录2 其他费用分摊对象对照参考表 ························· 300

附录3 电力建设项目竣工决算表格式 ························· 302

参考文献 ··· 310

Contents

Background ·········311

Study Program Ⅰ   Preparation for Construction Drawing Budget of 10kV Distribution Line ·········343

   Project case Ⅰ   Overview of A 10kV New Line Project ·········343

   Task 1   To Be Familiar with Project Breakdown Structure of Distribution Line Project 349

   Task 2   Measurement of Quantities ·········355

   Task 3   Apply the Quota and fill in the Table ·········377

   Task 4   Schedule of Project Cost ·········391

   Task 5   General Budget Sheet ·········415

   Task 6   Prepare A Budget Estimate ·········416

   Summary ·········417

   Practical Training project Ⅰ   Power Distribution and Installation Project of A Power Plant ·········418

Study Program Ⅱ   Preparation of Preliminary Budget Estimate for 220kV Overhead Transmission Line Project ·········424

   Project case Ⅱ   Overview of New Construction Project of 220kV Power Transmission Line ·········424

   Task 1   Be Familiar with the Composition of the Budget Estimate ·········439

   Task 2   Collecting Information On Site ·········456

   Task 3   Determining Quantities ·········467

   Task 4   Charge Calculation ·········508

   Task 5   Preparation Instructions for Budget Estimates ·········606

   Task 6   Proofreading and Review of Budget Estimate for Power Transmission Line Project ·········614

   Summary ·········622

   Practical Training project Ⅱ ·········623

Study Program Ⅲ　Preparation for Construction Estimate of 500kV Power Transmission Line················626
 Project Case Ⅲ　500kV New Power Transmission Line Project····························626
 Task 1　Preparation of Investment Estimation Data ·································628
 Task 2　Preparation of Investment Estimation ······································632
 Summary ··659
 Practical Training Ⅲ ···660

Study Program Ⅳ　Preparation for Project Settlement of 220kV Power Transmission Line················662
 Project Case Ⅳ　220kV Double-circuit Line Newly-built Project ·····················662
 Task 1　Preparation of Project Settlement Data ·····································664
 Task 2　Preparation of Project Settlement ··668
 Summary ··681
 Practical Training Ⅳ ···682

Study Program Ⅴ　Preparation for Project Final Account ·······················683
 Task 1　Preparations for Final Account upon Completion ····························683
 Task 2　Prepare the Final Account upon Completion ································690
 Summary ··705
 Practical Training Ⅴ ···706

Appendix 1　Budget for a 10kV New Line Project ······························710
Appendix 2　Comparison and Reference Sheet for Other Expense Allocations ······745
Appendix 3　Final Account Form upon Completion of Power Construction Project　748
References ··761

背景知识

工程造价是指完成某项建设工程需要花费的全部费用，包括从工程项目筹建到竣工验收交付使用的所有费用，是工程项目有计划地进行固定资产再生产和形成相应无形资产及铺底流动资金的一次性费用总和。在工程项目建设的不同阶段，具体体现为投资估算、概算、施工图预算以及工程结算和决算等技术经济文件。人们对它的认识，是随着生产力水平的发展——生产技术的进步和生产管理能力的提高——不断加深的。

工程建设预算是指在工程建设过程中，根据不同设计阶段的设计文件的具体内容和有关定额、指标及取费标准，预先计算和确定建设项目的全部工程费用的技术经济文件，是各阶段设计文件的重要组成部分。按照设计阶段的不同，工程建设预算可分为可行性研究阶段编制的投资估算、初步设计阶段编制的概算、施工图设计阶段编制的施工图预算等。工程建设预算常被称为工程建设概预算。

在实际工作中，特别是工程施工阶段，人们常常把两者等同。

一、国外工程建设预算制度形成和发展的三个阶段

国外工程建设预算制度最早是在英国出现，距今已有四百余年的历史，其形成和发展可分为下面三个阶段。

（1）在16世纪前，建筑业没有详细的分工，设计、施工等都是一体化的。随着建筑业的发展，建筑产品越来越复杂，设计和施工才逐步分离。施工工匠在工程完工后，为了确定其应得的报酬，必须对施工工程量进行测量并估价，但由于施工工匠文化水平较低，计算困难，因而一批有一定文化的人承担了此项任务，他们就是今天预算师的前身。当时，预算师只是在完工之后计算工程的投资额，也就是确定在人工、材料等方面支出后再算账。这是英国预算制度发展的初级阶段。

（2）1830年，英国政府为了规范建筑市场，在工程建设中实行总承包合同制，要求在工程招标之前，根据施工图纸计算出相应的工程量，作为承包商投标的基础，然

后通过投标报价，由承包商最后完成预算书的编制。预算书成为承包合同文件的重要组成部分。工程造价的确定是在开工以前，在工程施工过程中严格按照预算控制各项费用的支出，业主和承包商之间在工程竣工后按照预算办理工程结算。从此，预算制度在英国初步形成，并产生了一个独立的专业——预算专业。1868 年，英国成立了预算师学会，即现在的皇家预算师学会（也称皇家测量师学会），这标志着工程建设预算制度的发展实现了第一次飞跃，到了第二阶段。

（3）随着建筑业的不断发展，仅仅在施工招标阶段确定工程造价，已经远远不能适应工程建设发展的需要。由于在设计阶段对费用没有进行控制，到招标阶段才发现工程造价偏高、资金不足以致被迫停工或修改设计，这对业主极为不利。到 19 世纪末期，投资计划和控制的方法随之产生并得到广泛应用。这个投资计划就相当于现在的初步设计概算和按照概算控制施工图设计。特别在 1950 年以后，预算制度获得进一步完善：在业主提出工程建设任务或进行可行性研究时，预算师就同建筑师、工程师等一起对工程投资进行估算，供业主决策之用。即在设计的早期阶段，就对工程投资进行估价，经业主同意后，对设计的投资进行控制。至此，工程预算制度的发展实现了第二次飞跃，到了第三阶段。

目前，在英国等其他西方经济发达国家的预算师参与工程项目建设全过程之中，对工程投资实行全面管理：既负责工程投资预算书的编制，又负责对工程投资的使用实施监督控制，工程竣工后还负责办理竣工决算，从而为保证业主的投资取得良好的经济效益发挥了重要作用。

二、中国工程建设预算制度的形成

中国工程建设预算制度的形成历史最早可以追溯到 1000 多年前。我国古代各朝多大兴土木，在此过程中，不仅使工程技术不断提高，也逐步形成了一套工料限额管理制度，演变成现在的人工、材料定额。据《辑古篹经》等书记载，中国唐代就已有夯筑城台的用工定额——功；继宋代《营造法式》（1091 年编成）之后，清代官方颁布了《工程做法》（1734 年刊行），详细地阐述了各种房屋营造范例和应用工料估算额限，既是工匠营造房屋标准，又是主管部门验收工程、核定经费的明文依据。

中国现代工程建设预算制度形成于 20 世纪 50 年代初，即在"一五"计划期间（1953—1957 年）。当时，中国实施的预算制度与英国相比较，其相同之处是在初步设计阶段要求编制概算，作为控制基本建设投资的最高限额；施工图阶段要求编预算，作为甲乙双方结算的依据；其不同之处是，中国的概预算制度中还确定了工程造价的审批程序（即概预算的审批、审定程序）以及定额、费用标准、编制概预算依据的管理权限等，这反映了当时中国计划经济的特点。在此期间，基本建设管理制度比较健全，基本上做到了先确定工程造价再花钱，所以尽管当时的预算制度还有许多不完善的地方，但对于基本建设能够取得较好的经济效益还是起到了积极的作用。

1958—1976年，中国工程建设预算制度逐渐被破坏，概预算对设计和施工都失去了控制作用。

十一届三中全会以后，随着中国经济体制改革的深入，一套适应改革开放需要的预算制度逐步形成。1983年，国家计委和中国人民建设银行联合颁发了《关于改进工程建设概预算工作的若干规定（试行）》，国家计委、建设部、劳动人事部、中国人民建设银行颁布了《基本建设项目投资包干责任制办法》的通知；1984年，国务院颁发了《关于改革建筑企业和基本建设管理体制若干问题的暂行规定》；1988年，国家计委颁发了《关于控制建设工程造价的若干规定》的通知等文件，为中国工程造价管理工作的恢复、整顿和发展起到了积极的指导作用。

改革开放40多年来，中国在工程建设预算制度的建设方面取得了十分可喜的成绩：一是形成了粗具规模的工程定额体系，这对于在建设工程中合理地使用人力、物力科学决策和宏观调控，提高经济效益具有重要意义；二是实施了工程造价的动态管理，随着中国经济体制，特别是价格体制改革不断深化，将工程造价静态管理改革为动态管理，这对新形势下工程造价的合理确定和有效控制发挥了积极作用；三是加强了对工程造价的监督审查，保证了建设资金的合理使用；四是建立了工程造价管理机构，专业人员数量不断增多，素质逐步提高，培育了一支思想好、作风正、业务过硬的专业队伍。当然我们也应注意到，改革开放以来，为了适应经济体制改革的需要，虽然工程造价管理方式有所改变，但从总体上看，仍然没有从根本上脱离原有体制的束缚，不能充分适应社会主义市场经济的发展需要。工程建设领域是市场机制相当活跃的领域，特别是在工程造价方面充满了强烈的竞争性。因此，加快工程造价改革步伐，推动工程造价管理工作更快更好地向前发展，是摆在我们面前的一项重要任务。

三、中国电力建设简介

（一）中国电力建设概况

中国电力建设始于1882年，由英国商人开办的"上海电光公司"于同年7月26日正式供电，从对电能的商业性使用时间来看，中国仅次于英、法两国。到1949年，中国电力发展了67年，电力事业的经营模式经历了由最初的外商投资、清朝政府经营"电灯厂"，到后来的民族、官僚资本经营办电的发展过程，全国发电设备总容量185万千瓦，年发电量43亿千瓦时；最大的火电机组单机为5万千瓦，最大的水电机组单机为10万千瓦，最大的火电厂容量不超过20万千瓦，最大的水电站容量不超过30万千瓦。

新中国电力建设60年来，其间经历了恢复、增长、调整和发展的四个重要历史时期："一五"计划期间，中国电力建设属于"恢复"期，主要是将原国民党统治期间的发电设备修复再使用；随之而来是中国电力建设的"增长"期，为满足当时国民经济高速发展的要求，在全国各地开始推进各基础性行业建设，从苏联引进了一大批发电设备；从20世纪60年代开始到80年代初期中国电力建设处于"调整"期；从20世纪80年代中期开始，中国电力建设进入了一个高速发展时期。

目前，中国电力工业的生产技术和装备水平逐步接近世界经济发达国家水平，在特高压、智能电网等领域已处于世界先进水平。截至2006年年底，中国已拥有的百万千瓦级以上发电厂171座，竣工于2009年的三峡水力发电厂总装机容量达到了2250万千瓦，年发电量约1000亿千瓦时。运行中的火电单机容量型号有20万、30万、50万、60万、80万千瓦，水电单机容量型号有10万、32万、55万、70万千瓦，能自主设计制造单机容量达到100万千瓦的超大型水轮发电机组。运行中的核电机组总容量超过1000万千瓦，占总装机约为1.1%；在建核电机组总容量达到2500万千瓦，居世界第一。计划到2020年，中国核电装机容量突破7000~8000万千瓦，占届时中国总装机容量15亿千瓦的4.6%~5.3%。风能和太阳能发电站建设也取得了长足的发展，建成由10 kV、35 kV、66 kV、110 kV、220 kV、330 kV、500 kV、±500 kV、750 kV、±800 kV、1000 kV电力线路组成的大规模输配电网络。并将建成由特高压骨干网架为支撑的"三华"（华北—华中—华东）、东北、西北、南方四大同步电网。

（二）电力建设在国家基本建设中的地位和作用

基本建设是指在国民经济中投资进行建筑、购置和安装固定资产以及与此相联系的其他经济活动。基本建设在国民经济中占有重要的地位，电力建设是国家基本建设中的重要组成部分。

电力是农业的命脉、工业的先行。电力工业是一个国家的基础产业，在国家基本建设中占据着重要的地位。

中国电力建设历经百年，粗具规模，但人均占有的发电装机容量和发电量水平仍居于世界落后水平。譬如，2007年的中国人均发电量为2484 kW·h，占世界排名的第73位，远远低于发达国家水平，缺电持续时间几乎等于电力建设的历史。新中国建立后，从1953年开始京-津-唐地区缺电，1958年就开始全国性缺电，长期以来全国有20%~30%的生产能力得不到正常开工，一直持续到20世纪90年代初期。到1996年，为解决原国有企业的管理体制固有的种种弊端，开始实施经济体制改革，相当部分的大中型国有企业严重开工不足，这才使得全国性缺电的局面有所扭转，在部分地区甚至出现了电力富裕的局面。但这种低水平上的电力富裕持续时间不长，2001年的夏季在全国又开始出现了"拉闸限电"，2003年出现了大范围的"拉闸限电"。

长期以来，中国电力建设滞后于经济社会对电力能源不断增长的需求。其原因有二：一是电力生产与施工技术进步缓慢；二是国家没有将电力工业作为主导性产业，资金投入严重不足，这也是最关键的原因。

"十二五"期间，在"建设小康社会""工业化、城镇化"加快进行的形势下，对能源电力的需求快速增长，电力建设以加快转变电力发展方式为主线，以保障安全、优化结构、节能减排、促进和谐为重点，着力提高电力供应安全，着力推进电力结构优化，着力推进资源优化配置，着力推进电力产业升级，着力推进电力和谐发展，努力构建安全经济、绿色、和谐的电力工业体系，满足经济社会科学发展的有效电力需求。加大非化石能源发电比重，在保护生态环境的前提下，优先开发水电；在确保安全的基础上，大力发展核电；积极推进风能、太阳能和生物质能等可再生能源发电，提高非化石能源比重。推行煤电一体化开发，加快建设大型煤电基地，坚持输煤输电并举。鼓励发展热电联产，统一规划高参数、环保型机组和符合国家政策的热电联产项目。推进煤电绿色开发，大力推行洁净煤发电技术。同时，继续加强电网建设，农网改造、智能电网建设将成为建设重点。

目前，中国电力供应支撑经济社会发展能力显著增强，电源结构和布局进一步优化，电网优化配置资源能力明显提高，绿色发展能力进一步增强，电力技术装备水平和自主创新能力显著提高。

（三）电力基本建设的投资

1. 电力基本建设投资的组成

电力工业是资金密集型行业，对电力工业的投资包括了对"电厂及电力网"的投资两个部分，而电力网的投资涉及对变电设备和输配电网络的投资。资金的筹集、投入与回收是制约电力工业发展的最根本的问题。

2. 中国电力基本建设的投资现状

国务院为发展电力工业制定了"政企分开、省为实体、联合电网、统一调度、集资办电"的20字方针，以及"因地因网制宜"的电力工业体制改革方针，改变了以前电力部门一家办电的体制，实行"多渠道、多模式、多层次"的集资办电和多家办电——国家投资、地方集资、中外合资、外商独资等多种形式，基本解决了电力工业发展的资金问题。

四、基本建设概述

（一）基本建设项目

基本建设项目，是指在行政上有独立的组织形式，在经济上实行独立核算，可直接与其他企业或单位建立经济往来关系，按照一个总体设计进行兴建的一项独立工程项目。

基本建设项目性质的不同可分为新建、扩建、改建、恢复、迁建、技术改造、更新项目等。新建项目，即原来没有的新开工建设的项目；扩建项目，即在原有的基础上为扩大产品生产能力或增加新的产品生产能力而新建的工程项目；改建项目，是指原有企业以提高劳动生产率、改进产品质量或改变产品方向为目的，对原有设备或工程进行改造的项目；恢复项目，是指企业、事业单位因自然灾害等原因，使原有固定资产全部或部分报废，以后又按原有规模恢复建设的项目；迁建项目，是指原有的企业、事业单位迁往外地建设的项目；技术改造项目，是指用水平较高的技术代替水平较低的现有技术，用先进技术对现有企业的机器、设备、生产工艺进行技术改造的项目；更新项目，是指当固定资产基本部分已经丧失使用价值，另行购置新的固定资产来进行替换，以保持它原有规模的项目。

基本建设项目按用途的不同可分为生产性和非生产性建设项目。生产性建设项目，是指直接用于生产或满足生产需要的建设项目，如工业、建筑业、农业、水利、气象、运输、邮电、商业、物资供应、地质资源勘探等建设项目；非生产性建设项目，是指用于人民物质生活和文化生活需要的建设项目，如文教、卫生、科研、公用事业、机关和社会团体等建设项目。

基本建设项目按建设规模或投资大小可分为大型项目、中型项目、小型项目；按隶属关系可分为国务院各部门直属项目、地方投资国家补助项目、地方项目、企事业单位自筹建设项目；按建设阶段可分为预备项目、筹建项目、施工项目、建成投产项目、收尾项目和竣工项目等。

（二）基本建设程序

基本建设的特点是投资多，建设周期长，涉及的专业和部门多，工作环节错综复杂。为了保证工程建设顺利进行，达到预期的目的，在基本建设的长期实践中，逐步摸索、总结出一套为广大工程建设人员共同遵守的工作程序，包含基本建设全过程中各项工作的先后顺序和工作内容及要求，即基本建设程序。基本建设程序是基建实践中的客观规律性反映，严格遵守基本建设程序是进行基本建设工作的一项重要原则，不按基本建设程序建设，势必给国民经济带来严重损失。我国的基本建设程序是1952年由国务院颁布实施的，60余年来，随着国家基本建设逐步进行及发展，基本建设程序也得到了进一步完善，现行的基本建设程序可分为项目建议书阶段、可行性研究阶段、设计阶段（初步设计、施工图设计）、开工准备阶段、施工阶段、生产准备阶段、竣工验收阶段、工程后评价阶段等八个阶段，下面分别加以简单阐述。

1.项目建议书阶段

建设项目建议书是国家规定的基本建设程序中最初阶段的工作。项目建议书是由投资者根据国家的长远规划和部门、行业、地区的发展规划，对准备建设的项目做出大体轮廓性设想和建议，为确定拟建项目是否有必要建设、是否具备建设的基本条件、是否需要再做出进一步的研究论证工作提供依据。

项目建议书可以有繁有简，一般包括以下内容：①建设项目提出的必要性和依据；②市场预测；③建设规模和产品方案设想；④建设地点设想；⑤资源供给的可能性和可靠性；⑥主要技术工艺设想；⑦外部协作条件；⑧投资估算和资金筹措方案；⑨建设工期预计；⑩经济效益和社会效益的初步评价。

建设项目建议书是国家主管部门或投资者选择项目进行投资的依据；准确地编制和实事求是地审核项目建议书，就能够掌握建设项目前期工作的主动权，为以后工作的深入开展奠定良好的基础。

在建设项目建议书编制过程中应注意以下事项。①应从符合国家当前的经济发展水平出发，确定合理的建设标准。②以尽量靠近原料、燃料和消费地以及工业项目适当聚集的原则选择建设地区。③建设地点（厂址）的选择，最根本的要求有两点：一是从保证建厂直接经济效益出发，满足该厂生产、建设和职工生活的需求；二是从保证间接的社会效益年活动出发，要求厂址布局有利于所在城镇和工业小区总体规划的实现，不要造成景观和生态环境的破坏。④项目的经济规模应达到国家主管部门或行业、地区的要求，使规模效益充分发挥。⑤坚持先进适用和经济合理地选择生产工艺。⑥尽量选用国产设备，必须引进进口设备时，要注意进口设备与国产设备、厂房之间的配套问题，同时应注意对技术资料的引进和消化。

2. 可行性研究阶段

可行性研究简称"可研"，是由建设单位及主管部门进行管理和操作，是国家或投资者对建设项目进行宏观决策、宏观预控的基础，包括对该项目相关的技术、经济、社会、环境等所有方面进行调查研究。可行性研究主要对工程项目在技术及经济两方面是否可行进行综合的、科学的分析和论证，做出多方案比较，提出评价意见，推荐最佳方案。从技术方面，主要研究一个工程项目在建设及投产后对资源、技术、人才的需求情况的合理程度，以及该工程项目建设及建成后对社会、环境的影响；从经济方面，研究一个工程项目建设过程中所花费的投资的合理程度，以及该工程项目是否符合当前的国家的基础建设投资政策，财务上是否盈利。当然，技术与经济两者之间不是相割离的，而是相互联系的。某项目的工程技术方案（涵盖施工技术和生产技术）的实施，决定了该工程在经济上的合理程度，即投资估算；反过来，投资估算对该项目的工程技术方案的实施又有能动的影响作用，因为它控制着工程项目的总体造价。

根据国家规定，所有国内投资项目和利用外资的建设项目，在批准项目建议书后，都要进行可行性研究，并编报出可行性研究报告。一般地，国内工业项目可行性研究报告应具备以下主要内容。

①总论，包括项目提出的背景，投资的必要性和经济效益，研究工作的依据和范围。

②需求预测和拟建规模，包括国内外需求情况的预测、销售预测、价格分析、进入国际市场的前景，国内现有工厂的生产能力的估计，对项目在规模、产品方案和发展方向上的技术经济比较和分析。

③资源、原材料、燃料和公用设施情况，包括原料、辅助材料、燃料的种类、数量、来源和供应可能性，所需的公用设施的数量、供应方式和供应条件。

④建厂条件和厂址方案，包括建厂的地理位置、气象、水文、地质地形条件和社会经济现状，交通、运输及水电气的现状和发展趋势，以及厂址比较与选择意见、厂址选择时的费用分析。

⑤设计方案，包括项目的构成范围、技术来源和生产方法，主要技术工艺和设备选型方案的比较，引进技术设备的来源，全厂布置方案的初步选择和土建工程量情况，公用辅助设施和厂内交通运输方式的比较与初步选择。

⑥环境保护，包括调查环境现状、预测项目对环境的影响、提出环境保护和"三废"治理的初步方案，提出劳动保护及安全生产等施工技术以及相应措施的方案。

⑦拟建企业组织设置、劳动设置和人员培训计划。

⑧项目建设实施进度建议。

⑨投资估算和资金筹措，包括主体工程和协作工程所需的投资、项目建成后所需流动资金的估算，项目资金来源、筹措方式及以后贷款偿还方式。

⑩项目经济评价。要采用现代经济分析方法（微观经济评价——财务评价、宏观经济评价——国民经济评价），对拟建项目在建设期、生产期内投入产出的诸多经济因素进行调查、预测、研究、计算和论证，从中选择最佳方案作为决策项目的重要依据。

对可行性研究报告编制的要求有：一是确保可行性研究报告的真实性和科学性；二是编制单位必须具备承担可行性研究的条件，有一定的经济和市场分析专家、工程技术人员、财务人员，有较完备的技术装备手段；三是可行性研究的内容、深度及计算指标必须达到标准要求，满足项目决策的需要；四是编制完成后，应有编制单位行政、技术、经济方面的负责人签字，并对研究报告的质量负责。

可行性研究结束后，可研报告须经过各行业主管机关及国家计委评审、立项，小型项目的可行性研究报告，按隶属关系由各主管部、各省、市、自治区审批。工程项目立项后，才可进行工程设计工作。例如：举世闻名的三峡工程就是在半个多世纪中经过多次的可行性考察、论证，考虑了水利、电力、航运、工程技术（电力和土建）、生态学、环境保护、工程地质、工程经济、系统工程、宏观经济等多方面的问题，才最终确定了移民较少、投资较少的"中坝方案"。

3. 设计阶段

主管单位成立建设单位负责筹建工作，委托设计单位进行勘测设计。承担设计的单位在进行设计以前，要认真研究可行性研究报告，并进行勘测、调查和试验研究工作。设计是对拟建工程的实施在技术和经济上所进行的、全面而详尽的安排，是工程建设计划的具体化，是组织施工的依据。设计是复杂的综合性很强的技术经济工作，它建立在全面正确的勘测、调查工作之上。设计工作是分阶段进行的，一般分为初步设计和施工图设计两个阶段。对重大项目和技术复杂项目，可根据不同行业的特点和需要，增加技术设计阶段。设计质量直接关系到建设项目的质量，关系到工程造价的计价与管理，是工程建设决定性的环节。

（1）初步设计

初步设计简称初设，它要求按批准的项目任务书及国家的经济政策，结合各地当时的具体规定，收集有关的设计资料，明确设计条件及设计原则，写出初步设计纲要，作为初步设计的依据，提出工程材料估算清单并编制概算数，作为投资及订货的依据。初步设计是解决建设项目的技术可靠性和经济合理性的问题，所以初步设计有一定的规划性质，是建设项目的"纲要"设计。其具体内容、组成则随不同的工程项目不尽相同，如输电线路工程的初步设计包括：线路的起讫点、路径、电压等级、导地线型号等的确定，线路沿线地质、地形、水文、气象条件调查，土石方量估算、主要材料消耗估算，主要经济技术指标、建设工期、设计概算等的确定。对特殊地质地形条件、气象条件下的输电线路工程，大型输电线路工程的施工、组织等方面的问题，应进行相应深度的科学研究，必要时应有模型试验成果的论证。例如针对"二滩"送出工程中个别地段覆冰严重的问题，西南电力设计院于1982年在相应地段建立了"黄茅根"大型观冰站，架设了3档试验线路，另有大型的雾凇塔，进行了约20年的"覆冰"数据观测试验，1994年进入工程建设阶段。

技术设计，又称扩大初步设计。为了进一步解决初步设计中的重大技术问题，如工艺流程、建筑结构、设备选型等，根据初步设计和进一步的调查研究资料进行技术设计，这样做可以使建设工程更具体、更完善，技术指标更合理。

（2）施工图设计

施工图设计是初设的具体化，是在初步设计的基础上，根据建筑安装工作的需要，针对各项工程的具体施工，绘制施工详图。它是进行工程施工的依据，对工程建成后的生产过程的长期维护起着重要的参考作用。根据施工图设计，编制施工图预算（即预算书）。

设计文件编好后，必须按照规定进行审核和批准。初步设计与概算应提交有关部门组织审批。施工图设计文件系已定方案的具体化施工安排，由设计单位负责完成。在交付施工单位时，须经建设单位技术负责人审查签字，设计人员应到现场与建设、施工单位共同会审设计图纸、设计文件，进行技术讨论和说明。

4. 开工准备阶段

项目开工准备阶段的工作较多，涉及面较广，主要内容包括：申请列入固定资产投资计划；开展各项施工准备工作，如编制建设项目的实施计划、工程施工招标和设备、材料的订货，开展征地、拆迁、"三通一平"工作，签订各类合同、协议。这一阶段的各项工作，对于保证项目开工后能否顺利进行具有决定性作用。

5. 施工阶段

施工阶段是建设项目付诸实施的重要阶段，必须按照施工顺序，结合实际情况合理组织施工。施工单位应全力以赴，保证工程质量，按期完成工程建设任务。

项目新开工时间，是指建设项目设计文件中规定的任何一项永久性工程第一次正式破土开槽的日期。不需要开槽的工程，以建筑物基础的正式打桩日期作为正式开工日。工程地质勘察、平整场地、拆除旧建筑物、临时建筑、施工用临时道路和水、电等施工不算正式开工。建设工期从新开工时算起。

当开工准备基本就绪后，应由建设单位提出申请开工报告，经主管部门批准后，才能开工兴建。根据国家规定，大中型项目的开工报告要报国家计委批准。

施工阶段一般包括土建、装饰、给排水、采暖通风、电气照明、工业管道及设备安装等工程项目。施工单位要严格履行合同，要与建设、设计单位和监理工程师密切配合。在施工过程中，各环节要相互协调，要加强科学管理，确保工程质量，全面按期完成施工任务。施工过程中，施工单位必须严格按照设计施工图施工，在确保工程质量的前提下，降低工程造价。施工中因工程需要变更时，应取得设计单位和建设单位的同意。按照设计和施工验收规范进行验收，对地下工程、隐蔽工程，特别是基础和结构的关键部位，必须经过检验合格，并做好原始记录，才能进行下一道工序。对不符合质量要求的工程，要及时采取措施，不留隐患。不合格的工程不得交工。

6. 生产准备阶段

在施工过程中，建设单位应当根据建设项目的生产技术特点，按时组成专门班子，有计划有步骤地做好各项生产准备，为竣工后投产创造条件。生产准备工作主要有：招收和培训必要的生产人员，落实原材料、燃料、动力等生产协作条件，组织工器具、备品、备件的制造和订货，组建有力的生产指挥管理机构，制定必要的管理制度和安全生产操作规程等。

7. 竣工验收阶段

竣工验收的目的是全面考核建设成果，检查设计和施工质量；及时解决投产的问题；办理移交手续，交付使用。

竣工验收程序，一般分为两个阶段：单项工程验收和整个工程项目的全部验收。对于大型工程，因建设时间长或建设过程中逐步投产，应分批组织验收。一般竣工验收之前，施工单位会进行工程预验收，有时监理单位也会组织初步验收。在竣工验收时，由建设单位组织竣工验收，参加的单位包括设计、施工单位，银行、环保及有关的政府监督部门等。要系统整理技术资料，绘制竣工图，分类立卷，在验收后作为档案资料，交生产单位保存。建设单位要认真清理所有财产和物资，编好工程竣工决算，报上级主管部门审批。

输电线路工程按照设计文件所规定的内容建成后，在办理竣工验收前，必须进行线路带电试运行，检查考核是否已达到设计标准和施工验收的质量要求。如工程质量不合格，应返工或加固。

8. 工程后评价阶段

工程后评价是在工程交付后生产运行一段时间内，对项目的立项决策、设计、施工、竣工验收、生产运行等全过程进行系统评价的一种技术经济活动，是基本建设程序的最后一环，力求以此达到肯定成绩、总结经验、研究问题、提高项目决策水平和投产效果的目的。评价主要包括以下内容。①影响评价。通过项目建成后投入生产后对社会、经济、政治、技术和环境等方面所产生的影响来评价项目决策的正确性。如项目建成后没达到决策时的目的，或背弃了决策目的，则应分析原因，找出问题，加以改进。②经济效益评价。通过项目建成投产后所产生的实际效益的分析，来评价项目投资是否合理，经营管理是否得当，并与可行性研究阶段的评价结果进行比较，找出二者之间的差异及原因，提出改进措施。③过程评价。前述两种评价是从项目投产后运行结果来分析评价的，过程评价则是从项目的立项决策、设计、施工、竣工投产等全过程进行系统分析，找出成败的原因。

上述基本建设程序的内容，基本上反映了基本建设的全过程。它大致可以分为三个阶段，即前期工作阶段、工程实施阶段、竣工投产阶段。从国内外的基本建设的经验来看，前期工作阶段最重要，一般占整个工程的50%～60%的时间。前期工作搞好了，其后各阶段的工作就容易顺利完成。目前国内对基础设施建设工程质量有了高度的重视，尤其要求严格执行建设程序，确保前期工作质量。

同我国基本建设程序相比，国外通常把工程建设的全过程分为三个时期，即投资前时期、投资时期、投资回收时期，主要包括投资机会研究、初步可行性研究、可行性研究、项目评估、基础设计、工程设计、详细设计、招标发包、施工、竣工投产、生产阶段、工程后评价、项目终止等步骤。

五、工程建设预算简介

工程建设预算是国家确定工程建设项目投资额、建设单位确定工程造价和编制建设计划、银行拨付工程价款、施工单位签订经济合同、推行投资包干制和招投标承包制的主要依据。工程造价管理的两大任务，一是工程造价的测算，即在合理确定工程造价构成和水平的基础上，在设计、建设各阶段正确编制估算、概算、预算、结算和竣工决算；二是工程造价的控制，即在投资决策阶段，设计、招投标、施工、竣工阶段，把技术与经济紧密结合起来，有效控制造价，使各阶段的实际投资不超上一阶段的投资额，使最终的造价不超过批准的造价限额。

工程建设预算包括投资估算、设计概算、施工图预算、施工预算、工程结算、竣工决算等几种，在基本建设程序中它们之间的关系如图0-0-1所示，从图中可以看出，工程建设预算从确定建设项目、确定和控制基本建设投资、进行基本建设经济管理和施工企业经济核算，到最后核定项目的固定资产，它们以价值形态贯穿于整个基本建设过程中，其中设计概算、施工图预算和竣工决算，通常简称基本建设的"三算"，是建设项目的重要内容，三者有机联系，缺一不可。设计要编制概算，施工要编制预算，竣工要编制决算。一般情况下，决算不能超过预算，预算不能超过概算。此外，施工企业还要编制反映工程最终造价并作为清算工程价款的竣工结算。竣工结算与施工图预算、施工预算一起被称为施工企业内部的"三算"。

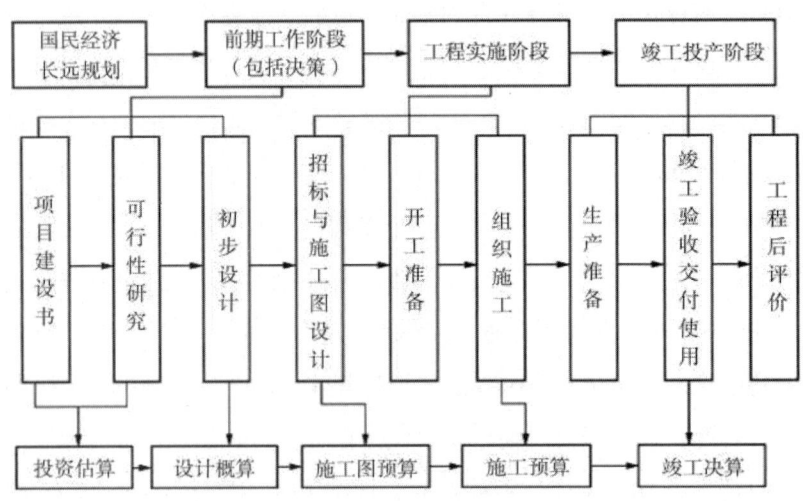

图 0-0-1 基本建设程序与概预算关系简图

一般认为，在建设项目施工招投标中编制的标底和标价也属于工程建设预算的范畴。建设单位编制的标底和施工企业编制的投标报价，是它们各自制订的基建产品的浮动价格，即市场价格。中标报价是基建产品的成交定价价格。

工程建设预算中的设计概算和施工图预算，在编制年度基本建设计划、确定工程造价、评价设计方案、签订工程合同、银行拨款和贷款、竣工结算等方面有着共同的作用，都是国家对基本建设进行科学管理和监督的有效手段。二者在编制方法上也有相似之处；但由于编制时间、依据、要求和编制单位不同，它们还是有所区别的。

（一）编制工程建设预算的必要性

工程建设预算，是确定工程费用的文件，其实质是计算和采用基本建设产品计划价格的一套程序和方法。编制工程建设预算的必要性，首先是由建设产品自身的特点所决定的。与一般工业生产相比，基本建设产品的生产有以下特点。

1. 基建产品的建设地点不固定性

基建产品都是在选定的地点上建造的，与一般工业产品在工厂里重复、批量地进行生产不同，工业产品的生产条件一般不受时间及气象条件限制。由于基建产品的施工地点不同，使得对于用途、功能规模、标准等基本相同的建设产品，因其建设地点的地质、气象、水文条件等不同，其造型、材料选用、施工方案等，都有较大的差异，从而影响到产品的造价。此外，不同地区工人的人工工资标准以及某些费用标准，例如材料运输费、冬雨季施工费等，都会由于建设地点的不同而不同，使基建产品的造价有很大的差异。

2. 基建产品的单件性

基建产品一般各不相同，每项工程中，都根据工程的具体要求进行单独设计，在设计内容、规模、造型、结构和材料等各方面都互不相同。同时，因为工程建设项目的性质（新建、改建、扩建或恢复等）不同，其设计要求也不同。即使工程的性质或设计标准相同，也会因建设地点的地质、水文条件不同，其设计也不尽相同。因此，基建产品的单件性，反映在基建产品的造价上互不相同。

3. 基建产品的露天性

基建产品的生产一般都是在露天进行的，季节的更替，气候、自然环境条件的变化，会引起产品设计的某些内容和施工方法的变化，也会造成防汛、防寒、防雨或降温等费用的变化，这些变化都会引起基建产品的造价发生相应的变动，使得各基建产品的造价并不相同。

基建产品的生产周期长，程序多，涉及面广，社会协作关系复杂，这些特点也决定了基建产品价值构成不可能一样。基建产品的上述特点，决定了它不可能像一般工业产品那样，可以采用统一的价格，而必须通过特殊的计划程序，对逐个产品单独编制建设预算来确定其价格。

另外，编制工程建设预算，是国家执行计划和调控市场的要求。国家根据国民经济计划对市场需求的预测，有计划地安排每个基建项目，每个基建项目又称基本建设产品。为了编制基本建设计划，需要根据基本建设产品及其生产特点，采取编制建设预算的方法，来确定基本建设产品的预算价格，然后根据其价格编制基本建设计划，确定每个建设项目的投资。

（二）投资估算

投资估算是指建设工程从前期工作开始到工程形成预定的生产能力，能够进行正常生产所需的全部建设费用的预期最大可能值。它是在规划阶段、项目建议书阶段、可行性研究阶段，建设单位向国家或主管部门申请基本建设投资时，为确定建设项目投资总额而编制的技术经济文件，是国家或主管部门确定基本建设投资计划的重要文件。

1. 国内工程项目的投资估算

项目投资估算是在做初步设计之前各工作阶段中的一项工作。在初步设计之前，应编制项目规划和项目建议书，同时应根据项目已明确的技术经济条件，编制和估算出精度不同的投资估算额。中国建设项目的投资估算分为以下几个阶段。

（1）规划阶段的投资估算。项目规划阶段，根据国民经济发展规划、地区发展规划和行业发展规划的要求，编制一个建设项目的建设规划。其误差率可大于或等于±30%。该估算作为否定一个项目或决定是否继续进行研究的依据之一。

（2）项目建议书阶段的投资估算。在项目建议书阶段，按项目建议书中的产品方案、项目建设规模、产品主要生产工艺、企业车间组成、初选建厂地点等，估算建设项目所需的投资额。估算误差率可在±30%以内。作为经济上判断工程项目是否应列入投资计划中的依据。根据此阶段估算的投资额，可以否定一个项目，但不能完全肯定一个项目是否真正可行。

（3）可行性研究阶段的投资估算。初步可行性研究阶段的投资估算，主要是在投资机会研究及其投资估算的基础上，进一步对建设项目的投资规模、工艺技术、材料来源、建址选择、组织机构和建设进度等情况，进行综合技术经济分析，以判断建设项目的可行性，并做出初步投资评价与决策。因为是经过技术经济论证后所做出的对投资数额的估计，所以误差率应在±20%以内。可作为编制设计任务书的参考依据。

（4）评审阶段的投资估算。这是在上一阶段投资估算的基础上，从技术、经济、财务制度等方面，对拟建项目的最佳投资方案进行评价，并对建设项目的可行性研究提出结论性意见。该阶段是进行全面、详细、深入的技术经济分析和论证阶段，投资估算的误差应控制在±10%以内。这一阶段的投资估算是决定拟建项目和选择最佳方案的主要依据，也是编制设计文件、控制初步设计及概算的重要依据。

（5）设计任务书阶段的投资估算。这是在评审的基础上，根据可靠的数据和资料,对工程项目投资数额所进行的最后估计和认可,误差率控制在±10%以内。该阶段的投资估算是编制投资计划、进行资金筹措及申请贷款的主要依据,是控制工程造价的最高限额。

2. 国外工程项目的投资估算

国外工程项目的投资估算与我国的不同,它不但包括项目建议书阶段、可行性研究阶段、设计任务书阶段的投资估算,还包括相当于我国初步设计阶段的概算和施工图设计阶段的预算。以英美为代表的西方国家,根据不同阶段研究的内容和深度,将投资估算分为以下五个阶段。

(1)数量级估算,又称毛估、比例估算。相当于我国项目建议书阶段的投资估算。这个阶段是对投资项目的机会研究阶段,此时的投资估算是根据已建成的类似工程的投资资料,采用综合比例法估计的,误差率可大于或等于±30%。

(2)研究性估算,又称粗估、评价性的估算。相当于我国的可行性研究阶段的投资估算。它是在已有主要设备表和流程图并已经初步选定厂址之后进行的投资估算。其误差率约为±30%。

(3)预算性估算,又称初步估算、拨款估算。相当于我国设计任务书阶段的投资估算。它是在已有设备材料的规格表、设备生产能力、工厂总平面图、建筑物的大致尺寸、公用设施的初步配置等较充足资料的基础上进行的估算。它可作为确定工程项目是否有发展前途,是否列入投资计划的参考依据。其误差率约为±20%。

(4)确定性估算,又称工程控制性估算。相当于我国初步设计阶段的概算,其误差率约为±10%,其可作为控制建设项目投资的依据。

(5)详细估算,又称投标估算、最终估算、工程预算。相当于我国施工图设计阶段的预算。它是根据整套施工图纸、技术说明文件和设备材料清单等资料编制的估算。这种估算的精度较高,误差率约为±5%,其可作为控制工程项目实施阶段投资的依据。

(三)设计概算

在初步设计(或扩大初步设计)阶段,根据初步设计图纸、概算定额(或指标)及其有关费用定额等编制的工程项目从筹建到竣工验收所需的全部建设费用,叫作设计概算,它是设计内容在经济上的体现,是设计文件的重要组成部分。

概算是国家基本建设投资的最高限额,是编制基本建设计划,实行基本建设投资大包干，控制其中建设拨款、贷款的依据；是考核设计方案和建设成本是否合理的依据。《工程建设项目施工招标投标方法》中规定：招标项目编制标底的，还根据批准的初步设计、投资概算，依据有关计价方法，参照有关工程定额，结合市场供求状况，综合考虑投资、工期和质量等方面的因素合理确定。概算不仅起着控制标底和投资的作用，还起着控制预算的作用，因为预算必须控制在概算的5%以内。概算一经主审机关批准，即作为建设项目投资的法定依据。设计概算总投资按同年度价格水平计算，不得超过计划任务书批准的总投资。一旦超过，必须详细分析原因，并重点说明超出原因及其合理性，或修改初步设计，直到满足要求为止。

（四）施工图预算

施工图预算是指在施工图设计阶段，根据施工图纸、施工组织设计、国家颁布的预算定额和工程量计算规则、地区材料预算价格、施工管理费标准、计划利润率、税金等，计算每项工程所需要人力、物力和投资额的文件。它是施工前组织物资、机具、劳动力，编制施工计划，统计完成工作量，办理工程价款结算，实行经济核算，考核工程成本，实行建筑工程包干和银行拨（贷）工程款的依据。一般建筑工程以施工图预算作为编制施工招标标底的依据。

预算书是施工图纸资料的重要组成部分，它延续了概算对设计的能动的影响作用，是设计单位进行工程造价管理的重要手段，是施工单位确定工程预算成本和考核工程实际成本的依据，是银行拨、贷款的依据，也可作为标底。

下面介绍预算与设计、施工、建设等各方面的关系。预算反映了工程设计在技术上的先进性和经济上的合理性；建设单位和施工单位之间的工程招、投标是在概算或预算的基础上进行的，已审定的预算是建设单位与施工单位工程结算的依据；预算是施工单位进行合理的施工组织，制定并采取先进的技术措施和施工方法，改善经营管理、降低工程成本的出发点。

施工图预算的构成基本与初步设计概算类似，下面介绍它们的区别。

区别一：编制费用的内容不完全相同。设计概算包括建设项目从筹建开始至全部项目竣工和交付使用前的全部建设费用。施工图预算的费用项目架构与概算基本一致，但由于设计深度的不同，施工图预算的费用项目更为细致，更接近工程项目建设最终状态。

区别二：编制的阶段不同。预算编制与概算编制有一定的时间间隔，在这段时间内，国家、地方的相关政策可能发生变化；设计可能出现设计变更，会导致施工图设计提出的工程量改变等因素的出现，最终导致概算与预算之间有着一定的差别。

区别三：审批过程及其作用不同。设计总概算是初步设计文件的组成部分，一并申报有关主管部门审批，作为建设项目和正式列入年度基本建设计划的依据。只有在初步设计图纸和设计总概算经审批同意后，施工图设计才能开始，因此它是控制施工图设计和预算总额的依据。施工图预算是先报建设单位初审，然后再送交银行经办审查认定，可作为拨付工程价款和竣工结算的依据。

区别四，概预算的分项大小和采用的定额不同。设计概算分项和采用定额，具有较强的综合性。设计概算采用概算定额，而施工图预算用的是预算定额。预算定额是综合概算定额的基础。另外设计概算和施工图预算采用的分级项目不同，设计概算一般采用三级项目，施工图预算一般采用比三级项目更细的项目。

投资估算、概算、预算三者属于技术经济的范畴，三者合称投资测算。在编制的过程中，它们相互影响、相互联系，对一个工程的建成不可或缺。但传统的编制过程中，多采用手工计算方法，计算工作量大，烦琐复杂、数字转移极多，易出差错且计算时间较长，目前已经广泛使用专用"概、预算"编制软件，它们一般有通用性强（包括输、配电线路）、灵活（可选用地方价目本或全国统一定额甚至于还包括行业外定额）、快速（编制一个工程的概、预算并打印出来可能就几个小时，是手工编制的20～50倍）、规范（表格形式规范统一，概、预算的成品容易实现标准化）、使用简便（一般的"概、预算"编制软件都采用Windows平台，操作界面良好，易于且便于使用）等优点，较好地解决了前述手工编制概、预算问题，所以目前在各电力公司及设计、基建企业已推广应用"概、预算"编制软件。

（五）工程结算

工程结算是指施工单位按照工程施工合同，对已完成的工程量向建设单位办理工程价格清算的经济文件。一般工程建设的周期较长，耗用的资金数量较多，为了使施工单位在施工过程中耗用的资金及时得到补偿，需要对工程价款进行结算，一般包括中间结算（进度款结算）、年终结算、全部工程竣工验收后进行的竣工结算。工程结算在工程项目承包中是一项十分重要的工作，主要作用表现在以下几方面。

1. 工程结算是反映工程进度的主要指标

在施工过程中，工程结算的一个重要依据就是已经施工完成的工程量，而通过累

计已结算的工程价款占合同总价款的比例,就可以近似反映出工程的进度情况。

2. 工程结算是加速资金周转的重要环节

施工单位尽快尽早地结算工程款,有利于偿还债务,有利于资金回笼,降低内部运营成本,通过加速资金周转提高资金的使用效率。

3. 工程结算是考核经济效益的重要指标

对于施工单位来说,只有工程款如数地结清,才意味着避免了经营风险,施工单位也才能够获得相应的利润,达到良好的经济效益。

(六)竣工决算

竣工决算,是指建设项目全部完工后,在工程竣工验收阶段,由建设单位编制的从项目筹建到建成投产全部费用的技术经济文件。它是建设投资管理的重要环节,是工程竣工验收、交付使用的重要依据,也是进行建设项目财务总结,银行对其实行监督的必要手段。其目的主要是考核工程项目投资使用效果的好坏,同时可将施工实践的技术经济数据,经过整理加工后,为修订定额提供可靠的依据。

竣工决算主要有以下几方面的作用。

一是建设项目竣工决算是综合、全面地反映竣工项目建设成果及财务情况的总结性文件,它采用货币指标、实物数量、建设工期和各种技术经济指标综合、全面地反映建设项目自开始建设到竣工为止的全部建设成果和财物状况,能够正确反映建设工程的实际造价和投资结果。

二是建设项目竣工决算是办理交付使用资产的依据,也是竣工验收报告的重要组成部分。

三是可以通过竣工决算与概算、预算的对比分析,考核投资控制的工作成效,总结经验教训,积累技术经济方面的基础资料,提高未来建设工程的投资效益。

(七)工程建设预算阶段划分及精度要求

由于在不同工程建设阶段所掌握的资料和具备条件不同,技术经济人员确定的工程造价的准确度就有了差异,它们的内容、目的、作用也就不同,见表0-0-2。

表0-0-2 建设预算阶段划分精度要求

序号	阶段划分	项目名称	投资额误差率（%）	备注
1	项目规划阶段	估算	≥±30%	1.按规划的要求和内容，初步确定项目所需投资额； 2.否定项目或决定是否进行深入研究的依据
2	项目建议书阶段	估算	±30%以内	1.主管部门审批项目建议书的依据； 2.否定或判断项目是否需要进行下阶段工作
3	初步可行性研究阶段	估算	±20%以内	据以确定项目是否进行详细可行性研究
4	详细可行性研究阶段	估算	±10%以内	1.决定项目是否可行； 2.可据此列入项目年度基建计划
5	评估审查阶段		±10%以内	1.作为可行性研究结果进行评价的依据； 2.作为对项目进行最后决定的依据
6	初步设计	概算	5%~10%	
7	施工图设计	预算	3%~5%	

学习项目一

编制10 kV配电线路施工图预算

案例工程一　10 kV某新建线路工程概况

一、总述

（一）设计依据

（1）受某市投资有限公司委托，对该市某10 kV配电工程进行勘察设计。
（2）《架空绝缘配电线路设计技术规程》DL/T 52002-2005。
（3）国家其他有关规程、规范。

（二）设计范围

某10 kV配电工程。

（三）工程概况

（1）在10 kV配电线路04号杆（高低压同杆）上搭火，新建12 m电杆3基，新建线路全长150 m。

（2）在新立的N3号杆上装高压真空断路器（12 kV，630 A）1台，敷设150 m电缆（YJV22-8.7/15 kV-3×50）下地至400 kVA干式变压器。

二、路径及交叉跨越

（一）路径概况

本工程路径见10 kV架空线路平面布置图，如图1-0-1所示。

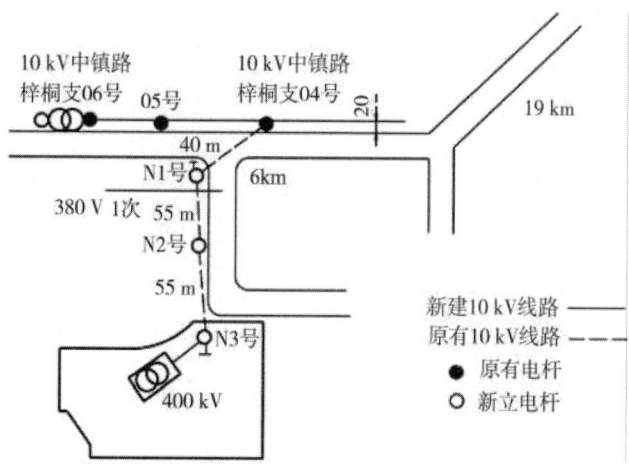

图 1-0-1　10 kV 架空线路平面布置图

（二）交叉跨越

本工程跨越公路 1 处，跨低压 380 V 线路 1 处。

（三）交通运输

本工程地处城镇，全线地形比例为平地 100%，运输地形图如图 1-1-1。
全线地质比例为普土 70%，坚土 20%，泥水 10%。

三、机电部分

（一）设计气象条件（略）

（二）导线

本工程架空线采用 JKLYJ-10 kV-50 绝缘导线。安全系数为 7.5，架空线与周围建筑物的安全距离应满足 10 kV 架空线路施工和验收规范。

（三）防雷保护、绝缘配合

1. 终端杆敷设人工接地体，接地电阻满足规程要求，绝缘子串悬挂点与接地体应有可靠电气连接。

2. 水泥杆架设段绝缘子型号为 FXBW2-10/45，直线绝缘子采用 FS-10/3 合成横担绝缘子。

3. 在装隔离开关处须装设氧化锌避雷器（HYW5-12.7/50）。

（四）金具

本工程全线采用国家标准电力金具。

四、杆塔及基础

（一）杆塔

本工程共使用电杆（Φ190×12000）3基，其中终端杆1基，转角杆1基，直线杆1基，组装图如图1-0-2、图1-0-3、图1-0-4所示。

（二）基础

本工程混凝土杆均采用D0.8×0.8×0.17的底盘基础，采用L0.8×0.4×0.15的拉线盘。

（三）其他

（1）本工程配隔离开关（12 kV 630 A）1组、避雷器1组。

（2）本工程图纸套用《城市电网10 kV及以下工程典型设计》。

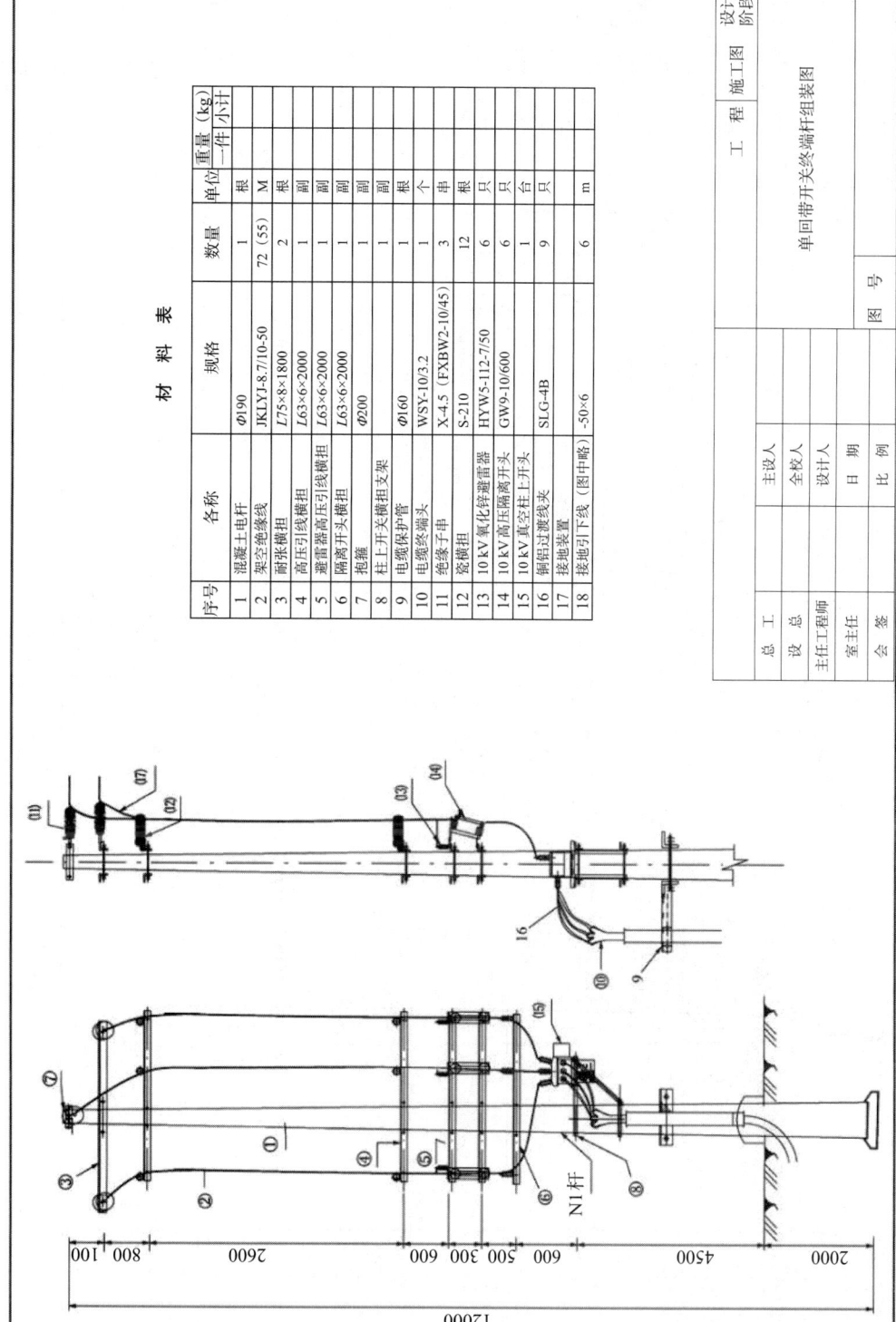

图 1-0-2 电缆终端杆组装图

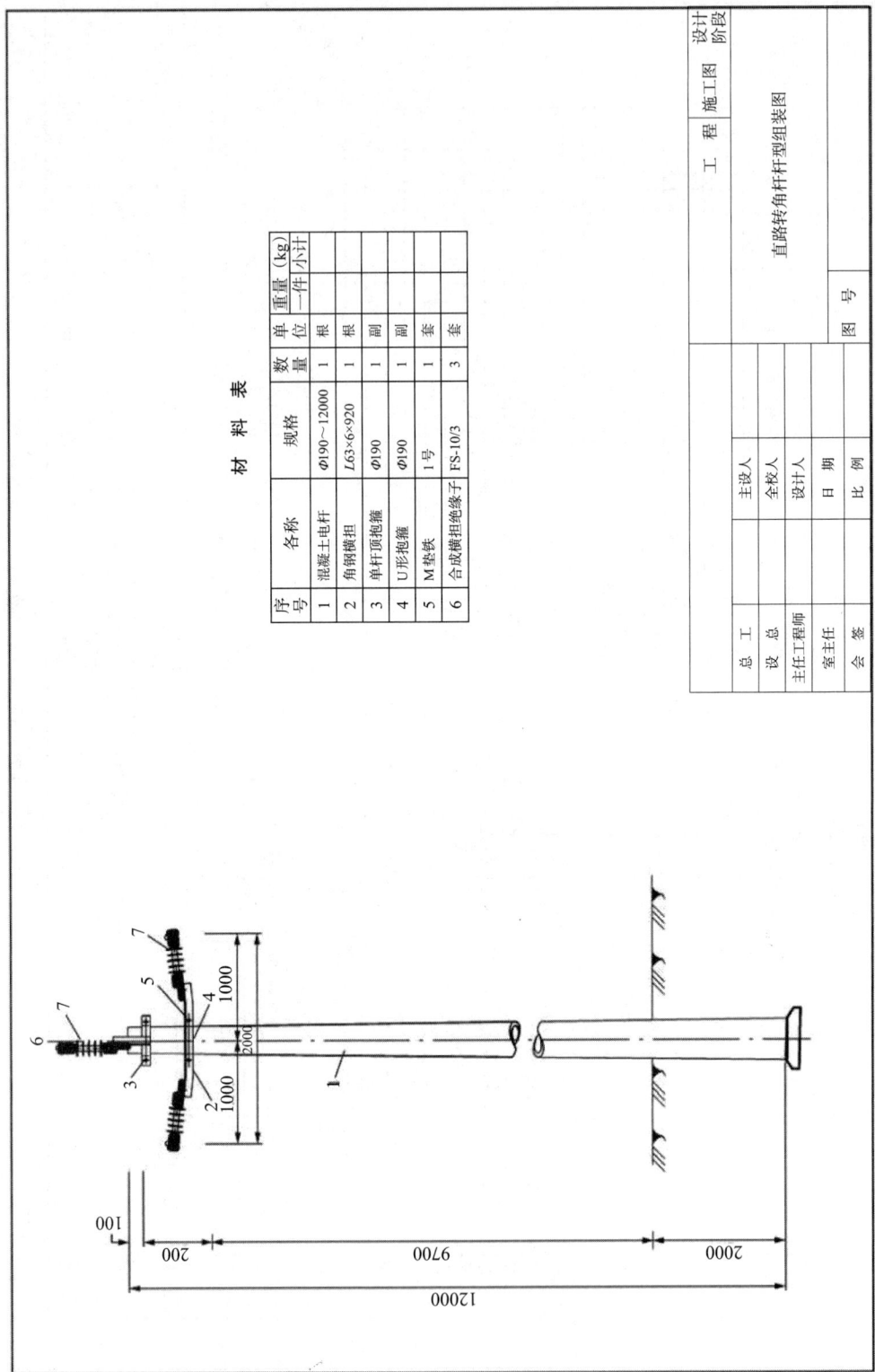

图 1-0-3 直线杆组装图

学习项目一 编制10kV配电线路施工图预算

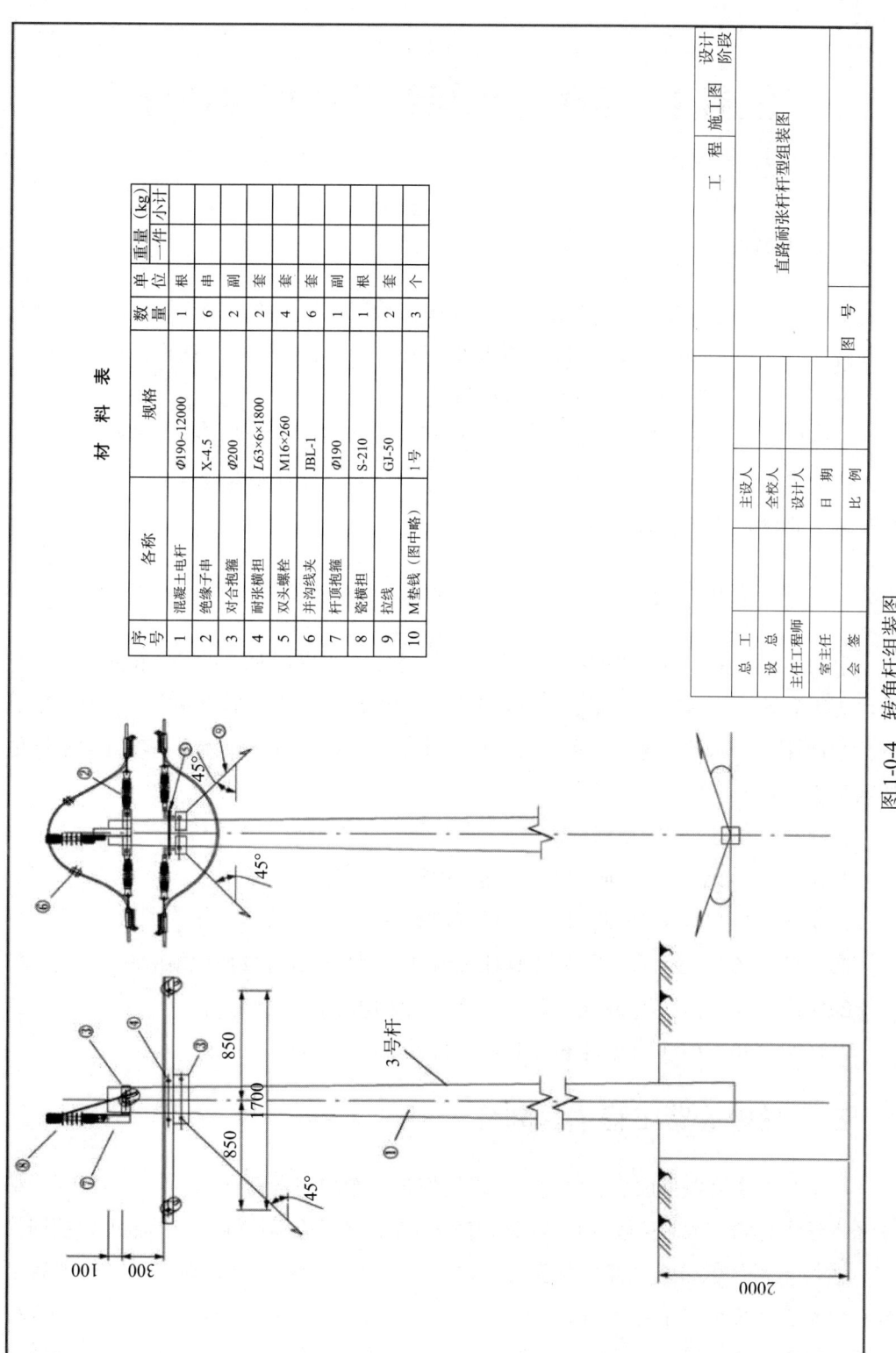

图1-0-4 转角杆组装图

任务1　熟悉配电线路工程项目划分

一、概念

施工图预算，是指在施工图设计和工程施工阶段，根据施工图设计文件、预算定额和费用计算有关规定，预先测算和确定的工程造价；也指在施工图设计和工程施工阶段编制、测算和确定施工图预算文件的过程。

一个建设项目是由各个不同专业，按生产特点系统综合起来的。为了便于统一管理，根据生产特点和专业分工以及设计的专业划分及分卷分册图的划分，对建设项目进行科学的分解，即为项目划分。

二、工程项目划分依据

电力工程计价体系是根据中国电力工业管理体制的变迁而逐步发展和完善的。目前电力工程计价依据体系按照电力工程造价管理的需要已逐步形成并完善了费用项目划分与计算方法体系、定额体系、价格信息体系、工程计价方法体系、项目实施评估体系。

新的配电线路工程项目划分依据是：

2016版《20 kV及以下配电网工程建设预算编制与计算标准》；

2016版《20 kV及以下配电网工程预算定额》；

2016版《20 kV及以下配电网工程建设预算编制与计算标准使用指南》；

2016版《20 kV及以下配电网工程预算定额使用指南》；

2016版《20 kV及以下配电网工程设备材料价格信息》。

三、配电线路工程项目划分

一个基本建设项目往往规模大、建设周期长、影响因素复杂。因此，为了便于编制基本建设计划、编制工程造价、组织材料供应、组织招标投标、安排施工和控制投资、拨付工程价款、进行经济核算等生产经营管理的需要，所以对工程进行项目划分。建设工程按项目本身的内部组成，将其划分为建设项目、单项工程、单位工程、分部工程和分项工程。建设项目，又称基本建设项目，是指在一个场地或几个场地上按一个总体设计进行施工的各个工程项目的总和。单项工程，是建设项目的组成部分，具有独立的设计文件，建成后可以独立发挥生产能力或效益。单位工程，是单项工程的组成部分，是指不能独立发挥生产能力，但具有独立施工条件的工程。分部工程，是单位工程的组成部分，一般以建筑物的主要部位或工种来划分。分项工程，是分部工程的细分，是建设项目的最基本的组成单元，也是最简单的施工工程。

由于电力系统是一个复杂的建筑系统，包含的建筑群体种类多，涉及面广，难以严格按单项工程、单位工程、分部工程和分项工程来确切划分，因此对电力系统基建工程项目，在编制各组成部分的概预算时，每部分从大到小又划分为一级项目、二级项目、三级项目等。一级项目相当于扩大单位工程，二级项目相当于单位工程，三级项目相当于分部、分项工程。

配电网工程属于单项工程，其下一般分为两级：第一级为扩大单位工程，第二级为单位工程。如表1-1-1所示，"1 站内房屋建筑"属于扩大单位工程，"1.1 一般土建"属于单位工程。

20 kV及以下配电线路工程项目按输送方式划分为架空线路工程、电缆线路工程。国家定额规定的具体划分情况如表1-1-1、表1-1-2、表1-1-3所示。

表1-1-1 建筑工程项目划分表

编号	项目名称	主要内容及范围说明	技术经济指标单位
一、配电站（开关站）工程			
1	站内房屋建设		元/m²
1.1	一般土建	包括设备基础及预埋槽钢	元/m³
1.2	采暖、通风及照明工程	包括事故照明	
2	箱它式变电站建筑		
2.1	土石方及基础工程		元/座
2.2	箱式变电站辅助设施		元/座
3	站内消防设施	包括变压器消防、建筑物消防等	元/座
4	站内电缆沟道		元/m
5	站内道路及地坪		元/座
5.1	站内道路		元/m²
5.2	栏栅及地坪		元/m²
6	站区辅助设施		
6.1	围墙及大门		

续表

编号	项目名称	主要内容及范围说明	技术经济指标单位
6.2	站区绿化		元/m²
6.3	站区排水	包括土建及设备管道	
6.4	挡土墙、护坡及防洪沟		
二、架空线路工程			
1	土石方工程		元/m³
2	基础工程	包括材料运输	元/m³
3	护坡、挡土墙及排洪沟砌筑	包括材料运输	
三、电缆线路工程			
1	电缆沟工程	包括材料运输、路面处理及土石方工程	元/km
2	电缆隧道工程	包括材料运输、路面处理及土石方工程	元/km
3	电缆排管工程	包括材料运输、排管敷设、混凝土浇制等	元/km
四、通信及调度自动化			
五、工程相关单项工程			
1	配电站外道路		元/m
2	施工防护措施		

表1-1-2 安装工程项目划分表

编号	项目名称	主要内容及范围说明	技术经济指标单位
一、配电站（开关站）工程			
1	变压器安装		元/kVA
2	配电装置安装		元/kVA
2.1	10 kV（20 kV）配电装置		
2.2	1 kV以下配电装置		
2.3	无功补偿装置		
3	成套式变电站		元/kVA
3.1	箱式变电站安装		
3.2	开闭及分接装置安装		
4	控制保护系统		元/kVA

续表

编号	项目名称	主要内容及范围说明	技术经济指标单位
5	直流系统	包括充电装置、直流屏、蓄电池	
6	站用电系统		元/kVA
6.1	站用配电装置		
6.2	站区照明		
7	站用电缆		
7.1	动力电缆		元/m
7.2	控制电缆		元/m
7.3	电缆辅助设施		
7.4	电缆防火		
8	全站接地		元/站
9	分系统调试与试验		元/站
9.1	系统调试		元/站
9.2	特殊试验项目		元/站
二、架空线路工程			
1	杆塔工程	包括材料运输、横担组合装配、拉线安装及接地安装	元/基
2	架线工程	含材料运输及附件安装	元/km
3	杆上变配电装置	包括运输及调试	元/套
三、电缆线路工程			
1	电缆桥（支、托）架安装		元/t
2	电缆敷设	包括电缆头制作	元/km
3	电缆防火		
4	避雷及接地工程		
4.1	避雷器安装		
4.2	接地装置安装		
5	调试与试验		
四、通信及调度自动化			
1	通信系统	包括载波、行政和调度电话	
2	调度自动化系统		
3	集中抄表系统		

表1-1-3 其他费用项目划分表

编号	项目名称	主要内容及范围说明
1	建设场地征用及清理费	
1.1	土地征用补偿费	
1.2	余物清理费	
1.3	施工场地租用费	
1.4	线路施工赔偿费	
2	项目建设管理费	
2.1	项目管理费	
2.2	招标费	
2.3	工程监理费	
3	项目建设技术服务费	
3.1	工程勘察费	
3.2	工程设计费	
3.3	设计文件评审费	
3.4	项目后评价费	
3.5	技术经济标准编制管理费	
4	工程建设监督检测费	
5	生产准备费	
6	基本预备费	

四、案例工程一的项目划分

根据工程设计资料可知，案例工程一中的单项工程包括架空线路工程、电缆线路工程。架空线路工程中扩大单位工程包括建筑工程和安装工程，建筑工程中单位工程包括土石方工程、基础工程；安装工程中单位工程包括杆塔工程、架线工程、杆上变配电装置。电缆线路工程中扩大单位工程也包括建筑工程和安装工程，建筑工程中单位工程包括电缆沟工程；安装工程中单位工程包括电缆敷设、电缆防火、调试与试验。

任务2　工程量计算

工程量的统计是施工图预算的重点，是以国家颁布的现行配电网工程预算定额及说明为依据，根据设计图纸进行计算。其计算内容根据项目划分内容分项进行。

一、架空线路工程

（一）工地运输

工地运输是指材料从集中材料堆放地点或分散仓库运至沿线杆塔位置的运输。根据现行定额规定工地运输需要统计的工程量有工地运输的重量和工地运输的距离，应根据其运输方式的不同进行分类统计。虽然20 kV及以下配电线路工程不同于更高电压等级的线路工程，其项目划分中未将工地运输单独列项，而是分散在各个项目中分别计算，但不同电压等级线路工程的工地运输计算是类同的，下面介绍其计算原则和方法。

1. 工地运输方式

依照运输工具的不同，工地运输主要分为人力运输、板车运输、马车运输、木船运输、汽车运输、索道运输。根据不同运输方式，选取不同的定额、不同的地形系数进行工程量统计。

2. 工地运输量的计算

（1）计算方法

$$预算重量=设计重量+损耗量=设计重量×（1+损耗率） \quad (1-2-1)$$

$$运输重量=预算重量×毛重系数（单位重量） \quad (1-2-2)$$

工地运输重量统计，应区别不同的运输方式（人力运输、汽车运输、船舶运输）和材料种类（混凝土杆、钢管杆、混凝土预制品、线材、金具、绝缘子、零星钢材、塔材、沙、石、石灰、水泥、砖、土水等）分别汇总。不同材料施工损耗率如表1-2-1所示。

表1-2-1　材料施工损耗率表

序号	材料名称			损耗率%	序号	材料名称		损耗率%
1	裸软导线（含良导体地线）	一般架线	其他地区	0.4	15	耐张压接线夹		2.0
			山地、高山、峻岭	0.6	16	预绞丝		2.0
		张力放、紧线		0.8	17	铝端夹		3.0
2	专用跨接线和引线			2.5	18	水泥压力管		2.0
3	电力电缆			1.0	19	混凝土杆（包括底盘、拉盘、卡盘、夹盘）		0.5
4	控制电缆			1.5	20	混凝土叉梁、盖板（方、矩形）		3.5
5	镀锌钢绞线（避雷线）			0.3	21	砖、条石、块石		2.5
6	镀锌钢绞线（拉线）			2.0	22	商品混凝土		1.5
7	电缆终端头瓷套			0.5	23	水泥、石灰、降阻剂	山地、高山、峻岭	7.0
8	绝缘子、瓷横担			2.0			平地、丘陵、河网、泥沼	5.0
9	合成绝缘子			0.5	24	石子	山地、高山、峻岭	15.0
10	钢筋、型钢（成品、半成品）			0.5			平地、丘陵、河网、泥沼	10.0
11	钢管			1.5	25	黄沙	山地、高山、峻岭	18.0
12	塑料制品（管材、板材）			5.0			平地、丘陵、河网、泥沼	15.0
13	金具			1.0	26	钢筋（加工制作）		6.0
14	螺栓、脚钉、垫片（不包括基础用地脚螺栓）			3.0				

注：1. 裸软导线、地线按送电线路设计用量计算，其施工损耗不包括线路弛度及跳线等长度。
　　2. 导线损耗率中不包括与电器设备连接应预留的长度。
　　3. 电力电缆和控制电缆损耗率中不包括备用预留的长度，以及因敷设有弯曲或有弧度而增加的长度。输电用电力电缆不计算施工损耗。按设备性材料对待，不应计入安装费内。
　　4. 拉线长度计算以拉线的展开长度（包括制作所需的预留长度）为准。

(2) 材料统计

1) 基础工程。配电网工程中多采用预制基础,少量使用现浇基础。预制基础按不同重量以"基""块""组"统计;现浇基础按不同等级(以单基混凝土方量为依据划分)以"m^3"统计,其中砂、石、水泥等预算用量计算公式为

$$预算用量=定额用量×（1+损耗率） \tag{1-2-3}$$

其他工程量的计算公式为

$$其他工程量=设计用量×（1+损耗率） \tag{1-2-4}$$

材料重量根据表1-2-2(由设计人员提供)统计。

在案例工程一中,基础只有预制基础,包括D0.8×0.8×0.17的底盘基础3块,L0.8×0.4×0.15的拉线盘2块。查表1-2-1,施工损耗率为0.5%,其重量为

底盘重量=3×274×(1+0.5%)=827(kg);

拉线盘重量=2×96×(1+0.5%)=193(kg);

底盘和拉线盘重量之和即为预制基础总重量,共计1020 kg。

2) 杆塔工程。杆塔组立按不同重量等级以"基"为单位统计;拉线制作以"根"为单位统计,应注意长度区别;接地安装以"根"为单位统计,附件金具包括所有的金具、绝缘子等。

混凝土杆重量为1482×3×(1+0.5%)=4476(kg);镀锌钢绞线重量为20.08kg;接地装置重量为107kg;铁附件重量为163kg;绝缘子重量为46.69kg。

3) 架线工程装置性材料统计。导线重量为159.5 kg。

4) 安装设备统计。案例工程一安装的设备包括箱式变压器、断路器、隔离刀闸、避雷器等。具体设备汇总如表1-2-3所示。

5) 电缆工程。电缆工程的主要材料包括150 m电缆(YJV22-8.7/15 kV-3×50),重524.19 kg;户内、户外电缆终端各一个,重20.2 kg;电缆保护管1根,重27.5 kg;电缆保护管热缩套1根,重4 kg;防火堵料30 kg。所有主要材料如表1-2-2所示。

3. 平均运距的计算方法

(1) 工地仓库(材料站)的位置是计算平均运距的基础。工地仓库(材料站)的合理设置,有利于节约运输费用。设置工地仓库一般应符合下列要求:

1) 靠近线路和线路中心;

2) 交通方便,运输费用省;

3) 地势较高,不易受淹;

表1-2-2 主材汇总表

编号	名称	单位	数量	价格/元 单价	价格/元 合价	重量/kg 单重	重量/kg 合重
	建筑主材						
一	基础工程						
	底盘 D0.8×0.8×0.17	块	3.02	47	141.94	274	827.48
	拉线盘 L0.8×0.4×0.15	块	2.01	48	96.48	96	192.96
	拉线棒	只	2.02	55	111.1	5	10.1
	小计				349.52		1030.54
	建筑主材合计				349.52		1030.54
	安装主材						
二	架空线路工程						
	混凝土杆 Φ190×12000	根	3.02	2015	6085.3	1482	4475.64
	10 kV线路铁附件 综合	t	0.163	7200	1173.6	163	163
	合成绝缘横担FS-10/3	根	10.2	126	1285.2	2.6	26.52
	合成绝缘子串FXBW2-10/45	串	9.18	145	1331.1	2.2	20.17
	联板类	t	0.005	15568	77.84	5	5
	挂环类	t	0.001	28945	28.95	1	1
	碗头挂环类	t	0.004	25858	103.43	4	4
	耐张线夹 NX-1	副	9.18	198	1817.64	1.2	11.02
	并沟线夹	只	6.12	13.7	83.84	1	6.12
	架空绝缘线	m	550	8	4400	0.29	159.5
	镀锌钢绞线 GJ-25～100	t	0.02	5500	110	20.08	20.08
	楔形线夹	只	2.04	18	36.72	1.76	3.59
	UT形线夹	只	2.04	33	67.32	3.2	6.528
	拉线标识管	根	2	24	48	2	4
	铜绞线 TJ16～120	kg	10.1	39.5	398.95	10.1	10.1
	镀锌接地扁钢	t	0.061	6200	378.2	61	61
	角钢接地体	t	0.046	6500	299	45.7	45.7
	小计				17725.09		4886.56

续表

编号	名称	单位	数量	价格/元		重量/kg	
				单价	合价	单重	合重
三	电缆工程						
	电缆 YJV22-8.7/15 kV-3×50	m	151.5	86	13029	3.46	524.19
	电缆终端户内型	套	1.01	570	575.7	10	10.1
	电缆终端户外型	套	1.01	1287	1299.87	10	10.1
	电缆保护管涂塑钢管	m	2.5	56	140	11	27.5
	电缆保护管热缩套	根	1	44	44	4	4
	防火堵料	t	0.03	15120	453.6	30	30
	小计				15542.17		605.89
	安装主材合计				33267.26		5492.45

表1-2-3 设备汇总表

编号	名称	单位	数量	价格		运杂费		合价/元
				单价/元	合价/元	费率/%	合价/元	
	安装设备							
二	架空线路工程							
	干式变压器 GB11-400kVA	台	1	122500	122500	1.25	1531.25	124031.25
	高压真空断路器 12 kV/630A	台	1	18800	18800	1.25	235.00	19035.00
	高压隔离开关 12 kV/630A	组	1	963	963	1.25	12.04	975.04
	氧化锌避雷器 YW5-12.7/50	组	1	890	890	1.25	11.13	901.13
	组合式电流互感器	套	1	20000	20000	1.25	250.00	20250.00
	小计				163153		2039.42	165192.42
	安装设备合计				163153		2039.42	165192.42

4）有足够的场地和就近可租赁的房屋；

5）通信和生活条件方便。

（2）卸料点的选择：依据线路的路径、地形，结合与通行车道、河道之间最短的人力运距为条件，将线路划分若干段和选定各段线路材料的卸料点。

（3）平均运距的计算方法。平均运距的计算是以线路路径图为基础，考虑材料运输方式、运输地形、运输距离、材料供应方式等因素，采用加权平均法计算出工程施工中某种运输方式的平均运距。若某工程施工中同时采用了汽车运输、人力运输等多种材料运输方式，则需要分别计算其平均运距。

人力运输平均运距的计算式为

$$Y=\sum k_i L_i R_i / \sum L_i \qquad (1\text{-}2\text{-}5)$$

式中，Y——平均运距（km）；

L_i——各段线路长度（材料量）；

R_i——各段线路材料的人力运输直线距离；

k_i——弯曲系数。道路弯曲系数取决于运输地形，平地取 1.05～1.1；河网、泥沼取 1.1～1.2；丘陵取 1.1～1.3；山地取 1.3～1.5；高山取 1.6～1.8。

车船运输平均运距的计算式为

$$Y=\sum L_i R_i / \sum L_i + C \qquad (1\text{-}2\text{-}6)$$

式中，Y——平均运距（km）；

L_i——各段线路材料量，预算中以各段线路长度为代表；

R_i——各段线路材料的车船运输距离，自工地仓库至各段材料的卸料点（其中道路或河流与线路平行的，则以该段的中心处为计算运距的卸料点）；

C——超过下站运距。超过下站运距指火车站或码头至工地仓库的运距超过装材价格中下站运距部分，可按装材价格中规定计入工地运输距离，无规定者不予计列。

根据材料运输实际，材料供应方式可分为折角供应方式、辐射供应方式、平行供应方式等，其相应的平均运距理论值计算公式如下。

1) 折角供应方式示意如图 1-2-1 所示。

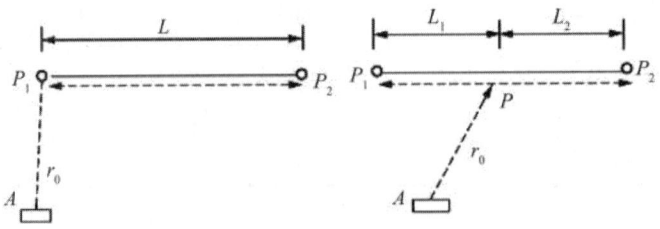

图 1-2-1　折角供应方式示意图

此时平均远距的计算公式为

$$R = \frac{L_1\left(r_0 + \dfrac{L_1}{2}\right) + L_2\left(r_0 + \dfrac{L_2}{2}\right)}{L_1 + L_2} \tag{1-2-7}$$

$$R = r_0 + \frac{L}{2} \tag{1-2-8}$$

式中，L_1，L_2，L——分别为 P_1P，PP_2，P_1P_2 控制线路工程的长度，线路路径可不是直线。

r_0——自材料站 A 到供应范围内的线路杆塔位上的最短里程。

2）线路工程路径为直线时，辐射供应方式如图 1-2-2 所示。

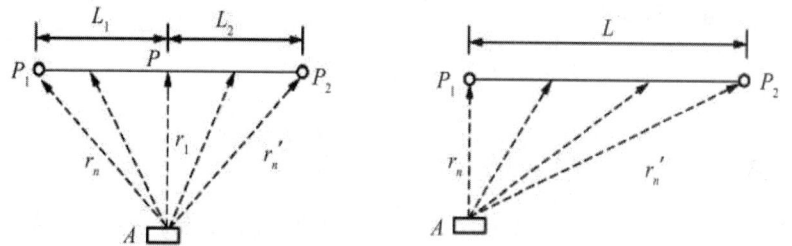

图 1-2-2　线路工程路径为直线时，辐射供应方式示意图

此时平均远距的计算公式为

$$R = \frac{L_1(r_1 + r_n) + L_2(r_1 + r_n')}{2(L_1 + L_2)} \tag{1-2-9}$$

$$R = \frac{r_n + r_n'}{2} \tag{1-2-10}$$

式中，r_0, r_n, r_n'——自材料站 A 到供应范围内的线路杆塔位上的最短里程。

3）线路工程路径为折线时，辐射供应方式如图 1-2-3 所示。

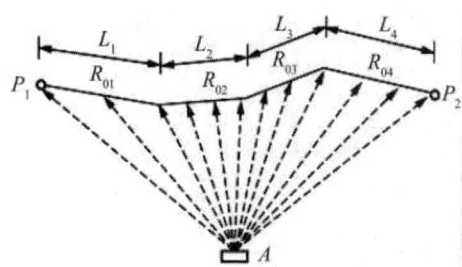

图 1-2-3　线路工程路径为折线时，辐射供应方式示意图

此时平均远距的计算公式为

$$R = \frac{L_1 R_{01} + L_2 R_{02} + L_3 R_{03} + L_4 R_{04}}{L_1 + L_2 + L_3 + L_4} \tag{1-2-11}$$

式中，$R_{01}, R_{02}, R_{03}, R_{04}$——各段直线线路对材料站的平均运输半径。

4）线路工程路径为直线时，平行供应方式如图1-2-4所示。

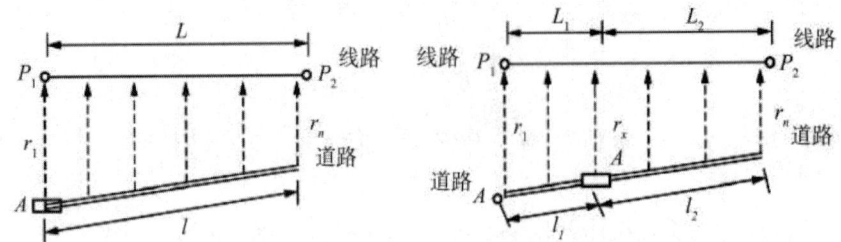

图1-2-4 线路工程路径为直线时，平行供应方式示意图

此时平均远距的计算公式为

$$R = \frac{l + r_1 + r_n}{2} \tag{1-2-12}$$

$$R = \frac{L_1(l_1 + r_1 + r_x)}{2(L_1 + L_2)} + \frac{L_2(l_2 + r_x + r_n)}{2(L_1 + L_2)} \tag{1-2-13}$$

式中，r_1, r_x, r_n——自材料运输道路分别到供应范围内的线路杆塔位上的最短里程。

5）线路工程路径为折线时，平行供应方式如图1-2-5所示。

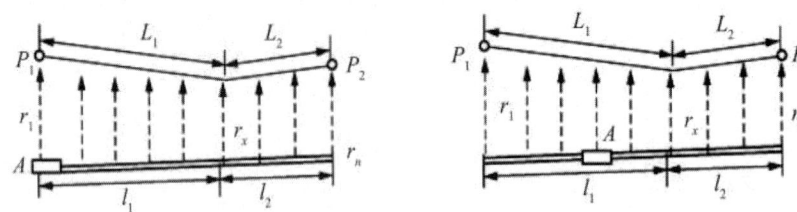

图1-2-5 线路工程路径为折线时，平行供应方式示意图

此时平均远距的计算公式为

$$R = \frac{L_1(l_1 + r_1 + r_x)}{2(L_1 + L_2)} + \frac{L_2(2l_1 + l_2 + r_x + r_n)}{2(L_1 + L_2)} \tag{1-2-14}$$

$$R = \frac{L_1(l_1 + r_1 + r_x)}{2(L_1 + L_2)} + \frac{L_2(l_2 + r_x + r_n)}{2(L_1 + L_2)} \tag{1-2-15}$$

（4）案例工程一的平均运距。

如图1-0-1，汽车平均运距为

$$19 + 6 = 25（km）$$

采用折角供应方式的人力平均运距理论值为

$$20 + (40 + 55 + 55)/2 = 95（m）$$

再考虑平地地形的道路弯曲系数取1.05，案例工程一的人力平均运距为

$$95 \times 1.05 = 100（m）$$

（二）土石方工程

土石方工程的计算是对尖峰、施工基面、基础坑、拉线坑、接地槽、开挖土石方量的统计，其计算方法与设计提供的具体尺寸及土质的类别相关。设计提供的尺寸是土石方量的静尺寸，还需要考虑施工操作裕度、边坡系数等。施工操作裕度及边坡系数的取值又取决于施工操作方法及土质类型。

1. 土、石质分类

（1）普通土：指种植土、黄土和盐碱土等，主要利用锹、铲即能挖掘的土质。

（2）坚土：指土质坚硬难挖掘的红土、板状黏土、重块土、高岭土，必须用铁镐、条锄挖松，再用锹、铲挖出的土质。

（3）松砂石：指碎石、卵石和土的混合体，各种不坚实的砾岩、页岩、风化岩。节理和列缝较多的岩石等（不需要用爆破方法开采的），需要用镐、撬棍、大锤、楔子等工具配合才能挖掘者。

（4）岩石：指不能用一般工具进行开挖的各类岩石，必须采用打眼、爆破或打凿才能开挖者。

（5）泥水：指坑的周围经常积水，坑的土质松散，如淤泥和泥沼等因水渗入和浸润而成泥浆，容易坍塌，需适量排水和用挡土板才能施工者。

（6）流沙：指坑的土质为沙质或分层沙质，挖掘过程中沙层有上涌现象并容易坍塌的体质，挖掘时需排水和采用挡土板才能施工者。不需排水者为干沙坑。

（7）水坑：指土质较为密实，开挖中坑壁不易坍塌，但有地下水涌出，挖掘过程中需用机械排水才能施工者。

2. 杆塔基坑、拉线坑、接地槽的开挖土石方量的计算

（1）正方体（不放边坡），其计算公式为

$$V = a^2 \times h \tag{1-2-16}$$

式中，V——土石方体积（m^3）；

h——坑深（m），其取值可参考表1-2-4；

$a(b)$——基坑的坑底宽（m），$a(b)$ = 基础底宽 + 2×每边操作裕度。

土石方开挖施工操作裕度（不包括垫层）取值列于表1-2-5。

表1-2-4　电杆埋深参考表

杆高/m	7	8	9	10	11	12	13	15	18
埋深/m	1.2	1.4	1.5	1.7	1.8	2.0	2.2	2.5	2.8

表1-2-5 施工操作裕度表

序号	名称	操作裕度/m
1	普通土、坚土坑、水坑、松砂石坑	0.2 m
2	泥水流、流沙坑、干沙坑	0.3 m
3	岩石坑有模板	0.2 m
4	岩石坑无模板	0.1 m

(2) 长方体（不放边坡，如图1-2-6所示），其计算公式为

$$V = a \times b \times h \tag{1-2-17}$$

(3) 平截方尖柱体（放边坡，如图1-2-6所示），计算公式为

$$V = \frac{h}{3} \times (a^2 + aa_1 + a_1^2) b \times h \tag{1-2-18}$$

式中，a_1（b_1）——基坑的坑口宽（m），a_1（b_1）= a（b）+ 2×h×边坡系数。

各类土、石质的边坡系数列于表1-2-6。

表1-2-6 各类土、石质的边坡系数表

坑深	土质			
	坚土 放坡系数	普通土、水坑 放坡系数	松砂石放 坡系数	泥水、流沙、岩石 放坡系数
2.0 m以内	1:0.10	1:0.17	1:0.22	不放边坡
3.0 m以内	1:0.22	1:0.30	1:0.33	不放边坡
3.0 m以上	1:0.30	1:0.45	1:0.60	不放边坡

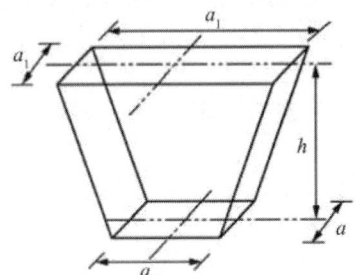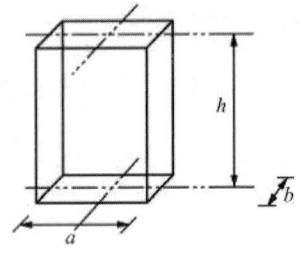

图1-2-6 长方体（不放边坡）、平截方尖柱体（放边坡）示意图

(4) 平截长方尖柱体（放边坡，如图1-2-7所示），其计算公式为

$$V = \frac{h}{6} \times [ab \times (a+a_1)(b+b_1) + a_1 b_1] \tag{1-2-19}$$

(5) 圆柱体（不放边坡，如图1-2-7所示），其计算公式为

$$V = \pi \times r^2 \times h] \tag{1-2-20}$$

式中，r——半径（m）。

（6）圆柱体连平截锥体（不放边坡，如图1-2-7所示），计算公式为

$$V = \pi r_1^2 h_1 + \frac{\pi h_1 (r_1^2 + r_2^2 + r_1 r_2)}{3} \quad (1\text{-}2\text{-}21)$$

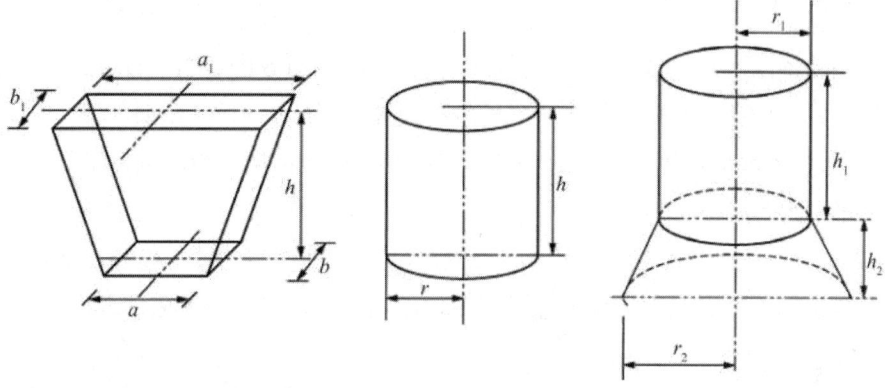

图1-2-7　平截方尖柱体（放边坡）、圆柱体（不放边坡）、圆柱体连平截圆锥体（不放边坡）示意图

（7）无底盘、卡盘的电杆坑，其计算公式为

$$V = 0.8 \times 0.8 \times h \quad (1\text{-}2\text{-}22)$$

如果$h \geqslant 1.5 \text{ m}$时，按放边坡处理。带卡盘的电杆，如原计算坑的尺寸不能满足安装时，因卡盘超长而增加的土石方量另计。

（8）接地槽土石方量，其计算公式为

$$V = 0.4 \times 长度 \times 槽深 \quad (1\text{-}2\text{-}23)$$

（9）马道的土石方量定额为0.2 m^3。

说明：

1）各类土、石质按设计地质资料确定，不做分层计算。同一坑、槽、沟内出现两种或两种以上不同土、石质时，则一般选用含量较大的一种确定其类型。出现流沙层时，不论其上层土质占多少，全坑均按流沙坑计算。

2）挖掘过程中因少量坍塌而多挖的，或石方爆破过程中因人力不易控制而多爆破的土石方工作量已包括在定额内。

3）接地槽土、石方量计算中，如遇接地装置需加降阻剂时，当设计无规定时，槽宽可按0.6 m计算。

4）回填土均按原挖原填和余土就地平整考虑，不包括100 m以上的取（换）土回填和余土外运。需要时可按设计规定的换土比例和平均运距，另行套用火峰挖方和工地运输定额。

5）余土处理，一般工程不予考虑，需要时，可考虑余土运至允许堆弃地，其运距超过100 m以上部分可列入工地运输。

余土运输量的计算：

①灌注桩钻孔渣土：按桩设计零米以下部分体积（m³）×1.7 t/m³（其中0.2 t/m³为含水量）计算；

②现浇和预制基础基坑余土：按混凝土体积（m³）×1.5 t/m³×30%计算；

③掏挖式、挖孔桩基础基坑余土：按混凝土体积（m³）×1.5 t/m³计算。

6）泥水、流沙坑的挖填方已分别考虑了必要的排水和挡土板的装拆工作量，套用定额时，不再另计。

7）人力开凿岩石坑是指在变电所、发电厂、通信线、电力线、铁路、居民点以及国家级的风景区等附近受现场地形或客观条件限制，设计要求不能采用爆破施工者。

8）几种特殊条件的规定：

①冻土厚度≥300 mm者，冻土层的挖方量，按坚土挖方定额乘以2.5的系数，其他土层仍按地质规定套用原定额；

②岩石坑挖填，如需要排水，可按挖填方（岩石）人工定额乘以1.05的系数；

③在线路复测分坑中遇到高低腿杆、塔，按相应定额乘以1.5的系数，三联杆定额乘以1.5的系数；跨越房屋每处另外增加0.7工日计算；

④挖孔桩基坑、掏挖式基础基坑若是岩石地质的，套用岩石嵌固基坑开挖的相应定额（原只针对自立式铁塔）；

⑤挖孔桩基坑、掏挖式基础基坑若是松砂石地质的，按相应的挖孔桩基坑、掏挖式基础基坑坚土定额乘以1.3的系数。

3. 案例工程一的土石方量统计

案例工程一包括3基电杆坑和2基拉线坑，杆高12 m。

底盘基础的尺寸为$D0.8×0.8×0.17$，

$$a=0.8+2×0.2=1.2 \text{（m）}$$

因杆高12 m，依据表1-2-4，h取2.0 m

因为$h>1.5$ m，考虑放坡系数（取$\mu=0.17$），

$$a_1=a+2×h×\mu$$
$$=1.2+2×2×0.17$$
$$=1.88 \text{（m）}$$
$$V=h/3（a^2+a×a_1+a_1^2）+0.2$$
$$=2/3（1.2^2+1.2×1.88+1.88^2）+0.2$$
$$=5.02 \text{（m}^3\text{）}$$

所以电杆坑 3 基土石方量共计 15.06 m³。

拉线盘尺寸为 $L0.8×0.4×0.15$，

$$a=0.8+2×0.2=1.2（m）$$
$$b=0.4+2×0.2=0.8（m）$$

h 取 1.8 m，所以

$$a_1=a+2×h×\mu$$
$$=1.2+2×1.8×0.17$$
$$=1.81（m）$$
$$b_1=b+2×h×\mu$$
$$=0.8+2×1.8×0.17$$
$$=1.41（m）$$
$$V=h/6[a×b+（a+a_1）×（b+b_1）+a_1×b_1]$$
$$=1.8/6[1.2×0.8+（1.2+1.81）×（0.8+1.41）+1.81×1.41]$$
$$=3.05（m^3）$$

所以拉线坑 2 基土石方量共计 6.10 m³。

（三）基础工程

基础工程涉及的内容包括预制基础、现浇基础、钢管桩基础等。预制基础需要统计底盘、卡盘、拉线盘个数；现浇基础需要统计钢筋混凝土用量。由于在 20 kV 及以下配电网工程中大量采用预制基础，在此主要介绍预制基础工程量统计，现浇基础及其他基础将在相关章节介绍。

案例工程一的基础工程包括 3 块底盘，2 块拉线盘。

（四）杆塔工程

杆塔组立内容包括木杆组立、混凝土杆组立、钢管杆组立、铁塔组立。在 20 kV 及以下配电网系统中大量采用的是混凝土杆，因而在此我们主要讲述混凝土杆的相关工程量统计。

混凝土杆杆塔工程的工程量首先要考虑的是混凝土杆组立有多少基，其中整根式有多少，分段式有多少，在案例工程一中 3 基混凝土杆组立，均为整根式；因为没有分段式混凝土杆，不需要考虑钢圈焊接的工程量；根据设计图纸统计横担、绝缘子安装数目，在此单根横担安装 5 组，双根横担安装 2 组；合成绝缘横担 10 组（直线杆 3 组，耐张杆 7 组），耐张绝缘子 9 只，并且有 2 根拉线；最后根据设计统计接地装置的数目，此项工程的案例工程一的接地装置为1套。

（五）架线工程

架线工程按照导线材质和架设方式的不同分为裸铝绞线、钢芯铝绞线、绝缘铜绞线、绝缘铝绞线、钢绞线、集束导线架设，低压架空电力电缆敷设，导线跨越及进户线架设。案例工程一采用铝芯交联聚乙烯绝缘导线（JKLYJ-10 kV-50），所以统计其全长3倍架设长度，在考虑导线松弛度及预留线长度增加20%，再考虑1.8%的损耗，导线量为

$$3\times150\times（1+20\%）\times（1+1.8\%）=550（m）$$

该工程还跨越公路1处，跨低压380 V线路1处。

（六）杆上变配电设备安装

杆上变配电设备安装的内容包括杆上油浸式变压器、非晶式变压器、单项变压器安装，杆上配电装置安装，接地环及绝缘护罩等安装。案例工程一牵涉的工作内容不多，仅包括杆上断路器1台、隔离刀闸1组、避雷器1组、电流互感器1台、干式变压器1台。

二、电缆工程

（一）电缆沟槽及保护管敷设

电缆沟槽及保护管敷设属于电缆建筑工程，其内容包括破路面、直埋电缆沟槽挖填土及移动盖板、电缆保护管铺设、顶过路钢管。

电力电缆的敷设方式有直埋敷设、穿管敷设、浅槽敷设、电缆沟敷设、电缆隧道敷设、空敷设等几种方式。根据敷设方式不同，其土石方量的计算有一定区别。由于该工程仅仅埋敷1根10 kV的电力电缆，且在道路边缘不易有经常性开挖的地段，采用直埋敷设方式。

1. 破路面

破路面的工程量统计主要考虑其路面材质，路面材质分别为混凝土路面，沥青混凝土路面，沙石、碎石路面，人行道预制板，人行道彩色预制板路面五种。

（1）混凝土路面，沥青混凝土路面，沙石、碎石路面，人行道（彩色）预制板路面，可根据实际路面种类分别按路面厚度，以"m^2"为单位计算。设计文件未说明的，可按下列公式计算。

直埋电缆沟槽开挖路面面积为

$$S=D \times L \tag{1-2-24}$$

式中，D——开挖沟槽路面宽度，一般宽度 $D=0.6+0.17(n-1)$，n 为敷设电缆根数；

L——开挖沟槽路面长度。

（2）人行步道预制板路面厚度按 60 mm 考虑，人行步道彩色预制板路面厚度按 120 mm 考虑，无论实际厚度的多少，均不做调整。以开挖面积"m^2"为单位计算。

（3）当市区人行步道预制板路面成"品"字形铺设，在开挖路面计算宽度时，可根据沟槽实际开挖平均宽度计算（包括交叉重叠部分）。

案例工程一电缆敷设于小区边缘，为沙石、碎石路面，其工程量为

$$D=0.6（m）$$

$$S=0.6 \times 150=90（m^2）$$

2. 直埋电缆沟槽挖填土及移动盖板

直埋电缆沟槽挖填土，直埋电缆除特殊要求外，可按表 1-2-7 计算土方量。

表 1-2-7　直埋电缆的挖土石方量

项目	电缆根数	
	1～2 根	每增 1 根
每米沟长挖方量/m^3	0.45	0.153

（1）两根以内的电缆沟，按上口宽度 600 mm，下口宽度 400 mm，深度 900 mm 计算，土方量为

$$(0.6+0.4) \times 0.9/2=0.45（m^3）$$

（2）每增加一根电缆，其宽度增加 170 mm，增加土方量为

$$0.17 \times 0.9=0.153（m^3）$$

案例工程一的土石方量为 $0.45 \times 150=67.5（m^3）$。

3. 密封电缆保护管安装

工程量统计其根数，在案例工程一中为 1 根。

（二）电缆敷设

1. 电力电缆敷设

电缆敷设属于电缆安装工程，其中电力电缆敷设内容包括直埋式电力电缆敷设，

电缆沟（隧）道内电力敷设，排管内电缆敷设，电力电缆沿支架、沿墙卡设。

案例工程一为直埋式电力电缆敷设，所以统计其工程量为 150 m。

2. 电缆头制作安装

电缆头制作安装的内容包括电力电缆终端头、电力电缆中间头、肘形电力电缆终端头的制作安装。其工程量统计分户内和户外的终端头制作安装，电力电缆中间头制作安装，或热（冷）缩头和肘形电力电缆终端头制作安装，以"套/三相"为单位计算。案例工程一包括户内与户外的终端头各 1 套。

（三）电缆防火

电缆防火内容包括防火堵料、防火隔板、防火槽盒、防火带、防火墙的安装。其中：

(1) 防火带按防火带设计长度以"100 m"为单位计算；

(2) 防火堵料以堵料的重量"t"为单位计算；

(3) 防火隔板以隔板的面积"m^2"为单位计算；

(4) 防火涂料以涂料的重量"kg"为单位计算；

(5) 防火槽盒按槽盒设计长度以"100 m"为单位计算；

(6) 防火墙按墙面的垂直投影面积以"m^2"为单位计算，不扣除孔洞面积。

案例工程一采用防火堵料，为 0.03 t。

（四）电缆试验

电缆试验内容包括电缆绝缘摇测、直流耐压试验、交流耐压试验、电阻比试验、电缆局放试验。电缆试验按"回路"为单位计算，在案例工程一中均为 1 回路。

1-2-8　工程量汇总表

序号	名称	单位	数量	备注
	工地运输——人力运输			
1	混凝土预制品	t·km	0.102	
2	混凝土杆	t·km	0.448	
3	金具、绝缘子、零星钢材	t·km	0.043	
4	线材	t·km	0.02	
5	电缆	t·km	0.052	
	工地运输——汽车装卸			

续表

序号	名称	单位	数量	备注
6	混凝土预制品	t	1.02	
7	混凝土杆	t	4.48	
8	金具、绝缘子、零星钢材	t	0.43	
9	线材	t	0.19	
10	电缆	t	0.52	
	工地运输——汽车运输			
11	混凝土预制品	t·km	25.5	
12	混凝土杆	t·km	112	
13	金具、绝缘子、零星钢材	t·km	10.75	
14	线材	t·km	4.75	
15	电缆	t·km	13	
	土石方工程			
16	电杆坑	m³	15.06	
17	拉线坑	m³	6.10	
	基础安装			
18	底盘安装	块	3	
19	拉盘安装	块	2	
	杆塔组立			
20	混凝土杆组立	基	3	
21	单根横担安装	组	5	
22	双根横担安装	组	2	
23	绝缘横担安装——直线杆	组	3	
24	绝缘横担安装——耐张杆	组	7	
25	绝缘子安装	只	9	
26	拉线安装	根	2	
27	角钢接地体制作	t	0.045	
28	接地极安装	根	6	
	架线工程			
29	导线架设	m	550	
30	导线跨越	处	2	

续表

序号	名称	单位	数量	备注
	杆上变配电设备			
31	隔离开关	组	1	
32	断路器	组	1	
33	避雷器	组	1	
34	电流互感器	组	1	
35	变压器	组	1	
	电缆工程			
36	破路面	m²	90	
37	电缆沟槽挖填土	m³	67.5	
38	密封电缆保护管	根	1	
39	电缆防火	t	0.03	

任务3 套用定额填表

定额是指根据一定时期的生产力水平，在正常施工条件下完成合格产品所必需的人工、材料、机械设备及资金消耗的数量标准。按照定额编制程序和用途可以将其分为投资估算指标、概算定额或概算指标、预算定额、施工定额。其中施工定额是指一种工种在一定时期内的建筑施工技术水平和条件下，完成某一计量单位的合格产品（如打桩、砌砖、浇筑混凝土等）所需的人工、材料和施工机械台班消耗量的标准，其反映该段时间劳动生产力水平。预算定额是在施工图设计阶段编制施工图设计预算的依据，由施工定额综合扩大而成。概算指标是编制初步设计概算和修正概算的依据，是以预算定额为基础，根据通用图和标准图等资料，经过适当综合扩大编制而成的。投资估算指标是在可行性研究阶段作为技术经济比较或建设投资估算的依据，是由概算定额综合扩大和统计资料分析编制而成的。

在施工图预算时选用预算定额。预算定额由人工定额、材料定额和施工机械台班定额组成。人工定额是指工序人工消耗量，包括基本用工和其他用工，单位为综合工日。人工单价包括人工基本工资及工资性补贴，人工定额乘以人工单价等于人工费。材料定额是指工序材料消耗量，即直接消耗在安装工作内容中的材料使用量和规定的损耗量，包括计价材料和未计价材料，材料数量乘以材料单价即得材料费。施工机械台班定额是指在某一工序施工中，按施工企业正常合理的机械配备——机械化程度所用各种机械（包括上下班用车）的数量，施工机械台班定额乘以台班单价等于机械费，或称施工机械使用费。

一、架空线路工程

架空线路工程的所用定额选择2016版《20 kV及以下配电网工程预算定额》（第三册 架空线路工程）。该定额于2017年1月3日由国家能源部发布，是现行配电网工程概预算的基础依据。定额基准工日单价为：普通工43.0元/工日，建筑工程技术工61.0元/工日，安装专业技术工65.0元/工日。线路专业技术工为68.0元/工日，带电作业技术工为120.0元/工日

土石方工程、基础工程属于建设工程项目，依据定额完成建筑工程单位工程预算表。而杆塔工程、架线工程、杆上变配电装置属于安装工程，依据定额完成安装工程

单位工程预算表。

(一) 土石方工程

依据定额，土石方工程内容包括线路复测及分坑，电杆坑、拉线坑、自立式铁塔坑的挖方（或爆破）及回填，接地槽的挖方（或爆破）及回填，排水沟开挖，尖峰及施工基面挖方。其中，该项目涉及的内容有线路复测及分坑，电杆坑、拉线坑的挖方（或爆破）及回填。

1. 线路复测与分坑

线路复测与分坑的工作内容包括：复测桩位及挡距，测定坑位、坑界及施工基面，主桩或辅助桩遗失或变动后的恢复，平、断面的校核，工器具的移运。

线路复测与分坑定额如表1-3-1所示。

表1-3-1 线路复测与分坑定额（摘至20kV及以下配电网工程预算定额第三册）

单位：基

定额编号		PX2-1	PX2-2	PX2-3	PX2-4	PX2-5	PX2-6
项目		单杆	直线双杆	耐张（转角）双杆	直线自立塔	耐张（转角）自立塔	跨越房屋（处）
基价/元		35.76	53.68	72.78	64.74	87.90	13.60
其中	人工费 材料费 机械费	14.19 20.36 1.21	20.34 31.52 1.82	30.27 40.08 2.43	35.00 27.01 2.73	52.50 31.45 3.95	13.60
名称	单位	数量					
人工	普通工 技术工（安装）	工日 工日	0.09 0.21	0.13 0.30	0.19 0.45	0.22 0.52	0.33 0.78	0.40
计价材料	圆钉 普通磁漆 木桩 竹桩	kg kg 个 个	0.010 0.020 5.000 16.000	0.010 0.020 8.000 24.000	0.010 0.030 9.000 35.000	0.010 0.025 8.000 16.000	0.010 0.030 10.000 16.000	
机械	送电专用载重汽车装载重量4t	台班	0.004	0.006	0.008	0.009	0.013	

案例工程一中均为单杆，所以选择定额PX2-1，即定额基价35.76元，其中人工费14.19元、定额材料费20.36元、机械费1.21元；将工程量3基带入，计算金额得107.28

元。其中人工费42.57元、定额材料费61.08元、机械费3.63元。填入建筑工程单位工程预算表，见表1-3-2。

表1-3-2 土石方工程——单位工程预算表

序号	编制依据	项目名称	单位	数量	设备单价	定额基价 金额	定额基价 其中工资	其中主要材料	设备费	费用合计 金额	费用合计 其中人工费	其中主要材料
二		架空线路工程										
1		土石方工程										
	PX2-1	线路复测与分坑 单杆	基	3.00		35.76	14.19			107.28	42.57	
	PX2-7	电杆坑挖方（或爆破）及回填 普通土 坑深2.0m以内	m³	15.06		11.46	10.37			172.59	156.17	
	PX2-7	拉线坑挖方（或爆破）及回填 普通土 坑深2.0m以内	m³	6.10		11.46	10.37			69.91	63.26	
		小计								349.78	262.00	

2. 电杆坑、拉线坑、铁塔坑挖方（或爆破）及回填

先根据土质选择定额，再依据所挖土方的坑深选定定额。（案例工程一主要为普通土，选择定额PX2-7、PX2-8、PX2-9，由于电杆坑与拉线坑坑深均在2.0m以内，因而都选定PX2-7（定额基价11.46元，其中人工费10.37元、机械费1.09元），再利用前面计算出的工程量，计算得出：电杆坑计算金额172.59元，其中人工费156.17元、机械费16.42元；拉线坑计算金额69.91元，其中人工费63.26元、机械费6.65元。填入表1-3-2。

通过计算可得到土石方工程的直接人工费是349.78元，其中人工费为262.00元、定额材料费为61.08元、机械费为26.70元。

（二）基础工程

1. 工地运输

因为在20kV及以下配电线路工程项目划分中没有将工地运输单独列项，而是分散在各个项目中分别计算，所以在有材料运输的项目中一一统计。基础工程的项目内容包括材料运输，于是将相应材料的工地运输内容添加在该项目中。

(1) 定额规定，工地运输定额内容包括人力运输、汽车运输、船舶运输。各种运输方式的平均运距均以"km"为单位，材料重量均以"t"为单位。

(2) 人力运输

根据平均人力运距选择所需定额。该工程平均人力运距为200m，选择定额PX1-2；其工作内容是：线路器材外观检查，绑扎及运送，卸至指定地点，运毕返回；单位是：t·km。

根据运输物品的种类，选定所需定额填入对应的表中，再将前面所计算的工程量填入。在基础工程中运输的主材主要是混凝土预制品（拉线棒属于零星钢材类，但工程量太小，仅0.01 t，在其放到杆塔工程工地运输一起统计），选定定额编号为PX1-2，前面已经算出其运输重量为1.02 t，运距为0.1 km，即为0.102 t·km，得出费用19.51元，其中人工费17.75元、机械费1.76元。填入表1-3-3中。

(3) 汽车运输

汽车运输定额内容包括装卸，运输。直接根据运输物品的种类，选定所需定额填表。因为运输的是混凝土预制品，所以选择定额PX1-24，PX1-25，带入其工程量（运输重量1.02t、运距25km）得出汽车运输及装卸的金额为84.27元，其中人工费16.52元、材料费0.52元、机械费67.23元。填入表1-3-3中。

2. 预制基础

预制基础包括底盘和拉线盘安装两部分，根据底盘单块重量为274kg，选择定额PX3-3，即底盘每块重量300kg以内；拉线盘（96kg）选择PX3-8（拉线盘每块重量200kg以内），根据其工程量计算出预制基础金额为78.80元，其中人工费57.16元、机械费21.64元。填入表1-3-3中。

3. 拉线棒防腐

拉线棒防腐根据其防腐方式选择PX3-80（沥青清漆防腐），得出拉线棒防腐的安装费是6.12元，其中人工费2.04元、材料费4.08元。

由前面的计算可以得出基础工程总费用是188.70元，其中人工费93.47元、材料费4.60元、机械费90.63元。填入表1-3-3中。

(三) 杆塔工程

定额规定杆塔工程的内容包括木杆组立，混凝土杆组立，撑杆及钢圈焊接，钢管杆组立，铁塔组立，横担及绝缘子安装，拉线制作及安装，接地安装。杆塔工程属于安装工程，其定额的选择及费用的计算填入安装工程单位工程预算表。

表1-3-3 基础工程——单位工程预算表

序号	编制依据	项目名称	单位	数量	设备单价	定额基价 金额	定额基价 其中工资	其中主要材料	设备费	费用合计 金额	费用合计 其中人工费	其中主要材料
二		架空线路工程										
2		基础工程										
	PX1-2	人力运输 平均运距500m以内 混凝土预制品	t·km	0.102		191.29	173.98			19.51	17.75	
	PX1-24	汽车运输 混凝土预制品 装卸	t	1.02		50.62	10.20			51.63	10.40	
	PX1-25	汽车运输 混凝土预制品 运输	t·km	25.5		1.28	0.24			32.64	6.12	
	PX3-3	预制基础 底盘安装 每块重量（kg）300以内	块	3.00		21.26	15.88			63.78	47.64	
	PX3-8	预制基础 拉线盘安装 每块重量（kg）300以内	块	2.00		7.51	4.76			15.02	9.52	
	PX3-80	拉线棒防腐 沥青清漆防腐	根	2.00		3.06	1.02			6.12	2.04	
		小计								188.7	93.47	

1. 工地运输

（1）人力运输

在杆塔组立项目中，运输的材料包括混凝土杆和金具、绝缘子、零星钢材，其中混凝土杆运输定额编号为PX1-1，根据材料汇总表算出其运输重量为4.48 t，运距为0.1 km，即为0.448 t·km，得出费用100.37元，其中人工费90.55元、机械费9.82元；金具、绝缘子、零星钢材运输定额选择PX1-6，案例工程一由于工程量较小，所以把各个项目中的零星钢材均在此进行统计，由主材汇总表可得出其运输重量为0.43 t，运距为0.1 km，即为0.043 t·km，得出费用4.42元，其中人工费4.01元、机械费0.41元。填入表1-3-4中。

(2) 汽车运输

汽车运输材料与人力运输一样包括混凝土杆和金具、绝缘子、零星钢材,其中混凝土杆装卸、运输选择定额编号为PX1-22、PX1-23,已知其装卸、运输的重量为4.48 t,运距为25 km,即为112 t·km,得出费用为527.16元,其中人工费73.43元、材料费32.97元、机械费420.76元。装卸、运输选择定额编号为PX1-34、PX1-35,已知其装卸、运输的重量为0.43 t,运距为25 km,即为10.75 t·km,计算出此项费用。填入表1-3-4中。

2. 混凝土杆组立

案例工程一为整根式12 m混凝土杆,选择定额PX4-4,定额规定线路一次施工工程量按5基以上电杆考虑的,如5基以内者,其人工、机械定额乘以系数1.3;所以在此进行定额调整。定额人工费调整为:215.22×1.3=279.79(元),机械费调整为:128.19×1.3=166.65(元),定额调整为450.79元。杆塔工程工程量为3基,可得出混凝土杆组立金额为1352.37元,其中人工费839.37元、材料费13.05元、机械费499.95元。填入表1-3-4中。

3. 横担及绝缘子安装

案例工程一需要安装5组单根横担,双根横担2组;合成绝缘横担10只,耐张绝缘子9串。所以选择定额PX4-33、PX4-34、PX4-35、PX4-36、PX4-49,算出其费用为381.75元,其中人工费345.53元、材料费33.52元、机械费2.7元。填入表1-3-4中。

4. 拉线制作及安装

案例工程一需要安装2组拉线,根据拉线的截面选择定额PX4-53(截面70 mm²以内)、PX4-58,算出拉线制作及安装项目金额是65.58元,其中人工费60.18元,材料费5.4元。填入表表1-3-4。

5. 接地安装

案例工程一的接地一处,选择定额PX-59(接地体加工及制作)、PX4-60、PX4-68、PX4-69,再带入工程量计算出所需金额并填入表1-3-4中。

(四)架线工程

1. 工地运输

(1) 人力运输

在架线工程中,运输的材料包括线材和一些金具、零星钢材,其中金具、零星钢

表1-3-4 杆塔工程——单位工程预算表

序号	编制依据	项目名称	单位	数量	单价 设备	单价 主要材料	单价 定额基价	单价 其中工资	合价 设备	合价 主要材料	合价 安装费	合价 其中工资
二		架空线路工程										
1		杆塔工程										
	PX1-1	人力运输 平均运距500m以内 混凝土杆	t·km	0.448			224.05	202.13			100.37	90.55
	PX1-22	汽车运输 混凝土杆 装卸	t	4.48			81.42	7.89			364.76	35.35
	PX1-23	汽车运输 混凝土杆 运输	t·km	112			1.45	0.34			162.4	38.08
	PX1-6	人力运输500m以内金具绝缘子零星钢材	t·km	0.043			102.76	93.23			4.42	4.01
	PX1-34	汽车运输 金具绝缘子零星钢材 装卸	t	0.43			38.5	9.04			16.56	3.89
	PX1-35	汽车运输 金具绝缘子零星钢材 运输	t·km	10.75			1.48	0.34			15.91	3.66
	PX4-4 调整	混凝土杆组立 整根式 13m以内	基	3			450.79	279.79			1352.37	839.37
	PX4-33	横担安装 铁、木横担 单根	组	5			20.6	16.86			103	84.3
	PX4-34	横担安装 铁、木横担 双根	组	2			31.67	26.57			63.34	53.14
	PX4-35	横担安装 瓷横担 直线杆	组	3			11.63	11.24			34.89	33.72
	PX4-36	横担安装 瓷横担 耐张杆	组	7			22.87	22.48			160.09	157.36
	PX4-49	绝缘子安装	只	9			2.27	1.89			20.43	17.01
	PX4-53	拉线制作安装 截面70mm²以内	根	2			28.72	26.02			57.44	52.04
	PX4-58	拉线制作安装 拉线保护管筒	根	2			4.07	4.07			8.14	8.14

续表

序号	编制依据	项目名称	单位	数量	单价 设备	单价 主要材料	单价 定额基价	单价 其中工资	合价 设备	合价 主要材料	合价 安装费	合价 其中工资
	PX-59	接地体加工及制作	t	0.045			228.64	132.08			10.29	5.94
	PX4-60	接地极安装 土	根	6			10.06	9.15			60.36	54.9
	PX4-62	接地体敷设 50以内	基	1			30.54	24.96			30.54	24.96
	PX4-68	混凝土杆高空接地引下线	根	1			44.74	13.73			44.74	13.73
	PX4-69	电阻测量	基	1			24.75	9.57			24.75	9.57
		小计									1389.25	850.92

材运输已放在杆塔工程中计算，线材的运输定额编号为PX1-5，根据材料汇总表算出其运输重量为0.19 t，运距为0.1 km，即为0.019 t·km，得出人力运输金额为5.42元。其中人工费4.86元、机械费0.56元。见附录1表三甲。

（2）汽车运输

线材的汽车运输与装卸定额为PX1-32、PX1-33，根据其工程量算出运输金额为23.12元，其中人工费3.76元、材料费0.23元、机械费19.13元。见附录1表三甲。

2. 导线架设

根据线路的种类和截面选择相应的定额。案例工程一采用JKLYJ-10kV-50绝缘导线，选择定额PX5-17（绝缘铝绞线截面95以内），根据前面计算的工程量算出此项金额为340.01元，其中人工费215.77元、材料91.68费、机械费32.56元。由于导线跨越公路1处，跨低压380V线路1处。选择定额PX5-40（导线跨越电力、公路、通信），可算出导线跨越金额为1095.14元，其中人工费700.30元、材料费325.52元、机械费69.32元。见附录1表三甲。

（五）杆上变配电设备安装

根据杆上安装的设备选择定额。案例工程一安装了断路器、避雷器、隔离刀闸，电流互感器，选择定额PX6-13，PX6-14，PX6-16，PX6-24，而干式变压器参考电气设备安装工程定额PD1-7（10kV干式变压器安装 容量500kVA以下），再根据工程量算出安装金额。见附录1表三甲。

二、电缆工程

电缆工程的所用定额选择2009版《20kV及以下配电网工程预算定额》(第四册 电缆工程)。电缆工程中电缆沟工程属于基础工程,而电缆敷设、电缆防火、调试与试验属于安装工程。

(一)电缆沟工程

1. 材料运输

(1)人力运输

电缆属于线材,因而选择定额PX1-5,根据材料汇总表算出其运输重量为0.52 t,运距为0.1 km,即为0.052 t·km,得出人力运输金额14.82元,其中人工费13.29元、机械费1.53元。见附录1 表三乙。

(2)汽车运输

电缆的汽车运输与装卸定额选择PX1-32,PX1-33,根据其工程量算出汽车运输金额。见附录1 表三乙。

2. 电缆沟工程

根据工程情况分析知道在案例工程一中所采用的定额包括破路面,直埋式电缆沟槽挖填土及移动盖板,密封电缆保护管安装。破路面根据路面的种类及厚度选择PL1-5(沙石、碎石路面厚度在150 mm以内),根据已经计算的工程量(90 m²)得出此项金额为558元,其中人工费554.4元、机械费3.6元;直埋式电缆沟槽挖填土根据土质的类型选择PL1-9(普通土)。根据其工程量(67.5 m³)可算出此项金额为834.30元,其中人工费749.93元、材料费2.70元、机械费81.67元。密封电缆保护管安装定额根据保护管尺寸选择PL1-39(Φ200以内),工程量为1根,所以金额为429.38元,其中人工费86.49元、材料费342.89元。见附录1 表三乙。

(二)电缆敷设

在案例工程一中所需要选用的定额包括直埋式电力电缆敷设(10kV)、户外热(冷)缩式电力电缆终端头制作安装(10kV)、户内热(冷)缩式电力电缆终端头制作安装(10kV)。根据电缆截面(50 mm²)选择PL3-1(截面50 mm²以内),PL4-1(截面50 mm²以内),PL4-5(截面50 mm²以内)。根据已经计算的工程量(150 m,因为此项定额单位为100m/三相,所以在此取值1.5)得出直埋式电力电缆敷设金额为560.28

元,其中人工费348.81元、材料费74.60元、机械费136.87元;1套户外热(冷)缩式电力电缆终端头制作安装金额158.80元,其中人工费124.40元、材料费34.40元;户内热(冷)缩式电力电缆终端头制作安装金额为74.29元,其中人工费39.89元、材料费34.40元。见附录1表三甲。

(三)电缆防火

电缆防火定额根据防火方式选择,案例工程一采用防火堵料,选择定额PL6-1(防火堵料),算出电缆防火金额70.12元,其中人工费59.57元、材料费10.55元。见附录1表三甲。

(四)电缆试验

电缆试验定额选择依据试验的类型,在案例工程一中选择了PL8-1(绝缘摇测),PL8-3(交流耐压试验),PL8-4(电阻比试验),PL8-5(局放试验)。其试验回路均为1,计算出电缆试验的金额。见附录1表三甲。

任务4　工程费用表

一、费用构成（根据预规）

配电网工程建设预算费用由建筑工程费、安装工程费、设备购置费、其他费用和动态费用构成，其中建筑工程费、安装工程费、设备购置费和其他费用之和称为静态投资。

二、取费标准

（一）建筑、安装工程费

建筑工程是指构成建设项目的各类建筑物、构筑物等设施工程。安装工程是指构成生产工艺系统的各类设备、管道、线缆及其辅助装置的组合、装配和调试工程。

建筑安装工程费是指对构成项目的基础设施、工艺系统及附属系统进行施工、安装、调试，使之具备生产功能所支出的费用。

建筑安装工程费由直接费、间接费、利润和税金组成。

计算公式为

$$建筑安装工程费=直接费+间接费+利润+税金 \qquad (1-4-1)$$

1. 直接费

直接费是指建筑安装产品生产过程中直接消耗在特定产品对象上的费用，由直接工程费和措施费组成。

计算公式为

$$直接费=直接工程费+措施费 \qquad (1-4-2)$$

（1）直接工程费。直接工程费是指按照正常的施工条件，在施工过程中耗费的构成工程实体的各项费用，包括人工费、材料费和施工机械使用费。

计算公式为

$$直接工程费=人工费+材料费+施工机械使用费 \qquad (1-4-3)$$

计算标准：依据《20 kV及以下配电网工程预算定额》计算，并按照电力工程定额管理规定，调整到建设预算编制年水平。详见附录1中表三甲、表三乙，建筑、安装工程单位工程预算表。

1）人工费。人工费是指直接为从事建筑安装工程施工的生产工人开支的各项费用，包括基本工资、工资性补贴、辅助工资、职工福利费、生产工人劳动保护费等。

①基本工资是指发放给生产人员基本工资，包括生产技术人员的岗职工资、工龄工资或工龄补贴、岗位津贴等。

②工资性补贴是指按规定标准发放的伙食补贴，物价补贴，煤、燃气补贴，交通补贴，以及流动施工津贴等。

③辅助工资是指生产工人年有效施工天数以外非作业天数的工资，包括职工学习、培训期间的工资，调动工作、探亲、休假期间的工资，因气候影响的停工工资，病假在六个月以内的工资，以及产、婚、丧假期间的工资，女工哺乳期间的工资。

④职工福利费是指按规定标准计提的职工福利费。

⑤生产工人劳动保护费是指按规定标准发放的劳动保护用品的购置费及修理费，服装补贴，防暑降温费，在有碍身体健康环境中施工的防护费用等。

人工费标准：普通工为34元/工日，建筑技术工48元/工日，安装技术工53元/工日，各地区、各年度人工费的调整应按照总站颁布的规定执行。

人工费的计算由建筑、安装工程单位工程预算表中的各项内容的人工费合计得出。比如土石方工程项目的人工费就是其人工费合计（见附录1表三乙土石方工程），为262元。

2）材料费。材料费是指施工过程中耗费的原材料、辅助材料、构配件、零件、半成品，以及施工过程中一次性消耗材料及摊销材料的费用。

配电网工程建设预算中的材料费包括主要材料费和消耗性材料费两部分。

①主要材料费。主要材料费是指构成工艺系统实体的原材料、辅助材料、构配件、零件、半成品等工艺性材料。一般情况下，主要材料指施工过程中必需的并在建设预算定额中未计价的材料，也称为未计价材料或装置性材料。

主要材料费的计算公式为

$$主要材料费=主要材料消耗量×材料信息价格 \qquad (1-4-4)$$

主要材料预算价格，应按照施工现场物料仓库的出库价格、项目管理单位集中存储仓库的出库价格或电力行业定额管理机构公布的材料信息价取定。

主要材料消耗量的统计由各项工程的建筑、安装工程单位工程预算表中主要材料合计算出。比如土石方工程没有主要材料，主要材料费为零。

②消耗性材料费。消耗性材料费是指施工过程中所消耗的、在建设成品中不体现其原有形态的材料，以及因施工工艺及措施要求需要进行摊销的材料。一般情况下，

消耗性材料指预算定额中，费用已经计入定额基价的材料，也称为计价材料费或定额材料费。

消耗性材料费的计算，根据《20kV及以下配电网工程预算定额》规定的原则计算，并根据相关价格水平调整规则调整到建设预算编制年水平。定额材料费是由各定额中材料费合价相加而获取的。例如土石方工程定额材料费为61.08元（见附录1表三乙土石方工程）。

3）施工机械使用费。施工机械使用费是指施工机械作业所发生的机械使用费以及机械的安拆和场外移动费用。内容主要包括：折旧费、大修理费、经常修理费、安装及拆卸费、场外运费、操作人员人工费、燃料动力费及车船税费等。

施工机械使用费按照《20 kV及以下配电网工程预算定额》规定的原则计算。

①折旧费是指施工机械在规定的使用年限内，陆续收回其原值及购置资金的时间价值，按照国家规定计提的成本费用。

②大修理费是指施工机械按规定的大修理间隔台班进行必要的大修理，以恢复其正常功能所需的费用。

③经常修理费是指施工机械除大修理以外的各级保养和临时故障排除所需的费用。包括为保障机械正常运转所需替换设备、零件的费用，随机配备工具、附具的摊销和维护费用，机械运转中日常保养所需润滑与擦拭的材料费用，以及机械停滞期间的维护和保养费用等。

④安装及拆卸费是指施工机械在现场进行安装与拆卸所需的人工、材料、机械费用，试运转费用，以及辅助设施的折旧、搭设、拆除等费用。

⑤场外运费是指施工机械整体或分体自停放地点运至施工现场或由原施工地点运至另一施工地点所发生的运输、装卸、辅助材料等费用。

⑥操作人员人工费是指机上司机（司炉）和其他操作人员的基本工资、工资性补贴、辅助工资、职工福利费、生产工人劳动保护费等。

⑦燃料动力费是指施工机械在运转作业中所消耗的固体燃料（煤、木柴）、液体燃料（汽油、柴油）、气体燃料，以及水、电、气体等所花费的费用。

⑧车船税费是指施工机械按照国家行政主管部门规定应缴纳的车船税、保险费及年检费等费用。

工程预算中机械费的获得由各项定额中机械费合价计算获得。例如土石方工程机械费为26.70元（见附录1表三乙土石方工程）。

根据已经得出的人工费、材料费、机械费，可算出直接工程费。例如土石方工程直接工程费为349.78元。将结果填入建筑、安装工程单位工程预算表，如表1-4-1所示。

表1-4-1 建筑工程单位工程预算表

单位：元

序号	编制依据	项目名称	单位	数量	设备单价	定额基价 金额	定额基价 其中工资	其中主要材料	设备费	费用合计 金额	费用合计 其中人工费	其中主要材料
二		架空线路工程										
1		土石方工程										
		小计								349.78	262.00	
(一)		直接费	%	100		400.37				400.37		
1		直接工程费	%	100		349.78				349.78		
1.1		人工费	%	100		262.00				262.00		
1.2		材料费	%	100		61.08				61.08		
1.2.1		定额材料费	%	100		61.08				61.08		
1.2.2		装材费	%	100								
1.3		施工机械使用费	%	100		26.70				26.70		
2		措施费	%	100		50.59				50.59		
2.1		临时设施费	%	8.83		262.00				23.13		
2.2		安全文明施工措施费	%	3.25		262.00				8.52		
2.3		施工工具用具使用费	%	2.28		262.00				5.97		
2.4		冬雨季施工增加费	%	4.95		262.00				12.97		
2.5		夜间施工增加费	%			262.00						
2.6		特殊地区施工增加费	%			262.00						
(二)		间接费	%	100		159.48				159.48		
1		规费	%	100		99.48				99.48		
1.1		社会保障费	%	25.93		262.00				67.94		
1.2		住房公积金	%	10.2		262.00				26.72		
1.3		危险作业意外伤害保险费	%	1.84		262.00				4.82		
2		企业管理费	%	22.9		262.00				60.00		
(三)		利润	%	15		262.00				39.30		
(四)		税金	%	3.41		599.15				20.43		
		合计	%	100		619.58				619.58		

（2）措施费。措施费是指为完成工程项目施工，发生于该工程施工前和施工过程中非工程实体项目的费用。

内容包括：临时设施费、安全文明施工措施费、施工工具用具使用费、冬雨季施工增加费、夜间施工增加费、特殊地区施工增加费。

计算公式为

措施费=临时设施费+安全文明施工措施费+施工工具用具使用费

+冬雨季施工增加费+夜间施工增加费+特殊地区施工增加费　（1-4-5）

1）临时设施费。临时设施费是指施工企业为满足工程现场正常的管理和施工作业需要，在现场必须搭设的办公、生产作业、轮班休息、物料（含工具）存放等用的临时建筑物、构筑物以及施工用移动电源、水电管线、简易防雨（防晒）遮挡等其他临时设施所发生的费用。

内容包括：临时设施的搭设、维修、拆除、折旧及摊销费，或临时设施的租赁费等。

计算公式为

$$临时设施费=人工费×费率 \quad (1-4-6)$$

临时设施费率见表1-4-2。

表1-4-2　临时设施费费率表

工程类别		建筑工程	安装工程
费率%	城区	8.83	13.14
	郊区	7.65	11.61
	乡村	6.32	10.42

例如，土石方工程的人工费为262.00元，则其临时设施费为

262.00×8.83%=23.13（元）

2）安全文明施工措施费。安全文明施工措施费是指根据电力行业安全文明施工与健康环境保护规范的要求，在施工现场所采取的安全文明保障措施所支出的补助费用。

计算公式为

$$安全文明施工措施费=人工费×费率 \quad (1-4-7)$$

表1-4-3　安全文明施工措施费费率（%）

工程类别	建筑工程	安装工程
费率%	3.25	6.56

以土石方工程为例，其安全文明施工措施费为

262.00×3.25%=8.52（元）

3）施工工具用具使用费。施工工具用具使用费是指施工企业生产、检验、试验部门使用的不属于固定资产的工具用具的购置、摊销和维护费用。此处所说的施工工具

用具不包括现场管理部门使用的管理工具和管理用具。

计算公式为

$$施工工具用具使用费 = 人工费 \times 费率 \quad (1-4-8)$$

表1-4-4 施工工具用具使用费费率

工程类别	建筑工程	安装工程
费率%	2.28	4.13

以土石方工程为例，施工工具用具使用费为

$$262.00 \times 2.28\% = 5.97（元）$$

4）冬雨季施工增加费。冬雨季施工增加费是指按照正常的施工组织计划安排，必须在冬季、雨季期间进行施工时需要增加的费用，包括在冬季施工期间，为确保工程质量而采取的保温及养护措施、为防风防寒而采取的遮挡和采暖措施等所发生的费用；雨季施工期间，采取防雨、防潮措施所增加的费用；因冬季、雨季施工增加的劳动保护措施费用；以及施工工效降低而发生的补偿费用。

计算公式为

$$冬雨季施工增加费 = 人工费 \times 费率 \quad (1-4-9)$$

表1-4-5 冬雨季施工增加费

地区分类		Ⅰ	Ⅱ	Ⅲ	Ⅳ	Ⅴ
费率%	建筑工程	4.46	4.95	5.63	6.84	8.12
	安装工程	6.22	6.63	7.45	8.66	9.88

案例工程一所属地区属于Ⅱ类地区，建筑及安装工程的冬雨季施工增加费率分别取4.95%和6.63%。

以土石方工程为例，冬雨季施工增加费为

$$262.00 \times 4.95\% = 12.97（元）$$

5）夜间施工增加费。夜间施工增加费是指按照规程要求，工程必须在夜间连续施工的单项工程所发生的夜班补助、夜间施工降效、夜间施工照明设备摊销及照明用电等费用。

计算公式为

$$夜间施工增加费 = 人工费 \times 费率 \quad (1-4-10)$$

案例工程一无夜间施工要求，不考虑此项费用。

6）特殊地区施工增加费。特殊地区施工增加费是指在高海拔、酷热、严寒等地区施工，因特殊自然条件影响而需额外增加的施工费用。

计算公式为

$$特殊地区施工增加费 = 人工费 \times 费率 \quad (1\text{-}4\text{-}11)$$

高海拔地区、高纬度寒冷地区、酷热地区：

①高海拔地区指平均海拔高度在3000 m以上的地区。

②高纬度寒冷地区指北纬45°以北地区。

③酷热地区指面积在10000 km²以上的沙漠地区，以及新疆吐鲁番地区。

案例工程一是普通城市工程，不属于特殊地区，不考虑此项费用。

2. 间接费

间接费是指建筑安装产品的生产过程中，为全工程项目服务而不直接消耗在特定产品对象上的费用，由规费和企业管理费组成。

计算公式为

$$间接费 = 规费 + 企业管理费 \quad (1\text{-}4\text{-}12)$$

（1）规费。规费是指按照国家行政主管部门规定必须缴纳的费用，电力工程应计列的规费内容主要包括：社会保障费、住房公积金和危险作业意外伤害保险费。

计算公式为

$$规费 = 社会保障费 + 住房公积金 + 危险作业意外伤害保险费 \quad (1\text{-}4\text{-}13)$$

1）社会保障费。社会保障费是指按照国家建立社会保障体系的有关要求，施工企业必须为职工交纳的保险、保障费用，由养老保险费、失业保险费和医疗保险费组成。

计算公式为

$$社会保障费 = 人工费 \times 0.85 \times 缴费费率 \quad (1\text{-}4\text{-}14)$$

①缴费费率是指工程所在省（自治区、直辖市）社会保障机构颁布的以工资总额为基数计取的基本养老保险、失业保险和基本医疗保险费率之和。

②此处的0.85系数也称为工资总额综合折算系数。

在此社会保障费率取25.93%。以土石方工程为例，社会保障费为

$$262 \times 25.93\% = 67.94（元）$$

2）住房公积金。住房公积金是指施工企业为职工缴纳的住房公积金。

计算公式为

$$住房公积金 = 人工费 \times 0.85 \times 住房公积金缴费费率 \quad (1\text{-}4\text{-}15)$$

案例工程一中企业住房公积金缴费费率为12%，住房公积金取费标准为0.85×

12%=10.2%。以土石方工程为例，住房公积金为

$$262×10.2\%=26.72（元）$$

3）危险作业意外伤害保险费。危险作业意外伤害保险费是指按照建筑法规定，企业为从事危险作业的建筑安装施工人员支付的意外伤害保险费。

计算公式为

$$危险作业意外伤害保险费=人工费×1.84\% \quad (1-4-16)$$

以土石方工程为例，危险作业意外伤害保险费为

$$262×1.84\%=4.82（元）$$

（2）企业管理费。企业管理费是指施工企业组织施工生产和经营管理所发生的费用，其费用内容包括管理人员工资，办公经费，差旅交通费，劳动补贴费，员工招募及队伍调遣费，工会经费，职工教育经费，固定资产使用费，财产保险费，办公车辆的车船税费、燃料费，管理机构工具用具使用费，建筑工程定点复测费，工程点交、场地清理费，检验试验费，工程排污费，工程保护与现场物资看管费，技术转让与技术开发费，公证费，法律顾问费，咨询费，广告费，业务招待费，劳动安全卫生检测费，企业按规定缴纳的房产税、土地使用税、印花税等。

计算公式为

$$企业管理费＝人工费×费率 \quad (1-4-17)$$

表1-4-6　企业管理费费率

工程类别	建筑工程	安装工程
费率%	22.9	35.2

1）管理人员工资是指支付给管理人员的基本工资、工资性补贴、辅助工资、职工福利费、劳动保护费等。

2）办公经费是指企业正常管理办公所使用的文具、纸张、账表、印刷、邮电、通信、书报等费用，以及施工现场的会议费、水电费、燃气费、集体取暖费、防暑降温费、卫生保洁等费用。

3）差旅交通费是指职工因公出差、调动工作的差旅费、住勤补助费，市内交通费和误餐补助费，职工探亲路费，劳动力招募费，职工离退休、退职一次性路费，工伤人员就医路费等。

4）劳动补贴费是指由企业支付离退休职工的易地安家补助费、职工退职金，六个月以上的病假人员工资，职工死亡丧葬补助费、抚恤费，按规定支付给离休干部的各

项经费。

5）员工招募及队伍调遣费是指施工企业招募员工所支出的费用，以及派遣施工队伍和施工机械到工程现场所发生的往返调遣费用。

6）工会经费是指施工企业根据国家行政主管部门有关规定，按照职工工资总额计提的工会经费。

7）职工教育经费是指为保证职工学习先进技术和提高文化水平，根据国家行政主管部门有关规定，施工企业按照职工工资总额计提的费用。

8）固定资产使用费是指施工企业管理和试验部门使用的属于固定资产的房屋、设备、仪器等折旧、大修、维修或租赁费。

9）财产保险费是指施工企业为管理用财产、车辆进行保险而支付的保险费用。

10）办公车辆的车船税费及燃料费是指施工企业为管理办公用车辆支付的车船税费及燃料费等。

11）管理机构工具用具使用费是指管理机构和人员使用的不属于固定资产的工具、器具、家具和检验、试验、测绘、消防用具等的购置、维修和摊销费。

12）建筑工程定点复测费是指规划部门对建筑物进行重新定位、检验所交纳的费用。

13）工程点交、场地清理费是指施工企业在工程竣工之后，对工程进行清点移交和现场清理所发生的费用。

14）检验试验费是指对建筑材料、构件和建筑安装产品进行一般性鉴定、检查所发生的费用。

15）工程排污费是指按照工程所在地行政主管部门的相关规定，对施工过程中产生污染物进行处理或向环境防治部门缴纳排污费所支出的费用。

16）工程保护与现场物资看管费是指施工企业从进场至工程竣工移交的正常施工期间，对已完工程、在建工程和现场物资等进行维护、看管所支出的费用。

17）劳动安全卫生检测是指按照国家劳动安全管理规定，施工企业接受劳动安全管理部门对企业进行安全资格认定、特种设备安全检测、劳动卫生检测、劳动安全培训考核所发生的费用。

以土石方工程为例，企业管理费为

$$262 \times 22.9\% = 60（元）$$

3. 利润

利润是指施工企业完成所承包工程获得的盈利。

计算公式为

$$利润 = 人工费 \times 利润率 \qquad (1\text{-}4\text{-}18)$$

表1-4-7 利润率

工程类别	建筑工程	安装工程
费率%	15	22

以土石方工程为例，利润为

$$262 \times 15\% = 39.30（元）$$

4. 税金

税金是指按照国家税法规定，应计入建筑安装工程造价内的营业税、城市维护建设税及教育费附加等。

计算公式为

$$税金 = （直接费 + 间接费 + 利润）\times 税率 \qquad (1\text{-}4\text{-}19)$$

税率按照工程所在地税务部门的规定计算，在此取3.41。

以土石方工程为例，税金为：

$$（400.37 + 159.48 + 39.30）\times 3.41\% = 20.43（元）$$

将架空线路工程的土石方工程、基础工程和电缆线路工程的电缆沟工程三个项目的费用算出后，汇总成建筑工程专业汇总表（见附录1表二乙）；而将架空线路工程的杆塔工程、架线工程、杆上变配电装置和电缆线路工程的电缆敷设、电缆防火、调试与试验六个项目的费用汇总成安装工程专业汇总表（见附录1表二甲）。

（二）设备购置费

设备购置费是指购置组成工艺流程的各种设备，并将设备由交货地点或项目管理单位集中储备仓库运至施工现场指定位置所支出的购置及运杂费用。

计算公式为

$$设备购置费 = 设备费 + 设备运杂费 \qquad (1\text{-}4\text{-}20)$$

1. 设备费

设备费是指按照设备供货价格（招标合同交货价格、协议交货价格）购买设备所支付的费用（包括包装费）。

设备费的计算原则：当设备供应方式为由项目管理单位集中储备仓库提货并配送

到安装地点时,设备价格可以取项目管理单位集中存储仓库的出库价格。

2. 设备运杂费

设备运杂费是指设备交货地点或项目管理单位集中储备仓库运至施工现场指定位置所发生的费用,其内容包括设备的装卸费、运输费、运输保险费以及保管费等。

计算公式为

$$设备运杂费=设备费×设备运杂费率 \quad (1-4-21)$$

设备运杂费率:运输距离在20km以内,费率为1.1%;运距超过20km时,每增加10km费率增加0.15%,不足10km按10km计取。供货商直接供货到现场的,只计取卸车费及保管费,按设备费的0.7%计算。

案例工程一汽车运距为25km,所以运杂费率取1.25%,填入表1-2-3得出设备购置费。再将设备购置费填入附录1表二甲,完成安装工程专业汇总表。

(三)其他费用

其他费用是指为完成工程项目建设所必需的不属于建筑工程费、安装工程费、设备购置费的其他相关费用,包括建设场地征用及清理费、项目建设管理费、项目建设技术服务费、工程建设监督检测费、生产准备费、基本预备费。

计算公式为

$$其他费用=建设场地征用及清理费+项目建设管理费+项目建设技术服务费$$
$$+工程建设监督检测费+生产准备费+基本预备费 \quad (1-4-22)$$

1. 建设场地征用及清理费

建设场地征用及清理费是指为获得工程建设所必需的场地并达到正常施工条件和施工环境而发生的有关费用,主要包括土地征用补偿费、余物清理费、施工场地租用费、线路施工赔偿费。

计算公式为

$$建设场地征用及清理费=土地征用补偿费+余物清理费+施工场地租用费$$
$$+线路施工赔偿费 \quad (1-4-23)$$

(1)土地征用补偿费。土地征用补偿费是指按照《土地法》和《物权法》的规定,项目法人为取得工程建设用地的使用权而发生的费用,包括土地补偿费、地上附着物和青苗补偿费、林木赔偿费、安置补助费、勘测定界费、征地管理手续费、证书费以及各种基金和税金等。

案例工程一中无此项支出。

(2) 余物清理费。余物清理费是指为满足工程建设需要,对所征用土地范围内原有的建筑物、构筑物等有碍工程建设的设施进行拆除、清理所发生的各种费用。

案例工程一中无此项支出。

(3) 施工场地租用费。施工场地租用费是指为保证工程建设期间的正常施工而临时租用场地所发生的费用,包括场地的租金、清理和复垦费等。

案例工程一中无此项支出。

(4) 线路施工赔偿费。线路施工赔偿费是指架空送电线路施工过程中,对线路走廊内非征用和租用土地上的建筑物、构筑物、林木、经济作物等造成不可避免的破坏而进行赔偿所发生的费用。或电缆线路工程施工中由挖掘地面、路面等发生的赔偿费用。

案例工程一中无此项支出。

2. 建设项目管理费

建设项目管理费是指建设项目经国家行政主管部门核准后,自项目筹建至竣工验收合格,并移交生产的合理建设期内对工程进行组织、管理、协调、监督等工作所发生的费用,包括项目管理经费、招标费、工程监理费。

计算公式为

$$项目建设管理费=项目管理经费+招标费+工程监理 \quad (1\text{-}4\text{-}24)$$

(1) 项目管理经费。项目管理经费是指项目管理单位在项目管理工作中发生的日常管理费用,主要包括项目建设相关手续的申办费,日常办公经费,差旅交通费,固定资产使用费、工具用具使用费,技术图书资料费、工程档案管理费、办公水电费,工程组织协调费,合同订立与公证费,法律顾问费,咨询费,工程审价(结算)费,会议费,业务接待费,印花税,以及设备材料的配送组织、建设项目劳动安全验收评价、工程竣工测量、交接验收、竣工审计、编制竣工决算等日常工作经费。

计算公式为

$$项目管理经费=(建筑工程费+安装工程费)\times 1.15\% \quad (1\text{-}4\text{-}25)$$

建筑工程费、安装工程费、设备购置费可以根据建筑、安装工程专业汇总表计算,案例工程一的建筑工程费与安装工程费之和为66909.47元,算出其项目管理费769.46元。

(2) 招标费。招标费是指按照国家有关规定,组织或委托具有资质的机构编制、审查标书、标底,以及委托具有招标代理资质的机构对各项采购及承包项目进行招标所发生的费用。

计算公式为

工程招标费=（建筑工程费+安装工程费+设备购置费）×0.32%　　（1-4-26）

案例工程一的建筑工程费、安装工程费与设备购置费之和为232101.89元，计算其招标费742.73元。

（3）工程监理费。工程监理费是指依据国家有关规定和规程、规范要求，委托工程监理机构对建设项目全过程实施监理所支付的费用。

计算公式为

工程监理费=（建筑工程费+安装工程费）×2.55%　　（1-4-27）

3. 项目建设技术服务费

项目建设技术服务费是指为工程建设提供技术服务和技术支持所发生的费用，包括工程勘察费、工程设计费、设计文件评审费、项目后评价费、技术经济标准编制管理费。

计算公式为

项目建设技术服务费=工程勘察费+工程设计费+设计文件评审费+项目后评价费
+技术经济标准编制管理费　　（1-4-28）

（1）工程勘察费。工程勘察费是指有资质的勘察机构按照勘察设计规范要求，对项目影响范围内地质断面、地形、水文、杆塔定位、交叉跨越等进行勘察、测量作业并编制相关勘察文件等所支付的费用。

计算公式为

工程勘察费=建筑工程费×4.5%　　（1-4-29）

（2）工程设计费。工程设计费是指委托有资质的设计机构，按照工程设计规范要求，对现场进行踏勘、测量，编制工程初步设计文件、施工图设计文件、竣工图文件，以及设计代表进行现场技术服务所支付的费用。

计算公式为

工程设计费=（建筑工程费+安装工程费）×设计费费率　　（1-4-30）

表1-4-8　设计费费率取定表

设备购置、建筑安装工程费之和	设计费费率（%）
20万元以下执行最高标准	8.0
50万元以下	6.5~8.0
100万元以下	5.5~6.5
300万元以下	4.0~5.5
300万元以上	3.2~4.0
1000万元以上执行最低标准	3.2

案例工程一的设备购置、建筑安装工程费之和为23.21万元,使用插值法计算设计费费率过程如下。

假定设计费费率为x,则

$$(50-23.21)/(23.21-20)=(6.5-x)/(x-8.0)$$

$$x=7.84$$

案例工程一的设计费费率取7.84%,再代入建筑工程费与安装工程费之和66909.47元,算出工程设计费为

$$66909.47×7.84\%=5245.70(元)$$

(3) 设计文件评审费。设计文件评审费是指根据国家有关规定,项目管理单位组织或委托相关咨询、评审机构对工程项目的设计文件(包括初步设计文件、施工图设计文件)进行评审所发生的费用。

计算公式为

$$设计文件评审费=工程设计费×2.2\% \quad (1-4-31)$$

(4) 项目后评价费。项目后评价费是指根据国家有关规定,项目管理机构为了对项目决策提供科学、可靠的依据,指导、改进项目管理,提高投资效益,同时为政府决策提供参考依据,完善相关政策,在建设项目投产后对项目的决策、设计、建设管理、投资效益等方面进行综合分析、评价所支出的费用。

计算公式为

$$项目后评价费=(建筑工程费+安装工程费)×0.5\% \quad (1-4-32)$$

(5) 技术经济标准编制管理费。技术经济标准编制管理费是指为保证电力行业工程建设技术经济标准体系的正常运转,确保各项技术经济标准编制、修订、解释和研究工作的正常进行,须向电力行业技术经济标准编制管理机构支付的费用。

计算公式为

$$技术经济标准编制管理费=(建筑工程费+安装工程费)×0.2\% \quad (1-4-33)$$

4. 工程建设监督检测费

工程建设监督检测费是根据国家行政主管部门及电力行业有关规定,对工程质量、特种设备(如消防)等进行监督、检验、检测所发生的费用。

计算公式为

$$工程建设监督检测费=(建筑工程费+安装工程费)×0.3\% \quad (1-4-34)$$

5. 生产设备费

生产设备费是指为保证工程竣工验收合格后能够正常投产运行提供技术保证和资

源配备所发生的费用。主要包括工器具购置、必要的安全防护器具（不包括消防器具）、警示牌、标志牌等发生的费用。

计算公式为

$$生产准备费=（建筑工程费+安装工程费）\times 0.75\% \qquad (1-4-35)$$

6. 基本预备费。基本预备费是指为因设计变更（含施工过程中工程量增减、设备改型、材料代用）而增加费用，一般自然灾害可能造成的损失和预防自然灾害所采取的临时措施费用，以及其他不确定因素可能造成的损失而预留的工程建设资金。

计算公式为

$$基本预备费=[建筑工程费+安装工程费+设备购置费$$
$$+其他费用（不包括基本预备费）]\times 费率 \qquad (1-4-36)$$

表1-4-9 基本预备费费率

设计阶段	费率（%）
投资估算	3
初步设计概算	2
施工图预算	1

（四）动态费用

动态费用是指筹措债务资金时，在建设期内发生并按照规定允许在投产后计入固定资产原值的利息。

计算公式为

$$建设期贷款利息 = \sum[（年初借款本息累计+本年贷款/2）\times 年利率] \qquad (1-4-37)$$

输配电线路工程建设周期短、投资小，因此此项费用一般不发生。

表1-4-10 其他费用计算表

单位：元

编号	项目名称	主要内容及范围说明	合价
1	建设场地征用及清理费		
1.1	土地征用补偿费		
1.2	余物清理费		
1.3	施工场地租用费		
1.4	线路施工赔偿费		
2	项目建设管理费		3218.38
2.1	项目管理费	（建筑工程费+安装工程费）×1.15%	769.46
2.2	招标费	（建筑工程费+安装工程费+设备购置费）×0.32%	742.73
2.3	工程监理费	（建筑工程费+安装工程费）×2.55%	1706.19

续表

编号	项目名称	主要内容及范围说明	合价
3	项目建设技术服务费		6037.59
3.1	工程勘察费	建筑工程费×4.5%	208.12
3.2	工程设计费	（建筑工程费+安装工程费）×7.84%	5245.70
3.3	设计文件评审费	工程设计费×2.2%	115.41
3.4	项目后评价费	（建筑工程费+安装工程费）×0.5%	334.52
3.5	技术经济标准编制管理费	建筑工程费+安装工程费）×0.2%	133.82
4	工程建设监督检测费	（建筑工程费+安装工程费）×0.3%	200.73
5	生产准备费	（建筑工程费+安装工程费）×0.75%	501.82
6	基本预备费	[建筑工程费+安装工程费+设备购置费+其他费用（不包括基本预备费）]×1%	2420.60

任务5　总预算表

在完成了安装工程专业汇总表（表二甲）、建筑专业汇总表（表二乙）、其他费用预算表（表四）后，根据工程项目划分情况，从建筑专业汇总表取建筑工程费，从安装工程专业汇总表取设备购置费和安装工程费，再从其他费用预算表中取对应的各项费用，完成总预算表。详见附录1中相关表格。

任务6 编写预算说明

一份完整的预算书，还必须包括"编制说明"，用来交代清楚编制情况、编制依据以及一些需要说明的问题，为阅读与审核提供方便。

20kV及以下配电网工程预算书的编制说明要具体、确切、简练、规范。

其内容一般包括：

（一）工程概况。包括线路经过地区的地形、土质结构、风力、运输条件，线路型号、长度，杆塔类型，接地情况，电缆的长度、尺寸、敷设方式，等等。

（二）工程的建设范围、施工措施及费用。

（三）编制原则及依据。包括编制范围、工程量计算依据、取费定额和标准等。

（四）有关重大问题说明。

案例工程一的编制说明见附录1。

最后，按照封面、编审人员签字扉页、目录、编制说明、总预算表（表一）、安装工程专业汇总表（表二甲）、建筑专业汇总表（表二乙）、安装工程单位工程预算表（表三甲）、建筑工程单位工程预算表（表三乙）、其他费用预算表（表四）以及相应的附表、附件的顺序，编印为《20kV及以下配电网工程建设预算书》送审。

小 结

项目一主要以案例工程一为载体,介绍了编制10 kV配电线路施工图预算的方法:首先根据《20 kV及以下配电网工程建设预算编制与计算标准》进行项目划分;再针对具体项目进行各项工程量统计;然后选择定额、费率填写安装工程单位工程预算表和建筑工程单位工程预算表;依据安装工程单位工程预算表和建筑工程单位工程预算表完成总预算表、安装工程专业汇总表、建筑工程专业汇总表和其他费用预算表;最后编写预算说明,从而完成10 kV配电线路施工图预算。

实训项目一　某厂配电安装工程

一、总述

（一）设计依据

1. 受某市某厂委托，对该市某厂配电安装工程进行勘察设计。
2. 《架空绝缘配电线路设计技术规程》DL/T 601-1996。
3. 国家其他有关规程、规范。

（二）设计范围

某配电工程。

（三）工程概况

1. 在10kV某32#杆上搭火，新建12 m电杆2基，10 m电杆1基，新建线路全长125 m。

2. 在新立的N2#杆上装高压真空断路器（12 kV 630 A）1台，高压计量箱1台，油浸式变压器（S9-200 kVA/10）1台。

二、路径及交叉跨越

（一）路径概况

该工程路径见《10 kV架空线路平面布置图》，如图1-7-1。

（二）交叉跨越

本工程跨越河流1处。

（三）交通运输

本工程地处城镇，全线地形比例：平地100%；运输地形图见图1-7-1。

全线地质比例：普土80%，坚土20%。

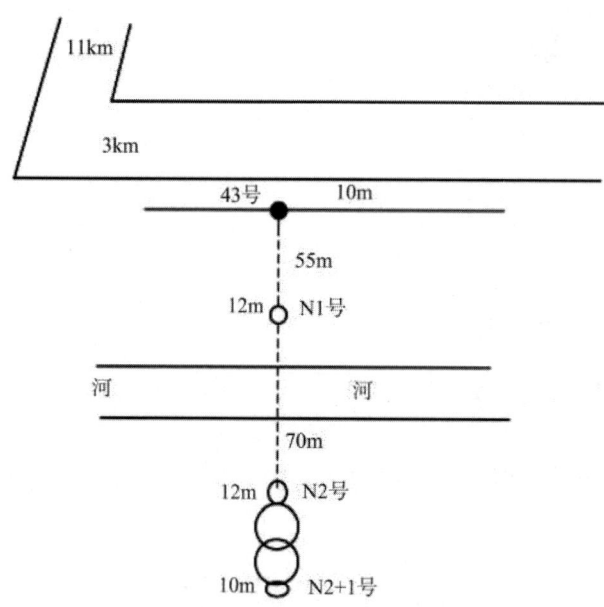

图 1-7-1　某厂配电工程架空线路平面布置图

三、机电部分

（一）设计气象条件（略）

（二）导线

本工程架空线采用 JKLYJ-10kV-50 绝缘导线。安全系数为 7.500，架空线与周围建筑物的安全距离应满足 10kV 架空线路施工和验收规范。

（三）防雷保护、绝缘配合

1. 终端杆敷设人工接地体，接地电阻满足规程要求，绝缘子串悬挂点与接地体应有可靠电气连接。

2. 水泥杆架设段绝缘子型号为 FXBW2-10/45，直线绝缘子采用 FS-10/3 合成横担绝缘子。

3. 在 N2#杆上装设氧化锌避雷器（HYW5-12.7/50）。

（四）金具

本工程全线采用国家标准电力金具。

四、杆塔及基础

（一）杆塔

本工程共使用电杆（Φ190×12000）2基，（Φ190×10000）1基。

（二）基础

本工程混凝土杆均采用D0.8×0.8×0.17的底盘基础，采用L0.8×0.4×0.15的拉线盘。

（三） 本线路配高压跌落式熔断器（12 kV 100 A）1组、避雷器1组。

（四） 本工程图纸套用《城市电网10 kV及以下工程典型设计》。

1. 施工图预算的概念是什么？
2. 什么是项目划分？项目划分的依据是什么？
3. 已知某线路工程全长18 km，运输地形为丘陵，汽车运送至B、D两点，如图1-7-3所示，试计算该工程汽车运输平均运距与人力运输平均运距。

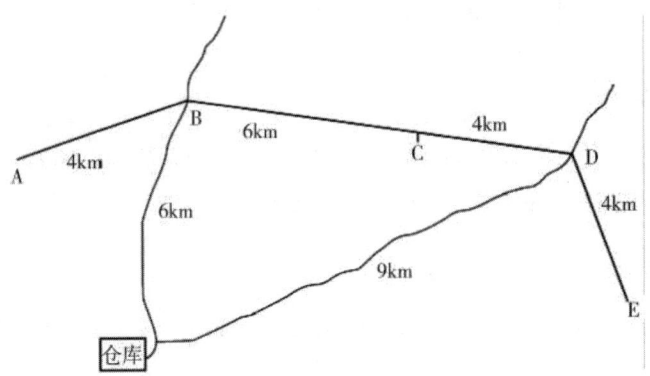

图1-7-3　某线路工程材料运输示意图

4. 某工程新立混凝土电杆11基，电杆坑深1.4 m，计算本工程的电杆土方量。
5. 新立混凝土15 m转角杆1基，拉线盘2个，埋深1.6 m，计算该混凝土杆的土石方量。
6. 某架空线路工程，路径长度5 km，跨越10 kV单回线路3处，10 kV双回线路1处，低压线路2处，计算其安装工程费。

学习项目一 编制10kV配电线路施工图预算

材 料 表

序号	名称	规格	数量	单位	重量(kg) 一件 小计
1	混凝土电杆	Φ190×12000	1	根	
2	架空绝缘线	Φ190×10000	1	根	
3	高压引线横担	JKLYJ-8.7/10-6	550	m	
4	跌落式熔断器横担	L63×6×2000	1	副	
5	避雷器横担台架	L63×6×2000	1	副	
6	避雷器横担支架	L63×6×2000	2	副	
7	台架抱箍	10×2246	2	根	
8	绝缘子	Φ266	12	只	
9	跌落式熔断器	FS-10/3	3	只	
10	避雷器	FRC-10/50	3	只	
11	变压器	HY5W-12.7/50	1	台	
12	铜铝过度线夹	S9-10/200	18	只	
13	低压引线横担	SLB-1B	1	根	
14	高压计量装置	L50×5×1000	1	套	
15	针式绝缘子	XJ-01	1	只	
16	铜绞线	PD-1T	4		
17	低压配电箱	TJ-25	40	m	
18	槽钢		1	台	
19	组合式互感器	12×12×800	2	根	
20	合成绝缘子	JLSZV-10	1	台	
21		FXBW2-10/45	3	串	

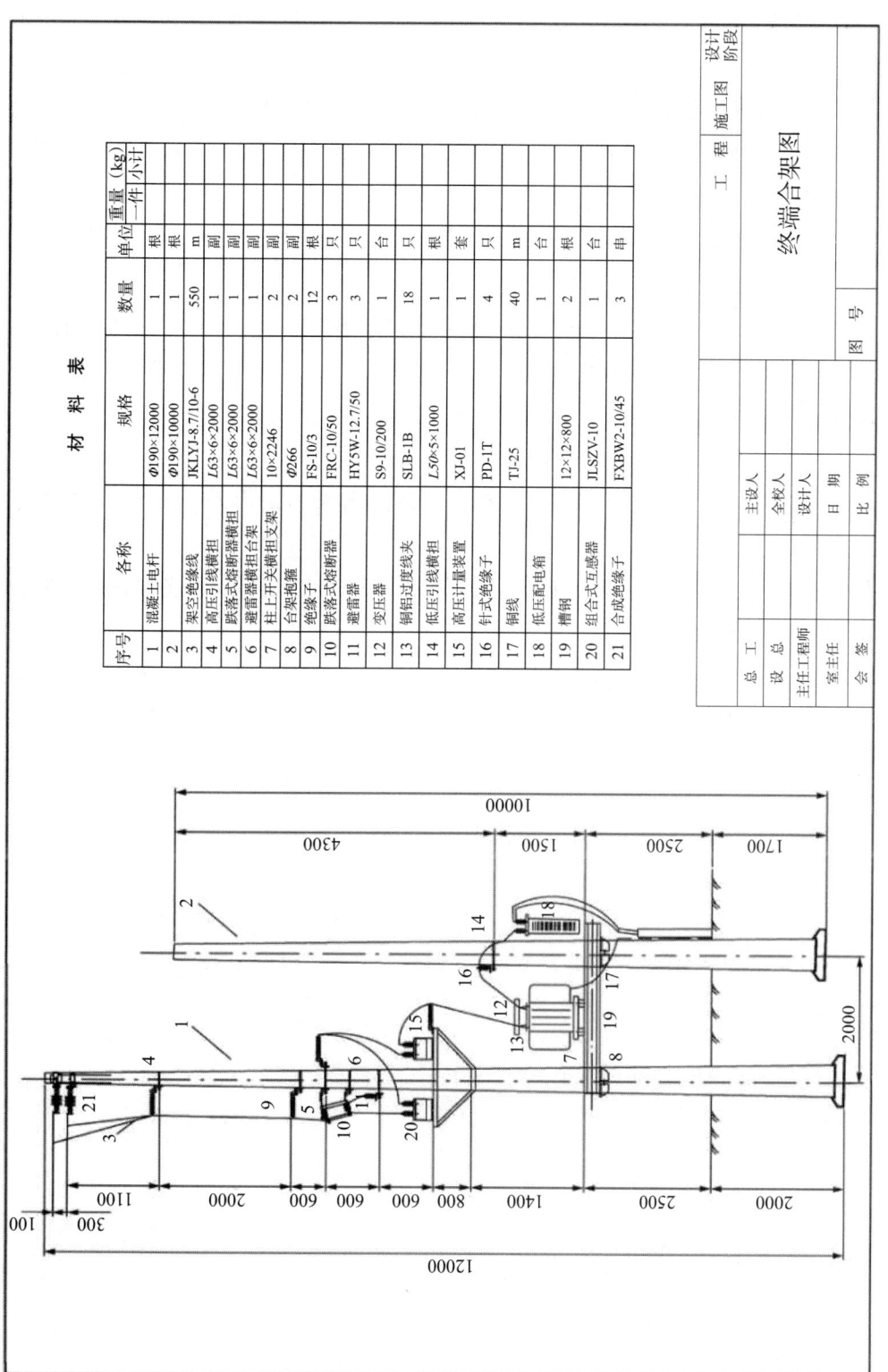

图 1-7-2 终端变压器台区

7. 某 1 kV 架空线路工程，路径长度 5 km，导线采用四芯集束 35 mm²，金具 0.1 t，计算安装工程费。

8. 某电缆工程，路径长 1 km，需同沟敷设 2 根 YJV22-3*120 mm²-10 kV 电缆，其中 100 m 路面为钢筋混凝土路面，其余为沥青路面厚度均为 150 mm，计算其路面开挖。

9. 路径长 1.5 km，需同沟敷设 4 根 YJV22-3*120 mm²-10 kV 电缆，计算其土石方开挖。

10. 某电缆工程，路径长 1 km，需同沟敷设 3 根 YJV22-0-3*120 mm²-电缆，土质全部为坚土，计算其建筑工程费用。

11. 配电网工程建设预算费用由哪些构成？

12. 建筑、安装工程费由哪些构成？

13. 某配电网工程建筑工程费为 30 万元，安装工程费为 20 万元，设备购置费为 50 万元。计算其设计费支出。

14. 配电网工程建筑工程费为 10 万元，安装工程费为 20 万元，设备购置费为 50 万元。计算其设计费支出。

15. 静态工程费与动态工程费是什么？

学习项目二

编制220 kV架空送电线路工程初步设计概算书

案例工程二 220 kV某送电线路新建工程概况

一、总述

1. 设计依据

(1) 与四川省电力公司签订的勘测设计合同。

(2) 四川省电力公司《关于某市220千伏某送电线路新建工程可行性研究报告的批复》。

(3) 某设计院对《某市220千伏某送电线路新建工程》的可行性研究报告和投标技术文件。

2. 设计范围

从某220 kV变电站（小号侧）出线构架至某220 kV变电站（大号侧）进线构架长51.8 km的220 kV单回（其中小号侧变电站出线3 km采用同塔双回设计，本期单侧挂线）2×LGJ-400/35导线送电线路本体设计，并完成工程投资概算，辅助设施工程只在本工程中列入所需费用。全线加挂OPGW（地线复合光缆）、OPGW材料及安装费计入通信工程。

二、路径及交叉跨越

线路全长约51.8 km，曲折系数1.20，途经三个县（市）行政区域，线路路径如图2-0-1。全线海拔高程为300~600 m。沿线地形北高南低，局部地段地形起伏较大，相对高差达100 m以上。地形划分为：平地7.4%，丘陵51.4%，山地41.2%。

线路沿线地层简单，主要为侏罗系遂宁组鲜红、紫红色泥岩，钙质泥岩第四系残积、残坡积黏性土。岩石一般较完整，松散堆积层状态也较好，地基土条件较好。地质划分为：岩石25%，松砂石55%，普通土16%，泥水4%。

本工程交通运输主要以区乡公路为主，全线与线路平行和交叉的机耕道较多，个别地段运输条件较差。全线汽车运输距离28 km，人力运输距离0.8 km。

全线主要交叉跨越如表2-0-1。

表2-0-1 全线主要交叉跨越表

序号	被跨越物	跨越次数
1	110kV电力线	3
2	35kV配电线	6
3	10kV配电线	32
4	380V及以下线路	146
5	广播线、通信线	86
6	公路、机耕道	44
7	小河及河沟	11
8	堰塘	7
9	嘉陵江	1

三、机电部分

1. 设计气象条件组合（略）

2. 导地线型号

导线采用2×LGJ-400/35（GB1179-83）型钢芯铝绞线。大号侧变电站进线段约8.0km采用OPGW-100与另一根良导体LBGJ-100-30AC（YB/T124-1997）铝包钢绞线成双地线，其他地段采用GJX-80（1×7-11.4-1270-A-YB/T183-2000）稀土锌铝合金镀层钢绞线与OPGW-100配合，OPGW挂在线路右侧地线支架上。

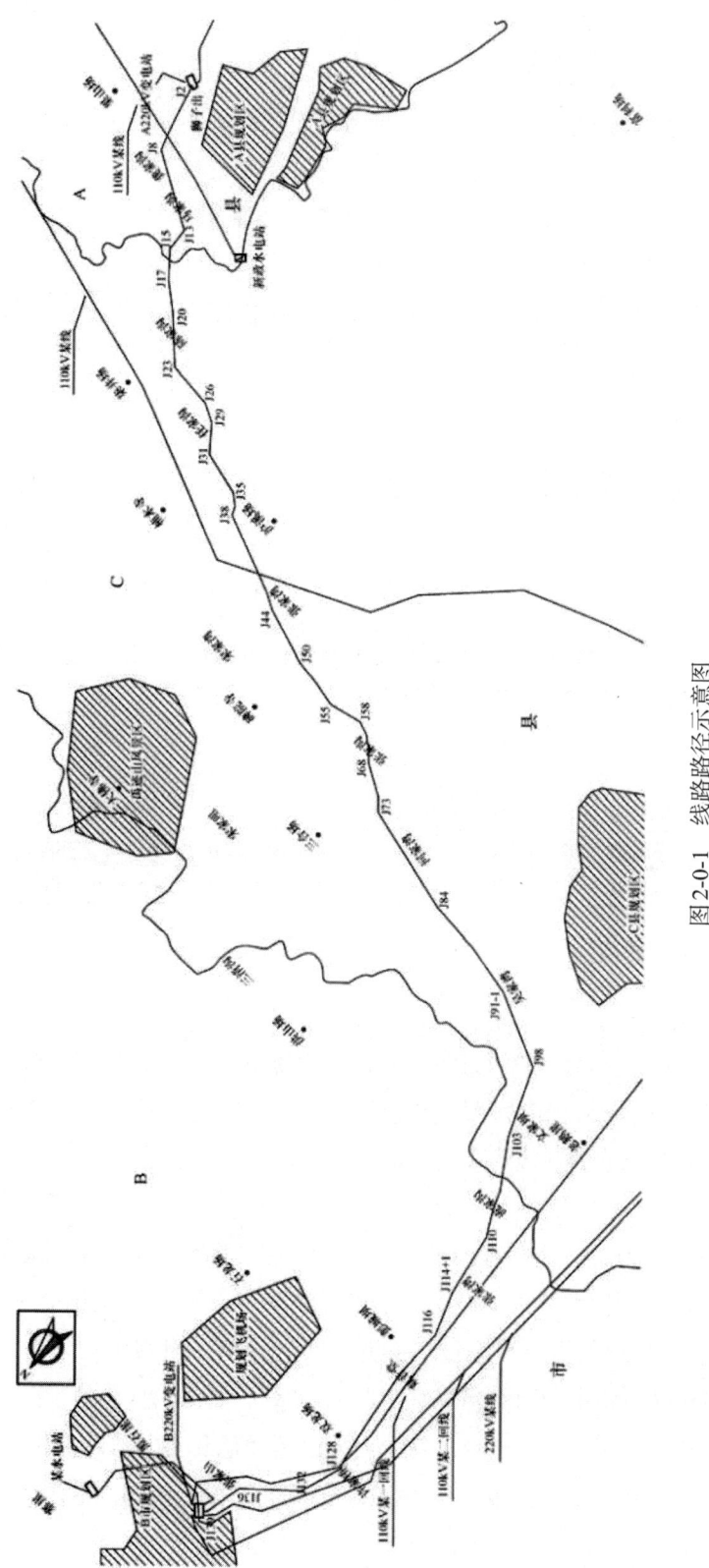

图 2-0-1 线路路径示意图

3. 相分裂导线排列形式及间距

导线为垂直排列双分裂，一般不安装间隔棒，档距大于700 m时的加装间隔棒，分裂间距为400 mm。

为方便引下线的施工，变电站进出线档分裂导线采用水平排列方式，加装间隔棒，分裂间距为400 mm。

耐张塔中相跳线采用垂直排列方式，边相跳线采用水平排列方式，加装跳线间隔棒，分裂间距为200 mm。

4. 导地线的防振

本工程导线和地线一般采用防振锤防振，对于重要的交叉跨越（包括35 kV及以上电压等级的高压送电线路，I级通讯线路，主干公路、嘉陵江等）的直线塔，除防振锤外，加装预绞丝护线条进行联合保护。防振锤使用型号及安装个数见表2-0-2。

表2-0-2　防振锤使用型号及安装个数表

线型	型号	1	2	3	4
LGJ-400/35	FD-5F	$L \leqslant 450$ m	450 m$<L \leqslant 800$ m	800 m$<L \leqslant 1200$ m	
LBGJ-100-30AC	FR-2	$L \leqslant 300$ m	300 m$<L \leqslant 600$ m	600 m$<L \leqslant 900$ m	900 m$<L \leqslant 1200$ m
GJX-80	FG-70	$L \leqslant 300$ m	300 m$<L \leqslant 600$ m	600 m$<L \leqslant 900$ m	900 m$<L \leqslant 1200$ m

5. 绝缘配合及防雷保护

（1）污秽等级的确定

本工程线路所经地区无大的污染源，根据四川省电力公司2006年出版的《四川省电力系统污区分布图》，结合现场实地调查收资情况，确定大号侧变电站进线段5 km为Ⅲ级污秽区，其余部分为Ⅱ级污秽区，按Ⅲ级污秽区下限设计。

（2）绝缘配合

本工程线路所经地带海拔高程不超过600 m，绝缘子串绝缘子片数按能耐受长期工频电压作用确定，受污秽等级的控制。本工程线路多位于丘陵、山区，运行维护条件差，为方便运行维护，设计推荐Ⅱ、Ⅲ级污区悬垂串、耐张串均采用玻璃绝缘子U100BP2，Ⅱ级污区悬垂串和耐张串分别为14和15片，Ⅲ级污区各增加一片。两端进线构架侧采用瓷质绝缘子，防止玻璃绝缘子因故自爆而危及变电站设备和运行人员。

按设计规程的规定，铁塔高度超过40 m，按高度每增加10 m，绝缘子串增加一片绝缘子设计。

本工程线路所经地段海拔高程均在600m以下，不需要特殊考虑增加空气间隙，本工程所取空气间隙值见表2-0-3。

表2-0-3　空气间隙值表

工作状态	运行电压	内过电压	外过电压	带电作业
间隙值（cm）	55	145	190	180

注：带电作业人员需要停留工作的部位，带电作业还应考虑人体活动范围30～50cm。

（3）防雷保护与接地

本工程线路所经地区年平均雷电日为40天，属中雷区。线路全线采用架设双避雷线进行防雷保护，地线采用直接接地方式。为便于线路两端变电站接地电阻的准确量测，进出线档靠门型构架侧地线耐张金具串加一片XDP-70C型无裙瓷质绝缘子。非测量状态下，应将该绝缘子短接。

接地装置。根据本工程的地质情况，接地装置采用典型设计，即环形加风车式放射形浅埋水平布置接地形式，如图2-0-2所示，与杆塔基础自然接地相结合。除甲型接地装置外，乙、丙、丁、戊、己型的形式相同，仅A取值不同，$A_乙$为5 m、$A_丙$为20 m、$A_丁$为30 m、$A_戊$为60 m、$A_己$为78 m。接地装置按土壤电阻率选用，如表2-0-4，其中丙型占10%、丁型占35%、戊型占50%、己型占5%。接地体采用Φ10圆钢，引下线采用Φ12圆钢，均要求热镀锌处理、接地引下线不得露出地面过长。按照设计规程和反措细则规定，杆塔接地电阻在雷雨季节干燥时的工频接地电阻不得超过表2-0-5中所示数值。

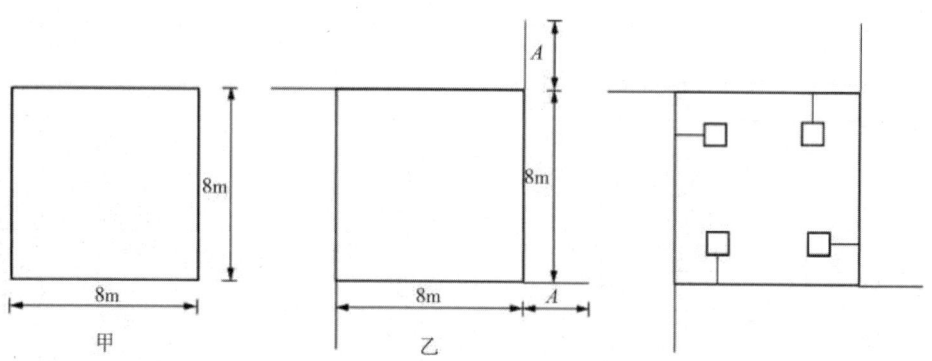

图2-0-2　接地装置形式及其与铁塔连接示意图

6. 绝缘子串及金具

玻璃绝缘子的主要尺寸及特性见表2-0-6。

导地线接续均采用液压方式。见表2-0-7，本工程使用的金具绝缘子串型及其具体使用范围，详见图2-0-5、2-0-6绝缘子金具串组装一览图。

表2-0-4 接地装置选用及其材料表

适用土壤电阻率（Ω·m）			≤100	100~300	300~500	500~1000	1000~2000	>2000
接地装置型号			甲	乙	丙	丁	戊	己
材料表	圆钢	Φ12 长度（m）	10.0	10.0	10.0	10.0	10.0	10.0
		Φ12 重量（kg）	8.88	8.88	8.88	8.88	8.88	8.88
		Φ10 长度（m）	40	60	120	160	280	352
		Φ10 重量（kg）	24.50	36.76	73.52	98.02	171.53	215.64
	扁钢 130×50×5	长度（m）	0.52	0.52	0.52	0.52	0.52	0.52
		重量（kg）	1.230	1.230	1.230	1.230	1.230	1.230
	铁塔用M16×45 镀锌螺栓及螺母	套	4	4	4	4	4	4
		重量（kg）	0.584	0.584	0.584	0.584	0.584	0.584
接地土石方量（m³）			9.6	14.4	28.8	38.4	67.2	84.5

表2-0-5 工频接地电阻取值表

土壤电阻率（Ω·m）	≤100	100~300	300~500	500~1000	1000~2000	>2000
工频接地电阻（Ω）	5	10	12	15	20	27

表2-0-6 绝缘子主要尺寸及特性表

绝缘子型号	主要尺寸			机电特性		额定机械破坏负荷（kN）
	高度（mm）	盘径（mm）	爬距（mm）	工频湿闪放电电压（kV）	全波冲击闪络电压（kV）	
U100BP2	146	280	450	45	120	100

表2-0-7 金具绝缘子串型及其具体使用范围表

序号	线型	型式	用途
1	导线	HX单联加护线条串（1′14′U100BP2）	重要跨越直线塔
2		SHX双联加护线条串（2′14′U100BP2）	大挡距直线塔
3		SHX1双联加护线条串（2′14′U100BP2）	重要跨越直线塔
4		CTX单联跳线串（1′14′U100BP2）	一般转角塔中相
5		N双联耐张串（2′15′U100BP2）	耐张转角塔
6		DN单联耐张串（1′15′U100BP2）	进出线档门型架侧
7		TDN单联耐张串加双调整板（1′15′U100BP2）	进出线档终端塔侧
8	地线	BX11单联悬垂串	一般直线塔 GJX-80
9		BX12单联悬垂串	一般直线塔 LBGJ-100-30AC
10		BN1单联耐张串	耐张、转角塔 GJX-80
11		BJN单联耐张串加绝缘子（1′1′XDP2-70C）	进线档门型架侧

7. 导线换位及相序配合

本工程线路长 51.8 km，按设计规程要求，导线不需要进行换位。因两端变电站不对应，在线路工程两侧终端塔调整相序。

8. 导线对地和交叉跨越距离

导线对地和交叉跨越距离见表 2-0-8。

表 2-0-8　导线对地和交叉跨越距离表

序号	被跨越物名称	间距（m）	备注
1	居民区	7.5	港口、城镇等人口密集地区
2	非居民区	6.5	车辆能到达的房屋稀少地区
3	交通困难地区	5.5	车辆不能到达地区
4	公路路面	8.0	
5	电力线	4.0	
6	通信线	4.0	
7	至最大自然生长高度树木顶部	4.5	
8	至最大自然生长高度果树顶部	3.5	
9	通航河流（4级）	3.0	最高航行水位的最高船桅顶
10	距百年一遇洪水位	4.0	

9. 通信保护

本工程属中性点直接接地系统，导线大多呈三角形排列。临近主要电信线路为架空光缆，经测算，本工程对影响范围内电信线路无危险、干扰影响，对临近无线电设施的危险和干扰影响均满足防护间距要求，无影响。

10. 杆塔及基础

（1）杆塔

本工程全部采用全方位不等高腿自立式铁塔，直线塔采用猫头型（呼称高为 21～42m），转角塔采用"干"字形（呼称高为 18～36 m），双回线路部分采用双回鼓形塔，塔身断面均为正方形，均选自 2005 年版《国家电网公司输变电工程典型设计》。全线选择 ZM1、ZM2、ZM3 等 12 种塔型，见表 2-0-9，参见图 2-0-3，杆塔一览图（其中，JC2、JC3、JC4 塔形同 JC1；SJ3、SJ4 塔形同 SJ1）。

表2-0-9 杆塔表选用一览表

序号	杆塔型号	适用线型截面	呼称高（m）	耗钢量（t）	备注
1	2A-ZM1	2′400复导线	27	4.88	套用（猫头形直线塔）
2	2A-ZM2	2′400复导线	33	6.32	套用（猫头形直线塔）
3	2A-ZM3	2′400复导线	39	8.04	套用（猫头形直线塔）
4	2A-ZMC3	2′400复导线	36	9.62	套用（猫头形直线塔）
5	2A-ZMC4	2′400复导线	39	11.74	套用（猫头形直线塔）
6	2A-JC1（0°~20°）	2′400复导线	30	10.47	套用（干字形耐张塔）
7	2A-JC2（20°~40°）	2′400复导线	30	11.28	套用（干字形耐张塔）
8	2A-JC3（40°~60°）	2′400复导线	30	12.49	套用（干字形耐张塔）
8	2A-JC4（60°~90°）	2′400复导线	30	14.10	套用（干字形耐张塔）
9	2I-SZ3	2′400复导线	38	14.70	套用（双回鼓形直线塔）
10	2I-SJ2（20°~40°）	2′400复导线	27	27.82	套用（双回鼓形耐张塔）
11	2I-SJ3（40°~60°）	2′400复导线	27	28.36	套用（双回鼓形耐张塔）
12	2I-SJ4（60°~90°）	2′400复导线	27	31.78	套用（双回鼓形耐张塔）

全线共计使用铁塔137基。平均挡距为0.38 km，平均耐张段长度为1.04 km，其中直线铁塔86基，平均呼称高28 m；耐张或转角铁塔51基，平均呼称高22 m。杆塔用钢材为Q235、Q345钢，连接螺栓M16螺栓为4.8级，M20和M24螺栓为6.8级。

各塔位最短腿基础立柱顶面以上、8.0m平面以下范围内的全部铁塔螺栓采用防盗螺栓，其余螺栓采取防松措施。

（2）基础

本工程所采用基础形式，是根据现场地形，结合工程地质和水文地质情况确定。沿线地震烈度为Ⅵ度，遵照《电力设施抗震设计规范》（GB50260-96），基础不考虑防震措施。全部采用钢筋混凝土现浇基础，其形式共有四大类（八种）：岩石嵌固式基础（QG）、直柱式全掏挖基础（TW）、斜柱式基础、直柱式柔性基础（LZ），如图2-0-4，基础一览图。

基础混凝土强度等级为C20和C25级，基础垫层和地脚螺栓保护帽为C10级。基础用钢材为HPB235（Q235）和HRB335（20Mnsi）级钢筋；地脚螺栓圆钢采用35号钢或16Mn钢、钢板采用Q235、Q345钢。混凝土沙、石、水、水泥（32.5普通硅酸盐水泥）均应符合相应标准规范的规定。

（3）施工说明及要求、运行维护注意事项、环境保护及水土保持措施（略）

图 2-0-3 杆塔一览图

基础材料一览表

序号	基础名称	基础代号	浇筑型式	单个基础钢材量 (kg)	单个基础砼量 (m³)	适用塔型
1	直柱式	LZ型	现浇基础	111.5~483.3	1.4~5.92	直线塔型
2	斜柱式	XC型		220.6~618.9	2.81~7.94	耐张塔型
		XCZ型		91.9~426.8	1.38~4.13	直线塔型
		XL型		276.1~1234.9	1.08~17.72	耐张塔型
		XY型		232.4~626.4	2.81~7.3	耐张塔型
3	掏挖式	TW型		43.4~118.4	2.25~4.13	所有塔型
4	嵌固式	QG型		27.0~58.3	2.51~5.33	所有塔型

说明：

（1）现浇混凝土基础钢筋采用HPB235（Ⅰ）、HRB335（Ⅱ）；底脚螺栓采用Q235、35#；混凝土强度等级：C20、C25；基础保护帽、基础垫层用C10。

（2）表中单个耗钢量未计入插入角钢和底脚螺栓的重量。

（3）表中单个耗混凝土量未计入保护帽方量。

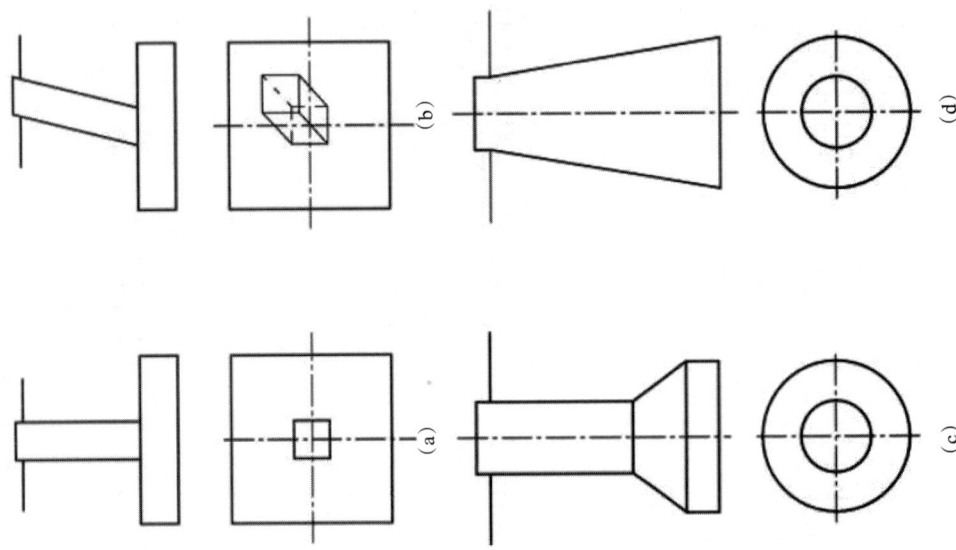

图 2-0-4 基础一览图

学习项目二 编制220kV架空送电线路工程初步设计概算书

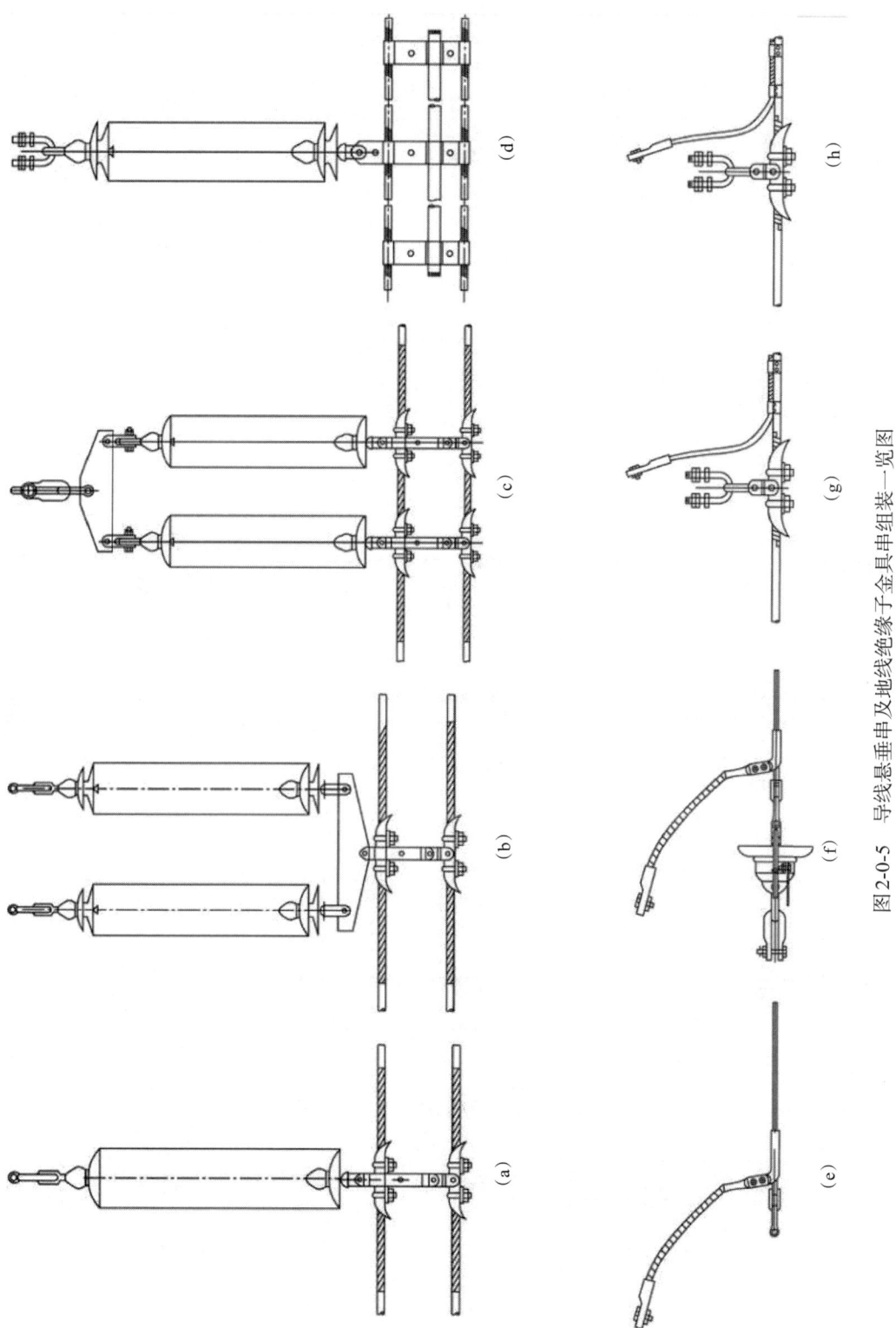

图 2-0-5 导线悬垂串及地线绝缘子金具串组装一览图

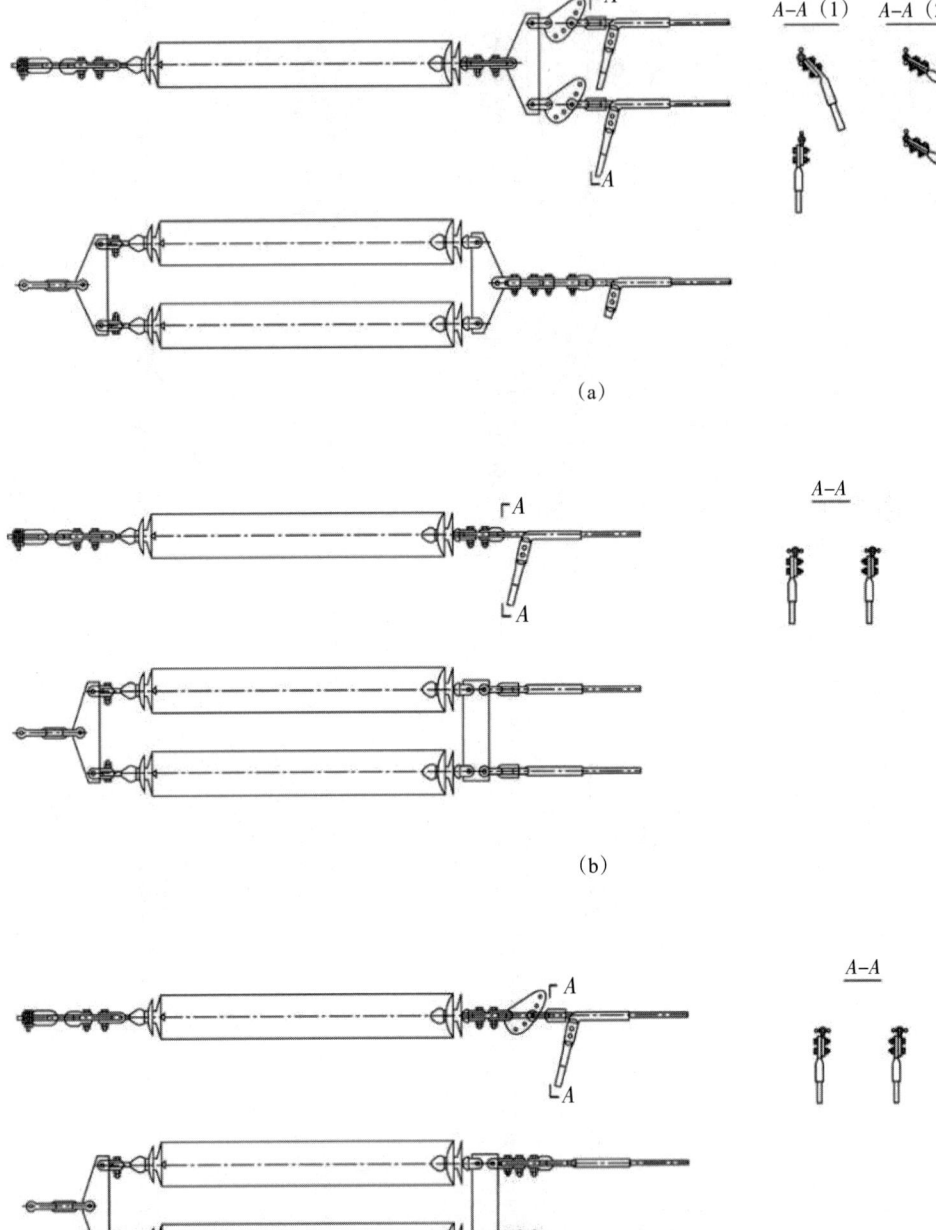

图 2-0-6 耐张绝缘子金具串组装一览图

学习项目二　编制220kV架空送电线路工程初步设计概算书

任务1　熟悉概算书的组成

要顺利完成编制送电线路工程概算书的任务，应掌握概算书的内容组成，特别是概算相关费用组成和计算标准，掌握概算编制方法和流程，明确工程项目划分，理解送电线路工程施工组织和施工方法。在具体工作中，还必须熟练使用工程定额。

一、《电网工程建设预算编制与计算标准》简介

《电网工程建设预算编制与计算标准（2007年版）》（以下简称《预标》）是电力建设预算系列标准之一，是根据《国家发展改革委关于开展电力工程造价与定额管理有关工作的函》（发改办能源〔2006〕427号）文件精神，遵照《中华人民共和国招投标法》、《建筑工程施工发包与承包计价管理办法》（建设部107号令）、《建筑安装工程费用项目组成》（建设部、财政部建标〔2003〕206号文），以及《电力建设工程量清单计价规范》（GB 50500-2003）和《电力建设工程量清单计价规范》（DL/T5205-2005）有关规定，以合理确定工程造价，提高投资效益，维护工程建设各方的合法权益，促进电力建设事业健康发展为目的，按照"国家宏观调控，市场竞争形成价格"的原则，并结合电网工程建设的特点制定的。"预规"由中国电力企业联合会提出，国家发展和改革委员会批准颁布，于2007年12月1日实施；由电力工程造价与管理总站归口管理并解释。

2007年版《预标》汲取了以往各版"预规"（即《电力工业基本建设预算管理制度和规定》）的编制经验和内容精华，继承和延续了电力工程建设预算管理体系，并充分考虑了当前电力建设管理体制下参与各方在工程建设中各自承担的职责和任务，以及各种项目管理模式的不同特点，体现了电力工程建设预算管理制度编制的适用性、时效性和公平公正性。

《预标》规定了电网工程建设预算的费用构成与计算标准、费用性质划分、预算项目划分、建设预算编制办法以及建设预算的计价格式。作为电网工程可行性研究投资估算、初步设计概算、施工图预算和电力建设工程量清单报价的编制和费用计算依据，应与电力工程投资估算指标、概算定额、预算定额和电力建设工程量清单计价规范配套使用；是编制电网工程招标标底、投标报价和工程结算的参考计算依据，同时也是调解处理工程建设经济纠纷、鉴定投标报价的基础依据。

《预标》适用于各种投资渠道新建、改建和扩建35 kV～750 kV交流送变电工

程、±500 kV及以下直流送电工程、换流站工程以及系统通信工程。

《预标》有关表内所称"××及以下",包括××在内,其下限截止低一档"××及以下"的上限之上。凡未注明"××及以下"的,适用于本电压等级工程。对于20 kV及以下配电网工程,则执行国家能源局颁布的《20 kV及以下配电网工程建设预算编制与计算标准》、《20kV及以下配电网工程预算定额》及其他相关规定。

二、建设预算内容组成

工程建设概算是初步设计阶段编制的工程建设预算。编制工程建设预算时,首先应制定统一的编制原则,确定统一的编制依据。编制原则的内容包括编制范围、价格水平年,定额、价格、取费标准的取定原则等。编制依据包括:工程量计算依据,人工、材料、机械等消耗量计算的依据(定额或指标),人工、材料、机械、设备等价格采用的依据、价格水平调整依据以及取费计算标准等。工程量的计算,应执行《预标》中的建设预算项目划分,根据定额(指标)所规定的工程量计算规则,按照设计图纸标示数据计算;采用的定额或指标必须是编制年现行适用的;人工、材料及机械价格以电力行业定额(造价)主管部门颁布的定额及相关规定为依据,并结合项目所在省(自治区、直辖市)的价格调整规定计算;取费计算标准应执行《预标》中的预算费用构成及计算标准,与所采用的定额或指标相匹配。

工程建设预算编制工作,也称为"工程造价的确定与控制",是指依据设计确定的某工程的建设工程量,进行取费相关系列计算,在此基础上履行编制、校核、审核和批准程序,确定工程合理投资金额的工程造价活动。编制人员被称为"工程造价员、工程造价师",统称工程造价人员。在工程造价确定活动中,要求工程造价人员努力提高自身业务水平,按相关造价文件的规定如实地编制工程概(预)算,采用合理的取费计算方式,提高所编工程建设预算的准确度。严禁在工程造价活动中高估冒算、弄虚作假,对严重违规者将按有关规定予以注销其执(从)业资格或不再续期注册。

按照《预标》规定,送电线路工程建设预算费用由安装工程费、其他费用和动态费用构成,其中前两项之和称为静态投资。对编制工程建设预算时已发生变化、或应项目法人提出要求对其中部分费用进行调整或作补充的部分,编制单位应予以具体说明原因,并提供调整的充分依据;在《预标》之外确有必要增列的费用项目,必须以国家行政主管部门、各省(自治区、直辖市)人民政府的规定为依据,经电力行业定额(造价)管理机构确认后计列。送电线路工程建设预算按费用性质不同分为安装工程费、辅助设施工程费和其他费用。架空线路工程的工地运输、土石方工程、基础工程、杆塔组立、架线、附件安装统称为安装工程,是针对线路工程本体的安装工程。

工程建设预算由编制说明、工程概况及总预算表(表一)、专业汇总预算表(表二)、单位工程预算表(表三)、其他费用预算表(表四)、主要技术经济指标表(表五)、建设场地征用及清理费用预算表(表七)以及相应的附表、附件组成,并应有预算造价水平分析。送电线路工程建设预算内容组成见表2-1-1。

表2-1-1 送电线路工程建设预算成品内容表

序号	内容组成名称	可行性研究估算	初步设计概算	施工图预算
1	编制说明(含造价水平分析)	√	√	√
2	工程概况及主要经济指标表(表五丙)	√	√	√
3	总预(估、概)算表(表一乙、丁)	√	√	√
4	送电线路建筑安装工程费用汇总预(估、概)算表(表二乙)	√	√	√
5	送电线路单位工程预(估、概)算表(表三丙、丁)	*	√	√
6	送电线路辅助设施工程预(估、概)算表(表三戊)	√	√	√
7	其他费用预(估、概)算表(表四)	√	√	√
8	建设场地征用及清理(估、概)算表(表七)	√	√	√
9	综合地形增加系数计算表(附表一)	√	√	√
10	送电线路工程装置性材料统计表(附表二)	*	√	√
11	送电线路土石方量计算表(附表三)	*	√	√
12	送电线路工程工地运输重量计算表(附表四)	*	√	√
13	送电线路工程工地运输工程量计算表(附表五)	*	√	√
14	送电线路工程杆塔分类一览表(附表六)	*	√	√

注:"*"标示内容作为编制单位的原始资料,可不出版;相关表格见附表。

建设预算的其他费用附表应完整,包括价差预备费计算表、建设期贷款利息计算表(可行性研究估算可不附)、编制年价差计算表等,还应有必要的附件。附件包括外委设计项目的建设预算表,特殊项目的依据性文件及建设预算表等。

三、概算编制方法

概算也称初步设计概算,是指在初步设计阶段,根据初步设计文件、预算定额和费用计算有关规定,预先测算和确定工程造价;也指在初步设计阶段编制、测算和确定概算文件的过程。

(一)准备工作

1. 了解工程总体情况

编制人员接受概算编制任务后,应对建设工程的设计情况进行全面了解。其内容如下：

（1）设计任务书（委托书）或项目建议书（文号、批准单位及内容——建设目的、规模、电压等级、设计范围及主要设计原则等）。

（2）工程的起讫（qi）地点及经过地区的地形、地貌、地质、地下水位、风力、地震烈度、线路亘（gen）长、导、地线型号，杆塔类型等。

（3）资金来源（融资单位的出资比例）及投资限额。各投资方的合营（合作）协议复印件，含资本平衡及分利水平，银行对融资部分的贷款意向承诺文件，包括融资成本、还贷方式及年限；其他融资渠道证明文件。

（4）建设方式（主要是招标形式）和建设单位名称、建设工期（含计划投产日期）。

（5）工程所在地有关政府部门颁发的相关文件、规定，如建设场地准备费及征地费用标准、项目所在地生活福利性建设工程造价标准及依据文件等。

（6）主要设备、材料的招标价及供货范围。

（7）网（省）电力公司承诺的代销电量协议书，有关部门对测算的上网电价的承诺文件。

（8）委托外部设计项目的正式概算（如公路、码头、航道等）。

（9）按协议规定的其他有关文件资料。

（10）勘测设计的初步安排及对本专业的要求。

（11）其他有关问题。

2. 现场搜集资料

了解工程总体情况后，再查阅参考本设计院所同类型或同地区工程资料，并编写调查搜资提纲，经相关负责人审查同意后，按搜资提纲外出搜资。

搜资结束后，对搜集到的资料进行分析整理，编制搜资报告。

（二）编制执行的规定及依据

1.《电网工程建设预算编制与计算标准》。

2.《电力建设工程预算定额（第四册 送电线路工程2006年版）》。

3. 某省电力建设装置性材料价格。

（三）编制概算流程

概算编制工艺流程如图2-1-1所示。

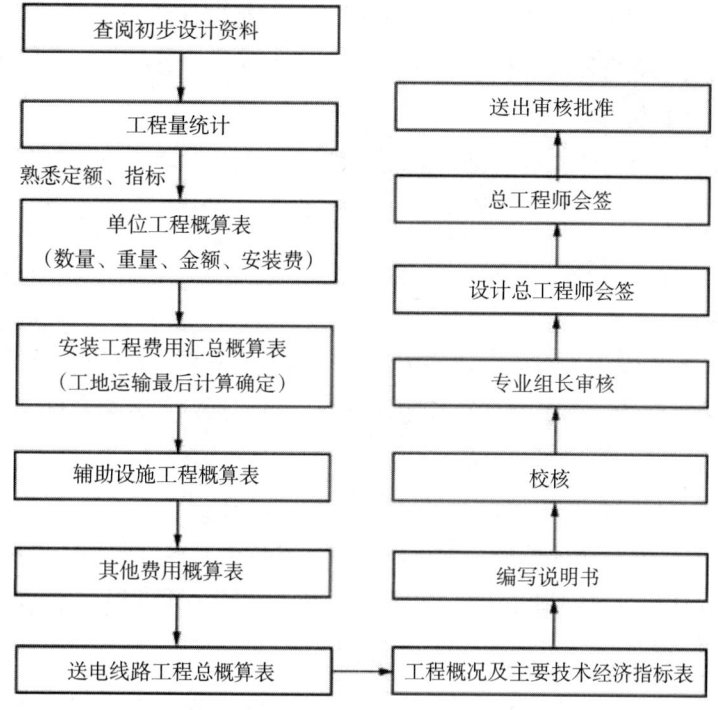

图 2-1-1 概算编制工艺流程示意图

(1) 确定概算工程量

概算工程量应根据初步设计的内容与深度规定,并按设计推荐的优化方案,由设计人员按概算编制的要求和深度提供。

(2) 熟悉相应的概算指标或预算定额(送电工程仅有预算定额),以及《预标》等相关规定。

(3) 取费计算

参照送电线路工程预算定额,执行《预标》等相关规定,对工程量进行取费计算,确定建筑安装工程费(含装置性材料费)、其他费用和动态费用等,最终计算出初步设计概算投资额。

初步设计概算的取费计算可以采用单位工程逐项取费、单位工程综合系数取费或单位工程汇总后逐项取费等方式,分别在案例工程概算确定过程中得以体现。

(4) 填写"工程概况及主要技术经济指标表"

(5) 编制编写说明书

(6) 校核、审核、审批

首先由编制人对包括说明书、表格、附表及附件等组成的概算书全部内容进行自行校核,其次由专业组长对概算书进行审核,再次是设计总工程师、总工程师会签,形成概算书成品。各级编制、校核、审核人员必须在正式的概算书上签字并加盖电力工程造价人员专用章。

概算书送交电力行业定额(造价)管理部门审核后,包括概算书在内所有设计文件送交工程项目甲方或甲方指定机构审批,基于审批文件,设计单位继续实施工程项目施工图设计,进而编制施工图预算。

(7) 注意事项

1) 概算必须根据选定的送电线路工程路径编制,取费符合规定,计算正确。

2) 对定额及取费中不包含的特殊施工项目,可根据设计方案及施工组织设计大纲中的工程量计算费用,列入工程概算。

3) 装置性材料、消耗性材料及机械台班价格按照电力行业定额(造价)管理部门颁发的规定计算,并按照项目所在地市场价格计算价差,该价差只记取税金。

4) 初步设计概算是在初步设计阶段确定工程总投资,原则上控制在已批准的可行性研究估算投资范围内。

5) 根据工程准备和建设程序的需要,"四通一平"或单项工程开工项目概算可先行编制。

(四) 编制概算的基本方法

1. 手工编制

即先画表格,再计算填表,形成概算书。随着计算机的普及应用,现已基本不再这样作业。

2. Excel 电子表格

Excel 是 Microsoft 公司开发的办公自动化软件的一个组件,它具有容易学习、容易实现表格的编辑及计算功能等特点。因为工程概预算的表现形式是表格,所以 Excel 电子表格特别适用于作概算编制的工具。考虑到一般电网工程技术人员所做的送电线路工程概算等级较为单一,工程数目较少,用 Excel 电子表格完全能满足需要,只要生成了一个较为完整的工程数据表格,在其基础上做同类型的工程的概预算,只要稍加修改,可以大大减轻工作量。

3. 专业预算软件

目前常见的有博微、鹏业、远东、筑业等多款电力工程造价软件,适用于电力行业发电、送变电工程估算、概算、预算、结算的编制与审核工作,均按照《预标》以及各省电力行业相关文件规定开发。这些专业预算软件功能相近，易学易用。

四、送电线路工程项目划分

送电线路工程与配电线路工程项目建筑安装作业内容不尽相同，配电线路工程包括配电装置和配电线路，而送电线路工程只含线路部分，因此在项目划分上不完全一样。送电线路又称送电线路，为符合技术经济工作习惯，以下均称送电线路。

送电线路工程是电网工程下的专业系统（工程），其项目划分为：第一级为扩大单位工程，如一般线路本体工程；第二级为单位工程，如工地运输；第三级为分部工程，如人力运输或汽车运输。

1. 架空送电线路工程

架空送电线路工程项目划分见表2-1-2。

2. 电缆线路工程项目划分

电缆线路工程项目划分见表2-1-3。

3. 送电线路辅助设施工程项目划分

送电线路辅助设施工程项目划分见表2-1-4。

编制送电线路工程建设预算时，对各级项目的工程名称不得任意简化，均应按照《预标》规定的全名填写。

如在本项目划分之外确有必要增列的工程项目，应以按照专业设计划分，在系统（工程）、扩大单位工程或单位工程项目序列之下，在已有项目之后顺序排列。比如，在工程中使用旧设备或改造设备，就需要在相应位置增加回收设备费、内部调拨设备费等。回收设备费是指施工设备、工程装置设备（如旧线路的导地线、杆塔等）处理后所得的款项。原有的旧的设备、装置及设施对新建工程来讲属于设备调拨的，则计入内部设备调拨费，均计入总投资，只有实物，作价但不拨款。

表2-1-2 架空送电线路工程项目划分表

编号	项目名称	主要内容及范围说明	技术经济指标单位
一	一般线路本体工程		元/km
1	土石方工程		元/m³
1.1	材料运输		
1.2	土石方开挖	包括杆塔坑、拉线坑、接地槽、风偏、施工基面的土石方	

续表

编号	项目名称	主要内容及范围说明	技术经济指标单位
2	基础工程	包括相应的材料运输	元/m³
2.1	材料运输		
2.2	基础工程	包括铺石灌浆，各种预制基础，现浇混凝土基础，打预制基础，灌注桩基础	
2.3	护坡、挡土墙及排洪沟砌筑		
3	杆塔工程		元/基
3.1	材料运输		
3.2	杆塔组立	包括各种杆塔的组立，拉线制作和安装	
3.3	接地安装		
4	架线工程		元/km
4.1	材料运输		
4.2	架线	包括导地线架设及一般跨越架设	
5	附件安装工程		元/基
5.1	材料运输		
5.2	附件安装	绝缘子、金具、均压屏蔽环等安装	
二	大跨越本体工程		元/km
1	土石方工程		元/m³
1.1	材料运输		
1.2	土石方开挖		
2	基础工程		元/m³
2.1	材料运输		
2.2	基础工程		
2.3	护坡、挡土墙及排洪沟砌筑		
3	杆塔工程		
3.1	材料运输		
3.2	杆塔组立		
3.3	接地安装		
4	架线工程		元/km
4.1	材料运输		
4.2	架线	包括导地线架设及一般跨越架设	
5	附件安装工程		元/基
5.1	材料运输		
5.2	附件安装	绝缘子、金具、均压屏蔽环等安装	

表 2-1-3　电缆送电线路工程项目划分表

编号	项目名称	主要内容及范围说明	技术经济指标单位
	电缆本体工程		
1	电缆沟、井、隧道、小间及保护管工程	土石方工程，电缆沟、隧道砌筑，电缆井，电缆小间，电缆保护管敷设及相应的材料运输	元/km
2	电缆支架、桥架及托架工程	包括相应的材料运输	元/t
3	电缆敷设工程		元/km
3.1	路面处理		
3.2	电缆敷设	包括电力电缆、控制电缆和电缆导管的敷设	
3.3	电缆头制作安装		
3.4	电缆防火		
4	避雷器及接地工程		
4.1	避雷器安装		
4.2	接地装置安装		
5	两端工程	包括送端和受端的设备及安装	
6	电缆常规试验		

表 2-1-4　送电线路辅助设施工程项目划分表

编号	项目名称	主要内容及范围说明	技术经济指标单位
1	巡线、检修站工程		元/m²
1.1	办公室、汽车库及仓库		
1.2	巡检修站征地		
1.3	室外工程		
2	巡线、检修道路工程		元/km
3	生产维护通信设备		元/km
4	生产作业工具		元/km

五、概算书的组成

概算书是送电线路工程概算的实体表现形式，是描述送电线路工程概况、工程量、工程造价及相关资料的文本文件。概算书由封面、签名、目录、编制说明、各类表格、附件和封底组成。

（一）封面

1. 封面上部应书写工程名称和初设概算、批准概算名称。

2. 右上角为工程代号，左上角为检索号。

3.封面下部应书写设计单位的全称,设计证号,勘测证号,编制年、月及编制地点。

案例工程二概算书封面如图2-1-2。

图2-1-2 案例工程二概算书封面

(二)签名(附案例工程二实物图片)

应由编制人、校对人、科(组)长、主任(专责)工程师、设计总工程师、总工程师逐级签字,并加盖电力工程造价人员专用章。

(三)目录

1.编制说明

2.工程概况及主要技术经济指标表

3.总概算表

4.送电线路建筑安装工程费用汇总概算表及单位工程概算表

5.送电线路辅助设施工程概算表

6.其他费用概算表

7.建设场地征用及清理概算表

8. 附表

附表包括综合地形增加系数、装置性材料、工程量计算表，送电线路杆塔分类一览表，其他费用附表等。

9. 附件

（四）编制说明

要求在"编制说明"部分简明扼要地叙述本工程概算编制的各项要点，并进行造价水平分析，内容必须完整。

编制说明的内容包括设计依据、工程概况、编制原则、编制方法、造价水平分析等。一般的，"工程概况及主要技术经济指标表"列于编制说明最后。

（五）各类表格

1. 总概算表（表一乙）
2. 送电线路建筑安装工程费用汇总概算表及单位工程概算表（表二乙、表三丙）
3. 送电线路辅助设施工程概算表（表三戊）
4. 其他费用概算表（表四）
5. 建设场地征用及清理概算表（表七）
6. 附表

（1）综合地形增加系数计算表（附表一）

（2）送电线路工程装置性材料统计表（附表二）

（3）送电线路土石方量计算表（附表三）

（4）送电线路工程工地运输重量计算表（附表四）

（5）送电线路工程工地运输工程量计算表（附表五）

（6）送电线路工程杆塔分类一览表（附表六）

上述表格样式详见以下内容中相应表格。

（六）附件

1. 设计依据和概算编制依据方面的主要文件。如：设计任务书（委托书）或项目建议书、初步设计审批文件或审查纪要的有关内容；工程主管部门、建设单位提供的有关文件。

2. 附件包括外委设计项目的建设预算表，特殊项目的依据性文件及建设预算表。

3. 涉及本工程项目签署的协议（合同）、议定的取费原则等，应写明全称及其编号。

任务2　现场搜集资料

在送电线路工程初步设计阶段，设计人员需要到可行性研究阶段确定的线路路径（可能不止一个路径方案）现场勘察并完成设计任务，并向概算编制人员提供概算工程量及相关资料。但考虑到设计人员和概算编制人员对同一个工程项目的关注点不尽相同，因此对概算编制人员来讲，除了可以向设计人员了解工程项目设计方案等相关资料外，还需要到现场搜集部分资料。

现场搜集资料是指概算编制人员向设计人员全面了解工程情况外，到送电线路工程沿线踏勘、核查并搜集编制概算所需资料的工作。视工作需要，概算编制人员可与设计人员同行，也可自行前往线路路径现场。搜集资料结束后，应及时整理并编制搜资报告。

一、现场搜集资料

（一）了解沿线地形、地貌、地质、水文、交通运输条件、障碍物情况和重要交叉跨越等

1. 地形

一般将送电线路工程地形分为：平地、丘陵、山地、高山、峻岭、泥沼、河网等。

（1）平地：指地形比较平坦广阔，地面比较干燥的地带。

（2）丘陵：指陆地上起伏和缓、连绵不断的矮岗、土丘，水平距离1 km以内地形起伏在50m以下的地带。

（3）山地：指一般山岭或沟谷等，水平距离250 m以内，地形起伏在50～150 m的地带。

（4）高山：指人力、牲畜攀登困难，水平距离250 m以内，地形起伏在150～250 m的地带。

（5）峻岭：指地势十分险峻，水平距离250 m以内，地形起伏在250 m以上的地带。

（6）泥沼：指经常积水的田地及泥水淤积的地带。

（7）河网：指河流频繁，河道纵横交叉成网，影响正常陆上交通的地带。

在实际工作中，首先将全线线路路径按地形的不同划分为若干区段，再计算出各种地形在工程全线中所占长度的百分比。还应确定因地形影响风偏，需要实施土石方开挖的位置及数量。

2. 地貌

指地面种植的植物种类。要求调查：

（1）沿线林木种类、数量、胸径和疏密程度。

（2）青苗种类、面积。

3. 土质分类

一般将土质分为：普通土、坚土、松砂石、岩石、泥水、流沙、水坑，应确定不同种类的土质在全线中所占的比例（根据地质报告确定）。

4. 交通运输条件

到各地的交通局或公路局了解送电线路工程沿线的公路等交通线的分布情况，以便布置材料站、卸料站等。交通运输条件是确定工地运输量方式及其平均运距的基础，是确定需要修建施工用临时道路和桥梁的位置和数量的基础。

5. 障碍物情况

掌握送电线路工程沿线需要拆迁的房屋类型、结构、面积，以及需迁移的坟墓的种类、数量，还有采石场、石灰窑、炸药库、油库等构筑物的结构、面积等。

6. 重要的交叉跨越

掌握送电线路工程沿线跨越的公路、铁路、通信线、电力线路、河流、湖泊、泥沼的位置、数量、跨距等。

上述内容原则上由设计人员提供，概算编制人员主要是做核查工作。

（二）向工程沿线人民政府相关部门搜集相关资料

需要向工程所在地人民政府相关部门搜集的资料包括：土地征用、场地租用、迁移补偿、送电线路走廊赔偿等有关规定、赔偿标准及计算办法。相关知识及确定方法详见"其他费用"中建设场地征用及清理费的说明，及案例工程概算的其他费用相关部分说明。

1. 土地征用相关资料

送电线路工程的土地征用，一般仅对杆塔基础（含拉线基础）一定范围的土地实施，具体参见电力行业主管部门的相关规定。其目的是确保对基础附近土壤实施耕作等行为不致影响基础稳定运行。

计算送电线路工程的土地征用费时，不同地区的土地价格标准不尽相同，若全线相差不大，取最高价格来计算；若不同地区的地价相差悬殊，则应分别计算后累加，汇总计入土地征用费。

概算编制人员需要到当地国土管理部门，详细了解征地费用标准，及其是否包含土地补偿费、安置补助费……税金等全部内容。

2. 林木迁移、清理及赔偿相关资料

以线路走廊为界，凡影响送电线路施工及运行的林木（竹、树）必须迁移或清理，需计算其赔偿费用，计入送电线路走廊赔偿费。

概算编制人员需要详细了解林木的种类、数量、胸径、疏密程度，并到当地林业主管部门收集相应的赔偿标准。原则上对于多年生长的经济林木，要尽量移植，由用地单位支付移植费，如必须砍伐的，则由用地单位按实际价值补偿；对于成材林木，由林权所有者自行砍伐，用地单位只付伐工工时费，不予补偿。具体赔偿标准，应根据当时当地实际情况而定，由工程业主方与林木所有者协商确定。

3. 青苗赔偿相关资料

青苗赔偿费是指征用土地或工程施工时，农作物正处在生长阶段而未能收获，工程业主方应给予土地承包者或土地使用者的经济补偿。送电线路工程建设常导致线路走廊及其附近一定范围的土地上种植的庄稼及其他经济作物损毁，需要对其进行赔偿，计入送电线路走廊赔偿费。导致青苗赔偿的原因具体分为土地征用和线路工程施工，青苗赔偿费在送电线路走廊赔偿费中常占有较大的比例。

青苗赔偿费标准：土地上长有的青苗，因征地或施工被毁掉的，应由用地单位按照在田作物一季产量、产值计算，给予补偿。对于刚刚播种的农作物，按其一季产值的1/3补偿工本费，对于成长期的农作物，最高按一季产值补偿；对于粮食、油料和蔬菜青苗，能够得到收获的，不予补偿，不能收获的按一季补偿。具体赔偿标准，应根据当时当地实际情况而定，由工程业主方与土地承包者或土地使用者协商确定。比如在具体操作中，土地征用或工程施工引起的青苗赔偿的年限就不一样的，前者一般较长，后者只赔一季。

概算编制人员须了解青苗的种类、面积、赔偿标准等相关资料。常见的青苗种类包括水稻、小麦、玉米及其他经济作物等。水稻分单季、双季，小麦分单种、间种、

青苗的面积通常以线路亘长、线路走廊宽度为基础，分段计算在预计施工期内种植的各种青苗面积，单独设置的施工场地面积另计，累计即为青苗赔偿面积（亩）。赔偿金额计算公式为

$$青苗赔偿面积=线路亘长×线路走廊宽度×沿线某种青苗比例 \qquad (2-2-1)$$
$$赔偿金额=青苗赔偿面积×亩产×市场价格 \qquad (2-2-2)$$

4. 建筑物、构筑物等迁移补偿相关资料

线路工程征用土地范围内以及线路走廊内影响送电线路正常施工及运行的机关、企业、住宅及有关建筑物和构筑物，以及电力线路、通信线路、铁路、公路、沟渠、管道、坟墓等需要迁移及清理，需要计算其赔偿费用，分别计入迁移补偿费和余物清理费。

概算编制人员需要到工程所在地政府建设委员会（拆迁办），了解相关赔偿标准，已签订迁移及清理协议（合同）的搜集协议（合同）价格。

5. 施工场地租用相关资料

材料站、卸料站及牵张场地租用，相关费用计入施工场地租用费。已签订协议（合同）的按协议价（合同价）计列，未签订协议（合同）参考同类型工程计列。

概算编制人员需向业主方或有关部门收集相关资料。

（三）搜集其他资料

（1）到当地的建材市场搜集工程所在地区的砂石资源的产地、产量、质量、价格或供应点的供应量及价格，了解沙、石就地取材的可能性，尽量减少运输距离以降低工程成本。

（2）对改扩建工程，应了解可以利用的部分或特殊条件。如旧塔的利用、改接点的情况、是否需要停电等。

（3）搜集工程沿线电力主管部门颁发的现行电力工程装置性材料预算价格。

（4）通过工程沿线的有关主管部门搜集统一定额、地区单位估价表和现行工资单价。

（5）向工程沿线电力定额（造价）管理部门搜集已计价材料费和施工机械使用费的调整系数。

（6）按《预标》中规定的应由建设和施工单位提供的资料。

概算编制人员在搜集资料过程中，应主动与建设单位、施工单位（若已经确定）搞好协调配合，对现场实际情况要及时核对记录，力求意见统一，避免事后发生分

歧。整理出的搜资报告中，应附相关协议书及会谈纪要，一并向上级行业主管部门汇报及提供审阅，再结合主管部门意见，主编人提出书面的工程概算技术组织措施初稿，经审查后与建设单位、主管部门、建设银行、施工单位等共同协商，形成意见一致的编制原则，以保证概算的编制质量。

（四）案例工程二现场搜资情况

(1) 某市220千伏A-B输变电新建工程可行性研究报告及批复；

(2) 水文气象报告；

(3) 工程地质报告；

(4) A县、C县、B市规划区域；

(5) 220千伏A变电站、B变电站出线规划；

(6) 某设计院完成的可行性研究报告和设计投标文件；

(7) 与地方政府签订的路径协议；

(8) 线路路径附近主要电信线路、无线电设施相关资料；

(9) 其他参见案例工程二线路工程概况。

二、计算地形增加系数

（一）关于地形增加系数

1. 采用地形增加系数的原因

采用地形增加系数，是因为预算定额均按平地施工考虑，如在其他地形条件下施工时，就应分别按预算定额的规定考虑实际地形对工程施工的影响，计算综合地形增加系数，对人工和机械费用进行调整。

2. 地形增加系数的计算方法

(1) 地形比例计算方法

根据现场搜资和设计人员提供的资料，按地形的定义将工程全线划分为若干段，再将各类地形的长度汇总，计算出各类地形长度占全线路长度的百分比。除高原台地外，各类地形段内夹杂着少量的其他地形时，可不予考虑，而按主要地形确定百分比例。

(2) 预算定额的地形增加系数（见表2-2-1）

表 2-2-1　　地形增加系数表（%）

序号	定额名称		项目	丘陵	山地	高山	峻岭	泥沼	河网	备注
1	工地运输	人力运输	（1）混凝土杆、混凝土预制品、钢管杆、线材的运输	40	150	300	400	70	-	不包括机械
			（2）金具、绝缘子、零星钢材、塔材、沙、石、石灰、土、水泥、降阻剂、水的运输	20	100	150	200	40	-	
			汽车、拖拉机运输	20	80	-	-	-	-	不包括装卸
2	土石方工程			5	10	20	25	10	5	不包括机械
3	基础工程			10	20	40	50	40	10	
4	杆塔工程			20	70	110	120	70	20	不包括高塔及接地工程
5	架线工程		一般放、紧线	15	100	150	170	40	10	不包括跨越架设、拦河线安装
			张力机械放、紧线	5	40	80	90	20	5	
			光缆接续	5	30	60	80	15	5	不包括测量
6	附件工程			5	20	50	60	10	5	
7	电缆工程		沟槽直埋	10	20	40	-	10	5	

注意：

①在确定运输地形时，应按运输路径的实际地形来划分，不同于工程地形。工程地形是指工程沿线线路路径的地形；工地运输地形可能与工程地形接近，但仍应分别按实际路径区分，"人力运输"的路径可以参考工程地形。

②"汽车运输"地形一般为平地、丘陵，有连续的弯道（盘山公路）时为"山地"。

③在高山、峻岭地带进行人力运输时，其平均运距的确定，应以山坡垂直高差的平均计算斜长和地形增加系数计列，不得按实际的运输距离计算。

④同一地段内，"泥沼"与"河网"并存时，仅可套用泥沼地形的增加系数，两者不可同时取用。

⑤西北高原台地沿线路平台长度 2 km 以内的工程地形按"山地"论，工程运输地形按运输路径的实际情况而定，上台运输按"山地"论，台上运输按"平地"论。

⑥在城市市区架空送电线路除人力运输外，参考丘陵地形计算。

（二）案例工程二的综合地形增加系数

（1）案例工程二综合地形增加系数计算表（见表2-2-2）

（2）计算说明

根据设计资料，案例工程二的工程地形划分为：平地7.4%、丘陵51.4%、山地41.2%。人力运输地形同工程地形；由于线路路径附近公路以区乡公路为主，多为盘山公路，因此汽车运输地形划分同工程地形；架线工程采用一般放、紧线方式。

表2-2-2 案例工程二综合地形增加系数计算表

序号	项目	地形增加系数（%）						地形比例（%）						综合增加系数（%）						合计
		丘陵	山地	高山	峻岭	泥沼	河网	丘陵	山地	高山	峻岭	泥沼	河网	丘陵	山地	高山	峻岭	泥沼	河网	
1	2	3	4	5	6	7	8	9	10	11	12	13	14	15	16	17	18	19	20	21
一	人力运输：线材及混凝土制品（不含机械费）	40	150	300	400	70		51.4	41.2					20.56	61.8					82.36
	人力运输：其他（不含机械费）	20	100	150	200	40	10	51.4	41.2					10.28	41.2					51.48
	汽车、拖拉机运输（不含装卸）	20	80			40	20	51.4	41.2					10.28	32.96					43.24
二	土石方工程	5	10	20	25	10	5	51.4	41.2					2.57	4.12					6.69
三	基础工程	10	20	40	50	40	10	51.4	41.2					5.14	8.24					13.38
四	杆塔工程	20	70	110	120	70	20	51.4	41.2					10.28	28.84					39.12
五	架线工程（一般放紧线）	15	100	150	170	40	10	51.4	41.2					7.71	41.2					48.91
	架线工程（张力机械放紧线）	5	40	80	90	20	5													
六	附件工程	5	20	50	60	10	5	51.4	41.2					2.57	8.24					10.81

注1：因平地无增加系数，故不计列。
注2：如果高山中人力运输按盘山道考虑，加长了运距，其他地形增加系数套用山地系数。
注3：(15) = (3) × (9)，(16) = (4) × (10)，…，以此类推。
注4：(15) + (16) + (17) + (18) + (19) + (20) = (21)。

任务3　确定工程量

工程量是指在送电线路工程建设中，基础工程、杆塔工程、架线工程及附件工程安装施工的工作量统计值，一般是指工作中完成安装的混凝土及其制成品、塔材、导地线、金具、绝缘子及附件等主要材料（简称主材，也称装置性材料）的数量，还包括土石方工程中土石方开挖量、线路复测及分坑工作数量，和工地运输工程中完成装卸及运输工作的数量。工程量的确定是下一步取费计算即确定工程造价的主要的基础性工作，应严格采用《预标》中附表规定的分类标准，与电力建设工程预算定额的定额子目一一对应。

初步设计阶段的工程量，由设计人员按概算编制的要求和深度提供，概算工程量应与初步设计图纸、说明书及设备、材料清册保持一致。对投资影响较大的项目，如电缆、桥架、土石方、地基处理、杆塔耗量、混凝土基础等，技术经济人员（概算编制人员）应根据掌握的资料，对设计人员提供的工程量参照相同自然条件的参考设计、类似工程施工图或预算工程量进行核查，并提出反馈意见。技经人员须对设计人员提供的工程量进行复核，施工损耗应按《电力建设工程预算定额（第四册 送电线路工程 2006年版）》规定的损耗率进行计算。工程量确有问题的，可要求设计人员说明原因或修改其提供的资料。工程量经分析确定后，不得再套用其他工程的估算或概算。

因为需要概算编制人员分析核算设计人员提供的工程量，所以在本学习任务中重点学习工程量计算方法。本学习项目所列工程量资料，未特别注明出处的，均来自由设计人员提供的案例工程二的工程量相关资料。

一、整理工程量资料

（一）设计人员提供的工程量

（1）线路名称、起讫点、电压等级、长度。
（2）导线和避雷线型号、回路数。
（3）基础型式种类（附一览图）、各型式数量。
（4）杆塔型式种类（附一览图）、各型式数量。
（5）附件安装型式及数量。
（6）接地安装型式及数量。

(7) 防震锤型式及数量。

(8) 线路工程中拆迁各种障碍物的种类及数量。

(9) 风偏尖峰开挖（线档中导、地线因风偏而对地距离不够）、基础坑土石方开挖量或高低腿基础的开挖土石方量。

(10) 跨越架种类及数量（跨越距离及宽度，跨江河时的江河宽度）。

(11) 地质报告。

（二）整理工程量资料

接收设计人员提供的工程量资料后，概算编制人员须按照"预规"中规定的送电线路工程项目划分等相关要求，通过分析核查，将其整理成为符合取费计算要求的工程量表。具体包括以下六个方面的统计工作：土石方工程量计算、工地运输工程量计算、基础工程量计算、杆塔工程量计算、架线工程量计算、附件工程量计算。

二、土石方工程量的计算

送电线路工程中开挖的土石方工程量主要是指工程施工中涉及的尖峰、施工基面、基础坑、拉线坑、接地槽等开挖的土石方量，具体而言，包括电杆坑、拉线塔坑、拉线坑、电缆沟的挖方（或爆破）及回填，自立式铁塔坑的挖方（或爆破）及回填，接地槽的挖方（或爆破）及回填，岩石嵌固基坑爆破，坚土坑掏挖，挖孔桩基坑开挖，井点施工开挖及回填，排水沟开挖，尖峰及施工基面挖方等。土石方工程量的计算，与设计提供的尺寸及土质的类别相关。设计提供的尺寸是土石方量的静尺寸，还需要考虑施工操作裕度、边坡系数等。施工操作裕度及边坡系数的取值又取决于施工操作方法及土质类型。此处仅介绍尖峰及施工基面开挖土石方量计算方法，土、石质分类，及杆塔基坑、拉线坑、接地槽的开挖土石方量的计算方法等详见本书学习项目一相关内容。

（一）尖峰及施工基面开挖土石方量计算

1. 尖峰及施工基面开挖的原因及计算原则

尖峰开挖一般出现在弧垂最低点附近，导线因风偏等原因对地安全距离不够时，对相关部位土石进行开挖。施工基面开挖一般是指杆塔基础位于山坡、山顶、山梁等位置时的施工基面平整，或基础位于水田、泥沼等软弱土质较薄处降低施工基面需要的土石方开挖。尖峰及施工基面开挖的土石方量一般由设计人员提供，直接计入概算。尖峰及施工基面土、石方量计算，应按设计提供的基面标高并按地形、地貌实际情况进行计算。

2. 尖峰及施工基面开挖土石方量的计算公式

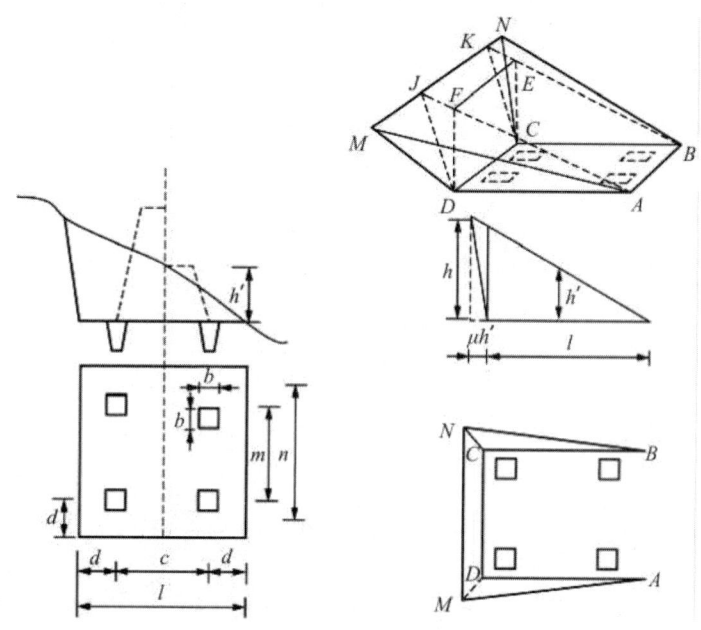

图 2-3-1　山坡施工基面示

（1）塔位位于山坡的施工基面（如图 2-3-1）

1）不放边坡部分的体积（ABCDEF 体积）

$$V_a = l \times n \times h' \tag{2-3-1}$$

2）放边坡部分体积由三部分组成（μ 为放坡系数），即上坡方向部分的体积（CDEFJK 体积）

$$V_2 = \frac{\mu \times h^2 \times n}{2} \tag{2-3-2}$$

左右两侧（ADMJA+BCKNB）体积

$$V_3 = \frac{\mu \times h^2 \times l}{3} \tag{2-3-3}$$

3）基面总体积

$$V = V_a + V_2 + V_3 \tag{2-3-4}$$

（2）塔位位于圆形山顶上的施工基面（如图 2-3-2，可按近似椭圆球体积的一半计算）

$$V = \frac{\pi \times l \times n \times h}{6} \tag{2-3-5}$$

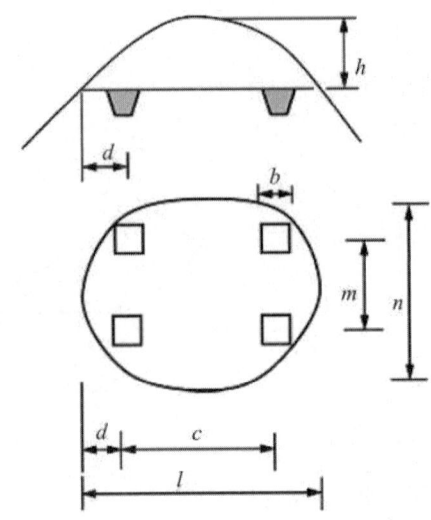

图 2-3-2　圆形山顶施工基面示意图

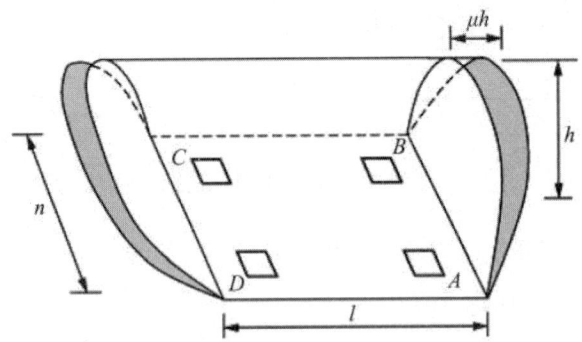

图 2-3-3　山脊施工基面示意图

（3）塔位位于山脊的施工基面（如图 2-3-3）

由于山脊两侧坡度的陡缓不同，可按近似长方体体积计算，但应乘以小于 1 的修正系数 K，一般可取 $0.4 \sim 0.6$。因而：

$$V = K \times l \times n \times h + \mu \times h^2 \times n \tag{2-3-6}$$

式中，V 为土、石方体积，m³；h、h' 为降基面值（施工基面高度），m；l 为施工基面底长，m；n 为施工基面底宽，m；c、m 分别为基础正、侧面根开，m；b 为基础坑口尺寸，m；d 为操作裕度及边坡预留尺寸，m；μ 为放坡系数。

（二）余土处理

一般工程不考虑余土处理，需要时，可考虑将余土运至允许堆弃地，其运距超过 100 m 以上部分可列入工地运输。余土运输量计算如下。

1. 灌注桩钻孔渣土

$$\text{余土运输量} = \text{桩设计零米以下部分体积} (m^3) \times 1.7 t/m^3 \quad (2\text{-}3\text{-}7)$$

其中，1.7 t/m³中包括0.2 t/m³的含水量。

2. 现浇和预制基础基坑余土

$$\text{余土运输量} = \text{混凝土体积} (m^3) \times 1.5 t/m^3 \times 30\% \quad (2\text{-}3\text{-}8)$$

3. 掏挖式、挖孔桩基础基坑余土

$$\text{余土运输量} = \text{混凝土体积} (m^3) \times 1.5 t/m^3 \quad (2\text{-}3\text{-}9)$$

（三）回填土

回填土均按原挖原填考虑，需要100 m以外的取（换）土回填时，可按设计规定的换土比例和平均运距，另行套用尖峰挖方和工地运输定额。

（四）案例工程二中土石方量的计算

1. 案例工程二土石方量表

见表2-3-1，土石方工程量汇总表。

2. 计算说明

本案例工程全部采用钢筋混凝土现浇基础，设计了直柱柔性基础、斜柱式基础、掏挖式基础和岩石嵌固式基础等四种基础类型，详见图2-0-3。根据工程设计资料，本工程主要采用前三种基础类型，下面就三种基础各取其一列出土石方量计算过程，填入表2-3-2，以说明基础开挖土石方量计算方法。本案例工程中，一般情况下，铁塔基础立柱露出地面高度：旱地200 mm、水旱田300 mm。

（1）直柱柔性基础的土石方量计算

某铁塔基础A、B、C、D四腿均采用直柱柔性基础LZG2026，丘陵地形，地质条件：0～0.5 m为耕土，0.5m以下为粉砂质泥岩（褐红或紫红色，强风化）。采用人力开凿方式开挖。

LZG2026基础底板为正方形2×2 m，坑底不支设模板，立柱顶面距离坑底2.6 m，扣除立柱露出地面高度200 mm，基础坑深为2.4 m。

表2-3-1　案例工程二土石方工程量汇总表

名称	单位	数量
自立式铁塔坑的挖方（爆破）及回填　普通土　坑深3.0m以内	m³	643.20
自立式铁塔坑的挖方（爆破）及回填　普通土　坑深4.0m以内	m³	775.20
自立式铁塔坑的挖方（爆破）及回填　普通土　坑深4.0m以上	m³	3372.00
自立式铁塔坑的挖方（爆破）及回填　松砂石　坑深3.0m以内	m³	2210.40
自立式铁塔坑的挖方（爆破）及回填　松砂石　坑深4.0m以内	m³	2665.20
自立式铁塔坑的挖方（爆破）及回填　松砂石　坑深4.0m以上	m³	11590.80
自立式铁塔坑的挖方（爆破）及回填　岩石（爆破）　坑深3.0m以内	m³	804.00
自立式铁塔坑的挖方（爆破）及回填　岩石（爆破）　坑深4.0m以内	m³	968.40
自立式铁塔坑的挖方（爆破）及回填　岩石（爆破）　坑深4.0m以上	m³	4214.40
自立式铁塔坑的挖方（爆破）及回填　岩石（人凿）　坑深3.0m以内	m³	200.40
自立式铁塔坑的挖方（爆破）及回填　岩石（人凿）　坑深4.0m以内	m³	242.40
自立式铁塔坑的挖方（爆破）及回填　岩石（人凿）　坑深4.0m以上	m³	1053.60
自立式铁塔坑的挖方（爆破）及回填　泥水坑　坑深3.0m以内	m³	160.80
自立式铁塔坑的挖方（爆破）及回填　泥水坑　坑深4.0m以内	m³	194.40
自立式铁塔坑的挖方（爆破）及回填　泥水坑　坑深4.0m以上	m³	843.60
接地槽挖方（或爆破）及回填　普通土	m³	1187.10
接地槽挖方（或爆破）及回填　松砂石	m³	4080.04
接地槽挖方（或爆破）及回填　泥水土	m³	296.28
接地槽挖方（或爆破）及回填　岩石（爆破）	m³	1483.38
接地槽挖方（或爆破）及回填　岩石（人凿）	m³	371.09
排水沟开挖　普通土	m³	55.00
排水沟开挖　松砂石	m³	186.00
排水沟开挖　泥水沟	m³	14.00
排水沟开挖　岩石（爆破）	m³	68.00
排水沟开挖　岩石（人凿）	m³	17.00
尖峰及施工基面挖方　普通土	m³	196.00
尖峰及施工基面挖方　松砂石	m³	537.00
尖峰及施工基面挖方　岩石（爆破）　尖峰	m³	147.00
尖峰及施工基面挖方　岩石（人凿）　尖峰	m³	49.00

根据上述条件，查表1-2-5、1-2-6，施工操作裕度为0.1 m，边坡系数为1∶0.33，由式（1-2-14），

LZG2026基础基坑的坑口宽为

$$a_1 = a + 2 \times h \times 0.33$$
$$= 2 + 2 \times 0.1 + 2 \times 2.4 \times 0.33$$
$$= 3.784 \text{（m）}$$

LZG2026 基础开挖土石方量为

$$a_1 = a + 2 \times h \times 0.33$$
$$= \frac{24}{3} \times [(2+2\times 0.1)^2 + (2+2\times 0.1)\times 3.784 + 3.784^2]$$
$$= 21.987 \text{ (m}^3\text{)}$$

（2）斜柱式基础的土石方量计算

某铁塔基础A、B、C、D四腿均采用斜柱式基础XJG2742，山地地形，地质条件：0～0.5 m为耕土，0.5 m以下为粉砂质泥岩（褐红或紫红色，强风化）。采用人力开凿方式开挖。

XJG2742基础底板为正方形2.7×2.7 m，坑底不支设模板，立柱顶面距离坑底4.2m，扣除立柱露出地面高度200 mm，基础坑深为4 m。

根据上述条件，查表1-2-5、1-2-6，施工操作裕度为0.1 m，边坡系数为1∶0.33，由式（1-2-14），

XJG2742基础基坑的坑口宽为

$$a_1 = a + 2 \times h \times 0.33$$
$$= 2.7 + 2 \times 0.1 + 2 \times 4 \times 0.33$$
$$= 5.54 \text{ (m)}$$

LZG2026 基础开挖土石方量为

$$V = \frac{h}{3} \times (a^2 + aa_1 + a_1^2)$$
$$= \frac{4}{3} \times [(2.7+2\times 0.1)^2 + (2.7+2\times 0.1)\times 5.54 + 5.54^2]$$
$$= 73.557 \text{ (m}^3\text{)}$$

（3）掏挖式基础的土石方量计算

某铁塔基础A、B、C、D四腿均采用掏挖式基础TWG1630，山地地形，地质条件：0～0.4m为残积粉质黏土，0.4 m以下为粉砂质泥岩（褐红或紫红色，强风化）。采用人力开凿方式开挖。

如图2-3-4，底板为圆形Φ1.6 m，高0.3 m；立柱为圆形Φ0.8 m，高2.2 m；立柱与底板间为平截圆锥体，高0.5 m。坑底不支设模板，立柱顶面距离坑底3m，扣除立柱露出地面高度200 mm，基础坑深为2.8 m。

TWG1630基础开挖土石方量为

$$V = \pi r_2^2 h_1 + \frac{\pi h_2(r_2^2+r_2^2+r_1r_2)}{3} + \pi r_2^2 h_3$$
$$= \pi \times 0.8^2 \times 0.3 + \frac{\pi \times 0.5 \times (0.8^2+0.4^2+0.8\times 0.4)}{3} + \pi \times 0.4^2 \times 2$$
$$= 2.194 \text{ (m}^3\text{)}$$

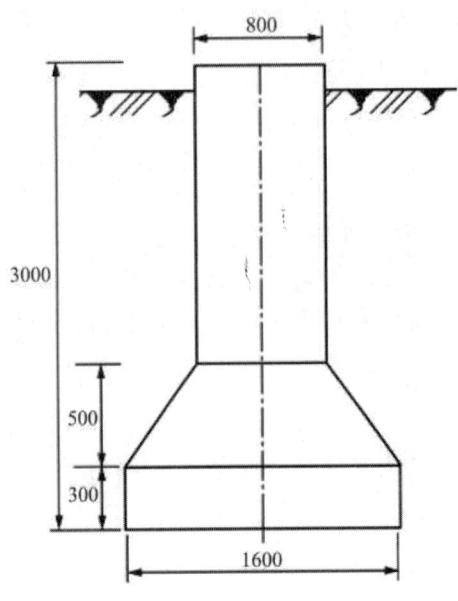

图2-3-4 TWG1630基础结构

（4）接地装置的土石方量计算

根据"铁塔接地装置安装图"，接地装置埋深一般取0.6 m，耕地应埋在耕作深度以下，岩石地区不小于0.3 m。

如图2-0-2，乙型接地装置埋设Φ10圆钢长度为60 m（表2-0-5），其接地槽开挖土石方量为

$$V=0.4×长度×槽深$$
$$=0.4×60×0.6$$
$$=14.4 \text{ m}^3$$

查表2-0-5，丙、丁、戊、己型接地装置土石方量分别28.8 m³、38.4 m³、67.2 m³、84.5 m³，137套接地装置中，丙型占10%、丁型占35%、戊型占50%、己型占5%。本案例工程接地装置土石方量计算为

（28.8×10%+38.4×35%+67.2×50%+84.5×5%）×137=7417.9（m³）

根据设计资料，本案例工程地质划分为：岩石25%，松砂石55%，普通土16%，泥水4%。根据同类型工程经验，岩石地质开挖，爆破方式占80%，人力开凿方式占20%。因此，接地装置土石方量——接地槽挖方（或爆破）及回填工程量分解为：普通土1187.10 m³，松砂石4080.04 m³，泥水土296.28 m³，岩石（爆破）1483.38 m³，岩石（人凿）371.09 m³，填入表2-3-1。

表 2-3-2　案例工程二土石方计算表

单位：m³

地形	土质	基础型式	坑底长×宽 m	坑深 m	每坑土石方量 m³ 杆坑	每坑土石方量 m³ 马道	每基坑数 个	每基土石方量 m³	坑深2m以内 基数	坑深2m以内 合计	坑深3m以内 基数	坑深3m以内 合计	坑深3m以上 基数	坑深3m以上 合计	备注
1	2	3	4	5	6	7	8	9	10	11	12	13	14	15	
丘陵	松砂石	LZG2026	2×2	2.4	21.987		4	87.948							
山地	松砂石	XJG2742	2.7×2.7	4.0	73.557		4	294.227					1	294.227	
山地	松砂石	TWG1630	Φ1.6	2.8	2.194		4	8.776			1	8.776			
其余略															

注1：[（6）+（7）]×（8）=（9）。
注2：（9）×（10）=（11），（9）×（12）=（13）或（9）×（14）=（15）。
注3：根据（4），（5）数据查表，取决于不同种类土石方开挖对应的定额子目的分类要求，填入（6）。
注4：坑深分类，取决于不同种类土石方开挖对应的定额子目的分类要求，统计土石方量时以基为单位；统计土石方量，应以坑为单位加以区分。
注5：本表中铁塔基础按每基4个基坑计，考虑到现在设计中多出现同一基铁塔四个腿基础形式不同的情况，统计时应注意加以区分，应以坑为单位统计土石方量。

三、装置性材料的数量、重量统计

装置性材料是指安装工程中构成工艺系统实体的原材料、辅助材料、构配件、零件、半成品等工艺性材料。在统计基础、杆塔、导地线及附件等装置性材料时，应计入其施工损耗量，主要的装置性材料施工损耗率详见表1-2-1。从前面的讲述可知，装置性材料统计的目的，一是为了计算装置性材料费，二是为了计算其相应的安装费，所以统计时设置的口径必须满足两个方面的需要。前者注意区别材料名称及规格、单位和损耗率即可，而后者则必须考虑相应定额子目的项目划分。

（一）基础工程

基础工程包括预制基础、现浇基础、岩石基础、灌注桩基础、预制桩基础、人工挖孔桩基础的安装，护坡、挡土墙及排洪沟砌筑，混凝土基础防腐，拉线棒防腐等，前六者是不同种类基础的安装，后三者是基础附属设施及构件处理。不同种类基础因其材料、结构和施工工艺不同，其相应安装费不同；不同的基础组成部分如钢筋制作及加工、基础垫层、基础本体安装费也不同；同理，不同种类的基础附属设施及构件处理的安装费也不同，但为了后续工作中便于套用定额，完成取费计算，在填写"附表二 送电线路工程装置性材料统计表"时，除了考虑材料名称及规格、单位和损耗率的不同外，还应充分考虑基础工程定额子目的项目划分。

1. 几种常见基础型式的装置性材料统计相关要求

（1）预制基础

预制基础，多为钢筋混凝土预制，根据其结构的不同分为底盘、套筒、卡盘及拉线盘，"预制基础"定额子目的项目划分也分为底盘安装、套筒安装、卡盘安装和拉线盘安装，统计口径较简单，按不同种类和重量以"基""块""组""根"为单位统计。统计时，底盘区分单杆和双杆，分为每基一块、每基两块；套筒分为每基一根、每基二根；卡盘分为每基一块、每基两块、每基四块；拉线盘分为每组一块、每组两块，定额子目步距均取决于重量。

（2）现浇基础

现浇基础按不同等级（单基混凝土方量）以"m³"为单位统计，其组成材料分为钢筋、沙、石、水泥、水，也有在工程中直接使用商品混凝土的，不同种类材料预算单价、损耗率、包装系数均不同，应区别统计。"现浇基础"定额子目中基础钢筋加工及制作不包括热镀锌。

现浇基础的基础垫层，分为铺石，铺石并灌浆，铺石并加浇混凝土，灰土和素混凝土垫层，应分类统计，其石、石灰、砂浆或混凝土的用量应按设计规定计算。如设计未作规定时，其石灰、砂浆的用量可以按垫层体积的20%计列，混凝土的用量可以按垫层体积的30%计列。

（3）灌注桩基础

灌注桩钻孔土质分类：

1)"砂土、亚黏土"：指亚砂土和中、轻亚黏土；

2)"黏土"指重亚黏土、黏土和松散的黄土；

3)"砂砾土"，指重亚黏土、僵石黏土，并伴有含量不超过20%，粒径不大于15cm的砾石或卵石；

4）凡一孔中有不同土质时，应按设计提供的地质资料分层计算。

（4）预制桩基础。打预制桩的体积，按设计全长乘以桩的截面积，扣除桩尖的虚体体积。送桩按桩截面面积乘以设计桩顶面标高至自然地坪另加0.5m长度计算。接桩按接头个数计算。截桩按根数计算。

（5）几种现浇基础超灌量的规定

各类现浇基础的超灌量应按设计规定执行，如设计无规定时，其超灌量为：①灌注桩基础，超灌量为设计计算量的17%；②掏挖式基础、岩石嵌固基础、挖孔桩基础，超灌量为设计计算量的7%；③岩石灌浆基础，超灌量为设计计算量的8%；④现浇护壁，超灌量为现浇护壁设计计算量的17%。

（6）混凝土和砂浆用料按下列配合比计算

现浇混凝土配合比表见表2-3-3，砂浆配合比表见表2-3-4。

表2-3-3　现浇混凝土配合比表

单位：m³

序号	混凝土强度	水泥强度等级	水泥 t	中沙 m³	碎石 m³	水 t	备注
1	C10	32.5	0.250	0.550	0.830	0.180	碎石粒径为40mm以内
2	C15	32.5	0.310	0.490	0.840	0.180	
3	C20	32.5	0.344	0.460	0.850	0.180	
4	C25	32.5	0.405	0.410	0.850	0.180	
5	C30	42.5	0.383	0.420	0.860	0.180	
6	C35	42.5	0.411	0.400	0.860	0.180	
7	C40	42.5	0.460	0.370	0.860	0.180	
8	C20	32.5	0.397	0.460	0.790	0.215	灌注桩用，碎石粒径为15mm以内
9	C25	32.5	0.470	0.400	0.800	0.215	
10	C30	42.5	0.451	0.410	0.800	0.215	
11	C35	42.5	0.479	0.400	0.800	0.215	
12	C40	42.5	0.536	0.370	0.790	0.215	
13	C45	52.5	0.512	0.390	0.790	0.215	

表2-3-4 砂浆配合比表

项目	单位	水泥砂浆				
		砂浆标号				
		M15	M10	M7.5	M5	M2.5
		数量				
32.5水泥	t	0.455	0.331	0.268	0.210	0.150
中沙	m³	1.180	1.180	1.180	1.180	1.180
水	t	0.220	0.220	0.220	0.220	0.220

2. 案例工程二基础工程装置性材料统计

(1) 案例工程二基础工程装置性材料统计表

1) 基础工程装置性材料统计计算表，见表2-3-5。

表2-3-5 案例工程二基础工程装置性材料统计计算表

序号	材料名称及规格	单位	单重	单价	设计用量	损耗率%	总重	总价
1	2	3	4	5	6	7	8	9
一	LZG2026型 10以内				9.568 m³			
	钢筋	t	1.000	3500	0.872	0.5	0.88	3065.85
	地脚螺栓	t	1.000	5700	0.260	3	0.27	1528.57
	水泥	t	1.000	350	3.291	5.824	3.48	1219.08
	中沙	m³	1.550	85	4.401	16.236	7.93	434.85
	碎石	m³	1.600	60	8.133	12.06	14.58	546.82
	水	t	1.000		1.722			
	小计						27.14	6795.17
二	XJG2742型 40以内				24.052 m³			
	钢筋	t	1.000	3500	2.982	0.5	3.00	10489.19
	地脚螺栓	t	1.000	5700	0.790	3	0.81	4640.44
	水泥	t	1.000	350	8.274	5.824	8.76	3064.52
	中沙	m³	1.550	85	11.064	16.236	19.93	1093.12
	碎石	m³	1.600	60	20.444	12.06	36.66	1374.59
	水	t	1.000		4.329			
	小计						69.16	20661.85
三	TWG1630型 10以内				8.776 m³			
	钢筋	t	1.000	3500	0.372	0.5	0.37	1308.51
	地脚螺栓	t	1.000	5700	0.260	3	0.27	1528.57

续表

序号	材料名称及规格	单位	单重	单价	设计用量	损耗率%	总重	总价
	水泥	t	1.000	350	3.554	5.824	3.76	1316.45
	中沙	m³	1.550	85	3.598	16.236	6.48	355.50
	碎石	m³	1.600	60	7.460	12.06	13.37	501.55
	水	t	1.000		1.580			
	小计						24.26	5010.59
四	拉盘 LP-1.2	块	0.45	158	1	0.5	0.45	160.00
…								
C10					38.2 m³			
	水泥	t	1.000	350	9.550	5.824	10.11	3537.17
	中沙	m³	1.550	85	21.010	16.236	37.85	2075.80
	碎石	m³	1.600	60	31.706	12.06	56.85	2131.78
	水	t	1.000		6.876			
	小计						129.52	12915.34
C20					2430.92 m³			
	钢筋	t	1.000	3500	174.875	0.5	175.75	615121.41
	地脚螺栓	t	1.000	5700	36.114	3	37.20	212024.12
	水泥	t	1.000	350	836.236	5.824	884.94	309728.61
	中沙	m³	1.550	85	1118.223	16.236	2014.66	110481.12
	碎石	m³	1.600	60	2066.282	12.06	3704.76	138928.54
	水	t	1.000		437.566			
	小计						6817.30	1386283.80
	合计						6947.28	1399359.14

注：(8) = (4) × (6) ×[1+ (7)]，(9) = (5) × (6) ×[1+ (7)]

注：价格单位为元，单价为示例预算价格，实际工程中应以工程设计当时当地装置性材料预算价或合同价为准。

2) 钢筋加工及制作工程量统计。

汇总表2-3-5表中各型现浇基础的钢筋和地脚螺栓设计用量，再乘以各型基础数量，即得到本案例工程的钢筋加工及制作工程量统计数据：210988.4 kg（见表2-3-5，参见设计资料中"设备材料汇总表"，其中，基础钢筋Ⅰ级60721.5 kg，Ⅱ级114153.1 kg；地脚螺栓Q235钢36113.8 kg）。

3) 基础垫层工程量统计无设计用量。

4) 现浇混凝土基础混凝土搅拌及浇制工程量统计。

根据表2-3-5中数据及各型基础数量，列出表2-3-6，以方便计算安装费。

表 2-3-6 现浇混凝土基础混凝土搅拌及浇制情况统计表

型号（基数） \ 每基混凝土量（m³）	10以内	20以内	40以内	80以上	120以内	120以上
LZG2026型（1基）	9.568					
XJG2742型（1基）			24.052			
TWG1630型（1基）	8.776					
……	……					
合计	18.344		24.052			

见表 2-3-5，参见设计资料中"设备材料汇总表"，本案例工程混凝土设计用量为 2469.12 m³，其中，C10 级为 38.20 m³，C20 级为 2430.92 m³。C10 级混凝土主要用于基础保护帽浇制。

5）护坡、挡土墙及排洪沟砌筑工程量统计。

根据设计图纸中"设备材料汇总表"，本案例工程护坡、挡土墙及排洪沟砌筑等工程量按同类工程估计值为：土石方开挖 950 m³，条石堡坎 510 m³，护坡面积 240 m³，挡土墙 79.1 m³，排水沟 17.55 m³。余土外运 750 m³。

将表 2-3-5、2-3-6 数据汇总，填入表 2-3-7。

表 2-3-7 案例工程二基础工程工程量统计表

名称	单位	数量
基础钢筋加工及制作　一般钢筋	t	174.88
混凝土搅拌及浇制　每基混凝土量 10 m³ 以内	m³	1003.74
混凝土搅拌及浇制　每基混凝土量 20 m³ 以内	m³	785.63
混凝土搅拌及浇制　每基混凝土量 40 m³ 以内	m³	641.55
保护帽浇制　每基方量 0.5 m³ 以内	基	137.00
排洪沟　浆砌	m³	132.00
护坡或挡土墙　斜坡形　浆砌	m³	995.80
基础防腐　混凝土基础	m³	2740.00

（2）计算说明

本工程初步设计时，根据设计经验并参考同类型工程，初步确定使用 137 基铁塔及其塔型和呼称高，再根据塔型和呼称高选定基础形式。下面以几种选用的基础形式为例，分步统计计算其装置性材料数量，以说明基础工程装置性材料统计计算方法。

1）LZG2026 基础

如图 2-3-5，LZG2026 基础结构图。根据设计资料，LZG2026 基础采用 C20 混凝土，单个（腿）基础混凝土 2.39 m³，钢筋设计用量（主筋Φ16、箍筋Φ6、支撑筋Φ8、底板筋Φ14）共计 217.9 kg。

根据"铁塔基础根开表"，查出使用 LZG2026 基础的某铁塔（ZM1-18）的地脚螺栓根开（正侧面）为 220 mm，地脚螺栓规格为 M36；根据"直柱式基础地脚螺栓加工图"，查出 M36 地脚螺栓使用材料如表 2-3-8。

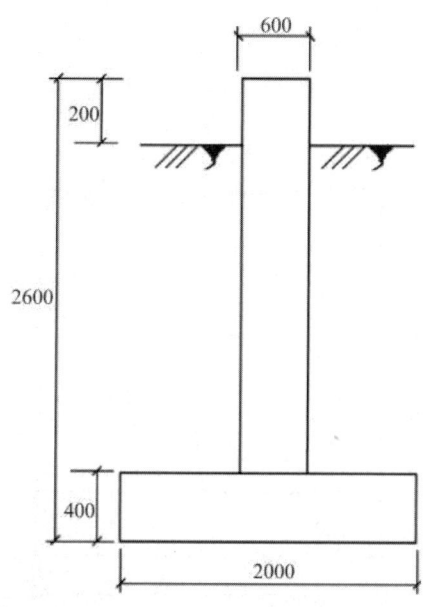

图 2-3-5　LZG2026 基础结构

此时应注意复核设计图纸提供的工程量数据，包括混凝土方量、钢筋及地脚螺栓使用量等。LZG2026 基础单个（腿）基础混凝土方量计算为

$$V = 2 \times 2 \times 0.4 + 0.6 \times 0.6 \times 2.2 = 2.392 \ (m^3)$$

设计提供的 LZG2026 基础单个（腿）基础混凝土方量为 2.39m³，而复核计算值为 2.392m³，在以下工程量计算中应使用后者。

根据表 2-3-3，C20 混凝土采用 32.5 水泥，配合比为 0.344∶0.460∶0.850∶0.180。LZG2026 基础单腿使用混凝土 2.392 m³，因此其水泥、沙、石、水用量为 0.823 t、1.117 m³、2.033 m³、0.431 t。根据表 2-3-10，中沙的单位运输重量 1.55 t/m³，碎石的单位运输重量 1.6 t/m³；按现行装置性材料预算价格确定单价；查表 1-2-1，综合考虑本案例工程地形划分为：平地 7.4%，丘陵 51.4%，山地 41.2%，分别计算水泥、石、沙等材料的施工损耗率，钢筋、螺栓等材料直接应用表 1-2-1 中数据。

水泥的施工损耗率为

$$(7.4\% + 51.4\%) \times 5.0\% + 41.2\% \times 7.0\% = 5.824\%$$

石的施工损耗率为

$$(7.4\%+51.4\%)\times10.0\%+41.2\%\times15.0\%=12.06\%$$

砂的施工损耗率为

$$(7.4\%+51.4\%)\times15.0\%+41.2\%\times18.0\%=16.236\%$$

将单腿基础工程量数据分别乘以4,得到整基基础工程量,填入表2-3-5中,再计算出总价和总重。

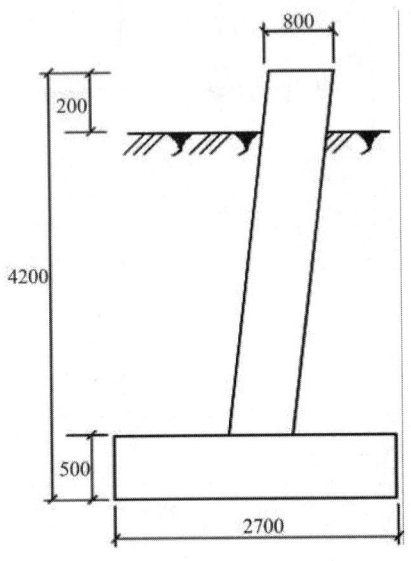

图2-3-6 XJG2742基础结构

2) XJG2742基础

如图2-3-6,XJG2742基础结构图。根据设计资料,XJG2742基础采用C20混凝土,单个(腿)基础混凝土6.03 m³,钢筋设计用量(主筋$\Phi25$、箍筋$\Phi8$、支撑筋$\Phi8$、底板筋$\Phi14$)共计745.5 kg;根据"铁塔基础根开表",查出使用LZG2026基础的N22号铁塔(JC1-18)的地脚螺栓根开(正侧面)为260 mm,地脚螺栓规格为M52;根据"斜柱式基础地脚螺栓加工图",查出M52地脚螺栓使用材料如表2-3-8。

XJG2742基础单个(腿)基础混凝土方量计算为

$$V=2.7\times2.7\times0.5+2.8\times0.8\times3.7$$
$$=6.013\ (m^3)$$

设计提供的XJG2742基础单个(腿)基础混凝土方量为6.03 m³,而复核计算值为6.013 m³,在以下工程量计算中应使用后者。

与LZG2026基础一样,同理确定其水泥、沙、石、水用量等数据分别填入表2-3-5中,计算出总价和总重。

3）TWG1630基础

如图2-3-4，TWG1630基础结构图。根据设计资料，TWG1630基础采用C25混凝土，单个（腿）基础混凝土2.32m³，钢筋设计用量（主筋$\Phi16$、外箍筋$\Phi8$、内箍筋$\Phi12$）共计90.3 kg；根据"铁塔基础根开表"，查出使用TWG1630基础的某铁塔（ZM1-30）的地脚螺栓根开（正侧面）为220mm，地脚螺栓规格为M36；根据"直柱式基础地脚螺栓加工图"，查出M36地脚螺栓使用材料如表2-3-8。

TWG1630基础单个（腿）基础混凝土方量计算为

$$V = \pi r_2^2 h_1 + \frac{\pi h_2(r_2^2 + r_1^2 + r_1 r_2)}{3} \pi r_2^2 h_3$$

$$= \pi \times 0.8^2 \times 0.3 + \frac{\pi \times 0.5\,(0.8^2 + 0.4^2 + 0.8 \times 0.4)}{3} + \pi \times 0.4^2 \times 2.2$$

$$= 2.194\,(\text{m}^3)$$

设计提供的TWG1630基础单个（腿）基础混凝土方量为2.32 m³，而复核计算值为2.194 m³，在以下工程量计算中应使用后者。

与LZG2026基础一样，同理确定其水泥、沙、石、水用量等数据分别填入表2-3-5中，计算出总价和总重。

表2-3-8 地脚螺栓使用材料表

地脚螺栓			地脚螺栓垫片			地脚螺栓钢箍			锚固端钢材（kg）	螺帽（kg）	每组螺栓合计（kg）
直径M（mm）	数量（件）	小计	数量（件）	小计	数量（件）	小计					
	单重（kg）		单重（kg）		单重（kg）						
36	4	44.76	4	6.36	5	1.40	9.59	2.98	65.09		
	11.19		1.59		0.28						
52	4	134.70	4	16.28	9	5.43	31.71	9.47	197.60		
	33.68		4.07		0.60						

（二）杆塔工程

杆塔工程包括混凝土杆组立、钢管杆组立、铁塔组立、高塔组立、拉线制作及安装、接地安装等。

1. 几种常见杆塔组立形式的装置性材料统计相关要求

（1）混凝土杆组立

定额中"每基重量"系指杆身自重与横担、叉梁、脚钉（爬梯）、拉线抱箍等全部杆身组合构件的总重量，不包括底、卡、拉盘的重量。

(2) 钢管杆组立

定额中"每基重量"系指钢管杆杆身自重与横担、螺栓等全部杆身组合构件的总重量。

(3) 铁塔组立

定额中"每基重量"系指铁塔总重量为

总重量=∑（铁搭本身所有的型钢、连板、螺栓、脚钉、爬梯等）×（1+3）　（2-3-8）

其中，3%为塔材以大代小增加量，钢管塔不计列。

(4) 高塔组立

适用于塔全高超过70 m的高塔组立。

杆塔组立按不同重量等级以"基"统计；拉线制作以"根"统计，应注意其长度区别；接地安装以"根"统计，应注意接地极（接地引下线）的长度。

2. 案例工程二杆塔工程装置性材料统计（附表二）

(1) 案例工程二杆塔工程装置性材料统计表

1) 杆塔工程装置性材料统计

根据设计资料，本工程全线使用铁塔137基，其中直线铁塔86基，耐张、转角铁塔51基，如表2-3-9。

表2-3-9　具体塔型及数量统计表

序号	回路数	冰区	用途	塔型	呼称高（m）	基数	小计	合计（基）
1	单回路	5mm	直线塔	2A-ZM1	21	4	22	85
					24	6		
					27	8		
					30	4		
				2A-ZM2	21	4	30	
					24	5		
					27	5		
					30	7		
					33	6		
					36	3		
				2A-ZM3	24	2	25	
					27	4		
					30	7		
					33	6		
					36	3		
					39	2		
					42	1		

续表

序号	回路数	冰区	用途	塔型	呼称高（m）	基数	小计	合计（基）
				2A-ZMC3	24	2	5	
					33	1		
					36	1		
					42	1		
				2A-ZMC4	27	2	3	
					42	1		
			转角塔	2A-JC1（0~20°）	21	11	30	
					24	10		
					27	9		
				2A-JC2（20~40°）	24	5	11	44
					27	4		
					30	2		
				2A-JC3（40~60°）	21	2	2	
				2A-JC4（60~90°）	21	1	1	
2	双回路	5mm	直线塔	2I-SZ3	27	1	1	1
			转角塔	2I-SJ2（20~40°）	24	2	3	
					27	1		
				2I-SJ3（40~60°）	24	2	3	7
					27	1		
				2I-SJ4（60~90°）	21	1	1	

通过查阅设计资料中"××型塔单线图及材料汇总表"，得出各型铁塔包括角钢、螺栓、脚钉、垫圈等材料的设计用量，填入表2-3-10。

表2-3-10 案例工程二杆塔工程装置性材料计算表

序号	材料名称及规格	单位	单重	单价	设计用量	损耗率%	总重	总价
1	2	3	4	5	6	7	8	9
一	ZM1-27型 9以内				7.0514t			
	塔材（角钢、钢板）	t	1	6800	6.4262	0.5	6.4583	43916.65
	螺栓、脚钉、垫片	t	1	6800	0.4324	3.5	0.4475	3043.23
	塔材代用3%	t	1	6800	0.1928	0.5	0.1937	1317.50
	小计						7.0996	48277.38
二	JC1-21型 11以内				10.9318t			
	塔材（角钢、钢板）	t	1	6800	10.0839	0.5	10.1343	68913.37
	螺栓、脚钉、垫片	t	1	6800	0.5454	3.5	0.5645	3838.53
	塔材代用3%	t	1	6800	0.3025	0.5	0.3040	2067.40
	小计						11.0028	74819.30
三	SJ2-24型 30以内				28.0390t			

续表

序号	材料名称及规格	单位	单重	单价	设计用量	损耗率%	总重	总价
	塔材（角钢、钢板）	t	1	6800	26.0113	0.5	26.1414	177761.22
	螺栓、脚钉、垫片	t	1	6800	1.2474	3.5	1.2911	8779.20
	塔材代用3%	t	1	6800	0.7803	0.5	0.7842	5332.84
	小计						28.2167	191873.26
…								
					1133.4914t			
	塔材（角钢、钢板）	t	1	6800	1059.423	0.5	1064.7201	7240096.78
	螺栓、脚钉、垫片	t	1	6800	74.0684	3.5	76.6608	521293.40
	塔材代用3%	t	1	6800	31.7827	0.5	31.9416	217202.90
	合计						1173.3225	7978593.08

注：(8) = (4) × (6) ×[1+ (7)]，(9) = (5) × (6) ×[1+ (7)]

注：价格单位为元，单价为示例预算价格，实际工程中应以工程设计当时当地装置性材料预算价或合同价为准。

根据表2-3-9中所列铁塔各塔型使用数量，以及表2-3-10中各塔型塔材、螺栓、脚钉、垫片设计用量，分类汇总即得到本案例工程杆塔工程的装置性材料量（见表2-3-10），此处限于篇幅不再赘述。

2）杆塔组立工程量统计

根据表2-3-9中所列铁塔各塔型使用数量，以及表2-3-10中各塔型塔材设计用量，按照铁塔安装定额子目划分，填入表2-3-11以方便计算安装费。

表2-3-11 杆塔组立工程量统计计算表

型号（基数） 每基重量t	5以内	7以内	9以内	11以内	30以内	小计
ZM1-27型（8基）			7.0514			56.4111
JC1-21型（11基）				10.9318		120.2500
SJ2-24型（2基）					28.0390	56.0781
……		……				
合计（t）			8基	11基	2基	232.7392

3）接地安装工程量统计

根据"初步设计总说明书"，本案例工程使用137套接地装置，其中丙型占10%，丁型占35%，戊型占50%，己型占5%。根据初步设计资料中"设备材料汇总表"，接地装置工程量统计如表2-3-12，注意计算复核工程量。

表2-3-12 接地安装工程量统计计算表

序号	材料名称及规格	单位	单价	设计用量	损耗率	总重	总价
1	圆钢F10	kg	4000	18934.2	0.5	19028.9	76115.57
2	圆钢F12	kg	4000	1216.6	0.5	1222.6	4890.57
3	扁钢130′50′5	kg	4000	168.5	0.5	169.4	677.41
4	镀锌螺栓M16′45	kg	5800	80.0	3.0	82.4	477.97
合计				20319.3		20503.3	82161.52

汇总表2-3-12中圆钢和扁钢设计用量为20319.3 kg，即为接地体加工及制作工程量，填入表2-3-13；如图2-0-2，本案例工程中使用的接地装置为丙、丁、戊、己型，每个接地装置敷设的F10接地圆钢4根，每根长度分别为28 m、38 m、68 m、86 m，根据各型接地装置使用比例计算接地圆钢根数，填入表2-3-13。将表2-3-11中"合计"栏数据，填入表2-3-13。

表2-3-13 案例工程二杆塔工程工程量统计表

名称	单位	数量
铁塔组立　每基重量5t以内	基	19
铁塔组立　每基重量7t以内	基	45
铁塔组立　每基重量9t以内	基	28
铁塔组立　每基重量11t以内	基	19
铁塔组立　每基重量13t以内	基	19
铁塔组立　每基重量27t以内	基	4
铁塔组立　每基重量30t以内	基	3
接地体加工及制作	kg	20319.3
接地体敷设　每基长度200m以内	根	247
接地体敷设　每基长度300m以内	根	274
接地体敷设　每基长度400m以内	根	28
电阻测量	基	137

(2) 计算说明

下面以本案例工程中使用的几种铁塔的装置性材料统计计算为例，说明杆塔工程装置性材料统计计算方法。

1) ZM1-27型直线塔

查阅设计资料中"ZM1型塔单线图及材料汇总表"，ZM1-27型直线塔各种材料设计用量分别为：角钢，Q345为2644.2 kg，Q235为3079.8 kg；钢板，Q345为365.0 kg，Q235为337.2 kg；螺栓，6.8级，M16为183.5 kg，M20为211.8 kg；脚钉，6.8级，

36 kg；垫圈（垫片）1.1 kg。将角钢和钢板量相加后填入表2-3-8"塔材"栏，将螺栓、脚钉、垫圈（垫片）量相加后填入表2-3-10。

2）JC1-21型转角塔

查阅设计资料中"JC1型塔单线图及材料汇总表"，JC1-21型转角塔各种材料设计用量分别为：角钢，Q345为4375 kg，Q235为4105.4 kg；钢板，Q345为1214.9 kg，Q235为388.6 kg；螺栓，6.8级，M16为99.5 kg，M20为284.1 kg，M24为129.2 kg；脚钉，6.8级，31.1 kg；垫圈（垫片）1.5 kg。同理填入表2-3-10。

3）SJ2-24型转角塔

查阅设计资料中"SJ2型塔单线图及材料汇总表"，SJ2-24型转角塔各种材料设计用量分别为：角钢，Q345为11239.7 kg，Q235为10342.8 kg；钢板，Q345为3454.2 kg，Q235为974.6 kg；螺栓，4.8级（M16）为220.4 kg，6.8级（M20）为933.9 kg；脚钉，4.8级（M16）为63.8 kg，6.8级（M20）为28.3 kg；垫圈（垫片）1.0 kg。同理填入表2-3-10。

4）接地装置材料

查表2-0-4，每套丙、丁、戊、己型接地装置使用$\varPhi$12圆钢均为8.88 kg，137套接地装置中，丙型占10%，丁型占35%，戊型占50%，己型占5%。本案例工程接地装置$\varPhi$12圆钢设计用量计算为

$$(8.88\times10\%+8.88\times35\%+8.88\times50\%+8.88\times5\%)\times137=1216.6（kg）$$

同理可得$\varPhi$10圆钢、扁钢和镀锌螺栓设计用量，填入表2-3-12。

（三）架线工程

架线工程包括导线、避雷线、光缆架设，导线、避雷线、光缆跨越架设，耦合屏蔽线安装，拦河线安装，光缆测量与接续。

1. 相关要求

定额分一般架设和张力架设两种，使用时应根据施工图设计要求套用。定额按导线和避雷线截面设置子目，并已包括跳线绝缘子串安装，不列电压等级。架线工程量以线路总长为准，且悬挂点高差角在10°范围以内。定额中导线是按三相交流单回线路工程考虑。

2. 案例工程二架线工程装置性材料统计

（1）案例工程二架线工程装置性材料统计表，见表2-3-14。

表2-3-14 案例工程二架线工程装置性材料统计表

序号	材料名称及规格	单位	单重	单价	设计用量	损耗率%	总重	总价
1	2	3	4	5	6	7	8	9
一	导线 LGJ-400/35	t	0.001349	16800	310800	0.4824	421.29	7077701.48
二	单根避雷线 GJX-80	t	0.000628	14000	43800	0.3	27.59	386244.87
	单根避雷线 LBGJ-100-30AC	t	0.00057393	14000	8000	0.4824	4.61	64590.25
	小计							

注：(8) = (4) × (6) ×[1+ (7)], (9) = (5) × (6) ×[1+ (7)]

注：价格单位为元。

(2) 计算说明

根据导线、避雷线和光缆的回路数，导线分裂数，导线、避雷线和光缆根数，单位长度重量，线路长度，再计及损耗得总重。计算公式为

$$总重量 = n_1 \times n_2 \times G_0 \times \sum l_i \times n_3 \times (1+损耗率\%) \tag{2-3-10}$$

式中，n_1 为导线、避雷线和光缆的回路数，分单、双、多回；n_2 为导线分裂数，分双分裂、四分裂、六分裂、八分裂等，避雷线和光缆则取1；n_3 为导线相数、避雷线和光缆根数；G_0 为导线、避雷线和光缆的单位长度重量，kg/km；$\sum l_i$ 为线路长度，即沿线各挡挡距之和，km。这里的线路长度本应是导线、避雷线或光缆的实际长度，因初步设计阶段各档的档距、高差、弧垂均未确定，一般用线路总长替代，施工图设计后即可计算出实际长度。存在的误差部分则根据经验并结合工程地形，通过适当放大工程量来处理，表2-3-14中数据未经放大处理。

损耗率为导线、避雷线和光缆的损耗率不同，同时与地形有关，详见《电力建设工程预算定额（第四册 送电线路工程2006年版）》；本案例工程导线（含良导体底线）的施工损耗率为0.4824%。计算式为

（7.4%+51.4%）×0.4%+41.2%×0.6%=0.4824%

$$总价 = 总重量 \times 单价 \tag{2-3-11}$$

根据设计资料，本案例工程亘长51.8 km，导线采用双分裂LGJ-400/35，避雷线采用单根避雷线配合OPGW，其中GJX-80型避雷线长43.8km，LBGJ-100-30AC型避雷线长8 km。

由式（2-3-10）、（2-3-11）计算导线避雷线的总重和总价。

1) 导线的总重为

1×2×1.349×51800×3×（1+0.4824%）=421291.75（kg）

2）GJX-80 避雷线的总重为

$$1×1×0.628×43800×1×（1+0.3\%）=27588.92（kg）$$

3）LBGJ-100-30AC 避雷线的总重为

$$1×1×0.57393×8000×1×（1+0.4824\%）=4613.59（kg）$$

同理计算总价。表 2-3-14 中单价为示例预算价格，实际工程中应以工程设计时当时当地装置性材料预算价或合同价为准。

（四）附件工程

附件工程包括绝缘子串悬挂，导线悬垂线夹安装，均压环、屏蔽环安装，防振锤、间隔棒安装，重锤安装，阻尼线安装，阻冰环安装。

1. 相关要求

绝缘子串悬挂适用于直线、直线转角及换位杆塔的绝缘子串安装，不包括耐张金具及耐张绝缘子串安装。耐张导、地线端头制作，跳线串安装，跨越跳线端头制作及安装，直线转角及换位杆（塔）地线的绝缘子串安装，这些工作内容均包括在架线工程中。

附件工程安装的装置性材料主要是指绝缘子和金具，分别按"串""个""套"统计。绝缘子分为导线用悬垂串、耐张串以及地线用绝缘子，金具包括联板类、挂环类、碗头挂板类和其他类，其他类金具包括线夹、均压环、屏蔽环、防振锤、间隔棒、重锤、阻尼线、阻冰环、接地螺栓、引下线等。

2. 案例工程二附件工程装置性材料统计表

（1）案例工程二附件工程装置性材料统计表，见表 2-3-15。

表 2-3-15 案例工程二附件工程装置性材料统计表

序号	材料名称及规格	单位	单重	单价	设计用量	损耗率%	总重	总价
1	2	3	4	5	6	7	8	9
一	绝缘子							
	U100BP2	片	4	85	15966	2.0	65141.28	1384252.2
	XDP-70CN	片	7	80	6	2.0	42.84	489.6
二	金具							
	联板类							
	联板 L-1640	块	9.54	144	926	1.0	8922.38	134677.44
	…							
	挂环类							
	U 形挂环 U-7	件	0.44	12	30	1.0	13.33	363.6

续表

序号	材料名称及规格	单位	单重	单价	设计用量	损耗率%	总重	总价
	…							
	碗头挂板类							
	碗头挂板 WS-10	件	1.2	34	1065	1.0	1290.78	36572.1
	…							
	其他类							
	悬垂线夹 XCS-6	件	15	234	346	1.0	5241.90	81773.64
	耐张线夹 NY-80G	件	1.3	43	214	1.0	280.98	9294.02
	防震锤 FDZ-5F	件	7.2	67	1726	1.0	12551.47	116798.42
	预绞丝护线条 FYH-400/35	件	2.8	274	176	1.0	497.73	48706.24
	…							
	合计						119706.40	2413711.00

注：(8) = (4) × (6) ×[1+ (7)]，(9) = (5) × (6) ×[1+ (7)]

注：重量单位为kg，价格单位为元，单价为示例预算价。

(2) 计算说明

1) 绝缘子数量的计算。

参考设计资料中"设备材料汇总表"，导线绝缘子U100BP2设计用量为15966片，地线绝缘子XDP-70CN设计用量为6片。根据表2-0-7金具绝缘子串型及其具体使用范围表和表2-3-9具体塔型及数量统计表，计算本案例工程中绝缘子和金具设计用量，以此对设计提供的材料量进行复核，然后填入表2-3-15。

2) 金具数量的计算。

方法同上。只是金具的种类和数量较多，表2-3-15只选取部分材料列表，其他限于本书篇幅不再赘述。

在统计绝缘子、金具数量时，应注意线路两端的门型构架或分支杆塔上的耐张绝缘子金具串是否遗漏。

根据表2-3-5、2-3-10、2-3-12、2-3-14、2-3-15，计算案例工程二主要装置性材料及工程量指标，见表2-3-16。

表2-3-16 主要装置性材料及工程量指标表

项目名称	导线	避雷线 GJX-80	避雷线 LBGJ	塔材	金具	基础钢筋	砼量	土石方量	绝缘子
单位	t/km	t/km	t/km	t/km	t/km	t/km	m³/km	m³/km	片/km
数量	8.13	0.63	0.58	22.65	2.31	3.38	47.67	745.68	315

四、工地运输工程量计算

（一）设备、材料的运输

设备、材料的运输是指将设备、材料从生产厂家运至施工现场。设备的运输费用计入设备购置费，按合同定价（含运杂费）或设备原价基础加运杂费（设备原价乘运杂费率）。线路工程的装置性材料运输分为大运输、小运输。

1. 大运输

大运输是指装置性材料从生产厂家经铁路或水路、公路运至工地的材料集散仓库的运输。

大运输的费用包括厂内运输费、铁路（水路、公路）运费，装卸费，进入仓库的运费，采购保管费，供销部门手续费等（不同材料、不同单位有相应的规定）。对装置性材料而言，其大运输费用则直接计入装置性材料的预算价格之中，装置性材料预算价格一般是执行全省统一价格，由各省电力定额（造价）管理站根据上一季度本省区域装置性材料市场价格制定本季度价格。

2. 小运输

小运输又称工地运输，是指装置性材料自工地集散仓库（材料站）运至沿线各杆、塔位的装卸、运输及空载回程等全部工作。

工地运输按运输方式分为人力运输、拖拉机运输、汽车运输、船舶运输、索道运输。之所以要区分不同运输方式，是因为采用不同运输方式运输单位重量消耗的人工、机械和材料是不同的，对应选取的定额子目不同。另外，还应注意不同运输方式的地形是不同的，比如人力运输的地形一般考虑与线路工程地形一致，而汽车运输又应该按实际汽车运输线路地形计。

（二）工地运输量的计算

$$概算量=设计用量+损耗量=设计用量×（1+损耗率） \qquad (2\text{-}3\text{-}12)$$

$$运输重量=概算量×单位运输重量 \qquad (2\text{-}3\text{-}13)$$

概算量的计算工作实际上在编制装置性材料数量统计计算表中完成，详见表 2-3-5、2-3-10、2-3-12、2-3-14、2-3-15，其中"总量"栏数值即为该种装置性材料的概算量；

设计用量是指由设计人员提供，经概算编制人员计算复核后，确定的包括各单位工程装置性材料种类和数量等在内的工程量数据。原则上概算编制人员不得擅自增减该数据种类和数量。但是，概算编制人员复核确定的该数据的数值常常大于设计提供的数值，根据经验视材料种类的不同分别放大5%~10%。其原因是初设概算控制整个工程投资额，而初步设计工程量数据较为粗略，为了确保预算投资额不突破概算投资额，只有适当放大工程量。本书中表2-3-5、2-3-10、2-3-12、2-3-14、2-3-15中数据均未作放大处理。

损耗量是指因搬运等施工原因导致装置性材料损坏的数量。损耗率详见表1-2-1，材料施工损耗率表。因施工损耗而准备的各种备件不计安装费，只计算其金额和重量计入"总量"和"总价"中。

计算运输重量时，直接取前述的装置性材料统计计算表中的概算量用于计算，材料的单位运输重量应执行预算定额的规定，见表2-3-17。

表2-3-17　装置性材料的单位运输重量表

材料名称		单位	运输重量（kg）	备注
混凝土制品	人工浇制	m³	2600	包括钢筋
	离心浇制	m³	2860	包括钢筋
线材	导线（有线盘）	kg	$W \times 1.15$	
	避雷线（有线盘）	kg	$W \times 1.10$	
	避雷线、拉线（无线盘）	kg	$W \times 1.04$	
	光缆（有线盘）	kg	$W \times 1.20$	
	电缆	kg	$W+G$	G为盘重
商品混凝土		m³	2560	
土方		m³	1500	实挖量
块石、碎石、卵石		m³	1600	
石灰		m³	1200	
黄沙（干中沙）		m³	1550	
水泥、降阻剂		kg	$W \times 1.01$	袋装
水		kg	$W \times 1.20$	
金具、绝缘子（瓷、玻璃）		kg	$W \times 1.07$	
合成绝缘子		kg	$W \times 2.00$	
螺栓、垫圈、脚钉		kg	$W \times 1.01$	

注：表中未列入的其他种类装置性材料按净重计算，W为理论重量。

预算定额中各类材料的含义：混凝土杆是指以离心机制的整根及分节混凝土杆、混凝土套筒及混凝土横担等；混凝土预制品是指以人工浇制、机械振捣的混凝土制成品及半成品，如底盘、拉盘、卡盘、叉梁、盖板等；线材是指导线、避雷线、耦合屏蔽线、电缆、光缆；塔材是指铁塔钢材；钢管杆是指以钢板压制、焊接形成的整根或分节钢管杆；金具、绝缘子、零星钢材是指金具、绝缘子、电杆用横担、地线支架、拉棒、拉杆、抱箍、连接金具、防振锤、间隔棒、铸铁重锤、接地管（带）材、螺栓、垫圈等。

工地运输的平均运距以千米为单位，凡用汽车、船舶运输时，其平均运距不足1 km者按1 km计算；用拖拉机、人力运输时，其平均运距保留两位小数。平均运距计算方法详见项目一中工程量计算相关内容。

（三）案例工程二的平均运距

本工程交通运输主要以区乡公路为主，全线与线路平行和交叉的机耕道较多，但个别地段运输条件较差。全线汽车运输平均运距28 km，人力运输平均运距0.80 km。

计算说明：经测算，沿本案例工程线路路径的用于材料运输的公路里程数为56 km，考虑将材料站设置在公路中点位置，所以取汽车运输平均运距28 km。因初步设计阶段杆塔位并未确定，人力运距参考同类型工程，估计为0.80 km。余土外运采用人力运输，参考同类型工程，平均运距为150 m。

（四）案例工程二的工地运输工程量计算

本案例工程工地运输重量和工程量计算见表2-2-18（格式同附表四），2-3-19（格式同附表五）。

计算说明：根据表2-3-5、2-3-10、2-3-12、2-3-14、2-3-15中数据等5个单位工程装置性材料数量统计数值，按照表2-3-18表材料类别分类汇总各种装置性材料的重量，填入表2-3-18（表中"材料类别"是依据预算定额中定额子目划分来确定的，本表中仅列出本案例工程中有的材料种类）。此时，应注意区分材料种类，因为不同材料的包装系数不同，这就需要将不同单位工程的同一种装置性材料汇总。

同样地，表2-3-19中"项目名称"是依据预算定额中定额子目划分来确定的。表中应注意区分装置性材料的人力运输和汽车运输工程量，还应注意余土外运采用人力运输，且其平均运距是不同的。表中现浇混凝土基础工程用水是按普通装置性材料同样的平均运距来计算其工地运输重量和工程量，实际工程施工中水一般是就地取用。定额中已考虑了混凝土的洗石、搅拌、养护、洗模板等所需的用水量的100 m范围内运输。

表 2-3-18　案例工程二工地运输重量计算表

材料类别	单位	全线概算量（含损耗）					合计	包装系数	运输重量 t
		土石方工程	杆塔工程	绝缘子及挂线金具安装	架线工程	接地工程			
混凝土预制品 500kg以内	kg	454.50					454.50	1.00	0.45
线材 1000kg以内导线	kg				421291.75		421291.75	1.15	484.49
线材 1000kg以内地线	kg				32202.51		32202.51	1.10	35.42
金属、绝缘子、零星钢材、塔材 金具	kg			119706.40			119706.40	1.07	128.09
绝缘子	kg			65184.12			65184.12	1.07	69.75
零星钢材	kg	175748.97				20420.90	196169.87	1.00	196.17
塔材	kg		1096661.70				1096661.70	1.00	1096.66
螺栓、垫圈、脚钉	kg	37197.21	76660.80			82.40	113940.41	1.01	115.08
砖、沙、石、土、水泥、石灰 沙	m³	1324.20					1324.20	1.55t/m³	2052.51
石	m³	2351.00					2351.01	1.60t/m³	3761.61
土（余土外运）	m³	750.00					750.00	1.50t/m³	1125.00
水	m³	444.44					444.44	1.20	533.33
水泥	kg	895045.08					895045.08	1.01	904.00
合计									10502.55

注1：拉线、避雷线、导线根据型号，每盘重量不同分栏填表，其包装系数按有关规定计算。

注2："运输重量"数填入附表五。

表 2-3-19 案例工程二工地运输工程量计算表

运距单位：km

材料站	项目名称	地形运输量 t	平地 运距	平地 t.km	丘陵 运距	丘陵 t.km	山地 运距	山地 t.km	高山 运距	高山 t.km	峻岭 运距	峻岭 t.km	泥沼 运距	泥沼 t.km
×站	人力运输	人力平均运距 800m												
	余土外运	1125	0.15	168.75										
	混凝土预制品													
	500kg 以内	0.45	0.80	0.36										
	线材													
	1000kg 以内	519.51	0.80	415.61										
	金具、绝缘子、零星钢材	431.66	0.80	345.32										
	塔材	1174.09	0.80	939.27										
	砖、沙、石、土、水、水泥、石灰	7251.44	0.80	5801.15										
	汽车运输	汽车平均运距 28km												
	混凝土预制品 500kg 以内	0.45	28.00	12.60										
	线材 1000kg 以内	519.51	28.00	14546.28										
	金具、绝缘子、零星钢材	431.66	28.00	12086.34										
	塔材	1174.09	28.00	32874.50										
	砖、沙、石、土、水、水泥、石灰	7251.44	28.00	203040.39										

注1：此处仅计算平地地形的运输工程量，在安装费费取费计算时再考虑综合地形调增系数。
注2：铁塔用螺栓、垫圈、脚钉重量计入塔材。

任务4　取费计算

上一个学习任务确定了线路工程的工程量。对编制工程初步设计概算工作来讲，知道工程量只是第一步，还必须执行《预标》规定的预算费用构成和计算标准，取定适用的装置性材料单价、安装费单价（基价）以及各种费率，依据工程量计算出工程概算投资金额数量，从而完成取费计算。这是取费计算的内涵，取费计算的外化表现为组成概算书的系列表格。

这些概算表格的填写，是依据上一个学习任务统计出来的各单位工程的工程量，套用定额确定各工程量对应的安装费单价，工程量乘以单价即得合价金额，再结合工程实际和现行相关规定考虑人工、机械、材料费的调整系数，采用加、乘、转移数据等多种方式，完成表格的填写工作。本学习任务侧重说明概算书的表一乙、表二乙、表三乙、表三丙、表四等表格的编制方法和过程。

在具体完成填写各种概算表格之前，首先应熟悉送电线路工程建设预算费用构成，它与项目一所述配电线路工程建设预算费用构成略有不同；其次，应进一步熟悉《电力建设工程预算定额》（第四册）《送电线路工程》（2006年版），以便取用适当的定额子目对应的安装费单价。本项目中所涉及费用内涵同项目一的，请查阅项目一中相关内容，此处不再赘述。

一、送电线路工程建设预算费用构成

送电线路工程建设预算费用由安装工程费、其他费用和动态费用组成。安装工程费和其他费用之和称为静态投资。

（一）安装工程费用的构成

安装工程费是指对构成项目的基础设施、工艺系统及附属系统进行施工、安装、调试，使之具备生产功能所支出的费用。它包括直接费、间接费、利润和税金。

1. 直接费

直接费指建筑安装产品生产过程中直接消耗在特定产品对象上的费用。它由直接工程费和措施费组成。

(1) 直接工程费包括人工费、材料费、施工机械使用费。

(2) 措施费包括冬雨季施工增加费、夜间施工增加费、施工工具用具使用费、特殊地区施工增加费、临时设施费、施工机构转移费、安全文明措施补助费。

2. 间接费

间接费指建筑安装产品生产过程中，为全工程项目服务而不直接耗用在特定产品对象上的费用。它由规费和企业管理费组成。

规费包括社会保障费、社会公积金、危险作业意外伤害保险费。

（二）其他费用构成

其他费用是指完成工程项目建设所必需的，不属于建筑安装工程费的其他相关费用。它包括以下费用。

1. 建设场地征用及清理费

(1) 土地征用费。

(2) 施工场地租用费。

(3) 迁移补偿费。

(4) 余物清理费。

(5) 送电线路走廊赔偿费。

(6) 通信设施防送电线路干扰措施费。

2. 项目建设管理费

(1) 建设项目法人管理费。

(2) 招标费。

(3) 工程监理费。

(4) 设备建造费。

(5) 工程保险费。

3. 项目建设技术服务费

(1) 项目前期工作费。

(2) 知识产权转让及研究试验费。

(3) 勘察设计费包括勘察费、设计费。

(4) 设计文件评审费，包括可行性研究设计文件评审费、初步设计文件评审费。

(5) 项目后评价费。

（6）工程建设监督检测费，包括工程质量监督检测费、特种设备安全监测费、环境监测验收费、水土保持项目验收及补偿费、桩基检测费。

（7）电力建设标准编制管理费。

（8）电力工程定额编制管理费。

4. 分系统调试及整套启动调试费

（1）分系统调试费。

（2）整套启动调试费。

（3）施工企业配合调试费。

5. 生产准备费

（1）管理车辆购置费。

（2）工器具及办公家具购置费。

（3）生产职工培训及提前进场费。

此外，其他费用中还包括大件运输措施费和基本预备费。

（四）动态费用的构成

动态费用是指对构成工程造价的各要素在建设预算编制年至竣工验收期间，因时间和市场价格变化所引起价格增长和资金成本增加所发生的费用，主要包括价差预备费和建设期贷款利息。

下面按照概算编制工作流程介绍各种概算表格的编制。

二、编制单位工程概算表

单位工程概算表在概算书中占的篇幅最多，包括土石方工程、基础工程、杆塔工程、架线工程、附件工程、工地运输等六个单位工程概算表。

单位工程概算表见表2-4-1，其中主要包括装置性材料费和安装费两类费用，分为单价和合价。编制单位工程概算表时，依据送电线路工程装置性材料统计表、土石方量计算表、工地运输工程量计算表，在"项目名称及规范"栏填入该单位工程安装的装置性材料的名称。若土石方工程和工地运输单位工程没有装置性材料，则填入土石方开挖工程量或工地运输工程量的名称，与此同时，在"单位"和"数量"栏中填入相应数据。查阅适用定额，在"编制依据"栏填入相应的定额子目编号，作为该工程量对应的定额安装基价（即单价）的确定依据。依据定额子目对应的定额安装"基价"，填入"单价"栏中安装费所属"合计、其中工资、其中机械"栏。依据选定的装置性材料预算价格,填入"单价"栏中装置性材料单价。"合价"等于"数量"乘以"单价"。

表2-4-1 架空送电线路单位工程概算表(表三丙)

序号	编制依据	项目名称及规范	单位	数量	单价(元)				合价(元)			
					装置性材料	安装费			装置性材料	安装费		
						合计	其中工资	其中机械		合计	其中工资	其中机械

一般的,表三丙直接填入合价(源于装置性材料统计计算表总价),不反映由单价到合价的计算过程。因为计算安装费时,使用的是装置性材料的设计用量,不包括施工损耗量,装置性材料合价包括施工损耗量。

(一)关于装置性材料费的计算

装置性材料的数量来自工程量统计数据,单价则取自工程所在地当时执行的"送变电工程设备材料信息价"或适用的"电力建设工程装置性材料预算价格",其余材料按工程所在地当前市场价格计。计算公式为

$$装置性材料费=装置性材料消耗量×装置性材料预算价格 \quad (2-4-1)$$

装置性材料预算价格按照电力行业定额(造价)管理机构公布的装置性材料预算价格或综合预算价格计算,一般由各省电力行业定额(造价)管理机构每季度公布上一季度的《电力建设工程装置性材料预算价格》。现行的装置性材料预算价格为上一季度价格水平,与现行的"电力建设工程预算定额"和"电网工程建设预算编制与计算标准"配套使用。材料到场检验试验费已包括在施工单位的企业管理费中。

(二)关于安装费的计算

单位工程概算表中的安装费包括定额直接费、地形调增、人工费调整和材机调整,它和装置性材料费相加构成直接工程费。安装费的计算公式为

$$安装费=定额直接费+地形调增+人工费调整+材机调整 \quad (2-4-2)$$

1. 定额直接费

定额直接费是安装费的主体部分,包含人工费、材料费(消耗性材料费)、机械费。计算公式为

$$定额直接费(合价)=各单位工程的工程量×定额安装基价(单价) \quad (2-4-3)$$

定额安装基价简称定额基价或基价,样例见表2-4-2,摘自《电力建设工程预算定额》(第四册)《送电线路工程》(2006年版)。

表2-4-2 线路复测及分坑定额子目样例表

工作内容：复测桩位及档距，测定坑位、坑界及施工基面，主桩或辅助桩遗失或变动后的恢复，平、断面的校核，工器具搬运。

单位：基

定额编号				YX2-1	YX2-2	YX2-3	YX2-4	YX2-5
项目				直线单杆	直线双杆及拉线塔	耐张（转角）双杆	直线自立塔	耐张（转角）自立塔
基价（元）				29.36	44.28	59.48	51.10	68.29
其中	人工费（元）			9.93	14.23	21.18	24.29	36.74
	材料费（元）			18.53	28.69	36.49	24.57	28.61
	机械费（元）			0.90	1.36	1.81	2.04	2.94
	名称		单位	数量				
人工	综合工日		工日	0.30	0.43	0.64	0.74	1.11
材料	木桩		个	5.000	8.000	9.000	8.000	10.000
	竹桩		个	16.000	24.000	35.000	16.000	16.000
机械	送电专用载重汽车4t		台班	0.004	0.006	0.008	0.009	0.013

（1）人工费已包含在定额基价内，见表2-4-2。根据送电线路工程预算定额（2006年版），定额的人工包括基本用工和其他辅助用工，不分工种、等级，均以综合工日表示；综合工日单价即定额基准工日单价，送电线路工程基准工日单价为33.1元/工日，其中已包括工资性补贴2.4元/工日。

（2）材料费，即消耗性材料费，又称计价材料费，一般是指在预算定额中，费用已经计入定额基价的材料。消耗性材料费根据定额规定的原则计算，已包含在定额基价内，见表2-4-2。

（3）机械费，即施工机械使用费，按照《电力建设施工机械台班费用定额（2006年版）》规定的原则计算，已包含在定额基价内，见表2-4-2。施工机械台班单价中，已考虑上下班用车；运输车辆的过路过桥费用在材机调整系数中已考虑；未计算运输机械的养路费及车船税，应根据各省（自治区、直辖市）规定标准在材机调整中予以考虑；大型施工机械是指起重量40t以上的吊装机械；大型机具的进出场费，按照机械台班定额的规定执行，预算定额中未包括且不属于施工机构转移费范围的，应在临时工程项目中单独列项，套用机械台班定额计算。

2. 地形调增

地形调增是指在定额直接费的人工费的基础上调增，调增系数（即综合地形增加系数）见任务2相关内容，表2-2-2。

3. 人工费调整

根据《电力建设工程概预算定额价格水平调整办法》(电定总造〔2007〕14号),各地区只调整工资性补贴并计入取费基数。人工费调整金额计算公式为

$$人工费调整金额 = 定额基价的人工费 \times \frac{当地工资性补贴 - 2.4}{定额基准工日单价} \tag{2-4-4}$$

各年度、各地区工资性补贴金额由各省(自治区、直辖市)电力建设定额站测算,经上级电力建设定额站平衡,报电力工程造价与定额管理总站(简称"定额总站")核定后发布实施。人工费调整金额应汇总计入概算编制年直接工程费的人工费,作为各项取费的取费基数。

4. 材机调整

材机调整是指安装工程定额材料、机械台班费用调整(简称材机调整),是针对定额基价中除人工费之外的材料与机械台班费用进行各地区概算编制水平年与定额基价水平年之间差值的调整。材机调整系数计算公式为

$$材机调整系数 = \frac{\sum(材料市场价格 \times 消耗量) + \sum(机械台班单价 \times 消耗量)}{\sum(定额内材料价格 \times 消耗量) + \sum(定额内机械台班单价 \times 消耗量)} \times 100\%$$

$$\tag{2-4-5}$$

送电线路工程分 750 kV、500 kV(含直流)、330 kV、220 kV、110 kV 及以下五个电压等级,分别测定各电压等级典型工程的材料及机械品种(见表 2-13)的材机调整系数。材机调整系数由各省(自治区、直辖市)电力建设定额站测算,经上级电力建设定额站平衡,报电力工程造价与定额管理总站(简称"定额总站")核定后,于每年第一季度末发布实施。

编制年材料市场价格的取定,按照各省(自治区、直辖市)编制水平年的第三季度材料价格为依据取定。编制年机械台班单价的取定,以《电力建设工程施工机械台班单价费用定额(2006年版)》为依据,水平运输机械需缴纳的养路费、车船使用税,按各地规定一并计入机械台班单价中予以调整;施工机械用油、电的市场价格与定额取定价格之差,按机械品种表(见表 2-4-3)中规定的消耗量计入机械台班费用中一并调整。材机价差的计算公式为

$$材机价差 = (定额基价 - 定额基价中的人工费) \times 材机调整系数 \tag{2-4-6}$$

在编制概算时,材机价差只计取税金,汇总进入编制年价差,不参与安装工程各项取费。

表 2-4-3 送电线路典型工程定额材料及机械品种构成表

编码	名称规格	单位	每公里含量				
			110kV	220kV	330kV	500kV	750kV
	材料						
C4101102	圆木 红白松 二等	m³	0.28	0.38	0.49	0.47	0.63
C4102102	方材 红白松 二等	m³	0.95	1.18	1.57	0.78	1.40
C4102202	板材 红白松 二等	m³	1.33	1.38	1.78	1.67	2.25
C5101101	电焊条 J422 综合	kg	21.00	44.00	63.65	110.00	138.16
C5206101	圆钉	kg					41.97
C5251101	镀锌铁丝 8号	kg	46.15	93.40	136.63	131.85	155.72
C6319101	硝铵炸药 2号	kg	14.41	50.72		139.18	161.30
C6319202	雷管 火雷管	个				385.67	
C6324201	焦炭	kg		150.65		506.83	
C6407101	沥青清漆	kg	4.41				
C7103104	镀锌钢绞线 GJ-70	kg		36.23			
C7103105	镀锌钢绞线 GJ-100	kg			25.49	29.03	
C7103106	镀锌钢绞线 GJ-120	kg					52.00
C7115701	铝包带 1×10	kg	2.70		12.95	11.43	16.52
C7208418	导线接续管 JTB-185	个	2.00				
C7208421	导线接续管 JYB-300	个		8.00	6.82		
C7208423	导线接续管 JYB-400	个				9.84	14.76
C8101101	钢管脚手架 包括扣件	kg	26.87	34.77	48.11	52.45	62.69
C8101801	安全网	m³	13.16	28.35		36.18	
	机械						
J1302202	送电专用汽车式起重机 8t	台班	1.21		2.57	4.58	4.93
J1302204	送电专用汽车式起重机 20t	台班			2.94	2.64	3.05
J1302205	送电专用汽车式起重机 25t	台班					3.05
J1401501	送电专用载重汽车 4t	台班	18.55	28.72	21.83	21.42	31.07
J1401502	送电专用载重汽车 5t	台班	14.98	29.96	41.04	45.02	62.69
J1802102	污水泵 100mm	台班		6.40	9.52	8.99	
J2101103	柴油发电机 60kW	台班			1.48	2.21	3.43
J2203102	牵引机组 一牵二	台班			1.09		
J2203103	牵引机组 一牵四	台班				0.91	
J2203104	牵引机组 一牵六	台班					1.04
J2203202	张力机组 一张二	台班			1.09		
J2203203	张力机组 一张四	台班				0.91	1.04
J2203301	机动绞磨	台班		8.33		11.42	
	汽油	kg	472.65	770.09	556.15	598.36	791.76
	柴油	kg	516.63	867.84	1705.80	1958.24	2799.65
	电	kwh		832.00	1237.97	1169.05	

(三) 案例工程二的单位工程概算表

1. 土石方工程单位工程概算表

除任务3中确定的土石方量需取费计算外，本单位工程还包括线路复测及分坑工程量的取费计算，见表2-4-4，土石方工程单位工程概算表。

取费计算说明：

（1）具体塔型及数量统计表参见表2-3-9，本案例工程使用铁塔137基，其中直线塔86基、耐张塔51基；再根据表2-3-1，土石方工程量汇总表，查阅《电力建设工程预算定额（第四册送电线路工程2006年版）》"土石方工程"一章，选择合适的定额子目，填入表2-4-4中对应"栏"中。根据表2-4-4中"数量"和"单价"所辖各项数据及式（2-4-3），计算出"合价"所辖各项数据（见表2-4-4，分为"装置性材料"费和"安装费"，安装费又分为合计、其中工资、其中机械三项费用）。

（2）汇总依据各定额子目计算出"合价"栏所辖"安装费"三项费用，得到土石方工程的定额直接费小计。

（3）查表2-2-2，案例工程二综合地形增加系数计算表，得土石方工程（不含机械费）对应的综合地形增加系数为6.69%。因此综合地形增加系数不含机械费，在"定额直接费小计"的"合计"栏数值扣减机械费后乘以6.69%，得"地形调增"安装费各项数据，从表2-4-4中看到，合价—安装费—其中机械对应的地形调增为0。

（4）将"定额直接费小计"和"地形调增"对应栏数据相加，得到定额直接费"合计"数据。

（5）本单位工程无装置性材料。

2. 基础工程单位工程概算表

（1）定额使用说明

1）预制基础

底盘安装定额中，如遇有胶结连接的底盘，每基应增加工日：单杆为0.37工日，双杆为0.74工日。"底盘安装""拉线盘安装"中的"每块重量"，取每组各块重量加权平均的原则计算。三联杆的预制基础安装定额，套相应的单杆定额乘以2.5的系数。"底盘安装""卡盘安装""拉线盘安装"定额中，如组合块（每基或每组）超过子目的规定时，可按单块重量和相应组合块的倍数乘以2.0的系数。套筒安装定额中，已包括二次灌浆工作，但未包括基础的底盘安装。如发生时应另外套相应的底盘安装定额。

表 2-4-4 土石方工程单位工程概算表

表三丙

序号	编制依据	项目名称及规范	单位	数量	单价(元) 装置性材料	单价(元) 合计	单价(元) 安装费	单价(元) 其中工资	单价(元) 其中机械	合价(元) 装置性材料	合价(元) 合计	合价(元) 安装费	合价(元) 其中工资	合价(元) 其中机械
1	YX2-4	线路复测及分坑 直线塔	基	86.00		51.10		24.49	2.04		4394.60		2106.14	175.44
2	YX2-5	线路复测及分坑 直线塔	基	51.00		68.29		36.74	2.94		3482.79		1873.74	149.94
3	YX2-34	自立式铁塔坑的挖方(爆破)及回填 普通土 坑深3.0m以内	m³	643.20		13.70		12.68	1.02		8809.91		8153.85	656.06
4	YX2-35	自立式铁塔坑的挖方(爆破)及回填 普通土 坑深4.0m以内	m³	775.20		16.12		14.70	1.42		12493.12		11392.34	1100.78
5	YX2-36	自立式铁塔坑的挖方(爆破)及回填 普通土 坑深4.0m以上	m³	3372.00		17.29		15.82	1.47		58308.62		53351.78	4956.84
6	YX2-42	自立式铁塔坑的挖方(爆破)及回填 松砂石 坑深3.0m以内	m³	2210.40		26.42		24.16	2.26		58405.40		53409.90	4995.50
7	YX2-43	自立式铁塔坑的挖方(爆破)及回填 松砂石 坑深4.0m以内	m³	2665.20		31.84		28.90	2.94		84849.31		77013.62	7835.69
8	YX2-44	自立式铁塔坑的挖方(爆破)及回填 松砂石 坑深4.0m以上	m³	11590.80		35.77		32.60	3.17		414649.28		377906.44	36742.84
9	YX2-46	自立式铁塔坑的挖方(爆破)及回填 岩石(爆破) 坑深3.0m以内	m³	804.00		65.51		53.42	5.20		52672.45		42952.09	4180.80
10	YX2-47	自立式铁塔坑的挖方(爆破)及回填 岩石(爆破) 坑深4.0m以内	m³	968.40		69.63		57.50	5.20		67424.85		55678.16	5035.68
11	YX2-48	自立式铁塔坑的挖方(爆破)及回填 岩石(爆破) 坑深4.0m以上	m³	4214.40		71.67		59.05	5.65		302046.05		248860.32	23811.36
12	YX2-50	自立式铁塔坑的挖方(人凿) 坑深3.0m以内	m³	200.40		137.21		122.37	12.44		27497.08		24523.15	2492.98

续表

序号	编制依据	项目名称及规范	单位	数量	单价(元) 装置性材料	单价(元) 合计	单价(元) 安装费 其中工资	单价(元) 安装费 其中机械	合价(元) 装置性材料	合价(元) 合计	合价(元) 安装费 其中工资	合价(元) 安装费 其中机械
13	YX2-51	自立式铁塔塔坑的挖方(爆破)及回填 岩石(人凿) 坑深4.0m以内	m³	242.40		145.57	130.28	12.89		35286.65	31580.36	3124.54
14	YX2-52	自立式铁塔塔坑的挖方(爆破)及回填 岩石(人凿) 坑深4.0m以上	m³	1053.60		153.79	137.60	13.79		162029.98	144972.20	14529.14
15	YX2-54	自立式铁塔塔坑的挖方(爆破)及回填 泥水坑 坑深3.0m以内	m³	160.80		60.40	28.60	17.99		9712.00	4598.56	2892.79
16	YX2-55	自立式铁塔塔坑的挖方(爆破)及回填 泥水坑 坑深4.0m以内	m³	194.40		78.57	37.37	27.39		15274.01	7264.73	5324.62
17	YX2-56	自立式铁塔塔坑的挖方(爆破)及回填 泥水坑 坑深4.0m以上	m³	843.60		87.49	44.26	29.42		73802.35	37333.52	24818.71
18	YX2-69	接地槽挖方(或爆破)及回填 普通土	m³	1187.10		8.32	7.51	0.81		9881.42	8919.87	961.55
19	YX2-71	接地槽挖方(或爆破)及回填 松砂石	m³	4080.04		19.62	18.60	1.02		80058.54	75896.90	4161.64
20	YX2-72	接地槽挖方(或爆破)及回填 泥水土	m³	296.28		14.55	13.74	0.81		4309.99	4070.00	239.99
21	YX2-73	接地槽挖方(或爆破)及回填 岩石(爆破)	m³	1483.38		54.31	43.43	1.42		80557.92	64418.74	2106.40
22	YX2-74	接地槽挖方(或爆破)及回填 岩石(人凿)	m³	371.09		82.98	77.65	4.07		30794.16	28816.25	1510.34
23	YX2-102	排水沟开挖 普通土	m³	55.00		4.58	4.17	0.41		251.96	229.41	22.55
24	YX2-104	排水沟开挖 松砂石	m³	186.00		8.63	8.04	0.59		1605.74	1496.00	109.74
25	YX2-105	排水沟开挖 泥水沟	m³	14.00		11.19	9.77	1.42		156.59	136.71	19.88
26	YX2-106	排水沟开挖 岩石(爆破)	m³	68.00		40.81	28.80	1.20		2774.88	1958.20	81.60

续表

序号	编制依据	项目名称及规范	单位	数量	单 价(元)				合 价(元)			
					装置性材料	安装费			装置性材料	安装费		
						合计	其中工资	其中机械		合计	其中工资	其中机械
27	YX2-107	排水沟开挖 岩石(人凿)	m³	17.00		63.78	58.82	3.62		1084.24	999.92	61.54
28	YX2-108	尖峰及施工基面挖方 普通土	m³	196.00		5.00	4.77	0.23		979.22	934.14	45.08
29	YX2-110	尖峰及施工基面挖方 松砂石	m³	537.00		11.42	10.92	0.50		6134.15	5865.65	268.50
30	YX2-111	尖峰及施工基面挖方 岩石(爆破) 尖峰	m³	147.00		38.14	29.69	2.49		5606.73	4364.58	366.03
31	YX2-112	尖峰及施工基面挖方 岩石(人凿) 尖峰	m³	49.00		39.92	31.25	2.71		1955.88	1531.05	132.79
		定额直接费小计								1617289.87	1382608.30	152911.34
		综合地形增加系数-土石方工程(不合机械费)	%	6.69								
		地形调增								97966.92	92496.50	0.00
		合计								1715256.79	1475104.80	152911.34

2）现浇基础

"现浇基础"定额中的基础垫层,如"铺石""铺石并灌浆""铺石并加浇混凝土""灰土垫层"定额,是以垫层的实际量为计算单位。"混凝土搅拌及浇制(包括商品混凝土浇制)"定额是按照有筋基础计算的,若为无筋基础时定额乘以0.95的系数。混凝土现场浇制中,洗石、养护、浇模用水的平均运距按100 m计算,如果运距超过部分可按每立方混凝土500 kg的用水量另套"工地运输"定额。混凝土搅拌及浇制(包括商品混凝土浇制)系数调整见表2-4-5。

表2-4-5　混凝土搅拌及浇制(包括商品混凝土浇制)系数调整

序号	名称	调整系数			说明
		人工	材料	机械	
1	高低腿基础	1.15	1	1.15	
2	基础立柱为斜、锥形	1.25	1	1.25	
3	基础是插入式角钢、斜式地脚螺栓	1.05	1	1.05	
4	基础立柱、承台、联梁高出地面1.0m以上,需要搭设平台施工	1.2	1.2	1.2	计算立柱、承台、联梁部分工程量

3）灌注桩基础

灌注桩基础定额中,不包括基础防沉台、承台和框梁的浇制工作;若有,则另套现浇基础定额。不包括余土的清理,需要时另套施工基面挖方和工地运输定额。挖孔桩基础、坑深5 m以上岩石嵌固基础套用桩基础混凝土浇灌定额;坑深5 m以内岩石嵌固基础套用现浇基础混凝土搅拌及浇制定额。灌注桩基础钻孔定额不足1 m按1 m计取,孔径超过1 m按实际尺寸根据相邻定额步距按插值法进行调整。

4）护坡、挡土墙及排洪沟砌筑

护坡、挡土墙及排洪沟砌筑定额内未包括挖土工作,需要时另套用"土、石方工程"中排水沟挖方定额。锥形护坡和挡土墙内侧如需要填土时,可套用"土、石方工程"中2.0m以内普通土定额和相应的运输定额。浆砌护坡和挡土墙砌筑中的砂浆用量,应按设计规定计算,如设计未做规定时,其砂浆用量为护坡和挡土墙体积的20%计列。

在施工中,存在预制基础和现浇基础时,造成跳跃施工,定额中的人工和机械可按基础总量(含高塔基础、护坡、挡土墙及排洪沟砌筑、基础防腐)乘以跳跃施工1.02的系数。

(2)基础工程单位工程概算表

基础工程单位工程概算表见表2-4-6。

取费计算说明：

1）根据表2-3-5、2-3-7，查阅《电力建设工程预算定额（第四册送电线路工程2006年版）》"基础工程"一章，选择合适的定额子目，填入表2-4-6中对应"栏"中；同理，据表2-4-4，计算出表2-4-6各栏数据。

2）根据表2-4-5，本案例工程中广泛使用高低腿基础和斜柱式基础，混凝土搅拌及浇制安装基价中人工费调整增加系数为0.4（0.15+0.25）；同理，机械费调整增加系数为0.4。

3）表2-4-6中计算"地形调增"时不扣减"机械费"。

4）表2-4-6中装置性材料费源于表2-3-5中"拉盘"和"C10、C20"混凝土对应的"总价"栏合计数据。

3. 杆塔工程单位工程概算表

（1）定额使用说明

由于杆与塔形式不同，造成跳跃施工，因而可将定额的人工、机械按杆、塔总量（不含高塔及接地）乘以1.02的系数。定额中不包括杆、塔上涂刷交通警示漆及其他航空标志安装。

1）混凝土杆组立

定额以杆型和组合重量的形式表示，已综合考虑了各种电压等级、结构形式、杆高和施工方法。使用时，不能因施工方法的不同而调整定额。使用中如出现三联杆组立，可按每根单杆重量套用相应定额乘以2.5的系数。钢环连接定额只包括钢环的连接与防腐处理。定额不适用于组合杆重在17 t或单杆高在42 m以上的电杆组立，如需要时，应按批准的施工组织设计另计。

2）钢管杆组立

定额已综合考虑了各种电压等级、结构形式、杆高和施工方法。使用时，不能因施工方法的不同而调整定额。

3）铁塔组立

定额对直线塔与耐张转角塔、自立塔与拉线塔做了综合考虑，适用于全塔高在70 m以内的各种形式的铁塔。紧凑型铁塔、钢管塔组立，按相应的铁塔组立定额的人工、机械乘以1.1的系数。混凝土塔的基础及筒身使用建筑工程预算定额的基础和烟囱部分。塔头部分的支架及横担（型钢）的吊、组装未专列定额，需要时可按塔头的总重量（t）与塔全高（m）的乘积计算工程量，其基价按每吨米5.4元计算，其中人工费占38%、材料费占15%、机械费占47%，并按塔位的所在地另计地形增加系数。

高塔组立时，定额适用于塔全高超过70 m的高塔组立。对于全塔每米重量平均超过1.2 t/m时，相应定额人工费和机械费按超重系数调整为

$$超重系数 = \frac{(设计每米重量t/m - 1.2t/m)}{1.2t/m} \qquad (2-4-7)$$

对于铁塔全高超过195 m时，以195 m高塔组立定额为基数，人工费和机械费按超高系数调整为

$$超高系数 = \frac{(设计高度m - 195m)}{195m} \qquad (2-4-8)$$

4）拉线制作及安装

定额对不同材质和规格已做了综合考虑，它适用于单根拉线的制作与安装，若安装"V"型、"Y"型或双拼拉线时，应按2根计算。定额内拉线上把高度按40 m以内考虑，如超过40 m时，按每增高10 m乘以1.10的系数，杆塔高不足10 m按10 m考虑。

5）接地安装

定额中不包括接地槽的挖方和填方。接地极长度按2.5 m考虑，如长度超过2.5 m时，定额乘以1.25的系数。接地极之间的连接套用相应接地体敷设定额。

（2）杆塔工程单位工程概算表

杆塔工程单位工程概算表见表2-4-7。

取费计算说明：

1）根据表2-3-13，查阅《电力建设工程预算定额（第四册送电线路工程2006年版）》"杆塔工程"一章，选择合适的定额子目，填入表2-4-7中对应"栏"中。同理，据表2-4-4，计算出表2-4-7各栏数据。

2）表2-4-7计算"地形调增"时不扣减"机械费"。

3）表2-4-7中装置性材料费源于表2-3-10、2-3-12中"总价"栏合计数据。

4. 架线工程单位工程概算表

（1）定额使用说明

1）定额中导线是按三相的交流单回路工程考虑，如遇下列情况时，按相应定额乘以系数调整：

①两相的直流线路工程可按同型号线材截面的定额乘以0.7的系数。

②同塔架设双回、多回线路工程和邻近有带电线路架线施工，定额按表2-4-8系数调整，其中：临近有带电线路架线，边线平行接近的控制距离见表2-4-9。

表三丙

表2-4-6 基础工程单位工程概算表

序号	编制依据	项目名称及规范	单位	数量	单价（元）				合价（元）			
					装置性材料	合计	安装费		装置性材料	合计	安装费	
							其中工资	其中机械			其中工资	其中机械
1	YX3-29	拉线盘安装 每组一块 每块重量500kg以内	组	1.00		18.64	15.72	2.92		18.64	15.72	2.92
2	YX3-37	基础钢筋加工及制作 一般钢筋	t	174.88	160.00	365.85	256.16	102.36	1399199.14	63978.02	44796.15	17900.21
3	YX3-51 调 人工1.4 机械1.4	混凝土搅拌及浇制 每基 混凝土量 10m³以内	m³	1003.74		212.10	136.37	18.57		275103.85	191634.84	26095.23
4	YX3-52 调 人工1.4 机械1.4	混凝土搅拌及浇制 每基 混凝土量 20m³以内	m³	785.63		190.56	121.81	16.90		193297.35	133974.43	18588.01
5	YX3-53 调 人工1.4 机械1.4	混凝土搅拌及浇制 每基 混凝土量 40m³以内	m³	641.55		161.75	95.33	16.52		132471.86	85620.75	14837.77
6	YX3-63	保护帽 每基方量0.5m³以内	基	137.00		114.86	83.41	8.14		15736.09	11427.44	1115.18
7	YX3-133	排洪沟 浆砌	m³	132.00		50.90	46.94	3.96		6718.27	6195.55	522.72
8	YX3-137	护坡、挡土墙 锥形 浆砌	m³	995.80		51.03	46.64	4.39		50813.68	46442.12	4371.56
9	YX3-140	混凝土基础防腐 沥青	m²	2740.00		2.35	1.66	0.23		6425.30	4534.70	630.20
		定额直接费小计								744563.08	524641.71	84063.79
		综合地形增加系数-基础工程	%	13.38						99622.54	70197.06	11247.74
		地形调增										
		合计							1399359.14	844185.62	594838.78	95311.53

表三丙

表 2-4-7 杆塔工程单位工程概算表

序号	编制依据	项目名称及规范	单位	数量	单价（元）					合价（元）			
					装置性材料	安装费			装置性材料	合价	安装费		
						合计	其中工资	其中机械		合计	其中工资	其中机械	
1	YX4-39	铁塔组立 每基重量 5t以内	基	19.00		1542.64	1267.73	247.12	7978593.08	29310.16	24086.87	4695.28
2	YX4-40	铁塔组立 每基重量 7t以内	基	45.00		2139.24	1721.20	377.67		96265.80	77454.00	16995.15
3	YX4-41	铁塔组立 每基重量 9t以内	基	28.00		2772.96	2273.97	449.00		77642.88	63671.16	12572.00
4	YX4-42	铁塔组立 每基重量 11t以内	基	19.00		3167.49	2644.69	466.70		60182.31	50249.11	8867.30
5	YX4-43	铁塔组立 每基重量 13t以内	基	19.00		3634.99	3038.58	535.48		69064.81	57733.02	10174.12
6	YX4-50	铁塔组立 每基重量 27t以内	基	4.00		7612.91	6332.03	1171.72		30451.64	25328.12	4686.88
7	YX4-51	铁塔组立 每基重量 30t以内	基	3.00		8200.98	6818.60	1266.85		24602.94	20455.80	3800.55
8	YX4-75	楔形线夹式 拉线截面 100mm² 以内	根	1.00		13.08	9.93	0.90		13.08	9.93	0.90
9	YX4-79	接地体加工及制作	t	20.32		186.69	105.09	76.96		3793.47	2135.42	1563.77
10	YX4-84	接地体敷设 每基长度 200m以内	基	247.00		46.39	39.72	3.39		11458.33	9810.84	837.33
11	YX4-85	接地体敷设 每基长度 300m以内	基	274.00		58.21	49.65	4.52		15949.54	13604.10	1238.48
12	YX4-86	接地体敷设 每基长度 400m以内	基	28.00		70.63	59.58	6.33		1977.64	1668.24	177.24
13	YX4-94	电阻测量	根、基	137.00		18.92	7.61	11.31		2592.45	1042.98	1549.47
		定额直接费小计							82161.52	423305.05	347249.59	67158.47
		综合地形增加系数-杆塔工程	%	39.12						165596.94	135844.04	26272.39
		地形调增											
		合计							8060754.60	588901.99	483093.63	93430.87

2）避雷线及光缆架线单独施工临近有带电线路（主要针对改建线路），按表2-4-8参照单回路调整系数。

3）张力架线定额中已包括牵张设备在施工过程中的装、拆和转移。

4）导线架设定额中综合考虑了耐张杆塔的耐张终端头制作和挂线、耐张（转角）杆塔的平衡挂线、跳线及跳线串的安装等工作，若工程中耐张杆塔每公里实际数量超过基准数量在10%以内时，定额不作调整，超过10%部分，定额基价调整系数按式2-4-9计算。

$$m = 1 + n \times [B - C \times (1 + 10\%)] \quad (2\text{-}4\text{-}9)$$

式中，m 为耐张杆塔调整系数，保留三位小数；n 为架线修正系数，一般放线1.25，张力放线0.52；B 为每千米实际耐张杆塔数量，它等于耐张杆塔数量除以线路长度，保留三位小数，如果工程包括两个终端，则耐张杆塔数量减1；C 为每千米耐张杆塔基准数量，电压220 kV以下按0.250综合取定，电压220 kV以上按0.200综合取定。

表2-4-8　同塔架设双回、多回线路工程和临近有带电线路架线系数调整表

序号	同塔回路数	同时架设			临近带电线路			序号	同塔二次架设回路数	同时架设			临近带电线路		
		人工	材料	机械	人工	材料	机械			人工	材料	机械	人工	材料	机械
1	一回路	1	1	1	1.1	1	1.1	5	一回路	1.1	1	1.1	1.21	1	1.21
2	二回路	1.75	2	1.75	1.92	2	1.92	6	二回路	1.92	2	1.92	2.11	2	2.11
3	三回路	2.8	3	2.8	3.08	3	3.08	7	三回路	3.08	3	3.08	3.38	3	3.38
4	四回路	3.9	4	3.9	4.29	4	4.29								

表2-4-9　临近带电线路架线边线平行接近控制距离表

已建线路电压（kV）	220	330	500	750
接近距离≤（m）	30	40	50	70

5）耐张杆塔调整系数如与本章内其他系数同时计列，与其他系数相乘。

6）导线、避雷线、光缆跨越架设

①定额计量单位"处"系指在一个档距内，对一种被跨越物所必须搭设的跨越架而言。如同一档距内跨越多种（或多次）跨越物时，应根据跨越物种类分别套用定额。

②高压电力线跨越不同电压等级的电力线路应按表2-4-10系数调整计算。

表2-4-10 跨越系数调整表

被跨越电力线电压（kV） 新建线路电压（kV）	10	35	110	220	330	500	750
35	0.67	1					
110	0.56	0.83	1				
220	0.45	0.68	0.82	1			
330	0.4	0.6	0.72	0.88	1		
500	0.36	0.54	0.64	0.79	0.89	1	
750	0.32	0.48	0.58	0.71	0.81	0.91	1

③单根线（避雷线、光缆）跨越架设只适用于单独架设或更换避雷线、光缆时使用，其中：跨越35kV以下电力线按跨越相应电压等级的定额乘以0.25的系数；跨越35kV以上电力线按跨越相应电压等级的定额乘以0.15的系数。

当带电跨越时，带电跨越措施费用按表2-4-11相应电压等级措施费的10%计列。

④本章定额子目中所列电压等级均指待建线路。

⑤本章定额仅考虑因跨越而多耗的人工、材料和机械台班。在计算总体架线工程量，其跨越长度不应扣除。

跨越架设定额不包括被跨越物产权部门提出的咨询、监护、路基占用等。如需要时，可按政府或有关部门的规定另计。

⑥跨越铁路定额如遇电气化铁路时，跨越铁路定额乘以1.2的系数。

⑦跨越电力线定额是按停电跨越考虑的。如需带电跨越，另列带电跨越措施费，按表2-4-11规定计列。如被跨越电力线为双回路、多回路时，措施费均乘以1.5的系数。

表2-4-11 带电跨越措施费用

单位：元/处

被跨越电压（kV）	10	35	110	220	330	500	750
措施费	3500	12000	20000	32000	45000	65000	100000

⑧跨越河流架线定额仅适用于有水的河流、湖泊（水库）的一般跨越。在架线期间，凡属能涉水而过的河道或正值干涸时的河流、湖泊（水库），均不作为跨越河流计。对于水面宽度虽然不大，但属通航河道、必须采取封航手段或水流湍急以及施工

难度较大的峡谷，其跨越架线可按审定的施工组织设计，由工程主审部门另行核定。

⑨定额中未列跨越房屋、果园、经济作物的项目。施工中遇到不拆迁的房屋及不砍伐的果园、经济作物等，架线时须采取防护措施，可按下述方法计算。

果园、经济作物按60 m为一处，套用跨越低压弱电线路定额乘以0.8的系数。跨越房屋，以独立房屋为一处，套用跨越低压弱电线路定额，房屋高度10 m以下乘以0.8的系数，房屋高度10 m以上乘以1.5的系数。

⑩跨越架设定额按单回路线路建设考虑，若为同塔同时架设双回路、多回路时，人工、机械均乘以1.5的系数。

7）耦合屏蔽线安装

屏蔽线按良导体考虑。如采用钢绞线作屏蔽线时，消耗材料定额乘以0.2的系数。

8）拦河线安装

定额中不包括拦河线所用器材的运输和混凝土杆的焊接。需要时可套本册"工地运输"和"杆塔工程"钢环焊接的相应定额。

9）光缆测量与接续

①单盘测量在编制初步设计概算时，如果尚未进行光缆招标的工程，可按每轴（盘）4km计算。

②光缆定额是按双窗口测试条件下考虑的，设计要求单窗口时，"接续"有关子目乘以0.85的系数。

③接续工程量按接头的个数计算，只计算架空部分的连接头，前后两段的光纤进线或出线的架构接线盒至通信机房部分按《电力建设工程预算定额 第三册 电气设备安装工程》执行。

④全程测试定额是按100 km为一基本段考虑的，超过100 km，每增加50km，其人工、机械增加40%，不足50 km按50 km计。

（2）架线工程单位工程概算表

见表2-4-12，架线工程单位工程概算表。

取费计算说明：

1）根据表2-0-1、2-3-14，查阅《电力建设工程预算定额（第四册送电线路工程2006年版）》"架线工程"一章，选择合适的定额子目，填入表2-4-12中对应"栏"中。对高压电力线跨越不同电压等级的电力线路时按表2-4-10系数调整计算。同理，据表2-4-4，计算出表2-4-12各栏数据。

2）表2-4-12计算"地形调增"时不扣减"机械费"。

3）表2-4-12中装置性材料费源于表2-3-14中"总价"栏数据。

表 2-4-12 架线工程单位工程概算表

表三丙

序号	编制依据	项目名称及规范	单位	数量	单价（元） 装置性材料	单价（元） 安装费 合计	单价（元） 安装费 其中工资	单价（元） 安装费 其中机械	合价（元） 装置性材料	合价（元） 安装费 合计	合价（元） 安装费 其中工资	合价（元） 安装费 其中机械
1	YX5-5	一般架线 单根避雷线 100mm² 以内 钢绞线	km	43.80		636.06	500.34	101.38		27859.43	21914.89	4440.44
2	YX5-7	一般架线 单根避雷线 100mm² 以内 良导体	km	8.00		723.88	528.34	117.17		5791.06	4226.74	937.36
3	YX5-18	一般架线 导线 2×400mm²以内	km/三相	51.80		6277.64	4162.59	1232.81	386244.87	325181.75	215622.16	63859.56
4	YX5-65	导线/避雷线 一般公路 220kV	处	44.00		2781.01	1645.07	354.77	64590.25	122364.44	72383.08	15609.88
5	YX5-78调 10kV*0.45	导线/避雷线 跨越高压电力线 220kV	处	32.00		3427.22	2591.73	442.62		49351.97	37320.91	6373.73
6	YX5-78调 35kV*0.68	导线/避雷线 跨越高压电力线 220kV	处	5.00		3427.22	2591.73	442.62		11652.55	8811.88	1504.91
7	YX5-78调 110kV*0.82	导线/避雷线 跨越高压电力线 220kV	处	3.00		3427.22	2591.73	442.62		8430.96	6375.66	1088.85
8	YX5-85	导线/避雷线 跨越低压、弱电线 220kV	处	232.00		1264.66	771.23	194.98	7077701.48	293401.12	178925.36	45235.36
9	YX5-98	导线/避雷线 跨越河流 导线截面 500mm²以内 河宽 50m以内	处	11.00		544.82	393.89	150.93		5993.02	4332.79	1660.23
10	YX5-100	导线/避雷线 跨越河流 导线截面 500mm²以内 河宽 300m以内	处	1.00		1380.58	999.62	380.96		1380.58	999.62	380.96
		定额直接费小计								851406.87	550913.09	141091.27
		综合地形增加系数-架线工程（一般放紧线）	%	48.91						416423.10	269451.59	69007.74
		地形调增								1267829.97	820364.68	210099.01
		合计							7528536.60			

表三丙

表 2-4-13 附件安装单位工程概算表

序号	编制依据	项目名称及规范	单位	数量	单价（元）				装置性材料	合价（元）			
					合计	安装费				合计	安装费			装置性材料
							其中工资	其中机械				其中工资	其中机械	
1	YX6-6	绝缘子串悬挂 直线（直线换位、直线转角）杆塔 220kV 双串	单相	411.00	41.17	27.80	11.78		16922.51	11427.44	4841.58	2413711.00
2	YX6-28	悬垂线夹安装（直线换位、直线转角）杆塔 220kV 双分裂	单相	411.00	30.97	18.21	6.81		12726.62	7482.26	2798.91	
3	YX6-38	预绞丝（或护线条）安装 直线（直线换位、直线转角）杆塔 220kV 双分裂导线	单相	411.00	30.27	28.47	1.80		12439.33	11699.53	739.80	
4	YX6-53	防震锤、间隔棒安装 防震锤 双分裂导线	个	2369.00	3.91	2.65	0.23		9258.05	6273.11	544.87	
5	YX6-72	阻尼线安装 导线 截面 2×500mm² 以内	单相	411.00	245.32	146.96	55.41		100828.16	60402.20	22773.51	
		定额直接费小计							152174.67	97284.54	31698.67	
		综合地形增加系数-附件工程	%	10.81					16450.08	10516.46	3426.63	
		地形调增										
		合计							168624.75	107801.00	35125.30	2413711.00

表三丙

表 2-4-14 工地运输单位工程概算表

序号	编制依据	项目名称及规范	单位	数量	单价（元）					合价（元）			
					装置性材料	合计	安装费			装置性材料	合计	安装费	
							其中工资	其中机械				其中工资	其中机械
1	YX1-19	人力运输 平均运距500m以内 余土外运	t.km	168.75		81.47	75.50	5.97			13748.23	12740.79	1007.44
2	YX1-27	人力运输 平均运距1000m以内 混凝土预制品 每件重500kg以内	t.km	0.36		139.47	129.09	10.38			50.21	46.47	3.74
3	YX1-33	人力运输 平均运距1000m以内 线材 每件重1000kg以内	t.km	415.61		162.62	148.19	14.43			67585.76	61588.53	5997.22
4	YX1-36	人力运输 平均运距1000m以内 金具、绝缘子、零星钢材	t.km	345.32		89.84	83.31	6.53			31024.58	28769.65	2254.94
5	YX1-37	人力运输 平均运距1000m以内 塔材	t.km	939.27		107.87	99.23	8.64			101322.81	93207.52	8115.29
6	YX1-38	人力运输 平均运距1000m以内 砂、石、石灰、水泥、砖、土、水	t.km	5801.15		77.93	72.16	5.77			452072.02	418599.38	33472.64
7	YX1-106	汽车运输 混凝土预制品 每件重500kg以内 装卸	t	0.45		42.02	9.93	31.63			18.91	4.47	14.23
8	YX1-107	汽车运输 混凝土预制品 每件重500kg以内 运输	t.km	12.60		1.01	0.23	0.78			12.75	2.92	9.83
9	YX1-118	汽车运输 线材 每件重1000kg以内 装卸	t	519.51		52.62	8.18	43.33			27334.54	4247.51	22510.37
10	YX1-119	汽车运输 线材 每件重1000kg以内 运输	t.km	14546.28		1.22	0.33	0.89			17761.01	4814.82	12946.19

续表

序号	编制依据	项目名称及规范	单位	数量	单价(元) 装置性材料	单价(元) 合计	单价(元) 安装费 其中工资	单价(元) 安装费 其中机械	合价(元) 装置性材料	合价(元) 合计	合价(元) 安装费 其中工资	合价(元) 安装费 其中机械
11	YX1-130	汽车运输 金具、绝缘子、零星钢材 装卸	t	431.66		30.97	8.81	22.16		13366.35	3800.77	9565.59
12	YX1-131	汽车运输 金具、绝缘子、零星钢材 运输	t.km	12086.34		1.19	0.33	0.86		14394.83	4000.58	10394.25
13	YX1-132	汽车运输 塔材 装卸	t	1174.09		42.16	8.90	31.51		49504.33	10454.10	36995.58
14	YX1-133	汽车运输 塔材 运输	t.km	32874.50		1.22	0.36	0.86		40238.39	11966.32	28272.07
15	YX1-134	汽车运输 砂、石、砖、土、水泥 装卸	t	7251.44		21.81	6.69	15.12		158124.90	48483.13	109641.77
16	YX1-135	汽车运输 砂、石、砖、土、水泥 运输	t.km	203040.39		0.92	0.27	0.65		185781.96	53805.70	131976.25
		定额直接费小计								1172341.58	756532.66	413177.39
		综合地形增加系数-工地运输人力运输线材及混凝土预制品(不含机械费)	%	82.36								
		综合地形增加系数-工地运输人力运输其他(不含机械费)	%	51.48								
		综合地形增加系数-工地运输汽车、拖拉机运输(不含装卸)	%	43.24								
		地形调增								447251.25	367863.22	79388.03
		合计								1619592.83	1124395.88	492565.43

5. 附件工程单位工程概算表

(1) 定额使用说明

1) 本章定额中不包括耐张金具及耐张绝缘子串安装。耐张导、地线端头制作，跳线串安装，跨接跳线端头制作及安装，直线转角及换位杆塔地线的绝缘子串安装，以上工作内容均包括在架线工程相关定额子目中。

2) 同塔非同时架设多回路或临近有带电线路时，在架设下一回时相应定额人工、机械乘以1.1的系数。

3) 阻尼线安装是按一般情况考虑，遇到大跨越、大档距杆塔，需采用超长阻尼线（每相扎花边13个以上）时，其人工、机械按相应定额乘以3.0的系数。

(2) 附件工程单位工程概算表

附件工程单位工程概算表见表2-4-13。

取费计算说明：

1) 根据表2-3-15，查阅《电力建设工程预算定额（第四册送电线路工程2006年版）》"附件工程"一章，选择合适的定额子目，填入表2-4-13中对应"栏"中。值得注意的是，附件工程对应的定额子目大多是以"单相"为单位，本案例工程共137基铁塔，共计411个"单相"。同理，据表2-4-4，计算出表2-4-13各栏数据。

2) 表2-4-13计算"地形调增"时不扣减"机械费"。

3) 表2-4-13中装置性材料费源于表2-3-15中"总价"栏合计数据。

6. 工地运输单位工程概算表

(1) 定额使用说明

1) 船舶、拖拉机、汽车运输中均已综合考虑了车、船形式，路面、河流级别和一次装、分次卸等因素，使用定额时不得另行换算。

2) 钢管塔按塔材机械运输及装卸相应定额乘以1.3的系数。

3) 采用张力架线，线材不计人力运输。

4) 计算塔材装卸、运输重量时，铁塔用螺栓、脚钉、垫圈等计入塔材重量。

(2) 工地运输单位工程概算表

见表2-4-14，工地运输单位工程概算表。

取费计算说明：

1) 根据表2-3-19，查阅《电力建设工程预算定额（第四册送电线路工程2006年版）》"工地运输"一章，选择合适的定额子目，填入表2-4-14中对应"栏"中。同理，据表2-4-4，计算出表2-4-14各栏数据。

2) 表2-4-14计算"地形调增"时,人力运输"线材及混凝土制品"和"其他"的综合地形增加系数是不同的,都需要扣减"机械费";汽车运输不调增"装卸"部分费用,只调增"运输"部分费用,不扣减"机械费"。

3) 本单位工程无装置性材料。

三、编制安装工程费用汇总概算表

安装工程费用汇总概算表,详见附录表二乙。

(一)安装工程费的组成

安装工程费由直接费、间接费、利润和税金组成。
计算公式为

$$\text{安装工程费}=\text{直接费}+\text{间接费}+\text{利润}+\text{税金} \tag{2-4-10}$$

(二)直接费

1. 直接费

直接费由直接工程费和措施费组成。计算公式为

$$\text{直接费}=\text{直接工程费}+\text{措施费} \tag{2-4-11}$$

2. 直接工程费

直接工程费由人工费、材料费、施工机械使用费组成。计算公式为

$$\text{直接工程费}=\text{人工费}+\text{材料费}+\text{施工机械使用费} \tag{2-4-13}$$

因为材料费包括装置性材料费和消耗性材料费,所以直接工程费的计算公式也可表示为

$$\text{直接工程费}=\text{装置性材料费}+\text{安装费} \tag{2-4-14}$$

计算公式中装置性材料费、安装费均来自于各单位工程概算表中装置性材料费、安装费的"小计"数值的汇总。值得注意的是,在实际工作中,为方便查看,常常在装置性材料统计表中直接计算出装置性材料费,单位工程概算表中就不会出现装置性材料费数值。

3. 措施费

措施费由冬雨季施工增加费、夜间施工增加费、施工工具用具使用费、特殊地区施工增加费、临时设施费、施工机构转移费、安全文明措施补助费组成。计算公式为

措施费=冬雨季施工增加费+夜间施工增加费+施工工具用具使用费+特殊地区施工

增加费+临时设施费+施工机构转移费+安全文明措施补助费 (2-4-15)

（1）冬雨季施工增加费

冬雨季施工增加费是指按照合理工期要求，建筑安装工程必须在冬季及雨季期间连续施工，而需要增加的费用。包括在冬季施工期间，为确保工程质量而采取的养护措施所发生的费用（如混凝土现浇基础的蒸汽养护），以及因冬雨季施工时增加施工工序、增加机械及材料消耗、降低工效而发生的补偿费用。

计算公式为

$$冬雨季施工增加费 = 人工费 \times 费率 \quad (2\text{-}4\text{-}16)$$

费率见表2-4-15。

表2-4-15 冬雨季施工增加费率表（%）

地区分类	I	II	III	IV	V
费率（%）	4.91	6.95	10.63	13.90	17.14

注1：随架空送电线路同时架设的光缆工程取费执行架空线路工程费率，下同。
注2：地区分类见表2-4-16。

表2-4-16 地区分类表

地区分类	省、自治区、直辖市名称
I	上海、江苏、安徽、浙江、福建、江西、湖北、湖南、广西、广东、海南
II	北京、天津、河北（张家口、承德以南地区）、山东、河南、重庆、四川（甘孜、阿坝州除外）、云南（迪庆州除外）、贵州
III	辽宁（盖县及以南地区）、陕西（榆林以南地区）、山西、河北（张家口、承德以北地区）
IV	辽宁（盖县以北）、陕西（榆林及以北地区）、内蒙古（锡林郭勒盟锡林浩特市以南各盟、市、旗，不含阿拉善盟）、乌兰察布盟、哲里木盟、新疆（伊犁、哈密地区以南）、吉林、甘肃、宁夏、四川（甘孜、阿坝州）、云南（迪庆州）
V	黑龙江、青海、新疆（伊犁、哈密地区及以北地区）、西藏、内蒙（除四类地区以外的其他地区）

冬雨季施工增加费中不包括为确保工程质量而需要添加在冬季施工所采取的混凝土添加防冻剂费用，防雨遮盖措施费用已综合考虑；不考虑台风、暴雨、暴风雪等恶劣天气影响，前述不可抗力因素所导致的损失费用在基本预备费中考虑。

（2）夜间施工增加费

夜间施工增加费是指按照规程要求，工程必须在夜间连续施工的单项工程所发生的夜班补助、夜间施工降效、夜间施工照明设备摊销及照明用电等费用。

送电线路工程一般不进行夜间施工，原则上不计列。大跨越工程和电缆线路工程除外。

计算公式为

$$夜间施工增加费 = 人工费 \times 1.05\% \qquad (2\text{-}4\text{-}17)$$

（3）施工工具用具使用费

施工工具用具使用费是指施工企业生产、检验、试验部门使用的不属于固定资产的工具、用具的购置、摊销和维修费。

计算公式为

$$施工工具用具使用费 = 人工费 \times 费率 \qquad (2\text{-}4\text{-}18)$$

费率标准：架空送电线路工程取5.38%。

（4）特殊地区施工增加费

特殊地区施工增加费是指在高海拔、酷热、严寒等地区施工，因特殊自然条件的影响，而需要额外增加的施工费用。

计算公式为

$$特殊地区施工增加费 = 人工费 \times 费率 \qquad (2\text{-}4\text{-}19)$$

费率见表2-4-17。

表2-4-17　特殊地区施工增加费费率

工程类别	高海拔地区	高纬度寒冷地区	酷热地区
费率（%）	6.5	5.5	4.75

注1：高海拔地区指平均海拔高度在3000m以上的地区。
注2：高纬度寒冷地区指北纬45°以北地区。
注3：酷热地区指面积在$1 \times 10^4 km^2$以上的沙漠地区（塔克拉玛干沙漠、古尔班通古特沙漠、巴丹吉林沙漠、腾格里沙漠、柴达木沙漠、库姆达格沙漠、库布齐沙漠、乌兰布和沙漠）以及新疆吐鲁番地区。

（5）临时设施费

临时设施费是指施工企业为满足现场正常生产、生活需要，在现场必须搭设的生活、生产用临时建筑物、构筑物和其他临时设施所发生的费用，其内容包括临时设施的搭设、维修、拆除、折旧及摊销费或临时设施的租赁费等。

临时设施包括职工宿舍，办公、生活、文化、福利等公用房屋，仓库、加工场、工棚、围墙等建、构筑物，站区围墙范围内的临时施工道路、水、电（含380V降压变压器）分支管线，以及建设期间的临时隔墙等。但不包括下述内容。

1）施工电源：施工、生活用380V变压器高压侧以外的装置及线路。

2）水源：场外供水管道及装置，水源泵房，施工、生活区供水母管。

3）施工道路：场外道路，施工、生活区的建筑安装共用主干道路。

计算公式为

$$临时设施费=直接工程费\times费率 \qquad (2\text{-}4\text{-}20)$$

费率见表2-4-18。

表2-4-18 临时设施费费率

地区分类	Ⅰ	Ⅱ	Ⅲ	Ⅳ	Ⅴ
费率（%）	1.87	1.95	2.04	2.18	2.55

注：扩建工程乘以0.9系数。

临时设施费中不包括现场工人生活所用的水电费及物业管理、卫生清理等费用，该费用在企业管理费统筹考虑；已经包括380V施工、生活变压器费用；已经包括工程完工后施工临时设施的拆除、清理费用；已经综合考虑了现场临时建筑及构筑物建设标准化并可多次使用、施工企业机械化水平和管理水平提高使现场人员大幅减少以及工期缩短等因素。

（6）施工机构转移费

施工机构转移费是指施工企业派遣施工队伍，到所承建工程现场所发生的搬迁费用，包括职工调遣差旅费和调遣期间的工资，以及施工机械、办公设备、工具、用具、材料用品的搬运费用。

计算公式为

$$施工机构转移费=人工费\times费率 \qquad (2\text{-}4\text{-}21)$$

费率见表2-4-19。

表2-4-19 施工机构转移费费率

电压等级(kV)	110及以下	220	330	500	750
费率(%)	3.59	3.37	2.84	2.71	2.44

费率中已经包括施工机构在进场过程中发生的过路过桥费。

（7）安全文明施工措施补助费

安全文明施工措施补助费是指根据电力行业安全文明施工与健康环境保护规范，在施工现场所采取的安全文明保障措施所支出的补助费用。

计算公式为

$$\text{安全文明施工措施补助费} = \text{人工费} \times \text{费率} \qquad (2\text{-}4\text{-}22)$$

费率标准：架空送电线路工程取2.52%。

近年来文明施工程度提高和安全措施的加强，导致定额中按照一般施工规范要求所考虑的费用不够，此项费用是对预算定额中安全文明施工措施费的补差。

安全文明施工措施与健康环境保护措施，主要是指现场安全文明设施（安全围栏、临边防护栏杆、孔洞盖板、安全网、安全操作规程牌、安全标志牌、安全文明施工责任牌、脚手架工程牌等）、现场健康环境保护措施（施工现场的淋水降尘、区域清理、垃圾清运、材料的遮盖、安全帽、防尘面罩、毛巾、工作服等），以及安全文明施工管理、监督制度、体系及机构建设等。

扩建工程应考虑停电措施费及施工安全特殊措施费用，应按照实际采取的防护措施，作为工程项目在"临时工程"项目下计列。

（三）间接费

间接费由规费和企业管理费组成。计算公式为

$$\text{间接费} = \text{规费} + \text{企业管理费} \qquad (2\text{-}4\text{-}23)$$

1. 规费

规费主要包括社会保障费、住房公积金和危险作业意外伤害保险费。计算公式为

$$\text{规费} = \text{社会保障费} + \text{住房公积金} + \text{危险作业意外伤害保险费} \qquad (2\text{-}4\text{-}24)$$

（1）社会保障费

社会保障费是指按照国家建立社会保障体系的有关要求，施工企业必须为职工缴纳的保险、保障费用，由养老保险费、失业保险费和医疗保险费组成，缴费费率按照工程所在地当地政府部门规定标准执行，跨省（自治区、直辖市）送电线路应分段计算或按照线路长度计算加权平均费率。

计算公式为

$$\text{架空送电线路工程社会保障费} = \text{人工费} \times 1.12 \times \text{缴费费率} \qquad (2\text{-}4\text{-}25)$$

$$\text{电缆线路及光缆线路工程社会保障费} = \text{人工费} \times 1.2 \times \text{缴费费率} \qquad (2\text{-}4\text{-}26)$$

（2）住房公积金

住房公积金是指企业按照当地政府部门规定为职工缴纳的住房公积金。缴费费率按照工程所在地当地政府部门公布的费率执行。

计算公式为

$$\text{架空送电线路工程住房公积金} = \text{人工费} \times 1.12 \times \text{缴费费率} \qquad (2\text{-}4\text{-}27)$$

$$\text{电缆线路及光缆线路工程住房公积金} = \text{人工费} \times 1.2 \times \text{缴费费率} \qquad (2\text{-}4\text{-}28)$$

(3) 危险作业意外伤害保险费

危险作业意外伤害保险费是指按照建筑法规定，企业为从事危险作业的建筑安装施工人员支付的意外伤害保险费。

计算公式为

$$危险作业意外伤害保险费 = 人工费 \times 费率 \quad (2\text{-}4\text{-}29)$$

费率标准：架空送电线路工程取 2.53%，电缆线路工程取 2.31%，光缆线路工程取 2.53%。

2. 企业管理费

企业管理费是指建筑安装施工企业组织施工生产和经营管理所发生的费用。内容包括管理人员工资、办公费、差旅交通费、固定资产使用费、工具用具使用费、劳动补贴费、工会经费、职工教育经费、财产保险费、劳动安全卫生检测费、财务费、税金，其他还包括工程排污费、建筑工程定点复测、工程点交、场地清理费、检验试验费、技术转让费、技术开发费、业务招待费、绿化费、广告费、公证费、法律顾问费、咨询费等。

工程排污费是指施工现场按规定交纳的排污处理费用。建筑工程检验试验费是指对建筑材料、构件和建筑安装物进行一般鉴定、检查所发生的费用，包括自设试验室进行试验所耗用的材料和化学药品等费用，以及技术革新和研究试制试验费。

计算公式为

$$企业管理费 = 人工费 \times 费率 \quad (2\text{-}4\text{-}30)$$

费率标准：架空送电线路工程取 46.52%，电缆线路工程取 47.91%，光缆线路工程取 23.70%，通信站工程建筑取 8.14%、安装取 67.63%。

（四）利润

利润是指施工企业完成所承包工程获得的盈利。

计算公式为

$$利润 = （直接费 + 间接费） \times 5\% \quad (2\text{-}4\text{-}31)$$

（五）税金

税金包括营业税、教育费附加和城市维护建设税。计算公式为

$$税金 = （直接工程费 + 简接费 + 计划利润） \times 税率 \quad (2\text{-}4\text{-}32)$$

税率按工程所在地税务部门的规定计算。

1. 营业税应纳税额计算公式

$$应纳税额=营业额×税率 \qquad (2-4-33)$$

送电线路工程属于建筑业中安装工程作业，营业税率取3%，营业额即工程承包额（工程总包的需扣除工程分包或转包的部分承包额）。

2. 教育附加计算公式

$$应纳税额=实际缴纳的营业税税额×税率 \qquad (2-4-34)$$

国家规定税率取3%，地方教育附加另计。

3. 城市维护建设税计算公式

$$应纳税额=实际缴纳的营业税税额×税率 \qquad (2-4-35)$$

城市维护建设税的税率，市区取7%，县城、镇取5%，其他取1%。

（二）案例工程二的安装工程费用汇总概算表

表2-4-20所示为安装工程费用汇总概算表。

取费计算说明如下。

1. 转移数据

将表2-4-4、2-4-6、2-4-7、2-4-12、2-4-13、2-4-14六个单位工程概算表"合计"栏数据填入表2-4-20"直接工程费"所辖对应栏中，包括定额直接费（其中人工费和机械费）、装置性材料费。

2. 确定费率

（1）人工费调整。根据"关于公布各地区工资性补贴的通知 电定总造[2007]12号"，四川地区工资性补贴为3.12元/工日，定额中送电线路工程基准工日单价为33.1元/工日，其中工资性补贴2.4元/工日，由式2-4-4，人工费调整系数为2.18%，填入表2-4-20中，计算人工费调整金额，并将其计入直接工程费人工费，作为各项取费的取费基数。

（2）查表2-4-15、2-4-16，本案例工程位于四川境内，属于Ⅱ级地区，冬雨季施工增加费费率取6.95%。

（3）本案例工程为架空送电线路工程，施工工具使用费费率取5.38%。

（4）本案例工程不属于特殊地区，特殊地区施工增加费费率为0。

（5）查表2-4-18，本案例工程位于四川境内，属于Ⅱ级地区，临时设施费费率取1.95%。

(6) 查表2-4-19，本案例工程为220kV送电线路工程，施工机构转移费费率取3.37%。

(7) 本案例工程为架空送电线路工程，安全文明施工措施费费率取2.52%。

(8) 经向本案例工程施工单位人力资源部查询，社会保障费费率为28%，乘以1.12后为31.36%；住房公积金费率为15%，乘以1.12后为16.8%。

(9) 本案例工程为架空送电线路工程，危险作业意外伤害保险费费率取2.53%。

(10) 本案例工程为架空送电线路工程，企业管理费费率取46.52%。

(11) 根据"预规"，利润率取值为5%。

(12) 根据"预规"和地方政府规定的地方教育附加税率，税金取值为3.37%。

根据转移数据和费率，计算并填表2-4-20。

四、编制辅助设施工程概算表

（一）辅助设施工程

辅助设施工程是指为提高线路安全运行水平，便于维护和检修而设置的工程项目。它包括：拦河（江）线标志，维护用通信工程，巡线检修站工程，巡线检修道路维护用设备、工器具购置等。

（1）拦江（河）线标志指送电线路跨越通航的河流或江面而设立的防护安全的明显标志。其材料据设计提供；安装定额参照《电力建设工程预算定额（第四册 送电线路工程2006年版）》关于拦河线定额计算或参照以往工程。拦河项目：带人行索道、不带人行索道；还应区分拦河线的河流宽度。拦河线数量单位为：道。

（2）维护用通信工程指线路工区与线路工段，巡线站检修站间安全可靠的通信联络用设备工程。包括：专用通信线、载波、便携式电话、电台、对讲机，其费用按有关价格执行。地线载波通信和架空明线通信，只有在大山区交通不便并缺乏通信手段的地区采用，其他通信设备则按沿线附近的通信条件考虑配备。

（3）巡线检修站工程指为线路运行维护及检修所需设立的巡线站、检修站及相应的工器具设备。

为了保证电力系统具备较高的供电可靠性，需要对建成的各电力线路进行定期巡视，检查线路各组成设备的完好状态，由线路运行检修单位根据线路运行状态制订运行检修计划，适时进行运行检修工作，确保建成投运的各条电力线路具有良好的机械和电气性能。为了便于对运行线路的管理，常常将长距离电力线路分为几个部分，每一部分均设立相应的巡线站和检修站。巡线站和检修站作为线路运行的基层组织，设置于线路附近，负责维护一定的线路。通常，每一巡线站或检修站负责的线路长度一

表二乙

表 2-4-20 架空送电线路安装工程费用汇总概算表

序号	工程或费用名称	取费基数	费率%	土石方工程	基础工程	杆塔工程	架线工程	附件工程	工地运输	合计	各项占总计%	单位投资 元/km
一	直接费			2056027.18	2411222.41	8918972.47	9138810.25	2655150.53	1885431.19	27065614.04	78.81%	522502.20
1	直接工程费 (B)	1)+2)		1747343.66	2256483.85	8660164.97	8814211.37	2584680.67	1644050.99	25706935.50		
1)	定额直接费			1747343.66	857124.71	599410.37	1285674.77	170969.67	1644050.99	6304574.16		
	其中：人工费 (A)			1507191.67	607777.87	493602.01	838209.47	110145.92	1148854.04	4705780.97		
	人工费调整		2.18%	32086.87	12939.09	10508.38	17844.79	2344.92	24458.16	100182.21		
	装置性材料费			152911.34	95311.53	93430.87	210099.01	35125.30	492565.43	1079443.47		
2)	措施费			0.00	1399359.14	8060754.60	7528536.60	2413711.00	0.00	19402361.34		
2	措施费			308683.52	154738.56	258807.50	324598.89	70469.86	241380.20	1358678.54		
1)	冬雨季施工增加费	A	6.95	104749.82	42240.56	34305.34	58255.56	7655.14	79845.36	327051.78		
2)	施工工具使用费	A	5.38	81086.91	32698.45	26555.79	45095.67	5925.85	61808.35	253171.02		
3)	特殊地区施工增加费	A	0	0.00	0.00	0.00	0.00	0.00	0.00	0.00		
4)	临时设施费	B	1.95	34073.20	44001.44	168873.22	171877.12	50401.27	32058.99	501285.24		
5)	施工机构转移费	A	3.37	50792.36	20482.11	16634.39	28247.66	3711.92	38716.38	158584.82		
6)	安全文明施工措施补助费	A	2.52	37981.23	15316.00	12438.77	21122.88	2775.68	28951.12	118585.68		
二	间接费			1465141.02	590820.86	479830.51	814823.43	107072.84	1116801.01	4574489.68	13.32%	88310.61
1	规费			763995.46	308082.60	250206.86	424888.38	55832.96	582354.11	2385360.38		
1)	社会保障费	A	31.36	472655.31	190599.14	154793.59	262862.49	34541.76	360280.63	1475732.91		
2)	住房公积金	A	16.8	253208.20	102106.68	82925.14	140819.19	18504.51	193007.48	790571.20		
3)	危险作业意外伤害保险费	A	2.53	38131.95	15376.78	12488.13	21206.70	2786.69	29066.01	119056.26		
2	企业管理费	A	46.52	701145.56	282738.26	229623.65	389935.05	51239.88	534446.90	2189129.31		

续表

序号	工程或费用名称	取费基数	费率%	土石方工程	基础工程	杆塔工程	架线工程	附件工程	工地运输	合计	各项占总计%	单位投资元/km
三	利润	一十二	5	176058.41	150102.16	469940.15	497681.68	138111.17	150111.61	1582005.19	4.61%	30540.64
四	税金	一十二+三	3.37	124596.54	106227.30	332576.64	352209.33	97741.27	106233.99	1119585.07	3.26%	21613.61
	安装工程费费合计	一十二+三+四		3821823.15	3258372.74	10201319.78	10803524.69	2998075.82	3258577.80	34341693.98		
	各项占总计（%）			11.13%	9.49%	29.71%	31.46%	8.73%	9.49%		100.00%	
	单位投资（元/km）			73780.37	62902.95	196936.68	208562.25	57877.91	62906.91	662967.07		

一般在40~60 km，它的配置取决于线路所处自然条件、电压等级、杆塔位的重要性及交通运输条件。

巡线检修站工程包括宿舍、办公室及仓库、汽车库、室外工程等。

（1）宿舍面积

职工宿舍包括带家属和单身职工宿舍，其面积按因新建线路新增的线路运行维护和检修人员数乘以面积指标计算。

1）新增人员数的确定

新增人员数按《国家电网公司供电企业劳动定员标准（第1部分：输电）》Q/GWD247.1-2008执行，见表2-4-21、2-4-22。

表2-4-21 送电线路运行维护定员标准

自然条件	计算单位回长	定员（人）							
		1000kV	±800kV	750/±660 kV	500 kV	330 kV	220 kV	110/66 kV	35 kV
平原区	百千米	5.8	5.6	4.0	3.2	2.4	1.9	1.4	1.3
丘陵区		6.4	6.2	4.2	3.5	2.9	2.3	1.7	1.5
山区		10.0	10.0	8.0	6.2	4.3	3.8	2.7	2.2
原始森林区		14.0	14.0	10.5	7.9	5.4	4.9	4.1	3.1

注1：500kV直流送电线路按500 kV交流线路的定员标准乘以0.9的系数计算定员；多雷区、严寒地区与污秽、河网地段按对应的定员标准乘以1.1的系数计算定员；强雷区、覆冰区、沙漠区按对应的定员标准乘以1.2的系数计算定员；同杆架设双回及以上的送电线路，以该线路总长度为基数按对应的定员标准乘以0.7的系数计算定员；需专人值班的大跨越过江塔按每塔1人计算定员。

注2：丘陵区指电力线路经过的峰谷水平高差在0.2~0.3 km之间的地段；山区指电力线路经过的峰谷水平高差在0.3km及以上的地段；原始森林区指由国家划定或确认的原始森林；严寒地区指最冷月份的月平均温度低于-15℃的地区；污秽地段指电力线路所处环境达到国家规定的B级污秽环境标准及以上的地段；河网地段指每千米电力线路跨越的河道平均在1.5条以上的地段；覆冰区指电力线路经过的每年平均有三个月覆冰期的地段；多雷区和强雷区指年雷暴日在40~90天的地区属多雷区，年雷暴日在90天以上的地区属强雷区；送电线路指电压为35kV及以上的电力线路；线路回长指具备传输电力条件的一回电力线路的长度。

表2-4-22 送电线路检修定员标准

自然条件	计算单位回长	定员（人）							
		1000kV	±800kV	750/±660 kV	500 kV	330 kV	220 kV	110/66 kV	35 kV
平原区	百千米	4.0	3.8	2.8	2.4	2.1	1.6	1.3	1.2
丘陵区		4.8	4.6	3.2	2.6	2.5	1.9	1.6	1.4
山区		8.0	8.0	5.5	4.1	3.0	2.5	2.5	1.8
原始森林区		9.0	9.0	7.0	5.2	3.5	3.0	2.7	2.6

注：500kV直流送电线路按500 kV交流线路的定员标准乘以0.9的系数计算定员；多雷区、严寒地区与污秽、河网地段按对应的定员标准乘以1.1的系数计算定员；强雷区、覆冰区、沙漠区按对应的定员标准乘以1.2的系数计算定员。

例：某供电机构管辖的某220 kV线路284 km，按地理条件划分为：平原120 km，丘陵84 km，山区80 km。在平原的120 km中有50 km处于B级以上污秽地段，有25 km为同杆架设双回线路；山区80 km中有20 km处于强雷区。试计算该线路需要的运行维护和检修人员。

解：

平原地区的运行维护和检修人员分别为

$$((120-50-25)+50\times1.1+25\times2\times0.7)\div100\times1.9=2.565（人）$$

$$((120-50-25)+50\times1.1+25\times2)\div100\times1.6=2.4（人）$$

丘陵地区的运行维护和检修人员为

$$84\div100\times(2.9+1.9)=4.032（人）$$

山区的运行维护和检修人员为

$$((80-20)+20\times1.2)\div100\times(3.8+2.5)=5.292（人）$$

该线路需要的运行维护和检修人员为

$$2.565+2.4+4.032+5.292=14.289（人）$$

将计算出的人数进整后，该220 kV线路需要的运行维护和检修人员为15人。

2）人均宿舍面积指标

确定人均宿舍面积的办法，一种是按关内28 m²/人，关外30 m²/人；另一种是按站上职工单身及带家属区分，单身7 m²/人，带家属50 m²/人；或者按照工程所在地人民政府或行业主管部门相关规定执行。

（2）辅助建筑面积

辅助建筑包括办公室、仓库、汽车房等，其面积以新增人员数乘以表2-4-23中的指标。

表2-4-23 辅助建筑面积指标表

序号	电压（kV）	面积定额（m²/人）
1	500	14
2	330	12
3	220	10
4	110	8

宿舍面积加上辅助建筑面积即为巡线检修站建筑面积。征用土地时，征地面积取建筑面积的2.5倍。

（3）室外工程

室外工程是指室外的围墙和围墙内道路，给排水、化粪池、电源等建筑和安装工程。

（4）巡线检修站工程费用计算

巡线检修站工程费用包括土地征用费，宿舍、辅助建筑及室外工程建筑和安装费用。宿舍及辅助建筑工程费为宿舍及辅助建筑面积乘以建筑造价。室外工程已设计的按设计预算计列，未设计的按宿舍及辅助建筑工程费之和乘上室外工程费率计算，若无规定，一般取15%。

土地征用费标准应执行工程所在地地方人民政府的规定标准，根据现场搜资结果确定。

（4）巡线检修道路工程

巡线检修道路一般与施工用道路和桥梁的修筑一并考虑，初期为施工服务，工程竣工试运转后为运行服务。一般平丘地段不发生，只在山地和高山大岭地段考虑修筑。

巡线检修道路工程费用计算：按修筑道路的长度乘"临时道路修筑拓宽定额"中的一般山地定额计费。

（5）维护用设备、工器具购置，执行相应的规定。

在总投资中列出一定比例的费用作为备品备件购置。

（二）辅助设施工程概算表

（1）案例工程二的辅助设施工程概算表

表 2-4-24 所示为辅助设施工程概算表。

表 2-4-24 送电线路辅助设施工程概算表

表三戊

序号	工程或费用名称	编制依据及计算说明	总价（元）
1	巡线检修站工程费用		
1.1	建筑工程直接费	3人×（28+10）m²/人×1000元/m²	114000.00
1.2	土地征用费	3人×（28+10）m²/人×2.5÷667×180000	76911.54
1.3	室外工程费	114000×15%	17100.00
	小计		208011.54
2	运行维护用通信设备费	4只×6000元/只	24000.00
合计			232011.54

注：各项费用必须写明编制和计算依据，以及必要的计算方法说明。

（2）取费计算说明

近年来，随着国家加大了在公路、通信方面的基建投资力度，全国各地交通运输和通信条件大为改善，再加之电网企业生产技术和管理水平稳步提高，除个别重点杆塔位和少部分交通运输和通信条件较差的电力线路外，大部分线路工程不再实际修建巡线检修站，但仍计列相关费用，由线路运行维护单位统筹使用。

本案例工程的辅助设施工程费用中，包括巡线检修站工程费用和通信设备费用，无其他辅助设施。经咨询搜资，本案例工程所在地土地征用费标准为18万元/亩，建筑造价为1000元/m^2。拟购买4只对讲机作为线路运行维护用通信设备。

（1）巡线检修站工程费用计算

从工程概况可知，本案例工程为220kV单回送电线路，线路全长约51.8 km，地形划分为：平地7.4%，丘陵51.4%，山地41.2%。

本案例工程的运行维护和检修人员：

51.8÷100×[（1.9+1.6）×7.4%+（2.9+1.9）×51.4%+（3.8+2.5）×41.2%]=2.7567（人）

将计算出的人数进整后，该220 kV线路需要的运行维护和检修人员为3人，按照关内28 m^2/人的面积指标计算职工宿舍面积为：3人×28 m^2/人=84（m^2）

查表2-4-23，辅助建筑面积分别如下。

220kV线路辅助建筑面积指标为10 m^2/人，3人×10 m^2/人=30（m^2）

征地面积为：（84+30）×2.5=285（m^2）

土地征用费为：（285 m^2÷667 m^2/亩）×180000元/亩=76911.54（元）

建筑工程直接费为：（84+30）m^2×1000元/m^2=114000.00（元）

室外工程费为：114000×15%=17100.00（元）

巡线检修站工程费用为：76911.54+114000+17100=232011.54（元）

（2）通信设备费计算

拟选用30兆频段短波调频对讲机（最大通话距离5 km），其对讲机本体加附件预算价为6000元/只。

$$4×6000=24000.00（元）$$

（3）本案例工程无巡线检修道路，不计列费用。

（4）本案例工程不计列其他维护用设备及工器具相关费用。

将上述费用填入表2-4-24中。

五、编制其他费用概算表

其他费用包括建筑场地征用及清理费、项目建设管理费、项目建设技术服务费、分系统调试及整套启动试运费、生产准备费、大件运输措施费、基本预备费。计算公式为

其他费用=建筑场地征用及清理费+项目建设管理费+项目建设技术服务费+分系统

调试及整套启动试运费+生产准备费+大件运输措施费+基本预备费　（2-4-36）

（一）建设场地征用及清理费

建设场地划拨及清理费由土地征用费、施工场地租用费、迁移补偿费、余物清理费、送电线路走廊赔偿费、通信设施防送电线路干扰措施费等组成。计算公式为

建设场地划拨及清理费=土地征用费+施工场地租用费+迁移补偿费

+余物清理费+送电线路走廊赔偿费+通信设施防送电线路干扰措施费　（2-4-37）

1. 土地征用费

土地征用费包括土地补偿费、安置补助费、耕地开垦费、勘测定界费、征地管理费、证书费、手续费以及各种基金和税金等。

计算标准：按批准的征用数量，根据有关法律、法规、国家行政主管部门以及省（自治区、直辖市）人民政府规定标准计算。

2. 施工场地租用费

施工场地租用费包括场地租金、清理和复垦费等。

计算标准：根据有关法律、法规、国家行政主管部门以及工程所在地人民政府规定，按照项目法人与土地所有者签订的租用合同计算。

3. 迁移补偿费

迁移补偿费是指为满足工程建设需要，对所征用土地范围内的机关、企业、住宅及有关建筑物、构筑物、电力线路、通信线路、铁路、公路、沟渠、管道、坟墓、林木等进行迁移所发生的补偿费用。

计算标准：按照工程所在地人民政府规定计算。

4. 余物清理费

余物清理费是指为满足工程建设需要，对所征用土地范围内原有的建筑物、构筑物等有碍工程建设的设施进行拆除、清理所发生的各种费用。

计算标准：按表2-4-25中的费率计算，并应扣除残余物回收金额。

上表中，工程新建直接费是指概算编制年的新建直接费，其中措施费项目中只计安全文明施工措施补助费。残余物是指拆除工程中包含在建筑安装定额中的材料的回收价值。旧设备以及线路工程中的铁塔、导线等由于已经形成固定资产，因而应按照固定资产处理的相关规定执行。

表 2-4-25　余物清理费费率

项目名称			计算公式	费率%
建筑工程		一般砖木结构	建筑工程新建直接费×费率	10
		混合结构	建筑工程新建直接费×费率	20
	混凝土及钢筋混凝土结构	有条件爆破的	建筑工程新建直接费×费率	20
		无条件爆破的	建筑工程新建直接费×费率	30~50
		临时简易建筑	建筑工程新建直接费×费率	8
	金属结构	拆除后金属结构能利用的	安装工程新建直接费×费率	55
		拆除后金属结构不能利用的	安装工程新建直接费×费率	38
安装工程		金属结构及工业管道	安装工程新建直接费×费率	45
		机电设备	安装工程新建直接费×费率	32
	送电线路及通信线路	拆除后能利用	安装工程新建直接费×费率	62
		拆除后不能利用	安装工程新建直接费×费率	35
铁路工程		铁路站	工程新建直接费×费率	18
		铁道线	工程新建直接费×费率	10

注1：费率中不包括运距超过5km部分的渣土运杂费。
注2：安装工程新建直接费中不包括未计价材料费。

5. 送电线路走廊赔偿费

送电线路走廊赔偿费是指按照送电线路有关规范要求，对线路走廊内非征用土地上需清理的建筑物、构筑物、林木、经济作物等进行赔偿所发生的费用。城市电缆工程施工中的城市道路挖掘和破路费、绿化赔偿费列入本项费用。

计算标准：按照工程所在地人民政府规定计算。

6. 通信设施防送电线路干扰措施费

通信设施防送电线路干扰措施费是指拟建送电线路与现有通信线路交叉或平行时，为消除干扰影响，对通信线迁移或加装保护设施所发生的费用。本费用中不包括线路交叉跨越所发生的费用。

计算标准：依据设计方案以及项目法人与通信部门签订的合同或达成的补充协议计算。

（二）项目建设管理费

项目建设管理费是指建设项目经国家行政主管部门核准后，自项目法人筹建至竣工验收合格移交生产的合理建设期内对工程进行组织、管理、协调、监督等工作所发生的费用。包括建设项目法人管理费、招标费、工程监理费、设备监造费、工程保险费。

计算公式为

$$项目建设管理费=项目法人管理费+招标费+工程监理费$$
$$+设备监造费+工程保险费 \quad (2\text{-}4\text{-}38)$$

1. 建设项目法人管理费

建设项目法人管理费是指项目法人在项目管理工作中发生的机构开办费及经常性费用。

（1）项目机构开办费包括相关执照及相关手续的申办费，必要办公家具、生活家具、用具及交通工具购置费用。

（2）项目法人工作经费是指建设项目法人机构在工程建设期间发生的工作人员基本工资、工资性补贴、辅助工资、职工福利费、劳动保护费、养老保险费、失业保险费、医疗保险费、住房公积金、办公费用、差旅交通费、固定资产使用费、工具用具使用费、技术图书资料费、工程档案管理费、水电费、教育及工会经费、施工图文件审查费、工程审价（结算）费、合同订立与公证费、法律顾问费、咨询费、会议费、董事会经费、业务接待费、消防治安费、采暖及防暑降温费、印花税、房产税、车船税、车船保险费、养路费，设备材料的催交验货、工程主要材料的监造、建设项目劳动安全验收评价费，工程竣工交付使用及清理及验收费等日常经费。

计算公式为

$$建设项目法人管理费=安装工程费 \times 费率 \quad (2\text{-}4\text{-}39)$$

费率见表2-4-26。

表2-4-26　建设项目法人管理费率表

电压等级（kV）	220及以下	330	500	750
架空线路工程	1.35		1.22	
电缆线路工程	1.64			

2. 招标费

招标费是指项目法人按照国家有关规定，组织或委托具有资质的机构编制、审查标书、标底，组织编制设备技术规范书，以及委托具有招标代理资质的机构对设计、施工、设备材料采购、工程监理、调试等承包项目进行招标所发生的费用。

计算公式为

$$招标费=安装工程费 \times 费率 \quad (2\text{-}4\text{-}40)$$

费率见表2-4-27。

表2-4-27　招标费费率表

电压等级（kV）	110及以下	330及以下	500及以上
架空线路工程	0.53	0.45	0.35
电缆线路工程	1.65		

3. 工程监理费

工程监理费是指依据国家有关规定和规程规范要求，项目法人委托工程监理机构对建设项目全过程实施监理所支付的费用。

计算公式为

$$电缆线路工程监理费=安装工程费×2.15\% \qquad (2-4-41)$$

架空送电线路工程监理费根据线路长度，按照表2-4-28所列标准计算。

表2-4-28　工程监理费费率表

万元/km

电压等级（kV）	单回路	同杆（塔）双回
750	2.00	/
500	1.55	2.05
330	1.25	1.60
220	1.00	1.25
110	0.60	0.75
35	0.50	0.60

注1：线路长度不足5 km的按5 km计算。
注2：架空线路的费率以平地、丘陵为标准地形考虑，其他地形按本标准乘相应系数，河网泥沼、一般山地1.1，高山1.2，峻岭1.3。
注3：大跨越工程，按安装工程费的1.5%计算。
注4：穿越城区的电网工程，可根据其施工难度，按本标准乘1.1～1.2系数。
注5：高海拔地区、酷热地区架空线路工程按本标准乘1.1系数。

对双回以上的多回路线路，以同杆塔双回为基础，每增加一回，按照同电压等级费用标准的20%增加。例如，220 kV同塔四回线路监理费标准计算式为

$$1.25+1.00×20\%×2=1.25+0.4=1.65（万元/km）$$

4. 设备监造费

设备监造费是指为保证设备质量，按照国家行政主管部门公布的设备建造管理办法的要求，项目法人在主要设备的制造、生产期间对原材料质量以及生产、检验环节进行必要的见证、监督所发生的费用。

送电线路工程铁塔、导线等材料的建造费用在项目法人管理法中已经考虑。

5. 工程保险费

工程保险费是指项目法人对项目建设过程中可能造成工程财产、安全等直接或间接损失的要素进行保险所支付的费用。

计算标准：根据项目法人要求及工程实际情况，按照实际保险范围和费率计算，从基本预备费中支付。

工程保险的内容和品种由项目主管单位审核确定。在可研阶段和初设阶段，工程保险费可以参照同类工程计列，从基本预备费中支付。

（三）项目建设技术服务费

项目建设技术服务费是指为工程建设提供技术服务和技术支持所发生的费用，包括项目前期工作费、知识产权转让及研究试验费、勘察设计费、设计文件评审费、项目后评价费、工程建设监督检测费、电力建设标准编制管理费、电力工程定额编制管理费。

计算公式：

$$项目建设技术服务费 = 项目前期工作费 + 知识产权转让及研究试验费 + 勘察设计费、设计文件评审费 + 项目后评价费 + 工程建设监督检测费 + 电力建设标准编制管理费 + 电力工程定额编制管理费 \quad (2\text{-}4\text{-}42)$$

1. 项目前期工作费

项目前期工作费是指项目法人在项目前期阶段（包括可行性研究阶段）所发生的费用，包括进行项目可行性研究设计、土地预审、环境影响评价、劳动安全卫生预评价、地质灾害评价、地震灾害评价、编制水土保持大纲、矿产压覆评估、林业规划勘测、文物普探等工作所发生的费用，以及分摊在本工程中的电力系统规划设计的咨询费与设计文件评审费等。

可行性研究阶段按式（2-4-42）计算为

$$项目前期工作费 = （勘察费 + 基本设计费）\times 费率 \quad (2\text{-}4\text{-}43)$$

费率见表2-4-29。初步设计阶段根据项目法人与有关单位签订的各项协议费用计列。

架空送电线路工程项目前期工作费的计算采用累进制，当线路长度超过100 km时，超过部分费率按照9.3%计算。例如，当线路长度为150 km，其项目前期工作费费率计算为为

$$11.2\% \times (100/150) + 9.3\% \times [(150-100)/150] = 7.47\% + 3.1\% = 10.57\%$$

表2-4-29　项目前期工作费费率表

工程类别	架空线路长度（km）		电缆线路工程
	100及以下	100以上	
费率%	11.2	9.3	5.6

2. 知识产权转让与研究试验费

知识产权转让费是指项目法人在本工程中使用专项研究成果、先进技术所支付的一次性转让费用；研究试验费是指为本建设项目提供或验证设计数据进行必要的研究试验所发生的费用，以及按照设计规定在施工过程中必须进行的研究试验费用。不包括：应由科技三项费用（即新产品试制费、中间试验费和重要科学研究补助费）开支的项目；应由管理费开支的鉴定、检查和试验费；应由勘察设计费中开支的项目。

计算标准：根据项目法人提出的项目和费用计列（一般送电线路工程中没有此项费用）。

3. 勘察设计费

勘察设计费是指对工程建设项目进行勘察设计所发生的费用。包括项目的各项勘探、勘察费用，初步设计、施工图设计费，竣工图文件编制费，施工图预算编制费，以及设计代表的现场技术服务费。分为勘察费和设计费。

计算公式为

$$勘察设计费=勘察费+设计费 \tag{2-4-44}$$

（1）勘察费是指项目法人委托有资质的勘察机构按照勘察设计规范要求，对项目进行工程勘察作业以及编制勘察文件和岩土工程设计文件等所支付的费用。

计算标准：依据国家行政主管部门颁发的工程勘察收费标准计算。

根据国家计委、建设部颁布的《工程勘察设计收费管理规定》（计价格〔2002〕10号），电力工程勘察费包括初步设计和施工图设计阶段的工程勘察费用支出。工程勘察工作范围包括工程测量、岩土工程勘察、工程水文气象，以及相应的测试、试验工作。架空送电线路工程勘察工作内容包括下述方面。

1）初步设计阶段：搜集可供利用的各种资料，编写勘察大纲；参加选线、水文调查、工程地质调查、拥挤地段和重要交叉跨越测量、影响范围内必要的通信线相对位置测量；资料整理、编写报告，提交勘察成果。

2）施工图设计阶段：研究任务、编写勘察大纲；进行定线、纵横断面、平面、交叉跨越、边线及风偏测量、塔位定测、塔位断面和弧垂危险点监测、配合岩石勘察、水文专业的测量，工程地质调查、勘探、试验、塔位水文鉴定；资料整理、编写报告，提交勘察成果。

计算公式为

$$电力工程勘察费=工程勘察设计费基准价+工程勘察作业准备费 \quad (2\text{-}4\text{-}45)$$

（2）设计费是指项目法人委托有资质的设计机构按照工程设计规范要求，编制建设项目初步设计文件、施工图设计文件、施工图预算、非标准设备设计文件、竣工图文件等，以及设计代表进行现场技术服务等所支付的费用。

计算标准：依据国家行政主管部门颁发的工程勘察设计收费标准计算。

根据国家计委、建设部颁布的《工程勘察设计收费管理规定》（计价格〔2002〕10号），电力工程设计的工作范围包括编制和提供初步设计文件、施工图设计文件、非标准设备设计文件、施工图预算文件、竣工图文件等。

计算公式为

$$电力工程设计费=基本设计费+其他设计费 \quad (2\text{-}4\text{-}46)$$

其他设计费是指除基本设计费包括的费用外，根据工程设计实际需要或者项目法人要求，设计单位提供相关服务收取的费用，包括总体设计费、主体设计协调费、采用标准设计和复用设计费、非标准设备设计文件编制费、施工图预算编制费、竣工图文件编制费。其中，

$$施工图预算编制费=基本设计费\times 10\% \quad (2\text{-}4\text{-}47)$$

$$竣工图文件编制费=基本设计费\times 8\% \quad (2\text{-}4\text{-}48)$$

4. 设计文件评审费

设计文件评审费是指项目法人根据国家有关规定，对工程项目的设计文件进行评审所发生的费用。按其内容分为可行性研究设计文件评审费和初步设计文件评审费。

计算公式为

$$设计文件评审费=可行性研究设计文件评审费+初步设计文件评审费 \quad (2\text{-}4\text{-}49)$$

可行性研究设计文件评审费是指项目法人委托有资质的评审机构，依据法律、法规和行业标准，从政策、规划、技术和经济等方面对工程项目的必要性和可行性进行全面评审并提出可行性评审报告所发生的费用。计算标准见表2-4-17。

初步设计文件评审费是指项目法人委托有资质的咨询机构依据法律、法规和行业标准，对初步设计方案的安全性、可靠性、先进性和经济性进行全面评审并提出评审报告所发生的费用。计算标准见表2-4-30。

表 2-4-30　送电线路工程设计文件评审费费用标准

电压等级（kV）	规模范围（km）	费用标准（万元/km）	
		可行性研究	初步设计
35	100 以内	0.11	0.15
110	100 以内	0.17	0.24
220	100 以内	0.22	0.31
330	100 以内	0.24	0.34
	100～300	0.13	0.19
	300 以上	0.10	0.13
500	100 以内	0.34	0.49
	100～300	0.18	0.26
	300 以上	0.12	0.17
750	100 以内	0.50	0.70
	100～300	0.29	0.42
	300 以上	0.19	0.27

注1：同塔双回线路工程（段）乘以1.8系数。
注2：覆冰20 mm及以上线路工程（段）乘以1.3系数。
注3：设计风速超过35 m/s时，乘以1.1系数。
注4：直流送电线路工程乘以1.2系数。
注5：500 kV采用630 mm^{2}及以上大截面导线时乘以1.2系数。
注6：送电线路长度不足5 km的按5 km计算；送电线路长度按本期本电压等级总长度计算，不得分段计费。

5. 项目后评价费

项目后评价费是指根据国家行政主管部门的有关规定，项目法人为了对项目决策提供科学、可靠的依据，指导、改进项目管理，提高投资效益，同时为政府决策提供参考依据，完善相关政策，在建设项目投产后对项目的决策、设计、建设管理、投资效益等方面进行综合分析、评价所支出的费用。

计算公式为

$$项目后评价费 = 安装工程费 \times 费率 \qquad (2\text{-}4\text{-}50)$$

费率标准：220 kV及以下送变电工程0.5%，330 kV及以上送变电工程0.35%。在实际过程中，项目是否需要做后评价，由项目的投资决策机构决定。

6. 工程建设监督检测费

工程建设监督检测费是指根据国家行政主管部门及电力行业的有关规定，对工程质量、环境保护、水土保持措施、特种设备（消防、电梯、压力容器等）安装进行监督、检验、检测所发生的费用。主要费用项目包括工程质量监督检测费、特种设备安全监测费、环境监测验收费、水土保持项目验收及补偿费、桩基检测费。

计算公式为

$$工程建设监督检测费=工程质量监督检测费+特种设备安全监测费$$
$$+环境监测验收费+水土保持项目验收及补偿费+桩基检测费 \quad (2-4-51)$$

（1）工程质量监督检测费

工程质量监督检测费是指根据电力行业有关规定，由国家行政主管部门授权的电力工程质量监督机构对工程质量进行监督、检查、检测所发生的费用。

计算公式为

$$工程质量监督检测费=安装工程费×费率 \quad (2-4-52)$$

费率标准：架空送电线路工程取0.23%，电缆线路工程取0.35%，系统通信工程取0.18%。

（2）特种设备安全检测费

特种设备安全检测费是指根据国务院《特种设备安全监察条例》规定，委托特种设备检验检测机构对工程所安装的特种设备进行检验、检测所发生的费用。

计算标准：500kV直流换流站按3万元/站计列。

（3）环境监测验收费

环境监测验收费是指根据国家环境保护法律、法规，环境检测机构对工程建设阶段进行监督检测以及对工程环保设施进行验收所发生的费用。

计算标准：根据工程所在省、自治区、直辖市行政主管部门规定的标准计算。

（4）水土保持项目验收及补偿费

水土保持项目验收费是指根据《水土保持法》及其《实施条例》对电力工程水土保持设施项目进行检测、验收所发生的费用；水土保持补偿费是指根据《水土保持法》及其《实施条例》对电力工程占用或损坏水土保持设施、破坏地貌植被、降低水土保持功能以及水土流失防治等给予补偿所发生的费用。

计算标准：根据工程所在省、自治区、直辖市行政主管部门规定的标准计算。

（5）桩基检测费

桩基检测费是指项目法人根据工程需要，组织对特殊地质条件下使用的特殊桩基进行检测所发生的费用。

计算标准根据工程实际情况确定。

7. 电力建设标准编制管理费

电力建设标准编制管理费是指根据国家有关规定，为保证电力工程各项标准、规范的测定、编制和管理工作正常进行，需向电力行业标准化管理部门缴纳的费用。

计算公式为

$$电力建设标准编制管理费=（勘察费+基本设计费）\times 1.5\% \qquad (2-4-53)$$

8. 电力工程定额编制管理费

电力工程定额编制管理费是指根据国家行政主管部门规定，为保证电力工程建设预算定额、劳动定额的测算、编制和管理工作正常进行，需向电力行业工程定额（造价）管理部门缴纳的费用。

计算公式为

$$电力工程定额编制管理费=安装工程费\times 0.12\% \qquad (2-4-54)$$

（四）分系统调试及整套启动试运费

分系统调试及整套启动试运费包括分系统调试、整套启动试运费和施工企业配合调试费。

计算公式为

$$分系统调试及整套启动试运费=分系统调试+整套启动试运费+施工企业配合调试费 \qquad (2-4-55)$$

1. 分系统调试费

分系统调试费是指工艺系统安装完毕后进行系统联动调试所发生的费用。
计算标准按照电力行业调试定额执行。

2. 整套启动试运费

整套启动试运费是指输变电工程项目投产前进行整套启动试运所发生的费用。
计算标准按照电力行业调试定额执行。

3. 施工企业配合调试费

施工企业配合调试费是指输变电工程整套启动试运阶段，施工企业按照专业配合调试所发生的费用。

计算公式为

$$施工企业配合调试费=安装工程费\times 费率 \qquad (2-4-56)$$

费率见表2-4-31。

表2-4-31　施工企业配合调试费费率

电压等级（kV）	110及以下	220	330	500	750
费率%		0.17		0.13	

注1：35kV及以下架空线路工程不列此项费用。
注2：电缆线路工程、通信工程、光缆工程不列此项费用。

（五）生产准备费

生产准备费是指为保证工程竣工验收合格后能够正常投产运行提供技术保证和资源配备所发生的费用，包括管理车辆购置费，工器具及办公家具购置费，生产职工培训及提前进场费。

1. 管理车辆购置费

管理车辆购置费指生产运行单位进行生产必须配备车辆的购置费用，包括车辆原价、运杂费及车辆附加费。

计算公式为

$$管理车辆购置费 = 安装工程费 \times 费率\% \quad (2\text{-}4\text{-}57)$$

费率见表2-4-32。

表2-4-32　管理车辆购置费费率

	电压等级（kV）	110及以下	220	330	500	750
费率%	架空线路工程		0.25		0.20	
	电缆线路工程			1.35		

车辆购置的具体品种及数量，由概算审批单位在上述计算标准所确定的投资范围内核定，在概算书中明确。

2. 工器具及办公家具购置费

工器具及办公家具购置费是指为满足电力工程投产初期生产、生活和管理需要，购置必要的家具、用具、标志牌、警示牌、标示桩等发生的费用。

计算公式为

$$工器具及办公家具购置费 = 安装工程费 \times 费率\% \quad (2\text{-}4\text{-}58)$$

费率见表2-4-33。

3. 生产职工培训及提前进场费

生产职工培训及提前进厂费指为保证电力工程正常投产运行，对生产和管理人员培训以及提前进场进行生产准备所发生的费用，包括培训人员和提前进场人员的培训费、基本工资、工资性补贴、辅助工资、职工福利费、劳动保护费、养老保险费、失业保险费、医疗保险费、差旅费、资料费、取暖费、教育经费和工会经费等。

表2-4-33 工器具及办公家具购置费费率

电压等级（kV）		110及以下	220	330	500	750
费率%	架空线路工程	0.21		0.15		0.11
	电缆线路工程	1.07				

计算公式为

$$\text{生产职工培训及提前进场费} = \text{安装工程费} \times \text{费率\%} \quad (2\text{-}4\text{-}59)$$

费率见表2-4-21。

表2-4-34 生产职工培训及提前进场费费率

电压等级（kV）	110及以下	220	330	500	750
费率%	0.10		0.08		0.06

（六）大件运输措施费

大件运输措施费是指超限的大型电力设备在运输过程中发生的路、桥加固、改造，以及障碍物迁移等措施费用。

计算标准按照实际运输条件及运输方案计算。

（七）基本预备费

基本预备费是指因设计变更（含施工过程中工程量增减、设备改型、材料代用等）而增加的费用，以及为预防一般自然灾害和其他不确定因素可能造成的损失而预留的工程建设资金。

计算公式为

$$\text{基本预备费} = [\text{安装工程费} + \text{其他费用（不包括基本预备费）}] \times \text{费率} \quad (2\text{-}4\text{-}60)$$

费率见表2-4-22。

表2-4-35 基本预备费费率

设计阶段	费率%	
	220kV及以下	330kV及以上
可行性研究估算	4	3
初步设计概算	2.5	2
施工图预算	1.0	1.0

基本预备费的计算基数包括编制年价差。

（八）动态费用

动态费用是指对构成工程造价的各要素在建设预算编制年至竣工验收期间，因时间和市场价格变化所引起价格增长和资金成本增加所发生的费用，主要包括价差预备费和建设期贷款利息。

计算公式为

$$\text{动态费用} = \text{价差预备费} + \text{建设期贷款利息} \quad (2\text{-}4\text{-}61)$$

1. 价差预备费

价差预备费是指建设工程项目在建设期间内由于价格等变化引起工程造价变化的预测预留费用。

计算公式为

$$C = \sum_{i=1}^{n_2} F_i \left[(1+e)^{n_1+i-1} - 1 \right] \quad (2\text{-}4\text{-}62)$$

式中，C 为价差预备费；e 为年度造价上涨指数；n_1 为建设预算编制水平年至工程开工年的时间间隔，年；i 为从开工年开始的第 i 年；n_2 为工程建设周期，年；F_i 为第 i 年投入的工程建设资金。

注：年度造价上涨指数依据国务院综合管理部门及电力行业主管部门颁布的有关规定执行。

2. 建设期贷款利息

建设期贷款利息是指筹措债务资金时在建设期内发生并按照规定允许在投产后计入固定资产原值的利息。

计算公式为

$$\text{建设期贷款利息} = (\text{年初贷款本息累计} + \text{本年贷款}/2) \times \text{年利率} \quad (2\text{-}4\text{-}63)$$

注：以工程年度资金使用计划为依据确定贷款额。年利率应根据实际（按年或月）结算利率折算的年利率计算，动态费用计算示例见表2-4-36，2-4-37。

表 2-4-36 价差预备费计算表示例

序号	项目	编制水平年 2006	开工年度 2009	建设期 第1年 (2009)	建设期 第2年 (2010)	建设期 第3年 (2011)	价差合计	备注
1	编制年静态投资额 万元	A						
2	建设资金投入比例 %							
3	建设资金投入金额 万元			$F_1=A\times B_1/100$	$F_2=A\times B_2/100$	$F_3=A\times B_3/100$		
4	年度造价上涨指数 %			e	e	e		年度造价上涨指数为 e
5	年度价差额 万元			$E_1=F_1\times[(1+e)^{2+1-1}-1]$	$E_2=F_2\times[(1+e)^{2+2-1}-1]$	$E_3=F_3\times[(1+e)^{2+3-1}-1]$	$E_1+E_2+E_3$	
6	价差预备费 万元						$E_1+E_2+E_3$	

注：1. 计划2009年开工，间隔年为2007/2008两年，因此，$n_1=2$。
2. 以上年度指日历年。

表2-4-37 建设期贷款利息计算表示例

序号	项目	开工年度 2007	建设期 第1年	建设期 第2年	建设期 第3年	利息合计	备注
1	编制年静态投资额+价差预备费 万元	A					
2	注册资本金额 万元	B					资本金比例20%
3	贷款金额 万元	A−B					
4	年度贷款比例%						
5	年度贷款金额 万元		$F_1=(A-B)\times E_1/100$	$F_2=(A-B)\times E_2/100$	$F_3=(A-B)\times E_3/100$		应视资本金的投入方式调整
6	实际贷款利率%	R					年名义利率 $r=7\%$ 按季度结算 实际利率 $r=7.186\%$
7	年贷款利息 万元		$L_1=(F_1/2)\times R/100$	$L_2=(D_1+F_2/2)\times R/100$	$L_3=(D_2+F_3/2)\times R/100$	$L_1+L_2+L_3$	
8	贷款本息累计 万元		$D_1=F_1+L_1$	$D_2=D_1+F_2+L_2$			

注：
1. 本表中把开工年度视为概算编制年，由于概算水平年实际为概算编制日历年的前一年，因而可作为利息计算起始年。
2. 以上年度指周期年，即工程开工满12个月即为一年。
3. 实际利率计算：$(1+r/4)^4-1=(1+7\%/4)^4-1=7.186\%$

（九）案例工程二的其他费用概算表

1. 其他费用概算表

见表2-4-38，案例工程二的其他费用概算表。

2. 取费计算说明

其他费用中，"预规"中有明确规定的费用按照规定的取费基础和费率进行取费计算；建筑场地征用及清理费、项目建设管理费中的工程保险费、项目建设技术服务费中的勘察设计费以及"预规"中其他费用名录中未包括的其他项目费用（如本案例工程的跨越措施费）等，必须根据工程实际情况，按照有关法律、法规、国家行政主管部门以及省（自治区、直辖市）人民政府规定标准进行计算，或依据业主与相关单位签订的协议（合同）价格确定，或参考同类型工程确定。下面将重点介绍建筑场地征用及清理费的计算。

（1）建筑场地征用及清理费

1）土地征用费

送电线路工程土地征用费是指杆塔占用土地面积的征用相关费用，辅助设施工程中土地征用费计入辅助设施工程费。本案例工程只使用了铁塔。铁塔占地面积计算原则：通常情况下，按基础立柱外边缘每边向外增加1 m计，遇有挡土墙、土石方开挖、护坡、排水沟等附属设施处，按实际占地面积征地。

铁塔按截面形状分为正方形和矩形两种，分别简称为方塔和扁塔。铁塔占地面积计算公式如下。

①方塔

$$(A+2B)^2 \qquad (2\text{-}4\text{-}64)$$

式中，A为铁塔根开；$B=\dfrac{b}{2}+1$，B为混凝土基础柱宽。

②扁塔

$$(A+2B)\times(C+2B) \qquad (2\text{-}4\text{-}65)$$

A、C分别为铁塔正侧面根开，B同上。

③举例说明。

某铁塔A、B、C、D腿均使用LZG2026基础，正方形布局，铁塔根开为4.372 m，基础立柱为600×600正方形截面，计算其占地面积为

$$[4.372+2\times(0.6\div2+1)]^2=48.61 \text{（m}^2\text{）}$$

某铁塔A、B、C、D腿均使用LZG2333基础,矩形布局,铁塔正侧面根开为6.166×5.036 m,基础立柱为600×600正方形截面,计算其占地面积为

$$[6.166+2×(0.6÷2+1)]×[5.036+2×(0.6÷2+1)]=66.94（m^2）$$

④关于砼杆占地面积问题

砼杆占地面积计算原则,不打拉线单杆,杆根外缘向四周延伸2 m;打拉线单杆,杆根外缘向四周延伸2 m,拉线以拉线入地点为中心向四周延伸1 m;不打拉线双杆,横线路方向各向外延伸2 m,打拉线双杆再加拉线占地面积（以拉线入地点为中心向四周延伸1 m）。

按照上述原则计算砼杆占地面积数值较小,在工程实际中不考虑因砼杆占地面征用土地。按照电力行业主管部门规定,仅计列适当的赔偿费（800~1000元/基,含拉线）。

2）施工场地租用费

本案案例工程无牵张场,组塔场地相关赔偿费用计入青苗赔偿中,此处仅计购买恢复植被用草籽,当时当地市场价为200元/kg。

3）迁移补偿费

本案例工程迁改10 kV电力线路1 km,按照电力行业主管部门规定补偿标准为10万元/km;迁改220/380V低压线2km,补偿标准为3万元/km。

4）余物清理费

按照工程所在地地方政府建委（拆迁办）规定标准执行,本案例工程计入房屋拆迁费中,不单独计列。

5）送电线路走廊赔偿费

①青苗赔偿

青苗赔偿是送电线路走廊赔偿费的重要组成部分,关系着线路工程沿线居民的切身利益。青苗赔偿包括因主材运输及砂石堆放,杆塔组立,导线、避雷线放紧线施工过程等因素导致青苗损毁的赔偿。

参见式2-2-1,青苗赔偿面积计算公式为

$$S=L×A×(1-B)÷667 \qquad (2\text{-}4\text{-}66)$$

S为青苗赔偿面积,亩;L为线路亘长,m;A为计入青苗赔偿的线路走廊宽度,35 kV、3 m,110 kV、4.5 m,220 kV、6 m,330 kV、7 m,500 kV、8 m;B为沿线无青苗地段（如铁路、公路、河流、成片林木区、果园、茶地等）占全线长度比例。

本案例工程中无青苗地段占全线长度比例为40%,参照同类型工程赔偿单价为2.5元/平方米。

②林木砍伐赔偿

统计需砍伐的种类及数量，分成片林木区及零星林木，又分为国家森林公园、防护林带、用材林、原始森林。本案例工程分为果树（主要是柑橘树）、松柏树及杂树两类，工程所在地地方政府林业局规定标准一般较低，且不能及时根据市场价格调整，实际执行与林木所有权人的协议价。参照近期同类型工程赔偿标准为果树120元/棵·年，赔偿年限为3年；松柏树及杂树50元/颗。

③房屋拆迁费

按照地方行业主管部门规定，220 kV架空线路工程边线垂直投影2.5 m内建筑物均需拆迁。由设计人员量测并编制"房屋拆迁卡"，统计房屋拆迁量；工程所在地地方政府建委（拆迁办）规定标准为420元/m²。

6）通信设施防送电线路干扰措施费

本案例工程迁改通信线1.5 km，与产权单位协议价格为1.5万元/km。

(2) 项目建设管理费

1）查表2-4-26，220 kV及以下架空线路工程的建设项目法人管理费费率为1.35%；

2）查表2-4-27，330 kV及以下架空线路工程的招标费费率为0.45%；

3）查表2-4-28，220 kV架空线路工程以平地、丘陵为标准地形，工程监理费为1万元/km，山地乘以1.1的系数。本案例工程地形比例为：平地7.4%，丘陵51.4%，山地41.2%。因此工程监理费标准为

$$1\times（7.4\%+51.4\%）+1.1\times1\times41.2\%=1.0412（元/km）$$

4）工程保险费

工程保险费应根据项目法人要求及工程实际情况，按照与保险公司协议价格确定。本案例工程参照同类型工程计列，从基本预备费中支付。

(3) 项目建设技术服务费

1）项目前期工作费

项目前期工作费包括可行性研究阶段的项目前期工作费和设计阶段的项目前期工程报告费。初步设计阶段的项目前期工作费根据项目法人与有关单位签订的各项协议费用计列，书中所列费用可作为计算基数。

①查表2-4-29，可行性研究阶段的项目前期工作费费率为11.2%。

②项目前期工程报告费

按照电力行业主管部门规定"输变电项目前期工作费用暂行标准（川电建[2007]436号文）"，项目前期工程报告费包括核准专题报告编制和评审费和其他专题报告编制和评审费。核准专题报告编制和评审费包括环境影响报告及评估费、水土保持专题

报告编制和评审费、用地预审费；其他专题报告编制和评审费包括其他专题报告编制和评审费、压覆矿评估费、地质灾害评估费、文物评估费、拟使用林地可行性报告费（林堪费）等，详见表2-4-38，此处限于篇幅，不再赘述。

2）知识产权转让与研究实验费，本案例工程不计列。

3）勘察设计费

按照按国家行政部门颁布工程勘察设计收费标准计算勘察设计费，当前执行"工程勘察设计收费管理规定（计价格〔2002〕10号）"。根据该规定计算出来的勘察设计费可作为基数，实际按照工程勘察设计招标价计列。书中列出根据本案例工程实际情况计算得出的勘察设计费基数，详见表2-4-38，此处限于篇幅，不再赘述。

4）设计文件评审费

查表2-4-30，220 kV架空线路工程可研设计文件评审费、初步设计文件评审费标准分别为0.22万元/km、0.31万元/km。

5）根据《预标》，220 kV架空线路工程项目后评价费费率为0.5%。

6）工程建设监督检测费

①根据《预标》，本案例工程的工程质量监督检测费费率取0.23%。

②环境监测验收费根据"关于规范环境影响咨询收费有关问题的通知（计价格〔2002〕125号）"，水土保持项目验收及补偿费根据"关于开发建设项目水土保持咨询服务费用计列的指导意见（保监〔2005〕22号）"，以及工程所在地政府行政和电力行业主管部门规定的标准计算收费基数，实际按照与有相关资质的咨询评估机构"服务合同（协议）价"执行。因概算编制阶段尚未与相关检测机构签订合同（协议），可参照同类型工程计列，本书中未计列。

7）根据《预标》，本案例工程的电力建设标准编制管理费费率取1.5%。

8）根据《预标》，本案例工程的电力工程定额编制管理费费率取0.12%。

（4）分系统调试及整套启动调试费

按照电力行业调试定额执行，本案例工程不计列分系统调试费，计列整套启动调试费。

查表2-4-31，220 kV架空线路工程施工企业配合调试费费率取0.17%。

（5）生产准备费

查表2-4-32、2-4-33、2-4-34，220 kV架空线路工程管理车辆购置费费率取0.25%，工器具办公家具购置费费率取0.21%、生产职工培训及提前进厂费费率取0.10%。

（6）其他项目费

其他项目费是指在《预标》其他费用名录中未包括的工程其他项目费，如带电跨越电力线、铁路、公路、江河等采取必要的未包含在安装费中的其他措施费用，或业主要求增加的其他项目费用。

本案例工程包括带电跨越电力线路和跨越嘉陵江相关措施费，查表2-4-11或按照电力行业主管部门规定执行，详见表2-4-38，此处限于篇幅，不再赘述。

（7）编制年价差

材机调整，执行电力行业主管部门规定"关于发布四川地区工程概预算定额价格水平调整系数的通知川电定造〔2008〕6号"，220 kV架空线路工程定额材机调整系数取22.90%。

装置性材料价差按照当时当地本案例工程耗用的装置性材料价差计列。

（8）基本预备费

查表2-4-35，220kV及以下架空线路工程在初步设计阶段的基本预备费费率取2.5%。

（9）动态费用

价差预备费，因本案例工程设计到施工阶段时间差极短，施工周期短，不计列。建设期贷款利息按照工程实际发生计列，本案例工程参照同类型工程计列。

六、编制总概算表

表2-4-39所示为总概算表。

汇总安装工程费用汇总概算表（表二乙）、辅助设施工程概算表（表三戊）、其他费用概算表（表四）各表数据，填入表2-4-39（表一乙），得架空送电线路工程总概算表。

表四

表2-4-38 其他费用表

序号	工程费用名称	编制依据及计算说明			总价（元）
一	建设场地占用及清理费				14647460
1	土地征用费	工程所在地政府征地标准18万元/亩	22.59亩	× 18万元/亩	4066200
2	施工场地租用费	购买恢复植被用草籽	40kg	× 200元/kg	8000
3	迁移补偿费				160000
3.1	10kV线路改造费用		1km	× 10万元/km	100000
3.2	低压线改造费用		2km	× 3万元/km	60000
4	余物清理费				
5	送电线路走廊赔偿费				10368260
5.1	果树砍伐赔偿费		350棵	× 120元/棵·年 *3年	126000
5.2	松柏树、杂树砍伐赔偿费		(21000+7000)颗	× 50元/颗	1400000
5.3	青苗赔偿费		51800m²*6m	× 2.5元/m²*60%	466200
5.4	房屋拆迁费		19943m²	× 420元/m²	8376060
6	通信设施防送电线路干扰措施费	通讯线改造	1.5km	× 3万元/km	45000
二	项目建设管理费				1169631
1	建设项目法人管理费	安装工程费×费率	35016103	× 1.35%	472717
2	招标费	安装工程费×费率	35016103	× 0.45%	157572
3	工程监理费	2007年《电网工程建设预算编制与计算标准》	51.8km	× 1.0412 万元/km	539342
4	工程保险费	参照同类型工程计列，从基本预备费支付			
三	项目建设技术服务费				3009834

续表

序号	工程费用名称	编制依据及计算说明			总价(元)
1	项目前期工作费				481600
1.1	项目前期工作费	(勘察费+基本设计费)×费率	1675719	11.20%	187680
1.2	项目前期工程报告费				293920
1.2.1	核准专题报告编制和评审费	输变电项目前期工作费用暂行标准 川电建[2007]436号文			169600
1.2.1.1	环境影响报告及评估费	20km以内4万元，超过20km部分0.12万元/km	51.8km	×	78160
1.2.1.2	水土保持专题报告编制和评审费		51.8km	× 0.08万元/km	41440
1.2.1.3	用地预审费		5万元		50000
1.2.2	其他专题报告编制和评审费	输变电项目前期工作费用暂行标准 川电建[2007]436号文			124320
1.2.2.1	压覆矿评估费		51.8km	× 0.10万元/km	51800
1.2.2.2	地质灾害评估费		51.8km	× 0.10万元/km	51800
1.2.2.3	文物评估费		51.8km	× 0.04万元/km	20720
1.2.2.4	拟使用林地可行性报告费(林堪费)	根据工程具体情况确定	60000元		
2	知识产权转让与研究实验费	无			0
3	勘察设计费				1930921
3.1	勘察费	按国家行政部门颁布工程勘察设计收费标准计算	51.8km	× 2469.66 元/km	257929
3.2	设计费				1672992
3.2.1	基本设计费	按国家行政部门颁布工程勘察设计收费标准计算	35016103	× 1.2	1417790
3.2.2	施工图预算编制费	按国家行政部门颁布工程勘察设计收费标准计算	10.00%	×	141779

续表

序号	工程费用名称	编制依据及计算说明			总价(元)
3.2.3	竣工图编制费	按国家行政部门颁布工程勘察设计收费标准计算	8.00%		113423
4	设计文件评审费	2007年《电网工程建设预算编制与计算标准》			274540
4.1	可研设计文件评审费		51.8km	0.22万元/km	113960
4.2	初步设计文件评审费		51.8km	0.31万元/km	160580
5	项目后评价费	安装工程费×费率	35016103	× 0.50%	175081
6	工程建设监督检测费				80537
6.1	工程质量监督检测费	安装工程费×费率	35016103	× 0.23%	80537
6.2	环境监测验收费				0
6.3	水土保持项目验收及补偿费		? m²	× 0.8元/m²	0
7	电力建设标准编制管理费	输变电项目前期工作费用暂行标准川电建[2007]436号文 (勘察费+基本设计费)×费率	1675719	× 1.50%	25136
8	电力工程定额编制管理费	安装工程费×费率	35016102.8	× 0.12%	42019
四	分系统调试及整套启动调试费				152839
1	整套启动调试费	按电力建设工程预算定额（第六册 调试标准 2006年版）执行	192工日	270元/工日	93312 *1.5*(1+0.2)
2	施工企业配合调试费	安装工程费×费率	35016103	× 0.17%	59527
五	生产准备费				196090
1	管理车辆购置费	安装工程费×费率	35016103	× 0.25%	87540
2	工器具办公家具购置费	安装工程费×费率	35016103	× 0.21%	73534
3	生产职工培训及提前进厂费	安装工程费×费率	35016103	× 0.10%	35016
六	跨越施工措施费				344000
1	带电跨越电力线措施费				244000

续表

序号	工程费用名称	编制依据及计算说明		总价（元）
	10kV	32处	3500元/处	112000
	35kV	6处	12000元/处	72000
	110kV	3处	20000元/处	60000
2	跨嘉陵江协议费及措施费	1处	100000元/处	100000
七	编制年价差	×	×	6750000
1	材机调整	1598793	×	353173
2	装置性材料价差（含税金）	6396827	×	6396827
	小计	×	×	19519855
	基本预备费	54535958	2.5%	1363399
八	合计	×	×	20883254
九	动态费用			2005000
1	价差预备费	本案例工程不计列		0
2	建设期贷款利息	200.5万元		2005000

注1：各项费用必须写明编制和计算依据，以及必要的计算方法和说明。
注2：本表适用于变电、送电工程。

表2-4-39 架空送电线路工程总概算表

表一乙　　　　　　　　　　　　　　　　　　　　　　　　　　　　　　　51.8km

序号	工程或费用名称	费用金额 万元	各项占总计 %	单位投资 万元/km
一	架空送电线路本体工程	3434	53.52%	66.30
（一）	一般线路本体工程	3434		
（二）	大跨越本体工程	0		
二	辅助设施工程	23	0.36%	0.45
	小计	3457		
三	编制年价差	675	10.52%	13.03
四	其他费用	2084	32.48%	40.24
	其中：1.建设场地征用及清理费	1465		
	2.基本预备费	135		
	静态投资（一～四项合计）	6217		120.01
五	动态费用	201	3.12%	3.87
（一）	价差预备费	0		
（二）	建设期贷款利息	201		
	动态投资（一～五项合计）	6417		123.88

注：本表金额除单位投资外，均以万元为单位，均不留小数，有小数时四舍五入。

任务5 编写概算编制说明

一、概算编制说明的内容和要求

概算编制说明,要求叙述本工程概算编制的各项要点,并对投资进行对比分析。简明扼要,内容须完整。

1. 编制说明的内容

(1) 设计依据;
(2) 工程概况;
(3) 编制原则;
(4) 编制方法;
(5) 投资分析。

2. 设计依据

设计依据指批准的设计任务书和设计委托书及文号、名称及有关内容,如工程名称、建设性质、计划建设工期、投资来源、批准的投资额等。

3. 工程概况

工程概况简要叙述以下内容:线路起讫点,单、双或者多回路数,线路亘长,电压等级,气象条件,导线、避雷线型号,避雷线绝缘方式,每公里杆塔基数,杆塔分类、型号、数量及各占总量的百分比,基础分类、形式、数量及各占总量的百分比,基坑土(石)方量分类及各占总量的百分比。

沿线地貌概况,各类地形长度及百分比,交通运输条件,工地仓库的数量及设置地点,工地运输方式及其平均运距,各类运输地形长度及所占的百分比等。

4. 编制原则

着重说明以下重要的原则和依据:
(1) 定额或指标的选定;
(2) 概算指标中安装费调整的依据;
(3) 人工费单价和调整系数的依据;

(4) 计价材料及机械台班费调整的依据；

(5) 装置性材料价格的取定及依据；

(6) 辅助设施工程的编制依据；

(7) 其他费用标准和依据；

(8) 其他重要原则问题。规定以外的特殊费用，调整或修正概算的重要原则等。

5. 编制方法

(1) 工程量计算依据；

(2) 超出定额（或指标）规定范围的调整换算方法；

(3) 大跨越特殊杆塔及地基处理费的计算方法；

(4) 特殊工程量和特殊费用的计算方法和来源；

(5) 编制中已处理的其他问题；

(6) 尚存在的问题。

6. 投资分析

对工程设计概算，应做简要的经济分析比较与分析。

(1) 初设概算，一般应与设计任务书或项目建议书批准的总投资额和同类型工程投资额对比分析，或与《国家电网公司输变电工程典型造价》（2006年版）进行比对分析，以说明本工程投资的合理性和存在的问题。

(2) 批准概算，应列出与原概算的对照分析表，并着重说明投资变化的主要原因。

7. 填写"送电工程概况及主要技术经济指标表"（表五丙）

表五丙列于说明最后，参见表2-4-40。可与同类型工程相比较，明确材料消耗指标先进与否。

二、案例工程二的概算编制说明

（一）工程概况

1. 线路起止点：从220 kV变电站（小号侧）出线构架至220 kV变电站（大号侧）进线构架。

2. 线路长度：共计51.8 km，220 kV单回（其中小号侧变电站出线3 km采用同塔双回设计，本期单侧挂线）。

3. 电压等级：220千伏。

4. 导线型号：2×LGJ-400/35。地线型号：GJX80，LBGJ-100-30AC，OPGW-100。

5. 杆塔：全线共使用铁塔137基，其中直线塔86基（占62.8%），耐张或转角塔51基（占37.2%）。

6. 地形划分

地形划分	平地	丘陵	山地	高山	峻岭	泥沼
比例	7.4%	51.4%	41.2%	/	/	/

7. 地质划分

地质划分	普通土	坚土	松砂石	岩石	泥水	流沙
比例	16%	/	55%	25%	4%	/

8. 气象条件：最大风速：25（30）m/s；导线最大设计冰厚5 mm。

9. 工地运输：人力运距0.8 km，汽车运距28 km。

10. OPGW架设费用计入通信工程。

（二）编制依据

1. 《电力建设工程预算定额—第四册 送电线路工程》2006年版。

2. 《电网工程建设预算编制与计算标准》2007年7月发布。

3. 《电力建设工程预算定额—第四册 送电线路工程》2006年版使用指南。

4. 《电网工程建设预算编制与计算标准》使用指南。

5. 川电定〔2008〕7号关于印发《四川省电网工程建设预算编制与计算程序》的通知。

6. 定额人工费调整：调增系数2.18%。

7. 定额材料与机械费调增：四川220 kV送电工程材机调整系数22.09%。

8. 建设期贷款利息：200.5万元。

9. 主要材料价格

单位：元

序号	名称	型号	原价	本体价格	材料价差	总价
1	导线	LGJ-400/35	/	16800	700	17500
4	塔材	角钢塔	/	6800	2200	9000

10. 工程量按设计资料。

11. 塔材代用只计列工地运输。

(三) 经济指标

项目名称	本体投资		静态投资		动态投资	
	费用金额	单位投资	费用金额	单位投资	费用金额	单位投资
单位	万元	万元/km	万元	万元/km	万元	万元/km
经济指标	3434	66.30	6217	120.01	6417	123.88

本案例工程概况及主要技术经济指标表见表2-4-40。

表五丙

表2-4-40 架空送电线路工程概况及主要技术经济指标表

工程概况	起点：A220kV变电站		终点：B220kV变电站		电压等级 220kV		输送容量 MVA			海拔高度 300~600m		
	折单回总长度 51.8km		单回 51.8km		双回 3 km		三回 0km		四回 0km		公路 44处	
	线路参数	杆塔总数 137	气象条件	最高气温 40℃	主要覆冰 5mm		平地 7.4%		山地 41.2%		铁路处	河流 12处
		转角次数		最低气温 -5℃			丘陵 51.4%		高山 %	地形分布	高速公路处	
		曲折系数 1.20		主要风速 m/s			河网 %		峻岭 %		加挂导线 0km	
		污秽等级 Ⅱ、Ⅲ		最大风速 25 (30) m/s	保护角 °		泥沼 %		交叉跨越		高压线 41处	低压线 232处
导线	牌号 2×LGJ-400/35		每相根数 2		地线	牌号 LBGJ-100-30AC	牌号 OPGW-100		根数 1	1	拉线	每组根数
			每相根数			牌号 GJX-80	牌号		芯 OPGW 芯 24	根数	牌号	每组根数
工程参数	角钢塔 137基		其中：直线塔 86基 62.8%		其中：耐张塔 51基 37.2%		光缆	根数 1	基 %			
	钢管杆塔基		其中：钢管塔基 %		其中：基 %			根数 1	基 %			
	混凝土杆基											
基础	大块式		配筋式		插入式	V形串 0.8km	悬垂串	基 掘挖式	耐张串	桩基础	跳线串 0.15km
	基坑	普通土 4790.40m³	松砂石 16466.40m³		干沙坑	水坑		水坑 m³	泥水坑 1198.80m³	排水沟 17.55m³	
	基面	普通土 196m³	松砂石 537m³		干沙坑	水坑		水坑 m³	泥水坑 m³	岩石坑 483.20m³	
											岩石坑 196 m³	
绝缘子悬挂方式												
	运距		人力运距		汽车运距		余土运距 28km				
主要技术经济指标	导线	420.95t	8.13t/km		t	t/km	845.79t	16.33t/km	挂线金具 119.71t	2.31t/km		
	OPGW地线	32.2t	0.62t/km	插入材	36.11t	0.70t/km	1139.23m³	21.99m³/km	拉线金具	t	组/km	
	钢绞地线	t	t/km	地脚栓	174.88t	3.38t/km	碎石 2097.99m³	40.50m³/km	间隔棒 1726只	33.32只/km		
	拉线	t	t/km	基础钢	20.32t	0.39t/km	瓷绝缘子 15966片	0.12片/km	防振锤	t		
	角钢塔	1173.32t	22.65t/km	接地钢			玻璃绝缘子 片	308.22片/km	降阻剂		m³/km	
	钢管塔	t	t/km	现浇混凝土	2469.12m³	47.67m³/km	合成绝缘子 串	串/km	预制混凝土	m³		
主要材料价格
	塔材	16800元/t		瓷绝缘子	6800元/t		瓷绝缘子	80元/片	合成绝缘子	元/串		
	基础钢材	元/t		玻璃绝缘子	3500元/t		玻璃绝缘子	85元/片	OPGW 24芯	24000元/km		
	导线											
	导线											

任务6 送电线路工程概算校审

一、成品校审程序

1. 自校出手。成品须认真自校，在"校审单"上签名，连同有关的原始资料，计算底稿送交科（组）内指定的全校人进行全面校核。

2. 复校、初审出科（组）。成品经全校人校核后交编制人进行第一次修改，全校人复校签字后送科（组）长审核。对成品评定质量等级后，退交编制人进行第二次修改，再由科（组）长核对签名出科（组）。校审中应逐级填写校审单。编制人应根据校审意见认真修改，并在校审单上填写执行情况，有意见分歧时应与校审人研究统一，不能统一时提请上一级研究解决。

3. 复审出室。成品经主任工程师（专工）进行综合性复审，要求编制者根据复审意见修改，复审人再对成品评定质量等级并签名出室。

4. 成品出室后送交设总、总工逐级审定，并签署意见和评级后，交付打印出版。

经过以上四步校审，提高概预算的质量，以防高估而浪费材料和资金，低估施工单位无经济效益。其主要目的是促使施工企业改善经营管理，提高劳动生产率水平，保证施工企业有合理利润，具备可持续发展的基础。

校审的主要依据包括电网工程建设预算编制与计算标准、全国统一安装工程预算定额、经批准的装置性材料预算价格、当地规定的工资标准及计算系数、工程就地取材的价格依据、设计图纸及说明书。

二、成品校审提纲

1. 封面、编制说明及工程概况

（1）工程名称、代号、索引号、电压等级是否与设计文件相一致；

（2）设计依据是否完整正确，是否已明确建设单位、施工单位及建设工期；是否已明确投资来源，投资限额；

（3）线路起讫点名称是否确切；

（4）线路亘长及单回、双回、双回共塔各多少千米；

（5）杆塔数量、种类、形式、平均每千米杆塔数量及各类杆塔占总量的百分比；

（6）导线、避雷线规格、型号，单导线或是分裂导线以及避雷线的绝缘方式；

（7）基础形式、数量及占总量的百分比；

（8）沿线地形划分，各多少千米及所占百分比；

（9）沿线交通情况：是方便、一般、困难；运输方式，地形系数，平均运距的计算是否正确；

（10）土石方工程：计算及分类是否准确，是否有余土外运及取土回填；

（11）基础施工是否需考虑施工用水运输及平均运距；

（12）杆塔工程是否已包括接地工程在内；

（13）是否有一般跨越、特殊跨越及跨越地点以及是否采用特殊导地线，特殊杆塔或基础；

（14）附件安装的绝缘子串数量是否计算正确。

2. 编制原则及依据

（1）定额的选定和使用原则是否正确。应特别注意人工工资调整的依据及计算方法有无差错；

（2）主要材料预算价格的依据，是否符合规定的使用范围及使用方法；

（3）辅助设施工程费的计算依据和方法；

（4）其他工程和费用的计算依据和方法；

（5）特殊费用的取定及依据；

（6）暂（估）列的费用是否恰当；

（7）选用的定额或指标，是否根据工程具体实际按规定进行了调查；

（8）选用的定额或指标子目是否有错项、漏项。

3. 工程量

（1）导地线型号、规格，单位重量、公里数、总重量，是否按规定计入了损耗；

（2）杆塔形式、数量是按规定计入了损耗；

（3）混凝土杆的封顶是否计算；

（4）基础工程量的校核，包括基础钢材、混凝土量、预制基础规格、数量；

（5）钻孔灌注桩基础的孔径、桩长，其混凝土量是否按规定增加了超灌量；

（6）爆扩桩基础混凝土量是否按规定增加了超灌量；

（7）基础保护帽的混凝土量是否已计算；

（8）根据工程地形、地质情况，设计是否考虑了基础垫层、护坡、排水（洪）沟及其他措施；

（9）挂线金具、防震金具，绝缘子规格及数量的校核，是否按规定计入了损耗；

（10）是否设计有重锤；

（11）接地材料校核；

（12）土石方量的核对；

（13）主材工地运输量，是否包括损耗和包装重量。

4. 核对各表格

5. 校核重点

（1）有无漏项：本体、辅助工程、各单项工程；

（2）单价选用是否正确；

（3）定额（价目本）是否正确；

（4）费用齐全否；

（5）计算有无差错；看计算数据的整数位对不对。

三、技术经济分析

（一）主要技术经济指标简介

技术经济分析是校审的最后一步。其目的是：弄清工程投资额、造价分配比例是否经济上合理、技术上安全可靠，判明设计质量的好坏并指出存在的问题。摸索送电工程的技术、经济相关的规律性，达到设计布置合理，技术上可靠，造价的经济先进的目的。

送电线路工程主要技术经济指标如下所述。

（1）单位造价

$$送电线路单位造价（元/km）=\frac{全部建设费用}{线路直长}$$

$$线路本体单位造价（元/km）=\frac{线路本体工程建设费用}{线路直长}$$

（2）特殊设计工程单位造价$（元/km）=\frac{特殊设计工程项目建设费用}{特殊设计工程线路长度}$

（3）主材消耗量：钢材、水泥、导线、避雷线等。

（4）曲折系数$（\%）=\frac{线路直长}{线路起始点航空直线距离}$

(5) 档距利用系数（%）= $\dfrac{平均档距}{计算档距}$

以上经济技术指标最终汇总在"送电工程概况及主要技术经济指标表"（参见表2-4-40）中，以资分析比较。

（二）案例工程二的技术经济分析

送电线路工程技术经济分析，可将实际工程的主要技术经济指标与《电网工程限额设计控制指标》或《国家电网公司输变电工程典型造价》做对比分析，本书选用《电网工程限额设计控制指标（2009年水平）》做具体分析。220 kV送电工程限额设计控制指标对比分析表见表2-4-41。

表2-4-41　220kV送电工程限额设计控制指标对比分析表

单位：万元/km

序号	项目名称	导线规格2×LGL-400/35（28.5m/s，10mm）					案例工程指标	
		平地	丘陵	河网泥沼	山地	高山	计算值	实际值
1	本体工程	45.68	48.59	53.76	58.00	65.82	52.25	66.30
	其中：材料	32.81	33.67	33.79	35.20	35.36	34.24	37.46
2	其他	22.39	22.91	25.28	25.63	27.92	23.99	57.59
	其中：价差	2.44	2.60	2.92	3.23	3.42	2.85	13.03
	合计	68.07	71.50	79.04	83.63	93.74	76.24	123.88

本案例工程设计气象条件：5 mm覆冰，25（30）m/s风速，地形比例为平地7.4%、丘陵51.4%、山地41.2%。根据计算风速28.5 m/s、覆冰10 mm标准条件下220 kV送电线路2×LGJ-400/35导线限额设计控制指标，计算本案例工程综合限额设计控制指标为

$$68.07 \times 7.4\% + 71.50 \times 51.4\% + 83.63 \times 41.2\% = 76.24（万元/km）$$

同理计算本体工程和其他费用数据，查表2-4-39，将相应数据填入表2-4-41。

同表2-4-41计算方法，将相应数据填入表2-4-42，220 kV送电工程限额设计基本技术组合方案对比分析表。

表2-4-42　220kV送电工程限额设计基本技术组合方案对比分析表

导线型号		2×LGL-400/35					案例工程指标	
地线型号		GJ-80					计算值	实际值
杆塔基数		3.2	3.2	3.2	2.4	2.2	2.87	2.64
运距	人力（km）	0.3	0.6	0.7	0.9	1.3	0.70	0.80
	汽车（km）	25	25	25	25	25	25.00	28.00

同表2-4-41计算方法,查表2-4-40,将相应数据填入表2-4-43,220kV送电工程主要材料单位公里指标对比分析表。

表2-4-43 220kV送电工程主要材料单位公里指标对比分析表

材料名称	单位	导线规格2×LGL-400/35(28.5m/s,10mm)					案例工程指标	
		平地	丘陵	河网泥沼	山地	高山	计算值	实际值
导线	t	8.09	8.09	8.09	8.09	8.09	8.09	8.13
地线	t	1.26	1.26	1.26	1.26	1.26	1.26	0.62
杆塔钢材	t	15.52	16.59	15.52	19.40	19.73	17.67	22.65
基础钢材	t	2.16	2.31	3.52	2.91	3.00	2.55	3.38
挂线金具	t	0.41	0.41	0.41	0.41	0.41	0.41	2.31
接地钢材	t	0.19	0.19	0.19	0.19	0.19	0.19	0.39
间隔棒	组							
防振锤	只	26.00	26.00	26.00	26.00	28.00	26.00	33.32
绝缘子(导线)	片	258.06	258.06	258.06	195.84	183.60	232.43	315.00
现浇混凝土	m³	30.90	32.96	39.14	36.40	37.44	34.22	47.67
水泥	t	10.63	11.34	15.74	12.52	12.88	11.77	16.33
中砂	m³	14.21	15.16	16.92	16.74	17.22	15.74	21.99
碎石	m³	26.27	28.02	32.36	30.94	31.82	29.09	40.50

表2-4-41、2-4-42、2-4-43中"案例工程指标"栏下"计算值",是根据《电网工程限额设计控制指标(2009年水平)》中相应指标结合案例工程实际情况(重点考虑地形划分,参考导、地线型号和主要设计气象条件),得出案例工程限额设计指标值,"实际值"是根案例工程初步设计概算数据。经过对比,可以看出本案例工程初步设计的"主要材料单位公里指标"均高于限额设计控制指标,导致初步设计概算指标也高于限额设计控制指标,设计方案不够经济先进,需要对技术方案设计部分中基础和杆塔设计部分实施严格审核,进一步改进和完善设计方案,确保技术方案可靠先进,造价指标经济合理。

小　　结

学习项目二主要以案例工程二为载体，介绍了编制220kV送电线路初步设计概算书的方法：首先根据《电网工程建设预算编制与计算标准（2007年版）》明确送电线路工程项目划分，熟悉其费用构成和计算标准；再经过现场收集资料，落实地域性取费标准；结合工程设计情况核算具体工程项目各单位工程量；然后选择适用的定额、费率编制单位工程概算表，汇总形成安装工程概算表，完成编制辅助设施概算表、其他费用概算表；依据安装工程概算表、辅助设施概算表、其他费用概算表汇总形成总概算表；最后编写概算说明书。从而确定220kV送电线路初步设计概算。

实训项目二

根据案例工程二初步设计相关资料，完成初步设计概算书；根据本案例工程施工图设计资料，完成施工图设计预算书。

复习与思考

1. 某110kV新建线路工程地形划分为：平地30%，丘陵40%，山地30%。工地运输地形为：平地38%，丘陵44%，山地18%，公路无连续弯道。求其各单位工程的综合地形增加系数。

2. 某新建送电线路工程地形为：平地50%，泥沼30%，丘陵20%；汽车运输地形为：平地80%，丘陵20%。请计算下列工程项目的综合地形增加系数：①现浇砼基础；②汽车运输；③护线条安装。

3. 试计算案例工程二中几种基础的土石方量。

（1）某铁塔基础A、B、C、D四腿均采用直柱柔性基础LZG2230，丘陵地形，地质条件：0~0.3 m为残积粉质黏土，0.3 m以下为粉砂质泥岩（褐红或紫红色、强风化、组织机构大部分破坏，矿物成分显著变化、裂隙发育、岩体破碎）。采用人力开凿方式开挖。

LZG2230基础底板为正方形2.2×2.2 m，坑底不支设模板。A、B、C、D腿基础立柱分别露出地面0.2、0.4、0.6、1.2 m，试计算该铁塔基础土石方开挖方量。

（2）某铁塔基础A、B、C、D四腿均采用斜柱式基础YJG2539、YJG2539、XJG2747、XJG2747，山地地形，地质条件：0~0.5 m为耕土，0.5 m以下为粉砂质泥岩（褐红或紫红色、强风化、组织机构大部分破坏，矿物成分显著变化、裂隙发育、岩体破碎）。A、D腿基面分别降0.4、0.6 m，B、C腿露出地面高度0.2 m。采用人力开凿方式开挖。试计算该铁塔基础土石方开挖方量。

（3）某铁塔基础A、B、C、D四腿均采用掏挖式基础TWG1630、TWG1837、TWG1733、TWG1630，山地地形，地质条件：0~0.4 m为残积粉质黏土，0.4 m以下为粉砂质泥岩（褐红或紫红色，强风化）。TWG1837、TWG1733基础底板和圆锥台部分高度同TWG1630，B、C腿分别露出地面高度1.0、0.6 m。采用人力开凿方式开挖。试计算该铁塔基础土石方开挖方量。

4. 某铁塔A、B、C、D腿均使用XJG2742基础，正方形布局，铁塔根开为5.15m，基础立柱为800×800正方形截面，试计算其占地面积。

5. 某铁塔A、B、C、D腿均使用TWG2035基础，矩形布局，铁塔正侧面根开为6.874×5.644m，基础立柱为Φ900圆形截面，试计算其占地面积。

6. 为什么在施行新版预规的最初一段时间里，会出现工程建设预算继续使用旧版预规的情况？

7. 巡线站、检修站相关费用如何计列？试举例说明。

8. 如何计算基础工程的装置性材料？

9. 如何计算杆塔工程的装置性材料？

10. 如何计算架线工程的装置性材料？

11. 如何计算附件安装工程的装置性材料？

12. OPGW地线复合光缆的施工损耗率如何确定？

13. 某架空送电线路工程地形划分为：平原25%、丘陵17%、山地44%、泥沼14%，试计算水泥、沙、石、导线的施工损耗率。

14. 为什么概算工程量与设计资料中"设备材料汇总表"不完全一致？

15. 初步设计阶段时人力运距如何确定？

16. 送电线路工程概算税金税率如何确定？

17. 概算中，土地征用费用如何确定？

18. 送电线路走廊赔偿费可能包含哪些具体项目费用？青苗赔偿费如何确定？

19. 试收集一份工程保险合同，说明项目建设管理费中工程保险费的确定过程。

20. 通信设施防送电线路干扰措施费可能包含哪些具体项目费用，如何确定？

21. 试根据本案例工程项目情况，计算勘察设计费。

22. 简述材机调整系数存在的意义，在线路工程初步设计阶段概算编制中如何使用？

23. 余物清理费如何计算？

24. 环境监测验收费如何确定？

25. 水土保持项目验收费及补偿费如何确定？

学习项目三

编制500kV送电线路工程估算

案例工程三　500kV某新建送电线路工程

一、工程概况

（一）本工程系500 kV新建送电线路工程，由某500 kV变电站（小号侧）—某500 kV变电站（大号侧），全长99公里，单回线路架设，10 mm覆冰设计。

（二）导地线型号

1. 导线

采用4×LGJ-400/50。

2. 地线

小号侧变电站进出线段约10 km采用LBGJ-100-40AC，其余采用LB-GJ-100-20AC，与OPGW配合组成双地线。OPGW的投资不含在本估算中。

二、杆塔形式及数量

本工程杆塔形式及数量见表3-0-1。

表3-0-1　建筑工程项目划分

项目名称	线路长度	铁塔数量	耐张塔	直线塔	耐张比例
10mm冰区	99km	222	44	178	19.82%

三、主要经济指标

本工程主要经济指标见表3-0-2。

表3-0-2　主要经济指标

项目名称	安装工程费（万元）	单位造价（万元/km）
本体投资	14688	148.36
其他费用	6023	60.84
其中：建设场地征用及清理	2732	27.59
基本预备费	662	6.69
静态投资	22492	227.19
动态投资	23038	232.71

任务1 投资估算资料准备

一、投资估算的概念

投资估算是指在项目投资决策过程中,依据现有的资料和特定的方法,对建设项目的投资数额(包括工程造价和流动资金)进行估计。投资估算总额是指从筹建项目、工程施工直至建成投产的全部建设费用,其包括的内容因项目的性质和范围而有所不同。

在项目决策前期,在编制项目建议书和可行性研究报告阶段,投资估算是其中重要的组成部分,是重要经济指标之一,是建设前期从决策直至初步设计以前的重要工作环节。

二、收集投资估算资料

投资估算的编制准确程度与该阶段资料收集、主要依据的完备是分不开的。资料越具体,越完备及详细,依据越充分齐全,编制的投资估算准确程度就越高。案例工程三收集的资料如下。

(1)由某院勘测设计人员提供资料及现场收资,相关资料见表3-1-1、3-1-2、3-1-3、3-1-4。

表3-1-1 沿线地形划分表

项目名称	丘陵	山地	高山
全线	15.00%	50.00%	35.00%

表3-1-2 沿线土质划分表

项目名称	普通土	坚土	松沙石	岩石	泥水
全线	10.00%	10.00%	42.00%	35.00%	3.00%

3-1-3 工地运输表

项目名称	人力运距(km)			汽车运距(km)	
	主要材料	毛石	水	沙石	其他材料
10mm冰区	1.00	1.00	1.00	25.00	25.00

表 3-1-4 主要材料或工程量指标表

序号	项目名称	单位	工程每公里指标				
			全线	10mm冰区	15mm冰区	20mm冰区	30mm冰区
1	线路长度	km	99.00	99.00			
2	风速	m/s					
3	导线	t/km	18.13	18.13			
4	避雷线	t/km	0.65	0.65			
5	杆塔钢材	t/km	58.20	58.20			
6	基础钢材	t/km	7.34	7.34			
7	导地线金具	t/km	3.09	3.09			
8	接地钢材	t/km	0.61	0.61			
9	导线间隔棒	组/km	60.77	60.77			
10	防振锤	只/km	50.00	50.00			
11	绝缘子	片/km	524.51	524.51			
12	合成绝缘子	支/km					
13	现浇混凝土	m³/km	91.67	91.67			
14	土石方	m³/km	506.13	506.13			
	其中：基坑	m³/km	251.28	251.28			

注：1. 以上工程量均不含损耗；
  2. 基础钢材不含插入式角钢，铁塔不含5%的以大代小；
  3. 砼量未包括超灌量，未包括护坡、保坎、排水沟、基础垫层、保护帽等用量；
  4. 土石方量为基坑、排水沟、接地槽、尖峰及施工基面等土石方量之和。

（2）关于发布《××电网建设工程概预算定额价格水平调整办法》的通知（云电定〔2008〕4号）。

（3）关于颁布《某电网地区2007年送变电安装工程定额材机调整系数》的通知（××电网定额〔2008〕11号）。

（4）《××工程造价信息》（2009年第1/6期）。

三、投资估算编制依据

（一）编制投资估算常用的主要依据

（1）国家或地方专门机构发布的建设工程造价费用构成、估算指标、计算方法、有关的其他工程造价文件及相关的工程造价资料等。

（2）国家或地区专门机构发布的工程建设其他费用计算办法、费用标准以及物价指数等。

（3）拟建项目的各单项工程或单位工程的全部内涵和特征、设计意图和设计工程量等。

（4）已建同类工程项目的投资档案资料。

（5）影响工程项目投资的动态因素，如利率、汇率、税率等。

（二）案例工程三的编制依据

（1）国家经济贸易委员会发布的《电力工程建设投资估算指标：送电线路工程》（2001年版）。

（2）《电网工程建设预算编制与计算标准》（2007年版）。

（3）《电网工程限额设计控制指标》（2008年水平）。

（4）基础钢筋、水泥等地方材料价格按《××工程造价信息》（2009年第1/6期）计列。

（5）按静态投资的80%计算建贷利息，年利率5.94%（按季付息）。

（6）税金按3.38计。

（7）基本预备费按3%计。

任务2 投资估算编制

一、投资估算的内容

根据国家规定,从满足工程建设项目投资设计和投资规模确定的角度,投资估算由工程建设投资、建设期利息和流动资金估算等组成,如图3-2-1。

工程建设投资估算按照费用的性质划分,包括建筑工程费、设备及工器具购置费、安装工程费、工程建设其他费用、基本预备费、涨价预备费。其中,建筑工程费、设备及工器具购置费、安装工程费直接形成实体固定资产,被称为工程费用;工程建设其他费用可分别形成固定资产、无形资产及其他资产。基本预备费、涨价预备费,在可行性研究阶段为简化计算,一并计入固定资产。

建设期利息是指债务资金在建设期内发生并应计入固定资产原值的利息,包括借款(或债券)利息及手续费、承诺费、管理费等。建设期利息单独估算,便于对建设项目进行融资前和融资后财务分析。

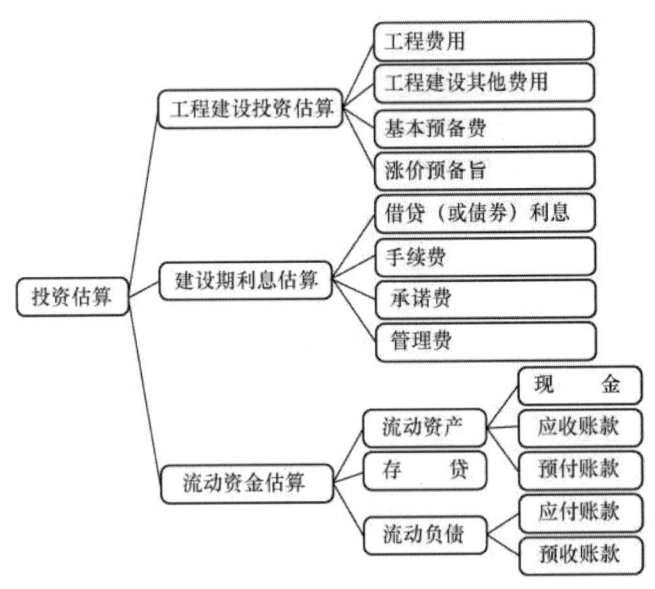

图3-2-1 投资估算的组成

流动资金是指生产经营性项目投产后,用于购买原材料、燃料、支付工资及其他经营费用等所需的周转资金。它是伴随着工程建设投资而发生的长期占用的流动资产投资，流动资金为流动资产与流动负债之间差额部分。其中，流动资产主要考虑现金、应收账款、预付账款和存货；流动负债主要考虑应付账款和预收账款。

二、建设项目投资估算要求

编制投资估算时，要求工程内容和费用构成要齐全，计算合理，不漏项、不少算。选用指标与具体工程之间存在标准或者条件差异时，可以进行必要的换算或调整。投资估算的精度要能满足控制初步设计概算的要求，具体要求如下。

（1）根据主体专业设计的阶段和深度，结合各自行业的特点，所采用生产工艺流程的成熟性，以及编制单位所掌握的国家及地区、行业或部门相关投资估算基础资料和数据的合理、可靠、完整程度，采用合适的方法进行建设项目投资估算。

（2）应做到工程内容和费用构成齐全，计算合理，不重复计算，不提高或者降低估算标准，不漏项、不少算。

（3）应充分考虑拟建项目设计的技术参数和投资估算所采用的估算系数、估算指标，在质和量方面所综合的内容，应遵循口径一致的原则。

（4）应将所采用的估算系数和估算指标价格、费用水平调整到项目建设所在地及投资估算编制年的实际水平，对于建设项目的边界条件，如建设用地费和外部交通、水、电、通信条件，或市政基础设施配套条件等差异所产生的与主要生产内容投资无必然关联的费用，应结合建设项目的实际情况修正。

（5）对影响造价变动的因素进行敏感性分析，注意分析市场的变动因素，充分估计物价上涨因素和市场供求情况对造价的影响。

（6）投资估算精度应能满足控制初步设计概算要求，并尽量减少投资估算的误差。

三、投资估算方法

投资估算的方法非常多，比较常用的有资金周转率法、生产能力指数法、比例估算法、综合指标投资估算法等。在实际项目中，需要结合项目特点，仔细分析有关资料，选用合适的估算方法。如果某些项目比较复杂，则需要运用几种方法进行投资估算，以确保相对的准确。同时，还需考虑建设周期问题，注意分析资金的时间价值，因为指标是过去的、静态的，一般估算的时间按开工前一年为基准年，再结合所在地区的价格水平，作相应的换算及调整。下面就上述几种方法做简要介绍。

（一）资金周转率法

资金周转率法是一种用资金周转率来推测投资额的简便方法。一般可以根据已建同类项目的有关数据进行分析，根据拟建项目的预计产品的年产量及单价，对拟建项目的投资额进行估算。其公式为。

$$C = \frac{Q \times P}{T} \quad (3\text{-}2\text{-}1)$$

式中，C 为拟建项目总投资；Q 为拟建项目预计产品年产量；P 为拟建项目预计产品单价；T 为同类项目资金周转率，等于年销售总额/总投资。

这种方法的优点是计算速度快、比较简便，但误差较大，一般用于投资机会研究及项目建议书阶段的投资估算。

（二）生产能力指数法

生产能力指数法是根据已建成的、性质类似的建设项目的生产能力和投资额与拟建项目的生产能力，来估算拟建项目投资额。其公式为

$$C_2 = C_1 \cdot \left(\frac{Q_2}{Q_1}\right)^x \cdot f \quad (3\text{-}2\text{-}2)$$

C_2 为拟建项目投资额；C_1 为已建类似项目投资额；Q_1 为已建类似项目的生产能力；Q_2 为拟建项目的生产能力；f 为综合调整系数；x 为生产能力指数，正常情况下，$0 \leq x \leq 1$。

生产能力指数法估算优点是简单快速，误差较小（一般可控制在±20%以内），这种方法不需要详细的类似工程资料，只知道工艺流程及规模就可以。所以，承包商经常在进行工程报价时采用这种方法估价。但这种方法要求类似工程资料可靠，与拟建项目比较，基本条件相差不大。

例3-1 某化工厂年产10万吨某化工产品，其静态投资额为5000万元，现拟建年产相同产品20万吨类似项目。生产能力指数为0.6，综合调整系数为1.2，则采用生产能力指数法，确定拟建项目静态投资额为多少万元？

解：根据题意有 C_1=5000万元，Q_2=20万吨，Q_1=10万吨、x=0.6、f=1.2

将已知数据代入（3-1）式，得

$$C_2 = 5000 \times \left(\frac{20}{10}\right)^{0.6} \times 1.2 \approx 9094 \text{万元}$$

（三）比例估算法

比例估算法需要已建成的同类项目大量的统计资料，这是一种在经济活动分析中经常应用的方法。一般有两种计算方法。

1. **以拟建项目的设备购置费为基数进行估算**

这种方法是根据已建成的同类项目的建筑工程费、安装工程费占设备购置费的百分比，估算出拟建项目的建筑工程费和安装工程费，再估算出拟建项目的其他有关费用（包括工程建设其他费用和预备费等），最终构成拟建项目的建设投资额。其表达式为

$$C = E(1 + f_1 p_1 + f_2 p_2) + I \tag{3-2-3}$$

式中，C 为拟建项目的建设投资额；E 为拟建项目根据当时当地价格计算的设备购置费；p_1、p_2 分别为已建项目中建筑工程费、安装工程费和其他有关费用占设备购置费的百分比；f_1、f_2 为由于时间因素引起的定额、价格、费用标准等综合调整系数；I 为拟建项目的其他费用。

2. **以拟建项目的工艺设备投资为基数进行估算**

这种方法是以拟建项目的工艺设备投资为基数，分析同类型已建项目有关统计资料，计算出各专业工程占工艺设备投资的百分比，然后估算出拟建项目各专业工程的投资，并把每一部分投资额（包括工艺设备投资）相加，再加上拟建项目的其他有关费用，最终构成拟建项目建设投资额。其表达式为

$$C = E(1 + f_1 p'_1 + f_2 p'_2 + f_3 p'_3 + \cdots\cdots) + I \tag{3-2-4}$$

式中，C 为拟建项目的建设投资额；E 为拟建项目根据当时当地价格计算的工艺设备投资；p'_1、p'_2、p'_3 为已建项目各专业工程费用占工艺设备投资的百分比；I 为拟建项目的其他费用。

（四）指标估算法

估算指标是一种比概算指标更为扩大的单项工程指标或单位工程指标，它是以单项工程或单位工程为对象，综合估算项目建设中的各类成本和费用，具有较强的概括性和综合性。

估算指标一般以单项（或单位）工程生产能力单位投资表示，如：元／m，元／m^2，元／m^3，元／t，元/km、t/kV.A 等。在使用估算指标时，应根据不同地区、不同时期的实际情况进行适当调整和修正，最终以"量"和"价"相结合的形式来表示。

指标估算法是较常用的一种估算方法。在估算时，需要采用适合拟建工程的估算指标，同时要注意工程建设地域、建设时间、工程特点及技术标准的差异等，做好相应的修正或调整，不能盲目生搬硬套指标；否则，会使得估算结果不符合实际工程情况，误差较大。使用指标估算法进行估算的关键点是选择合适的估算指标。

（五）建设投资分类估算法

建设投资分类估算法是对组成建设投资的各项费用，即工程费用（包括建筑工程费、安装工程费、设备购置费）、工程建设其他费用和预备费（包括基本预备费、涨价预备费）分类进行估算。下面简单介绍各类费用的估算方法。

1. 建筑工程费估算

建筑工程费估算一般有三种方法，包括单位建筑工程投资估算法、单位实物工程量投资估算法和概算指标投资估算法。前两种方法相对较简单，而后一种方法要求以较为详细的、准确的工程资料为基础，工作量非常大，在实际工作中选用哪种方法，可按具体条件和要求进行选择。

（1）单位建筑工程投资估算法：是用每单位建筑工程量投资额与建筑工程总量相乘，来进行估算建筑工程费的方法。例如送电线路工程是以单位长度（公里）投资额，乘以相应的送电线路总长来估算建筑工程费。

（2）实物工程量投资估算法：是用单位实物工程量投资额与实物工程量总量相乘，来估算建筑工程费的方法。例如，土石方工程以每立方米投资额，乘以相应的土石方工程总量来估算建筑工程费。

（3）概算指标投资估算法：一般采用前面两种指标估算建筑工程费，如果没有前两种估算指标，或者不适合采用上述两种方法（如：建筑工程费占建设投资比例较大的项目），可采用概算指标估算法。具体方法参照项目二。

2. 安装工程费估算

安装工程费的估算一般有三种方式，公式为

$$安装工程费 = 设备原价 \times 安装费率 \qquad (3\text{-}2\text{-}5)$$

$$安装工程费 = 设备吨位 \times 每吨安装费 \qquad (3\text{-}2\text{-}6)$$

$$安装工程费 = 安装工程实物量 \times 安装费用指标 \qquad (3\text{-}2\text{-}7)$$

3. 设备购置费估算

设备购置费包括国内设备购置费、进口设备购置费和工器具及生产家具购置费。其中国内设备购置费指本建设项目购置或自制的达到固定资产标准的所有国产设备的购置费用。它由设备原价和设备运杂费构成。进口设备购置费是由进口设备货价（需注意区别离岸价FOB和到岸价CIF）、进口从属费用及国内运杂费组成。

总的来说，估算一般在可行性研究阶段，不同性质的项目，采用什么方法进行投资估算更好，比较重要的因素是估算人员的业务水平、专业素质及有关的工程造价实际经验，因此需引起高度重视，并采取相应的措施预防个人主观因素对投资估算的影响，以保证投资估算的合理性。

四、编制步骤

（1）分别估算各单项工程所需的安装工程费、设备及工器具购置费；在案例工程三中，采用的是投资估算方法中的分类估算法，其中，安装工程费估算是按照"实物工程量投资估算法"，首先估算出实物工程量和单位实物工程量投资额，进而估算出安装工程费。详见表3-2-1。

（2）在汇总各单项工程费用的基础上，形成"架空送电线路安装工程费用汇总估算表"，进而估算工程建设其他费用和基本预备费，见表3-2-2、表3-2-3。

（3）估算涨价预备费。涨价预备费一般是针对建设工期比较长的项目设置的，因为建设周期长，有可能在建设期间发生材料、人工、设备、施工机械等价格上涨，以及费率、利率、汇率等变化，造成项目费用的增加，所以需要事先预留一定的费用，也称为涨价预备费或价格变动不可预见费。案例工程三因为建设期较短，所以没有考虑这笔费用。

（4）估算建设期贷款利息。一般建设项目的建设资金除了自有资金外，还需要通过其他方式筹集资金，例如通过银行贷款、募集债券、出口信贷等，而采取这些方式都会产生贷款利息、借款利息以及融资费用等费用，这项费用归入建设期贷款利息。案例工程三根据工程资金计划，估算本项费用为546万元。

（5）估算流动资金。流动资金是指建设项目投产后，为维持正常经营，用于购买原材料、燃料、支付工资及其他生产经营费用等所必不可少的周转资金。其估算方法比较多，目前国际上通行的流动资金估算方法是分项详细估算法，其公式为

$$流动资金 = 流动资产 - 流动负债 \tag{3-2-8}$$

$$流动资产 = 现金 + 应收（及预付）账款 + 存货 \tag{3-2-9}$$

$$流动负债 = 应付（及预收）账款 \tag{3-2-10}$$

$$流动资金本年增加额 = 本年流动资金 - 上年流动资金 \tag{3-2-11}$$

本案例工程未考虑流动资金。

（6）总估算表。这是最后一个步骤，将前面估算的数据进行汇总，并计算出各项费用所占百分比，以及各项费用的单位投资额，与相应的限额设计控制指标相比较，则可以大致判断投资是否合理，如不合理需对投资做出修正。案例工程三的总估算表如表3-2-4。

在表3-2-4中，其本体工程单位投资估算为148.36万元，其他费用为60.84万元。与《电网工程限额设计控制指标》（2009年水平）比较，同类项目比较接近的500 kV，导线规格为4×LGJ-400/50（27 m/s，20 mm）的送电线路工程，山地的本体工程单位投资为181.2万元，其他费用为66.9万元。因本项目有山地、丘陵、高山，以及覆冰厚度（10 mm）与限额设计指标的项目情况有一定偏差，但总的来说是控制在限额设计指标以内，故可以判断本项目的投资估算比较合理。

表 3-2-1 案例工程三单位估算表

序号	编制依据	项目名称	单位	数量	单价(元) 合计	单价安装 人工费	单价安装 材料费	单价安装 机械费	装置性材料费	合价(元) 合计	合价安装 人工费	合价安装 材料费	合价安装 机械费
一		土石方工程											
1		材料运输											
1.1		人力运输1000m以上											
	ZX1-2	砂、石、水泥、水	10t.km	362.0	830.21	754.42		75.79		300536	273100	0	27436
		地形调整	%	106		273100		27436		289486	289486	0	0
		小 计								590022	562586	0	27436
1.2		汽车运输											
	ZX1-3	装 卸	10t	316	671.60	109.32	251.42	548.79		212226	34545	0	173418
	ZX1-4	运 输	10t.km	475	14.63	3.43		11.20		6949	1629	0	5320
		装卸小计								207963	34545	0	173418
		运输小计								6949	1629	0	5320
		地形调整	%	38		1629		5320		2641	619	0	2022
		小 计								217553	36793	0	180759
2		线路复测及分坑											
	ZX2-1	直线塔、耐张塔	10基	22.2	548.80	269.99	251.42	27.39		12183	5994	5582	608
3		线路杆塔坑挖方及回填		2712						0	0	0	0
	ZX2-2	普通土坑	10m³	503	164.37	148.31		16.06		82678	74600	0	8078
	ZX2-3	松沙石坑	10m³	1302	323.38	293.63		29.75		420911	382189	0	38723
	ZX2-5	岩石坑	10m³	864	884.57	694.75	120.16	69.66		764534	600472	103854	60207
	ZX2-4	泥水坑	10m³	43	983.96	456.98	290.96	236.02		42310	19650	12511	10149
4		其他土石方开挖		257									
	ZX2-7	普通土	10m³	51.50	60.54	55.11	0.00	5.43		3118	2838	0	280

续表

序号	编制依据	项目名称	单位	数量	单价（元） 合计	单价（元）安装 人工费	单价（元）安装 其中 材料费	单价（元）安装 其中 机械费	装置性材料费	合价（元） 合计	合价（元）安装 人工费	合价（元）安装 其中 材料费	合价（元）安装 其中 机械费
	ZX2-9	坚土	10m³	39.60	398.85	275.68	95.31	27.86		15794	10917	3774	1103
	ZX2-8	松沙石	10m³	166.32	115.06	104.43	0.00	10.63		19137	17369	0	1768
		小计								1360666	1114029	125721	120916
		地形调整	%	13		1114029		120916		144824	144824	0	0
		小计								1505490	1258853	125721	120916
		定额直接费（不含人工费调整）								2313065	1858232	125721	329111
二		基础工程											
1		材料运输											
1.1		人力运输1000m以上											
	ZX1-2	零星钢材、沙、石、水泥、水	10t·km	378.8	830.21	754.42		75.79		314484	285774	0	28709
		地形调整	%	106		285774.30				302921	302921		
		小计								617404	588695	0	28709
1.2		汽车运输											
	ZX1-3	零星钢材、沙、石、水泥、降阻剂	10t	374.1	671.60	109.32		548.79		251225	40893	0	205286
	ZX1-4	装卸运输	10t·km	1435.2	14.63	3.43		11.20		20997	4923	0	16074
		地形调整	%	38		4923		16074		7979	1871	0	6108
		小计								7979	1871	0	6108
2		基础钢筋加工及制作											
	ZX3-5	基础钢筋加工及制作	t	774.11	551.14	307.00	118.06	126.08		426643	237652	91391	97600

续表

序号	编制依据	项目名称	单位	数量	单价（元）				装置性材料费	合价（元）			
					合计	安装 其中				合计	安装 其中		
						人工费	材料费	机械费			人工费	材料费	机械费
调	ZX3-8	500kV垫层、护坡	10m³	75.00	516.71	432.40	0.00	84.31		38753	32430	0	6323
	ZX3-4	现浇砼基础	10m³	492.70	2514.11	1332.33	838.59	342.20		1238702	656439	413173	168602
	ZX3-6	灌注桩基础	10m³	368.50	9853.17	3698.38	530.16	5624.63		3630893	1362853	195364	2072676
	ZX3-8	排洪沟砌、护坡浆砌	m³	3465	516.71	432.40	0.00	84.31		1790400	1498266	0	292134
		小计								7124904	3787640	699929	2637335
		地形调增	%	25.50		3787640		2637335		1638369	965848	0	672520
		小计								8763272	4753488	699929	3309856
		定额直接费（不含人工费调整）							6007629	9388656	5344054	699929	3344673
三		杆塔工程											
1		材料运输											
1.1		人力运输1000m以上											
	ZX1-1	塔材	10t.km	375.1	1927.16	1751.01		176.15		722878	656804		66074
		地形调整	%	106		656804		66074		766250	696212		70038
		小计								1489128	1353016		136112
1.2		汽车运输											
	ZX1-3	装卸	10t	385.4	671.60	109.32		548.79		258835	42132		211504
	ZX1-4	运输	10t.km	925.9	14.63	3.43		11.20		13546	3176		10370
		地形调整	%	38		3176		10370		5147	1207		3941
		小计								272329	46515		225814
2		杆塔组立											

续表

序号	编制依据	项目名称	单位	数量	单价（元） 合计	单价（元）安装 人工费	单价（元）安装 其中 材料费	单价（元）安装 其中 机械费	装置性材料费	合价（元） 合计	合价（元）安装 人工费	合价（元）安装 其中 材料费	合价（元）安装 其中 机械费
3	ZX4-13	500kV铁塔导线4*500	基	222	7210.79	5553.76	167.49	1489.54		1600795	1232935	37183	330678
	YX4-85	接地安装											
		接地杆塔数量	10基	9.6	1714.97	1474.11	92.82	148.05		16464	14151	891	1421
		小　计								1617259	1247086	38074	332099
		地形调增（不含高塔）	%	77		1247086				1215973	960256	38074	255716
		小　计								2833232	2207343	38074	587816
		定额直接费调整（不含人工费调整）								4594689	3606873	38074	949742
四		架线工程							39572139				
1		材料运输											
	ZX1-1	人力运输线材	10t·km	279.3	1927.16	1751.01		176.15		150573	24510	0	123039
	ZX1-3	装　卸	10t	224.2	671.60	109.32		548.79		81987	19222	0	62765
	ZX1-4	汽车运输	10t·km	5604.0	14.63	3.43		11.20		147548	24510	0	123039
		装卸小计								81987	19222	0	62765
		运输小计	%	38		19222				31155	7304	0	23851
		地形调整						62765		260690	51036	0	209654
		小　计（1）											
2		架线											
2.1		导、地线架设											
	ZX5-14	截面4×400/120以内	km	99	19567.00	5116.61	1997.07	12453.32		1937133	506544	197710	1232879
	ZX5-2	单根避雷线	km	99	2548.03	1753.66	292.63	501.74		252255	173612	28970	49672

续表

序号	编制依据	项目名称	单位	数量	单价（元）				装置性材料费	合价（元）				
					合计	安装				合计	安装			
						人工费	材料费	机械费			人工费	材料费	机械费	
2.2		架设												
	ZX5-3	OPGW光缆	km	99	3691.55	2349.81	578.96	762.78		365463	232631	57317	75515	
		小 计								2554851	912788	283997	1358066	
		地形调增	%	49		912787.92		1358066.16		1112718	447266		665452	
		小 计（2）								3667570	1360054	283997	2023519	
2.3		导、地线跨越架设												
	ZX5-18	跨铁路	处	53	6824.90	4008.30	1918.06	898.54		361720	212440	101657	47623	
	ZX5-21	跨低压或弱电线	处	18	1941.68	1172.63	445.43	323.62		34950	21107	8018	5825	
		跨河流，导线4x720mm²以内			0.00					0	0	0	0	
	ZX5-25	跨河流，导线4x720mm²以内	处	2	1168.96	760.88		408.08		2338	1522	0	816	
		小 计（3）								399008	235069	109675	54264	
		定额直接费（不含人工费调整）								32171049	4327267	1646159	393672	2287437
3		附件工程												
五		材料运输												
1		人力运输1000m以上												
1.1	ZX1-2	金具、绝缘子	10t.km	85.7	830.21	754.42		75.79		71149	64654		6495	
		地形调整	%	106		64654		6495		75418	68533		6885	
		小 计								146567	133187		13380	
1.2		汽车运输												
		金具、绝缘子												

续表

序号	编制依据	项目名称	单位	数量	单价（元）					装置性材料费	合价（元）				
					合计	安装					合计	安装			
						人工费	材料费	机械费				人工费	材料费	机械费	
	ZX1-3	装 卸	10t	95.3	671.60	109.32		548.79			64003	10418		52300
	ZX1-4	运 输	10t.km	2382.2	14.63	3.43		11.20			34852	8171		26681
		地形调整	%	38		8171		26681			13244	3105		10139
		小 计									112099	21694		89119
2		附件安装												
1		直线塔及换位塔绝缘子串悬挂												
	ZX6-3	500kV线路	基	222	462.53	308.48	28.16	125.89			102682	68483	6252	27948
2		其他金具安装												
	ZX6-4	重锤安装	基	195	143.71	96.02	10.60	37.09			28023	18724	2067	7233
	ZX6-7	防振锤 四分裂导线	10套	925.6	48.49	20.49	5.95	21.72			44882	18966	5507	20104
	ZX6-9	间隔棒 四分裂导线	10套	587.6	85.21	65.14	13.46	6.61			50069	38276	7909	3884
		小 计									225657	144448	21735	59168
		地形调增系数	%	28		144448		59168			57013	40446		16567
		小 计									282669	184894	21735	75735
		定额直接费（不含人工费调整）								19305382	541335	339775	21735	178234

· 238 ·

表二乙

表 3-2-2 架空送电线路安装工程费用汇总估算表（10mm冰区）

99km 单位：元

序号	工程或费用名称	取费基数	费率%	土石方工程	基础工程	杆塔工程	架线工程	附件工程	合计	各项占总计%	单位投资元/km
一	直接费			2699361	16677738	45690342	37512286	20296114	122875841	83.66%	1241170
1	直接工程费（B）	1)+2)		2313065	15396285	44166828	36498316	19846717	118221211	80.49%	1194154
1)	定额直接费			2313065	9388656	4594689	4327267	541335	21165012	14.41%	213788
	其中：人工费(A1)			1858232	5344054	3606873	1646159	339775	12795093	8.71%	129243
	人工费调整(A2)	A1	4.56	84771	243792	164543	75097	15500	583704	0.40%	5896
	机械费			374346	3344673	1079987	2240234	104747	7143987	4.86%	72161
2)	装置性材料费				6007629	39572139	32171049	19305382	97056199	66.08%	980366
2	措施费			386296	1281453	1523514	1013970	449397	4654630	3.17%	47016
1)	冬雨季施工增加费	A1+A2	6.95	135039	388355	262113	119627	24692	929826	0.63%	9392
2)	施工工具用具使用费	A1+A2	5.38	104534	300626	202902	92604	19114	719779	0.49%	7270
3)	特殊地区施工增加费	A1+A2		0	0	0	0	0	0	0.00%	0
4)	临时设施费	B	1.95	45105	300228	861253	711717	387011	2305314	1.57%	23286
5)	施工机构转移费	A1+A2	2.71	52655	151431	102205	46646	9628	362565	0.25%	3662
6)	安全文明施工措施费	A1+A2	2.52	48964	140814	95040	43376	8953	337146	0.23%	3406
二	间接费			1806022	5193903	3505531	1599907	330228	12435591	8.47%	125612
1	规费			919623	2644728	1785011	814670	168152	6332184	4.31%	63961
1)	社会保障费	A1+A2	31.36	609326	1752349	1182716	539786	111414	4195591	2.86%	42380
2)	住房公积金	A1+A2	13.44	261140	751007	506878	231337	47749	1798110	1.22%	18163
3)	危险作业意外伤害保险费	A1+A2	2.53	49158	141373	95417	43548	8988	338484	0.23%	3419
2	企业管理费	A1+A2	45.62	886398	2549175	1720520	785237	162077	6103407		125612
三	利润	一+二	5	225269	1093582	2459794	1955610	1031317	6765572		
四	税金	一+二+三	3.38	159896	776225	1745962	1388092	732029	4802203	3.27%	48507
	安装工程费合计			4890548	23741448	53401628	42455894	22389689	146879207	100.00%	1483628
	各项占合计（%）			3.33%	16.16%	36.36%	28.91%	15.24%	100.00%		
	单位投资（元/km）			49399	239813	539410	428847	226158	1483628		

表 3-2-3 其他费用估算表

序号	工程或费用名称	编制依据及计算说明	总价（元）
一	项目建设管理费		4024644
1	建设项目法人管理费	本体 146879207×1.22%	1791926
2	招标费	本体 146879207×0.35%	514077
3	工程监理费	99.00km×15500元/km×1.12	1718640
二	项目建设技术服务费		19988263
1	前期工程费	（勘测费+基本设计费）×费率（11.2%，9.3%）	1497581
2	勘测设计费		16074702
2.1	勘测费		6760480
2.2	设计费		9314222
2.2.1	基本设计费		6610781
2.2.2	其他设计收费		2703441
	塔基勘界费（估列）	99.00km×7000元/km	693000
	海拉瓦及路径优化费用	99.00km×7500元/km	742500
	施工图预算编制费	基本设计费 6622158×10.00%	661078
	竣工图编制费	基本设计费 6622158×8.00%	528862
	林业勘察费	68km×2250元/km	78000
3	设计文件评审费（可研）	99.00km×3400元/km	336600
	（初设）	99.00km×4900元/km	485100
4	项目后评价费	本体 146879207×0.35%	514077
5	工程建设监督检测费		786444
	工程质量监督检测费	本体 146879207×0.23%	337822
	环境监测验收费（环评+验收）	50000元（20km以内）+（99-20）km×1500元/km	165500
	水土保持项目验收及补偿费	99km×2100元/km+征地面积×2元/㎡	283122
6	电力工程技术经济标准编制管理费	146879207×0.20%	293758
7	电力工程定额编制管理费	按电定总造（2009）3号文取消	0
三	分系统调试及整套启动试运费		259103
1	整套启动试运费	400元/工日×142工日×1.2	68160
2	施工企业配合调试费	本体 146879207×0.13%	190943
四	生产准备费		631581
1	管理车辆购置费	本体 146879207×0.20%	293758
2	工器具、办公、生产及生活家具购置费	本体 146879207×0.15%	220319
3	生产职工培训及提前进厂费	本体 146879207×0.08%	117503
五	其他		1311175
1	施工道路及桥梁补偿		324000
	施工道路修筑	19km×10000元/km	220000

续表

序号	工程或费用名称	编制依据及计算说明	总价（元）
	牵、张机场进场道路修筑费	19km×4000元/km	104000
2	跨越措施费		649000
	高速公路	1次×65000元/次	65000
	铁路	1次×65000元/次	65000
	主干公路	8次×25000元/次	250000
	河流或水库	2次×25000元/次	50000
	带电跨越（220kV）	1次×32000元/次	32000
	带电跨越（110kV）	6次×20000元/次	60000
	带电跨越（35kV）	8次×1200元/次	36000
	带电跨越（10kV）	12次×3500元/次	91000
3	余土外运	5994t×25元/t	338175
4	煤矿区塔位处理费	×7000000元/基	0
	其他费用合计		26214765
六	基本预备费	（本体+辅助设施+其他费用+价差）×2%	6623619
七	编制年价差		16648838
	材料价差及税金	16298700×1×1.0338	15728581
	材机费调整及税金	6223541×14.76%×1.0338	920258
八	静态投资		224921399
九	建设期贷款利息		5461092
十	动态投资		230382491

表3-2-4 总估算表

99.00km

序号	工程或费用名称	合计（万元）	各项占总计（%）	单位投资（万元/km）
一	送电线路本体工程	14688	65.30%	148.36
二	辅助设施费	116	0.52%	1.18
	小计	14804	65.82%	149.54
三	编制年价差	1665	7.40%	16.82
四	其他费用	6023	26.78%	60.84
	其中：1.建设场地划拨及清理费	2732	12.15%	27.59
	2.基本预备费	662	2.94%	6.69
	静态投资（一~四项合计）	22492	100.00%	227.19
五	动态费用	546		5.52
（一）	涨价预备费			0.00
（二）	建设期贷款利息	546		5.52
	动态投资（一~五项合计）	23038		232.71

表 3-2-5　辅助设施估算表

序号	项目名称及规范	编制依据及计算说明	总价（元）
1	巡线检修站工程		
1.1	宿舍		
1.2	办公室及仓库、汽车库	700元/m²×14m²/人×22人	215600
1.3	室外工程	215600×15%	32340
1.4	巡检站征地	0.924×150000元/亩	138531
2	巡线、检修道路		
2.1	人行道		
2.2	简易公路	15km×30000元/km×15元/亩	600000
2.3	便桥		
3	通信工程	99km×1000元/km	99000
4	带电作业工器具	99km×800元/km	79200
4	线检修道路工程		
(1)	人行道		
(2)	简易公路		
(3)	便桥		
	合　计		1164671

表 3-2-6　建设场地划拨及清理费估算表

序号	工程或费用名称	编制依据及计算说明	总价（元）
一	建设场地划拨及清理费		27,318,683
1	土地征用费		2,158,607
	塔基征地费	18.23亩×80000元/亩	1,458,122
	占用征用林地补偿费	38.1602亩×8500元/亩	324,375
	耕地占用税	56.39亩×6670元/亩	376,110
2	施工场地租用费		395,850
	集散仓库临时用地	材料站2个×80000元/个	160,000
		牵张场17个×8000元/个	136,000
	临时占地复耕费	200亩×500元/亩	99,850
3	房屋拆迁		15,489,574
	砖混结构	10098m²×700元/m²	7,068,600
	砖墙瓦顶	15147m²×500元/m²	7,573,500
	晒坝等附属面积	2524.5m²×120元/m²	302,940
	房屋拆迁配套费	126户×3000元/户	378,000
	宅基地	42亩×4000元/亩	166,534
4	林木砍伐		7,224,606
	轻冰区（松树）	40.2km×9000元/亩×9亩/km	3,256,200
	轻冰区（杂木）	26.8km×6000元/亩×9亩/km	1,447,200
	果树	300棵×360元/棵	108,000

续表

序号	工程或费用名称	编制依据及计算说明	总价（元）
	植被恢复费	603亩×4002元/亩	2,413,206
5	青苗赔偿	（99-67）km×8m/667m²/亩×40%×2000元/亩	307,046
6	三线迁移		325,000
	10kV线路	2.5km×120000元/km	300,000
	低压及弱电线	km×10000元/km	
	机耕道改迁	2.5km×10000元/km	25,000
7	坟墓拆迁	12处×1500元/处	18,000
8	厂矿拆迁		1,200,000
	小煤窑	处×150000元/处	
	小矿	2处×15000元/处	300,000
	采石场	6处×150000元/处	900,000
9	通信设施防送电线路干扰措施费		200,000

小　结

　　学习项目三主要以案例工程三为载体,介绍了编制500 kV送电线路工程估算的方法:首先是根据已明确的技术经济条件,以及估算的精度不同,将投资估算划分成不同的阶段。然后收集投资估算资料,确定编制依据,根据建设项目投资估算要求,采取相应的投资估算方法,按步骤进行估算。第一步是分别估算各单项工程所需的建筑工程费、设备及工器具购置费、安装工程费,形成"单位工程估算表";第二步是在汇总各单项工程费用的基础上,形成"架空送电线路安装工程费用汇总估算表",进而估算工程建设其他费用和基本预备费;第三步是估算涨价预备费、建设期贷款利息、流动资金,最后汇总成"总估算表",从而完成500 kV送电线路工程估算。

实训项目三

根据下面某送电线路工程的基本情况,在空格处填写估算金额。

1. 基本情况

某220kV同塔四回路2×400导线线路工程,具体情况如下表。

电压等级(kV)	220				
导线截面(mm²)	2×400				
线路长度	5.5km				
回路数	四回路设计双回路架设				
工程地形(%)	平地	丘陵	河网泥沼	山地	高山
	40	0	60	0	0
工程地质(%)	土坑	泥水坑	水坑	流沙坑	岩石
	40	30	30	0	0
导线型号	2×LGJ-400/35				
工地运输平均运距	人力运距(km)			0.35	
	汽车运距(km)			10	
全线杆塔(基)	22	直线杆塔(基)		16	
		耐张杆塔(基)		6	
工程设计年	2005~2006年				

2. 投资费用估算。

(1)建筑安装工程费用,按单位指标估算法估算如下:本体工程单位造价为341.09万元/km,其估算额为:_____。

(2)工程建设其他费用占本体工程造价的22.22%,其估算额为:_____。

(3)编制年价差的单位造价为30.55万元/km,其估算额为:_____。

(4)基本预备费占总的静态投资额的1.64%,其估算额为:_____,总的静态投资额为:_____。

复习与思考

1. 什么是投资估算?
2. 投资估算编制的依据是什么?
3. 建设项目投资估算的要求是什么?
4. 投资估算方法有几种?请简要叙述。
5. 简述投资估算的编制步骤。

学习项目四

编制220kV送电线路工程结算

案例工程四　220kV某双回新建线路工程

一、工程概况

220kV某双回线路新建工程起于某新建220 kV变电站（小号侧），止于某220 kV变电站（大号侧），线路全长46.626 km。

本线路基础采用原状土基础（掏挖式基础、人工挖孔桩基础）、板式斜柱式基础、其中原状土基础59基，板式斜柱基础34基，基础型号有81种。

本线路有铁塔93基（N1-N94，N4空号），其中转角37基（含2基终端塔），直线塔56基，塔型较多，共有17种塔型。

二、气象及地形情况

本工程最大设计风速为23.5 m/s，N14-N19导线设计覆冰为15 mm，地线设计覆冰为20 mm，其余段导线设计覆冰为10 mm，地线为10 mm。N1-N41为Ⅲ级污区，其余段为Ⅱ级污区。

本线路全线地形划分为：山地79%，高山大岭20.5%。全线地质划分：岩石76%，松沙石9%，普通土15%。

三、工程基本情况

本线路导线采用LGJ-300/40。N1-N79地线采用GJX-100；N79-N94地线采用LB-

JG-120-40AC，配合OPGW（悬挂于地线支架右侧）构成双地线。案例工程基本情况见表4-0-1。

表4-0-1 220 kV某双回线路新建工程基本情况表

工程名称	\multicolumn{4}{l}{220kV某双回线路新建工程}
起止点	\multicolumn{4}{l}{起于某220 kV变电站（小号侧）门架，止于某220 kV变电站（大号侧）门架}
电压等级	220kV	\multicolumn{2}{l}{主要气象条件}	地震烈度
		\multicolumn{2}{l}{最大设计风速25 m/s；最大设计冰厚20 mm；年平均雷电日45天}	VII度
线路长度	\multicolumn{4}{l}{全长2×46.626 km}

基础工程：共计93基，混凝土等级采用C10级、C20级和C25级		
基础型式	与铁塔连接	塔腿布置
插入式斜柱基础、岩石基础	插入角钢、地脚螺栓	全方位长短腿

杆塔工程：共计93基；

架线工程：46.626 km；

导线型式	地线型式	绝缘子串型式
2×LGJ-300/40	LBGJ-120-40AC、GJX-100	U70BP、U70BP2、U100BP、XDP-70CN

\multicolumn{8}{c}{重要跨越与主要拆迁}							
序号	项目	单位	数量	序号	项目	单位	数量
1	110 kV电力线	处	4	7	通信线及光缆	处	17
2	35 kV电力线	处	4	8	改迁10 kV	m	500
3	10 kV线路	处	16	9	改迁220 V	m	600
4	380 V及220 V	处	56	10			
5	公路	处	7	11			
6	河流（大河）	处	6	12			

任务1 工程结算资料准备

一、工程结算的概念及意义

工程结算是指施工单位按照工程施工合同，对已完成的工程量向建设单位办理工程价清算的经济文件。一般工程建设的周期较长，耗用的资金数量较多，为了使施工单位在施工过程中耗用的资金及时得到补偿，需要对工程价款进行结算，一般包括：中间结算（进度款结算）、年终结算，全部工程竣工验收后进行的竣工结算。工程结算在工程项目承包中是一项十分重要的工作。

工程价款的及时结算和支付，对建设单位和施工单位都具有重要的意义。通过工程结算，对建设单位而言，能提高建设单位的资金管理，增强投资控制，有利于成本分析和造价管理；对施工单位而言，主要有下面三点意义。

（1）工程结算是反映工程进度的主要指标。在施工过程中，工程结算是根据施工单位完成的工程量进度情况来决定的，根据累计已结算的工程价款与合同总价款进行比较，能够近似反映出工程的进度情况，较为直观地对工程造价进行动态控制和管理。

（2）工程结算是加速资金周转的重要环节。施工单位尽快尽早地结算工程款，则有利于施工单位快速、及时、更多地收回工程价款，有利于偿还债务，有利于资金回笼，降低内部运营成本。对施工单位的经营管理、降低内部经营成本、提高资金的使用效率都非常重要。如果工程结算不及时或不及时支付，则会使工程进度款的支付金额与实际工程进度不相符，或者竣工结算后不支付尾款，或者质保金不按合同规定时间支付。一方面加大了施工单位的经营成本，不利于资金流通；另一方面也会影响工程进度按计划实施和工程质量得不到保证，进而影响到工程的竣工时间，最后导致建筑物的使用时间甚至使用效果等。

（3）工程结算是考核经济效益的重要指标。对于施工单位来说，只有工程款如数地结清，才意味着避免了经营风险，施工单位也才能够获得相应的利润，进而达到良好的经济效益。

所以，建设单位和施工单位双方都应以工程施工合同为依据，及时结清工程价款，以利于工程项目的顺利推进。

对于工程价款的结算和支付，在合同示范文本中都有约定。电力工业部在1996年

3月26日颁发了《电力建设工程施工合同范本》，其中就规定了关于工程结算的问题。建设部和国家工商行政管理局也于1999年12月颁布了新的《建设工程施工合同（示范文本）》。在国际工程项目的实施中，有多种施工合同标准文件，运用较多的是国际咨询工程师联合会（Fédération Internationale Des Ingénieurs Conseils）出版的《土木工程施工合同条件》（简称FIDIC合同条件）；英国土木工程师学会ICE制订的（新工程合同条件）（简称NEC合同）；美国建筑师学会AIA制订的《工程承包合同通用条款》（A201）等。这些合同标准文件都对工程结算做了清晰的规定。

二、结算基础资料的收集

在建设工程的实施过程中，广泛收集与结算工作相关的资料十分必要，因为这样可以保证结算编制内容的完备性，同时也可以保证结算审核工作的顺利进行，避免审核时产生过多疑问、争执和矛盾。因此，施工单位应注意以下几方面资料的收集。

（1）工程施工合同。这是结算编制的最根本、最直接的依据，因为在合同中明确了工程项目的承发包范围、双方的权利义务、价款结算方式和时间、风险分摊等，另外在工程实施过程中，哪些费用项目可以计入或调整、如何计算等也都需要按照合同规定执行。

（2）图纸及图纸会审记录。这是确定标底及合同价的依据之一。

（3）投标报价、合同价或原预算。这是实际做法发生变化或进行增减删项后调整有关费用的依据。

（4）工程或设计变更通知单、工程停工报告、监理工程师指令等。

（5）施工组织设计（方案）、施工记录、原始票据、形象进度及现场照片等。

（6）有关定额、费用调整的文件规定。

（7）经审查批准的竣工图、工程竣工验收单、竣工报告等。

在施工过程中，因不同行业、不同施工单位对项目管理方式不同，对上述这些资料的管理也有不同，但基本上这些资料的原始凭据分属于不同的管理部门和人员，因此从整个施工项目管理而言，项目部需要统筹安排，合理分工，确保资料的完整性，同时要及时、完整地提供给结算编制部门或人员，确保结算工作的顺利进行，并在其中发挥积极的作用。

三、确定编制依据

在收集完结算资料后，需分析整理，归纳出与结算相关的编制依据，除了合同、标准、规范、规定之外，已经完成的工程量也是依据之一。以案例工程四为例，其编制依据主要有以下几个方面。

（1）国家颁布的有关送电线路工程施工的现行标准、规范及规程。

（2）《电力建设工程施工技术管理导则》。

（3）《国家电网公司电力建设安全健康与环境管理工作规定》。

（4）《输变电工程达标投产考核办法》（2005版）。

（5）《某220 kV输变电工程施工招标文件》。

（6）某电力公司下发的其他招标资料及附图。

（7）本工程现场调查资料。

（8）某公司220 kV送电线路施工的有关资料。

（9）某公司依据GB/T19001-ISO9001-2000质量体系标准编制的《质量手册》和相关程序文件。

（10）某公司依据GB/T24001-ISO14001-1996《环境管理体系规范及使用指南》、《国家经贸委职业安全健康管理体系审核规范》-2001、《电力建设安全健康与环境管理工作规定》等规范标准的要求编制的《职业安全健康与环境管理手册》和《职业安全健康（OSH）和环境管理体系（EMS）程序文件》。

任务2　工程结算的编制

学习项目一中介绍的施工图预算，所分析的工料数量、确定的工程预算造价，都是在开工前进行编制的。一般工程在施工过程中，由于施工周期长，面临众多变化因素，如材料涨价、设计变更、不可抗力因素等，使原设计有所改变，使原有的施工图预算不能反映工程的实际成本，而工程结算恰好能弥补这点不足，一般工程结算分为中间结算和竣工结算。

中间结算一般在规模较大，施工工期较长，甚至跨年度的工程中使用，施工企业为了使某个施工期间的消耗，包括人工费、材料费和其他费用得到补充，保证施工进度不因资金的短缺受到影响，保证施工活动不间断而又顺利地进行，施工单位按合同规定日期，或此期间完成的工程量，向建设单位进行定期的工程结算，为工程财务拨款提供依据。

竣工结算是在工程竣工验收后，根据施工过程中实际发生的变更情况，修正原有施工图预算，重新确定的工程造价文件。它是调整工程计划、确定和统计工程进度、考核基本建设投资的效果，进行工程成本分析的依据。

工程结算是否编制得好，是否把已实施的工作内容，应该得到的利益，在工程结算中反映出来，将直接关系到施工单位的切身利益。因此，如何使自身利益不受损失，是每个施工企业应该重视的问题。同时，竣工结算是施工单位考核工程成本进行经济核算的依据，是总结和衡量企业管理水平的依据，通过竣工结算，可总结工作经验教训，找出施工浪费的原因，为提高施工管理水平服务。下面就编制工程结算做简要介绍。

一、工程结算的构成

工程建设资料繁多，为了防止漏项，工程施工企业应在工程建设预算的基础上，充分考虑工程的具体实施情况，重点关注下列因素导致的工程施工费用变化的部分。

（1）因政策变化而造成的费用调整。如人工工资标准、材料价差系数、间接费率、机械台班单价的调整等。

（2）投标报价时按常规计算，结算时应按实际发生调整的费用。如大型机械进出场费（需按实际进出场的机械及次数计算）、墙体加固筋、供水电费的扣除等。

(3) 设计变更、监理指令等导致的费用变化（建设单位主动提出的部分）。这部分费用包括工程实施中工程量的增加，以及因为这个变化影响到施工进度计划，造成对其他工作的影响而增加的费用（也可作为索赔费用）。如楼层和建筑面积的局部增加，会导致脚手架和垂直运输费用的增加。

(4) 施工索赔费用。在施工过程中，工程施工企业根据合同和法律法规的规定，对非自身过错所造成的损失，或者承担了合同规定之外的工作所付出的额外支出，工程施工企业向建设单位提出的经济补偿。譬如，建设单位违约（未按时支付工程款、苛刻检查、未按合同规定按时提供设备和场地等），合同调整（设计变更、指令工程施工企业加速施工、与勘探报告不符的地质情况等），不可预见因素（发生洪水、战争、地震等；建设单位提供的工程地质勘探报告及现场资料，并经过现场调查，都难以发现的地下或人为障碍，如：古井、墓坑、断层、溶洞及其他人工构筑障碍物等）。

(5) 合同规定的有关奖励费用：如提前竣工奖、赶工措施费、质量奖等。

(6) 由于工程变更，减少某些项目，导致原让利优惠部分的退还费用。

(7) 现场签证引起的相关费用，如零星用工、零星用机械量、设计变更或工程洽商所致的返工量、合同外新增零星工程量的确认。

二、工程结算方式

根据建设工程的规模、性质、进度和工期，按照签订合同的规定，工程结算（其中的中间结算）有多种方式，我国现在一般采用的结算方式主要有以下几种。

(1) 按月结算。是指在每月的旬末或月中预支一旬或半月工程款，月终再提出工程款结算账单和已完工程月报表后收取本月工程款的每月结算一次的方式，待竣工后清算。具体结算时间按合同规定执行。对于工期较长，跨年度竣工的工程，一般在每年年终进行工程盘点，办理年度结算。这种结算方式，目前在中国是较常采用的结算建设工程价款的方式。

(2) 竣工后一次结算。对于工程项目规模不大，建设期不长（一般在12个月以内），合同价值在100万元以下的工程，常采用竣工后一次结算。这种方式一般在合同中会明确：预支进度款的方式、时间及比例，通常情况是每月预支，这样较利于工程项目的实施。

(3) 分阶段结算。对于工程规模较大、建设周期较长（跨年度）的单项工程或单位工程，除了按月结算方式以外，还可以根据工程形象进度，划分成不同阶段进行结算，一般是按月预支工程价款，每完成的一个阶段再进行阶段结算，阶段的划分标准，由各部门、自治区、直辖市计划单列市自行规定。

（4）其他结算方式。结算双方按照约定的其他方式进行结算。

三、工程结算款的支付

在项目施工过程中，建设单位支付的工程款有几种情况：在开工前支付的一般叫预付款，工程施工过程中支付的叫工程进度款，竣工验收后支付的叫尾款；最后还有工程质量保证金（也简称质保金），在合同保修期满后支付。其中工程进度款和尾款是属于工程结算款，但在谈结算款时也涉及预付款和质保金。下面做简要介绍。

（一）预付款

本项目案例没有支付工程预付款。一般情况下，对于施工企业承包的包工包料工程，在开工前，建设单位要拨付给工程施工企业一定数额的工程预付款，以便备料周转。即工程施工企业为该工程项目储备主要设备及材料、结构构件等所需的流动资金，对于单包的工程（包工不包料），一般不预付备料款。

按照中国有关规定，实行工程预付款的，双方应当在专用条款内约定建设单位向工程施工企业预付工程款的时间和数额，开工后按约定的时间和比例逐步扣回。预付时间应不迟于约定的开工日期前7天。如建设单位不按约定预付，工程施工企业可在约定预付时间7天后向建设单位发出要求支付预付款的通知，建设单位收到通知后仍不能按要求预付，工程施工企业可在发出通知后7天停止施工，建设单位应从约定应付之日起向工程施工企业支付应付款的贷款利息，并承担违约的责任。

工程预付款仅用于工程施工企业支付施工开始时与本工程相关的费用。如工程施工企业不按规定滥用此款，建设单位有权立即收回。在工程施工企业向建设单位提交金额等于预付款数额（由发包方认可的银行开出）的银行保函后，建设单位按规定的金额和规定的时间向工程施工企业支付预付款，在建设单位全部扣回预付款前，该银行保函将一直有效。当预付款被建设单位扣回时，银行保函金额相应递减。

（二）工程进度款、质保金

下面用案例工程四来说明工程进度款、质保金。

本案例工程合同价为2933万元，是采取按月结算的方式。工程施工工期为8个月，前3个月，每月完成基础施工31基；中间2个月分别完成组立铁塔47基、46基；最后3个月每月架线18 km。每月工程进度款如下。

第一个月进度款：310万；

第二个月进度款：310万；

第三个月进度款：310万；

第四个月进度款：330万；

第五个月进度款：322万；

第六个月进度款：464万；

第七个月进度款：464万；

第八个月应付进度款：424万，但需预留尾款（质保金）为合同价的5%，即需扣留尾款147万，支付工程款为277万元。

对于工程质保金的计算与预留，一般是在工程竣工结算办理后，为了促使工程施工企业对工程质量按规定时间进行保修，工程项目总造价中需要预留一定比例的尾款作为质量保证金，待保修期结束后，按照合同要求再最后拨付。一般情况下，质保金的扣留比例及扣留方式是由建设单位及工程施工企业结合工程规模和工程性质等因素由双方协商，最后双方通过合同进行约定，通常中国建设工程按工程造价的3%～5%比例扣留，具体扣留方式有两种。

（1）最后一次按比例扣留。这种方式一般是对于工程造价不高，质保金金额不大的工程，当预付款及进度款累计达到工程造价一定比例（比如95%～97%，具体比例按合同约定执行）时，停止支付工程价款，将这部分价款作为质保金。（本项目案例工程就采用此种方式）

（2）分阶段按比例扣留。这种方式一般是对于工程造价高，质保金金额较大的工程，建设单位可以选择每次从支付的工程进度价款中按扣留比例扣留，直到质保金总额达到双方规定的限额为止，这种方式是与进度款支付同步扣留的，相当于总的质保金分阶段按其比例扣留的，这种方式对工期较长，投资较大的工程有必要，对于办理年度结算，年度投资额控制都十分可行。

（三）造价调整

在工程实施过程中，一般会发生设计变更、工程量变更、施工方法变化、工程师指令引起的变更等，就需要结合工程量计算过程存在的遗留、未定等事宜及时深入现场，或依据施工过程中的变更、洽商等文件，准确对这类问题进行处理；同时深入现场及时掌握工程施工企业在施工过程中自行变更的工程内容，并进行记载或补充资料，及时进行价款调整。如本案例工程在施工过程中，发生了许多超出预计情况以外的变化，进而进行价款调整，形成追加款，具体情况如下。

（1）在施工过程中，由不可抗力因素使正常工程进度受阻，引起费用增加和工程延期，填写如下工程联系单（本案例工程共计填写工程联系单21份，本书限于篇幅，只列出其中一张，见表4-2-1）。工程联系单主要涉及设计变更增加费用、征地费用增加费、地方工作经费、追加费用、停电损失费、自然灾害引起的费用等。

表4-2-1 工程联系单

工程名称：220kV某双回线路新建工程

表号：DJS-A13—01
编号：SG-S5TJ-OO2

致：四川××监理有限责任公司某220kV输变电工程 项目监理部： 　　事由：根据×市（乐府办发【2009】12号<关于加快电力通讯基础设施建设的实施意见>规定，××县和××县属于×市三类地区，土地征用标准为9～12万，经过与××县和××县政府相关部门交涉协商，确定本工程征地标准为11万元/亩，请审核。   　　　　　　　　　　　　　　　　　　　　　承包单位（章）： 　　　　　　　　　　　　　　　　　　　　　项目经理_____ 　　　　　　　　　　　　　　　　　　　　　日　　期_09.5.10._____
监理部意见：   　　　　　　　　　　　　　　　　　　　　　项目监理部（章）： 　　　　　　　　　　　　　　　　　　　　　总/专业监理工程师：_____ 　　　　　　　　　　　　　　　　　　　　　日　　期：_____
指挥部意见：   　　　　　　　　　　　　　　　　　　　　　指挥部（章）： 　　　　　　　　　　　　　　　　　　　　　指挥长：_____ 　　　　　　　　　　　　　　　　　　　　　日　　期：_____

本表一式三份，由承包单位填报，建设管理单位、项目监理部各一份、承包单位存一份。

(2)将联系单进行汇总,得出本案例工程追加费用汇总表,见表4-2-2。

表4-2-2 某220千伏线路新建工程追加费用汇总表

序号	项目名称	费用项目	合价（元）		合计（元）
			本体	建场及其他	
一	第一部分：设计变更增加费用		398647	0	398 647
1	设计更改通知单QEOR-A-01	增加导线	38647		38 647
2	设计更改通知单QEOR-D-01	新增电力线改迁	360 000		360 000
二	第二部分：其他原因增加费用		55800	5 626 694	5 682 494
1	工程联系单SG-S5TJ-OO2	征地费用增加		896 000	896 000
2	工程联系单SG-S5TJ-OO4	地方工作经费		419 634	419 634
3	工程联系单SG—S5TJ-005	暴雨自然灾害大运道路损毁抢修		341 505	341 505
4	工程联系单SG—S5TJ-005A	暴雨自然灾害小运道路损毁抢修		15 090	15 090
5	工程联系单SG—S5TJ-006	暴雨自然灾害基坑垮塌二次开挖		190 800	190 800
6	工程联系单SG—S5TJ-007	暴雨自然灾害大运道路损毁抢修		149 275	149 275
9	工程联系单SG—S5TJ-009	暴雨造成运输道路桥梁垮塌抢修		36 960	36 960
10	工程联系单SG-S5TJ-O10	房屋拆迁费用追加		1 280 720	1 280 720
12	工程联系单SG-S5TJ-O12	架设索道费用追加		225 000	225 000
13	工程联系单SG-S5TJ-O13	塔材供货造成窝工费用追加		96 355	96 355
15	工程联系单SG-S5TJ-O15	增加设备人力抢工期		815 630	815 630
18	工程联系单SG-S5TJ-O18	新增材料站费用追加		44 000	44 000
19	工程联系单SG-S5TJ-O19	森林植被恢复费		160 748	160 748
20	工程联系单SG-S5TJ-O20	停电损失		954 977	954 977
21	工程联系单SG-S5TJ-O22	刷色标漆	55800		55 800
	合计		454 447	5 626 694	6 081 141

（四）竣工结算

1.竣工结算编制的方法

如果工程项目是按工程量清单计价的单价合同,在办理结算时,对新增的清单项目的工程量及综合单价,按建设单位签证同意的工程量及价款进行调整。对于原合同约定清单项目工程量有增减时,应按时调整,以上两部分调整如果总额在总价包干合同的浮差以内时,这种合同一般不作总价调整。需要注意的是,在办理结算时一定要资料完备有效,以合同为依据,以计价规范为准则按实调整并办理竣工结算。

如果工程项目是按现行定额单价计价的工程,在办理结算时,主要是比较原施工图预算的构成内容与实际施工的变化,一般根据各种设计变更资料、现场签证、工程量核定单等相关资料,在原施工图预算基础上,计算增减,最后经过建设单位认可后办理竣工结算。

2. 工程竣工结算的要求

中国《建设工程施工合同（示范文本）》的通用条款中对竣工结算的办理做了如下规定。

（1）工程竣工验收报告经发包方认可后28天内，承包方向发包方递交竣工结算报告及完整的结算资料，双方按协议书约定的合同价款及专用条款约定的合同价款调整内容，进行竣工结算。

（2）发包方收到承包方递交的竣工结算报告及结算资料后28天内进行核实，给予确认或者提出修改意见。发包方确认竣工结算报告后通知经办银行向承包方支付工程竣工结算价款。承包方收到竣工结算后14天内将竣工工程交付发包方。

（3）发包方收到竣工结算报告及结算资料后28天内无正当理由不支付工程竣工结算价款，从第29天起按承包方同期向银行贷款利率支付拖欠工程价款的利息，并承担违约责任。

（4）发包方收到竣工结算报告及结算资料后28天内不支付工程竣工结算价款，承包方可以催告发包方支付结算价款，发包人在收到竣工结算报告及结算资料后，56天内仍不支付的，承包方可以与发包方协议将工程折价，也可以由承包方申请人民法院将该工程依法拍卖，承包方就工程折价或拍卖的价款优先受偿。

（5）工程竣工验收报告发包方认可后28天内，承包方未能向发包方递交竣工结算及完整结算资料，造成工程竣工结算不能正常进行或工程竣工结算价款不能及时支付，发包方要求支付工程的，承包方应当交付，发包方不要求交付工程的，承包方承担保管责任。

（6）发包方和承包方对工程竣工结算价款发生争议时，按解决争议的约定方式处理。

在实际工作中，当年开工、当年竣工的工程，只须办理一次性结算。跨年度的工程，在年终办理一次年终结算，将未完工程接转到下一年度，此时竣工结算等于各年度结算的总和。

四、结算审查与确定

1. 审查方法

常用的结算审查方法有：全面审查法、重点抽查法、分解对比审查法、筛选审查法、分组计算审查法等。几种主要工程结算审查方法的优缺点如下。

全面审查法的优点是全面、细致、审查结果误差小、质量比较高，缺点是工作量大、占用时间长、人员投入大。它适用于一些工程量小、工艺比较简单、对方预算力量比较薄弱等情况。

重点抽查法是抓住重点进行审查，优点是重点突出、审查时间短、效果好。它适用于工程量大、造价高、工程结构复杂、对方预算力量较强等情况。

分解对比审查法是对结算造价进行层层分解之后，再进行对比分析，寻找金额或工程量差距较大项目，进行审查的方法。

筛选审查法、分组计算审查法（内容缺）

要做好结算，工程施工企业除充分考虑自身因素外，还应正确处理与其他相关单位及人员的关系，具体包括建设单位、监理、设计、造价咨询等单位。工程施工企业应根据项目实施中所确定的组织结构关系，同他们建立必要的经济合同关系，在工作中建立友好的协作关系，在各方面能相互配合、相互支持，在合同履行上诚实守信，树立良好的自身形象，从而来润滑结算各环节，为搞好结算创造一个良好的外部环境。

案例工程四通过审查后的竣工结算价为：合同造价2933万元，追加工程款608万元，共计3541万元。

2. 审查内容

（1）审查竣工决算报告情况说明书。建设项目、基本建设投入、投资包干结余、施工结余资金的上缴分配情况是否真实、正确；资金来源及运行等财务分析计算是否正确。

（2）审查竣工财务决算报表。建设项目概况表是否编制完整、正确；建设项目竣工财务决算表是否编制完整、正确；建设项目交付使用资产总表是否编制完整、正确；建设项目交付使用资产明细表是否编制完整、正确。

（3）审查建设工程竣工图。审查竣工图绘制是否符合相关规定要求。

（4）审查造价比较指标。审查主要实物工程量指标、主要材料消耗量指标是否计算正确，并与概算确定指标对比分析。考核其他计取费用是否多列或少列并与概算比较分析。

审查完毕后，应提交竣工决算审查报告，审减（增）项目及原因分析。

小　结

学习项目四主要以案例工程四为载体,介绍了编制 220 kV 送电线路工程结算的方法:做好基础资料的收集,确定编制依据,仔细分析,不漏项,根据工程合同确定结算方式,并确定工程预付款、进度款和竣工结算款。另外尚须考虑在工程中随着工程进度的推进,根据设计变更、工程量变更、施工方法变化、工程师指令引起的变更等,实时对工程价款进行调整,形成工程追加费用汇总表,从而完成 220 kV 送电线路工程结算。

实训项目四

某建筑安装工程合同承包价为600万元,合同约定预付款比例为25%,当尚未完成工程价值的主材价值等于预付款时,开始按比例扣回预付款,工程主材和构件占工程价款的65%,预留5%为保修金。实际施工中,发生60万元为合同调增额,各月完成工程进度款分别为:一月30万元,二月80万元,三月120万元,四月200万元,五月120万元,六月50万元,试计算预付款、每月结算工程款、竣工结算价款、保留金各为多少?

1. 简述工程结算的概念及意义。
2. 结算时应收集哪些基础资料?
3. 工程结算的编制依据有哪些?
4. 工程结算方式有几种?请具体说明。
5. 如何支付工程结算款?
6. 竣工结算的审查内容是什么?

学习项目五

编制工程决算

任务1 竣工决算准备工作

一、基础资料的准备

财务管理和会计核算的基础工作非常重要,从建设项目开工之日起就需要重视,平时做好资料的收集和积累,为编制竣工决算打好基础工作。准备工作的内容如下。

1. 设置基建业务会计核算账户

基建业务会计核算账户的设置,需要充分考虑基本建设财务与生产经营财务并轨以后,要满足基建工程管理和编制竣工决算的需要。"在建工程"明细账账户的设置和分类要与基本建设概算口径相对应,所有单项工程也要和批准的工程概算项目一一对应。例如,建筑工程费用、在安装设备、安装工程费用、其他支出等,均须采用多栏式账页核算;若工程跨越不同的年份,则账册要历年结转使用,本期发生数须每月结出,至年末须结出本年累计数和历年累计数。

具体设置基建业务核算账户的方法为:建筑工程费用和安装工程费用应分专栏核算到每一个单位工程;在安装设备明细账也应按单位工程设明细账户,并按设备品种、数量、规格、价格进行明细核算;其他费用支出应按概(预)算项目设置费用明细项目,采用多栏式核算各项费用。这样在进行决算编制时,就可根据账面实际发生数直接填写到竣工决算报表中。

2. 参与并掌握工程进展情况

财务部门要随时掌握工程进展情况，并积极参加建设项目各个阶段的管理和控制，并做好日常资料的积累。

（1）要积极参加工程概（预）算的讨论和审核，随时掌握概（预）算中各单位工程的投资额增减变化情况，以及批准动用预备费的工程项目。

（2）要积极参加重要经济合同的准备及签订，及时掌握工程项目、主材、设备等招标情况，并随时了解有关合同执行情况。

（3）及时掌握各个阶段投资完成情况，关注工程进度情况，了解是否有重大设计变更，以及工程质量、工程事故鉴定情况等，掌控资金可能的变化情况。

（4）及时掌握单项工程价款结算、审计情况，与计划进行比较、分析单项工程超支原因或节约原因。

（5）及时掌握历年工程建设资金到位和使用情况。

（6）及时掌握有关开竣工报告、工程总结、会议纪要、工程简报等相关资料。

3. 设立辅助登记簿

（1）设立建设场地划拨及清理费用登记簿。主要用于记录：征地相关文件和单证编号、征用土地的面积、金额、地址、收款单位、土地占用税、旧有设施补偿、余物拆除清理计算标准等。

（2）设立设备、主要专用材料台账或卡片登记簿。主要用于记录：掌握专用设备和主要用料的采购、付款、保管和领用情况，设备卡片需要详细记录设备的型号、规格、厂家、数量、金额和安装地点。

电力行业的基本建设需要动用大量的资金，其中设备投资（包括安装工程费用）占总投资的比例一般都在50%以上，所以建设项目的设备投资是电力行业在建设成本管理和核算中的重点，也是编制竣工决算和控制投资的关键。在项目设备管理和核算方面，需要做好如下几个方面的工作。

1）设置好设备核算卡片，按概算中所列设备的明细项目填写。

2）记录设备招标和合同，及掌握设备订货情况。

3）设备监造监运工作，强化预付款大型设备款的管理与控制，严格控制到货验收和支付尾款，减少在途运输周转时间，及时验收。

4）库存设备收、发、存的管理和核算，按照转为"在安装设备"的三个条件，严格控制设备的领用，记录安装部位。实行委托施工企业、工程总承包企业代管设备方式的，需要明确责任，严格执行会计制度规定，按月进行财务稽核。

5）结余设备（包括现场在安装设备）的清点、分割记录，及时对多余设备进行处理。

（3）设立建设期移交的各项资产登记簿。其中固定资产和流动资产应记录名称、规格、单位、数量、金额、制造厂、供应单位、领用部门、领用人等。

二、编制前的准备工作

为了保证竣工决算报告的质量，在编制竣工决算报告前，根据财政部财建[2002]394号文第37条规定，"建设单位及其主管部门应加强对基本建设项目竣工财务决算的组织领导，组织专门人员，及时编制竣工财务决算。设计、施工、监理等单位应积极配合建设单位做好竣工财务决算编制工作。建设单位应在项目竣工后三个月内完成竣工财务决算的编制工作。在竣工财务决算未经批复之前，原机构不得撤销，项目负责人及财务主管人员不得调离"。

具体应当做好的准备工作，能源部颁发的《电力发、送、变电工程基本建设项目竣工决算报告编制规程（试行）》中明确规定如下。

（一）财务部门

（1）将历年批准决算数，各个工程项目的投资完成额，拨、贷款数，应交款项，结余资金等财务收支情况，进行一次全面整理和核对，特别是投资完成额，要与计划统计方面配合，结合现场施工情况进行细致的核对，做到工程款结清，设备不漏列、不多列，进度和统计相符。明确大型施工机械设备产权归属。

（2）清理现场、清理账务。

工程竣工，要督促有关部门进行一次仓库盘点和现场清理工作，多余的设备、材料要全部退库，债权债务要落实并及时清理；水电工程的大型临建回收金额较大，要全面清理回收入账。防止工程结束后无人处理。

（3）做好其他费用项目的分析分摊工作。

其他费用项目，因其性质不同，财务上有各种不同的处理方式。有的作为费用直接拨给其他单位；有的作为增加固定资产；有的作为流动资产移交给生产单位；有的不增加固定资产的价值；有的要增加固定资产价值但分不出为哪一个工程项目支付的共同费用，而要采取分摊的办法。即使分摊，也要按其不同性质，做出不同的分摊方法，具体说明如下。

1）建设场地占用及清理费，按占地面积或工作量比例摊入房屋及建筑物各工程项目。

2）"建设单位管理费"，按工作量比例摊入房屋及建筑物和需要安装的机械设备各工程项目。其中，属于车辆购置和零星固定资产购置的，作为固定资产移交给生产单位。

3）"研究试验费"，摊入有关研试服务对象。

4）"生产职工培训及提前进厂费"，不分摊，不增加固定资产造价。

5）"办公及生活家具购置费"，不分摊，作为流动资产移交给生产单位。

6）"联合试运转费"，摊入安装工程费。

7）"勘察设计费"，按工作量比例摊入房屋及建筑物和需要安装的机械设备各工程项目；其中，属固定资产购置的，不分摊，作固定资产移交生产单位。

8）"供电贴费"，不分摊，作为转出投资处理。

9）"通信设施防送电线路干扰措施费"，分摊到安装工程通信线路部分。

10）"电力施工企业基地建设贴费"，根据能源部能源基（1991）34号文关于颁发《火电、送变电工程建设预算费用构成及计算标准》的补充规定的通知，已并入"四、临时设施费"项目中，不再作"其他费用的构成"。

11）"基本预备费"，这是概算中一个资金来源，不是工程项目，除规定的使用范围外，要动用此款，须经一定的审批手续。

（4）"预计未完扫尾工程5%"在计划上列入投资计划，按概算项目留足投资额，落实承包单位包干使用的，在财务核算上，可列入"交付使用财产"科目。

（二）其他有关部门

编制竣工决算虽以财务部门为主，但其他有关部门如计划、统计、物资、劳资、施工、预算及工程施工企业必须密切配合，共同研究，提供有关资料，以满足报表编制的需要。

（1）批准的设计文件。

（2）经过批准的调整概算文件。

（3）建设单位对建设项目之间费用的相互调整资料。

（4）预备费动用的批准文件。

（5）5%扫尾工程投资包干合同。

（6）有关统计报表。

（7）土地征用、青苗赔偿等文件和合同。

（8）水电站库区淹没移民搬迁赔偿等资料。

（9）清理现场和核算投资完成额。

（10）盘点预计5%未完扫尾工程项目具体内容，根据概算中所列项目一一列出清单，做到不重列和漏列，进度和统计数相符。

（11）主要材料消耗数量。

（12）各项技术经济指标计划和实际数。

（13）采取措施使工程投资有明显节约的具体方法和总结资料。

（14）劳动生产率和工程的耗工数等。

任务2　编制竣工决算

一、编制竣工决算的原则及要求

1. 原则

凡新建、扩建、改建、迁建和恢复工程建设项目，在竣工验收合格后，都应及时组织工程竣工决算的编制，并在规定的时间内办理资产移交手续。

工程竣工决算应遵循的原则是：一个概算范围内的工程项目，只编制一个竣工决算报告。

工程竣工决算的成本范围，须包括建设工程前期费至竣工验收完毕交付使用的全部建设成本费用。即：建筑工程费、安装工程费、设备购置费、其他费用（包括建设工程前期费）、动态费用和不通过在建工程核算的直接形成的资产。但企业在工程竣工前，投入的生产性费用不能计入建设工程成本性支出。

经过验收合格，具备投入使用条件的工程项目，一般上不保留尾工；如确有未完收尾工程和费用的，必须经过工程竣工验收委员会审定后，方可预估纳入竣工决算，同时按照概算项目编报未完收尾工程明细表。必须注意的是，预计未完收尾工程的实物工作量和价值不得大于执行概算的5%。

2. 竣工决算的编制要求

为了加强竣工决算编制工作的规范化、标准化和科学化，严格执行建设项目竣工验收制度，正确考核投资效益，建立健全经济责任制，所有新建、扩建、改建、迁建和恢复工程等建设项目竣工后，建设单位都应及时组织竣工决算的编制，并落实竣工决算报告的及时性、真实性、合法性和完整性。能源部颁发的《电力发、送、变电工程基本建设项目竣工决算报告编制规程（试行）》中明确编制要求如下：

第三十七条　电力基本建设发、送、变电工程项目，应一律按照本《规程》规定的报表格式和内容编制竣工决算报告，不得随意减少应编的表格和内容。

第三十八条　竣工决算报告是建设项目重要的经济档案，表格中所列数据必须与有关部门核实，根据财务账面数字如实填报，做到账实相符，账表相符。

第三十九条　竣工决算是提供正确计算固定资产的依据，因此，在可能情况下，要尽量符合水利电力部1987年7月1日制定的"电力工业企业固定资产目录"的建卡要求（详见附录2：能源部新予规发电工程项目划分表与原水电部电力工业企业固定资产目录对照参考表）。

二、竣工决算的组成

（一）工程竣工决算报告的组成

（1）竣工决算报告封面。
（2）竣工决算的工程全景彩照及主体工程彩照。
（3）竣工决算报告目录。
（4）竣工决算报告情况说明书。
（5）竣工决算财务报表。
（6）工程项目核准文件（或可行性研究报告批准文件）、概算批准文件和竣工验收报告。
（7）审计报告及其他主要文件。
（8）工程大事记。

（二）竣工决算报告情况说明书的内容

竣工决算报告情况说明书，是概括反映竣工工程建设成果和管理经验，全面考核分析评价工程投资与造价的书面总结，是对竣工决算报表的进一步说明和补充，是竣工决算报告的重要组织部分。其主要内容如下。

（1）建设项目的依据和条件。建设项目的依据按照"可行性研究报告""项目建议书""设计任务书""概算批准书""修正概算批准书"等的批准单位、批准日期和文件号码进行说明。条件主要以厂址的地理、地貌、交通条件、水源、电源、原材料来源，三废处理等方面进行说明。

（2）建设项目概况及工程总的评价。主要从工程的进度、质量、安全和造价四方面来进行分析说明。进度主要说明开工和竣工时间，对照合理工期和要求工期是提前还是延期；质量要根据启动验收委员会或相当一级质量监督部门的验收评定等级，合格率和优良品率进行说明；安全根据劳动工资和施工部门记录，有无设备和人身事故进行说明；造价应对照概算造价，说明节约还是超支，用金额和百分率进行分析说明。

（3）建设规模、主设备和主体结构。说明主体工程结构和主设备方面的有关资料，说明工程概况、工程规模、主要建筑的布置和主体设备的合理性。

(4) 从工程筹建开始到竣工验收时为止的历年投资资金（包括资本金、投资借款及其他来源）到位和使用情况的说明，当资金有缺口或过剩情况时分析其产生的原因，并分析筹资成本；分析资金运用情况，一般包含专用工程物资、工程价款、会计账务处理、财产物资占用及债权债务清偿情况的分析；最后还须说明结余资金的占用形态及处理情况。

(5) 各项经济技术指标的分析。包括四个方面：概算执行情况分析，根据实际投资完成额与概算进行对比分析；新增生产能力的效益分析，说明交付使用财产占总投资额的比例，占交付使用财产的比例，移交其他单位固定资产和转出投资占总投资的比例，不增加固定资产造价占投资总数的比例，分析有机构成和因果；基本建设投资包干情况的分析，说明投资包干数、实际支用数和节约额、投资包干节余的有机构成和包干节余的分配情况；财务状况分析，列出历年资金来源和资金占用情况。

(6) 预留未完工程的说明。说明预留收尾工程的项目内容、原因和拟完成的时间等。

(7) 审计意见处理情况的说明。按照审计机构（部门）对竣工决算报告的审计意见，逐项说明对提出意见的整改情况。

(8) 工程项目管理经验和财务管理效果的说明。主要内容：施工中发生的问题和解决办法，施工技术组织措施是否恰当，现场布置是否合理，施工中采取了哪些合理化建议，采用了哪些技术，哪些先进科学方法，涌现了哪些先进事迹取得了哪些经验和教训；财务部门在整个工程建设过程中，制定了哪些规章制度，采取了哪些措施，促进了财务管理工作的开展，在控制和节约投资、支持和服务工程、提高经济效益等方面取得的成绩。

(9) 决算报表编制的说明。主要内容：编制竣工决算的主要依据，竣工决算的结账截止时间；其他费用分摊的依据、原则和计算方法，新老预算规定和会计制度变化对决算数据的影响；最后是竣工财务决算中有待解决的问题。

(10) 需要说明的其他事项。

三、竣工决算的编制内容及步骤

（一）竣工决算编制的各个阶段

建设工程竣工决算的编制一般划分为三个工作阶段，一般需要花费9~12个月的时间才能完成，对于大中型建设项目的竣工决算，则须做到在工程竣工验收交付使用后，一个年度内完成。

第一阶段：准备阶段。准备工作是否做好，直接关系到竣工决算的质量和进度，大概需要4～6个月。

第二阶段：编制阶段。成果是编制完成的竣工决算，并报送相关部门审稿，大概需要2～3个月。

第三阶段：内部审查阶段。通过权威部门的审计，修改定稿，然后装订成册，上报批复，大概需要3个月左右。

在第一阶段做好各项准备工作的基础上，对"在建工程"明细账进行核实、调整，并对没有完成收尾项目的工作量和预计投资进行测算，在核实各项工程投资的情况下，按照下面九个步骤编制竣工决算报告。

（二）竣工决算编制的步骤和方法

竣工决算的编制分下面九个步骤，同时介绍编制竣工决算的方法。

1. 编制"竣工工程决算一览表"

竣工工程决算一览表，详见附录3中"竣建02表"。该表反映了工程投资、造价、考核概算与实际或投资包干的执行情况，据以向生产使用单位移交财产总值。本表在竣工决算表中起总括作用，是决算报表的核心，其他表都是以此为基础进行延伸编制而成的。

（1）"项目"栏应先按总概算表分系统编制一张汇总表，然后再按批准概算扩大单位工程项目填列。先按照不同的系统工程（或扩大单位工程）分类，再按单位工程项目逐项填列。

（2）"概算价值"栏，按照最后一次相关部门批准的修正概算书进行分项填列。应与"竣建01表"的总造价中的"概算造价"数字相符。

（3）"实际价值"栏，根据"在建工程"明细账进行编制。应与"竣建01表"的总造价中的"实际造价"数字相符。本栏目内各项填列方法如下。

1）"建筑工程费""安装工程费"栏，根据建筑工程、安装工程明细账中的直接费用，按照"项目"填列的各"单位工程"名称，对应按照支出发生历年累计数填列。

2）"设备购置费"栏，应先将设备采购运输费、设备检验费等设备性费用，按照设备原价进行分摊，再加上设备价之后列入"设备购置费"中。

3）"其他费用"栏，是按照"在建工程——其他支出"明细账和"其他基建支出备查簿"登记的无形资产、长期待摊费用等明细项目填列。

4）"基本预备费"和"价差预备费"不填写。

2. 编制"预计未完收尾工程明细表"

预计未完收尾工程明细表,详见附录3中"竣建02附表"。该表反映工程已经竣工,但尚有少量尾工需要继续完成,预计的未完工程投资。按概算所列单项或分部工程及计划所需投资数填列,并写明所在部位、预计实物量。其中未完工程项目的工作量价值,应当按照已批准设计概算为依据,不能随意增加,而且其预计全部完成价值不应超过原批准修正总概算数(前提是没有考虑物价上涨因素)。本表的合计数应与"竣建02表"的"预计未完工程"行合计数相符。

3. 编制"其他费用明细表"

其他费用明细表详见附录3中"竣建03表"。该表反映列入概算的其他费用及不列入概算项目的既不构成投资完成额又不计入交付使用财产成本的"应核销其他支出"的费用。

"费用项目"栏,按照概算中所列项目填列。"概算数"栏的数字应与"竣建02表"的"其他费用"栏的概算数相符。实际数的"需分摊费用"栏是指按受益对象分摊计入移交使用固定资产价值的其他费用,其数字应当与"在建工程"其他支出明细账相对应;实际数的"固定资产""流动资产""无形资产"和"长期待摊费用"栏,与"其他基建支出备查簿"相对应填列。

4. 编制"其他费用分摊计算表"

其他费用分摊计算表详见附录3中"竣建03附表"。该表反映了需要分摊计入移交使用固定资产价值的各项其他费用。分摊原则是:分摊各项费用的计算基数为工程实际完成的工作量。当按照实际工作量计算有困难时,可直接使用概算工作量作为计算基数。

分摊的方法有两种:分步分摊法和一次分摊法,前者较复杂,一般为了简化计算量,多采用一次分摊法。其方法可按下列公式计算。

(1)按实际分配率分配,一般用于建设工期比较短,一次竣工没有尾工的建设项目。

$$实际分配率 = \frac{需分摊费用余额 - 其中可直接分配部分}{建筑工程余额 + 安装工程余额 + 在安装设备余额} \times 100\% \quad (5\text{-}2\text{-}1)$$

(2)按概算分配率分配,一般用于建设工期比较长,单项工程分期分批竣工,并交付使用的建设项目。

$$概算分配率 = \frac{概算中需分摊费用合计数 - 其中可直接分配部分}{概算中建筑工程、安装工程和需要安装设备价值合计} \times 100\% \quad (5\text{-}2\text{-}2)$$

（3）通过上面两种计算方法，针对不同的项目工期特点，选用相应的分配率，就可计算出分摊的费用，其公式为

$$某项固定资产应分摊的其他费用=该项固定资产的建筑工程、$$
$$安装工程和需要安装设备成本合计×分配率 \qquad (5\text{-}2\text{-}3)$$

需要说明的是，其他费用分摊一般不包括：已购入但不需要安装的机械设备、工器具及家具、无形资产、长期待摊费用，以及生活福利工程等。

本表最后一栏的合计数应与"其他费用明细表"（竣建03表）中实际数栏下的"需分摊费用"合计数相一致。本表各工程明细项目的分摊数，应分别填列到"竣建04-1""竣建04-2表"中"摊入费用"栏的对应工程项目中。

5. 编制"移交使用资产一览表"

移交使用资产一览表，详见附录3中"竣建04-1""竣建04-2""竣建04-3""竣建04-4表"。

（1）编制"移交使用的资产房屋及建筑物一览表"

移交使用的资产房屋及建筑物一览表，详见附录3中"竣建04-1表"。该表中"房屋及建筑物名称"栏，要按照固定资产目录登记的项目填列，如没有对应的项目，须按照《企业会计准则第4号——固定资产》第五条规定同时满足"与该固定资产有关的经济利益很可能流入企业；该固定资产的成本能够可靠地计量"两个条件的，可以确认为固定资产的建筑费用，可补充填列；否则，按建筑工作量摊入各登记项目，并汇总填入"建筑工程费"一栏。

"建筑工程费"栏，按照会计核算实际发生数填列，也可以通过"竣建02表"中的建筑工程费用减去"设备基座费"后，按照房屋、建筑物明细项目逐行填列。

"摊入费用"栏，是按照"竣建03附表""其他费用分摊计算表"计算分摊到建筑工程项目的费用。

"建筑工程费""摊入费用"和"移交资产价值"栏最后一行的合计数，分别填入"移交使用资产总表"（竣建04表）"建筑物""房屋"行的"建筑工程费""摊入费用"和"移交资产合计"各对应栏内。

如有预计未完收尾工程估列的资产，另行在"备注"中注明。

（2）编制"移交使用的资产安装机械设备一览表"

移交使用的资产安装机械设备一览表，详见附录3中"竣建04-2表"。该表中"机械设备名称"栏，须按照固定资产目录的登记项目填列，若没有对应的项目，则可以补充填列。

"设备价值"栏，按照会计核算资料填列，其中包括设备原价、运杂费和采保费等，对于进口设备还需包含关税、手续费等相关费用。

"设备基座价值"栏，是根据"竣建02表""建筑工程费"中的"设备基座价值"填列的，其值包含设备支架和管道的支墩等。

"安装费用"栏，按照会计核算资料填列，首先按单位工程列出安装费用，可以确认为固定资产的安装费用单独登记；否则，需摊入相关单位工程费用中，例如保温、油漆、设备照明、金属试验等费用；如果在同一个单位工程中有不同设备组成时，其安装费需要在不同设备之间进行分摊（其分摊比例一般以概算设备费的比例为准）。

"摊入费用"栏，与"竣建03附表""其他费用分摊计算表"相应项目对应。

"移交资产价值"栏为"设备价值""设备基座价值""安装费用""摊入费用"的合计。

将"设备价值""设备基座价值""安装费用""摊入费用"和"移交资产价值"各栏在最后一行进行合计，并将合计数分别填入"移交使用资产总表"（竣建04表）"安装的机械设备"行的"设备购置费""安装工程费"（包括设备基座价值）、"摊入费用"和"移交资产合计"各对应栏内。

如有预计未完收尾工程中有安装机械设备的资产，另行在"备注"中注明。

（3）编制"移交使用的资产不需要安装机械设备、工器具及家具一览表"

移交使用的资产不需要安装机械设备、工器具及家具一览表，详见附录3中"竣建04-3表"。该表中"资产名称"栏，按照不需安装机械设备、管理车辆、办公用具、工器具和家具进行分类，在每类下面再按资产名称逐项填列。

"移交资产价值"后的其中"属固定资产""属流动资产"栏，按照财务部门的"其他基建支出备查簿"的记录和相关会计核算资料填列。

"不需要安装机械设备小计""管理车辆小计"行的"移交资产价值"后的其中"属固定资产""属流动资产"栏的数字，填入"竣建04表""移交使用资产总表"中；行次为"5"的"不需安装机械设备"行中相对应栏，以及"移交资产合计"栏中。

"办公用品小计""工器具小计""家具小计"行的"移交资产价值"后的其中"属固定资产""属流动资产"栏的数字，填入"竣建04表""移交使用资产总表"中；行次为"6"的"工器具及家具"行中相对应栏，以及"移交资产合计"栏中。

（4）编制"移交使用的资产无形资产、长期待摊费用一览表"

移交使用的"资产无形资产、长期待摊费用一览表""竣建04-4表"。该表中"资产项目"栏，按资产或费用项目填列。

实际价值中的"无形资产"和"长期待摊费用"栏，按照财务部门的"其他基建支出备查簿"的记录和相关会计核算资料填列，在最后一行进行合计，其合计数填入"竣建04表""移交使用资产总表"中，行次分别为"18"和"20"的"无形资产""长期待摊费用"中相对应栏，以及"移交资产合计"栏中。

"备注"栏，是说明形成无形资产、长期待摊费用时，相关的文件、协议、资产移交或资金划拨的情况，主要是为了方便资产的管理。

6. 编制"移交使用资产总表"

移交使用资产总表，详见附录3中"竣建04表"。该表是"竣建04-1表""竣建04-2表""竣建04-3表"和"竣建04-4表"的汇总表，综合反映了移交使用资产的分类、价值构成和直接形成的资产情况。

"资产分类"栏，按照固定资产、流动资产、无形资产和长期待摊费用进行分类，并按移交使用资产一览表项目排序。

"建筑工程费""摊入费用"和"移交资产合计"栏，填列"竣建04-1表"最后一行合计数。

"设备购置费""安装工程费""摊入费用"和"移交资产合计"栏，是按照"竣建04-2表"中最后一行合计数填列。

"其他费用"栏下面的"作固定资产移交生产""作流动资产移交生产""作无形资产移交生产""作长期待摊销费用移交生产"等栏，是根据"竣建04-3表"和"竣建04-4表"相对应项目分析填列。

最后的"合计"行"移交资产合计"栏，与"竣建02表""竣工工程决算一览表"中最后的"合计"行的"实际价值"合计栏的合计数相同。

7. 编制"竣工工程财务决算表"

竣工工程财务决算表，详见附录3中竣建05表。该表反映了竣工工程历年基建拨款、投资贷款、基建支出、投资完成额和结余资金等综合情况。数字来源为历年经批准的建设单位年度决算。

本表是采用资金平衡表的形式，即全部资金来源必须等于全部资金占用，反映建设项目从工程筹建开始到竣工验收时为止的全部资金来源和资金运用情况，是考核和分析基本建设拨款、投资借款及投资完成交付使用和结余资金的依据。本表应按照批准企业历年财务决算和基本建设业务相关的会计核算资料分析填列。

8. 编制"竣工工程概况表"

竣工工程概况表，详见附录3中"竣建01表"。该表反映基本建设竣工工程的规模、工期、投资、质量、技术经济指标、特征等基本情况。为全面考核竣工工程主要技术经济指标，为工程投资分析提供依据，本表须按照最终批准的概算设计文件、计划和会计核算等相关资料填列。

本表根据发电、送电、变电、通信及自动化工程的建设内容和特点，将本表分为七种格式："火电竣工工程概况表"（竣建01—1表）、"水电竣工工程概况表"（竣建01—2表）、"核电竣工工程概况表"（竣建01—3表）、"送电竣工工程概况表"（竣建01—4表）、"变电竣工工程概况表"（竣建01—5表）、"通信及自动化竣工工程概况表"（竣建01—6表）、"其他基建项目竣工工程概况表"（竣建01—7表）。限于篇幅，"竣建01-1""竣建01-2""竣建01-3""竣建01-5表"略。

在栏目设置上除了有各表不同之处，也有相同的公共栏目。下面对这些栏目简述如下。

（1）"建设性质"栏，按建设项目属于新建、扩建、改建、恢复和迁建的性质填列。

（2）"主要工程特征"各栏，按照设计文件、最终实际建设情况填列。

（3）"工程进度"中"开工日期"栏，按照上级批准的开工报告中，建筑安装工程最先一个永久性工程开工项目的开工日期填列；"竣工日期"栏，按照经验收合格，并工程全部投产的日期填列。

（4）"概算投资"栏，按照有关部门最终批准的概算数填列，必须与"竣建02表""合计"行的"概算价值"栏合计数相符。

（5）"实际投资"栏，按照会计核算资料填列，必须与"竣建02表""合计"行的"实际价值"栏合计数相符。

（6）"招标总额"栏，反映的是中标单位与建设单位签订的工程合同中注明的金额，而不是建设单位招标的标的金额，如果一个工程有两个以上工程合同的，需要进行汇总后填列。

（7）"工程造价"栏，是工程全部固定资产投资，其值=工程总投资-（移交的流动资产+无形资产+长期待摊费用）。

（8）"固定资产形成率"栏是实际移交固定资产总额与实际总投资额之比的百分数。

计算公式为

$$固定资产形成率 = 实际移交固定资产总额 \div 实际总投资额 \times 100\% \quad (5\text{-}2\text{-}4)$$

（9）"工程质量鉴定"栏，按照竣工验收报告中相关部门鉴定的结果填列。

9. 编写"竣工决算报告情况说明书",完成竣工决算报告送审稿编制任务。

按照上面的步骤完成竣工决算报告后,将报送上级主管部门、有关投资方和审计部门(单位)审查,然后按照审查时给定的意见修改定稿,装订成册,再正式上报上级主管部门和各投资方。

根据财政部财建[2003]724号文规定,财政部对基本建设项目年度财务决算不再审批;对项目竣工决算按基本建设财务制度规定审批,即中央级大中型基本建设项目竣工财务决算,经主管部门审核后报财政部审批。

小　结

　　学习项目五介绍了编制工程竣工决算的方法：做好日常基础资料的准备工作，在编制前还需做相关的准备工作，然后根据编制竣工决算的原则及要求，分别编制"竣工工程决算一览表""预计未完收尾工程明细表""其他费用明细表""其他费用分摊计算表""移交使用资产一览表""移交使用资产总表""竣工工程财务决算表""竣工工程概况表""竣工决算报告情况说明书"，从而完成工程竣工决算。

实训项目五

某大、中型建设项目2001年开工建设，2002年底有关财务核算资料如下。

1. 已经完成部分单项工程，经验收合格后，已经交付使用的资产包括：

①固定资产价值67986万元。

②为生产准备的使用期限在一年以内的备品备件、工具、器具等流动资产价值27000万元。

③期限在一年以上，单位价值在1500元以上的工具54万元。

④建造期间购置的专利权、非专利技术等无形资产1800万元，摊销期5年。

⑤筹建期间发生的开办费72万元。

2. 基本建设支出的项目包括：

①建筑安装工程支出14400万元。

②设备工器具投资39600万元。

③建设单位管理费、勘察设计费等待摊投资2160万元。

④通过出比方式购置的土地使用权形成的其他投资99万元。

3. 非经营项目发生的待核销基建支出45万元。

4. 应收生产单位投资借款1260万元。

5. 购置需要安装的器材45万元，其中待处理器材14.4万元。

6. 货币资金423万元。

7. 预付工程款及应收有偿调出器材款16.2万元。

8. 建设单位自用的固定资产原值54495万元，累计折旧9019.8万元。

《资金平衡表》上的各类资金来源的期末余额是：

①预算拨款46800万元。

②自筹资金拨款52200万元。

③其他拨款468万元。

9. 建设单位向银行借入的借款99000万元。

10. 建设单位当年完成交付生产单位使用的资产价值中，180万元属于利用投资借款形成的待冲基建支出。

11. 应付销售商36万元贷款和尚未支付的应付工程款1724.4万元。

12 未缴税金27万元。

根据上述有关资料填写该项目竣工财务决算表（见下表）。

大、中型建设项目竣工财务决算表

建设项目名称：××建设项目　　　　　　　　　　　　　　　　　　　单位：万元

资金来源	金额	资金占用	金额	补充资料
一、基建拨款		一、基建支出		1.基建投资借款期末余额
1.预算拨款		1.交付使用资产		2.应收生产单位投资借款期末余额
2.基建基金拨款		2.在建工程		3.基建结余资金
3.进口设备转账拨款		3.待核销基建支出		
4.器材转账拨款		4.非经营项转出投资		
5.煤代油装用基金拨款		二、应收生产单位投资借款		
6.自筹资金拨款		三、拨款所属投资借款		
7.其他专款		四、器材		
二、项目资金		其中：待处理器材损失		
1.国家资本		五、货币资金		
2.法人资本		六、预付及应收款		
3.个人资本		七、有价证券		
三、项目资本公积金		八、固定资产		
四、基建借款		固定资产原值		
五、上级拨入投资借款		减：累计折旧		
六、企业债券资金		固定资产净值		
七、待冲基建支出		固定资产清理		
八、应付款		待处理固定资产损失		
九、未交款				
1.未缴税金				
2.未交基建收入				
3.未交基建包干节余				
4.其他未交款				
十、上级拨入资金				
十一、留成收入				
合　计				

1. 竣工决算在基础资料的准备方面应当做哪些工作？
2. 竣工决算编制前的准备工作应做哪些？
3. 编制竣工决算的原则及要求是什么？
4. 竣工决算由哪些部分组成？
5. 请简述竣工决算的各阶段的主要工作。
6. 竣工决算编制的步骤是什么？

附录1

10kV某新建线路工程预算书

10kV某新建线路工程

施工图预算

某电力工程公司

××年××月

设计单位：

建设单位：

编制单位：

编制：

审定：

校核：

批准：

编制说明

一、工程概况

（1）本工程为某地区 10 kV 新建线路工程。

（2）导线架设：新架设 JKLYJ-10 kV-50 绝缘导线 55 m；跨越电力、公路、通信 2 处；GJ-70 普通拉线 2 组。

（3）电缆敷设：敷设直埋 YJV22-8.7/15 kV-3×50 电缆 150 m，路面为沙石、碎石路面。

（4）杆塔组立：新立电杆（Φ190×12000）3 基。

（5）配电装置：新装真空断路器 1 组，隔离刀闸 1 组，避雷器 1 组，电流互感器 1 套，400 kVA 干式变压器 1 台。

（6）接地装置：角钢接地体 6 根，镀锌扁铁 30 m。

（7）全线地形：100%平地；全线地质比例：普土 70%，坚土 20%，泥水 10%。

二、编制依据

（1）2009 版《20 kV 及以下配电网工程建设预算编制与计算标准》

（2）2009 版《20 kV 及以下配电网工程预算定额》（第一册）

（3）2009 版《20 kV 及以下配电网工程预算定额》（第二册）

（4）2009 版《20 kV 及以下配电网工程预算定额》（第三册）

（5）2009 版《20 kV 及以下配电网工程预算定额》（第四册）

（6）2009 版《20 kV 及以下配电网工程预算定额》（第五册）

（7）2009 版《20 kV 及以下配电网工程预算定额》（第六册）

（8）2009 版《20 kV 及以下配电网工程设备材料价格信息》

三、其他说明

（1）本工程人力平均运距为 100 m，汽车运距为 25 km。

（2）基本预备费按 1%考虑。

表一　20kV及以下配电网工程总预算表

单位：元

序号	工程或费用名称	建筑工程费	设备购置费	安装工程费	其他费用	合计	各项占静态投资比例%	单位投资
一	配电站（开关站）工程							
二	架空线路工程	1268.15	165192.42	26053.48		192514.05	78.77%	
三	电缆线路工程	3356.68		36231.16		39587.84	16.20%	
四	通信与调度自动化							
五	工程相关单项工程	4624.83	165192.42	62284.64		232101.89	94.97%	
六	其他费用				12293.88	12293.88	5.03%	
（一）	建设场地征用及清理费							
（二）	项目建设管理费				3195.41	3195.41	1.31%	
（三）	项目建设技术服务费				5987.82	5987.82	2.45%	
（四）	工程建设监督检测费				199.01	199.01	0.08%	
（五）	生产准备费				497.54	497.54	0.20%	
（六）	基本预备费				2414.1	2414.1	0.99%	
七	特殊项目							
	小计	4624.83	165192.42	62284.64	12293.88	244395.77	100.00%	
	工程静态投资	4624.83	165192.42	62284.64	12293.88	244395.77	100.00%	
	各项占静态投资比例%	1.89%	67.59%	25.49%	5.03%	100.00%		
八	建设期贷款利息							
	小计	4624.83	165192.42	62284.64	12293.88	244395.77		
	工程动态投资	4624.83	165192.42	62284.64	12293.88	244395.77	100.00%	
	各项占动态投资比例%	1.89%	67.59%	25.49%	5.03%	100.00%		

表二甲 20kV及以下配电网安装工程专业汇总表

单位：元

序号	工程项目名称	设备购置费	安装工程费 金额	其中 主要材料费	其中 人工费	合计	技术经济指标 单位	技术经济指标 数量	技术经济指标 指标
	整个工程	165192.42	62284.64	33267.26	6301.20	227477.06			
二	架空线路工程	165192.42	26053.48	17725.09	2321.69	191245.90			
1	杆塔工程		14355.24	11423.61	657.21	14355.24	元/基		
2	架线工程		9231.24	6301.48	924.68	9231.24	元/套		
3	杆上变配电装置	165192.42	2467.00		739.80	167659.42			
三	电缆线路工程		36231.16	15542.17	3979.51	36231.16	元/km		
2	电缆敷设		19293.75	15088.57	1390.82	19293.75			
3	电缆防火		618.96	453.60	59.57	618.96			
5	调试与试验		16318.45		2529.12	16318.45			
	合计	165192.42	62284.64	33267.26	6301.20	227477.06			

表二乙 20kV及以下配电网建筑工程专业汇总表

单位：元

序号	工程项目名称	建筑工程费 金额	其中 设备费	其中 主要材料费	其中 人工费	合计	技术经济指标 单位	技术经济指标 数量	技术经济指标 指标
	整个工程	4624.83		349.52	1769.86	4624.83			
二	架空线路工程	1268.15		349.52	355.47	1268.15	元/km		
1	土石方工程	619.58			262.00	619.58	元/m³		
2	基础工程	648.57			93.47	648.57	元/m³		
三	电缆线路工程	3356.68			1414.39	3356.68			
1	电缆沟工程	3356.68			1414.39	3356.68			
	合计	4624.83		349.52	1769.86	4624.83			

表三甲 20kV及以下配电网安装工程预算表

单位：元

序号	编制依据	项目名称	单位	数量	单价 设备	单价 主要材料	单价 定额基价	单价 其中工资	合价 设备	合价 主要材料	合价 安装费	合价 其中工资
二		整个工程										
		架空线路工程										
1		杆塔工程										
	PX1-1	人力运输 平均运距500m以内 混凝土杆	t.km	0.448			224.05	202.13			100.37	90.55
	PX1-22	汽车运输 混凝土杆 装卸	t	4.48			81.42	7.89			364.76	35.35
	PX1-23	汽车运输 混凝土杆 运输	t.km	112			1.45	0.34			162.4	38.08
	PX1-6	人力运输500m以内金具绝缘子零星钢材	t.km	0.043			102.76	93.23			4.42	4.01
	PX1-34	汽车运输 金具绝缘子零星钢材装卸	t	0.43			38.5	9.04			16.56	3.89
	PX1-35	汽车运输 金具绝缘子零星钢材运输	t.km	10.75			1.48	0.34			15.91	3.66
		混凝土杆Φ190×12000	根	3		2015				6045		
	PX4-4 调整	混凝土杆组立 整根式 13m以内	基	3			450.79	279.79			1352.37	839.37
		10kV线路铁附件综合	t	0.161		7200				1159.2		
		合成绝缘横担FS-10/3	根	10		126				1260		
		合成绝缘子串FXBW2-10/45	串	9		145				1305		
		联板类	t	0.005		15568				77.84		
		挂环类	t	0.001		28945				28.95		
		碗头挂环类	t	0.004		25858				103.43		
	PX4-33	横担安装 横担、木横担 单根	组	5			20.6	16.86			103	84.3

附录1　10kV某新建线路工程预算书

续表

序号	编制依据	项目名称	单位	数量	单价 设备	单价 主要材料	单价 定额基价	单价 其中工资	合价 设备	合价 主要材料	合价 安装费	合价 其中工资
	PX4-34	横担安装 铁、木横担 双根	组	2			31.67	26.57			63.34	53.14
	PX4-35	横担安装 瓷横担 直线杆	组	3			11.63	11.24			34.89	33.72
	PX4-36	横担安装 瓷横担 耐张杆	组	7			22.87	22.48			160.09	157.36
	PX4-49	绝缘子安装 耐张	只	9			2.27	1.89			20.43	17.01
		镀锌钢绞线 GJ-25～100	t	0.02		5500				110		
		楔形线夹	只	2		18				36		
		UT形线夹	只	2		33				66		
		拉线标识管	根	2		24				48		
	PX4-53	拉线制作安装 截面70mm²以内	根	2			28.72	26.02			57.44	52.04
	PX4-58	拉线制作安装 拉线保护管筒	根	2			4.07	4.07			8.14	8.14
		铜绞线 TJ16～120	kg	10		39.5				395		
		镀锌接地扁钢	t	0.06		6200				372		
		角钢接地体	t	0.045		6500				292.5		
	PX-59	接地体加工及制作	t	0.045			228.64	132.08			10.29	5.95
	PX4-60	接地极安装 土	根	6			10.06	9.15			60.36	54.9
	PX4-62	接地体敷设 50以内	基	1			30.54	24.96			30.54	24.96
	PX4-68	混凝土杆高空接地引下线	根	1			44.74	13.73			44.74	13.73
	PX4-69	电阻测量	基	1			24.75	9.57			24.75	9.57
		主材损耗								124.69		
		主材小计								11423.61		
(一)		直接费	%	100			13072.05			11423.61	1389.254	850.92
1		直接工程费	%	100			13072.05				13072.05	
1.1		人工费	%	100			850.92				12812.86	850.92
1.2		材料费	%	100			11436.66				11436.66	

续表

序号	编制依据	项目名称	单位	数量	单价			合价			
					设备	主要材料	定额基价	其中工资	设备	主要材料	安装费	其中工资
1.2.1		定额材料费	%	100			13.05				13.05	
1.2.2		装材费	%	100			11423.61				11423.61	
1.3		施工机械使用费	%	100			525.28				525.28	
2		措施费	%	13.14			259.19				259.19	
2.1		临时设施费	%	6.56			850.92				111.81	
2.2		安全文明施工措施费	%	4.13			850.92				55.82	
2.3		施工工具用具使用费	%	6.63			850.92				35.14	
2.4		冬雨季施工增加费	%				850.92				56.42	
2.5		夜间施工增加费	%				850.92				0	
2.6		特殊地区施工增加费	%				850.92				0	
(二)		间接费	%	100			622.62				622.62	
1		规费	%	100			323.09				323.09	
1.1		社会保障费	%	25.93			850.92				220.64	
1.2		住房公积金	%	10.2			850.92				86.79	
1.3		危险作业意外伤害保险费	%	1.84			850.92				15.66	
2		企业管理费	%	35.2			850.92				299.52	
(三)		利润	%	22			850.92				187.20	
(四)		税金	%	3.41			13881.87				473.37	
		合计	%	100			14355.24				14355.24	
		架线工程										
		架空绝缘线	m	550		8				4400		
2		耐张线夹	副	9		198				1782		
		并沟线夹	只	6		13.7				82.2		

续表

序号	编制依据	项目名称	单位	数量	单价				合价			
					设备	主要材料	定额基价	其中工资	设备	主要材料	安装费	其中工资
	PX1-5	人力运输 平均运距500m以内 线材	t.km	0.02			285	255.6			5.42	4.86
	PX1-32	汽车运输 线材装卸	t	0.19			81.18	8.77			15.42	1.67
	PX1-33	汽车运输 线材运输	t.km	4.75			1.62	0.44			7.70	2.09
	PX5-17	导线架设 绝缘铝绞线 截面95mm²以内	100m	5.5			61.82	39.23			340.01	215.77
	PX5-40	导线跨越设 电力、公路、通信	处	2			547.57	350.15			1095.14	700.3
		主材损耗								37.28		
		主材小计								6301.48		
		小计								6301.48	1463.68	924.68
(一)		直接费	%	100			8046.82				8046.82	
1		直接工程费	%	100			7765.16				7765.16	
1.1		人工费	%	100			924.68				924.68	
1.2		材料费	%	100			6718.92				6718.92	
1.2.1		定额材料费	%	100			417.44				417.44	
1.2.2		装材费	%	100			6301.48				6301.48	
1.3		施工机械使用费	%	100			121.57				121.57	
2		措施费	%	13.14			281.66				281.66	
2.1		临时设施费	%	6.56			924.68				121.50	
2.2		安全文明施工措施费	%	4.13			924.68				60.66	
2.3		施工工具用具使用费	%	6.63			924.68				38.19	
2.4		冬雨季施工增加费	%				924.68				61.31	
2.5		夜间施工增加费	%				924.68					
2.6		特殊地区施工增加费	%				924.68					
(二)		间接费	%	100			676.59				676.59	

续表

序号	编制依据	项目名称	单位	数量	单价 设备	单价 主要材料	单价 定额基价	单价 其中工资	合价 设备	合价 主要材料	合价 安装费	合价 其中工资
1		规费	%	100			351.1				351.1	
1.1		社会保障费	%	25.93			924.68				239.77	
1.2		住房公积金	%	10.2			924.68				94.32	
1.3		危险作业意外伤害保险费	%	1.84			924.68				17.01	
2		企业管理费	%	35.2			924.68				325.49	
(三)		利润	%	22			924.68				203.43	
(四)		税金	%	3.41			8926.84				304.41	
		合计	%	100			9231.24				9231.24	
3		杆上变配电装置										
	PX6-13	高压真空断路器 12kV630A	台	1	18800				18801			
	PX6-14	高压隔离开关 12kV630A	组	1	963				964			
	PX6-16	氧化锌避雷器 HYW5-12.7/50	组	1	890				891			
	PX6-24	组合式电流互感器	套	1	20000				20001			
		干式变压器 SGB11-400kVA	台	1	122500				122500			
		杆上变配电装置隔离开关	组	1			198.29	126.94			198.29	126.94
		杆上变配电装置断路器	组	1			482.22	132.35			482.22	132.35
		杆上变配电装置避雷器	组	1			132.61	65.93			132.61	65.93
		杆上变配电装置电流互感器	组	1			71.32	28.63			71.32	28.63
	PD1-7	10kV干式变压器安装 容量500kVA以下	台	1			571.8	385.95			571.8	385.95
		设备运杂费	%	1.25	163153				2039.42			
		设备购置费小计							165192.42			
		主材损耗										
		主材小计										

附录1 10kV某新建线路工程预算书

续表

序号	编制依据	项目名称	单位	数量	单价 设备	单价 主要材料	单价 定额基价	单价 其中工资	合价 设备	合价 主要材料	合价 安装费	合价 其中工资
		小计	%	100					165192.42		1456.2	739.8
(一)		直接费	%	100			1681.58				1681.58	
1		直接工程费	%	100			1456.24				1456.24	
1.1		人工费	%	100			739.8				739.8	
1.2		材料费	%	100			289.27				289.27	
1.2.1		定额材料费	%	100			289.27				289.27	
1.2.2		装材费	%									
1.3		施工机械使用费	%	100			427.17				427.17	
2		措施费	%	100			225.34				225.34	
2.1		临时设施费	%	13.14			739.8				97.21	
2.2		安全文明施工措施费	%	6.56			739.8				48.53	
2.3		施工工具用具使用费	%	4.13			739.8				30.55	
2.4		冬雨季施工增加费	%	6.63			739.8				49.05	
2.5		夜间施工增加费	%				739.8					
2.6		特殊地区施工增加费	%				739.8					
(二)		间接费	%	100			541.31				541.31	
1		规费	%	100			280.90				280.90	
1.1		社会保障费	%	25.93			739.8				191.83	
1.2		住房公积金	%	10.2			739.8				75.46	
1.3		危险作业意外伤害保险费	%	1.84			739.8				13.61	
2		企业管理费	%	35.2			739.8				260.41	
(三)		利润	%	22			739.8				162.76	
(四)		税金	%	3.41			2385.65				81.35	
		合计	%	100			2467				2467	

续表

序号	编制依据	项目名称	单位	数量	单价 设备	单价 主要材料	单价 定额基价	单价 其中工资	合价 设备	合价 主要材料	合价 安装费	合价 其中工资
三		电缆线路工程										
2		电缆敷设										
		电缆YJV22-8.7/15kV-3×50	m	150		86				12900		
		电缆终端户内型	套	1		570				570		
		电缆终端户外型	套	1		1287				1287		
		电缆保护管涂塑钢管	m	2.5		56				140		
		电缆保护管热缩套	根	1		44				44		
	PL1-5	破路面沙石、碎石路面厚度在150mm以内	m2	90			6.2	6.16			558	554.4
	PL1-9	直埋式电缆沟槽挖填土 普通土	m3	67.5			12.36	11.11			834.3	749.93
	PL1-39	密封电缆保护管安装 φ200以内	根	1			429.38	86.49			429.38	86.49
		主材损耗								147.57		
		主材小计								15088.57		
(一)		直接费	%	100			17333.89			15088.57	17333.89	1390.82
1		直接工程费	%	100			16910.25				16910.25	
1.1		人工费	%	100			1390.82				1390.82	
1.2		材料费	%	100			15437.76				15437.76	
1.2.1		定额材料费	%	100			349.19				349.19	
1.2.2		装材费	%	100			15088.57				15088.57	
1.3		施工机械使用费	%	100			81.68				81.68	
2		措施费	%	13.1			423.64				423.64	
2.1		临时设施费	%				1390.82				182.75	
2.2		安全文明施工措施费	%	6.56			1390.82				91.24	

续表

序号	编制依据	项目名称	单位	数量	单价 设备	单价 主要材料	单价 定额基价	单价 其中工资	合价 设备	合价 主要材料	合价 安装费	合价 其中工资
2.3		施工工具用具使用费	%	4.13			1390.82				57.44	
2.4		冬雨季施工增加费	%	6.63			1390.82				92.21	
2.5		夜间施工增加费	%				1390.82				0	
2.6		特殊地区施工增加费	%				1390.82				0	
(二)		间接费	%	100			1017.66				1017.66	
1		规费	%	100			528.09				528.09	
1.1		社会保障费	%	25.9			1390.82				360.64	
1.2		住房公积金	%	10.2			1390.82				141.86	
1.3		危险作业意外伤害保险费	%	1.84			1390.82				25.59	
2		企业管理费	%	35.2			1390.82				489.57	
(三)		利润	%	22			1390.82				305.98	
(四)		税金	%	3.41			18657.53				636.22	
		合计	%	100			19293.75	1985.53			19293.75	
3		电缆防火										
	PL6-1	电缆防火 防火堵料	t	0.03		15120	2337.2			453.6	70.12	59.57
		主材损耗										
		小计	t	0.03						453.6	70.12	59.57
(一)		直接工程费	%	100			541.86			453.6	541.86	
1		直接工程费	%	100			523.71				523.71	
1.1		人工费	%	100			59.57				59.57	
1.2		材料费	%	100			464.15				464.15	
1.2.1		定额材料费	%	100			10.55				10.55	

续表

序号	编制依据	项目名称	单位	数量	单价 设备	单价 主要材料	单价 定额基价	单价 其中工资	合价 设备	合价 主要材料	合价 安装费	其中工资
1.2.2		装材费	%	100			453.6				453.6	
1.3		施工机械使用费	%	100			0				0	
2		措施费	%	100			18.144				18.14	
2.1		临时设施费	%	13.14			59.57				7.83	
2.2		安全文明施工措施费	%	6.56			59.57				3.91	
2.3		施工工具用具使用费	%	4.13			59.57				2.46	
2.4		冬雨季施工增加费	%	6.63			59.57				3.95	
2.5		夜间施工增加费	%				59.57					
2.6		特殊地区施工增加费	%	100			43.58				43.58	
(二)		间接费	%	100			22.62				22.62	
1		规费	%	25.93			59.57				15.45	
1.1		社会保障费	%	10.2			59.57				6.08	
1.2		住房公积金	%	1.84			59.57				1.10	
1.3		危险作业意外伤害保险费	%	35.2			59.57				20.97	
2		企业管理费	%	22			59.57				13.10	
(三)		利润	%	3.41			598.55				20.41	
(四)		税金	%	100			618.96				618.96	
5		调试与试验										
	PL8-1	电缆试验 绝缘遥测	回路	1			35.1	27.03			35.1	27.03
	PL8-3	10kV电缆试验 交流耐压试验	回路	1			4037.72	737.19			4037.72	737.19
	PL8-4	10kV电缆试验 电阻比试验	回路	1			200.18	159			200.18	159
	PL8-5	10kV电缆试验 局放试验	回路	1			8330.01	1605.9			8330.01	1605.9
		主材损耗										

续表

序号	编制依据	项目名称	单位	数量	单价					合价				
					设备	主要材料	定额基价	其中工资		设备	主要材料	安装费	其中工资
		主材小计											
		小计	%	100			13373.38					12603	
(一)		直接费	%	100			12603.01					13373.38	
1		直接工程费	%	100								12603	
1.1		人工费	%	100			2529.12					2529.12	2529.12
1.2		材料费	%	100			580.79					580.79	
1.2.1		定额材料费	%	100			580.79					580.79	
1.2.2		装材费	%										
1.3		施工机械使用费	%	100			9493.1					9493.1	
2		措施费	%	100			770.37					770.37	
2.1		临时设施费	%	13.14			2529.12					332.33	
2.2		安全文明施工措施费	%	6.56			2529.12					165.91	
2.3		施工工具用具使用费	%	4.13			2529.12					104.45	
2.4		冬雨季施工增加费	%	6.63			2529.12					167.68	
2.5		夜间施工增加费	%										
2.6		特殊地区施工增加费	%				2529.12						
(二)		间接费	%	100			1850.56					1850.56	
1		规费	%	100			960.31					960.31	
1.1		社会保障费	%	25.93			2529.12					655.80	
1.2		住房公积金	%	10.2			2529.12					257.97	
1.3		危险作业意外伤害保险费	%	1.84			2529.12					46.54	
2		企业管理费	%	35.2			2529.12					890.25	
(三)		利润	%	22			2529.12					556.41	
(四)		税金	%	3.41			15780.34					538.11	
		合计	%	100			16318.45					16318.5	

表三乙 20kV及以下配电网建筑工程预算表

单位：元

序号	编制依据	项目名称	单位	数量	设备单价	定额基价			设备费	费用合计		
						金额	其中工资	其中主要材料		金额	其中人工费	其中主要材料费
二		架空线路工程										
1		土石方工程										
	PX2-1	线路复测与分坑 单杆	基	3.00		35.76	14.79			107.28	44.28	
	PX2-7	电杆坑挖方（或爆破）及回填 普通土 坑深2.0m以内	m³	15.06		11.46	10.37			172.59	156.17	
	PX2-7	拉线坑挖方（或爆破）及回填 普通土 坑深2.0m以内	m³	6.10		11.46	10.37			69.91	63.26	
（一）		小计				400.37				349.78	262.00	
1		直接工程费	%	100		349.78				400.37		
1.1		人工费	%	100		262.00				349.78		
1.2		材料费	%	100		61.08				262.00		
1.2.1		定额材料费	%	100		61.08				61.08		
1.2.2		装材料费	%	100						61.08		
1.3		施工机械使用费	%	100		26.70				26.70		
2		措施费	%	8.83		50.59				50.59		
2.1		临时设施费	%	3.25		262.00				23.13		
2.2		安全文明施工措施费	%	2.28		262.00				8.52		
2.3		施工工具用具使用费	%	4.95		262.00				5.97		
2.4		冬雨季施工增加费	%			262.00				12.97		
2.5		夜间施工增加费	%			262.00						
2.6		特殊地区施工增加费	%	100		159.48				159.48		
（二）		间接费										

续表

序号	编制依据	项目名称	单位	数量	设备单价	定额基价 金额	定额基价 其中工资	定额基价 其中主要材料	设备费	费用合计 金额	费用合计 其中人工费	其中主要材料费
1		规费	%	100		99.48				99.48		
1.1		社会保障费	%	25.93		262.00				67.94		
1.2		住房公积金	%	10.2		262.00				26.72		
1.3		危险作业意外伤害保险费	%	1.84		262.00				4.82		
2		企业管理费	%	22.9		262.00				60.00		
(三)		利润	%	15		262.00				39.30		
(四)		税金	%	3.41		599.15				20.43		
		合计	%	100		619.58				619.58		
2		基础工程										
	PX1-2	人力运输 平均运距500m以内 混凝土预制品	t.km	0.102		191.29	173.98			19.51	17.75	
	PX1-24	汽车运输 混凝土预制品 装卸	t	1.02		50.62	10.20			51.63	10.40	
	PX1-25	汽车运输 混凝土预制品 运输	t.km	25.5		1.28	0.24			32.64	6.12	
	PX3-3	预制基础底盘安装 每块重量（kg）300以内	块	3.00		21.26	15.88			63.78	47.64	
		底盘 D0.8×0.8×0.17	块	3.00				47.00				141.00
		拉线盘 L0.8×0.4×0.15	块	2.00				48.00				96.00
	PX3-8	预制基础拉线盘安装 每块重量（kg）300以内	块	2.00		7.51	4.76			15.02	9.52	
		拉线棒	只	2.00				55.00				111.00
	PX3-80	拉线棒防腐 沥青清漆防腐	根	2.00		3.06	1.02			6.12	2.04	1.52
		主材损耗费								188.7	93.47	349.52
		主材费小计										349.52

续表

序号	编制依据	项目名称	单位	数量	设备单价	定额基价			设备费	费用合计		
						金额	其中工资	其中主要材料		金额	其中人工费	其中主要材料费
(一)		直接费	%	100		556.27				556.27		
1		直接工程费	%	100		538.22				538.22		
1.1		人工费	%	100		93.47				93.47		
1.2		材料费	%	100		354.12				354.12		
1.2.1		定额材料费	%	100		4.60				4.60		
1.2.2		装材费	%	100		349.52				349.52		
1.3		施工机械使用费	%	100		90.63				90.63		
2		措施费	%	100		18.05				18.05		
2.1		临时设施费	%	8.83		93.47				8.25		
2.2		安全文明施工措施费	%	3.25		93.47				3.04		
2.3		施工工具用具使用费	%	2.28		93.47				2.13		
2.4		冬雨季施工增加费	%	4.95		93.47				4.63		
2.5		夜间施工增加费	%			93.47						
2.6		特殊地区施工增加费	%			93.47						
(二)		间接费	%	100		56.89				56.89		
1		规费	%	100		35.49				35.49		
1.1		社会保障费	%	25.93		93.47				24.24		
1.2		住房公积金	%	10.2		93.47				9.53		
1.3		危险作业意外伤害保险费	%	1.84		93.47				1.72		
2		企业管理费	%	22.9		93.47				21.40		
(三)		利润	%	15		93.47				14.02		
(四)		税金	%	3.41		627.18				21.39		
		合计	%	100		648.57				648.57		

续表

序号	编制依据	项目名称	单位	数量	设备单价	定额基价			设备费	费用合计		其中主要材料费
						金额	其中工资	其中主要材料		金额	其中人工费	
三		电缆线路工程										
1		电缆沟工程										
	PX1-5	人力运输 平均运距500m以内线材	t.km	0.052		285.03	255.61			14.8216	13.29	
	PX1-32	汽车运输 线材装卸	t	0.52		81.18	8.77			42.2136	4.56	
	PX1-33	汽车运输 线材运输	t.km	13		1.62	0.44			21.06	5.72	
	PL1-5	破路面沙石、碎石路面厚度在150mm以内	m²	90		6.20	6.16			558	554.4	
	PL1-9	直埋电缆沟槽挖填土普通土	m³	67.5		12.36	11.11			834.3	749.9	
	PL1-39	密封电缆保护管安装 φ200以内	根	1		429.38	86.49			429.38	86.49	
(一)		小计				2172.89				1899.78	1414	
1		直接工程费	%	100		1899.78				2172.89		
1.1		人工费	%	100		1414.39				1899.78		
1.2		材料费	%	100		349.82				1414.39		
1.2.1		定额材料费	%	100		349.82				349.82		
1.2.2		装材费										
1.3		施工机械使用费	%	100		135.56				135.56		
2		措施费	%	8.83		1414.39				273.12		
2.1		安全文明施工措施费	%	3.25		1414.39				124.89		
2.2		临时设施费										
2.3		施工工具用具使用费	%	2.28		1414.39				45.97		
2.4		冬雨季施工增加费								32.25		
2.5		夜间施工增加费	%	4.95		1414.39				70.01		
2.6		特殊地区施工增加费	%			1414.39						

续表

序号	编制依据	项目名称	单位	数量	设备单价	定额基价 金额	定额基价 其中工资	定额基价 其中主要材料	设备费	费用合计 金额	费用合计 其中人工费	费用合计 其中主要材料费
(二)		间接费	%	100		860.94	537.04			860.94		
1		规费	%	100		537.04				537.04		
1.1		社会保障费	%	25.93		1414.39				366.75		
1.2		住房公积金	%	10.2		1414.39				144.27		
1.3		危险作业意外伤害保险费	%	1.84		1414.39				26.02		
2		企业管理费	%	22.9		1414.39				323.90		
(三)		利润	%	15		1414.39				212.16		
(四)		税金	%	3.41		3245.99				110.69		
		合计	%	100		3356.68				3356.68		

表四 其他费用计算表

单位：元

编号	项目名称	主要内容及范围说明	合价
1	建设场地征用及清理费		3218.38
1.1	土地征用补偿费		
1.2	余物清理费		
1.3	施工场地租用费		
1.4	线路施工赔偿费		
2	项目建设管理费		769.46
2.1	项目管理费	（建筑工程费+安装工程费）×1.15%	742.73
2.2	招标费	（建筑工程费+安装工程费+设备购置费）×0.32%	1706.19
2.3	工程监理费	（建筑工程费+安装工程费）×2.55%	6037.59
3	项目建设技术服务费		208.12
3.1	工程勘察费	建筑工程费×4.5%	5245.70
3.2	工程设计费	（建筑工程费+安装工程费）×7.84%	115.41
3.3	设计文件评审费	（建筑工程费+安装工程费）×2.2%	334.52
3.4	项目后评价费	（建筑工程费+安装工程费）×0.5%	133.82
3.5	技术经济标准编制管理费	（建筑工程费+安装工程费）×0.2%	200.73
4	工程建设监督检测费	（建筑工程费+安装工程费）×0.3%	501.82
5	生产准备费	（建筑工程费+安装工程费）×0.75%	2420.60
6	基本预备费	[建筑工程费+安装工程费+设备购置费+其他费用（不包括基本预备费）]×1%	

附录2

其他费用分摊对象对照参考表

其他费用分摊对象对照参考表

编制单位：

	其他费用	会计科目	摊入范围	备 注
一	建设场地征用及清理费			
1	建设场地征用费	在建工程—其他支出	建筑	
2	旧有设施迁移补偿费	在建工程—其他支出	建筑	
3	余物拆除清理费	在建工程—其他支出	建筑	
二	项目建设管理费			
1	建设项目法人管理费	在建工程—其他支出	建筑、安装、设备	
2	前期工程费	在建工程—其他支出	建筑、安装、设备	
3	设备成套服务费	在建工程—在安装设备	设备	在设备内分摊，如实际支出列入设备费
4	备品备件购置费	在建工程—其他支出	建筑、安装、设备	
5	其他	在建工程—其他支出	建筑、安装、设备	
三	项目建设技术服务费			
1	研究试验费	在建工程—其他支出	建筑、安装、设备	剔除能分清服务对象的部分
2	勘察设计费	在建工程—其他支出	建筑、安装、设备	
3	工程监理费	在建工程—其他支出	建筑、安装、设备	
4	设备监理费	在建工程—其他支出	设备	
5	中介机构费	在建工程—其他支出	建筑、安装、设备	
6	其他	在建工程—其他支出	建筑、安装、设备	
四	生产准备费			
1	管理车辆购置费	固定资产		不分摊
2	工器具、办公、生产及生活家具购置费	固定资产、低值易耗品		不分摊
3	生产职工培训及提前进厂费	长期待摊费用		不分摊
4	整套启动试运费及分系统调试费	在建工程—其他支出	安装	
五	其他			

续表

	其他费用	会计科目	摊入范围	备注
1	施工安全措施补助费	在建工程—其他支出	建筑、安装、设备	
2	工程质量监督检测费	在建工程—其他支出	建筑、安装、设备	
3	预算定额编制管理费、劳动定额测定费	在建工程—其他支出	建筑、安装、设备	
4	其他	在建工程—其他支出	建筑、安装、设备	
六	建设期筹资费	在建工程—其他支出	建筑、安装、设备	
七	引进项目费用	在建工程—其他支出	在引进范围内分摊	剔除直接形成资产的费用

附录3

电力建设项目竣工决算表格式

基本建设工程竣工决算报告

（财务报表部分）

工程名称：＿＿＿＿＿＿＿＿＿＿＿＿＿＿＿＿＿＿＿＿＿＿＿＿＿＿＿＿＿＿

编制单位：＿＿＿＿＿＿＿＿＿＿＿＿＿＿＿＿＿＿＿＿＿＿＿＿＿＿＿＿＿＿

单位负责人：＿＿＿＿＿＿＿＿＿＿＿＿＿＿ 财务负责人：＿＿＿＿＿＿＿＿＿＿＿＿＿＿

编制日期： 年 月 日   报送日期： 年 月 日

送电竣工工程概况表（竣建01-4表）

编制单位：　　　　　编制日期：　年　月　日　　　　　　　　单位：元

工程名称				设计单位			
建设地址				主要工程施工企业			
建设性质				监理单位			
				概算批准机关、文号			
主 要 工 程 特 征				工程进度、投资及造价			
线路长度及导线型号	线路起止地点			工程进度	计划	考核	实际
	线路长度（km）			开工日期			
	电压等级及回路			竣工日期			
	导线型号			工程投资	总投资	每公里投资	
	地线型号			概算投资			
				实际投资			
地形及比重	平原	km	%	招标总额			
	丘陵	km	%	工程造价	总造价	单位造价	
	山地	km	%	概算造价			
地形及比重	泥沼、河网	km	%	实际造价			
				固定资产形成率（%）			
杆塔	铁塔（基）			工程质量鉴定			
	混凝土杆（基）						
	钢管塔（基）						

通信及自动化竣工工程概况表（竣建01-6表）

编制单位：　　　　　编制日期：　年　月　日　　　　　　　　单位：元

工程名称			设计单位			
建设地址			主要工程施工企业			
建设性质			监理单位			
			概算批准机关、文号			
主要工程特征			工程进度、投资及造价			
通信方式			工程进度	计划	考核	实际
线路长度	线路起止地点		开工日期			
	线路长度（km）		竣工日期			
			工程投资	总投资	每公里安投资	
电路容量和方式	电路容量		概算投资			
	电路制式		实际投资			
	电路频串		招标总额			

续表

电路容量和方式	电路站址数				
		工程造价		总造价	单位造价
杆塔及基数	微波铁塔（基）	概算造价			
	线路杆塔（基）	实际造价			
		固定资产形成率（%）			
主要设备型号、产地、制造厂					
设备名称		工程质量鉴定			
规格型号					
产地厂家					

其他基建项目竣工工程概况表（竣建 0l-7 表）

编制单位：　　　　　　编制日期：　　年　月　日　　　　　　单位：元

工程名称			设计单位			
建设地址			主要工程施工企业			
建设性质			监理单位			
			概算批准机关、文号			
主要工程特征			工程进度、投资及造价			
占地面积	征地面积（m²）		工程进度	计划	考核	实际
	建筑面积（m²）	地上	开工日期			
		地下	竣工日期			
	征地文号、证号		工程投资	概算投资（万元）		实际投资（万元）
			建筑装饰工程投资			
建筑结构特征	建筑名称		设备工具投资			
	建筑结构		其他投资			
建筑结构特征	建筑层次		合计			
			工程造价	总造价（万元）		单位造价（万元）
其他特征			概算造价			
			实际造价			
			固定资产形成率（%）			
			工程质量鉴定			

附录3 电力建设项目竣工决算表格式

竣工工程决算一览表（竣建02表）

编制单位：　　　　　　　　　　　　编制日期：　　年　　月　　日　　　　　　　　　　　单位：元

行次	项目	概算价值（元）						实际价值（元）					实际较概算	
		建筑工程费	其中：设备基座	安装工程费	设备购置费	其他费用	合计	建筑工程费	其中：设备基座	安装工程费	设备购置费	其他费用	合计	增减额（元）	增减率（%）
栏次	1	2	3	4	5	6	7=2～6	8	9	10	11	12	13=8～12	14=13-7	15=14÷7
一	主辅生产工程														
二	与厂址有关的单项工程														
三	其他														
四	其他费用														
五	差价预备费														
六	基本预备费														
七	建设期贷款利息														
八	铺底生产流动资金														
	合　计														
	其中：预计未完工程														

预计未完收尾工程明细表（竣建02附表）

编制单位： 　　　　编制日期： 年 月 日　　　　单位：元

栏次\行次	工程项目	所在地部位	计量单位	数量	概算价值	已完工作量		预计未完部分价值				说明
						金额	百分比	建筑工程	安装工程	设备购置费	其他费用	合计	
行次	1	2	3	4	5	6	7	8	9	10	11	12	13
1													
2													
…													
3	合计												

其他费用明细表（竣建03表）

编制单位： 　　　　编制日期： 年 月 日　　　　单位：元

行次	费用项目	概算数	实际数					备注
			需分摊费用	固定资产	流动资产	无形资产	长期待摊费用	合计	
1									
2									
…									
3	合计								

其他费用分摊计算表（竣建03附表）

编制单位： 　　　　编制日期： 年 月 日　　　　单位：元

栏次\行次	工程项目	工作量	建设场地占用及清理费	旧有设施迁移补偿费	余物拆除清理费	建设项目法人管理费	……			合计
行次	1	2	3	4	5	6				
1										
2										
…										
3	合计									

移交使用资产总表（竣建04表）

编制单位： 　　　　　编制日期： 　年　月　日　　　　　单位：元

栏次\行次	资产分类	建筑工程费	设备购置费	安装工程费	其他费用					移交资产合计
					摊入费用	作固定资产移交生产	作流动资产移交生产	作无形资产移交生产	作长期待摊费用移交生产	小计	
		1	2	3	4	5	6	7	8	9=4~8	10=1+2+3+9
1	一、固定资产										
2	1.建筑物										
3	2.房屋										
4	3.安装的机械设备										
5	4.不需要安装的机械设备										
6	5.工器具及家具										
…											
7	二、流动资产										
8	1.工器具及家具										
9	2.备品备件										
10	3.铺底流动资金										
…											
11	三、无形资产										
12											
13	四、长期待摊费用										
14	合　计										

移交使用的资产房屋及建筑物一览表（竣建04-1表）

编制单位： 　　　　　编制日期： 　年　月　日　　　　　单位：元

栏次\行次	房屋及建筑物名称	结构及层次	所在地、部位或使用、保管部门	计量单位	数量	建筑工程费	摊入费用	移交资产价值	备注
	1	2	3	4	5	6	7	8=6+7	9
1									
2									
…									
3	房屋合计								
4									
5									
…									
6	建筑物合计								
7	房屋建筑物总计								

移交使用的资产安装机械设备一览表（竣建04-2表）

编制单位：　　　　　　　　　编制日期：　　年　月　日　　　　　　　　　　单位：元

栏次\行次	机械设备名称	规格型号	供应单位制造厂	安装部位或使用者	计量单位	数量	单价	设备价值	设备基座价值	安装费用	摊入费用	移交资产价值	备注
	1	2	3	4	5	6	7	8	9	10	11	12=8+9+10+11	
1													
2													
...													
3	合计												

移交使用的资产不需安装机械设备、工器具及家具一览表（竣建04-3）

编制单位：　　　　　　　　　编制日期：　　年　月　日　　　　　　　　　　单位：元

栏次\行次	资产名称	规格型号	供应单位及制造厂	所在部位或使用者	计量单位	数量	单价	移交资产价值	其中		备注
									属固定资产	属流动资产	
	1	2	3	4	5	6	7	8	9	10	
1	一、不需要安装设备小计										
2											
...											
4	二、管理车辆小计										
5	三、办公用品小计										
6											
7											
...											
8	四、工器具小计										
9											
10											
...											
11	五、家具小计										
12	合　计										

移交使用的资产无形资产、长期待摊费用一览表（竣建04-4表）

编制单位：　　　　　　　　　编制日期：　　年　月　日　　　　　　　　　　单位：元

栏次\行次	资产项目	所在地或使用单位	计量单位	数量	实际价值		备注
					无形资产	长期待摊费用	
	1	2	3	4	5	6	7
1							
2							
...							
3	合　计						

注：备注中说明移交协议文号、资产移交或资产划拨。

竣工工程财务决算表（竣建05表）

编制单位：　　　　　　　　　编制日期：　　年　月　日　　　　　　　　单位：元

资金来源	行次	金额	资金占用	行次	金额
一、资本金	1		一、建筑工程	21	
1.	2		二、安装工程	22	
2.	3		三、在安装设备	23	
3.	4		四、其他费用	24	
二、投资借款小计	5		五、直接形成资产的其他基建	25	
1.	6		1.固定资产	26	
2.	7		2.流动资产	27	
三、债券资金	8		3.无形资产	28	
1.	9		4.长期待摊费用	29	
2.	10		六、基建工程投资合计	30	
四、应付款项	11		七、结余资金小计	31	
1.应付工程教	12		1.库存设备	32	
2.应付设备款	13		2.库存材料	33	
3.其他应付款	14		3.货币资金	34	
	15		4.应收款	35	
	16			36	
	17			37	
	18			38	
	19			39	
资金来源合计	20		资金占用合计	40	

参 考 文 献

[1] 四川省电力公司.四川省电力公司生产人员岗位培训标准.成都：电子科技大学出版社，2005.
[2] 汤晓青.送电线路施工.北京：中国电力出版社，2008.
[3] 汤晓青.送电线路施工实训教程.北京：中国电力出版社，2009.
[4] 《电网工程建设预算编制与计算标准》.中电联技经[2007]139号.
[5] 《电网工程建设预算编制与计算标准使用指南》.电定总造[2007]10号.
[6] 《20kV及以下配电网工程建设预算编制与计算标准》.国能电力[2009]23号.
[7] 《20kV及以下配电网工程建设预算编制与计算标准使用指南》.电定总定[2009]30号.
[8] 《电力建设工程预算定额（2006年版）》.中电联技经[2007]15号.
[9] 《电力建设工程预算定额使用指南》.电定总定[2007]11号.
[10] 《20kV及以下配电网工程预算定额》.国能电力[2009]123号.
[11] 《20kV及以下配电网工程预算定额使用指南》.电定总定[2009]30号.
[12] 电力工程造价与定额管理总站.电力建设工程概预算定额2009年价格水平调整文件汇编.北京：中国电力出版社，2010.
[13] 电力规划设计总院.电网工程限额设计控制指标（2009年水平）.北京：中国电力出版社，2010.
[14] DL/T 5168-2002《110kV～500kV架空电力线路工程施工质量及评定规程》.
[15] DL 5009.2-2004《电力建设安全工作规程 第2部分：架空电力线路》.
[16] DL/T 5092-1999《110kV～500kV架空送电线路设计技术规程》.
[17] 国家电网公司.《国家电网公司电力建设安全健康与环境管理工作规定》，2003.
[18] GB 50233-2005《110kV～500kV架空送电线路施工及验收规范》.
[19] GB50173-1992《35kV及以下架空电力线路施工及验收规范》.
[20] 《国家电网公司电力安全工作规程》（电力线路部分）.国家电网安监[2005]83号.
[21] 《电力建设施工技术管理导则》.国家电网工[2003]153号.
[22] GB175-1999《硅酸盐水泥、普通硅酸盐水泥》.
[23] GB1344-1999《矿渣硅酸盐水泥、火山灰质硅酸盐水泥及粉煤灰硅酸盐水泥》.
[24] GB12958-1999《复合硅酸盐水泥》.
[25] GB/T3608-93《高处作业分级》.
[26] 《电力发、送、变电工程基本建设项目竣工决算报告编制规程》.能源经（1992）960号
[27] 柴忠信.电力基本建设项目竣工决算报告编制办法.北京：中国电力出版社，2007.
[28] 中华人民共和国国家经济贸易委员会.电力工程建设投资估算指标：送电线路工程（2001年版）.北京：工人出版社，2002.
[29] 中华人民共和国国家经济贸易委员会.电力工业基本建设预算管理制度及规定（2002年版）.北京：中国电力出版社，2002.
[30] 国家电网公司.输变电工程达标投产考核办法.北京：中国电力出版社，2005.
[31] 章志刚等.高压输配电线路施工运行与维护专业人才培养方案与课程标准.北京：中国电力出版社，2011.
[32] 国家电网公司.国家电网公司生产技能人员职业能力培训规范.北京：中国电力出版社，2009.

Background

The project cost refers to all expenses used to complete a construction project, including all expenses from the engineering project preparation to the completion acceptance, delivery and use, and is a lump sum of one-time expenses for the engineering project including planned fixed asset reproduction, and formation of corresponding intangible assets and bottoming working fund. In different stages of the engineering project construction, it is manifested as such technical and economic documents as investment estimation, budget estimate, construction drawing budget, engineering settlement and final account. While the level of productive forces grows - the development of production technology and production management ability - people are deepening the understanding about it.

The project construction budget refers to the technical and economic documents used to pre-calculate and determine all project costs of the construction project according to specific contents of the design documents as well as related quotas, indicators and charge standards in different design stages, and is an important constituent part of the design documents in each stage. According to the differences of design stages, the project construction budget can be divided into the investment estimation prepared in the feasibility study stage, the budget estimate prepared in the preliminary design stage, the construction drawing budget prepared in the construction drawing design stage, etc. The project construction budget is often called the preliminary budget of project construction.

People often regard them equally in practical work, particularly in the project construction stage.

I. Three Stages for Formation and Development of Overseas Project Construction Budget System

The overseas project construction budget system first appeared in England over 400 years ago, and its formation and development can be divided into the following three stages.

(1) Before the 16th century, there was no detailed division of labor in the construction in-

dustry, and the design, construction, etc. are integrated. With the development of the construction industry, the construction products are more and more complicated, and then the design and construction are gradually separated. After the project is completed, the construction craftsmen must measure and valuate the construction quantities to determine their remuneration. However, due to their low educational level and difficult calculation, a batch of educated people have undertaken such task, who are the predecessor of the quantity surveyor nowadays. At that time, the quantity surveyor only calculated the engineering investment amount after project completion, namely accounting after determining the expenditures in manual work, materials, etc. This is a preliminary stage of the budget system development in England.

(2) In 1830, the British government implemented the EPC contract system in the project construction to standardize the construction market, requiring that corresponding quantities should be calculated according to construction drawings before the project bidding as the basis of bidding by contractors. Then, the contractors finally completed the budget statement preparation through tender offer. The budget statement is an important constituent part of the contract documents.

The determination of project cost refers to that various expenditures are controlled strictly during project construction before commencement and the project settlement is handled as per budget between the owner and the contract after the project is completed. Since then, the budget system was preliminarily formed in England and an independent discipline - budget discipline was formed. In 1868, a quantity surveyor academy was established in England, namely the current Royal Institution of Quantity Surveyors (also called Royal Institution of Chartered Surveyors), which has represented the first leap for the growth of project construction budget system and that the second stage was started.

(3) With the constant development of the construction industry, only determining the project cost in the construction tender stage has been far from meeting the needs of the development of project construction. Higher project cost and insufficient funds discovered in the tender stage, resulting in the forced shutdown or design modification due to no control on expenses in the design stage are very bad for the owner. By the end of the 19th century, the methods of investment plan and control were generated and widely applied. This investment plan is equivalent to the current preliminary design budget estimate and the construction

drawing design control as per budget estimate. Particularly, after 1950, the budget system has been further improved: when the owner proposes the project construction tasks or undertakes the feasibility study, the quantity surveyors would estimate the project investment with architects and engineers for decision-making by the owner. That is, the project investment is valuated in the early stage of design, and the design investment is controlled after the approved by the owner. So far, the second leap has been achieved for the project budget system, and the third stage is started.

At present, the quantity surveyor is involved in the whole process of engineering project construction in England and other western economically developed countries to be responsible for comprehensive management of the project investment: namely the preparation for project investment budget statement and also the supervision control for the project investment, and for handling the Final Account upon Completion after the project is completed, so as to play an important role in ensuring excellent economic benefit for the investment of the owner.

II. Formation of Project Construction Budget System in China

The project construction budget system in China can be traced back to over 1,000 years ago. A lot of buildings have been built in the ancient dynasties in China. In this process, the engineering technology has been constantly improved, and a set of labor and material quota management system has been gradually formed, evolved into the current labor and material quotas. As recorded in the Jigucuan Classics, the labor quota - work for gate tower platform construction appeared in the Tang Dynasty in China. After the Construction Methods (Yingzao Fashi) in the Song Dynasty (Completed in 1091), the Engineering Methods (Gongcheng Zuofa) was issued in the Qing dynasty officially (printed and published in 1734), detailing house construction examples and applied labor and material estimate limits, which were the standards of house construction by craftsmen and the explicit basis for competent departments in project acceptance and expense approval.

The modern project construction budget system in China was formed at the beginning of the 1950s, namely during "1st Five-year Plan" (1953-1957). At that time, if comparing the budget systems implemented in China and England respectively, the similarities lie in that the budget estimate is required in the preliminary design stage as the maximum quota to control the infrastructure investment and required in the construction drawing stage as the basis for the settlement by Party A and Party B. The differences lie in that the project cost approval procedures (namely examination and approval procedures of preliminary budget) and administration authority of quotas, expense standards and basis of preliminary budget preparation have been determined in the preliminary budget system of China, which have reflected the features of planned economy in China at that time. In this process, the infrastructure management system was relatively sound. Basically, the money was paid after determining the project cost first. Therefore, although there are many imperfect defects in the budget system at that time, it has played an active role in obtaining good economic benefit for infrastructure.

The project construction budget system in China has been gradually damaged from 1958 to 1976, and the preliminary budget has lost the control for design and construction.

After the Third Plenary Session of the 11th Central Committee of the Chinese Communist Party, a set of budget system suitable for the reform and opening-up policy has been gradually formed with the detailing of China's reform of the economic system. In 1983, the State Development Planning Commission and the Construction Bank of China jointly issued the Several Provisions on Improving Preliminary Budget of Project Construction (Trial). The State Development Planning Commission, the Ministry of Construction, the Ministry of Labor and Personnel and the Construction Bank of China issued the Notice on Investment Lump Sum Contracting Responsibility System of Infrastructure Project. In 1984, the State Council issued the Interim Provisions on Several Problems of Reforming Construction Enterprises and Infrastructure Management System. In 1988, the State Development Planning Commission issued such documents as Notice on Several Provisions on Controlling Construction Project Cost, playing a positive guiding role for the restoration, rectification and development of China's project cost management.

For more than 40 years of reform and opening-up, China has achieved very gratifying results in the construction for the project construction budget system: first, the engineering quota system of initial scale has been formed, which were of great significance to scientific decision-making and macro-control for rational use of the manpower and material resources in construction projects and the improvement of economic benefit; second, the dynamic management of project cost has been implemented. The static management of project cost has been reformed to dynamic management with the constant detailing of economic system in China particularly the price structure reform, which has played a positive role in the reasonable determination and effective control of the project cost under the new situations; third, the supervision review has been strengthened for the project cost, ensuring the reasonable use of construction funds; and fourth, the project cost management institution has been established, the number of professionals has been increasing with gradually improved quality, and an excellent professional team with good ideas, moral integrity and outstanding business has been cultivated. Of course, we have also noticed that the restraint of the former system has not be separated primarily still as a whole although the project cost management mode has been changed since the reform and opening-up to adapt to the need for economic restructuring, and the development of socialist market economy cannot be fully adapted to. The project construction field is quite active in the market mechanism, particularly that the project cost is strongly competitive. Therefore, the acceleration of project cost reform and promotion of the project cost management to step forwards better are important tasks for us.

III. Introduction To Power Construction in China

(I) Overview of Power Construction in China

The power construction in China was started in 1882. Shanghai Electric Company established by British businessmen formally supplied the power on July 26 in the same year. From the time of commercial use of electric energy, China is second only to England and France. The power in China has grown for 67 years till 1949. The power operation mode has been developed from the initial foreign investment, the "lamp factory" operated by the government of Qing Dynasty to the later power operation by national and bureaucratic capitals. The total capacity of power generation equipment in the whole country was 1.85 million kW, and the annual generating capacity was 4.3 billion kWh. The maximum capacity of the single thermal power generating unit was 50,000 kW, and the maximum capacity of the single hydroelectric generating set was 100,000 kW. The maximum capacity of the heat-engine plant was less than 200,000 kW, and the maximum capacity of the hydropower station was less than 300,000 kW.

Since the power construction in new China for 60 years, four important historical periods, namely recovery, growth, adjustment and development, have been experienced: during the "1st Five-year Plan", the power construction in China belonged to the "recovery" period that the power generation equipment during the former ruling period of the Nationalist Party was recovered and reused; then, the "growth" period of the power construction in China come that the basic industry construction was promoted all over the country, and a batch of power generation equipment had been introduced from the Soviet Union to meet the requirements of fast development of national economy at that time; the power construction in China was in the "adjustment" period from the 1960s to the early 1980s; and it stepped into a fast development period since the mid-1980s.

At present, the production technology and equipment level of the power industry in China are gradually approaching the level of the economically advanced countries in the world, and the UHV, smart power grids, etc. have been in the world-class advance. By the end of 2006, China has owned 171 power plants over 1 million kW, and the total installed capacity of Three-Gorge Hydropower Plant completed in 2009 has reached 22.5 million kW, with the annual generating capacity of about 100 billion kWh. The models of thermal power unit capacity in operation include 200,000, 300,000, 500,000, 600,000 and 800,000 kW. The models of hydropower unit capacity include 100,000, 320,000, 550,000 and 700,000 kW. China is capable of independent design and manufacturing of ultra-large type hydro-generator sets with unit capacity reaching 1 million kW. The total capacity of nuclear power units in operation has exceeded 10 million kW, approximately accounting for 1.1% of the total installed capacity. The total capacity of nuclear power units in construction has reached 25 million kW, ranking No. 1 in the world. It is planned that the installed capacity of nuclear power in China will exceed 70-80 million kW in 2020, accounting for 4.6%~5.3% of the total installed capacity of 1.5 billion kW in China at that time. The construction of wind and solar power stations has also made great progress, and a large scale power transmission and distribution network composed of 10kV, 35kV, 66kV, 110kV, 220kV, 330kV, 500kV, ±500kV, 750kV, ±800kV and 1000kV power lines has been built. Four synchronous power grids in "three parts of China" (North China-Central China-East China), the northeast, the northwest and the south supported by the UHV backbone network frame.

(II) Position and Role of Power Construction in National Capital Construction

The capital construction refers to the investment in national economy for construction, purchasing and installation of fixed assets and other economic activities related to them. The capital construction occupies an important position in the national economy, and the power construction is an important constituent part in the national capital construction.

The power is the lifeblood of agriculture and goes ahead of the industry. The power industry is the basis of a state, and occupies an important position in the national capital construction.

The power construction in China has grown for one hundred years of initial scale, but the per capita installed power generation capacity and the generating capacity still fall behind in the world. For example, the per capita generating capacity in China in 2007 was 2484kW·h, ranking No. 73 around the world, far lower than the level of developed countries, and the duration of power shortage has almost equaled to the history of power construction. After new China is founded, the power was short in Beijing-Tianjin-Tangshan in 1953, and in the country in 1958. 20%-30% of the normal production capability cannot be ensured for a long time, which has been continued to the early 1990s. The reform of the economic system was started till 1996 in order to solve the inherent malpractices of the original state-owned enterprise management system. A considerable number of large and medium-sized state-owned enterprises had short manpower, which slightly changed the power shortage in the whole country, and the power was sufficient in some areas. However, the low-level power sufficiency has not been continued for a long time. The "power rationing" started again nationwide in summer in 2001, and it occurred in 2003 in a large scope.

The power construction in China has lagged behind the increasing economic and social demand for electrical energy for a long time. There are two reasons: first, the electric power production and construction technology have progressed slowly; and second, the country failed to take the power industry as the leading industry, and the capital investment was seriously insufficient, which were also the most critical reasons.

During the "12th Five-year Plan", the demand for energy and electricity has been growing rapidly under the situation of "building a moderately prosperous society" and "accelerating the industrialization and urbanization". The acceleration of power development mode conversion has been taken as the main line of power construction, focusing on ensuring the safety, optimizing the structure, conserving energy and reducing emissions, and promoting the harmony, putting forth effort to improve the safety of power supply, promote the power structure optimization, boost the optimization of the resource allocation, carry forward the power industry upgrading, advance the harmonious development of power, and striving to build a safe, economic, green and harmonious power industry system to meet the effective power demand of economic and social science development. The proportion of non-fossil energy power generation has been enlarged, and the water and electricity has been developed preferentially on the premise of protecting ecological environment. On the basis of ensuring safety, the nuclear power has been rapidly developed. The power generation from renewable sources such as wind, solar and biomass has been actively promoted, and the proportion of non-fossil energy has been increased. The integrated development of coal and electricity has been carried out, the large coal and electricity base construction has been sped up, and the coal and power transmission have been developed simultaneously. The development of combined heat and power generation has been encouraged, and the large-parameter and environment-friendly units and the combined heat and power generation projects consistent with national policies have been planned uniformly. The green development of coal power has been promoted, and the clean coal power generation technology has been vigorously boosted. In the meantime, the power grid construction enhancement has been continued, and the upgrading of rural power grid and smart grid construction would be the focus of construction.

At present, the capability of power supply in China to support the socio-economic development has been obviously strengthened, and the power structure and layout have been further optimized.

The power grid optimization resource allocation capacity has been significantly enhanced, and the green development ability has been further strengthened. The level of power technology and equipment and the ability of independent innovation have been significantly improved.

(Ⅲ) Investment On Power Capital Construction

1. Composition of Power Capital Construction Investment

The power industry is fund-intensive, and the investment on the power industry includes two parts, namely the investment on "power plant and power grid". The investment on power grid involves the power transformation equipment and power transmission and distribution network. The capital raising, investment and return are fundamental problems to restrain the development of power industry.

2. Current Investment On Power Capital Construction in China

The State Council has formulated the 20-character policy of "separation of enterprise from administration, entity based on province, interconnected power system, unified dispatching and capital raising for electricity", and the reform policy of power industry system "based on local conditions and network conditions" to develop the power industry, changed the system that the electric power was operated by the power department before, and implemented the "multi-channel, multi-mode and multi-level" capital raising for electricity and power operation by multiple units.

—— Multiple forms, such as state investment, local financing, sino-foreign joint ventures and foreign sole proprietorship, have basically solved the financing problem for the development of the power industry.

Ⅳ. Overview of Capital Construction

(Ⅰ) Capital Construction Projects

The capital construction project refers to an independent engineering project built as per an overall design which has an independent form of organization in administration and the independent business accounting on economy and can directly establish economic relations with other enterprises or units.

According to the different nature of capital construction projects, it is possible to be divided into new construction, expansion, reconstruction, restoration, relocation, technical transformation, renewal project, etc. New projects refer to the projects which have not existed and will be newly built. Expansion projects refer to the engineering projects built to expand production capacity or increase new production capacity on the original basis. Reconstruction projects refer to the projects reconstructed fro original equipment or projects by the original enterprises aiming at increasing labor productivity, improving product quality or changing product direction. Restoration projects refer to the projects restored as per the former scale after the former fixed assets are scrapped completely or partially due to natural disasters and other reasons for enterprises and public institutions.Relocation projects refer to the projects of original enterprises and public institutions relocated to other places. Technical transformation projects refer to the projects with technical transformation by advanced technologies for machinery, equipment and production process of the existing enterprises. Renewal projects refer to the projects that new fixed assets are separately purchased for replacement to maintain its original scale when the basic part of fixed assets has lost its use value.

Capital construction projects can be divided into productive and non-productive construction projects according to different usage. Productive construction projects refer to the construction projects directly used in production or meet the production needs for industry, construction industry, agriculture, water conservancy, meteorology, transportation, post and telecommunications, commerce, material supply, geological resources exploration, etc. Non-productive construction projects to the construction projects used to meet the needs of people's material life and cultural life, such as culture and education, sanitation, scientific research, public utility, organs and social organization.

The capital construction projects can be divided into large projects, medium projects and small projects according to the scale of construction or investment scale; into the projects under direct control by various departments of the State Council, national subsidy projects locally invested, local projects and construction projects self-raised by enterprises and public institutions as per membership function; and into preparatory projects, projects preparing to construct, construction projects, projects constructed and put into operation, ending projects and completed projects as per construction stage.

(Ⅱ) Capital Construction Procedures

The characteristics of capital construction include more investment, long construction duration, many disciplines and departments involved, and complicated work links. In order to ensure the smooth progress of project construction and achieve the expected purpose, we have gradually explored and summarized a set of work procedures for the majority of project construction personnel to abide by in the long-term practice of capital construction, including the sequence, contents and requirements of work in the whole process of capital construction, namely capital construction procedures. The capital construction procedures reflect the objective regularity during capital construction practice, and strict observance of capital construction procedures is an important principle in capital construction. The construction inconsistent with capital construction procedures will definitely bring serious loss to national economy. The capital construction procedures in China were issued by the State Council for implemented in 1952. With the gradual development of national capital construction, the capital construction procedures have been further improved for over 60 years, and the existing capital construction procedures are divided into eight stages, including project proposal stage, feasibility study stage, design stage (preliminary design and construction drawing design), commencement preparation stage, construction stage, production preparation stage, completion acceptance stage and post-engineering evaluation stage, which are detailed below briefly.

1. Project Proposal Stage

The construction project proposal is the work in the initial stage of the capital construction procedures stipulated by the state. The project proposal refers to general outline assumptions and recommendations for the projects prepared to be built by investors according to the long-term planning of the state and the development planning of departments, industries and regions to provide basis for determining whether the proposed project is necessary to build, whether it has the basic conditions for construction, and whether it is necessary to make further research and demonstration.

The project proposal can be complicated or simple. Generally, it includes the following contents: ① necessity and basis of the construction project; ② market forecasting; ③ construction scale and product scheme plan; ④ construction site ideas; ⑤ availability and reliability of resource supply; ⑥ main technical ideas; ⑦ external collaboration conditions; ⑧ investment estimation and fund raising schemes; ⑨ construction period estimate; and ⑩ preliminary evaluation of economic and social benefits.

The construction project proposal is the basis for the national authority or investors to select the projects for investment. After accurate preparation and realistic review of the project proposal, we will grasp the initiative of the preliminary work of the construction project, and lay a good base for the further work.

The following items shall be noted during the preparation of the construction project proposal. ① Comply with the current economic development level of the state, and determine reasonable construction standards. ② Select the construction areas on the principles of being as close as possible to raw materials, fuel and consumption and appropriate clustering of industrial projects. ③ Two fundamental items required for selection of construction site (plant site): first, ensure direct economic benefits of plant and meet its needs of production, construction and staff's life; and second, ensure the yearly activities for indirect social benefit, and require the plant layout in favor of realizing the overall planning of tow and industrial district with damage to landscape and ecological environment. ④ The economic scale of the project shall meet the requirements of national competent departments or industries and regions, so as to bring the benefits of scale into full play. ⑤ Adhere to advanced, applicable, economic and reasonable selection of production process. ⑥ Choose domestic equipment as much as possible, pay attention to the supporting of imported equipment, domestic equipment and plants if the imported equipment must be introduced, and also concern about the introduction and absorption of technical information.

2. Feasibility Study Stage

The feasibility study is referred to as "FS" for short, which is managed and operated by the Client and competent departments. It is the basis for the state or investors to make macro decisions and pre-control on the construction projects, including the investigation and study on all aspects related to the project such as technology, economy, society and environment. The feasibility study mainly analyzes and demonstrates the feasibility of engineering project in technology and economy comprehensively and scientifically, compares multiple schemes, puts forward evaluation opinions and recommends the best scheme. From technology, it mainly studies the reasonable degree of an engineering project for the demands of resources, technology and talents after construction and production, as well as the impact of such project on society and environment after construction and completion. From economy, the reasonable degree of investment spent in the construction process of an engineering project, and whether the project conforms to the current national infrastructure investment policy and whether it is financially profitable are studied. Of course, technology and economy are not separate, but interrelated. The implementation of the engineering technical scheme of a project (covering construction technology and production technology) determines the reasonable degree of the project in economy, namely investment estimation. In reverse, the investment estimation has a positive influence on the implementation of the engineering technology scheme of the project, because it controls the overall cost of the engineering project.

As stipulated by the state, all domestic investment projects and construction projects by foreign capital shall be provided with feasibility study after approving the project proposal, and the feasibility study report shall be prepared. Generally, the feasibility study report of domestic industrial project shall include the following main contents.

① Overview, including background proposed for the project, necessity and economic benefits of investment, as well as basis and scope of the research.

② Demand forecast and proposed scale, including forecast of domestic and foreign demands, sales forecast, price analysis, prospect of entering the international market, estimation of the production capacity of the existing domestic factories, and technical and economic comparison and analysis of project scale, product scheme and development direction.

③ Resources, raw materials, fuels and utilities, including types, quantities, sources and supply availability of raw materials, auxiliary materials and fuels, number of utilities required, supply mode and supply conditions.

④ Plant construction conditions and plant site scheme, including geographical locations, meteorological, hydrological, geological and topographic conditions and current socio-economic status of plants, present situation and development trend of transportation, water and electricity, plant site comparison and selection opinions and expense analysis while selecting plant site.

⑤ Design scheme, including project scope, technical source and the production methods, comparison of main technical process and equipment selection scheme, source of the imported technical equipment, preliminary selection of the whole plant layout scheme and civil engineering quantities, as well as comparison and preliminary selection of public auxiliary facilities and in-plant transportation modes.

⑥ Environmental protection, including investigating the current situation of the environment, predicting the impact of projects on the environment, putting forward preliminary plans for environmental protection and treatment of "three wastes", and proposing plans for construction technologies such as labor protection and safe production and corresponding measures.

⑦ Planned business organizational setup, labor setup and personnel training plan.

⑧ Project construction implementation schedule suggestions.

⑨ Investment estimation and fund raising, including the investment required for main work and collaborative works, estimation of the working fund required after the completion of the project, source of the project fund, financing ways and repayment mode of the loan in the future.

⑩ Project economic evaluation. The investigation, prediction, research, calculation and demonstration are required for various economic factors of input-output of the proposed project during construction and production by modern methods of economic analysis (microeconomic evaluation - financial evaluation and macroeconomic evaluation - national economy evaluation) to select the best scheme as the important basis for the decision-making project.

Requirements for preparation of feasibility study report: first, it is required to ensure the authenticity and scientificity of feasibility study report; second, the preparation unit must have the conditions for feasibility study, certain economic and market analysis experts, engineering technicians and financial personnel, as well as relatively complete technical equipment and means; third, the content, depth and calculation indexes of feasibility study must meet the standards and meet the needs of project decision-making; and fourth, the persons in charge of administration, technology or economy of the preparation unit shall sign upon completion of the preparation, and be responsible for the quality of the research report.

After the completion of feasibility study, the feasibility study report must be reviewed and approved by the competent authorities of various industries and the State Development Planning Commission. Feasibility study reports of small projects shall be approved by the competent departments, provinces, municipalities and autonomous regions according to their subordinate relations. After the project is approved, the engineering design can be started. For example, the "scheme for the dam of medium-height" with less immigrants and investment has been finally determined for the world-famous Three Gorges Project after multiple feasibility study and demonstration and considering the problems of water conservancy, electric power, shipping, engineering technology (electric power and civil engineering), ecology, environmental protection, engineering geology, engineering economy, system engineering and macro economy lasting more than half a century.

3. Design Stage

The Administrator shall establish the Client to be responsible for the preparation and entrust the design unit to carry out survey and design. The unit in charge of design shall carefully study the feasibility study report with survey, investigation and experimental research before design. The design is a comprehensive and detailed arrangement for the implementation of the proposed project in technology and economy, and is the embodiment of the project construction plan and the basis for the construction organization. The design is a complex and particularly comprehensive technical and economic work based on a comprehensive and correct survey and investigation. It is carried out in stages, generally divided into two stages, namely preliminary design and construction drawing design. For major projects and technically complex projects, the technical design stage can be added according to the characteristics and needs of different industries. Design quality is directly related to the quality of construction projects and the pricing and management of project cost, and is a decisive link in project construction.

(1) Preliminary design

The preliminary design is called "preliminary design" for short. It requires following the approved project assignment and national economic policies, combining local specific provisions at that time, collecting relevant design information, defining the design conditions and design principles, preparing the preliminary design outline as its basis, proposing the engineering material estimate list and preparing the budget estimate number as the basis of investment and ordering. The preliminary design solves the problems of technical reliability and economic rationality of the construction project, therefore the preliminary design has a certain nature of planning and is the "outline" design of such project. Its specific contents and composition vary with different engineering projects. For example, the preliminary design of transmission line project includes determination of starting and ending points, paths, voltage classes and types of conductors or ground wires, etc., survey of geological, topographical, hydrological and meteorological conditions along the route, estimation of earthwork quantity and main materials consumed, and determination of main economic and technical indicators, construction period, and design budget, etc. For the transmission line projects under special geological, topographic and meteorological conditions, the construction and organization of large-scale transmission line projects shall be studied deeply accordingly and the results of model tests shall be proved when necessary. For example, for the serious icing in some sections in the "Ertan" Outgoing Project, Southwest Electric Power Design Institute established a large "Huangmaogen" ice observation station in corresponding section in 1982, and erected 3 test routes with large rime tower for the "icing" data observation test lasting about 20 years. In 1994, the project construction stage was started.

Technical design, also known as detailed preliminary design. In order to further solve major technical problems in the preliminary design, such as process flow, building structure and equipment selection, the technical design is carried out according to the preliminary design and further investigation and research data, which will enable the construction project more specific and improved and the technical indexes more reasonable.

(2) Construction drawing design

The construction drawing design is the embodiment of the preliminary design to draw the detailed construction drawings based on the preliminary design according to the needs of construction and installation for specific construction of works. It is the basis of engineering construction and plays an important reference role in the long-term maintenance during production after the completion of the project. According to the construction drawing design, the construction drawing budget (namely the "Budget") is prepared.

After the design documents are prepared, they must be reviewed and approved in accordance with the regulations. The preliminary design and budget estimate shall be submitted to the relevant departments for approval. The design documents of construction drawing are the specific construction arrangement of the determined scheme, which shall be completed by the design unit. While being delivered to the Builder, the review and signing are required by the technical leader of the Client, and the designers shall arrive at the site to jointly review the design drawings and design documents with technical discussion and descriptions with the Client and the Builder.

4. Commencement Preparation Stage

The project commencement preparation stage has more work and involves a wide range, mainly including application for being included in the fixed assets investment plan; carrying out various construction preparations, such as preparation for the implementation plan of construction projects, bidding for construction projects and ordering for equipment and materials; carrying on land expropriation, demolition, relocation and "three supplies and one leveling"; and signing various contracts and agreements. The work is this stage plays a decisive role in ensuring the smooth progress of the project after commencement.

5. Construction Stage

The construction stage is an important stage for the construction project to be put into practice, and the construction must be organized reasonably according to the construction sequence and the actual situation. The Builder shall spare no pains to ensure the project quality and complete the construction tasks on schedule.

The new commencement date of the project refers to the date on which any permanent works specified in the construction project design documents is first officially started. For the projects in no need of grooving, the official piling date of the building base is regarded as the official commencement date. Engineering geological survey, site leveling, demolition of old buildings, temporary buildings, construction of temporary roads, water and electricity used in construction are excluded in the formal construction. The construction period starts from the new commencement.

When the preparation for commencement is basically ready, the Client shall submit an application report for commencement, which is allowed after being approved by the competent departments. As specified by the state, the commencement reports of large and medium-sized projects must be submitted to the State Development Planning Commission for approval.

The construction stage generally includes the engineering works related to civil engineering, decoration, water supply and drainage, heating and ventilation, electrical lighting, industrial piping and equipment installation. The Builder shall strictly perform the contract and cooperate closely with the Client and design unit and the supervision engineers. During construction, all links shall be coordinated with each other, and it is required to strengthen scientific management, ensure the project quality, and complete the construction tasks on schedule.

During construction, the Builder must strictly follow the design construction drawings for construction, and reduce the project cost on the premise of ensuring the project quality. If the project needs to be changed in construction, the consent of the design unit and the Client is required. The acceptance is required according to the design and construction acceptance codes. The underground works and concealed works, especially key parts of base and structure, must be qualified in acceptance, and the original records shall be made properly before the next procedure is started. For the projects inconsistent with quality requirements, timely measures shall be taken, leaving no hidden dangers. Unqualified projects cannot be handed over.

6. Production Preparation Stage

During construction, the Client shall establish a special team on time according to the production and technical characteristics of construction project to make preparations for production in a planned and step-by-step manner so as to create conditions for operation after completion. Production preparations mainly include: recruiting and training necessary production personnel, implementing production coordination conditions for raw materials, fuel and power, organizing the manufacturing and ordering of tools, instruments and spare parts, establishing a strong production command and management organization, and formulating necessary management system and operating procedures for safe production.

7. Completion Acceptance Stage

The completion acceptance aims at comprehensive assessment of construction results, inspection of design and construction quality, production problem solving in time, handling of delivery formalities, delivery and use.

The completion acceptance procedures generally include two stages: single project acceptance and complete acceptance of the whole engineering project. For large projects, the acceptance shall be organized in batches due to long construction duration or gradual operation during construction. Before general completion acceptance, the Builder shall perform the pre-acceptance of projects, and the supervising unit sometimes will also organize the preliminary acceptance. During completion acceptance, the Client shall organize the completion acceptance, and participating units include design unit, Builder, banks, and environmental protection and related government supervision departments. It is required to systematically organize technical data, draw as-built drawings with classification and filing, use the data after acceptance as archival data, submit it to the production unit for preservation. The Client shall carefully sort out all property and materials, prepare the Final Account upon Completion, and submit it to the superior department in charge for approval.

After the transmission line project is completed in accordance with the contents specified in the design documents, it is a must to conduct live trial operation of the line and check whether the design standards and the quality requirements of construction acceptance have been met before completion acceptance. If the project quality is unqualified, reworking or reinforcement is required.

8. Post-engineering Evaluation Stage

The post-engineering evaluation refers to a technical and economic activity for systematic evaluation of the whole process, including approval decision-making, design, construction, completion acceptance and production operation of the project within a period of production after the project is delivered. It is the last link of capital construction procedures, striving to achieve result confirmation, summary of experience, problem research, project decision-making level improvement and production results.

The evaluation mainly includes the following contents. ① Impact assessment. The correctness of the project decision is evaluated by the impact on society, economy, politics, technology and environment after the project is completed and put into production. If the purposes during decision-making are not achieved after the project is completed, or if the purpose of decision-making is abandoned, it is required to analyze the reasons, find out the problems and improve them. ② Economic benefit assessment. It is necessary to evaluate whether the project investment is reasonable and operation management is proper through the analysis of practical effects generated after the project is completed and put into operation, compare with the evaluation results in the feasibility study stage, find out the difference between the two and propose improvement measures. ③ Process evaluation. The above two evaluations are undertaken from the operation results after the project is put into operation. The process evaluation systematically analyzes the whole process of project approval and decision-making, design, construction, completion and operation to find out the reasons for the success or failure.

The contents of above capital construction procedures basically reflect the whole process of capital construction. It can be roughly divided into three stages, namely the preliminary work stage, the project implementation stage, and the completion and operation stage. From the experience of domestic and foreign capital construction, the preliminary work stage is foremost, generally accounting for 50%-60% of the whole project duration. After the preliminary works are properly done, the work in the subsequent stages will be easily and smoothly completed. At present, China has attached great importance to the quality of infrastructure construction projects, especially the strict implementation of construction procedures to ensure the quality of preliminary work.

Compared with the domestic capital construction procedures, the whole process of project construction overseas is generally divided into three periods, namely pre-investment period, investment period and investment return period, mainly including study of investment opportunities, preliminary feasibility study, feasibility study, project evaluation, base design, engineering design, detailed design, bidding and contracting, construction, completion and operation, production stage, post-engineering evaluation, project termination and other steps.

V. Introduction To Project Construction Budget

The project construction budget is a major basis for the state to determine the investment amount of construction projects, the Client to determine the project cost and prepare the construction plan, the banks to appropriate the project cost, and the Builder to sign business contracts and promote the investment lump sum contracting system and bidding contracting system. The project cost management has two tasks, i.e. first, calculation of project cost, namely that the estimates, estimation, budget estimate, budget, settlement and Final Account upon Completion are correctly prepared based on reasonably determining the construction cost composition and level; and second, project cost control, namely that the technology is combined with economy closely in the investment decision-making, design, bidding, construction and completion stages to effectively control the cost, so that the actual investment of each stage will not exceed the investment amount of the last stage, and the final cost will not exceed the cost limit approved.

The project construction budget includes several items, namely investment estimation, design budget estimate, construction drawing budget, construction budget, engineering settlement and Final Account upon Completion. The relationship among them in the capital construction procedures is shown in Fig. 0-0-1. From the figure, the project construction budget is throughout the whole process of capital construction in the form of value from determining construction projects, determining and controlling the capital construction investment, conducting the economic administration of capital construction and economic calculation of construction enterprises to the final verification of fixed assets of the project. Among them, the design budget estimate, construction drawing budget and Final Account upon Completion are generally called "three calculations" of capital construction for short, which are important contents of the project construction and are organically connected and integral. The budget estimate, budget and final account shall be prepared for design, construction and completion respectively. Generally, the final account amount cannot exceed the budgeted amount, and the budgeted amount cannot exceed the amount after budget estimate. Besides, the construction enterprise shall also prepare the final accounts reflecting the final project cost and used for the project price liquidation. The final accounts and the construction drawing budget and construction budget are called "three calculations" of the construction enterprise together.

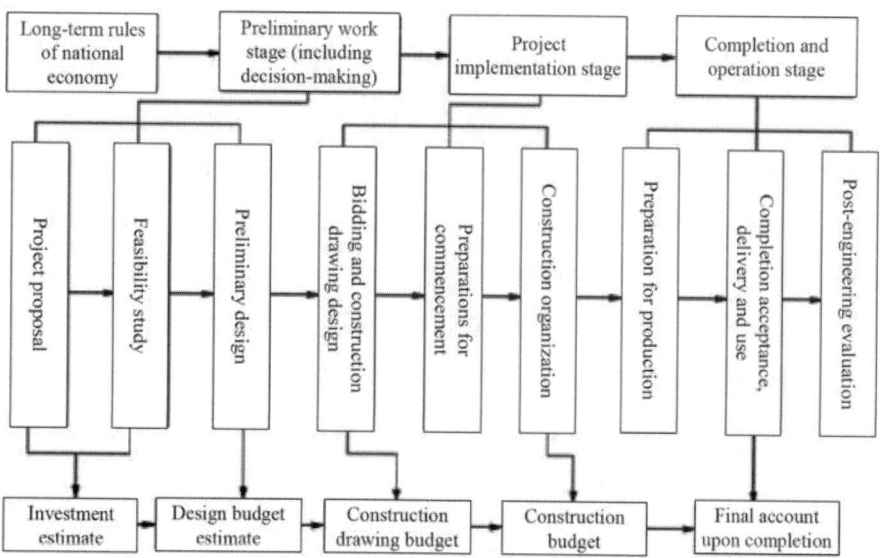

Fig. 0-0-1 Diagram for Capital Construction Procedures and Relationship of Preliminary Budget

Generally, the base number of a tender and bid price prepared in the construction bidding of construction projects also belong to the scope of project construction budget. The base number of a tender prepared by the Client and the tender offer prepared by the construction enterprise are floating for the capital construction products respectively prepared, namely market price. The winning offer is the dealt price of capital construction products.

The design budget estimate and construction drawing budget in the project construction budget play a joint role in preparing the annual capital construction plan, determining the project cost, evaluating the design scheme, signing the engineering contract, appropriation by and loan from banks and final accounts, and are effective means for the state in scientific management and supervision of capital construction. They have similarities in preparation mode as well. However, due to different preparation time, basis, requirements and preparation units, they are different.

(I) Necessity of Project Construction Budget Preparation

The project construction budget is the document to determine the project cost, and its essence lies in a set of procedures and methods used to calculate and adopt the planned prices of capital construction products. The necessity to prepare the project construction budget is first decided by own features of construction products. Compared with general industries, the production of capital construction products has the following features.

1. Construction Sites of Capital Construction Products Are Not Fixed

The capital construction products are built at the selected positions. Different from general industrial products which are produced repeatedly and in batches in the plant, the production conditions of industrial products will not be restrained by time and meteorological conditions. Due to different construction sites of capital construction products, the modeling, material selection, construction schemes, etc. are largely different for the construction products with basically same purposes, functional scale and standards because of diversified geological, meteorological and hydrological conditions of construction sites, so as to influence the product cost. Besides, the standard of wages for workers as well as certain cost standards in different areas, such as material freight and construction costs in winter and rainy season will vary with different construction sites, so that the costs of capital construction products will be largely different.

2. Singleness of Capital Construction Products

Generally, the capital construction products are different. In each works, separate design is required according to specific requirements of the works. Design contents, scale, shape, structure and materials are different. At the same time, due to different nature of the construction projects (new construction, reconstruction, expansion or restoration, etc.), the design requirements are also different. Even if the nature or design standards of the project is the same, the design will be different depending on the geological and hydrological conditions of the construction site. Therefore, the singleness of capital construction products is reflected in the costs of capital construction products.

3. Nature of Exposed Capital Construction Products

The capital construction products generally are produced in the open air. The change of seasons, climate and natural environmental conditions will cause the changes of certain contents and construction methods of product design, and also the expense changes in the prevention of flood, cooling and rain, or temperature reduction. These changes will cause the corresponding cost changes of capital construction products, so that the costs of the capital construction products will not be the same.

The capital construction products have long production cycle, many procedures, wide involved range, and complex social cooperation relation. These characteristics also decide that the value composition of capital construction products cannot be the same. The above characteristics of capital construction products determine that it is impossible to adopt the uniform price as general industrial products. But the price must be determined through a special planning procedure and a separate construction budget prepared for each product.

Besides, the preparation of project construction budget is the requirement for the state to execute the plan and control the market. According to the market demand forecast in the national economic plan, the state arranges each capital construction project in a planned way, and each capital construction project is also called capital construction product. In order to prepare the capital construction plan, it is required to adopt the method of preparing the construction budget according to the capital construction products and their production characteristics to determine the budgeted prices of the capital construction products, and then prepare the capital construction plan according to their prices to determine the investment of each construction project.

(Ⅱ) Investment Estimation

The investment estimation refers to the expected maximum possible value of all construction expenses necessary for the normal production for the construction products from preliminary work to formation of predetermined production capacity. It is the technical and economic documents prepared to determine the total investment amount of construction project when the Client applies for the capital construction investment to the state or the competent departments in the planning, project proposal and feasibility study stages, and the important documents for the state or competent departments to determine the capital construction investment plan.

1. Investment Estimation of Domestic Engineering Projects

The project investment estimation is one of the work phases prior to preliminary design. Before preliminary design, it is required to prepare the project planning and project proposal, and also prepare and estimate the investment estimation amount with different precision according to the clear technical and economic conditions of the project. The investment estimation of construction projects in China is divided into several stages below.

(1) Investment estimation in planning stage. In the project planning stage, the construction planning of a construction project shall be formulated according to the requirements of national economic development planning, regional development planning and industry development planning. The error rate may be greater than or equaling to $\pm 30\%$. This estimate serves as a basis for denying a project or deciding whether it is proceeded for study.

(2) Investment estimation in the project proposal stage. In the project proposal stage, the investment amount necessary for the construction project shall be estimated as per the product scheme, project construction scale, main production processes of products, workshop composition of enterprises, primary location for plant, etc. in the project proposal. Estimate error rate can be controlled within $\pm 30\%$. It is regarded as the economic basis to judge whether the engineering project will be included in the investment plan. According to the investment amount estimated at this stage, a project can be denied, but it is not completely certain whether a project is really feasible.

(3) Investment estimation of feasibility study stage. The investment estimation in the preliminary feasibility study stage mainly conducts a further comprehensive technical and economic analysis on the basis of investment opportunity study and investment estimation for investment scale of the construction project, technology, material sources, construction site selection, organization and construction schedule, to judge the feasibility of the construction project, and make a preliminary investment evaluation and decision. It is the estimate for invested amount after techno-economic demonstration, so the error rate can be controlled within ±20%. It can be regarded as the reference basis to prepare the design assignment.

(4) Investment estimation of review stage. This is the evaluation on the best investment scheme of the proposed project based on the investment estimation in the previous stage from technology, economy, financial system and other aspects, and the conclusive suggestions proposed for the feasibility study of construction project. This stage is for comprehensive, particular and detailed technical and economic analysis and demonstration, and the error of investment estimation shall be controlled within ±10%. The investment estimation in this stage is the main basis to decide the proposed project and select the best scheme, and important basis for preparing the design documents, and controlling the preliminary design and the budget estimate.

(5) Investment estimation of design assignment stage. It is the final estimate and recognition based on the review for the investment amount of engineering project according to reliable data and materials, and the error rate shall be controlled within ±10%. The investment estimation in this stage is the main basis for preparation of investment plan, fund raising and loan application, and is the maximum limit of project cost control.

2. Investment Estimation of Overseas Engineering Projects

The investment estimation of overseas engineering projects is different from that in China. It not only includes the investment estimation in project proposal stage, feasibility study stage and design assignment stage, but also includes the budgets of preliminary design stage and construction drawing design stage in China. In western countries, represented by Britain and the United States, the investment estimation is divided into the following five stages according to the content and depth of research in different stages.

(1) Estimation in the order of magnitudes, also called gross estimate and proportional

estimation. It is equivalent to the investment estimation in the project proposal stage in China. This stage is the opportunity research stage for the invested project. This investment estimation at this time is undertaken by the comprehensive proportion method according to the investment information on similar projects completed. The error rate may be larger than or equaling to ±30%.

(2) Research estimation, also called rough estimation and evaluating estimation. It is equivalent to the investment estimation in the feasibility study stage in China. It is an investment estimate made after the list of main equipment and flow chart have been available and the site has been preliminarily selected. The error rate is about ±30%.

(3) Budgetary estimation, also called preliminary estimate and appropriation estimate. It is equivalent to the investment estimation in the design assignment stage in China. It is estimated based on the existing specification table of equipment and materials, equipment production capacity, general layout of plant, approximate sizes of the building, initial configuration of public facilities and other sufficient information. It can be used as the reference basis to determine whether the engineering project has a future and whether it is included in the investment plan. The error rate is about ±20%.

(4) Determining estimation, also called engineering control estimation. It is equivalent to the investment estimation in the preliminary design stage in China. The error rate is about ±10% as the basis of controlling the construction project investment.

(5) Detailed estimation, also called bidding estimation, final estimation and engineering estimation. It is equivalent to the investment estimation in the construction drawing stage in China. It is based on a complete set of construction drawings, technical instruction documents, list of equipment and materials and other information. Such estimation has a high accuracy, and the error rate is about ±5%, which can be used as the basis to control the investment in the implementation stage of engineering projects.

(Ⅲ) Design Budget Estimate

In the preliminary design (or detailed preliminary design) stage, all construction expenses prepared from preparation to completion acceptance according to preliminary design drawings, budget estimate quotas (or indexes) and other related expenses and quotas are called design budget estimate, which embody the design contents in economy and are important part of design documents.

The budget estimate is the maximum quota of national capital construction investment, and the basis to prepare the capital construction plan, implement the lump sump of capital construction investment and control the construction appropriation and loan and also to assess whether the design scheme and construction cost are reasonable. As specified in the Measures for the Bid Invitation and Bid Tendering for Construction and Engineering Projects, if the base number of a tender is prepared for the bidding project, it can be reasonably determined according to the approved preliminary design, investment budget estimate and related pricing methods by reference to related project quotas combining the market supply and demand in consideration of investment, duration, quality and other factors. Budget estimate plays a role not only in controlling the base number of a tender and investments, but also in controlling the budget. This is because the budget must be kept within 5% of the budget estimate. As soon as the budget estimate is approved by the presiding authority, it shall be regarded as the legal basis for the investment in the construction project. The total investment of design budget estimate shall be calculated at the price level in the same year and cannot exceed the total investment approved in the planning assignment. Once exceeding, the reasons must be analyzed in detail and the reasons and their rationality for exceeding must be emphasized, or the preliminary design must be modified until the requirements are met.

(Ⅳ) Construction Drawing Budget

The construction drawing budget refers to the documents which calculate the manpower, material resources and investment amount required for each project according to construction drawings, construction organization design, budget quotas and project quantities calculation rules issued by the state, budgeted prices of regional materials, standards of construction management fee, planned profit margin, and taxes in the construction drawing design stage. It is the basis to organize material, tools and labor before construction, prepare construction plan, make statistic about the completed workload, deal with the project price settlement, execute the economic accounting, assess the project cost, implement the lump sump of construction projects and appropriation (loan) for engineering by banks. General construction projects take the budget of construction drawings as the basis for preparing the base number of a tender.

The Budget is an important part of the construction drawing materials, which continues the active impact of budget estimate on design. It is an important means for the project cost management by the design unit, the basis for the Builder to determine the project budget cost and assess the actual project cost, and the basis for the bank appropriation and loan, and it can also be used as a base number of a tender.

The relations among the budget and the design, construction, building, etc. are introduced below. The budget reflects the technical advancement and economic rationality of engineering design. The engineering tender and bidding between the Client and the Builder are undertaken based on budget estimate or budget, and the approved budget is the basis for project settlement between the Client and the Builder. The budget is the starting point for the Builder to make reasonable construction organization, formulate and adopt advanced technical measures and construction methods, improve management and reduce project costs.

The construction drawing budget composition is basically similar to that of the preliminary design budget. Their differences are introduced below.

Difference I: The contents of costs prepared are not identical. The design budget estimate includes all construction costs from the preparation to the completion of all items and before delivery. The expense item structure of construction drawing budget is basically consistent with the budget estimate. However, due to different design details, the expense items of construction drawing budget are more detailed and closer to the final construction state of the engineering project.

Difference II: The stages of preparation are different. There is a certain time interval between the preparation of budget and the preparation of budget estimate, during which relevant national and local policies may change. Design changes may occur during the design, which may lead to changes of quantities proposed for the construction drawing design and other factors, and finally cause a certain difference between the budget estimate and the budget.

Difference III: The approval process and its roles are different. The total design budget estimate is a constituent part of preliminary design documents, which shall be submitted to related competent departments for approval as the basis for the construction project and of being formally included in the annual capital construction plan. Only after the preliminary design drawings and total design budget estimate are approved, the construction drawing design can be started. Therefore, it is the basis to control the construction drawing design and total budget. The construction drawing budget is submitted for the preliminary review by the Client and then to the bank for handling, review and affirmation as the basis for appropriation of the project price and the final accounts.

Difference IV: The itemized sizes and quotas adopted for the preliminary budget are different. The design estimate items and quotas adopted are strongly comprehensive. The budget estimate quota is adopted for the design budget estimate, and the budget quota is adopted for the construction drawing budget. The budget quota is the basis for comprehensive budget estimate quota. Besides, the grading items adopted for the design budget estimate and the construction drawing budget are different, and Grade-III items are adopted generally for the design budget estimate. The items more detailed than the Grade-III items are adopted generally for the construction drawing budget.

The investment estimation, budget estimate and budget belong to the scope of technical economy, and they are called investment measurement together. During preparation, they mutually influenced and connected, and are necessary for the completion of a project. However, during traditional preparation, the manual calculation methods are adopted in most case. The calculation workload is large and complicated, and there are many numeric shifts. It is easy to have errors and the calculation lasts longer. Currently, the special "estimate and budget" preparation software has been widely applied. They are generally featured by strong universality

(including transmission and distribution lines), flexibility (local prices or national unified quotas and even the quotas beyond the industry), fastness (preparing and printing the estimate and budget of a project may cost several hours, which is 20-50 times manual preparation), standardization (the form is standardized and unified, and the finished estimate and budget are easy to achieve the standardization), and convenient use

(generally, the Windows platform is adopted for the "estimate and budget" preparation software, and the operation interface is good and easy for use), which has better solve the previous problems of manual preparation of estimate and budget. Therefore, the "estimate and budget" preparation software has been promoted and applied in the power companies and the design and capital construction enterprises at present.

(V) Project Settlement

Project settlement refers to the economic documents that the Builder conducts the project price settlement to the Client for the completed project quantity according to the project construction contract. Generally, the project construction period is long, and a number of funds is consumed. In order to compensate the funds consumed by the Builder in the construction process in a timely manner, it is necessary to settle the project price, generally including: intermediate settlement (progress payment settlement), year-end settlement, and completion settlement after the completion and acceptance of all the projects. The project settlement is a very important work in project contracting. The main function is shown in the following aspects.

1. The Project Settletment Is the Main Index Reflecting the Project Progress

During construction, an important basis of project settlement is the quantities completed, and the project schedule can be approximately reflected through the proportion of cumulatively settled project price in the total contract price.

2. The Project Settlement Is An Important Part of Accelerating Capital Turnover

The Builder shall settle the project payment as soon as possible, which is beneficial to repay the debts, withdraw the funds and reduce the internal operating cost. The service efficiency of funds will be improved by capital turnover acceleration.

3. The Project Settlement Is An Important Index To Evaluate Economic Benefit

For the Builder, only when the project funds are settled in full, it means that the operation risk is avoided, and the Builder can also obtain the corresponding profit, and then achieve good economic benefits.

(VI) Final Account Upon Completion

The Final Account upon Completion refers to the technical and economic documents regarding all expenses prepared by the Client from project preparation to completion and operation in the project completion acceptance stage after all construction items are completed. It is an important link of construction investment management, an important basis for project completion acceptance, delivery and use, and a necessary means for financial summary of construction project and the supervision by bank. It mainly aims at evaluating the investment effect of engineering project, and providing reliable basis for quota modification after sorting out and processing the technical and economic data of construction practice.

The Final Account upon Completion includes the following effects. First, the Final Account upon Completion of construction project is the summary documents

comprehensively and roundly reflect the construction achievements and financial situations of the completed project. Monetary indicators, physical quantity, construction period and various technical and economic indicators are adopted to comprehensively and roundly reflect all construction achievements and financial situations from the commencement to completion of the construction project, and can accurately reflect the actual costs and investment results of the construction project.

Second, the Final Account upon Completion of construction project is the basis for handling asset delivery and use, and also the important constituent part for the completion acceptance report.

Third, it is possible to assess the performance of investment control, draw lessons from the past, accumulate basic technical and economic data and improve the future investment benefit of construction projects through contrastive analysis of Final Account upon Completion with budget estimate and budget.

(VII) Division and Precision Requirements of Project Construction Budget

Due to different data and conditions in different project construction stages, there is differences for the precision of project cost determined by the technical and economic personnel. Their contents, purposes and effects are different, as shown in the Table 0-0-2.

Table 0-0-2　Division Precision Requirements in Construction Budget Stage

S/N	Stage division	Project name	Error rate of investment amount (%)	Remarks
1	Project planning stage	Estimation	≥±30%	1. According to the requirements and contents of the planning, the investment amount required for the project shall be preliminarily determined; 2. It is the basis for denying a project or deciding whether it is proceeded for study
2	Project proposal stage	Estimation	Within ±30%	1. Basis for the approval of project proposal by the competent authority; 2. Negate or determine if the work in the next phase is required for the project
3	Preliminary feasibility study stage	Estimation	Within ±20%	Determine whether a detailed feasibility study is required for the project on this account
4	Detailed feasibility study stage	Estimation	Within ±10%	1. Determine the feasibility of the project; 2. Include it in the annual capital construction plan of the project on this account
5	Evaluation review stage		Within ±10%	1. As the basis for the evaluation of feasibility study results; 2. As the basis for the final decision on the project
6	Preliminary design	Budget estimate	5% ~ 10%	
7	Construction drawing design	Budget	3% ~ 5%	

Study Program I

Preparation for Construction Drawing Budget of 10kV Distribution Line

Project case I Overview of A 10kV New Line Project

I. Overview

(I) Design Basis

(1) Entrusted by a investing company in a city, we carry out the survey and design of a 10kV power distribution project in this city.

(2) Standard for Distribution Line Design Overhead (DL/T 52002-2005).

(3) Other relevant regulations and norms of the state.

(II) Design Scope

A 10kV power distribution project.

(III) Project Overview

(1) Connect line on the #04 pole of the 10kV distribution line (in the same pole for HV and LV), build 3 x new 12m electric poles, and build a new line at a total length of 150m.

(2) Install a HV vacuum circuit breaker (12kV and 630 A) on the new #N3 pole, and bury the 150m cable (YJV22-8.7/15kV-3×50) with 400kVA dry-type transformer.

II. Route and Crossing

(I) Route Overview

Refer to the 10kV Overhead Line Layout Plan for the path of the Project, as shown in Fig. 1-0-1.

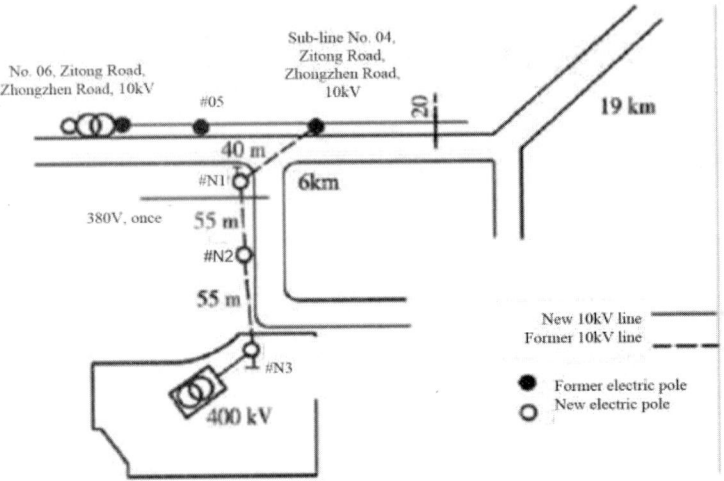

Fig. 1-0-1   10kV Overhead Line Layout Plan

(II) Crossing

The Project also crosses highway and low-voltage 380V line at 1 place respectively.

(III) Transportation

The Project is located in the town, and the terrain proportion of the whole line is 100% of flat ground. The topographic map of transportation is shown in Fig. 1-1-1. Geological proportions of the whole line are 70% for ordinary soil, 20% for pan soil and 10% for muddy water.

III. Mechanical and Electrical Part

(I) Design Meteorological Conditions (Omitted)

(II) Conductor

JKLYJ-10kV-50 insulated conductor is adopted for overhead line of the Project . The safety factor is 7.5, and the safe distance between the overhead line and the surrounding buildings shall meet the requirement of Erection and Acceptance Regulations for Overhead Distribution Lines of 10kV.

(Ⅲ) Lightning Protection and Insulation Coordination

1. The manual earthing body shall be laid on the terminal pole, and the grounding resistance shall meet the requirements of regulations. The suspension point of insulator string and the grounding body shall have reliable electrical connection.

2. The insulators for cement pole erection section shall be FXBW2-10/45, and insulators for intermediate support shall adopt FS-10/3 composite cross arm insulator.

3. Zinc-oxide arrester shall be installed at the place where the disconnector is installed (HYW5-12.7/50).

(Ⅳ) Armor Clamps

The Project adopt power armor clamps of national standard.

Ⅳ. Pole and Tower, and Base

(Ⅰ) Pole and Tower

There are three electric poles (Φ 190 × 12000), including one terminal pole, one angle pole and one straight pole. The assembly drawing is shown in Fig. 1-0-2, Fig. 1-0-3 and Fig. 1-0-4.

(Ⅱ) Base

The concrete pole of the Project adopts the chassis base of D0.8 × 0.8 × 0.17, and the anchor plate of L0.8 × 0.4 × 0.15.

(Ⅲ) Others

(1) The Project is provided with 1 set of disconnector (12kV630A) and 1 set of arrester.

(2) The project drawing applies Typical Design of 10kV and below Urban Power Grid Project.

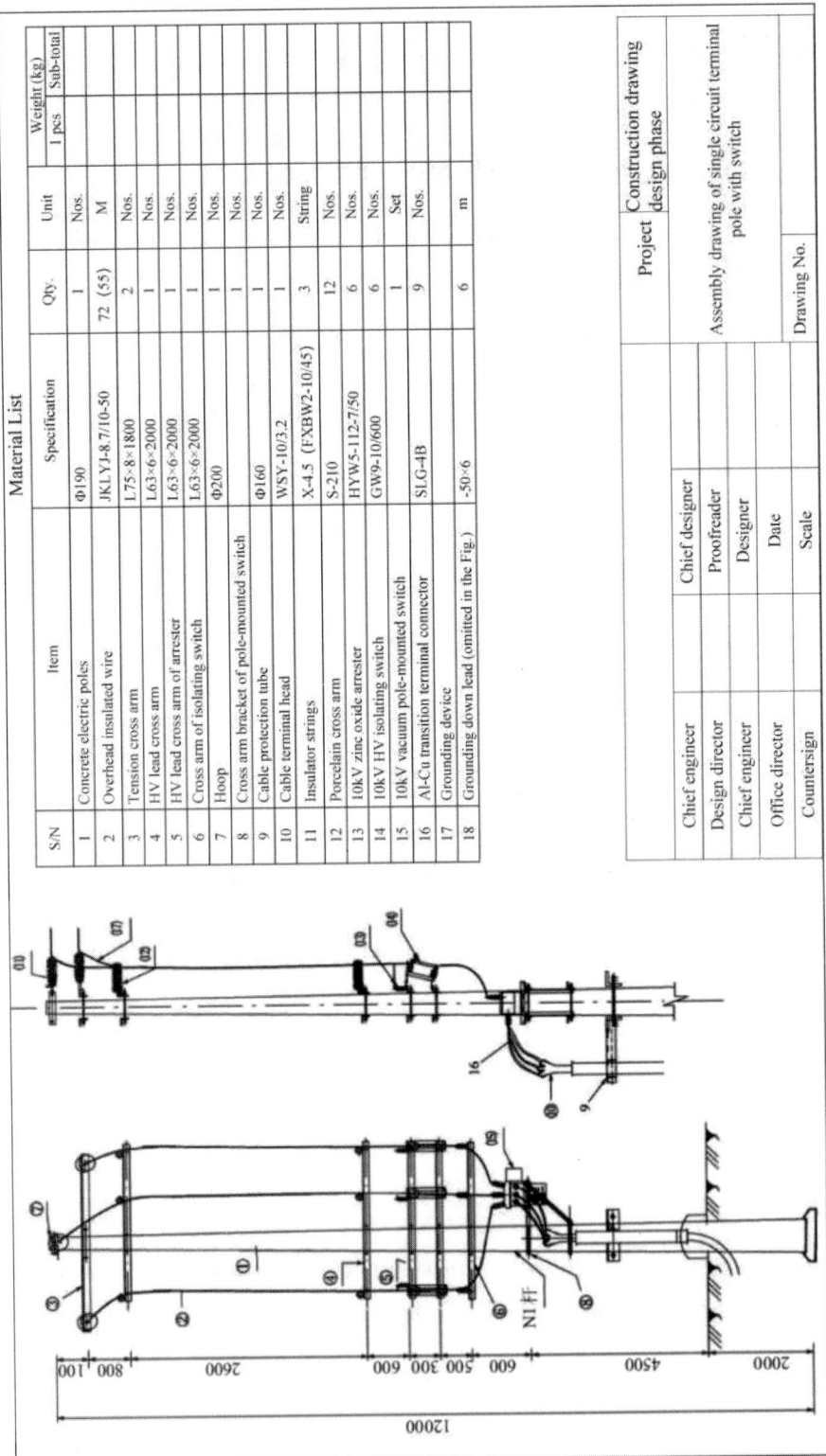

Fig. 1-0-2 Assembly Drawing of Terminal Pole

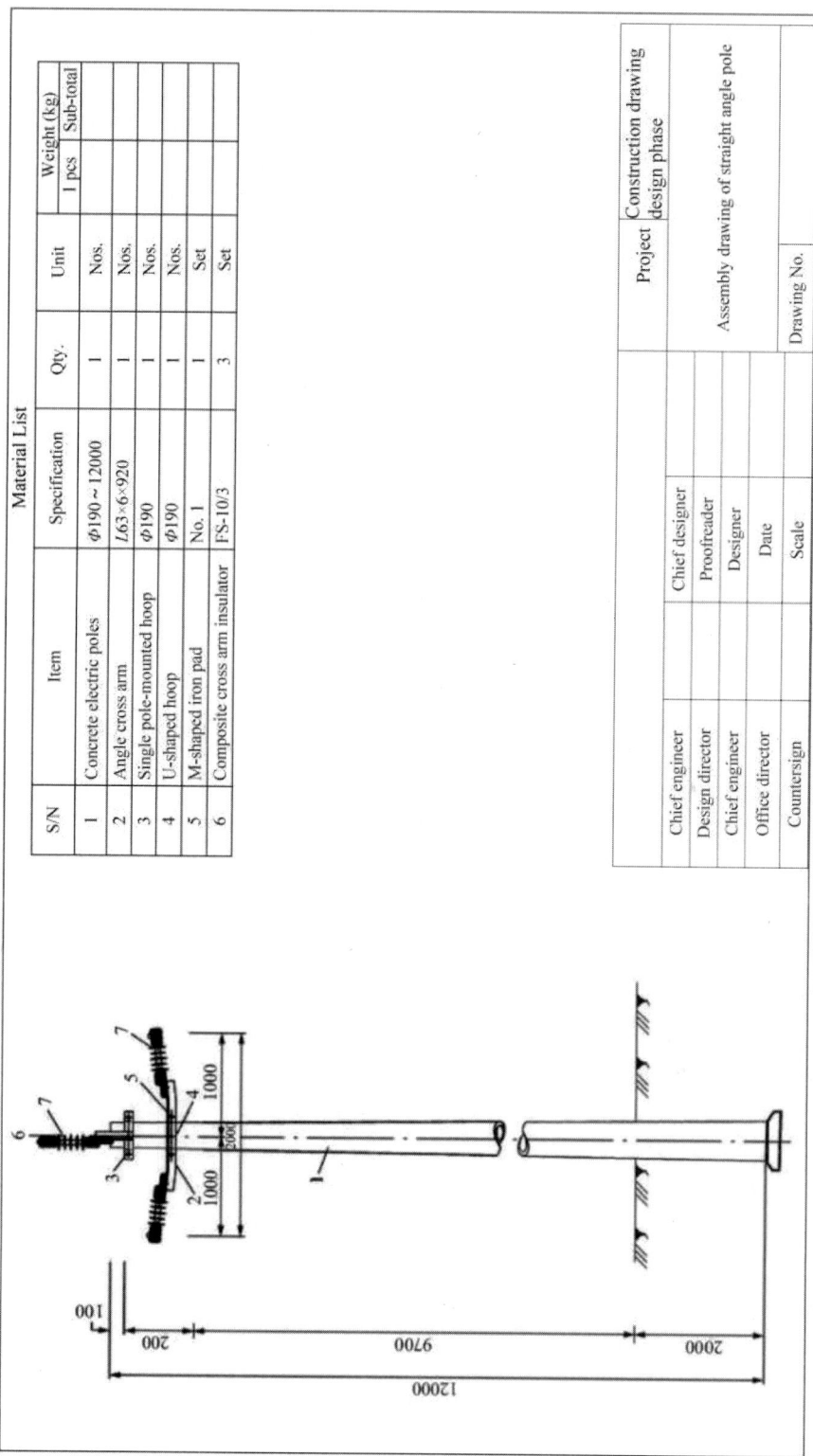

Fig.1-0-3 Assembly Drawing of Straight Corner Pole

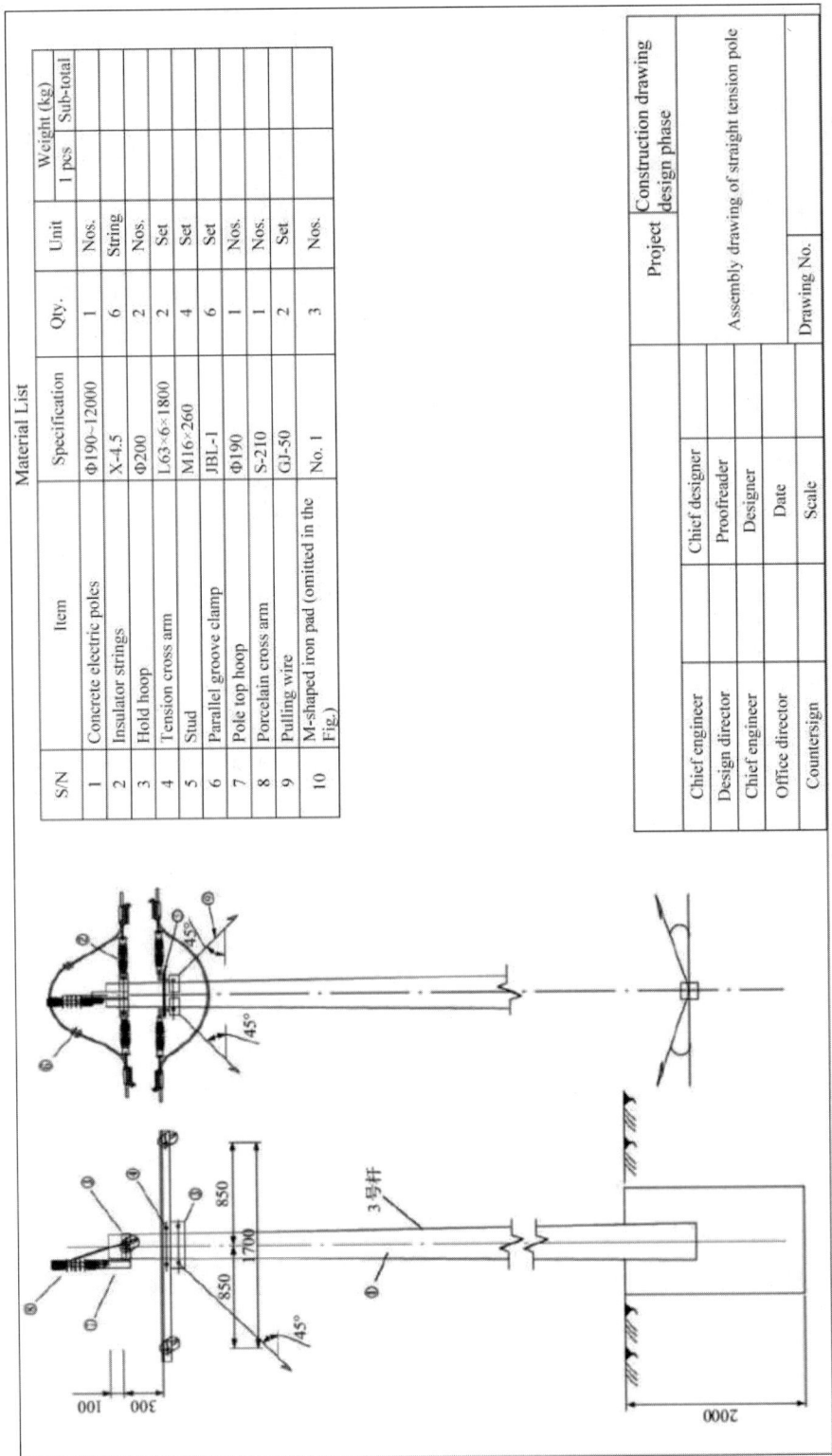

Fig.1-0-4　Assembly Drawing of Angle Pole

Task 1 To Be Familiar with Project Breakdown Structure Of Distribution Line Project

I. Concept

Working drawing estimate refers to the Project cost estimated and determined in advance according to the relevant provisions of construction drawing design documents, detailed estimate norm and cost calculation in the stage of construction drawing design and construction stage; It also refers to the process of preparing, estimating and determining working drawing estimate documents in the stage of construction drawing design and construction.

A construction project is a comprehensive system of different specialties according to production characteristics. Project breakdown is to decompose the construction project scientifically according to the production characteristics, division of labor, as well as the professional division of design and division of drawings so as to facilitate the management.

II. Project Breakdown Basis

The pricing system of power engineering is gradually developed and perfected according to the change of management system of electric power industry in China. At present, in the light of the needs of power project cost management, the pricing basis system of power engineering has gradually formed and improved the Project breakdown and calculation method system, quota system, price information system, project pricing method system and project implementation and evaluation system.

The project breakdown basis of new distribution line project include:

Budget Preparation and Calculation Standard for 20kV and below Distribution Network Engineering Construction, 2016 Edition;

Budget Quota for 20kV and below Distribution Network Engineering Construction,

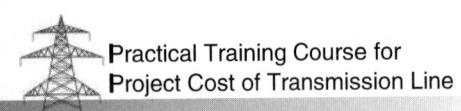

2016 Edition;

Instruction for the Construction Budget Preparation and Calculation Standard for 20kV and below Distribution Network Engineering Construction, 2016 Edition;

Instruction for Budget Quota for 20kV and below Distribution Network Engineering Construction, 2016 Edition;

Price Information of Equipment and Materials for 20kV and below Distribution Network Engineering Construction, 2016 Edition.

III. Project Breakdown Structure of Distribution Line Project

A infrastructure construction project is often large in scale, long in construction period and complex in influencing factors. Therefore, the Project breakdown is carried out so as to facilitate the preparation of infrastructure construction plan, preparation of project cost, organization of material supply, organization of tender & bid, arrangement of construction, control of investment, project payment, economic accounting and other production and operation management needs. According to the internal composition of the Project itself, the construction project is divided into building project, single project, work units, divisional work and subdivisional work. Building project, also known as infrastructure construction project, refers to that all engineering projects constructed at one site or several sites according to one overall design. Single project is part of the construction project. It has independent design documents and can play its production capacity or benefit independently after completion. Work unit is part of the single project. It refers to a project that cannot develop its production capacity independently but has independent construction conditions. Divisional work is part of work unit, which is generally divided by main parts of buildings or types of work. Subdivisional work is the subdivision of divisional work, the most basic constitutional unit of the construction project, and also the simplest construction work.

As the power system is a complex building systems, which contains many types of building groups and covers a wide range, it is difficult to divide it exactly according to the single project, work unit, divisional work and subdivisional work. Therefore, when preparing the preliminary budget of each part of the power system infrastructure project, each part is divided into the first level project, the second level project, the third level project and so on from large to small. The first level project is equivalent to expanded unit project, the sec-

Study Program I Preparation for Construction Drawing Budget of 10kV Distribution Line

ond level project is equivalent to work unit, and the third level project is equivalent to divisional work and subdivisional work.

The distribution network project is the single project, which is generally divided into two levels: the first level is expanded unit project, and the second level is work unit. As shown in Table 1-1-1, "1 station building" belongs to the expanded unit project, "1.1 general civil engineering" belongs to the work unit.

Power distribution line project of 20kV and below are divided into overhead line project and cable line project according to transmission mode. See Table 1-1-1, Table 1-1-2 and Table 1-1-3 for the specific division of national quota.

Table 1–1–1 Table for Construction Project Breakdown

No.	Project name	Major content and scope of work	Technical and economic indicator unit
I. Distribution station (switch station) works			
1	Building construction of the station		Yuan /m^2
1.1	General civil engineering	Including equipment base and pre-embedded steel channel	Yuan /m^3
1.2	Light, ventilation and heating works	Including accidental lighting	
2	Building of complete substation		
2.1	Earthwork and base works		Yuan/set
2.2	Auxiliary facilities of box-type substation		Yuan/set
3	Fire-fighting equipment in station	Including transformer fire fighting, building fire fighting, etc.	Yuan/set
4	Cable trench in station		Yuan/m
5	Road and terrace in station		Yuan/set
5.1	Road in station		Yuan /m^2
5.2	Barrier and terrace		Yuan /m^2
6	Auxiliary facilities in station area		
6.1	Wall and gate		
6.2	Greening in station area		Yuan /m^2
6.3	Drainage in station area	Including civil engineering and equipment piping	
6.4	Retaining wall, slope and flood control ditch		

Table (Cont'd)

No.	Project name	Major content and scope of work	Technical and economic indicator unit
II. Overhead line works			
1	Earthwork		Yuan /m³
2	base works	Including material transportation	Yuan /m³
3	Construction of revetment, retaining wall and drainage ditch	Including material transportation	
III. Cable line works			
1	Cable trench work	Including material transportation, pavement treatment and earthwork	Yuan/km
2	Cable tunnel work	Including material transportation, pavement treatment and earthwork	Yuan/km
3	Cable piping work	Including material transportation, pipe laying, and concrete casting, etc.	Yuan/km
IV. Communication and dispatching automation			
V. Project-related individual works			
1	Road of outside the station		Yuan/m
2	Construction protection measures		

Table 1-1-2 Table for Installation Works Breakdown

No.	Project name	Major content and scope of work	Technical and economic indicator unit
I. Distribution station (switch station) works			
1	Transformer installation		Yuan/kVA
2	Installation of power distribution unit		Yuan/kVA
2.1	10kV (20kV) power distribution device		
2.2	Power distribution device under 1kV		
2.3	Reactive power compensation device		
3	Complete set of substation		Yuan/kVA
3.1	Mounting of box substation		
3.2	Installation of opening / closing and tapping device		
4	Control protection system		Yuan/kVA
5	DC system	Including charging device, DC panel and storage battery	
6	Station power system		Yuan/kVA

Study Program I Preparation for Construction Drawing Budget of 10kV Distribution Line

Table (Cont´d)

No.	Project name	Major content and scope of work	Technical and economic indicator unit
6.1	Station power distribution device		
6.2	Station lighting		
7	Station cable		
7.1	Power cable		Yuan/m
7.2	Control cable		Yuan/m
7.3	Cable ancillary facilities		
7.4	Fire protection of cables		
8	Total station grounding		Yuan / station
9.	Subsystem debugging and test		Yuan / station
9.1	System commissioning		Yuan / station
9.2	Special test items		Yuan / station
II. Overhead line works			
1	Pole and tower works	Including material transport, cross arm assembly, pull wire installation and grounding installation	Yuan / site
2	Stringing works	Including material transport and accessories installation	Yuan/km
3	Pole-mounted power transformation and distribution device	Including transport and commissioning	Yuan/set
III. Cable line works			
1	Installation of cable tray (support and bracket)		Yuan/t
2	Cable laying	Including cable head fabrication	Yuan/km
3	Fire protection of cables		
4	Lightning protection and grounding works		
4.1	Arrester Installation		
4.2	Installation of grounding devices		
5	Commissioning and test		
IV. Communication and dispatching automation			
1	Telecommunication system	Including carrier, administration and dispatching telephone No.	
2	Dispatching automation system		
3	Concentrated reading system		

Table 1-1-3 Table for Other Cost Item Breakdown

No.	Project name	Major content and scope of work
1	Construction site requisition and clearing costs	
1.1	Compensation for land acquisition	
1.2	Waste cleaning cost	
1.3	Construction site rental	
1.4	Compensation for line construction	
2	Construction management cost of the project	
2.1	Project management cost	
2.2	Bidding cost	
2.3	Engineering supervision fee	
3	Technical service cost for project construction	
3.1	Survey fees	
3.2	Engineering design expense	
3.3	Design document review fee	
3.4	Project post evaluation fee	
3.5	Technical and economic standard preparation and management fee	
4	Project construction supervision and testing fee	
5	Production preparation cost	
6	Basic reserve cost	

IV. Project Breakdown of Project Case I

The single project in project case I includes overhead line project and cable line project according to the engineering design data. In the overhead conductor and ground wire installation works, the expanded work unit includes the construction work and the installation work. The work unit of the construction work includes earthwork and base. The work unit of the installation work includes the pole & tower work, line erection work and pole-mounted transformation and distribution device. In the cable line project, the expanded work unit also includes construction work and installation work. The work unit of the construction project includes cable trench work. The work unit of the installation works includes cable laying, cable fire prevention, debugging and test.

Task 2 Measurement of Quantities

The statistics of quantities is the key point of working drawing estimate and is calculated according to the design drawing based on the current budget quota and description of distribution network project issued by the State. The calculation shall be carried out according to the contents of project breakdown.

I. Overhead Line Works

(I) Site Transport

Site transport refers to the transport of materials from the centralized material storage site or scattered warehouse to the pole and tower along the line. According to the current quota provisions, the quantities for site transport include the site transport weight and the site transport distance, which shall be classified and calculated according to the different modes of transport. The 20kV and below distribution line project is different from the line project of higher voltage class, site transport is not listed separately in the Project breakdown, but it is calculated separately in each work. However, the calculation for site transport of different voltage line project is similar. The calculation principle and method are introduced below.

1. Site Transport Mode

The site transport is mainly divided into human-powered transport, cart transport, carriage transport, wooden ship transport, automobile transport and cableway transport. The quantities are calculated according to different modes of transport with selection of different quotas and terrain factors.

2. Calculation of Transport Weight On Site

(1) Calculation method

Budget weight = design weight + loss weight = design weight × (1 + loss rate)   (1-2-1)

Transport weight = budget weight × gross weight coefficient (unit weight) （1-2-2）

Statistics of site transport weight shall be summarized separately according to different transport modes (human-powered transport, automobile transport, ship transport) and material types (concrete pole, steel pipe pole, precast concrete, wires, armor clamp, insulator, sporadic steel, tower materials, sand, stone, lime, cement, brick, earth, water, etc.). The construction loss rate of different materials is as shown in Table 1-2-1.

Table 1-2-1 Table for Construction Loss Rate of Materials

S/N	Material name			Loss Rate/%	S/N	Material name		Loss Rate/%
1	Bare flexible conductor (including good conductor ground wire)	Installation of overhead conductor and ground wire	Other areas	0.4	15	Tension cable clamp		2.0
			Hilly area, high mountain, steep	0.6	16	Preformed armor rods		2.0
		Tension stringing, stringing		0.8	17	Aluminum end clamp		3.0
2	Special jumpers and leads			2.5	18	Cement pressure pipe		2.0
3	Power cable			1.0	19	Concrete pole (including chassis, pull plate, chuck and clamping chuck)		0.5
4	Control cable			1.5	20	Concrete X-beam and cover plate (square, rectangular)		3.5
5	Galvanized steel strand (lightning wire)			0.3	21	Brick, strip stone, block stone		2.5
6	Galvanized steel strand (pull wire)			2.0	22	Commercial concrete		1.5
7	Cable terminal porcelain bushing			0.5	23	Cement, lime, friction reducer	Hilly area, high mountain, steep	7.0
8	Insulator, porcelain cross arm			2.0			Flat ground, hills, river network, swamp	5.0
9	Composite insulator			0.5	24	Stone	Hilly area, high mountain, steep	15.0
10	Reinforcement, section steel (finished product, semi-finished product)			0.5			Flat ground, hills, river network, swamp	10.0

Study Program I Preparation for Construction Drawing Budget of 10kV Distribution Line

S/N	Material name	Loss Rate/%	S/N	Material name		Loss Rate/%
11	Steel conduits	1.5	25	Yellow sand	Hilly area, high mountain, steep	18.0
12	Plastic products (pipes, plates)	5.0			Flat ground, hills, river network, swamp	15.0
13	Fitting	1.0	26	Reinforcement (processing and fabrication)		6.0
14	Bolt, shackles and gasket (excluding anchor bolt of base)	3.0				

Note: 1. The bare flexible conductor and ground wire are calculated according to the design quantity of power transmission line, and the construction loss does not include such length as line sag, jumper etc.
2. The conductor loss rate does not include the length reserved for connection with the electrical equipment.
3. The loss rate of power cables and control cables does not include the length reserved for standby and the length increased due to bending or radian. The power cable for transmission is not calculated with construction loss. It shall be treated as equipment materials and shall not be included in the installation costs.
4. The length of pull wire shall be calculated based on the unfolded length of pull wire (including the reserved length required for fabrication).

(2) Material statistics

1) base works. Prefabricated base is often used in distribution network project, while a small amount of cast-in-place base is used. The prefabricated base shall be counted by "Nos.", "piece" and "group" for different weights; The cast-in-place base is calculated by "m^3" for different grades (based on the concrete volume of single base), and the calculation formula for the estimated consumption of sand, stone and cement is

$$\text{Estimated quantity} = \text{quota quantity} \times (1 + \text{loss rate}) \quad (1\text{-}2\text{-}3)$$

The calculation formula of other quantities is

$$\text{Other quantities} = \text{design quantity} \times (1 + \text{loss rate}) \quad (1\text{-}2\text{-}4)$$

Material weight shall be calculated according to Table 1-2-2 (provided by the designer).

In project case I, there are only prefabricated bases, including 3 chassis bases of D0.8 × 0.8 × 0.17 and 2 anchor plates of L0.8 × 0.4 × 0.15. According to Table 1-2-1, the construction loss rate is 0.5%, and its weight is

Chassis weight = 3 × 274 × (1 + 0.5%) = 827 (kg);

Anchor plate weight = 2×96×(1+0.5%)=193 (kg);

The total weight of the prefabricated base is the sum of the weight of chassis and the weight of anchor plate, 1020kg in total.

2) Pole and tower works. Pole and tower assembly and erection shall be counted by "Nos." according to different weight grades; Pull wire fabrication shall be counted by "Nos.", and the length difference shall be noted; Earthing installation shall be counted by "Nos.", and accessories and armor clamps include all fittings, insulators, etc.

The weight of concrete pole is $1482 \times 3 \times (1 + 0.5\%) = 4476$ (kg); The weight of galvanized steel strand is 20.08kg; The weight of grounding device is 107kg; The weight of iron accessories is 163kg; The weight of insulator is 46.69kg.

3) Statistics for installation materials of overhead conductor and ground wire installation works. The weight of conductor is 159.5kg.

4) Statistics for installation equipment. The equipment installed in project case I includes box-type transformer, circuit breaker, disconnector, lightning arrester, etc. The specific equipment list is shown in table 1-2-3.

5) Cable works. The main materials of cable works include 150m cable (YJV22-8.7/15kV-3×50) with the weight of 524.19kg; One indoor and outdoor cable terminal with the weight of 20.2kg; one cable protection pipe with the weight of 27.5kg; one heat shrinkable sleeve for cable protection pipe with the weight of 4kg; and fire proof blockage with the weight of 30kg. All main materials are as shown in table 1-2-2.

3.Calculation method of average load distance

(1) The location of the site warehouse (material station) is the basis for calculating the average load distance. The reasonable setting of the warehouse (material station) at the construction site is good for saving the transportation cost. The site warehouse shall generally meet the following requirements:

1) Close to the line and the center of the line;

2) Convenient traffic and low transport cost;

3) The site is high and not easy to be flooded;

Study Program I Preparation for Construction Drawing Budget of 10kV Distribution Line

Table 1-2-2 List of Main Materials

No.	Name	Unit	Qty.	Price / Yuan		Weight/kg	
				Unit price	Combined price	Unit weight	Total weight
	Main materials for building						
I	base works						
	Base plate D0.8×0.8×0.17	Piece	3.02	47	141.94	274	827.48
	Anchor plate L0.8×0.4×0.15	Piece	2.01	48	96.48	96	192.96
	Pulling rod	Nos.	2.02	55	111.1	5	10.1
	Sub-total				349.52		1030.54
	Total of main building materials				349.52		1030.54
	Main materials for installation						
II	Overhead line works						
	Concrete pole Φ190×12000	Nos.	3.02	2015	6085.3	1482	4475.64
	Combined iron accessories for 10kV line	t	0.163	7200	1173.6	163	163
	Composite insulator cross arm FS-10/3	Nos.	10.2	126	1285.2	2.6	26.52
	Synthetic insulator string FXBW2-10/45	String	9.18	145	1331.1	2.2	20.17
	Yoke plate	t	0.005	15568	77.84	5	5
	Ring	t	0.001	28945	28.95	1	1
	Socket eye	t	0.004	25858	103.43	4	4
	Strain cable clamp NX-1	Nos.	9.18	198	1817.64	1.2	11.02
	Parallel groove clamp	Nos.	6.12	13.7	83.84	1	6.12
	Overhead insulated wire	m	550	8	4400	0.29	159.5
	Galvanized steel strand GJ-25 ~ 100	t	0.02	5500	110	20.08	20.08
	Wedge clamp	Nos.	2.04	18	36.72	1.76	3.59
	UT-type clamp	Nos.	2.04	33	67.32	3.2	6.528
	Marking tube for pull wire	Nos.	2	24	48	2	4
	Copper strand TJ16 ~ 120	kg	10.1	39.5	398.95	10.1	10.1
	Galvanized grounding flat steel	t	0.061	6200	378.2	61	61
	Angle steel grounding body	t	0.046	6500	299	45.7	45.7
	Sub-total				17725.09		4886.56
III	Cable works						
	Cable YJV22-8.7/15kV-3×50	m	151.5	86	13029	3.46	524.19

Table (Cont´d)

No.	Name	Unit	Qty.	Price / Yuan		Weight/kg	
				Unit price	Combined price	Unit weight	Total weight
	Cable terminal (indoor type)	Set	1.01	570	575.7	10	10.1
	Cable terminal (outdoor type)	Set	1.01	1287	1299.87	10	10.1
	Plastic-coated steel pipe for cable protection pipe	m	2.5	56	140	11	27.5
	Heat shrink sleeve for cable protection pipe	Nos.	1	44	44	4	4
	Fire proof blockage	t	0.03	15120	453.6	30	30
	Sub-total				15542.17		605.89
	Total of main installation materials				33267.26		5492.45

Table 1-2-3 Equipment List

No.	Name	Unit	Qty.	Price		Freight and other charges		Combined / Yuan
				Unit price / Yuan	Combined / Yuan	Rate /%	Combined / Yuan	
	Equipment for installation							
II	Overhead line works							
	Dry type transformer GB11-400kVA	Set	1	122500	122500	1.25	1531.25	124031.25
	High-voltage vacuum breaker12kV/630A	Set	1	18800	18800	1.25	235.00	19035.00
	High voltage disconnector 12kV/630A	Group	1	963	963	1.25	12.04	975.04
	Zinc-oxide lightning arresterYW5-12.7/50	Group	1	890	890	1.25	11.13	901.13
	Combined current transformer	Set	1	20000	20000	1.25	250.00	20250.00
	Sub-total				163153		2039.42	165192.42
	Sum for Installation Equipment				163153		2039.42	165192.42

4) There are enough places and houses that can be rented nearby;

5) Communication and living conditions are very convenient.

(2) Selection of unloading point: The line is divided into several sections and unloading points of the materials are selected according to the route and terrain of the line with combination to the shortest manpower load distance between the traffic lane and the river.

(3) Calculation method of average load distance. The average load distance is calculated with basis to the route map and the weighted averages method is adopted to calculate the average load distance of a certain transport mode in engineering construction with consideration to the factors such as material transport mode, transport topography, transport distance, material supply mode, etc. If many kinds of material transport modes such as automobile transport and human-powered transport are used in the construction of the project, the average load distance should be calculated separately.

The calculation formula for the average load distance of human-powered transport is

$$Y=\sum k_i L_i R_i / \sum L_i \qquad (1\text{-}2\text{-}5)$$

Wherein, Y - average load distance (km);

L_i——Length of each section of line (material quantity);

R_i——Straight-line distance of human-powered transport for materials of each section of line;

k_i——Curvature coefficient. The curvature coefficient of road depends on the transport topography, 1.05-1.1 for flat ground, 1.1-1.2 for river network and swamp, 1.1-1.3 for hills, 1.3-1.5 for mountainous region and 1.6-1.8 for high mountains.

The calculation formula for the average load distance of vehicle and ship transport is

$$Y=\sum L_i R_i / \sum L_i + C \qquad (1\text{-}2\text{-}6)$$

Wherein, Y - average load distance (km);

L_i——Material quantity of each section of the line, represented by the length of each section of the line in the budget;

R_i——Vehicle and ship haul distance of materials for each section of the line from the site warehouse to the unloading point of materials for each section (where if the road or river is parallel to the line, the center of the section shall be taken as the unloading point for calculating the load distance);

C——Exceeding the load distance of the next stop. Exceeding the load distance of the next stop refers to the load distance from the railway station or wharf to the site warehouse exceeding that of next stop in the material-loading price, which can be included in the site load distance according to the provisions in the material-loading price, otherwise, it will not be included.

The material supply mode can be divided into corner supply mode, radiation supply mode, parallel supply mode, etc. according to the actual transport of materials, and the corresponding theoretical calculation formula of average load distance is as follows.

1) See Fig. 1-2-1 for the corner supply mode.

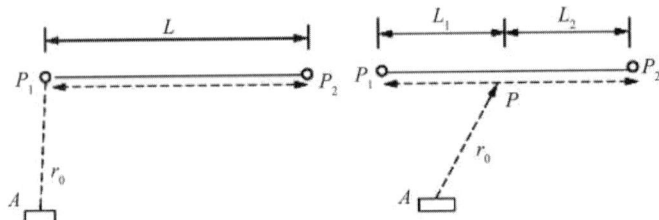

Fig. 1-2-1   Diagram of Corner Supply Mode

TAt this time, the calculation formula of the average load distance is

$$R = \frac{L_1\left(r_0 + \frac{L_1}{2}\right) + L_2\left(r_0 + \frac{L_2}{2}\right)}{L_1 + L_2} \quad (1\text{-}2\text{-}7)$$

$$R = r_0 + \frac{L}{2} \quad (1\text{-}2\text{-}8)$$

Wherein, L_1, L_2, L—— are the length of P_1P, PP_2 and P_1P_2 control line works, and the line path is not a straight line.

r_0——Shortest mileage from material station A to pole and tower location of the line within the scope of supply.

2) When the route of the line project is straight, the radiation supply mode is shown in Fig. 1-2-2.

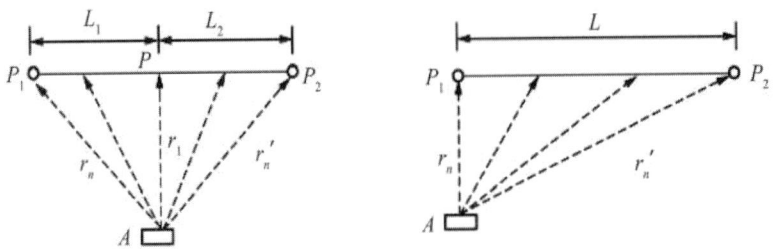

Fig. 1-2-2   Diagram of Radiation Supply Mode when the Route of Line Project is a Straight Line

At this time, the calculation formula of the average load distance is

$$R = \frac{L_1(r_1+r_n) + L_2(r_1+r_n')}{2(L_1+L_2)} \quad (1\text{-}2\text{-}9)$$

$$R = \frac{r_n+r_n'}{2} \quad (1\text{-}2\text{-}10)$$

Wherein, r_0, r_n, r_n' ——shortest mileage from material station A to pole and tower location of the line within the scope of supply.

3) When the route of the line project is corner, the radiation supply mode is shown in Fig. 1-2-3.

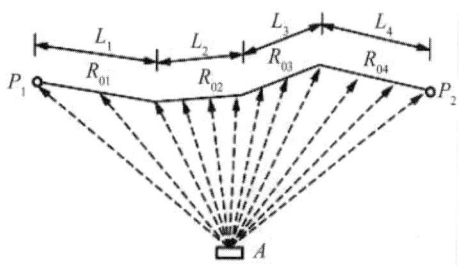

Fig. 1-2-3 Diagram of radiation supply mode when the route of line project is a corner line

At this time, the calculation formula of the average load distance is

$$R = \frac{L_1 R_{01} + L_2 R_{02} + L_3 R_{03} + L_4 R_{04}}{L_1+L_2+L_3+L_4} \quad (1\text{-}2\text{-}11)$$

Wherein, $R_{01}, R_{02}, R_{03}, R_{04}$ ——Average transport radius of each straight line to the material station.

4) When the route of the line project is straight, the parallel supply mode is shown in Fig. 1-2-4.

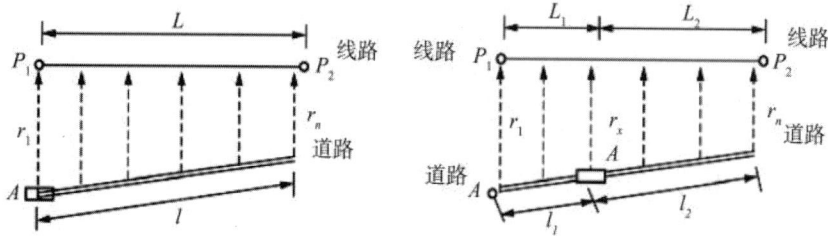

Fig. 1-2-4 Diagram of parallel supply mode when the route of line project is a straight line

At this time, the calculation formula of the average load distance is

$$R = \frac{l+r_1+r_n}{2} \quad (1\text{-}2\text{-}12)$$

$$R = \frac{L_1(l_1+r_1+r_x)}{2(L_1+L_2)} + \frac{L_2(l_2+r_x+r_n)}{2(L_1+L_2)} \quad (1\text{-}2\text{-}13)$$

Wherein, r_1, r_x, r_n ——shortest mileage from material transport path to pole and tower location of the line within the scope of supply.

5) When the route of the line project is a fold line, the parallel supply mode is shown in Fig. 1-2-5.

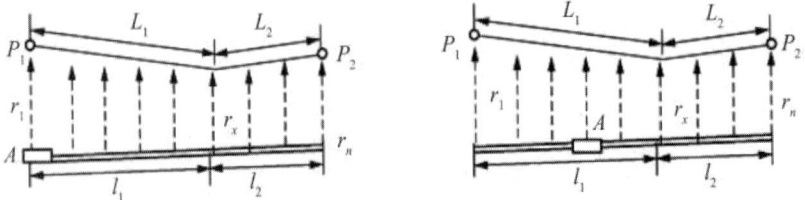

Fig. 1-2-5 Diagram of corner supply mode when the route of line project is a straight line

At this time, the calculation formula of the average load distance is

$$R = \frac{L_1(l_1+r_1+r_x)}{2(L_1+L_2)} + \frac{L_2(2l_1+l_2+r_x+r_n)}{2(L_1+L_2)} \quad (1\text{-}2\text{-}14)$$

$$R = \frac{L_1(l_1+r_1+r_x)}{2(L_1+L_2)} + \frac{L_2(l_2+r_x+r_n)}{2(L_1+L_2)} \quad (1\text{-}2\text{-}15)$$

(4) Average load distance of project case I.

As shown in Fig. 1-0-1, the average load distance of automobile is

19+6=25 (km)

The theoretical value of average manpower load distance with the fold line supply mode is

20+ (40+55+55) /2=95 (m)

Considering the road curvature coefficient of the flat ground is 1.05, and the average load distance of project case I is

95×1.05=100 (m)

(Ⅱ) Earthworks

The calculation of earthwork is to calculate the volume of earthworks for the peak, construction surface, base pit, pull wire pit, grounding groove. The calculation method is related to the specific dimensions and soil type provided by the design. The dimension provided by the design is the static dimension of earthwork volume, and the construction & operation margin, slope coefficient, etc. shall be considered. The value of construction & operation margin and slope coefficient depend on construction & operation method and soil type.

1. Classification of Soil and Stone

(1) Ordinary soil: refers to planting soil, loess, saline-alkali soil, etc., which can be mainly excavated with spade or shovel.

(2) Hard soil: refers to the red soil, tabular clay, heavy block soil and kaolin which are hard to excavate, which shall be loosened with pickaxes and spades and be excavated with spades and shovels.

(3) Loose sandstone: refers to the mixture of break stone, pebble and soil, and various unstable conglomerate, shale and weathered rock. For rocks with many joints and cracks (which do not need to be mined by blasting), it is necessary to use pickaxes, crowbars, sledgehammers, wedges and other tools to excavate.

(4) Rock: refers to all kinds of rocks that cannot be excavated with common tools, and can only be excavated by drilling, blasting or chiseling.

(5) Muddy water: refers to the water often accumulated around the pit, and the soil of the pit is loose, such as mud and mire, which are easily collapsed due to the infiltration of water. The construction can only be carried out with proper drainage and retaining board.

(6) Quicksand: refers to the pit with sand or layered sand, the sand layer has the phenomenon of upwelling and is easy to collapse during excavation, and the construction can only be carried out with drainage and retaining board. If there is no need for drainage, it is a dry sand pit.

(7) Water pit: refers to the one with dense soil, the pit wall is not easy to collapse during excavation, but there is groundwater gushing out, and mechanical drainage is required for construction during excavation.

2. Calculation of Earthwork Excavation Volume of Pole & Tower Base Pit, Pull Wire Pit and Grounding Groove

(1)Cube (without slope), whose calculation formula is

$$V = a^2 \times h \qquad (1\text{-}2\text{-}16)$$

Wherein, V——earthwork volume (m^3);

h——pit depth (m), whose value can refer to table 1-2-4;

a (b) ——pit bottom width of the base pit (m), $a(b)$ = base bottom width + 2 × operation margin on each side.

Table 1-2-5 shows the value of operation margin (excluding cushion) of earthwork excavation.

Table 1-2-4 Reference Table for Buried Depth of Electric Pole

Pole height/m	7	8	9	10	11	12	13	15	18
Buried depth /m	1.2	1.4	1.5	1.7	1.8	2.0	2.2	2.5	2.8

Table 1-2-5 Table of Construction Operation Margin

S/N	Name	Operation margin/m
1	Plain soil pit, hard soil pit, water pit, loose sand pit	0.2m
2	Muddy water pit, quicksand pit, dry sand pit	0.3m
3	Rock pit with formwork	0.2m
4	Rock pit without formwork	0.1m

(2) Cuboid (without side slope, as shown in Fig. 1-2-6), its calculation formula is

$$V = a \times b \times h \quad (1\text{-}2\text{-}17)$$

(3) Frustum (with side slope, as shown in Fig. 1-2-6), its calculation formula is

$$V = \frac{h}{3} \times (a^2 + aa_1 + a_1^2) b \times h \quad (1\text{-}2\text{-}18)$$

Where, a_1 (b_1) ——pit width of base pit (m), a_1 (b_1) = a (b) + 2×h×slope coefficient.

The slope coefficients of all kinds of soil and stone are listed in table 1-2-6.

Table 1-2-6 Slope Coefficient of all Kinds of Soil and Stone

Pit depth	Soil quality			
	Slope coefficient of hard soil	Slope coefficient of plain soil and water pit	Slope coefficient of loose sand and stone	Slope coefficient of muddy water, quicksand and rock
Within 2.0m	1:0.10	1:0.17	1:0.22	No side slope
Within 3.0m	1:0.22	1:0.30	1:0.33	No side slope
3.0m or above	1:0.30	1:0.45	1:0.60	No side slope

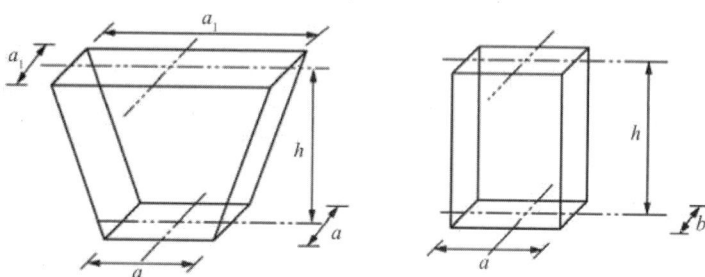

Fig. 1-2-6 Diagram of Cuboid (without Slope) and Frustum (with Slope)

(4) Frustum cylinder (with side slope, as shown in Fig. 1-2-7), its calculation formula is

$$V=\frac{h}{6}\times[ab\times(a+a_1)(b+b_1)+a_1b_1] \quad (1\text{-}2\text{-}19)$$

(5) Cylinder (without side slope, as shown in Fig. 1-2-7), its calculation formula is

$$V=\pi\times r^2\times h] \quad (1\text{-}2\text{-}20)$$

Where, r——Radius (m).

(6) Cylinder frustum (without side slope, as shown in Fig. 1-2-7), its calculation formula is

$$V=\pi r_1^2 h_1+\frac{\pi h_1(r_1^2+r_2^2+r_1r_2)}{3} \quad (1\text{-}2\text{-}21)$$

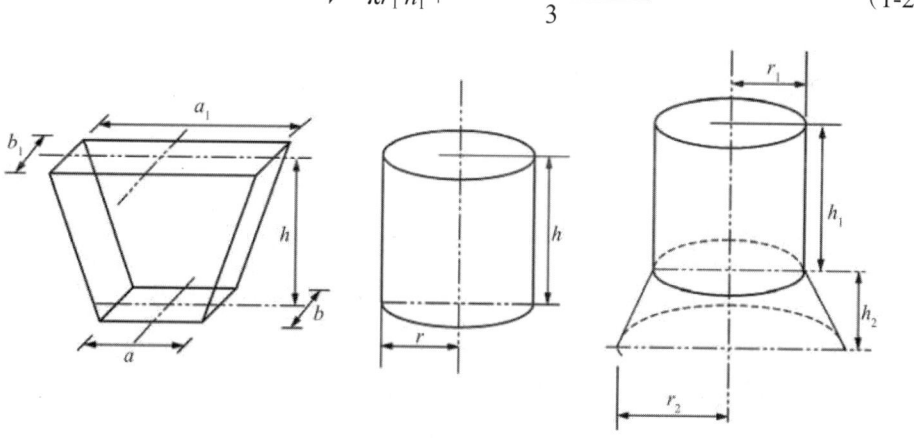

Fig. 1-2-7 Diagram of Frustum Cylinder (with Side Slope), Cylinder (without Side Slope) and Cylinder Frustum (without Side Slope)

(7) For electric pole pit without chassis or chuck, the calculation formula is

$$V=0.8\times0.8\times h \quad (1\text{-}2\text{-}22)$$

If $h\geqslant 1.5$ m, it shall be treated as side slope. For electric pole with chuck, if the original pit size calculated cannot meet the installation requirements, additional earthwork volume due to the extra long chuck shall be calculated separately.

(8) The calculation formula for earthwork volume of the grounding groove is

$$V=0.4\times \text{length} \times \text{groove depth} \tag{1-2-23}$$

(9) Earthwork volume quota of bridle path is $0.2m^3$

Description:

1) All kinds of soil and stone are determined according to the design geological data and there is no need for layered calculation. When there are two or more kinds of soil and stone in the same pit, groove and ditch, the one with higher content is generally selected. In case of quicksand layer, the whole pit is calculated as quicksand pit no matter how much soil is at the upper layer.

2) The volume of earthwork, which is over excavated due to a small collapse in the process of excavation, or that is over blasted due to the difficulty of human control in the process of rock blasting, has been included in the quota.

3) For the calculation of earthwork volume of the grounding groove, if the grounding device needs the friction reducer, the groove width can be calculated as 0.6m when there is no provision in the design.

4) The backfilled soil shall be considered as the original excavation, original filling and remaining soil leveling, excluding the backfilling of soil taken (replaced) and outward transport for the surplus soil above 100m. When necessary, the peak excavation and site transport quota can be applied separately according to the soil replacement proportion and average load distance specified in the design.

5) The disposal of surplus soil shall not be considered for the general project. If necessary, the surplus soil can be considered to be transported to the allowable dump land, and for the transport distance more than 100m, it can be included in the site transport.

Calculation of surplus soil transport weight:

① Drilling muck of cast-in-place concrete pile: It is calculated according to the volume (M^3) $\times 1.7t/m^3$ ($0.2t/m^3$ is the water content) of the part below the design zero meter of the pile;

② Cast-in-place and prefabricated base pit residual soil: it is calculated by the volume of concrete (m^3) $\times 1.5t/m^3 \times 30\%$;

③ Digging and excavated pile base pit residual soil: It shall be calculated by the volume of concrete (m^3) $\times 1.5t/m^3$.

6) For the excavation and filling volume of muddy water and quicksand pit, the necessary drainage and the installation and removal of retaining board have been considered respectively. When the quota is applied, it will not be calculated separately.

7) The manual excavation of rock pit refers to those in the vicinity of substations, power plants, communication lines, power lines, railways, residential areas and national scenic spots, etc., which can not be blasted as required by the design with restriction to the site topography or objective conditions.

8) Provisions for several special conditions:

① If the thickness of frozen soil is ≥300mm, the excavation volume of frozen soil layer shall be the excavation quota of hard soil multiplied by the coefficient of 2.5, and other soil layer shall still apply the original quota according to the geological regulations;

② Excavation and filling of rock pit, if drainage is required, is the manpower quota of excavation and filling (rock) multiplied by coefficient of 1.05;

③ When high and low leg poles and towers are encountered in the line resurvey pit, the corresponding quota shall be multiplied by the factor of 1.5, and the quota of triple pole shall be multiplied by the factor of 1.5; When crossing the houses, 0.7 working days shall be added;

④ If the base pit of digging pile and excavated base pit are of rock, the corresponding quota of rock-embedded base pit excavation shall be applied (originally only for self-supporting tower);

⑤ If the base pit of digging pile and excavated base pit are of loose sandstone, the coefficient of 1.3 shall be multiplied by the hard soil quota of the corresponding digging pile base pit and excavated base pit.

3. Earthwork Volume Statistics of Project Case I

Project case I includes three pole pits and two pull wire pits with the pole height of 12m. The size of chassis base is D0.8×0.8×0.17,

$$a = 0.8 + 2 \times 0.2 = 1.2 \text{ (m)}$$

As the pole height is 12m, h is taken as 2.0m according to table 1-2-4

As $h > 1.5$ m, the slope coefficient takes ($\mu = 0.17$),

$$a_1 = a + 2 \times h \times \mu$$
$$= 1.2 + 2 \times 2 \times 0.17$$
$$= 1.88 \text{ (m)}$$

$$V = h/3 \ (a^2 + a \times a_1 + a_1^2) + 0.2$$
$$= 2/3 \ (1.22 + 1.2 \times 1.88 + 1.88^2) + 0.2$$
$$= 5.02 \ (m^3)$$

Therefore, the total earthwork volume for 3 bases of the pole pits is 15.06m³.

The size of anchor plate is $L0.8 \times 0.4 \times 0.15$,

$$a = 0.8 + 2 \times 0.2 = 1.2 \ (m)$$
$$b = 0.4 + 2 \times 0.2 = 0.8 \ (m)$$

h is taken as 1.8m, therefore

$$a_1 = a + 2 \times h \times \mu$$
$$= 1.2 + 2 \times 1.8 \times 0.17$$
$$= 1.81 \ (m)$$
$$b_1 = b + 2 \times h \times \mu$$
$$= 0.8 + 2 \times 1.8 \times 0.17$$
$$= 1.41 \ (m)$$
$$V = h/6[a \times b + (a + a_1) \times (b + b_1) + a_1 \times b_1]$$
$$= 1.8/6[1.2 \times 0.8 + (1.2 + 1.81) \times (0.8 + 1.41) + 1.81 \times 1.41]$$
$$= 3.05 \ (m^3)$$

Therefore, the total earthwork volume for 2 bases of the pull wire pits is 6.10m³.

(Ⅲ) Base Works

The base works includes the prefabricated base, cast-in-place base, steel pipe pile base, etc. For prefabricated base, the number of chassis, chuck and pull wire shall be calculated; For cast-in-place base, the quantities of reinforced concrete shall be calculated. Since prefabricated base is widely used in 20kV and below distribution network project, the statistics of prefabricated base quantities are mainly introduced hereinafter. Cast-in-place base and other bases will be introduced in relevant chapters.

The base work of project case I includes 3 chassis and 2 anchor plates.

(Ⅳ) Tower Works

The pole & tower assembly and erection includes the wooden pole assembly, concrete pole assembly, steel tube pole assembly and tower assembly. Concrete poles are widely used in 20kV and below distribution network system, so hereinafter we mainly talk about the statistics of relevant quantities of concrete poles.

The first thing to be considered for the quantities of concrete pole and tower project is how many bases there are for concrete pole assembly, including the number of integral type and that of segmented type. In project case I, 3 concrete poles for assembly and erection are integral type; As there is no segmented concrete pole, it is not necessary to consider the quantity of steel ring welding; The installation number of cross arms and insulator shall be calculated according to the design drawings and 5 sets of single cross arm and 2 sets of double cross arm shall be installed here; There are 10 sets of composite insulated cross arms (3 sets of straight poles and 7 sets of tension poles), 9 strain insulators and 2 pull wires; Finally, the number of grounding devices shall be calculated according to the design, and there is only 1 set of grounding devices in project case I.

(V) Overhead Conductor and Ground Wire Installation Works

Overhead Conductors and Ground Wire Installation Works is divided into erection of bare aluminum stranded conductor, steel-cored aluminum stranded conductor, insulated copper strand, insulated aluminum strand, steel strand and bundle conductor, laying of low-voltage overhead power cable, conductor crossing and household wire erection according to different conductor materials and erection methods. In project case 1, XLPE insulated conductor with aluminum core (JKLYJ-10kV-50) is adopted, so the total length of the conductor is calculated to be 3 times of the erection length. With consideration to 20% of the total length increased for conductor relaxation and reserved wire length and 1.8% of the loss, the quantity of conductor is

$$3 \times 150 \times (1+20\%) \times (1+1.8\%) = 550 \text{ (m)}$$

The project also crosses highway and low-voltage 380V line at 1 place respectively.

(VI) Installation of Pole-mounted Power Transformation and Distribution Equipment

The installation of pole-mounted transformer and distribution equipment includes the installation of pole-mounted oil-immersed transformer, amorphous transformer, single-phase transformer, installation of pole-mounted distribution device, installation of grounding ring and insulation shield. Project case I only involves 1 pol-mounted circuit breaker, 1 set of disconnector, 1 set of arrester, 1 set of current transformer and 1 set of dry-type transformer.

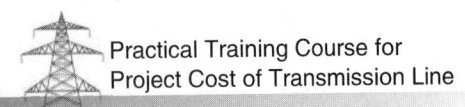

II. Cable Works

(I) Cable Trench and Protection Pipe Laying

Cable trench and protection pipe laying belongs to cable construction works, which includes breaking the road surface, digging and filling of directly buried cable trench and moving cover plate, laying of cable protection pipe and jacking of steel pipe on the way.

The installation methods of power cables include direct burying, pipe laying, shallow trench laying, cable trench laying, cable tunnel laying, overhead laying and so on. There are some differences in the calculation of earthwork volume according to different laying methods. As there is only one 10kV power cable to be buried in the project, and at the road edge which is not to be excavated frequently, the direct buried laying method is adopted.

1. Breaking the Road Surface

Five kinds of pavement are considered for the quantity calculation of breaking the road, namely concrete pavement, asphalt concrete pavement, sand and break stone pavement, precast slab pavement of walkway, and colorful precast slab pavement of walkway.

(1) Concrete pavement, asphalt concrete pavement, sand and gravel pavement, (colorful) precast slab pavement of walkway shall be calculated in "m^2" according to the pavement thickness of actual pavement type. If it is not specified in the design document, it can be calculated according to the following formula.

The excavated pavement area of directly-buried cable trench is

$$S = D \times L \qquad (1\text{-}2\text{-}24)$$

Where, D——width of trench-excavated pavement, general width $D = 0.6 + 0.17(n-1)$, n is the number of cables to be laid;

L——Length of trench-excavated pavement.

(2) The thickness of precast slab pavement for walkway is considered as 60mm, and the thickness of colorful precast slab pavement for walkway is considered as 120mm. No matter what the actual thickness is, no adjustment will be made. It is calculated in "m^2" of excavated area.

(3) When the precast slab pavement of urban walkway is laid in the shape of "triangle",

the width of the excavated pavement can be calculated according to the average width of the actual excavated trench (including the overlapping part).

Project case 1: The cable is laid under sand and break stone pavement at the edge of the housing estate, and the quantity is

$$D=0.6 \text{ (m)}$$
$$S=0.6\times150=90 \text{ (m}^2\text{)}$$

2. Excavation and Filling of Directly-buried Cable Trench and Moving Cover Plate

Earthwork volume for excavation and filling of directly-buried cable trench can be calculated according to Table 1-2-7 except for special requirements.

Table 1-2-7 Earthwork Volume for Excavation of Directly-buried Cable

Item	No. of cable	
	1~2	Each additional cable
Excavation volume per meter of trench /m³	0.45	0.153

(1) For cable trench with two cables, the earthwork volume shall be calculated as per the width of upper opening of 600mm, the width of lower opening of 400mm and the depth of 900mm

$$(0.6+0.4) \times 0.9/2 = 0.45 \text{ (m}^3\text{)}$$

(2) 4 For each additional cable, its width is increased by 170mm, and the increased earthwork volume is

$$0.17 \times 0.9 = 0.153 \text{ (m}^3\text{)}$$

The earthwork volume of project case I is $0.45\times150=67.5$ (m³).

3. Installation of Sealed Cable Protection Pipe

The quantity shall be calculated as "Nos." and there is only 1 in project case I.

(II) Cable Laying

1. Power Cable Laying

Cable laying belongs to cable installation works. Power cable laying includes directly-buried power cable laying, power cable laying in cable trench (tunnel), cable laying in electricity channel, power cable laying along bracket and wall.

Project case I is directly-buried power cable, and the quantity is calculated as 150m.

2. Fabrication and Installation of Cable Head

The manufacturing and installation of cable head includes the manufacturing and installation of power cable terminal head, middle head of power cable and terminal head of elbow power cable. The quantity is calculated as fabrication and installation of indoor and outdoor terminal head, fabrication and installation of power cable middle head or fabrication and installation of hot (cold) shrink head and elbow power cable terminal head with "set / three-phase" unit. Project case I includes 1 set of indoor and 1 set of outdoor terminal head.

(Ⅲ) Cable Fire Protection

The fire protection of cable includes the installation of fire proof blockage, fireproof barrier, fireproof slot box, fire belt and firewall. Wherein:

(1) The fire belt is calculated in "100m" according to the design length;

(2) The fire-proof blockage is calculated by the weight "t" of the plugging material;

(3) The fire baffle plate is calculated by the area "m^2" of the baffle plate;

(4) The fire retardant coating is calculated by the weight "kg" of the coating;

(5) The fireproof slot box is calculated in "100 m" according to the design length;

(6) The firewall is calculated by the vertical projected area of the wall in "m^2" without deducting the hole area.

(7) Project case I adopts fire proof blockage, which is 0.03t.

(Ⅳ) Cable Test

Cable test includes cable insulation shake test, DC withstand voltage test, AC withstand voltage test, resistance ratio test and cable partial discharge test. The cable test is calculated by "loop" and there is 1 loop in project case I.

Table 1-2-8 List of Quantities

S/N	Name	Unit	Qty.	Remarks
	Site transport - human-powered transport			
1	Precast concrete products	t·km	0.102	
2	Concrete pole	t·km	0.448	
3	Armor clamp, insulator and sporadic steel	t·km	0.043	
4	Wire rods	t·km	0.02	
5	Cable	t·km	0.052	
	Site transport - automobile load			
6	Precast concrete products	t	1.02	
7	Concrete pole	t	4.48	
8	Armor clamp, insulator and sporadic steel	t	0.43	
9	Wire rods	t	0.19	
10	Cable	t	0.52	
	Site transport - automobile transport			
11	Precast concrete products	t·km	25.5	
12	Concrete pole	t·km	112	
13	Armor clamp, insulator and sporadic steel	t·km	10.75	
14	Wire rods	t·km	4.75	
15	Cable	t·km	13	
	Earthwork			
16	Pole pit	m^3	15.06	
17	Pull wire pit	m^3	6.10	
	Base installation			
18	Installation of base plate	Piece	3	
19	Pull plate installation	Piece	2	
	Tower erection			
20	Assembly and erection of concrete pole	Site	3	
21	Installation of single cross arm	Group	5	
22	Installation of double cross arm	Group	2	
23	Installation of insulated cross arm —— straight pole	Group	3	
24	Installation of insulated cross arm —— tension pole	Group	7	
25	Insulator installation	Nos.	9	
26	Installation of pull wire	Nos.	2	

S/N	Name	Unit	Qty.	Remarks
27	Fabrication of angle steel grounding body	t	0.045	
28	Installation of grounding electrodes	Nos.	6	
	Stringing works			
29	Installation of conductor	m	550	
30	Conductor cross	Position	2	
	Pole-mounted power transformation and distribution device		1	
31	Disconnector	Group	1	
32	Circuit breaker	Group	1	
33	Arrester	Group	1	
34	Current transformer	Group	1	
35	Transformer			
	Cable works			
36	Breaking the Road Surface	m^2	90	
37	Cable trench Excavating & backfilling	m^3	67.5	
38	Sealing of cable protection tube	Nos.	1	
39	Fire protection of cables	t	0.03	

Task 3 Apply the Quota and Fill in the Table

Quota refers to the quantity standard of labor, materials, mechanical equipment and fund required to complete the qualified products under normal construction conditions according to the productivity level of a certain period. It can be divided into investment estimate target, budget estimate quota or budget estimate target, budget quota and construction quota according to quota preparation procedure and purpose. Among them, the construction quota refers to the standard of labor, material and construction machinery required by a certain type of work to complete the qualified products (such as piling, bricklaying, concrete pouring, etc.) of a certain measurement unit under the construction technology level and conditions within a certain period, and reflects the labor productivity level of that period. Budget quota is the basis for preparing the budget of construction drawing design at the construction drawing design stage and is formed by comprehensive expansion of construction quota. The budget estimate target is the basis for the preparation of preliminary design estimate and revised estimate. It is based on budget quota and is prepared through appropriate comprehensive expansion based on general drawings, standard drawings and other data. The investment estimate target is used as the basis for technical and economic comparison or construction investment estimation in the feasibility study stage. It is prepared by the comprehensive expansion of budget estimate quota and the analysis of statistical data.

Budget quota is selected for working drawing estimate. Budget quota consists of labor quota, material quota and construction machinery quota. Labor quota refers to the labor consumption of working procedure, including basic labor and other labor, and the unit is the comprehensive working day. Labor unit price includes basic labor wage and wage subsidy. Labor quota multiplied by labor unit price is the labor cost. Material quota refers to the materials consumption of working procedure, that is, amount of materials directly consumed in the installation work and the specified loss, including the priced materials and unpriced materials. The material cost is obtained by multiplying the material quantity by the material unit price. Construction machinery one-shift quota refers to the number of all kinds of machinery

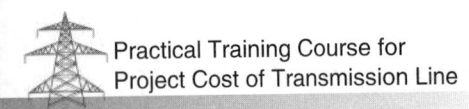

(including vehicles for going to and getting off the work) used by the normal and reasonable allocation of mechanical equipment ——mechanization degree of the construction enterprise for a certain working procedure. The construction machinery one-shift quota multiplied by the unit price of one shift equals to the machinery cost, or the cost of using construction machinery.

I. Overhead Line Works

The quota for overhead line works shall be selected from Budget Quota for 20kV and below Distribution Network Engineering Construction (Volume III Overhead Line Works), 2016 Edition. The quota was issued by National Energy Administration on January 3, 2017, which is the basis for the preliminary budget of current distribution network project. The base unit price per work day in the quota is: 43.0 Yuan / work day for unskilled workers, 61.0 Yuan / work day for construction skilled workers, and 65.0 Yuan / work day for installation skilled workers. 68.0 Yuan / work day for professional skilled workers of the line and 120.0 Yuan / work day for live-working skilled workers. Earthwork and base work belong to construction works, and budget sheet of work units of construction project shall be completed according to the quota. Pole and tower works, overhead conductor and ground wire installation works, pole-mounted power transformation and distribution devices belong to installation works and budget sheet of work units of installation project shall be completed according to the quota.

(I) Earthworks

According to the quota, the earthwork include line resurvey and pit division, excavation (or blasting) and backfilling of pole pit, pull wire pit and self-supporting tower pit, excavation (or blasting) and backfilling of grounding groove, excavation of drainage ditch, excavation of peak and construction base surface. Among them, the Project involves line resurvey and pit division, excavation (or blasting) and backfilling of pole pit and pull wire pit.

1. Line Resurvey and Pit Division

The contents of line resurvey and pit division include: Resurvey of pile position and span length, determination of pit position, pit boundary and construction base surface, recov-

Study Program I Preparation for Construction Drawing Budget of 10kV Distribution Line

ery of main pile or auxiliary pile after loss or change, verification of plane and section, and transport of tools and instruments.

Quota for line resurvey and pit division is shown in table 1-3-1.

Table 1–3–1 Line Resurvey and Pit Division Quota (from Volume III of Budget Quota for 20kV and below Distribution Network Project)

Unit: site

Quota No.			PX2-1	PX2-2	PX2-3	PX2-4	PX2-5	PX2-6
Item			Single pole	Double straight pole	Tension (corner) double pole	Straight self-supporting tower	Tension (corner) self-supporting tower	Crossing the houses (Place)
	Base price/ Yuan		35.76	53.68	72.78	64.74	87.90	13.60
Where	Labor cost		14.19	20.34	30.27	35.00	52.50	13.60
	Material expenses		20.36	31.52	40.08	27.01	31.45	
	Machinery cost		1.21	1.82	2.43	2.73	3.95	
	Name	Unit	Qty.					
Labor	Unskilled workers	Man-day	0.09	0.13	0.19	0.22	0.33	0.40
	Skilled workers (installation)	Man-day	0.21	0.30	0.45	0.52	0.78	
Priced-materials	Round nail	kg	0.010	0.010	0.010	0.010	0.010	
	Common enamel paint	kg	0.020	0.020	0.030	0.025	0.030	
	Wood pipe	Nos.	5.000	8.000	9.000	8.000	10.000	
	Bamboo pile	Nos.	16.000	24.000	35.000	16.000	16.000	
Machinery	Special truck for power transmission with loading weight of 4t	Set/shift	0.004	0.006	0.008	0.009	0.013	

In project case I, all is single pole, so the quota PX2-1 is selected, that is, the base price of quota is 35.76 Yuan, including labor cost of 14.19 Yuan, material cost of 20.36 Yuan, and mechanical cost of 1.21 Yuan; Then quantity 3 is taken, the calculated amount is 107.28 Yuan.

Among which, labor cost is 42.57 Yuan, material cost is 61.08 Yuan and machinery cost is 3.63 Yuan. Fill in the budget sheet of work units of construction project and see table 1-3-2.

Table 1-3-2 Earthworks——Work Unit Budget Sheet

S/N	Basis of preparation	Project name	Unit	Qty.	Equipment unit price	Quota base price Amount	Quota base price Where in: Salary	Main materials	Equipment expenses	Total expenses Amount	Total expenses Where in: Labor cost	Main materials
II		Overhead line works										
1		Earthwork										
	PX2-1	1. Line resurvey and pit division (single pole)	Site	3.00		35.76	14.19			107.28	42.57	
	PX2-7	Excavation (or blasting) of electric pole pit and backfilling of common soil pit with the depth less than 2.0m	m³	15.06		11.46	10.37			172.59	156.17	
	PX2-7	Excavation (or blasting) of pull wire pit and backfilling of common soil pit with the depth less than 2.0m	m³	6.10		11.46	10.37			69.91	63.26	
		Sub-total								349.78	262.00	

2. Excavation (Or Blasting) and Backfilling of Pole Pit, Pull Wire Pit and Tower Pit

First, select the quota according to the soil quality, and then select the quota according to the excavated pit depth. (It is mainly plain soil in project case I, select the quota PX2-7, PX2-8 and PX2-9. As the depth of pole pit and pull wire pit is within 2.0m, PX2-7 (the base price of quota is 11.46 Yuan, including labor cost of 10.37 Yuan and machinery cost of 1.09 Yuan) is selected. Then, with the quantities calculated above, it is calculated that amount of pole pit is 172.59 Yuan, including labor cost of 156.17 Yuan and machinery cost of 16.42 Yuan; The amount of pull wire pit is calculated to be 69.91 Yuan, including labor cost of 63.26 Yuan and machinery cost of 6.65 Yuan. Fill in Table 1-3-2.

Through calculation we can get that the direct labor cost of earthwork is 349.78 Yuan, including 262.00 Yuan of labor cost, 61.08 Yuan of material cost and 26.70 Yuan of machinery cost.

(Ⅱ) Base Engineering

1. Site Transport

As site transport is not listed separately in the Project breakdown of 20kV and below distribution line project and it is calculated separately in each work, statistics are made one by one in the Project with material transportation. The content of base work includes the material transport, so the site transport of corresponding materials is added to the project.

(1) According to the quota, the site transport quota includes human-powered transport, automobile transport and ship transport. The average load distance of various transport mode is in "km" and the weight of materials is in "t".

(2) Human-powered transport

Select the required quota according to the average human-powered transport distance. The average human-powered transport distance of the Project is 200m, and the quota PX1-2 is selected; The work content is: visual inspection of line and equipment, binding and transport, unloading to the specified place and return after transport; The unit is: t·km.

According to the type of goods to be transported, select the required quota and fill in the corresponding table, and then fill in the quantities calculated previously. The main material transported in the base works is mainly the precast concrete products (Pull wire belongs to sporadic steel, quantities is too small and is just 0.01t, it will be calculated together with the site transport of tower and pole works), and the quota selected is PX1-2. It has been calculated that the transport weight is 1.02t, the load distance is 0.1km, then it should be 0.102t·km, and the cost is 19.51 Yuan, including labor cost of 17.75 Yuan and machinery cost of 1.76 Yuan. Fill in Table 1-3-3.

(3) Automobile transportation

Automobile transport quota includes loading, unloading and transport. Select the required quota according to the type of goods to be transported. As the precast concrete product is to be transported, PX1-24 and PX1-25 quota are selected, and by putting the quantities (transport weight of 1.02t and load distance of 25km), we can get that automobile transport and load & unload is 84.27, among which, labor cost of 16.52 Yuan, material cost of 0.52 Yuan and machinery cost of 67.23 Yuan. Fill in Table 1-3-3.

2. Prefabricated Base

The prefabricated base consists of two parts: chassis and anchor plate. The weight of single chassis is 274kg, the quota PX3-3 is selected, that is, the weight of each chassis is less than 300kg; Px3-8 (weight of each pull wire plate is less than 200kg) is selected for pull wire plate (96kg), and the prefabricated base is calculated as 78.80 Yuan according to its quantities, including labor cost of 57.16 Yuan and machinery cost of 21.64 Yuan. Fill in Table 1-3-3.

3. Pulling Rod Anticorrosion

PX3-80 (asphalt varnish anticorrosion) is selected according to the anticorrosion method of pulling rod. It is concluded that the installation cost of pulling rod anticorrosion is 6.12 Yuan, including labor cost of 2.04 Yuan and material cost of 4.08 Yuan.

From the previous calculation, the total cost of base is 188.70 Yuan, including labor cost of 93.47 Yuan, material cost of 4.60 Yuan and machinery cost of 90.63 Yuan. Fill in Table 1-3-3.

(Ⅲ) Tower And Pole Works

It is stipulated in the quota that the contents of pole and tower works include the wooden pole assembly and erection, concrete pole assembly and erection, stay pole and steel ring welding, steel tube pole assembly, tower assembly, cross arm and insulator installation, pull wire fabrication and installation, and grounding installation. Pole and tower works belongs to the installation works, and the quota selected and cost calculated shall be filled in the budget sheet of work units of installation project.

Study Program I Preparation for Construction Drawing Budget of 10kV Distribution Line

Table 1-3-3 Base Works——Work Unit Budget Sheet

S/N	Basis of preparation	Project name	Unit	Qty.	Equipment unit price	Quota base price - Amount	Quota base price - Where in: Salary	Main materials	Equipment expenses	Total expenses - Amount	Total expenses - Where in: Labor cost	Main materials
II		Overhead line works										
2		base works										
	PX1-2	Prefabricated concrete products, with average human-powered transport distance within 500m	t·km	0.102		191.29	173.98			19.51	17.75	
	PX1-24	Loading and unloading of prefabricated concrete products transported by truck	t	1.02		50.62	10.20			51.63	10.40	
	PX1-25	Transport of prefabricated concrete products by truck	t·km	25.5		1.28	0.24			32.64	6.12	
	PX3-3	Installation of prefabricated base chassis Within 300 (kg) / pcs	Piece	3.00		21.26	15.88			63.78	47.64	
	PX3-8	Installation of prefabricated base chassis within 300 (kg) / pcs	Piece	2.00		7.51	4.76			15.02	9.52	
	PX3-80	Anti corrosion asphalt varnish of pulling rod	Nos.	2.00		3.06	1.02			6.12	2.04	
		Sub-total								188.7	93.47	

1. Site Transport

(1) Human-powered transport

For the pole and tower assembly and erection project, materials transported include the concrete pole and armor clamp, insulator and sporadic steel. The quota for transport of concrete pole is PX1-1. According to the material list, the transport weight is 4.48t, the load distance is 0.1km, that is 0.448t·km, and the cost is 100.37 Yuan, including labor cost of 90.55 Yuan and machinery cost of 9.82 Yuan; The quota for transport of armor clamp, insulator and sporadic steel shall select PX1-6. As the quantities of project case I is small, steel for each works are calculated here. According to the material list, the transport weight is 0.43t, the load distance is 0.1km, that is 0.043t·km, and the cost is 4.42 Yuan, including labor cost of 4.01 Yuan and machinery cost of 0.41 Yuan. Fill in table 1-3-4.

(2) Automobile transportation

Automobile transport is the same as the human-powered transport, including concrete pole and armor clamp, insulator and sporadic steel. The quotas for transport, load and unload of concrete pole are PX1-22 and PX1-23. It is known that the transport, load and unload weight is 4.48t, the load distance is 25km, that is 112t·km, and the cost is 527.16 Yuan, including labor cost of 73.43 Yuan, material cost is 32.97 Yuan and machinery cost is 420.76 Yuan. The quotas for transport, load and unload are PX1-34 and PX1-35. It is known that the transport, load and unload weight is 0.43t, the load distance is 25km, that is 10.75t·km, and the cost is then calculated. Fill in table 1-3-4.

2. Concrete Pole Assembly and Erection

Project case I is complete concrete poles of 12m, and the quota PX4-4 is selected. The quota is considered that construction quantity of the line is more than 5 poles, and if it is less than 5, the labor and machinery quota shall be multiplied by a factor of 1.3; Therefore, the quota shall be adjusted here. The labor cost is adjusted to $215.22 \times 1.3 = 279.79$ (Yuan), the mechanical cost is adjusted to $128.19 \times 1.3 = 166.65$ (Yuan), and the quota is adjusted to 450.79 Yuan. For pole and tower works, the quantities is 3 poles, and amount of concrete pole assembly and erection is 1352.37 Yuan, including labor cost of 839.37 Yuan, material cost of 13.05 Yuan and machinery cost of 499.95 Yuan. Fill in table 1-3-4.

3. Cross Arm and Insulator Erection

In project case 1, 5 groups of single cross arms, 2 groups of double cross arms, 10 composite insulated cross arms and 9 strain insulators need to be installed. So PX4-33, PX4-34, PX4-35, PX4-36 and PX4-49 are selected and the cost calculated is 381.75 Yuan, including labor cost of 345.53 Yuan, material cost of 33.52 Yuan and machinery cost of 2.7 Yuan. Fill in table 1-3-4.

4. Pull Wire Fabrication and Installation

In project case I, two sets of pull wires need to be installed. Quota PX4-53 (section is within 70mm^2) and PX4-58 are selected according to the section of pull wires. It is calculated that the amount of pull wire fabrication and installation is 65.58 Yuan, including labor cost of 60.18 Yuan and material cost of 5.4 Yuan. Fill in table 1-3-4.

5. Earthing Installation

In project case I, there is one ground connection. Quota PX-59(for processing and manufacturing the grounding body), PX4-60, PX4-68 and PX4-69 are selected, which are brought into the quantities to calculate the required amount and are filled in table 1-3-4.

(IV) Overhead Conductor and Ground Wire Installation Works

1. Site Transport

(1) For overhead conductor and ground wire installation works, the materials transported by manpower include wires, some armor clamps and sporadic steel. Among them, the transport of armor clamps and sporadic steel have been calculated in the tower and pole works. The quota for wire transport is PX1-5. According to the material list, the transport weight is 0.19 t, the load distance is 0.1 km, that is 0.019 t · km, and the human-powered transport amount is 5.42 Yuan. Among which, labor cost is 4.86 Yuan and machinery cost is 0.56 Yuan. See Appendix 1, Table 3A.

Table 1-3-4 Pole and Tower Works——Work Unit Budget Sheet

S/N	Basis of preparation	Project name	Unit	Qty.	Unit price				Combined price			
					Equipment	Main materials	Quota base price	Where in: Salary	Equipment	Main materials	Installation fee	Where in: Salary
II		Overhead line works										
1		Pole and tower works										
	PX1-1	Prefabricated concrete poles, with average human-powered transport distance within 500m	t·km	0.448			224.05	202.13			100.37	90.55
	PX1-22	Loading and unloading of prefabricated concrete poles transported by truck	t	4.48			81.42	7.89			364.76	35.35
	PX1-23	Transport of prefabricated concrete poles by truck	t·km	112			1.45	0.34			162.4	38.08
	PX1-6	Armour clamp, insulator and sporadic steel with average human-powered transport distance within 500m	t·km	0.043			102.76	93.23			4.42	4.01
	PX1-34	Loading and unloading of armor clamp, insulator and sporadic steel transported by truck	t	0.43			38.5	9.04			16.56	3.89
	PX1-35	Transport of armor clamp, insulator and sporadic steel by truck	t·km	10.75			1.48	0.34			15.91	3.66

Table (Cont'd)

S/N	Basis of preparation	Project name	Unit	Qty.	Unit price				Combined price			
					Equipment	Main materials	Quota base price	Where in: Salary	Equipment	Main materials	Installation fee	Where in: Salary
	PX4-4 Adjustment	Assembly and erection of complete concrete pole within 13m	Site	3			450.79	279.79			1352.37	839.37
	PX4-33	Cross arm mounting-single iron and wood cross arm	Group	5			20.6	16.86			103	84.3
	PX4-34	Cross arm mounting-double iron and wood cross arm	Group	2			31.67	26.57			63.34	53.14
	PX4-35	Cross arm mounting-porcelain cross arm straight rod	Group	3			11.63	11.24			34.89	33.72
	PX4-36	Cross arm mounting-Porcelain cross arm strain rod	Group	7			22.87	22.48			160.09	157.36
	PX4-49	Insulator installation	Nos.	9			2.27	1.89			20.43	17.01
	PX4-53	Fabrication and installation of pull wire with the section less than 70mm^2	Nos.	2			28.72	26.02			57.44	52.04
	PX4-58	Fabrication and installation of pull wire-pull wire protective tube	Nos.	2			4.07	4.07			8.14	8.14
	PX-59	Processing and manufacturing of grounding body	t	0.045			228.64	132.08			10.29	5.94
	PX4-60	Installation of earth electrode	Nos.	6			10.06	9.15			60.36	54.9

Table (Cont´d)

S/N	Basis of preparation	Project name	Unit	Qty.	Unit price				Combined price			
					Equipment	Main materials	Quota base price	Where in: Salary	Equipment	Main materials	Installation fee	Where in: Salary
	PX4-62	Laying of grounding body within 50 Within	Site	1			30.54	24.96			30.54	24.96
	PX4-68	High-altitude grounding downlead of concrete pole	Nos.	1			44.74	13.73			44.74	13.73
	PX4-69	Measurement of resistance	Site	1			24.75	9.57			24.75	9.57
		Sub-total										

(2) Automobile transportation

The quota for automobile transport, loading and unloading of wire is PX1-32 and PX1-33. According to the quantity, the transport amount is 23.12 Yuan, including labor cost of 3.76 Yuan, material cost of 0.23 Yuan and machinery cost of 19.13 Yuan. See Appendix 1, Table 3A.

2. Conductor Erection

Corresponding quota shall be selected according to the type and section of the line. In project case 1, JKLYJ-10kV-50 insulated conductor is used and the quota PX5-17 (insulated aluminum strand with section less than 95) is selected. According to the quantity calculated above, it is 340.01 Yuan, including labor cost of 215.77 Yuan, material cost of 91.68 Yuan and machinery cost of 32.56 Yuan. As the conductor also crosses highway and low-voltage 380V line at 1 place respectively. By selecting quota PX5-40 (conductor crossing electric power, highway and communication), it can be calculated that amount of conductor crossing is 1095.14 Yuan, including labor cost of 700.30 Yuan, material cost of 325.52 Yuan and machinery cost of 69.32 Yuan. See Appendix 1, Table 3A.

(V) Installation of Pole-mounted Power Transformation and Distribution Equipment

The quota shall be selected according to the equipment installed on the pole. In project case I, circuit breaker, lightning arrester, disconnector and current transformer are installed, and quota PX6-13, PX6-14, PX6-16 and PX6-24 are selected, while the dry-type transformer refers to quotas PD1-7 (10kV dry-type transformer with the installation capacity less than 500KVA) of electrical equipment installation works, and then the installation amount is calculated as per the quantities. See Appendix 1, Table 3A.

II. Cable Works

The quota for cable works shall be selected from Budget Quota for 20kV and below Distribution Network Engineering Construction (Volume IV Cable Works), 2009 Edition. In cable works, cable trench works belongs to base works, while cable laying, fire protection for cable, commissioning and test belong to installation works.

(I) Cable Trench Works

1. Material Transportation

(1) Human-powered transport

The cable belongs to wire, so the quota PX1-5 is selected. According to the material list, the transport weight is 0.52t, the load distance is 0.1km, that is, 0.052 t·km, and human-powered transport is 14.82 Yuan, including 13.29 Yuan of labor cost and 1.53 Yuan of machinery cost. See Appendix 1, table 3B.

(2) Automobile transportation

The quota for automobile transport, loading and unloading of cable is PX1-32 and PX1-33. The transport amount is calculated according to the quantity. See Appendix 1, table 3B.

2. Cable Trench Works

According to the analysis of the project, it is known that quotas adopted in project case I include breaking the pavement, digging and filling the directly-buried cable trench, moving the cover plate, and installing the sealed cable protection pipe. PL1-5 (sand and gravel pavement with thickness less than 150 mm) is selected for breaking the pavement according to the type and thickness of pavement, and according to the quantities calculated (90m^2), the amount is 558 Yuan, including labor cost of 554.4 Yuan and machinery cost of 3.6 Yuan; PL1-9 (ordinary soil) shall be selected for the excavation and filling of directly-buried cable trench according to the type of soil. According to the quantity (67.5m³), this item is 834.30 Yuan, including labor cost of 749.93 Yuan, material cost of 2.70 Yuan and machinery cost of 81.67 Yuan. According to the size of protection pipe, PL1-39 (within Φ200) is selected as the installation quota of sealed cable protection pipe, the quantity is 1, so it is 429.38 Yuan, including labor cost of 86.49 Yuan and material cost of 342.89 Yuan. See Appendix 1, table 3B.

(Ⅱ) Cable Laying

The quotas to be selected in project case I include laying of directly-buried power cable (10kV), fabrication and installation of outdoor hot (cold) shrinkable power cable terminal head (10kV), and fabrication and installation of indoor hot (cold) shrinkable power cable terminal head (10kV). PL3-1 (section within 50mm²), PL4-1 (section within 50mm²) and PL4-5 (section within 50mm²) are selected according to the section of cable (50mm²). According to the calculated quantities (150m, the quota unit is 100m / three-phase, so the value here is 1.5), amount for directly-buried power cable laying is 560.28 Yuan, including labor cost of 348.81 Yuan, material cost of 74.60 Yuan and machinery cost of 136.87 Yuan; Fabrication and installation amount for one set of outdoor hot (cold) shrinkable power cable terminal is 158.80 Yuan, including labor cost of 124.40 Yuan and material cost of 34.40 Yuan; Fabrication and installation amount for indoor heat (cold) shrinkable power cable terminal is 74.29 Yuan, including labor cost of 39.89 Yuan and material cost of 34.40 Yuan. See Appendix 1, Table 3A.

(Ⅲ) Cable Fire Prevention

The quota for cable fire prevention is selected according to the fire protection mode. For project case I, fireproof blockage is adopted and quota PL6-1 (fireproof blockage) is selected. It is calculated that amount for cable fire prevention is 70.12 Yuan, including 59.57 Yuan of labor cost and 10.55 Yuan of material cost. See Appendix 1, Table 3A.

(Ⅳ) Cable Test

According to the type of test, PL8-1 (insulation shake test), PL8-3 (AC withstand voltage test), PL8-4 (resistance ratio test) and PL8-5 (partial discharge test) are selected in project case I. The test loop is 1, and amount of cable test is calculated. See Appendix 1, Table 3A.

Task 4 Schedule of Project Cost

I. Cost Composition (According To Budget Regulations)

The budget cost of distribution network project consists of construction work cost, installation work cost, equipment procurement cost, other cost and dynamic cost. The sum of construction project cost, installation project cost, equipment procurement cost and other costs is called static investment.

II. Charging Standard

(I) Construction Work and Installation Work Cost

Construction works refers to all kinds of buildings, structures and other facilities that constitute the project. Installation works refers to the combination, assembly and commissioning of various equipment, pipelines, cables and auxiliary devices that constitute the production process system.

The construction and installation work cost refers to the cost of construction, installation and commissioning of infrastructure, process system and auxiliary system, which form the project, to make them have production functions.

The construction and installation work cost incorporates direct cost, indirect cost, profit, and tax.

The equation for calculation is:

Construction and installation work cost = direct cost + indirect cost + profit + tax (1-4-1)

1. Direct Cost

Direct cost refers to the cost on specific product objects, which is directly consumed during the production process of construction and installation products, and consists of direct

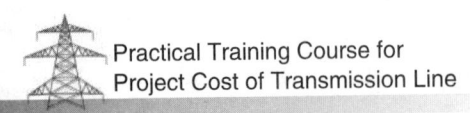

construction cost and measure cost.

The equation for calculation is:

$$\text{Direct cost} = \text{direct construction cost} + \text{measure cost} \quad (1\text{-}4\text{-}2)$$

(1) Direct construction cost. Direct construction cost refers to the various costs expended in the construction process for the Project entity according to the normal construction conditions, including labor cost, material cost and cost of using construction machinery.

The equation for calculation is:

$$\text{Direct construction cost} = \text{labor cost} + \text{material cost} + \text{cost of using construction machinery} \quad (1\text{-}4\text{-}3)$$

Calculation standard: Calculate according to *Budget Quota for 20kV and below Distribution Network Engineering Construction*, and adjust to the level of budget-making year in accordance with regulations on quota management of electric power engineering. The details is shown in Table 3A, Table 3B of Appendix 1, budget sheet of work units of construction and installation project

1) Labor cost. Labor cost refers to various expenses directly spent on production workers engaged in construction and installation works, including basic wage, wage subsidy, supplementary wage, employee welfare expense, labor protection fees for production workers, etc.

① The basic wage refers to the basic wage paid to the production personnel, including the post wage, working age wage or working age subsidy, post allowance, etc.

② Wage subsidy refers to meal subsidy, price subsidy, coal and gas subsidy, transportation subsidy, and mobile construction subsidy paid according to the prescribed standards.

③ Supplementary wage refers to the wage for non-working days other than the annual effective construction days of the production workers, including the wage at the period of study and training of the employees, the wage during the period of work transfer, home visit and vacation, the wage for work stoppage due to the influence of climate, the wage for sick leave within six months, the wage during the period of maternity leave, marriage leave and funeral leave, and the wage during the breastfeeding of the female workers.

④ Employee welfare expense refers to the employee welfare expenses accrued according to the prescribed standards.

⑤ Labor protection fees for production workers refers to the procurement and repair costs of labor protection articles, clothing subsidies, heatstroke prevention subsidy, and the construction protection cost in the environment that is harmful to physical health, etc. paid according to the specified standards.

Labor cost standard: 34 Yuan / workday for unskilled workers, 48 Yuan / workday for construction skilled workers, 53 Yuan / workday for installation skilled workers. The labor cost in each region and each year shall be adjusted in accordance with the regulations issued by the Power Engineering Cost and Quota Management Station.

Labor cost is calculated from the sum of labor cost of each item in the budget sheet of work units of construction works and installation works. For example, the labor cost of the earthworks is the sum of labor cost (see Appendix 1 Table 3B- Earthworks), and is 262 Yuan.

2) Material cost. Material cost refers to the cost of raw materials, auxiliary materials, components, parts and semi-finished products consumed in the construction process, as well as the cost of disposable consumable materials and amortized materials in the construction process.

Material cost in the budget of distribution network construction project includes the main material cost and consumable material cost.

① Main material cost. Main material cost refers to the raw materials, auxiliary materials, components, parts, semi-finished products and other technological materials that constitute the entity of the process system. Under ordinary circumstances, main materials refer to the materials which is necessary in the construction process and is not priced in the construction budget quota, also known as unpriced materials or installation materials. The calculation formula of main material cost is

Main material cost = main material consumption × material information price (1-4-4)

The budget price of main materials shall be determined according to the ex-warehouse price of the warehouse at the construction site, the ex-warehouse price of the centralized storage warehouse of the Project management unit or the material information price published by the quota management organization of the power industry.

Main material consumption is calculated from the sum of main materials in budget sheet of work units of construction project and installation project. For example, there is no main material for earthworks, and the main material cost is zero.

② Consumable material cost. Consumable material cost refers to the materials consumed in the construction process without reflecting their original form in the finished construction products, and the materials that need to be amortized due to the requirements of construction technology and measures. Generally speaking, consumable materials refer to the materials whose cost has been included in the base price of quota in the budget quota, also known as priced material cost or quota material cost.

The cost of consumable materials shall be calculated according to the principles specified in the Budget Quota for 20kV and below Distribution Network Engineering Construction and is adjusted to the level of budget-making year in accordance with relevant price level adjustment rules. The quota material cost is obtained by adding the combined price of material cost in each quota. For example, the quota material cost of the earthworks is 61.08 Yuan (see Appendix 1 Table 3B- Earthworks).

3) Cost of using construction machinery. Cost of using construction machinery refers to the cost for using the construction machinery, and the cost for installation, disassembly and off-site transportation. It mainly includes: depreciation cost, overhaul cost, regular repair cost, installation and disassembly cost, off-site transportation cost, operator labor cost, fuel and power cost, vehicle and vessel tax, etc..

Cost of using construction machinery shall be calculated according to the principles stipulated in the Budget Quota for 20kV and below Distribution Network Engineering Construction.

① Depreciation cost refers to the cost accrued in accordance with national regulations for the original value and the time value of purchase funds of construction machinery recovered in succession within the specified service life.

② Overhaul cost refers to the cost needed by necessary overhaul of construction machinery according to the specified overhaul interval to restore its normal function.

③ Regular repair cost refers to the cost needed by maintenance and temporary troubleshooting of construction machinery at all levels except overhaul. Including the cost for replacing the equipment and parts required to ensure the normal operation of the machinery, the amortization and maintenance cost of tools and accessories at random, the cost of lubrication and wiping materials required for daily maintenance during the operation of the machinery, and the cost of maintenance and repair during the period of stagnation of the machinery.

④ Installation and disassembly cost includes the costs for labor, materials, machinery and commissioning required by the installation and disassembly of construction machinery and equipment, as well as the costs for the depreciation, erection and demolition of auxiliary facilities.

⑤ Off-site transportation cost include the cost for transportation, loading and unloading and auxiliary materials incurred by the construction machinery and equipment, either in whole or in part from the parking place to the construction site or from one construction site to another construction site.

⑥ Labor cost refers to various expenses directly spent on driver (stoker) and other operators, including basic wage, wage subsidy, supplementary wage, employee welfare expense, labor protection fees for production workers, etc.

⑦ Fuel and power cost refers to the cost of solid fuel (coal, firewood), liquid fuel (gasoline, diesel), gas fuel, water, electricity, gas, etc. consumed by construction machinery in operation.

⑧ Vehicle and vessel tax refers to the vehicle and vessel tax, insurance expense, annual inspection fee and other fees payable for construction machinery in accordance with the provisions of the national administration authority.

The machinery cost in the Project budget is obtained by calculating the combined machinery cost in each quota. For example, the machinery cost of the earthworks is 26.70 Yuan (see Appendix 1 Table 3B- Earthworks).

According to the labor cost, material cost and machinery cost obtained, the direct construction cost can be calculated. For example, the direct construction cost of earthwork is 349.78 Yuan. Fill the result in the budget sheet of work units for construction project and installation project, just as shown in table 1-4-1.

Table 1-4-1 Construction Works——Work Unit Budget Sheet

Unit: Yuan

S/N	Basis of preparation	Project name	Unit	Qty.	Equipment unit price	Quota base price		Main materials	Equipment expenses	Total expenses		Main materials
						Amount	Where in: Salary			Amount	Where in: Labor cost	
II		Overhead line works										
1		Earthwork										
		Sub-total								349.78	262.00	
(I)		Direct cost	%	100		400.37				400.37		
1		Direct engineering cost	%	100		349.78				349.78		
1.1		Labor cost	%	100		262.00				262.00		
1.2		Material expenses	%	100		61.08				61.08		
1.2.1		Quota material cost	%	100		61.08				61.08		
1.2.2		Installation material expense	%	100								
1.3		Charge for use of construction machines	%	100		26.70				26.70		
2		Measures expenses	%	100		50.59				50.59		
2.1		Temporary facilities	%	8.83		262.00				23.13		
2.2		Expenses in safe and civilized construction measurement	%	3.25		262.00				8.52		
2.3		Use cost for construction tools	%	2.28		262.00				5.97		
2.4		Additional cost for winter and rainy season construction	%	4.95		262.00				12.97		

Study Program I   Preparation for Construction Drawing Budget of 10kV Distribution Line

Table (Cont'd)

S/N	Basis of preparation	Project name	Unit	Qty.	Equipment unit price	Quota base price		Main materials	Equipment expenses	Total expenses		Main materials
						Amount	Where in: Salary			Amount	Where in: Labor cost	
2.5		Additional fee for night time construction work	%			262.00						
2.6		Extra charge for special site construction	%			262.00						
(II)		Indirect costs	%	100		159.48				159.48		
1		Levies and charges	%	100		99.48				99.48		
1.1		Social security fee	%	25.93		262.00				67.94		
1.2		Housing provident fund	%	10.2		262.00				26.72		
1.3		Accidental injury premium for hazardous operation	%	1.84		262.00				4.82		
2		Administrative expenses	%	22.9		262.00				60.00		
(III)		Margin	%	15		262.00				39.30		
(IV)		Tax	%	3.41		599.15				20.43		
		Total	%	100		619.58				619.58		

(2) Measure cost. Measure cost refers to the cost occurred on the non-engineering entity before and during the construction of the Project so as to complete the construction of the project. It includes: fees for construction site facilities, measure cost of safe and civilized construction, expenses for using tools and appliances, additional cost for construction in winter and rainy season, additional cost for working at night, and additional cost for construction in special areas.

The equation for calculation is:

Measure cost = fees for construction site facilities + cost of safe and civilized construction measures + expenses for using tools and appliances + additional cost for construction in winter and rainy season + additional cost for working at night + additional cost for construction in special areas (1-4-5)

1) Fees for construction site facilities. Fees for construction site facilities refers to the cost of temporary buildings, structures, mobile power supply, water and electricity pipelines, simple rainproof (sunscreen) shelter and other temporary facilities erected by the construction company at site for office, production, shift rest, materials (including tools) storage, etc. so as to meet the normal management and construction needs of the Project site. Contents include: expenses for the erection, maintenance, demolition, depreciation and amortization of temporary facilities, or rental of temporary facilities, etc.

The equation for calculation is:

$$\text{Fees for construction site facilities} = \text{labor cost} \times \text{rate} \quad (1\text{-}4\text{-}6)$$

The rate for temporary facilities is shown in Table 1-4-2.

Table 1–4–2 Rate for Fees for Construction Facilities on–site

Category of engineering		Construction works	Installation works
Rate%	Urban area	8.83	13.14
	Peri-urban	7.65	11.61
	Rural	6.32	10.42

For example, the labor cost of the earthworks is 262.00 Yuan, then fees for construction site facilities is

$$262.00 \times 8.83\% = 23.13 \text{ (Yuan)}$$

2) Measure cost for safe and civilized construction. Measure cost for safe and civilized construction refers to the subsidy for the safety and civilization guarantee measures taken at the construction site according to the requirements of safe and civilized construction and health and environmental protection code of electric power industry.

The equation for calculation is:

$$\text{Measure cost for safe and civilized construction} = \text{labor cost} \times \text{rate} \quad (1\text{-}4\text{-}7)$$

Table 1-4-3 Measure Cost Rate for Safe and Civilized Construction (%)

Category of engineering	Construction works	Installation works
Rate%	3.25	6.56

Taking earthworks for example, the measure cost of safe and civilized construction is

$$262.00 \times 3.25\% = 8.52 \text{ (Yuan)}$$

3) Expenses for using tools and appliances. Expenses for using tools and appliances refers to the purchase, amortization and maintenance costs of tools and appliances not belonging to fixed assets used by the production, inspection and test departments of construction enterprises. The construction tools and instruments mentioned here do not include the management tools and management appliances used by the site management department.

The equation for calculation is:

$$\text{Expenses for using tools and appliances} = \text{labor cost} \times \text{rate} \quad (1\text{-}4\text{-}8)$$

Table 1-4-4 Rate of Expenses for Using Tools and Appliances.

Category of engineering	Construction works	Installation works
Rate%	2.28	4.13

Taking earthworks for example, expenses for using tools and appliances is

$$262.00 \times 2.28\% = 5.97 \text{ (Yuan)}$$

4) Additional cost for construction in winter and rainy season. Additional cost for construction in winter and rainy season refers to the cost that needs to be added for construction carried out in winter and rainy season according to the normal construction organization plan, including the expenses incurred in the heat preservation and maintenance measures taken to ensure the Project quality, and shelter and heating measures taken to prevent wind and cold during the construction in winter; The cost that needs to be added for taking rainproof and moisture-proof measures during construction in rainy season; The cost that needs to be added for labor protection measures due to construction in winter and rainy season; As well as the compensation cost incurred due to the reduction of construction efficiency.

The equation for calculation is:

$$\text{Additional cost for construction in winter and rainy season} = \text{labor cost} \times \text{rate} \quad (1\text{-}4\text{-}9)$$

Table 1-4-5 Additional Cost for Construction in Winter and Rainy Season

Area classification		I	II	III	IV	V
Rate%	Construction works	4.46	4.95	5.63	6.84	8.12
	Installation works	6.22	6.63	7.45	8.66	9.88

The project case I belongs to class II area, and for construction and installation works, the rates of additional cost for construction in winter and rainy season take 4.95% and 6.63% respectively.

Taking earthworks for example, additional cost for construction in winter and rainy season is

$$262.00 \times 4.95\% = 12.97 \text{ (Yuan)}$$

5) Additional cost for working at night. Additional cost for working at night refers to the cost for night shift subsidy, efficiency reduction for working at night, amortization of lighting equipment, lighting power consumption and other expenses incurred by the single project which shall be carried out continuously at night according to the requirements of the regulations.

The equation for calculation is:

$$\text{Additional cost for working at night} = \text{labor cost} \times \text{rate} \quad (1\text{-}4\text{-}10)$$

There is no requirement for working at night in the Project case I, so this cost will not be considered.

6) Additional cost for construction in special areas. Additional cost for construction in special areas refers to the additional construction cost due to the influence of special natural conditions when the construction is carried out in high altitude, extremely hot, severe cold and other areas.

The equation for calculation is:

$$\text{Additional cost for construction in special areas} = \text{labor cost} \times \text{rate} \quad (1\text{-}4\text{-}11)$$

High altitude region, high latitude and cold region, extremely hot region:

① High altitude region refers to the area with an average altitude of more than 3000m.

② High latitude and cold region refers to the area north of north latitude 45°.

③ Extremely hot region refers to the desert area with an area of more than 10000km² and the Turpan area of Xinjiang. The project case I is an ordinary urban project, which does not belong to special area, and there is no need to consider this cost.

2. Indirect Cost

Indirect cost refers to the cost, which serve for the whole project during the production process of construction and installation products and is not directly consumed in specific product objects. It consists of the stipulated fees and enterprise administration expense.

The equation for calculation is:

$$\text{Indirect cost} = \text{stipulated fees} + \text{enterprise administration expense} \quad (1\text{-}4\text{-}12)$$

(1) Stipulated fees. The stipulated fees refer to the fees that must be paid according to the regulations of the national administration authority. The stipulated fees that should be calculated and listed for electric power projects mainly include: social security fee, housing fund and accidental injury insurance expense for dangerous operations.

The equation for calculation is:

$$\text{Stipulated fees} = \text{social security fee} + \text{housing fund} + \text{accidental injury insurance expense for dangerous operations} \quad (1\text{-}4\text{-}13)$$

1) Social security fee. Social security fee refers to the insurance and security expenses that construction enterprises must pay for the employees according to the relevant requirements of the state to establish the social security system, which is composed of endowment insurance expenses, unemployment insurance expense and medical insurance expense.

The equation for calculation is:

$$\text{Social security fee} = \text{labor cost} \times 0.85 \times \text{contribution rate} \quad (1\text{-}4\text{-}14)$$

① Contribution rate refers to the sum of rates for the basic pension insurance, unemployment insurance and basic medical insurance calculated based on the total wage issued by the social security institution of the province (autonomous region, municipality directly under the central government) where the Project is located.

② Coefficient 0.85 here is also known as the comprehensive conversion coefficient of total wages. The rate for social security fee here takes 25.93%. Take earthwork as an example, the social security fee is

$$262 \times 25.93\% = 67.94 \text{ (Yuan)}$$

2) Housing provident fund. Housing provident fund refers to the housing fund paid by the construction enterprises for employees.

The equation for calculation is:

Housing provident fund = labor cost ×0.85× housing fund contribution rate   (1-4-15)

In project case I, the contribution rate of enterprise's housing provident fund is 12%, and the housing provident fund charge standard is 0.85 × 12% = 10.2%. Taking the earthwork as an example, the housing fund is

$$262\times10.2\%=26.72 \text{ (Yuan)}$$

3) Accidental injury insurance expense for dangerous operations. Accidental injury insurance expense for dangerous operations refers to the accidental injury insurance premium paid by the enterprise for the construction and installation personnel engaged in dangerous operations according to the provisions of the construction law.

The equation for calculation is:

Accidental injury insurance expense for dangerous operations = labor cost ×1.84%   (1-4-16)

Taking the earthwork as an example, accidental injury insurance expense for dangerous operations is

$$262\times1.84\%=4.82 \text{ (Yuan)}$$

(2) Enterprise administration expense. The enterprise administration expense refers to the expenses incurred by the construction enterprise in organizing the construction and operation management, including the executive salaries, office expense, travel expenses, labor subsidies, employee recruitment and team dispatching expenses, labor union expenditure, personnel education fund, expenses for using fixed assets, premiums for property insurance, vehicle and vessel tax and fuel expense of the company vehicles, expenses for using tools and appliances, fixed-point retest fee of construction project, fixed-point retest fee of construction project, expenses for project hand over item by item and site clearing, inspection and test fees, project pollutant discharge cost, project protection and on-site material supervision fee, technology transfer and technological development expense, notarial fee, advisory and legal expenses, consulting fee, advertising cost, business reception expense, labor safety and health inspection fee, property tax, land use tax, stamp duty etc. paid by the enterprise according to regulations.

The equation for calculation is:

Enterprise administration expense=labor cost × rate   (1-4-17)

Study Program I Preparation for Construction Drawing Budget of 10kV Distribution Line

Table 1-4-6 Enterprise Administration Expense Rate

Category of engineering	Construction works	Installation works
Rate%	22.9	35.2

1) Executive salaries refer to basic wage, wage subsidy, supplementary wage, employee welfare expense, labor protection fees, etc. paid to the management personnel.

2) Office expenses refer to the expenses of stationery, paper, account book, printing, post and telecommunications, communication, books and newspapers used in the normal management of enterprises, as well as conference expenses, utilities, gas charges, collective heating fees, heatstroke prevention and cooling fees and cleaning expenses, etc. at the construction site.

3) Travel expenses refer to the travel expenses of employees for business trips, transfer of work, living expenses, urban transport costs and overtime meal allowances, costs of visiting certain family member of staff, labor recruitment fees, retirement costs of labor force, nonrecurring travelling expenses for retirement and resignation, and medical treatment fees for employees with occupational injuries, etc.

4) Labor subsidy refers to the payment of retired and resigned employees' subsidy for settling in another place, employee retirement allowance, wage for employees applied for sick leave for over six months, funeral expenses for death of employees and pension costs, and various expenses paid to retired cadres according to regulations.

5) Employee recruitment and team dispatching expenses refer to the expenses incurred by the construction enterprises in recruiting employees, as well as the round-trip expenses incurred by dispatching construction teams and construction machinery to the project site.

6) The labor union expenditures refer to the labor union expenditures accrued by the construction enterprises according to the relevant provisions of the national administration authority and according to the total wages of the employees.

7) The personnel education fund refers to the expenses accrued by the construction enterprises according to the total wages of the employees in order to ensure that the employees learn advanced technology and improve their cultural level according to the relevant regulations of the national administration authority.

8) Expenses for using fixed assets refer to the depreciation, overhaul, maintenance or

lease fees of houses, equipment and instruments belonging to fixed assets used by the construction enterprises' management and testing departments.

9) Premiums for property insurance refer to the insurance premiums paid by the construction enterprises for the management of property and vehicles.

10) The vehicle and vessel taxes and fuel expenses for office vehicles refer to the vehicle and vessel taxes and fuel expenses paid by the construction enterprises for the management of office vehicles.

11) The expenses for using tools and appliances of the management organization refer to the purchase, maintenance and amortization fees of tools, appliances, furniture and inspection, testing, mapping, fire fighting equipment, etc. that are not fixed assets used by the management organization and personnel.

12) The fixed-point retest fees of construction projects refer to the fees of re-positioning and inspection of buildings by the planning department.

13) Expenses for project hand over item by item and site clearing refer to the expenses incurred by the construction enterprises after the project is completed for handover of works and site clearing.

14) Inspection and test fees refer to the costs incurred in the general identification and inspection of building materials, components and building installation products.

15) Project pollution discharge costs refer to the expenses incurred for the treatment of pollutants in the construction process or the payment of sewage charges to the environmental protection department in accordance with the relevant regulations of the administrative department in charge of the project.

16) Project protection and on-site material supervision fees refer to the expenses incurred for the maintenance and supervision of completed projects, construction in progress and on-site materials during the normal construction period from the mobilization to the completion and handover of the project.

17) Labor safety and health inspection fees refer to the expenses incurred by the construction enterprises in accepting the safety qualification certification, special equipment safety inspection, labor hygiene inspection and labor safety training assessment by the construction safety management department in accordance with the national labor safety management regulations.

Taking the earthwork as an example, the enterprise administration expense is

$$262×22.9\%=60 \text{ (Yuan)}$$

3. Profits

Profits refer to the profits earned by the construction enterprises to complete the contracted project.

The equation for calculation is:

$$\text{Profit} = \text{labor cost} \times \text{profit margin} \qquad (1\text{-}4\text{-}18)$$

Table 1–4–7 Profit Margin

Category of engineering	Construction works	Installation works
Rate%	15	22

Take the earthwork as an example, the profit is

$$262×15\%=39.30 \text{ (Yuan)}$$

4. Tax

Tax refers to business tax, urban maintenance and construction tax and education surcharge specified by the national tax law and included in the cost of construction and installation.

The equation for calculation is:

$$\text{Tax} = (\text{direct cost} + \text{indirect cost} + \text{profit}) \times \text{tax rate} \qquad (1\text{-}4\text{-}19)$$

The tax rate is calculated according to the regulations of the taxation department where the project is located, and is taken as 3.41.

Take the earthwork as an example, the tax is:

$$(400.37+159.48+39.30)×3.41\%=20.43 \text{ (Yuan)}$$

The costs of the three types of works: earthwork, base works and the cable trench works of the cable line works in the overhead line project are calculated, and then summarized into the summary table of the construction project discipline (see Table II-B, Appendix 1); and the costs of six projects such as pole and tower works, installation of overhead conductor and ground wire, power transformation and distribution devices on pole, cable laying, cable fire protection, commissioning and test for cable line project in the overhead line project are summarized into the summary table of installation project discipline (see Table II-A, Appendix 1).

(II) Equipment Procurement Cost

The equipment procurement cost refers to the procurement cost and freight and miscellaneous charges incurred in purchasing various equipment that constitutes the process flow and transporting the equipment from the delivery location or the centralized management warehouse of the project management unit to the designated location on the construction site.

The equation for calculation is:

$$\text{Equipment procurement cost} = \text{equipment cost} + \text{equipment freight and miscellaneous charges} \qquad (1\text{-}4\text{-}20)$$

1. Equipment Costs

The equipment cost refers to the fee (including the packing expense) paid for the purchase of equipment at the equipment supply price (the delivery price of the tender contract and the negotiated delivery price).

Calculation principle of equipment cost: When the equipment is delivered by the centralized storage warehouse of the project management unit to the installation site, the equipment price can be taken as the ex-warehousing price of the centralized storage warehouse of the project management unit.

2. Equipment Freight and Miscellaneous Charges

Equipment freight and miscellaneous charges refer to the expenses incurred by transporting the equipment from the delivery place or the centralized storage warehouse of the project management unit to the designated location on the construction site, including the handling costs, transportation costs, transportation premiums and storage fees of the equipment.

The equation for calculation is:

$$\text{Equipment freight and miscellaneous charges} = \text{equipment cost} \times \text{rate of equipment freight and miscellaneous charges} \qquad (1\text{-}4\text{-}21)$$

Rate of equipment freight and miscellaneous charges: When the haul distance is within 20km, the rate is 1.1%; when the haul distance exceeds 20km, the rate increases by 0.15%

Study Program I Preparation for Construction Drawing Budget of 10kV Distribution Line

for each additional 10km, and the haul distance less than 10km is taken as 10km. If the supplier directly supplies the equipment to the site, only the unloading charges and storage fees will be calculated, which are calculated at 0.7% of the equipment cost.

In the Project Case I, the automobile haul distance is 25km, so the rate of freight and miscellaneous charges is 1.25%. Fill in Table 1-2-3 to obtain the equipment procurement cost. Then fill the equipment procurement cost in Table II-A, Appendix 1, and complete the summary table of installation project discipline.

(III) Other Expenses

Other expenses refer to other related expenses that are not construction project costs, installation project costs, and equipment procurement costs but are necessary for construction project construction, including construction site requisition and clearing costs, project construction administrative costs, project construction technical service costs, project construction supervision and testing fees, production preparation costs and basic reserve costs.

The equation for calculation is:

Other expenses = construction site requisition and clearing costs + project construction administrative costs + project construction technical service costs + project construction supervision and testing fees + production preparation costs + basic reserve costs (1-4-22)

1. Construction Site Requisition and Clearing Costs

Construction site requisition and clearing costs refer to the relevant expenses incurred by obtaining the necessary site for the construction of the project and reaching the normal construction conditions and construction environment, mainly including compensation for land acquisition, clearance costs, construction site rental, and compensation for line construction. The equation for calculation is:

Construction site requisition and clearing costs = compensation for land acquisition + clearance cost + construction site rental + compensation for line construction (1-4-23)

(1) Compensation for land acquisition. The compensation for land acquisition refers to the expenses incurred by the project legal person in order to obtain the right to use the construction land in accordance with the provisions of the Land Law and the Property Law, including land compensation, compensation for ground attachments and young crops, forest compensation, resettlement subsidy, surveying and demarcation fees, land acquisition man-

agement fees, certificate fees, and various funds and taxes.

There is no such expenditure in the Project Case I.

(2) Clearance cost. The clearance cost refers to the various expenses incurred in dismantling and cleaning up the existing buildings, structures, and other facilities that hinder the construction of the project within the scope of the land requisitioned for the project.

There is no such expenditure in the Project Case I.

(3) Construction site rental. The construction site rental refers to the expenses incurred in temporarily renting the site to ensure the normal construction during the construction period, including the rent, cleaning and reclamation fees of the site.

There is no such expenditure in the Project Case I.

(4) Compensation for line construction. The compensation for line construction refers to the expenses incurred in compensation for the inevitable damages to the buildings, structures, trees, cash crops, etc. on the land not expropriated and leased in the line corridor during the construction of the overhead transmission line. Or it may be compensation for the ground excavation, pavement, etc. during the construction of the cable line project.

There is no such expenditure in the Project Case I.

2. Construction Project Management Fee

The construction project management fee refers to the expenses incurred in the organization, management, coordination and supervision of the project after the construction project has been approved by the national administration authority during the reasonable period from the preparation of the project to the completion acceptance and handover for production, including project management funds, bidding costs, and project supervision costs.

The equation for calculation is:

$$\text{Project construction management fee} = \text{project management funds} + \text{bidding costs} + \text{engineering supervision} \quad (1\text{-}4\text{-}24)$$

(1) Project management funds. Project management funds refer to the daily management fees incurred by the project management unit in the project management, mainly including the application fees for the project construction related procedures, daily office expenses, travel expenses, expenses for using fixed assets, expenses for using tools and appliances, technical book and data fees, project file management fees, office utilities, project or-

Study Program I Preparation for Construction Drawing Budget of 10kV Distribution Line

ganization and coordination fees, contract conclusion and notary fees, advisory and legal expenses, consulting fees, project price appraisal (settlement) fees, conference expenses, business entertainment fees, stamp duties, as well as daily work expenses such as equipment and material distribution organization, construction project labor safety acceptance evaluation, project completion measurement, handover acceptance, completion audit, and preparation of Final Account upon Completion.

The equation for calculation is:

Project management funds = (construction project costs + installation project costs) × 1.15%

(1-4-25)

The construction project costs, installation project costs, and equipment procurement costs can be calculated according to the summary table of construction and installation project discipline. The sum of the construction project costs and the installation project costs for the Project Case I is 66,909.47 Yuan, and the project management fee is calculated to be 769.46 Yuan.

(2) Bidding costs. Bidding cost refers to the expenses incurred when relevant personnel, in accordance with the related national regulations, organize or authorize the qualified organ to prepare and review the bidding documents and tender estimate, and authorize the organ having the qualification of bidding agency to call for bids for procurement and subcontract project.

The equation for calculation is:

Project bidding costs = (construction project costs + installation project costs
+ equipment procurement costs) × 0.32%   (1-4-26)

The sum of the construction project costs, the installation project costs and the equipment procurement costs of Project Case I is 232,101.89 Yuan, and the bidding cost is calculated to be 742.73 Yuan.

(3) Project supervision cost. Project supervision cost refers to the payment made by authorizing a project supervision organ to supervise the whole process of the construction project in accordance with the related national regulations, procedures and specifications.

The equation for calculation is:

Project supervision cost = (construction project cost + installation project cost) × 2.55%

(1-4-27)

3. Project Construction Technical Service Cost

Project construction technical service cost refers to the expenses incurred to provide technical services and technical support for the project construction, including project survey fee, design document review fee, post evaluation fee of the project, and technical and economic standard preparation and management fee.

The equation for calculation is:

Project construction technical service cost = project survey fee + project design fee

+ design document review fee + post evaluation fee of the project + technical

and economic standard preparation and management fee   (1-4-28)

(1) Project survey fee. The project survey fee refers to the fees paid to qualified surveying agencies for surveying and measuring geological sections, terrain, hydrology, pole and tower positioning, cross-over, etc. in accordance with the requirements of survey and design specifications within the scope of the project and compiling relevant survey documents.

The equation for calculation is:

$$\text{Project survey fee} = \text{construction project cost} \times 4.5\% \quad (1\text{-}4\text{-}29)$$

(2) Engineering design fee. The project design fee refers to the payment made for authorizing qualified design institution to conduct site reconnaissance and survey, prepare the preliminary design document for the project, construction drawing design document, as-built drawing document, etc. as required in the project design specifications, and for the field technical services from the design representative.

The equation for calculation is:

Project design fee = (construction project cost + installation project cost) × design fee rate

(1-4-30)

Table 1–4–8 Selection Table of Design Fee Rate

Sum of equipment procurement, construction and installation project costs	Design fee rate (%)
Execute the highest standard of less than 200,000 Yuan	8.0
Less than 500,000 Yuan	6.5 ~ 8.0
Less than 1 million Yuan	5.5 ~ 6.5
Less than 3 million Yuan	4.0 ~ 5.5
More than 3 million Yuan	3.2 ~ 4.0
Execute minimum standards if more than 10 million Yuan	3.2

The sum of the equipment procurement and construction and installation project costs of Project Case I is 232,100 Yuan. The process of calculating the design fee rate using the interpolation method is as follows.

Assuming the design fee rate is x, then

$$(50-23.21) / (23.21-20) = (6.5-x) / (x-8.0)$$

$$x=7.84$$

the design fee rate of Project Case I is 7.84%, and the sum of the construction project and the installation project cost of 66,909.47 Yuan is brought into the formula to calculate that the project design fee is

$$66909.47 \times 7.84\% = 5245.70 \text{ (Yuan)}$$

(3) Design document review fee. The design document review fee refers to the expenses incurred by the project management unit in organizing or entrusting relevant consulting and evaluation agencies to review the design documents of the project (including preliminary design documents and construction drawing design documents) in accordance with relevant national regulations.

The equation for calculation is:

$$\text{Design document review fee} = \text{project design fee} \times 2.2\% \qquad (1\text{-}4\text{-}31)$$

(4) Post evaluation fee of the project. Post evaluation fee of the project refers to the expenses paid by the project management organization for carrying out the comprehensive analysis and evaluation of the project's decision-making, design, construction management, investment benefits and other aspects in accordance with the related national regulations in order to provide scientific and reliable basis to the project's decision-making, guide and improve the project management, improve the investment benefits, and meanwhile provide reference basis to the government's decision-making.

The equation for calculation is:

$$\text{Post evaluation fee of the project} = (\text{construction project cost} + \text{installation project cost}) \times 0.5\% \qquad (1\text{-}4\text{-}32)$$

(5) Technical and economic standard preparation and management fee. The technical and economic standard preparation and management fee refers to the fee payable to the management body for the preparation of technical and economic standards of the power industry to ensure normal operation of the technical and economic standard system for ensuring the

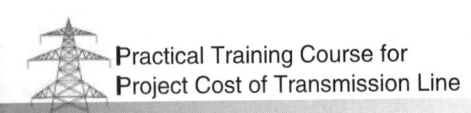

construction of the power industry, ensure the normal preparation, revision, interpretation and research of various technical and economic standards.

The equation for calculation is:

$$\text{Technical and economic standard preparation and management fee} = (\text{construction project cost} + \text{installation project cost}) \times 0.2\% \quad (1\text{-}4\text{-}33)$$

4. Project Construction Supervision and Testing Fee

Project construction supervision and testing fee refers to the expenses incurred for supervising, inspecting and testing the project quality, and special equipment (fire control facilities, etc.) in accordance with the related provisions of national administration authority and power industry.

The equation for calculation is:

$$\text{Project construction supervision and testing fee} = (\text{construction project cost} + \text{installation project cost}) \times 0.3\% \quad (1\text{-}4\text{-}34)$$

5. Production Equipment Cost

Production equipment cost refers to the expenses incurred for providing the technical assurance and resource allocation in order to guarantee the normal production and operation after the completion and acceptance of a project.

It mainly includes the expenses incurred in the purchase of tools, necessary safety protective equipment (excluding fire-fighting equipment), warning boards, signs and so on.

The equation for calculation is:

$$\text{Production preparation costs} = (\text{construction project costs} + \text{installation project costs}) \times 0.75\% \quad (1\text{-}4\text{-}35)$$

6. Basic reserve cost. Basic reserve cost refers to the cost increased for design changes (including the increase or decrease of quantities, equipment modification, and material substitution), project construction fund reserved for possible losses caused by all natural disasters and expenses for temporary measure costs for preventing natural disasters, as well as the project construction fund reserved for the possible losses caused by general natural disasters and other uncertainties.

The equation for calculation is:

Basic reserve cost = [construction project cost + installation project cost + equipment procurement cost + other expenses (excluding basic reserve cost)] × rate　　(1-4-36)

Table 1–4–9　Rate of Basic Reserve Cost

Design stage	Rate (%)
Investment estimate	3
Preliminary design budget estimate	2
Construction drawing budget	1

(IV) Dynamic Cost

Dynamic cost refers to the interests incurred during the construction period for raising debt capital and accounted into the original value of fixed assets after the project is put into production as allowed by the related provisions.

The equation for calculation is:

Interest for loans during construction = (year opening amount of accumulated principal and interest + loan of that year /2) × annual interest rate　　(1-4-37)

The construction period of the transmission and distribution line project is short and the investment is small, so this cost generally does not occur.

Table 1–4–10 Calculation of Other Costs

Unit: Yuan

No.	Project name	Major content and scope of work	Combined price
1	Construction site requisition and clearing costs		
1.1	Compensation for land acquisition		
1.2	Waste cleaning cost		
1.3	Construction site rental		
1.4	Compensation for line construction		
2	Construction management cost of the project		3218.38
2.1	Project management cost	(construction project costs + installation project costs) × 1.15%	769.46

Table (Cont'd)

No.	Project name	Major content and scope of work	Combined price
2.2	Bidding cost	(construction project costs + installation project costs + equipment procurement costs) × 0.32%	742.73
2.3	Engineering supervision fee	(construction project cost + installation project cost) × 2.55%	1706.19
3	Technical service cost for project construction		6037.59
3.1	Survey fees	construction project cost × 4.5%	208.12
3.2	Engineering design expense	(construction project cost + installation project cost) × 7.84%	5245.70
3.3	Design document review fee	Project design fee × 2.2%	115.41
3.4	Project post evaluation fee	(construction project cost + installation project cost) × 0.5%	334.52
3.5	Technical and economic standard preparation and management fee	(construction cost + installation cost) × 0.2%	133.82
4	Project construction supervision and testing fee	(construction project cost + installation project cost) × 0.3%	200.73
5	Production preparation cost	(construction project costs + installation project costs) × 0.75%	501.82
6	Basic reserve cost	[construction project cost + installation project cost + equipment procurement cost + other expenses (excluding basic reserve cost)] × 1%	2420.60

Task 5 General Budget Sheet

After completing the summary table of installation project discipline (Table II B), the summary table of construction discipline (Table II B), and the budget sheet of other costs (Table IV), according to the project breakdown, the construction project cost is taken from the summary table of construction discipline, the equipment procurement cost and installation project cost are taken from the summary table of installation project discipline, and then the corresponding expenses are taken from the budget sheet of other costs to complete the total budget sheet. See Appendix 1 for relevant forms.

Task 6　Prepare a budget estimate

A complete Budget Estimate must also include a "compilation note" to explain the preparation, the basis for preparation, and some issues that need to be explained, to facilitate reading and review.

The compilation note of the Budget Estimate for the distribution network project of 20kV and below shall be specific, exact, concise and standardized.

Its contents generally include:

(I) Project overview. Including the terrain where the line passes, soil structure, wind power, transportation conditions, line model, length, pole and tower type, grounding, cable length, size, and laying method

(II) Construction scope, construction measures and costs of the project.

(III) Principles and basis for preparation. Including the scope of preparation, calculation basis of quantities, quota of charges and standards.

(IV) Description of major issues. See Appendix 1 for the preparation instructions of the project case 1.

Finally, it is compiled and printed as the Budget Estimate for Construction of Power Distribution Network Project of 20kV and Below in the order of the cover, the editor signature page, catalogue, preparation instructions, total budget sheet (Table I), summary table of installation project discipline (Table II A), summary table of construction discipline (Table II B), budget sheet of work units of installation project (Table III A), budget sheet of work units of construction project (Table III B), and budget sheet of other costs (Table IV), as well as the corresponding schedules and attachments.

Study Program I Preparation for Construction Drawing Budget of 10kV Distribution Line

Summary

Project 1 mainly introduces the method of compiling the construction drawing budget of 10kV distribution line with the project case 1 as the carrier: firstly, project breakdown was carried out according to the Preparation and Calculation Standards for Budget of Power Distribution Network Construction of 20kV and Below; quantity statistics were obtained for specific items; then the quota and rate were selected and the budget sheet of work units of installation project and the budget sheet of work units of construction project were completed; the general budget sheet, the summary table of installation project discipline, the summary table of the construction project discipline and the budget sheet of other costs were completed; finally a budget statement was prepared to complete the construction drawing budget for the 10kV distribution line.

Practical Training project I   Power Distribution and Installation Project of A Power Plant

I. Overview

(I) Design Basis

1. Entrusted by a certain factory in a city, we carry out the survey and design of the power distribution and installation project of a certain factory in a city.

2.2. Standard for Distribution Line Design Overhead (DL/T601-1996).

3. Other relevant regulations and norms of the state.

(II) Design Scope

A power distribution project.

(III) Project Overview

1. Connect line on a 32# pole of 10kV line, build two 12m poles and one 10m pole, and build a new line with a total length of 125m.

2. One high-voltage vacuum circuit breaker (12kV; 630A), one high-voltage measuring box and one oil-immersed transformer (S9-200kVA/10) are installed on the N2# pole newly erected.

II. Route and Crossing

(I) Route Overview

The project path can be found in the 10kV Overhead Line Layout Plan, as shown in Fig. 1-7-1.

(II) Crossing

The project spans 1 river.

(Ⅲ) Transportation

The project is located in a town; the proportion of the terrain in the whole line: 100% flat ground; the topographic map of transportation is shown in Fig. 1-7-1.

Geological proportion of the whole line: 80% general soil and 20% hard soil.

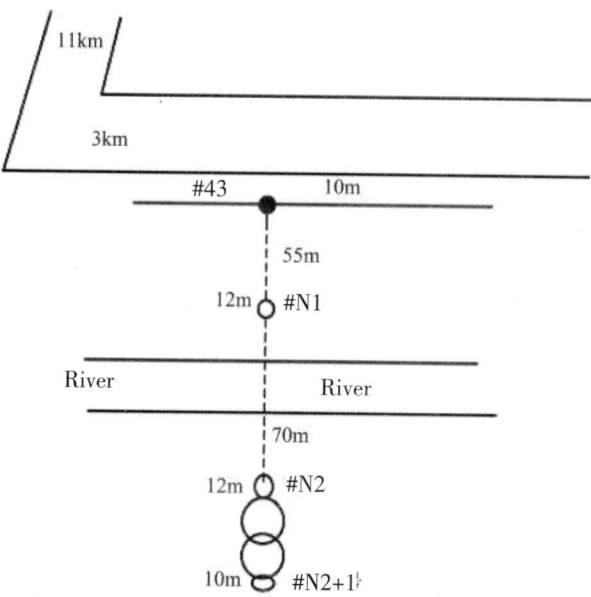

Fig. 1-7-1 Layout Plan of Overhead Line for Power Distribution Project of a Power Plant

Ⅲ. Mechanical and Electrical Part

(Ⅰ) Design Meteorological Conditions (Omitted)

(Ⅱ) Conductor

JKLYJ-10kV-50 insulated conductor is adopted for overhead line of the Project. The safety factor is 7.500, and the safe distance between the overhead line and the surrounding buildings shall meet the requirement of Erection and Acceptance Regulations for Overhead Distribution Lines of 10kV.

(Ⅲ) Lightning Protection and Insulation Coordination

1. The manual earthing body shall be laid on the terminal pole, and the grounding resis-

tance shall meet the requirements of regulations. The suspension point of insulator string and the grounding body shall have reliable electrical connection.

2. The insulators for cement pole erection section shall be FXBW2-10/45, and insulators for intermediate support shall adopt FS-10/3 composite cross arm insulator.

3. A zinc-oxide arrester shall be installed on the N2# pole (HYW5-12.7/50).

(IV) Armor Clamps

The Project adopt power armor clamps of national standard.

IV. Pole and Tower, and Base

(I) Pole and Tower

In this project, two ($\Phi 190 \times 12000$) poles and one ($\Phi 190 \times 10000$) pole are used.

(II) Base

The concrete pole of the Project adopts the chassis base of $D0.8 \times 0.8 \times 0.17$, and the anchor plate of $L0.8 \times 0.4 \times 0.15$.

(III) This Line Is Equipped with A Group of High-voltage Drop-out Fuses (12kV 100A) and A Group of Arresters.

(IV) The Project Drawing Applies Typical Design of 10kV and Below Urban Power Grid Project.

Review and Reflection

1. What is the concept of the construction drawing budget?

2. What is project breakdown? What is the basis for the project breakdown?

3. It is known that a certain line project has a total length of 18km, the terrain is hill, and automobiles are used to transporting to points B and D. As shown in Fig. 1-7-3, the average haul distance of the project and the average haul distance of the human-powered transport are calculated.

Study Program I Preparation for Construction Drawing Budget of 10kV Distribution Line

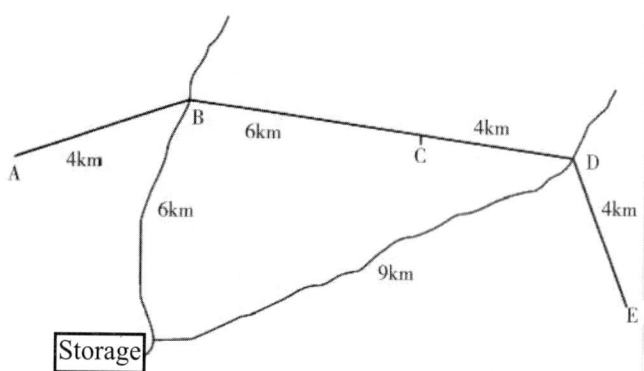

Fig. 1-7-3 Diagram of Transportation of Materials for a Certain Line Project

4.11 new concrete poles are erected in a project, and the pole depth is 1.4m. The earthwork of the pole of the project is calculated.

5.One 15m concrete angle pole and 2 anchor plates are erected, with a buried depth of 1.6m. The earth and stone volume of the concrete pole is calculated.

6.For an overhead line project, the path length is 5km, spanning three 10kV single-circuit lines, one 10kV double-circuit line, and two low-voltage lines. The installation work cost is calculated.

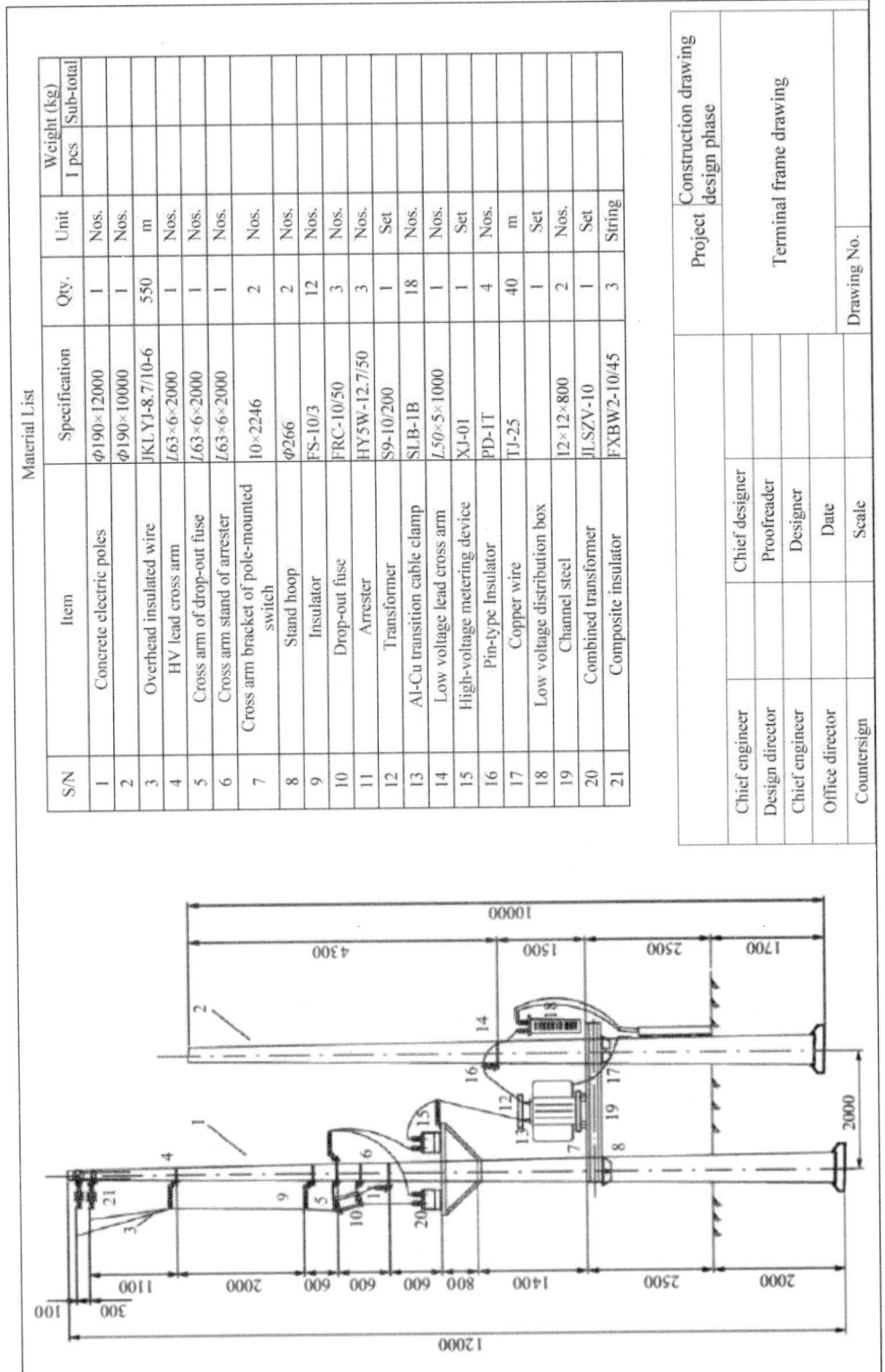

Fig. 1-7-2　Terminal Transformer Platform Area

7. For a 1kV overhead line project with a path length of 5km, the wire is a four-core bundle of 35mm², and the metal fittings are 0.1t. The installation work cost is calculated.

8. For a cable project with a path length of 1km, two YJV22-3*120 mm²-10 kV cables are required to be laid in the same trench. The 100 m pavement is reinforced concrete pavement, and the rest is asphalt pavement with thickness of 150mm. The pavement excavation is calculated.

9. When the path length is 1.5km, four YJV22-3*120 mm²-10 kV cables are required to be laid in the same trench. The earthwork excavation is calculated.

10. For a cable project with the path length of 1km, three YJV22-0-3*120 mm²-cables are required to be laid in the same trench. The soil is all solid. The construction work cost is calculated.

11. What is the composition of the budget for the construction of the distribution network project?

12. What is the composition of the construction and installation work costs?

13. The construction work cost of a distribution network project is 300,000 Yuan, the installation work cost is 200,000 Yuan, and the equipment procurement cost is 500,000 Yuan. The design fee is calculated.

14. The construction work cost of the distribution network project is 100,000 Yuan, the installation work cost is 200,000 Yuan, and the equipment procurement cost is 500,000 Yuan. The design fee is calculated.

15. What are the static project costs and dynamic project costs?

Study Program II

Preparation of Preliminary Budget Estimate for 220kV Overhead Transmission Line Project

Project case II Overview of New Construction Project of 220kV Power Transmission Line

I. Overview

1. Design Basis

(1) Survey and design contract signed with Sichuan Electric Power Corporation.

(2) Sichuan Electric Power Corporation's Reply on the Feasibility Study Report on a New Construction Project of 220kV Power Transmission Line in a City.

(3) A feasibility study report and bidding technical documents of a design institute for the New Project of a 220kV Power Transmission Line in a City.

2. Design Scope

Design of 220kV single circuit (the 3km outgoing line of the small side substation adopts the same tower double-circuit design, and the line is hung on one side in this phase) 2×LGJ-400/35 conductor power transmission line from the outgoing line frame of a 220kV substation (small side) to the incoming line frame of a 220kV substation (large side) at 51.8km, and completion of the project investment estimate. For the auxiliary facilities works, the required cost is only included in this project. OPGW (optical fiber composite overhead ground wire) is hung on the entire line, OPGW material and installation costs are included in the communication works.

II. Route and Crossing

The total length of the line is about 51.8km, and the buckling factor is 1.20. It passes through the administrative areas of three counties (cities). The route is shown in Fig. 2-0-1. The altitude of the entire line is 300-600m. The terrain along the line is high in the north and low in the south. The terrain of the local area is undulating and the relative height difference is more than 100m. The terrain is divided into: 7.4% flat ground, 51.4% hills, and 41.2% mountainous areas.

The strata along the line are simple, mainly the bright red and purple-red mudstones of the Jurassic Suining Formation, the Quaternary calcareous mudstone residuals, and the residual slope accumulation cohesive soil. The rock is generally intact, the loose accumulation layer is also in good condition, and the base soil condition is good. The geology is divided into: 25% rock, 55% loose sand, 16% ordinary soil, and 4% muddy water.

The transport of the project is mainly district and township roads. There are many tractor roads parallel and crossing the whole line. However, the transport conditions in some sections are poor. The average haul distance of the whole line is 28km by automobile and 0.8km by manpower.

The main crossover of the whole line is as shown in Table 2-0-1.

Table 2-0-1 Main Crossings of the Whole Line

S/N	Crossed object	Crossing times
1	110kV power line	3
2	35kV power distribution line	6
3	10kV power distribution line	32
4	Lines of 380V and below	146
5	Broadcasting line and communication line	86
6	Road and farm track	44
7	Small river and river ditch	11
8	Pond	7
9	Jialing River	1

III. Mechanical and Electrical Part

1. Design Meteorological Condition Combination (Omitted)

2. Models Of Conductor and Ground Wire

The conductor is $2 \times$ LGJ-400/35 (GB1179-83) steel-cored aluminum stranded conductor. The incoming line section of the large side substation is connected to another good conductor LBGJ-100-30AC (YB/T124-1997) aluminum-clad steel stranded wire with OPGW-100 at about 8.0km to form a double ground wire. The other sections adopt GJX-80 ($1 \times$ 7-11.4-1270-A-YB/T183-2000) rare-earth zinc-aluminum alloy coated steel strand to be matched with OPGW-100, and OPGW is hung on the right ground wire bracket of the line.

3. Phase Split Conductor Arrangement and Spacing

The conductors are vertically arranged and double-split. Generally, spacers are not installed. When the span is more than 700m, the spacers are installed, and the split spacing is 400mm.

In order to facilitate the construction of the down lead, the split conductors of the incoming and outgoing line span of the substation are arranged horizontally, and spacers are installed with a split spacing of 400mm.

The phase jumpers in the resisting-tensile tower are vertically arranged, and the side phase jumpers are horizontally arranged. A jumper spacer is installed, and the split spacing is 200mm.

4. Anti-vibration of the Conductor Or Ground Wire

The conductor and ground wire of this project are generally treated with anti-vibration with a vibration damper. For the important crossing (including high-voltage power transmission lines of 35kV and above voltage class, class I communication lines, trunk roads, Jialing River, etc.), in addition to the vibration damper, the armor rods for the preformed armor rods are installed for joint protection. See Table 2-0-2 for the type of vibration dampers and the number of vibration dampers to be installed.

Study Program Ⅱ　Preparation of Preliminary Budget Estimate for 220kV Overhead Transmission Line Project

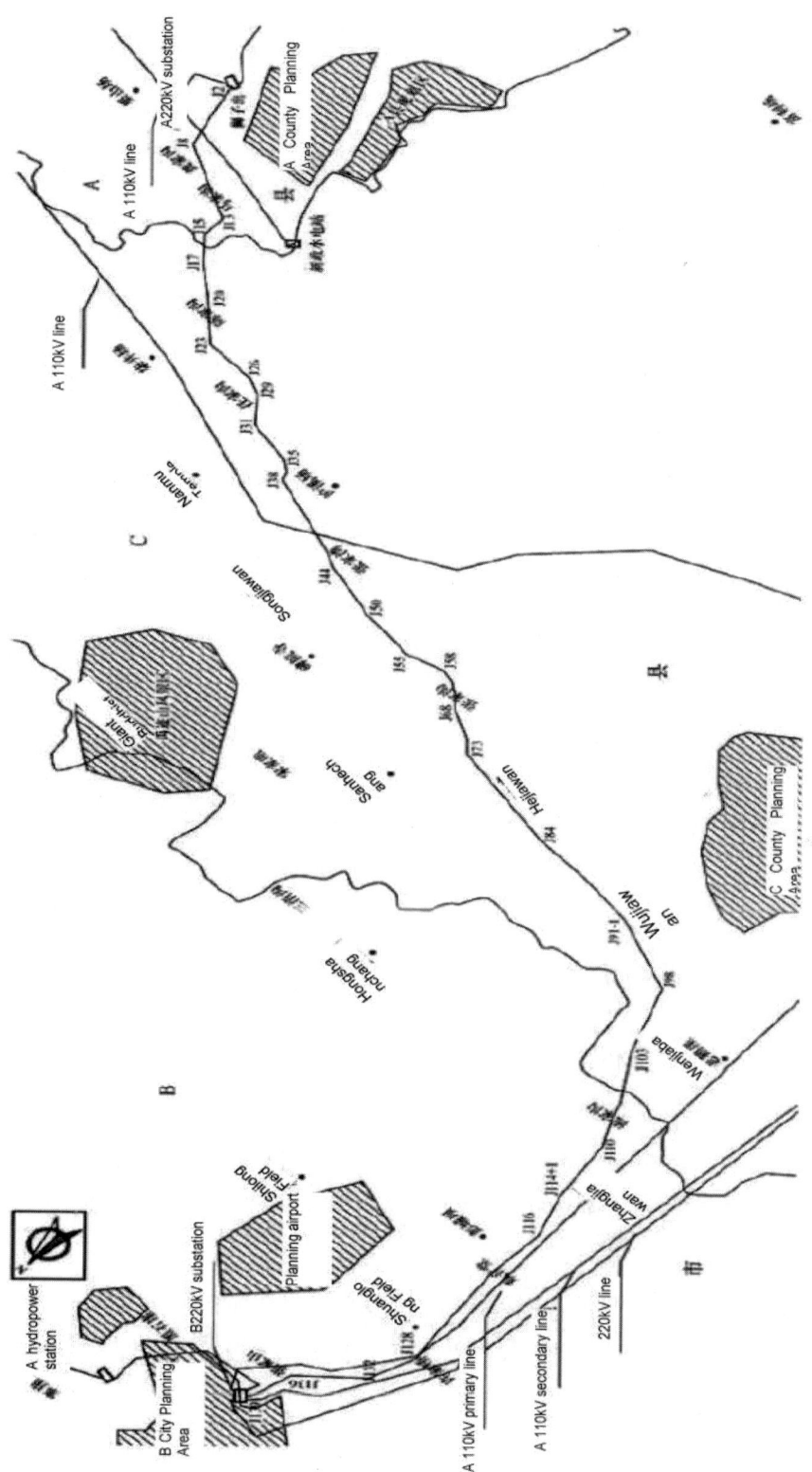

Fig. 2-0-1　Diagram of the Line Path

Table 2-0-2 Type of Vibration Dampers and the Number of Vibration Dampers to Be Installed

Line type \ Model	Qty.	1	2	3	4
LGJ-400/35	FD-5F	$L \leqslant 450$m	$450\text{m} < L \leqslant 800\text{m}$	$800\text{m} < L \leqslant 1200\text{m}$	
LBGJ-100-30AC	FR-2	$L \leqslant 300$m	$300\text{m} < L \leqslant 600\text{m}$	$600\text{m} < L \leqslant 900\text{m}$	$900\text{m} < L \leqslant 1200\text{m}$
GJX-80	FG-70	$L \leqslant 300$m	$300\text{m} < L \leqslant 600\text{m}$	$600\text{m} < L \leqslant 900\text{m}$	$900\text{m} < L \leqslant 1200\text{m}$

5. Insulation Coordination and Lightning Protection

(1) Determination of pollution grade

There is no major pollution source in the area where the project passes. According to the Distribution Map of Polluted Areas of Sichuan Power System published by Sichuan Electric Power Corporation in 2006, it is determined that the 5km part of the incoming line section of the large side substation is Grade III polluted area, and the rest is Grade II polluted area, designed according to the lower limit of the Grade III polluted area combined with field investigation and information collection.

(2) Insulation coordination

The altitude above sea level of the zone where this project passes shall not exceed 600m, and the number of insulator strings and insulators shall be determined according to the long-duration power frequency voltage, and shall be controlled by the pollution grade. The lines of this project are mostly located in hills and mountainous areas where the operation and maintenance conditions are poor. For the convenience of operation and maintenance, it is recommended to use the glass insulators U100BP2 as the suspension strings and the strain insulator strings of the Grade II and III polluted areas. There are 14 suspension strings and 15 strain insulator strings respectively, and another one is added for Grade III polluted area. Porcelain insulators are used on the side of the incoming line frame to prevent the glass insulators from spontaneously exploding to endanger the substation equipment and operating personnel.

According to the design regulations, the height of the tower exceeds 40m, and for each 10m increase in height, the insulator string is provided with an additional insulator.

The altitude above sea level of the section where the project passes is below 600m. No special consideration is needed to the increase of the air gap. The air gap value obtained in this project is shown in Table 2-0-3.

Table 2–0–3 Air Gap Value Table

Working status	Operating voltage	Internal overvoltage	External overvoltage	Live working
Gap value (cm)	55	145	190	180

Note: 30-50mm human activity range shall be considered for the position for the operators of live working to stand and work.

(3) Lightning protection and grounding

The annual average lightning day in the area where the project passes is 40 days, so it belongs to a middle thunderstorm region. Double lightning wires are used for the entire line for lightning protection, and the ground wire is directly grounded. In order to facilitate the accurate measurement of the grounding resistance of the substation at both ends of the line, one piece of XDP-70C skirtless porcelain insulator is added for the strain fitting string of ground wire at the side of the portal frame in the incoming and outgoing line span. In the non-measuring state, the insulator shall be shortened.

Grounding device. According to the geological conditions of the project, the grounding device adopts a typical design, that is, the grounding is arranged in ring-shaped and windmill-type radial shallow-buried horizontal arrangement form, as shown in Fig. 2-0-2. It is combined with the tower base by natural grounding. Except for the type A grounding device, the forms of types B, C, D, E, and F are the same. Only the value of A is different, A B is 5m, A C is 20m, A D is 30m, A E is 60m, and A F is 78m. The grounding device is selected according to the soil resistivity, as shown in Table 2-0-4, in which type C accounts for 10%, type D accounts for 35%, type E accounts for 50%, and type F accounts for 5%. The grounding body shall be $\Phi 10$ round steel, and the down lead shall be $\Phi 12$ round steel. Both of them require hot-dip galvanizing treatment, and the grounding down lead shall not be exposed to the ground too long. According to the design specifications and countermeasure rules, the power frequency grounding resistance of the pole and tower grounding resistor during the thunderstorm season shall not exceed the values shown in Table 2-0-5.

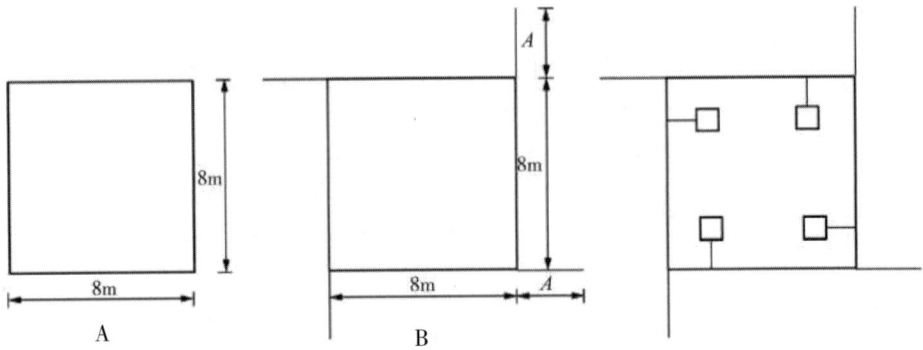

Fig. 2–0–2 Diagram of Form of Grounding Device and Its Connection with the Tower

6. Insulator String and Fittings

The main dimensions and characteristics of glass insulators are shown in Table 2-0-6.

The conductor or ground wire shall be connected by hydraulic way. See Table 2-0-7. The type of fitting insulator strings used in this project and the specific use range are shown in Fig. 2-0-5 and Fig. 2-0-6 General Chart of Assembly of Insulator Fitting String

Table 2–0–4　Grounding Device Selection and Material Table

Applicable soil resistivity (Ω·m)				≤100	100 ~ 300	300 ~ 500	500 ~ 1000	1000 ~ 2000	>2000
Grounding device model				A	B	C	D	E	F
Material List	Round steel	Φ12	Length (m)	10.0	10.0	10.0	10.0	10.0	10.0
			Weight (kg)	8.88	8.88	8.88	8.88	8.88	8.88
		Φ10	Length (m)	40	60	120	160	280	352
			Weight (kg)	24.50	36.76	73.52	98.02	171.53	215.64
	Flat steel 130×50×5		Length (m)	0.52	0.52	0.52	0.52	0.52	0.52
			Weight (kg)	1.230	1.230	1.230	1.230	1.230	1.230
	M16×45 Galvanized bolts and nuts for tower		Set	4	4	4	4	4	4
			Weight (kg)	0.584	0.584	0.584	0.584	0.584	0.584
Grounded earthwork volume (m³)				9.6	14.4	28.8	38.4	67.2	84.5

Study Program II Preparation of Preliminary Budget Estimate for 220kV Overhead Transmission Line Project

Table 2-0-5 Power Frequency Grounding Resistance Value Table

Soil resistivity ($\Omega \cdot m$)	≤100	100~300	300~500	500~1000	1000~2000	>2000
Power frequency grounding resistance (Ω)	5	10	12	15	20	27

Table 2-0-6 Main Dimensions and Characteristics of Insulators

Insulator type	Main Dimensions			Electromechanical characteristics		Rated mechanical failure load (kN)
	Height (mm)	Coil diameter (mm)	Creepage distance (mm)	Power frequency wet flash discharge voltage (kV)	Full wave impulse flashover voltage (kV)	
U100BP2	146	280	450	45	120	100

Table 2-0-7 Fitting Insulator String Type and Its Specific Range of Use

S/N	Line type	Type	Use
1	Conductor	HX single connection with armor rod string (1′14′U100BP2)	Important crossing tangent tower
2	Conductor	SHX double connection with armor rod string (2′14′U100BP2)	Large span tangent tower
3	Conductor	SHX1 double connection with armor rod string (2′14′U100BP2)	Important crossing tangent tower
4	Conductor	CTX single connection jumper string (1′14′U100BP2)	General angle tower mid-phase
5	Conductor	N double connection strain insulator string (2′15′U100BP2)	Tension angle tower
6	Conductor	DN single connection strain insulator string (1′15′U100BP2)	At the side of door frame of incoming and outgoing line span
7	Conductor	TDN single connection strain insulator string with double adjustment plate (1′15′U100BP2)	At the side of terminal tower of incoming and outgoing line span
8	Ground Wire	BX11 single suspension string	General tangent tower GJX-80
9	Ground Wire	BX12 single suspension string	General tangent tower LBGJ-100-30AC
10	Ground Wire	BN1 single strain insulator string	Strain and angle tower GJX-80
11	Ground Wire	BJN single strain insulator string and insulator (1′1′XDP2-70C)	At the side of door frame of incoming line span

7. Conductor Transposition and Phase Sequence Matching

The length of the line is 51.8km. According to the design specifications, the conductors do not need to be transposed. Because the substations at both ends do not correspond, the phase sequence is adjusted on the terminal towers on both sides of the line project.

8. Conductor-to-ground and Crossing Distance

The wire-to-ground and crossing distances are shown in Table 2-0-8.

Table 2-0-8 Conductor-to-Ground and Crossing Distance Table

S/N	Crossed object	Spacing (m)	Remarks
1	Residential area	7.5	Densely populated areas such as ports and towns
2	Non-residential area	6.5	Building rare areas where vehicles can reach
3	Areas with transport difficulties	5.5	Areas where vehicles cannot reach
4	Highway pavement	8.0	
5	Power line	4.0	
6	Communication line	4.0	
7	To the top of the tree with maximum natural growth height	4.5	
8	To the top of the fruit tree with the maximum natural growth height	3.5	
9	Navigation river (Level 4)	3.0	To the top of the highest mast with the highest navigation level
10	To the flood level of a hundred-year flood	4.0	

9. Communication Protection

This project is a neutral point direct grounding system, and the conductors are mostly arranged in a triangle shape. The main adjacent telecommunication line is an overhead optical cable. It is estimated that the project has no danger and interference to the telecommunication lines within the affected area, and the hazard and interference effects on the adjacent radio facilities meet the protection spacing requirements, so there is no impact.

10. Pole & Tower and Base

(1) Pole and tower

In this project, all-round self-supporting iron towers with legs of different height are used. The straight tower is of cat head type (nominal height is 21~42m), the angle tower is in "干" shape (nominal height is 18~36m), and the double-circuit line adopts double-circuit drum towers. The tower body sections are all square, all of which are according to the 2005 Typical Design of Transmission and Transformation Project of State Grid Corporation of China. 12 types of towers such as ZM1, ZM2 and ZM3 are used for the whole line, as shown in Table 2-0-9. See Fig. 2-0-3 for the General Chart of Poles and Towers (where JC2, JC3, and JC4 towers are the same as JC1 in shape; SJ3 and SJ4 towers are the same as SJ1 in shape).

Table 2-0-9 List of Poles and Towers

S/N	Tower model	Applicable line section	Line length (m)	Steel consumption (t)	Remarks
1	2A-ZM1	2′400 compound conductor	27	4.88	Apply (cat head type tangent tower)
2	2A-ZM2	2′400 compound conductor	33	6.32	Apply (cat head type tangent tower)
3	2A-ZM3	2′400 compound conductor	39	8.04	Apply (cat head type tangent tower)
4	2A-ZMC3	2′400 compound conductor	36	9.62	Apply (cat head type tangent tower)
5	2A-ZMC4	2′400 compound conductor	39	11.74	Apply (cat head type tangent tower)
6	2A-JC1 (0°~20°)	2′400 compound conductor	30	10.47	Apply ("干" shaped resisting-tensile tower)
7	2A-JC2 (20°~40°)	2′400 compound conductor	30	11.28	Apply ("干" shaped resisting-tensile tower)
8	2A-JC3 (40°~60°)	2′400 compound conductor	30	12.49	Apply ("干" shaped resisting-tensile tower)
8	2A-JC4 (60°~90°)	2′400 compound conductor	30	14.10	Apply ("干" shaped resisting-tensile tower)
9	2I-SZ3	2′400 compound conductor	38	14.70	Apply (double-circuit drum tangent tower)
10	2I-SJ2 (20°~40°)	2′400 compound conductor	27	27.82	Apply (double-circuit drum-shaped resisting-tensile tower)

Table (Cont'd)

S/N	Tower model	Applicable line section	Line length (m)	Steel consumption (t)	Remarks
11	2I-SJ3 (40°~60°)	2'400 compound conductor	27	28.36	Apply (double-circuit drum-shaped resisting-tensile tower)
12	2I-SJ4 (60°~90°)	2'400 compound conductor	27	31.78	Apply (double-circuit drum-shaped resisting-tensile tower)

A total of 137 towers were used on the whole line. The average span distance is 0.38km, and the average length of the strain section is 1.04km. There are 86 linear towers with an average nominal height of 28m and 51 strain or angle towers with an average nominal height of 22m. The steel for the pole and tower is Q235 and Q345 steel, the connecting bolt M16 is Level 4.8, and the M20 and M24 bolts are Level 6.8.

All tower bolts above the top surface of the shortest leg base column and below the 8.0m plane of each tower are anti-theft bolts, and the remaining bolts are protected against loosening.

(2) Bases

The base form adopted in this project is determined based on the site terrain combined with engineering geology and hydrogeology. The seismic intensity along the line is degree VI in accordance with the Code for Design of Seismic of Electrical Installations (GB50260-96), and anti-seismic measures are not considered for the base. All of them are reinforced concrete cast-in-place bases, which are in four types of forms (eight kinds): rock-embedded base (QG), straight-column full-excavating base (TW), inclined column base, and straight-column flexible base (LZ), as shown in Fig. 2-0-4 General Chart of Base.

The base concrete strength grades are C20 and C25, and that of the base cushion and anchor bolt protection caps is C10. The base steel is HPB235 (Q235) and HRB335 (20Mnsi) grade reinforcement; the anchor bolt round steel is made of 35 steel or 16Mn steel, and the steel plate is Q235 and Q345 steel. Concrete sand, stone, water, and cement (32.5 ordinary Portland cement) shall meet the requirements of the corresponding standard specifications.

(3) Construction instructions and requirements, operation and maintenance precautions, environmental protection and soil and water conservation measures (omitted)

Fig. 2-0-3 General Chart of Poles and Towers

List of Base Materials

S/N	Base Name	Base Code	Pouring Type	Single base steel quantity (kg)	Single base concrete quantity (m³)	Applicable tower type
1	Straight column type	LZ type	Cast-in-place base	111.5~483.3	1.4~5.92	Tangent tower type
		XC type		220.6~618.9	2.81~7.94	Resisting-tensile tower type
2	Inclined column type	XCZ type		91.9~426.8	1.38~4.13	Tangent tower type
		XL type		276.1~1234.9	1.08~17.72	Resisting-tensile tower type
		XY type		232.4~626.4	2.81~7.3	Resisting-tensile tower type
3	Excavating type	TW type		43.4~118.4	2.25~4.13	All tower types
4	Embedded type	QG type		27.0~58.3	2.51~5.33	All tower types

Description:

(1) The cast-in-place concrete base reinforcement is HPB235(I) and HRB335(II); the anchor bolts are Q235 and 35#; the concrete strength grades are C20 and C25; the base protection cap and the base cushion are C10.

(2) The individual steel consumption in the table does not include the weight of steel inserted into the steel angle and the anchor bolt.

(3) The single concrete consumption in the table does not include the amount of protection caps.

Fig. 2-0-4 General Chart of Base

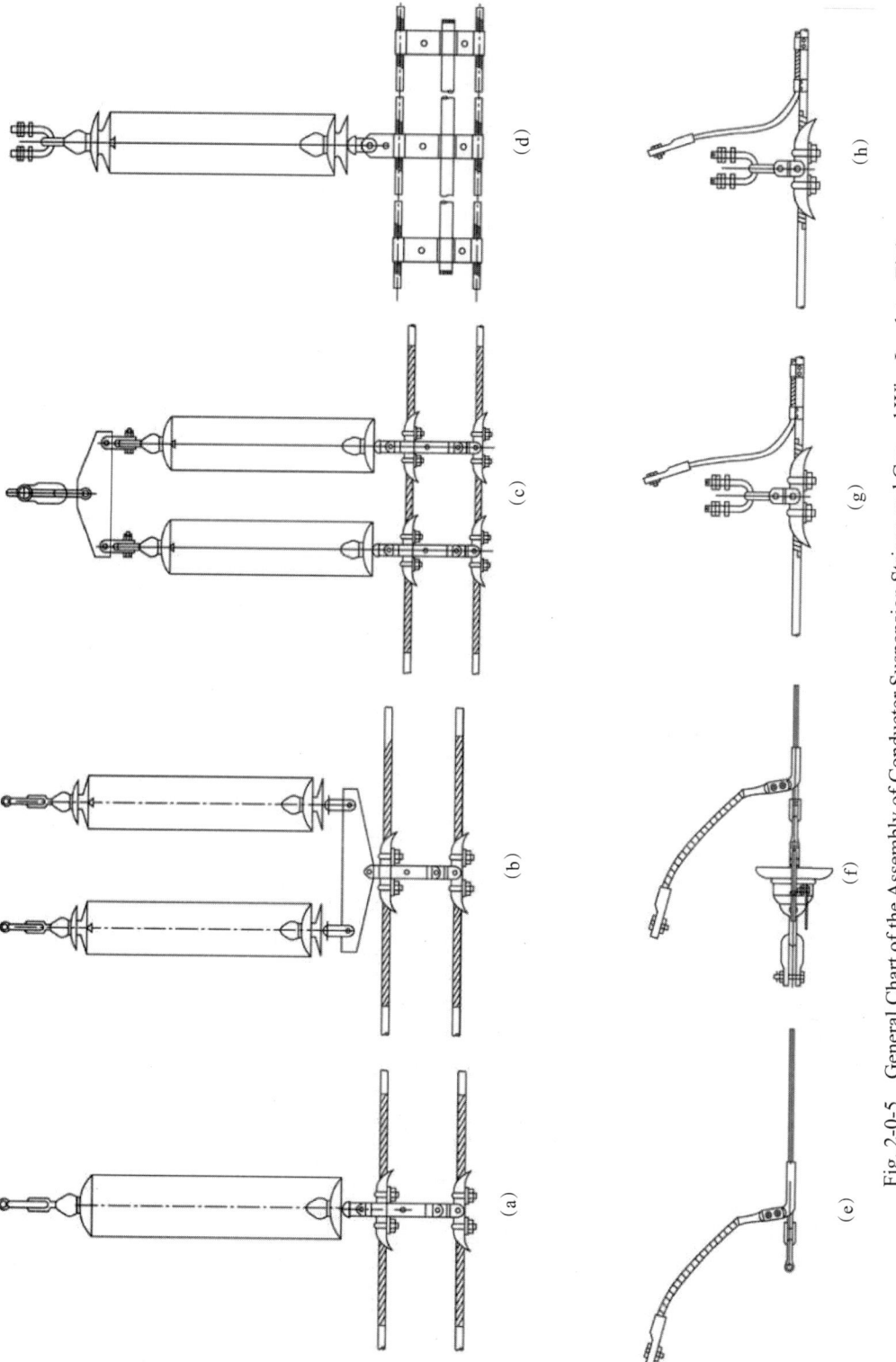

Fig. 2-0-5　General Chart of the Assembly of Conductor Suspension Strings and Ground Wire Insulator Fittings

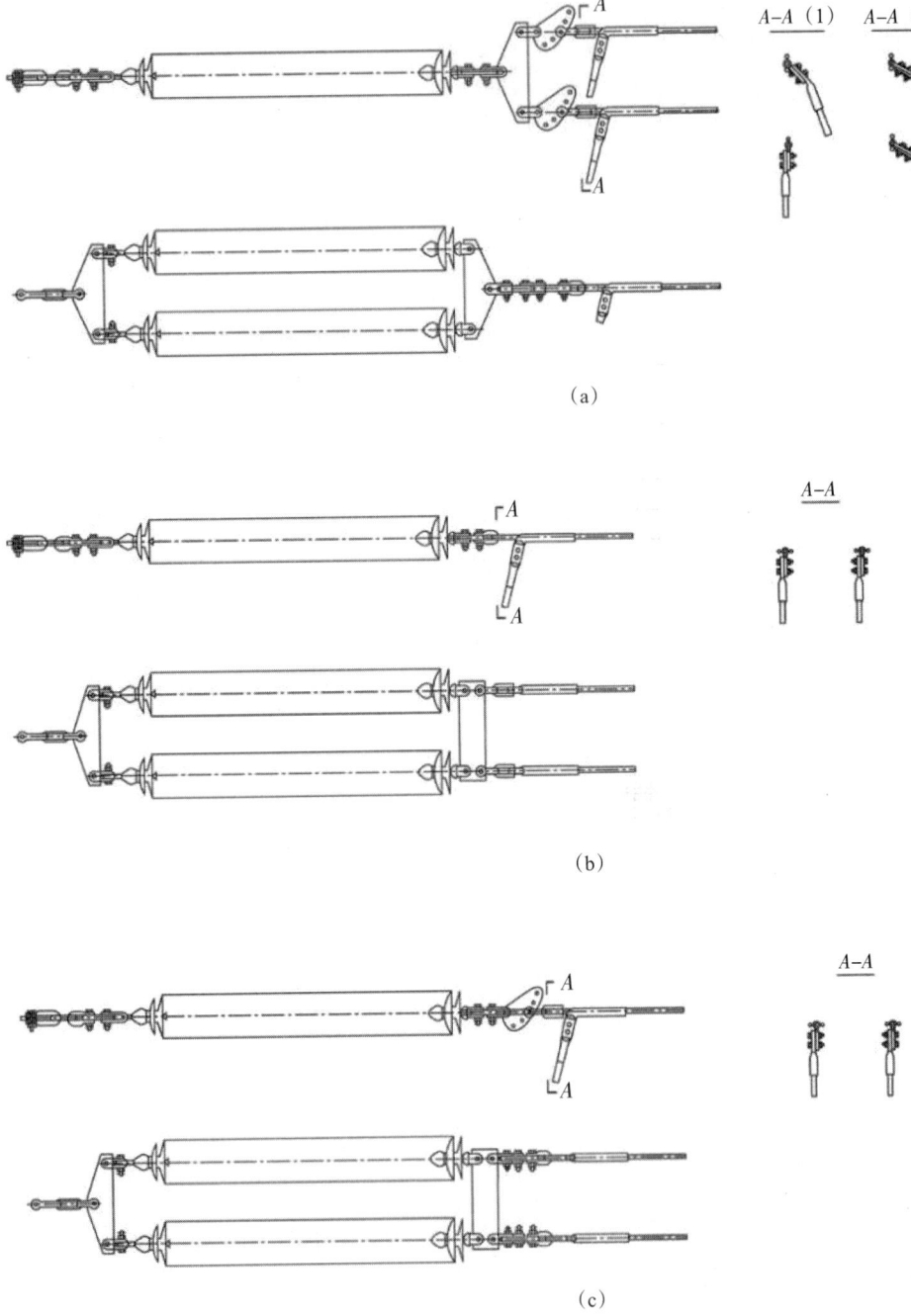

Fig. 2-0-6 List of Strain Insulator Fittings

Task 1 Be Familiar with the Composition of the Budget Estimate

In order to successfully complete the task of preparing the Budget Estimate for the power transmission line project, the content of the Budget Estimate shall be mastered, especially the cost-related composition and calculation standards of the budget estimate, the method and process of preparing the budget estimate, the division of the project, and the construction organization and construction methods of the transmission line project. In the specific work, operators must also be skilled in using project quotas.

I. Introduction To Standard for Budget Preparation and Calculation of Grid Project Construction

The Standard for Budget Preparation and Calculation of Grid Project Construction (2007 Edition) (hereinafter referred to as Budget Standard) is one of the series of power construction budget standards. It is prepared in accordance with the spirit of the Letter from the National Development and Reform Commission on the Development of Power Engineering Cost and Quota Management (FGBNY [2006] No. 427), the Law of the People's Republic of China on Tenders and Bids, Valuation Management Method for Contract Awarding and Contracting of Construction of Architectural Engineering (Order No. 107 of the Ministry of Construction), Construction and Installation Project Cost Composition (Ministry of Construction and Ministry of Finance, JB [2003] No. 206), as well as Code of Valuation with Bill Quantity of Electric Power Construction Works (GB50500-2003) and Code of Valuation with Bill Quantity of Electric Power Construction Works (DL/T5205-2005) combined with the features of construction of power grid projects in order to reasonably determine the project cost, improve the investment efficiency, safeguard the legitimate rights and interests of all parties involved in the project construction, and promote the healthy development of the power construction industry, in accordance with the principle of "national macro-control, market competition to form prices". The "Budget Regulations" was proposed by the China Electricity Council, approved by the National Development and Reform Commission, and implemented on December 1, 2007; it is managed and explained by the Power Engineering Cost and Quota Management Station.

The 2007 Budget Standard draws on the experience and content of the previous editions of "Budget Regulations" (i.e. Basic Construction Budget Management System and Regulations of the Electric Power Industry), inherits and continues the power project construction budget management system, and fully considers the different responsibilities and tasks of the participants in the current power construction management system and the different characteristics of various project management modes, reflecting the applicability, timeliness and fairness of the power project construction budget management system.

The Budget Standard stipulates and cost composition and calculation standard of the power grid construction budget, the division of the nature of the cost, the division of budget items, the preparation method of the construction budget, and the pricing method of the construction budget. As the basis for preparation and cost calculation for feasibility study investment estimation of power grid projects, preliminary design budget estimate, construction drawing budget and power construction project quantity list quotation, it shall be used along with the power project investment estimation indicators, budgetary quotas, budget quotas and pricing specifications of power construction quantity list, and it is also the basis for mediating and handling economic disputes and appraising the tender offer.

The Budget Standard is applicable to construction, reconstruction and expansion of 35kV-750kV AC transmission and transformation projects with various investment channels, ±500kV and below DC power transmission projects, converter station projects and system communication projects.

The reference to "xx and below" in the relevant table of the Budget Standard includes xx, and the lower limit is above the upper limit of "×× and below". Those that do not indicate "×× and below" shall apply to this voltage class project. For distribution network projects of 20kV and below, the Preparation and Calculation Standards for Budget of Power Distribution Network Construction of 20kV and Below, Budget Quota for 20kV and below Distribution Network Engineering Construction and other relevant regulations that are promulgated by the National Energy Administration are implemented.

II. Composition of the Construction Budget

The project construction budget estimate is the project construction budget prepared in the preliminary design stage. When preparing the project construction budget, it is first necessary to formulate a unified compilation principle and determine a unified basis for preparation. The principles of the preparation shall include the scope of preparation, the price level, and the principle of determining the quota, price and fee collection standards. The basis for preparation includes: calculation basis for quantities, basis for calculation of consumption of labor, materials and machinery, etc. (quota or index), basis for price of labor, materials, machinery and equipment, basis for price level adjustment and calculation standard for charges. The calculation of quantities shall be carried out according to the construction budget item division in the Budget Standard. According to the calculation rules of the quantities specified by the quota (index), the data shall be calculated according to the design drawing; the quota or index used must be the current ones applicable for the preparation year. The price of labor, materials and machinery shall be calculated on the basis of the quotas and relevant regulations promulgated by the competent authorities of the power industry quota (cost), in accordance with the price adjustment regulations of the province (autonomous region and municipality directly under the Central Government) where the project is located; the charge calculation standard shall be the budget composition and calculation standard matched with the quotas or indexes used.

The project construction budget preparation, also known as "determination and control of project cost", refers to the calculation of the charge related items of quantities of construction works of a project determined according to the design, on which basis the preparation, verification, audit and approval procedures are handled to determine the project cost activity within the project's reasonable investment amount. The compilers are called "project cost engineers or cost engineers" and are collectively referred to as project cost personnel. In the project cost determination activities, the project cost personnel are required to strive to improve their own business level, prepare the project (estimate) budget in accordance with the relevant cost documents, and use reasonable charge calculation methods to improve the accuracy of the project construction budget prepared. It is strictly forbidden to overestimate or practice fraud in the project cost activities. For those who commit serious violations, the practicing certificate will be cancelled or renewal is impossible according to the relevant regulations.

According to the Budget Standard, the construction cost of the power transmission line project budget is composed of installation work cost, other expenses and dynamic cost, and the sum of the first two items is called static investment. The preparation unit shall specify the reasons for the changes that have occurred during the preparation of the project construction budget, or where the project legal person requests to adjust or supplement some of the costs, and provide sufficient basis for the adjustment; if it is indeed necessary to add additional cost items beyond the Budget Standard, they must be recorded based on the regulations of the national administration authority and the people's governments of all provinces (autonomous regions and municipalities directly under the Central Government), after being recognized by the power industry quota (cost) management agency. The project construction budget of the power transmission line project is divided into installation work cost, auxiliary facilities project cost and other expenses according to the nature of the cost. The site transport, earth and stone works, base works, pole and tower assembly and erection, installation of overhead conductor and ground wire and accessory installation of overhead line projects are collectively referred to as installation works, which are the installation works for the line project itself.

The project construction budget consists of preparation instructions, project overview and general budget sheet (Table I), professional summary budget sheet (Table II), Unit Work Budget Estimate (Table III), budget sheet of other costs (Table IV), main technical and economic indicators (Table V), budget sheet of construction site requisition and clearing costs (Table VII) and the corresponding schedules and annexes, and there shall be an analysis of the budget cost level. The composition of the construction budget of the power transmission line project is shown in Table 2-1-1.

Study Program II Preparation of Preliminary Budget Estimate for 220kV Overhead Transmission Line Project

Table 2-1-1 Summary of Contents of the Construction Budget of the Power Transmission Line Project

S/N	Content/Composition Name	Feasibility study estimation	Preliminary design budget estimate	Construction drawing budget
1	Preparation instructions (including cost level analysis)	√	√	√
2	Project Overview and Main Economic Indicator Table (Table V C)	√	√	√
3	General Budget (Estimate) Sheet (Table I-B and D)	√	√	√
4	Summary Budget (Estimate) Sheet of the Construction and Installation Work Costs of Power Transmission Lines (Table II B)	√	√	√
5	Summary Budget (Estimate) Sheet of the Unit Work Costs of Power Transmission Lines (Table II C and D)	*	√	√
6	Summary Budget (Estimate) Sheet of the Auxiliary Facilities Costs of Power Transmission Lines (Table III E)	√	√	√
7	Budget (Estimate) Sheet of Other Expenses (Table IV)	√	√	√
8	General Budget (Estimate) Sheet of Construction Site Requisition and Clearing (Table VII)	√	√	√
9	Calculating Table of Comprehensive Terrain Increase Coefficient (Schedule I)	√	√	√
10	Statistical Table of Installation Materials for Power Transmission Line Project (Schedule II)	*	√	√
11	Calculating Table of Earthwork Volume for Power Transmission Lines (Schedule III)	*	√	√
12	Calculating Table of Site Transport Weight of Power Transmission Line Project (Schedule IV)	*	√	√
13	Calculating Table of Site Transport Quantities of Power Transmission Line Project (Schedule V)	*	√	√
14	List of Categories of Poles and Towers of Power Transmission Line Project (Schedule VI)	*	√	√

Note: The content marked with "*" is the original data of the preparation unit and may not be published; the relevant form is attached to the schedule.

The schedules for other expenses of the construction budget shall be complete, including the calculating table of reserve cost for price difference, the calculating table of interest for loans during construction (the feasibility study estimate may not be attached), the annual price difference calculating table, and the necessary annexes. The annexes include the construction Budget Estimate of the external design project, the basis of the special project and the construction Budget Estimate.

III. Budget Estimate Preparation Method

The budget estimate, also referred to as the preliminary design estimate, refers to the pre-calculation and determination of project cost based on preliminary design documents, budget quotas and cost calculations in the preliminary design stage. It also refers to the process of preparing, calculating and determining the budget estimates in the preliminary design stage.

(I) Preparations

1. Understand the Overall Situation of the Project

After the compiler accepts the budget preparation task, the compiler shall have a comprehensive understanding of the design of the construction project. The content is as follows:

(1) Design assignment (power of attorney) or project proposal (document number, approval unit and content - construction scale, voltage class, design scope and main design principles, etc.).

(2) The location of the project start and end points and the terrain, geomorphology, geology, groundwater level, wind power, seismic intensity, line extending length, conductor and ground line type, and pole and tower type.

(3) Source of funds (ratio of contributions of financing units) and investment limits. A copy of the joint venture (cooperation) agreement of each investor, including the capital balance and the level of interest in dividend, the bank's commitment to the loan of the financing, including financing costs, repayment methods and years; other documents of financing channels.

(4) The construction method (mainly the form of bidding) and the name of the Employer and the construction period (including the planned production date).

(5) Relevant documents and regulations issued by relevant government departments at the project site, such as construction site preparation fee and land acquisition fee standards, cost standards and basis of the project welfare in construction on project site.

Study Program II Preparation of Preliminary Budget Estimate for 220kV Overhead Transmission Line Project

(6) The bid price and scope of supply of major equipment and materials.

(7) The consignment power agreement promised by the network (provincial) power company, and the commitment document of the relevant department on the estimated on-grid price.

(8) Formal budget estimates for entrusting external design projects (e.g. roads, terminals, waterways, etc.).

(9) Other relevant documents and materials as specified in the agreement.

(10) The preliminary arrangement of the survey and design and the requirements for the discipline.

(11) Other related issues.

2. Collecting Information On Site

After understanding the overall situation of the project, refer to the engineering materials of the same type or the same area provided by the design institute, and compile the survey and search outline. After the relevant responsible person has reviewed and approved, collect the information according to the outline.

After the information collection is completed, the collected information will be analyzed and compiled, and an information collection report will be prepared.

(II) Provisions and Basis for the Preparation

1.Standard for Budget Preparation and Calculation of Grid Project Construction.

2.User Guide to Power Construction Engineering Budget Norm (Book IV: Transmission Line Works 2006).

3.The price of installation materials for a province's power construction.

(III) Procedure for Preparation of the Budget

The process flow of the budget estimate preparation is shown in Fig. 2-1-1.

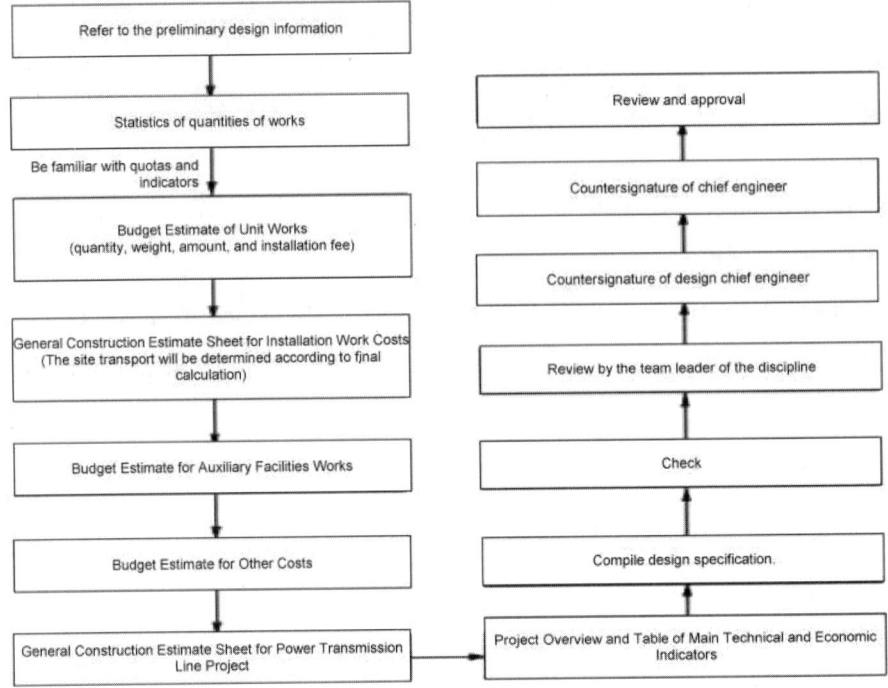

Fig. 2-1-1 Diagram of the Process Flow of the Budget Estimate Preparation

(1) Determine the quantities of budget estimate

The estimated quantities shall be determined based on the content and depth of the preliminary design, and in accordance with the optimization plan recommended in the design, and provided by the designer according to the requirements and depth of the budget estimate preparation.

(2) Be familiar with the corresponding budget estimate indicators or quotas (only budget quota for power transmission projects), as well as related provisions such as Budget Standard.

(3) Charge calculation

Refer to the budget quota of the transmission line project, implement the relevant regulations such as the Budget Standard, calculate the charge of the quantities, determine the construction and installation work costs (including the installation material cost), other expenses and dynamic costs, and finally calculate the estimated investment amount of the preliminary design.

The calculation of the charge for the preliminary design budget estimate can be carried out in the process of determining the project case budget estimate by means of item-by-item charge, comprehensive coefficient charge for work units or item-by-item charge after work units summary.

(4) Fill out the "Project Overview and Table of Main Technical and Economic Indicators"

(5) Instructions for Preparation

(6) Check, review, and approval

Firstly, the compiler shall conduct self-checking of all the contents of the Budget Estimate including the specification, form, schedule and attachments. Secondly, the discipline team leader shall review the Budget Estimate, and again the design chief engineer and chief engineer shall countersign the statement.

Finish the Budget Estimate. The preparation, verification and review personnel at all levels must sign the formal Budget Estimate and affix the special seal of the electric power project cost personnel.

After the Budget Estimate is submitted to the power industry quota (cost) management department for review, all design documents including the Budget Estimate are sent to the project Party A or the designated organization of Party A for approval. Based on the approval documents, the design unit continues to implement the project project construction drawing design to prepare the construction drawing budget estimate.

(7) Notes

1) The budget estimate must be prepared according to the selected transmission line project path, and the charge is in accordance with the regulations and is calculated correctly.

2) For special construction projects not included in the quota and cost, the cost can be calculated according to the design plan and the quantities in the construction organization design outline, and shall be included in the project budget estimate.

3) The price of the installation materials, consumable materials and machinery is calculated according to the regulations issued by the power industry quota (cost) management department, and the price difference is calculated according to the market price of the project location. Only tax is recorded for the price difference.

4) The preliminary design estimate is to determine the total investment of the project at the preliminary design stage and, in principle, to control the estimated investment in the ap-

proved feasibility study.

5) According to the needs of the project preparation and construction procedures, the budget estimate for commenced works in "four connections and one leveling" or single works can be prepared first.

(Ⅳ) Basic Methods for Preparing the Budget Estimates

1. Manual Preparation

That is, draw a table first, then calculate and fill in the table to form a Budget Estimate. With the popularization of computers, this is no longer such a task.

2. Excel Spreadsheet

Excel is a component of office automation software developed by Microsoft Corporation. It is easy to learn and implement table editing and calculation functions, etc. Because the project budget estimate is expressed in the form of a table, the Excel spreadsheet is particularly suitable for use as a tool for budget estimate preparation. Considering that the budget estimate class of the power transmission line project by general grid engineering technicians is single and the number of projects is small, the Excel spreadsheet can fully meet the needs. As long as a relatively complete engineering data table is generated, the budget estimate for projects of the same type can be completed on its basis. The workload can be greatly reduced by moderate modifications.

3. Professional Budget Software

At present, there are many types of power engineering cost software such as Microcyber, Penge Software, Yuandon, and Zhuye, which are suitable for the compilation and review of estimate, budget estimate, budget and settlement of power generation, power transmission and transformation projects in the power industry. They are all developed according to Budget Standard and relevant documents in the power industry of provinces. The professional budget software has similar functions, so they are easy to learn and use.

Ⅳ. Project Breakdown of Power Transmission Line Project

The construction and installation work of the transmission line project and the distribution line project are not the same. The distribution line project includes the distribution equipment and the distribution line, while the transmission line project only contains the line part, so the project breakdown is not exactly the same. The power transmission line is also called the transmission line. In order to meet the technical and economic work habits, it is referred to as power transmission line.

The power transmission line project is a professional system (project) under the power grid project. The project breakdown is as follows: the first level is the expansion work units, such as the main works of general lines; the second level is the work units, such as site transport; the third level is divisional works, such as manpower transport or automobile transport.

1. Overhead Power Transmission Line Projects

The project breakdown of overhead transmission line projects is shown in Table 2-1-2.

2. Cable Line Project

The project breakdown of the cable line project is shown in Table 2-1-3.

3. Project Breakdown of Auxiliary Facilities Works of Power Transmission Line Project

The project breakdown of auxiliary facilities works of transmission line projects is shown in Table 2-1-4.

When the construction budget of the transmission line project is prepared, the names of the projects at all levels shall not be arbitrarily simplified, and shall be filled with the full names specified in the Budget Standard.

For projects that are necessary to be added in addition to the division of the project, they shall be arranged in accordance with the discipline design, under the system (project), expansion work units or work units or project following the existing projects. For example, if old equipment or transformation equipment is used in the project, the equipment recovery fee and internal allocation fee of equipment are required to be increased in the corresponding location. The equipment recovery fee refers to the payment of construction equipment, engineering equipment (such as the conductor or ground wire of the old line, pole and tower and so on) after treatment. If the original old equipment, devices and facilities belong to the equipment transfer for new project construction, they will be included in the internal equipment transfer fee, which is included in the total investment. There is only the material object, and the price is fixed but no fund is allocated.

Table 2–1–2 Project Breakdown Table of Overhead Power Transmission Line Project

No.	Project name	Major content and scope of work	Technical and economic indicator unit
I	General line main works		Yuan/km
1	Earthwork		Yuan/m³
1.1	Material transportation		
1.2	Earthwork excavation	Including the earthwork for pole and tower pits, pull wire pits, grounding trenches, wind reflection, and formation level	
2	base works	Including the corresponding material transport	Yuan /m³
2.1	Material transportation		
2.2	base works	Including stone paving and grouting, various prefabricated bases, cast-in-place concrete bases, driven prefabricated bases, cast-in-place pile bases	
2.3	Construction of revetment, retaining wall and drainage ditch		
3	Pole and tower works		Yuan / site
3.1	Material transportation		
3.2	Tower erection	Including the assembly of various powers and towers, pull wire production and Installation	
3.3	Ground installation		
4	Stringing works		Yuan/km
4.1	Material transportation		
4.2	Wiring	Including the erection of the conductor or ground wire and the general spanning erection	
5	Accessories installation works		Yuan / site
5.1	Material transportation		
5.2	Accessory installation	Installation of insulators, fittings, grading and shielding ring, etc.	
II	Main large span works		Yuan/km

Study Program II Preparation of Preliminary Budget Estimate for 220kV Overhead Transmission Line Project

Table (Cont´d)

No.	Project name	Major content and scope of work	Technical and economic indicator unit
1	Earthwork		Yuan/m³
1.1	Material transportation		
1.2	Earthwork excavation		
2	base works		Yuan/m³
2.1	Material transportation		
2.2	base works		
2.3	Construction of revetment, retaining wall and drainage ditch		
3	Pole and tower works		
3.1	Material transportation		
3.2	Tower erection		
3.3	Ground installation		
4	Stringing works		Yuan/km
4.1	Material transportation		
4.2	Wiring	Including the erection of the conductor or ground wire and the general spanning erection	
5	Accessories installation works		Yuan / site
5.1	Material transportation		
5.2	Accessory installation	Installation of insulators, fittings, grading and shielding ring, etc.	

Table 2–1–3 Project Breakdown Table of Cable Power Transmission Line Project

No.	Project name	Major content and scope of work	Technical and economic indicator unit
	Main cable works		
1	Cable trench, well, tunnel, cubicle and protection tube works	Earthworks, cable trenches, tunnel masonry, cable wells, cable cubicles, cable protection tube laying and corresponding material transportation	Yuan/km
2	Cable bearer, tray and bracket works	Including the corresponding material transport	Yuan/t
3	Cable laying project		Yuan/km

Table (Cont´d)

No.	Project name	Major content and scope of work	Technical and economic indicator unit
3.1	Pavement treatment		
3.2	Cable laying	Including the laying of power cables, control cables and cable ducts	
3.3	Cable head fabrication and installation		
3.4	Fire protection of cables		
4	Arrester and grounding works		
4.1	Arrester Installation		
4.2	Installation of grounding devices		
5	Works of two ends	Including equipment and installation at the sending end and the receiving end	
6	Cable routine test		

Table 2-1-4 Project Breakdown Table of Auxiliary Facilities Works of Power Transmission Line Project

No.	Project name	Major content and scope of work	Technical and economic indicator unit
1	Line inspection and repair station works		Yuan /m^2
1.1	Office, garage and warehouse		
1.2	Land requisition for inspection station		
1.3	Outdoor works		
2	Line inspection and repair road works		Yuan/km
3	Production maintenance communication equipment		Yuan/km
4	Production operation tool		Yuan/km

V. Composition of the Budget Estimate

The Budget Estimate is the real manifestation of the budget estimate of the transmission line project. It is a text file describing the overview of the transmission line project, the quan-

Study Program II Preparation of Preliminary Budget Estimate for 220kV Overhead Transmission Line Project

tities, the project cost and related materials. The Budget Estimate consists of a cover, signature, catalogue, preparation instructions, various forms, attachments and back covers.

(I) Cover

1. The name of the project and the preliminary design budget estimate and the approved budget estimate shall be written on the upper part of the cover.

2. The project code is at the upper right corner and the retrieval reference number is at the upper left corner.

3. The full name of the design unit, the design certificate number, the survey certificate number, and the year, month and place of preparation shall be written at the lower part of the cover.

The cover of the Budget Estimate of the project case 2 is shown in Fig. 2-1-2.

Retrieval reference No.: Project code:
XX-XXXXX-X

220kVA to transmission line new construction

Preliminary design

Technical and economic part

Budget Estimate

XX Power Design Consulting Co., Ltd.
Power Engineering Design X Level No. XXXXXX
July XX, 2008 (location)

Fig. 2-1-2 Cover of Budget Estimate of Project Case II

(II) Signature (with the Real Picture of Project Case 2)

It shall be signed by the compiler, proofreader, section (group) chief, director (special) engineer, design chief engineer and chief engineer, and shall be stamped with special seals

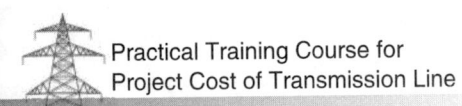

for power project cost personnel.

(Ⅲ) Catalogue

1. Preparation instructions
2. Project Overview and Table of Main Technical and Economic Indicators
3. General Construction Estimate Sheet
4. General Construction Estimate Sheet of Construction and Installation Works Costs of Power Transmission Lines and Budget Estimate for Unit Works
5. Budget Estimate for Auxiliary Facilities Works of Power Transmission Line Project
6. Budget Estimate for Other Costs
7. Budget Estimate for Construction Land Acquisition and Clearing
8. Schedule

The schedules include the comprehensive terrain increase coefficient, installation material and quantity calculating table, the list of categories of the power transmission line poles and towers, and the schedule of other expenses.

9. Appendix

(Ⅳ) Preparation Instructions

It is necessary to succinctly describe the main points of the preparation of the project budget estimate in the "preparation instructions" section, and analyze the project cost level. The content must be complete.

The contents of the preparation instructions include the analysis of design basis, project overview, preparation principles, preparation methods, and project cost level. In general, the "Project Overview and Table of Main Technical and Economic Indicators" is listed at the end of the preparation instructions.

(Ⅴ) Various Forms

1. General Construction Estimate Sheet (Table I B)
2. General Construction Estimate Sheet of Construction and Installation Works Costs of Power Transmission Lines and Budget Estimate for Unit Works (Table II-B and Table III C)
3. Budget Estimate of the Auxiliary Facilities Costs of Power Transmission Lines (Table III E)

4. Budget Estimate for Other Costs (Table IV)

5. Budget Estimate for Construction Land Acquisition and Clearing (Table VII)

6. Schedule

(1) Calculating Table of Comprehensive Terrain Increase Coefficient (Schedule I)

(2) Statistical Table of Installation Materials for Power Transmission Line Project (Schedule II)

(3) Calculating Table of Earthwork Volume for Power Transmission Lines (Schedule III)

(4) Calculating Table of Site Transport Weight of Power Transmission Line Project (Schedule IV)

(5) Calculating Table of Site Transport Quantities of Power Transmission Line Project (Schedule V)

(6) List of Categories of Poles and Towers of Power Transmission Line Project (Schedule VI)

The styles of the above tables are detailed in the corresponding tables below.

(VI) Appendix

1. The main documents on the design basis and the basis for the preparation of the budget estimate. Such as: design assignment (power of attorney) or project proposal, preliminary design approval documents or relevant content of the review minutes; relevant documents provided by the engineering competent department and the Employer.

2. The appendixes include the construction Budget Estimate of the external design project, the basis of the special project and the construction Budget Estimate.

3. The agreement (contract) signed for the project, the agreed principle of charging etc., with the full name and number indicated.

Task 2   Collecting Information On Site

In the preliminary design stage of the transmission line project, the designer needs to survey the site of the line path determined in the feasibility study stage (possibly more than one path plan) and complete the design task, and provide the budget estimate quantities and related data for the budget estimate compiler. However, considering that the designer and the budget estimate compiler have different concerns about the same project, the budget estimate compiler needs to go to the site to collect some information in addition to knowing about the project design plan and other relevant information from the designer.

The collection of information on the site refers to the work of the budget estimate compiler to survey, verify and collect the information required for the preparation of the budget estimate along the transmission line project in addition to fully understanding the engineering situation to the designer. As required by the work, the budget estimate compiler can go to the line path site with the designer or on his or her own. After the collection of the information, the information collection report shall be organized and prepared in time.

II. Collecting Information On Site

(I) Understand the Terrain, Geomorphology, Geology, Hydrology, Transportation Conditions, Obstacle Conditions and Important Crossings, Etc. Along the Line

1. Terrain

Generally, the terrain of the transmission line project is divided into: flat ground, hills, mountainous regions, high mountains, steep mountains, swamps, river networks, etc.

(1) Flat ground: refers to a flat area with a relatively flat terrain and a relatively dry ground.

(2) Hill: refers to the undulating and continually low-lying hills and mounds on the land and the area where the terrain is less than 50m within the horizontal distance of 1km.

(3) Mountainous region: refers to general mountains or valleys, with a horizontal dis-

tance of less than 250m and the area with topographic reliefs between 50 and 150m

(4) High mountain: refers to the area with difficulty of human and livestock climbing, a horizontal distance of less than 250m, and topographic reliefs between 150~250m

(5) Steep mountain: refers to the area with very dangerous terrain, a horizontal distance of less than 250m, and topographic reliefs of over 250m.

(6) Swamp: refers to the fields where water is often accumulated and the area where muddy water is deposited.

(7) River network: refers to the area with many rivers crossed into the network and affecting normal land transportation.

In actual work, the whole line path is first divided into several sections according to the terrain, and then the percentage of the length of various terrain in the whole line of the project is calculated. In addition, it shall also be determined that the location and quantity of earth and stone excavation needs to be implemented due to the influence of terrain on wind deviation.

2. Geomorphology

It refers to the types of plants planted on the ground. Required investigation:
(1) The type, quantity, DBH and density of forest trees along the line.
(2) The type and area of young crops.

3. Soil Classification

Generally, the soil is divided into: ordinary soil, hard soil, loose sand, rock, muddy water, quicksand, and puddle, and the proportion of different types of soil in the whole line shall be determined (according to the geological report).

4. Transportation Conditions

Know the distribution of traffic lines such as highways along the transmission line project to the local transportation bureau or highway bureau, so as to arrange material stations and unloading stations. The transportation conditions are the basis for determining the mode of transportation on the site and its average load distance, and are the basis for determining the location and number of temporary roads and bridges that need to be constructed.

5. Obstacle Situation

Master the type, structure, and area of the houses to be demolished along the transmission line project, and the types and quantities of graves to be moved, as well as the structure and area of structures such as quarries, lime kilns, explosives, and oil depots.

6. Important Crossings

Master the location, quantity, and span of roads, railways, communication lines, power lines, rivers, lakes, and mud that span the transmission line project.

The above content is provided by the designer in principle, and the budget estimate compiler is mainly responsible for carrying out verification work.

(Ⅱ) Collect Relevant Information From Relevant Departments of the People'S Government Along the Project Line

The information that needs to be collected from the relevant departments of the people's government where the project is located includes: relevant regulations, compensation standards and calculation methods for land acquisition, site lease, migration compensation, and compensation for transmission line corridors. For relevant knowledge and determination methods, please refer to the description of the construction site requisition and clearing costs in "Other Costs" and the relevant part of other costs for the Project Case budget estimates.

1. Land Acquisition Related Information

The land acquisition of the transmission line project is generally carried out only for a certain range of land on the pole and tower base (including the pull wire base). For details, refer to the relevant regulations of the competent department of the power industry. The purpose is to ensure that the cultivation of soil near the base does not affect the stable operation of the base.

When the land acquisition fee for transmission line projects is calculated, the land price standards in different regions are not the same. If the difference for the whole lines is not large, the highest price is used to calculate; if the land prices are very different in different regions, they shall be calculated separately and accumulated, and then summarized in the land acquisition fee.

The budget estimate compiler needs to go to the local land administration department to learn more about the land acquisition cost standard and whether it includes land compensation fees, resettlement subsidies, taxes, etc.

2. Forest Migration, Cleanup and Compensation Related Information

With the line corridor as the boundary, all forests (bamboo or trees) that affect the construction and operation of the transmission line must be moved or cleaned up, and the compensation cost must be calculated and included in the corridor compensation for the power transmission line.

The budget estimate compiler needs to know in detail the type, quantity, DBH, and density of the trees, and collect the corresponding compensation standards from the local forestry authorities. In principle, for perennate economic forests, they shall be transplanted as much as possible. The land use units shall pay the transplant fees. If they must be cut down, the land use units shall provide compensation according to the actual value. For the mature timber forests, the forest owners shall cut them by themselves, and the land use units pay only the man-hour costs of the cost of cutting workers, but not provide compensation. The specific compensation standard shall be determined according to the actual situation at the time, and shall be determined by the owner of the project and the owner of the forest.

3. Young Crop Compensation Related Information

The compensation for young crops refers to the economic compensation that shall be provided by the owner of the project for the land contractor where the crops are in the growing stage and cannot be harvested when the land is acquired or the project is constructed. The construction of power transmission line projects often leads to the destruction of crops and other economic crops planted on a certain area of the corridor and its vicinity. Compensation shall be provided and included in the compensation for the power transmission line corridor. The reasons for the compensation for young crops are specifically divided into land acquisition and line construction. The compensation for young crops often accounts for a large proportion of the compensation fees for power transmission line corridors.

Yong crop compensation standard: If the young crops on the land are destroyed due to land acquisition or construction, the land use unit shall compensate according to the output and output value of the crops in one season. For the crops that have just been planted, the compensation cost of 1/3 of the output value of one season is compensated, not exceeding the output value of one season. For the young crops of grain, oil and vegetables, it they can be harvested, they shall not be compensated. If they cannot be harvested, compensation of the output value of one season shall be provided. The specific compensation standard shall be determined according to the actual situation at the time, and shall be determined by the owner of the project and the land contractor or land user. For example, in specific operations, the years of compensation for young crops caused by land acquisition or construction are not the same, the former is generally longer, while the latter is only compensated for one season.

The budget estimate compiler must understand the types, areas, and compensation standards of young crops. Common young crop species include rice, wheat, corn and other cash crops. Rice is divided into single season and double season rice, and wheat is divided into single crop and intercropping wheat.

The area of young crops is usually based on the length of the line and the width of the line corridor. The areas of various young crops planted during the expected construction period are calculated in sections. The area of the construction site separately set up is calculated separately, which is accumulated to the total compensation area (mu) for young crops. The compensation amount is calculated as

$$\text{Yong crop compensation area} = \text{line length} \times \text{line corridor width} \times \text{proportion of a certain type young crops along the line} \qquad (2\text{-}2\text{-}1)$$

$$\text{Compensation amount} = \text{young compensation area} \times \text{yield per mu} \times \text{market price} \qquad (2\text{-}2\text{-}2)$$

4. Relocation Compensation Related Information On Buildings and Structures

Institutions, enterprises, houses and related buildings and structures that affect the normal construction and operation of transmission lines within the land acquisition and line corridors, as well as power lines, communication lines, railways, highways, ditches, pipelines, graves, etc. need to be relocated and cleaned up. It is necessary to calculate the compensation costs, which are included in the relocation compensation and the clearance cost, respectively.

The budget estimate compiler needs to know the relevant compensation standards in the government construction committee (demolition and relocation office) where the project is located, and collect the migration and clean-up agreement (contract) price in case the agreement (contract) has been signed.

5. Construction Site Lease Related Information

The material station, the unloading station and the stretching site are rented, and the related expenses are included in the Construction site rental. The fee is recorded as the agree-

Study Program II Preparation of Preliminary Budget Estimate for 220kV Overhead Transmission Line Project

ment (contract) price in case the agreement (contract) has been signed, and it is recorded with reference to the same type of projects in case no agreement (contract) has been signed. The budget estimate compiler needs to collect relevant information from the owner or relevant departments.

(III) Collecting Other Information

(1) Go to the local building materials market to collect the origin, output, quality, price of sand and gravel resources in the project area, or supply and price of the supply station, understand the possibility of purchasing sand and stone in local areas, and minimize the haul distance to reduce the project cost.

(2) For the reconstruction and expansion project, the compiler shall also know some or special conditions that can be utilized, such as the use of old towers, the situation of changing and connecting, whether there is a need for power outages and so on.

(3) Collect the current budget price of electric power project installation materials issued by the power authority along the project.

(4) Collect the unified quota, the regional unit valuation form and the current wage unit price through the relevant competent authorities along the project.

(5) Collect the adjustment coefficient of the material fees and the cost of using construction machinery from the power quota (cost) management department along the project.

(6) Information provided by the Builder and the Employer as specified in the Budget Standard. In the process of collecting data, the budget estimate compiler shall take the initiative to coordinate with the Employer and the Builder (if they have been determined), and check the records in real time for the actual situation on the site, and strive to unify the opinions to avoid disagreements afterwards.

The collated information collection report shall be accompanied by the relevant agreement and the minutes of the meeting, and shall be reported to reviewed by the superior competent department of the industry. Then, in conjunction with the opinions of the competent department, the editor-in-chief shall submit the first draft of the technical organization measures for the budget estimate in writing. After review, consult with the Employer, the competent department, the construction bank, and the Builder to form a consensus preparation principle to ensure the preparation quality of the budget estimate.

(Ⅳ) Site Information Collection Of Project Case 2

(1) Feasibility study report and reply of a 220kV A-B power transmission and transformation project in a city;

(2) Hydrometeorological report;

(3) Engineering geological report;

(4) Planning areas of counties A and C, and city B;

(5) Outgoing line planning for 220kV substations A and B;

(6) Feasibility study report and design bidding documents completed by a design institute;

(7) A path agreement with the local government;

(8) Information on major telecommunication lines and radio facilities near the line;

(9) See the overview of the line project in the project case 2 for other information.

Ⅱ. Calculating the Terrain Increase Coefficient

(Ⅰ) About the Terrain Increase Coefficient

1. Reasons for Using the Terrain Increase Coefficient

The terrain increase coefficient is adopted because the budget quota is considered consuming the construction is carried on the flat ground. If the construction is carried out under other terrain conditions, the impact of the actual terrain on the construction shall be considered according to the budget quota, and the comprehensive terrain increase coefficient shall be calculated. The labor and mechanical costs shall be adjusted.

2. Calculation Method of the Terrain Increase Coefficient

(1) Terrain proportion calculation method

According to the information collected on site and provided by the designer, the whole line of the project is divided into several sections according to the definition of the terrain, and then the lengths of various terrains are summarized to calculate the percentage of the length of each terrain to the length of the whole line. Except for the plateau and platform, when there are a small amount of other terrains in various terrain sections, they may not be

Study Program II Preparation of Preliminary Budget Estimate for 220kV Overhead Transmission Line Project

considered, and the percentage is determined according for the main terrain.

(2) Terrain increase coefficient for budget quota (see Table 2-2-1)

Table 2-2-1 Terrain Increase Coefficient Table (%)

S/N	Quota name			Item	Hill	Mountain land	High mountain	Steep mountain	Swamp	River network	Remarks
1	Site transportation	Human-powered transport		(1) Transportation of concrete poles, concrete prefabricated products, steel pipe poles and wires	40	150	300	400	70	-	Excluding machinery
				(2) Transportation of fittings, insulators, sporadic steel, towers, sand, stone, lime, earth, cement, friction reducer, and water	20	100	150	200	40	-	
		Automobile and tractor transportation			20	80	-	-	-	-	Excluding loading and unloading
2	Earthwork				5	10	20	25	10	5	Excluding machinery
3	base works				10	20	40	50	40	10	
4	Pole and tower works				20	70	110	120	70	20	Excluding high towers and grounding works
5	Stringing works			General release and stringing	15	100	150	170	40	10	Excluding crossing erection and overhead warning line installation
				Release and stringing of tension machinery	5	40	80	90	20	5	
				Optical cable connection	5	30	60	80	15	5	Excluding survey
6	Accessory project				5	20	50	60	10	5	
7	Cable works			Direct burial of trenches	10	20	40	-	10	5	

Note:

① When the transport terrain is determined, it shall be divided according to the actual terrain of the transport route, which is different from the engineering terrain. The engineering terrain refers to the terrain of the route along the project; the terrain of the site transport may be close to the engineering terrain, but they shall still be distinguished according to the actual path. The path of "human transport" can refer to the engineering terrain.

② "Automobile transport" terrain is generally flat, hilly, and when there is a continuous bend (winding road), it is a "mountainous region".

③ When human-powered transport is carried out in high and steep mountains, the average haul distance shall be determined by the average calculated dip length and the terrain increase coefficient of the slope vertical height difference, and shall not be calculated according to the actual haul distance.

④ In the same section, when the "mud" and "river network" coexist, only the increase coefficient of the mud terrain can be applied, and the two cannot be used at the same time.

⑤ The terrain of the project with platform length within 2km in northwest plateau and platform along the line is considered as "mountainous region". The transport terrain of the project is determined according to the actual situation of the transportation route. The transport terrain on the platform is considered as the "mountainous region", and the that of transport on the platform is considered as "flat ground".

⑥ Except for the human-powered transport, the terrain of the power transmission line in the urban area is calculated with reference to the hilly terrain.

(Ⅱ) Comprehensive Terrain Increase Coefficient of Project Case 2

(1) Comprehensive Terrain Increase Coefficient Calculation Table of Project Case II (see Table 2-2-2)

(2) Statement of calculation

According to the design data, the project terrain of project case 2 is divided into: 7.4% flat ground, 51.4% hills, and 41.2% mountainous regions. The terrain of human-powered transport is the same as the engineering terrain; since the roads near the route are mainly township roads, mostly the winding roads, the terrain of the automobile transport is divided same as the engineering terrain; the overhead conductor and ground wire installation works adopt the general release and stringing method.

Study Program II Preparation of Preliminary Budget Estimate for 220kV Overhead Transmission Line Project

Table 2–2–2 Comprehensive Terrain Increase Coefficient Calculation Table of Project Case II

S/N	Item	Terrain increase coefficient (%)						Terrain ratio (%)						Comprehensive increase coefficient (%)						
		Hill	Mountain land	High mountain	Steep mountain	Swamp	River network	Hill	Mountain land	High mountain	Steep mountain	Swamp	River network	Hill	Mountain land	High mountain	Steep mountain	Swamp	River network	Total
1	2	3	4	5	6	7	8	9	10	11	12	13	14	15	16	17	18	19	20	21
I	Human-powered transport: wire and concrete products (excluding machinery fee)	40	150	300	400	70		51.4	41.2					20.56	61.8					82.36
	Human-powered transport: other (excluding machinery fee)	20	100	150	200	40		51.4	41.2					10.28	41.2					51.48
	Automobile and tractor transportation (excluding loading and unloading)	20	80					51.4	41.2					10.28	32.96					43.24
II	Earthwork (excluding machinery fee)	5	10	20	25	10	5	51.4	41.2					2.57	4.12					6.69
III	base works	10	20	40	50	40	10	51.4	41.2					5.14	8.24					13.38
IV	Pole and tower works	20	70	110	120	70	20	51.4	41.2					10.28	28.84					39.12

Table (Cont'd)

S/N	Item	Terrain increase coefficient (%)							Terrain ratio (%)							Comprehensive increase coefficient (%)						
		Hill	Moun-tain land	High moun-tain	Steep moun-tain	Swamp	River net-work		Hill	Moun-tain land	High moun-tain	Steep moun-tain	Swamp	River net-work		Hill	Moun-tain land	High moun-tain	Steep moun-tain	Swamp	River net-work	Total
V	Stringing works (General release and stringing)	15	100	150	170	40	10		51.4	41.2						7.71	41.2					48.91
	Stringing works (Release and stringing of tension machinery)	5	40	80	90	20	5															
VI	Accessory project	5	20	50	60	10	5		51.4	41.2						2.57	8.24					10.81

Note 1: Since there is no coefficient in the flat ground, it is not counted.

Note 2: If the human-powered transport in the high mountains is considered as being carried out on winding roads, the load distance is lengthened, and the mountain coefficient is applied to other terrain increase coefficients.

Note 3: $(15) = (3) \times (9)$, $(16) = (4) \times (10)$, ..., and so on.

Note 4: $(15) + (16) + (17) + (18) + (19) + (20) = (21)$.

Task 3　Determining Quantities

The quantities refer to the statistical value of the workload of installation and construction of the base works, the pole and tower works, the wiring works and the accessory project during the construction of the transmission line project, generally refers to the quantity of main materials (referred to as main materials, also called installation materials) such as concrete and its finished products, tower materials, conductors or ground wires, fittings, insulators and accessories installed in the work, and also include earthwork excavation volume in earthworks, line resurvey and pit division workload, and quantity of loading and unloading and transportation work completed for site transport. The determination of the quantities is the main basic work for determining the cost of the project in the next step. The classification standard specified in the Schedule of the Budget Standard shall be strictly adopted, and they shall correspond to the quota sub-item for the budget quota of the power construction project.

The quantities in the preliminary design stage shall be provided by the designer in accordance with the requirements and depth of the budget estimate preparation. The estimated quantities shall be consistent with the preliminary design drawings, specifications and equipment and material inventory. For projects that have a major impact on investment, such as cables, cable trays, earthwork, ground treatment, pole and tower consumption, concrete base and so on, technical and economic personnel (budget estimate compilers) shall verify them against the reference design, construction drawings of similar projects or estimated quantities with the same natural conditions according to the information available, and shall provide feedback. The technical and economic personnel shall review the quantities provided by the designer, and the construction loss shall be calculated according to the loss rate specified in the Detailed Budget Quota in Electric Power Construction Projects - Volume IV Power Transmission Line Engineering (2006 Version). If the quantities are indeed problematic, the designer may be asked to explain the reason or modify the information provided. After the quantities are determined through analysis, no other project estimates or budget estimates may be applied.

Because the budget estimate compiler needs to analyze and verify the quantities provided by the designer, this study task focuses on quantity calculation method. The quantity data listed in this study project, unless specifically indicated, are from quantity related data of the project case 2 provided by the designer.

I. Organizing Quantity Data

(I) Quantities Provided By the Designer

(1) Line name, starting and ending point, voltage class and length.

(2) Conductor and lightning wire number and number of circuits.

(3) Base type (with a general chart) and the number of each type.

(4) Type of pole and tower (with general chart), and the number of each type.

(5) Accessory installation type and quantity.

(6) Grounding installation type and quantity.

(7) Anti-vibration hammer type and quantity.

(8) The types and quantities of various obstacles removed during the line project.

(9) Wind-deviated peak excavation (the distance from the conductor and ground wire in the line span to the ground is not enough due to wind deviation), the earthwork excavation volume of the base pit or the excavation earthwork volume of the high and low leg bases.

(10) The type and number of crossing structures (crossing distance and width, and the width of the river when crossing the river).

(11) Geological report.

(II) Organizing Quantity Data

After receiving the engineering quantity data provided by the designer, the budget estimate compiler must, in accordance with the relevant requirements of the power transmission line project breakdown as specified in the "Budget Regulations", analyze and verify it to form an bill of quantities that meets the calculation requirements of the charge. Specifically, it includes the following six aspects of statistical work: earthwork quantity calculation, site transport quantity calculation, base quantity calculation, pole and tower quantity calculation, overhead conductor and ground wire quantity calculation, and accessory quantity calculation.

II. Calculation of the Earthwork Quantities

The earthwork quantities excavated in the power transmission line project mainly refer to the earthwork quantities excavated in the peaks, formation levels, base pits, pull line pits and grounding grooves involved in the construction of the power transmission project. Specifically, they include excavation (or blasting) and backfilling of electric pole pits, pull line tower pits, pull line pits and cable trenches, excavation (or blasting) and backfilling of self-supporting tower pits, blasting of rock-embedded base pits, solid soil pit excavation, excavation of digging pile base pits, excavation and backfilling of well points, excavation of drainage ditches, peak and formation level excavation. The calculation of the quantities of earthworks is related to the size designed in the design and the type of soil. The dimension provided by the design is the static dimension of earthwork volume, and the construction & operation margin, slope coefficient, etc. shall be considered. The value of construction & operation margin and slope coefficient depend on construction & operation method and soil type. Here, only the calculation method of earthwork quantities for excavation of peaks and formation level is described, soil and stone classification, and the calculation method of excavation earthwork quantities of base pits, pull line pits and grounding grooves are shown in detail in the study project part of this book.

(I) Calculation of Earthwork Quantities for Excavation of Peaks and Formation Level

1. Reasons for the Excavation of Peaks and formation Level and Calculation Principles

The peak excavation generally occurs near the lowest point of the sag. When the safe distance between the conductor and the ground is not enough due to wind deviation, etc., the earth and stone of the relevant part are excavated. The excavation of the formation level generally refers to the levelling of the formation level when the base of the pole and tower is located at the positions such as the hillside, the mountaintop, the mountain ridge, etc., or the base is located in the thin area of soft soil of the paddy field, the muddy soil and so on, where the earthwork excavation is required to lower the formation level. The earthwork quantities of the peaks and formation level are generally provided by the designer and directly included in the budget estimate. The calculation of the peak and formation level soil and stone volume shall be calculated according to the elevation of the formation level provided by the designer and according to the actual situation of the topography and landform.

2. Calculation Formula for Excavation of Earthwork In Peak and Formation Level

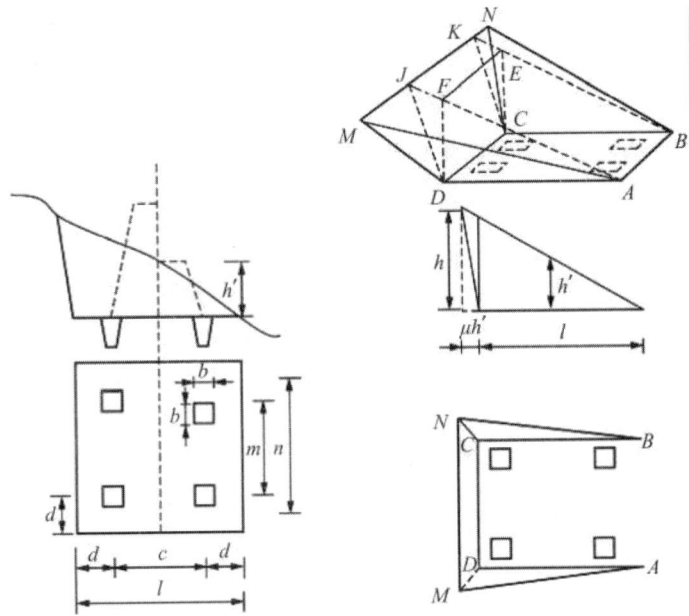

Fig. 2-3-1 Diagram of Hillside Formation Level

(1) The tower is located on the formation level of the hillside (Fig. 2-3-1)

1) Volume of the part without slope (ABCDEF volumes)

$$V_a = l \times n \times h' \qquad (2\text{-}3\text{-}1)$$

2) The volume of the part with slope is composed of three parts (μ is the grading coefficient), that is, the volume of the uphill direction part (CDEFJK volumes).

$$V_2 = \frac{\mu \times h^2 \times n}{2} \qquad (2\text{-}3\text{-}2)$$

Left and right side (ADMJA+BCKNB) volumes

$$V_3 = \frac{\mu \times h^2 \times l}{3} \qquad (2\text{-}3\text{-}3)$$

3) Total volume of the formation level

$$V = V_a + V_2 + V_3 \qquad (2\text{-}3\text{-}4)$$

(2) The tower is located on the formation level of the circular mountain top (as shown in Fig. 2-3-2, which can be calculated as approximately half of the volume of the elliptical ball)

$$V = \frac{\pi \times l \times n \times h}{6} \quad (2\text{-}3\text{-}5)$$

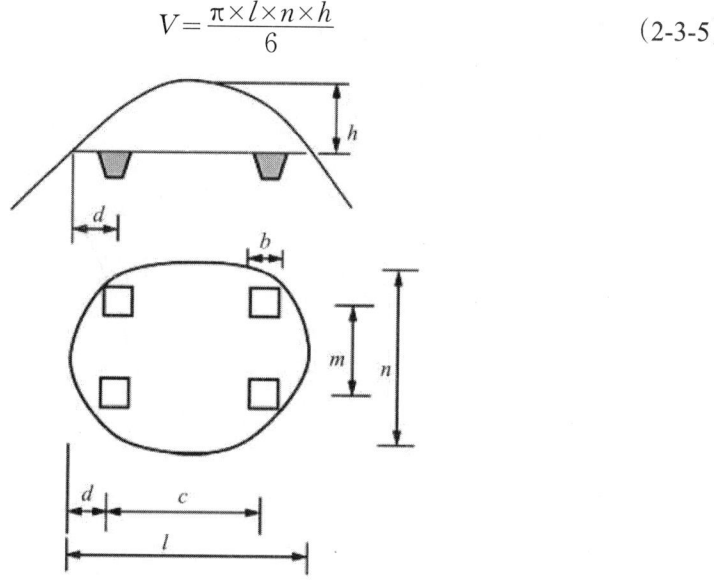

Fig. 2-3-2　Diagram of the Circular Mountain Top Formation Level

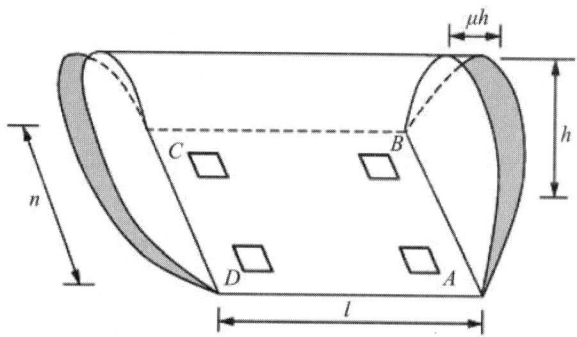

Fig. 2-3-3　Diagram of Ridge Formation Level

(3) The tower is located on the ridge formation level (as shown in Fig. 2-3-3). It can be calculated according to the approximate cuboid volume due to the different steepness of the slope on both sides of the ridge, but it shall be multiplied by a correction coefficient K of less than 1, generally 0.4 to 0.6, thus:

$$V = K \times l \times n \times h + \mu \times h^2 \times n \quad (2\text{-}3\text{-}6)$$

Wherein, V is soil and stone volume, m³; h and h' are the descending formation level value (formation level height), m; l is the formation level bottom length, m; n is the formation level width, m; c and m are the front and lateral foot distance of the base, m; b is the base pithead size, m; d is the operation margin and the reserved size of the slope, m; μ is the grading coefficient.

(Ⅱ) Surplus Soil Treatment

The disposal of surplus soil shall not be considered for the general project. If necessary, the surplus soil can be considered to be transported to the allowable dump land, and for the transport distance more than 100m, it can be included in the site transport. Calculation of surplus soil transport weight is as follows.

1. Drilling Muck Of Cast-in-place Pile

$$\text{Surplus soil transportation volume} = \text{volume of the part below zero meter in the pile design (m}^3) \times 1.7 \text{t/m}^3 \quad (2\text{-}3\text{-}7)$$

Wherein, a water content of 0.2 t/m^3 is included in 1.7 t/m^3.

2. Surplus Soil Of Cast-in-place and Prefabricated Base Pit

$$\text{Surplus soil transportation volume} = \text{concrete volume (m}^3) \times 1.5 \text{t/m}^3 \times 30\% \quad (2\text{-}3\text{-}8)$$

3. Surplus Soil of Excavated and Digging Pile Base Pit

$$\text{Surplus soil transportation volume} = \text{concrete volume (m}^3) \times 1.5 \text{t/m}^3 \quad (2\text{-}3\text{-}9)$$

(Ⅲ) Backfilling

The backfilled soil shall be considered as the original excavation. When the borrowing (replacement) of soil beyond 100m is required, the peak excavation and site transport quota can be applied separately according to the soil replacement proportion and average load distance specified in the design.

(Ⅳ) Calculation of Earthwork Volume In Project Case 2

1. Earthwork Volume Table of Project Case 2

See Table 2-3-1 Summary of Earthwork Volume.

2. Calculation Description

This project case uses reinforced concrete cast-in-place base, and has designed four base types of bases: straight column flexible base, inclined column base, digging base and rock embedded base. See Fig. 2-0-3 for details. According to the engineering design data, the first three base types are used in this project. Next the calculation process of earthwork volume is listed for one of each of the three bases, and it is filled in Table 2-3-2 to explain the calculation method of base excavation earthwork volume. In this project case, under normal circumstances, the base column of the tower is exposed to the ground by: 200mm in dry land and 300mm in paddy and dry land.

(1) Earthwork volume calculation of straight column flexible base

An iron tower adopts straight flexible base LZG2026 as the four feet A, B, C and D of its base, the terrain is hill, and the geological conditions are: cultivated soil for 0~0.5m, and silty mudstone below 0.5m (in browny red or purplish red, strongly weathered). Excavation is carried out by manual digging.

The base slab of LZG2026 is a 2×2m square. The bottom of the pit is not supported by the form. The top surface of the column is 2.6m away from the bottom of the pit. After the height of the column exposing the ground of 200mm is deducted, the depth of the base pit is 2.4m.

Table 2-3-1 Summary of Earthwork Quantities of Project Case II

Name	Unit	Qty.
Excavation (or blasting) of self-supporting tower pit and backfilling of common soil pit with the depth of less than 3.0m	m^3	643.20
Excavation (or blasting) of self-supporting tower pit and backfilling of common soil pit with the depth of less than 4.0m	m^3	775.20
Excavation (or blasting) of self-supporting tower pit and backfilling of common soil pit with the depth of more than 4.0m	m^3	3372.00
Excavation (or blasting) of self-supporting tower pit and backfilling of light sand and stone pit with the depth of less than 3.0m	m^3	2210.40
Excavation (or blasting) of self-supporting tower pit and backfilling of light sand and stone pit with the depth of less than 4.0m	m^3	2665.20
Excavation (or blasting) of self-supporting tower pit and backfilling of light sand and stone pit with the depth of more than 4.0m	m^3	11590.80
Excavation (or blasting) of self-supporting tower pit and backfilling of rock (blasting) pit with the depth of less than 3.0m	m^3	804.00
Excavation (or blasting) of self-supporting tower pit and backfilling of rock (blasting) pit with the depth of less than 4.0m	m^3	968.40

Table (Cont´d)

Name	Unit	Qty.
Excavation (or blasting) of self-supporting tower pit and backfilling of rock (blasting) pit with the depth of more than 4.0m	m³	4214.40
Excavation (or blasting) of self-supporting tower pit and backfilling of rock (manual digging) pit with the depth of less than 3.0m	m³	200.40
Excavation (or blasting) of self-supporting tower pit and backfilling of rock (manual digging) pit with the depth of less than 4.0m	m³	242.40
Excavation (or blasting) of self-supporting tower pit and backfilling of rock (manual digging) pit with the depth of more than 4.0m	m³	1053.60
Excavation (or blasting) of self-supporting tower pit and backfilling of muddy water pit with the depth of less than 3.0m	m³	160.80
Excavation (or blasting) of self-supporting tower pit and backfilling of muddy water pit with the depth of less than 4.0m	m³	194.40
Excavation (or blasting) of self-supporting tower pit and backfilling of muddy water pit with the depth of more than 4.0m	m³	843.60
Excavation (or blasting) of grounding groove and backfilling of common soil	m³	1187.10
Excavation (or blasting) of grounding groove and backfilling of light sand and stone	m³	4080.04
Excavation (or blasting) of grounding groove and backfilling of muddy water soil	m³	296.28
Excavation (or blasting) of grounding groove and backfilling of rock (blasting)	m³	1483.38
Excavation (or blasting) of grounding groove and backfilling of rock (manual digging)	m³	371.09
Excavation of common soil from drainage ditches	m³	55.00
Excavation of light sand and stone from drainage ditches	m³	186.00
Excavation of muddy water pit from drainage ditches	m³	14.00
Excavation of rock (blasting) from drainage ditches	m³	68.00
Excavation of rock (manual digging) from drainage ditches	m³	17.00
Excavation of common soil from peak and formation level	m³	196.00
Excavation of light sand and stone from peak and formation level	m³	537.00
Excavation of rock (blasting) from peak and formation level Peak	m³	147.00
Excavation of rock (manual digging) from peak and formation level Peak	m³	49.00

Study Program II Preparation of Preliminary Budget Estimate for 220kV Overhead Transmission Line Project

According to the above conditions, look up Tables 1-2-5 and 1-2-6 to know the construction operation margin is 0.1 m, and the slope coefficient is 1:0.33. Using the formula (1-2-14),

the pithead width of LZG2026 base pit is

$$a_1 = a + 2 \times h \times 0.33$$
$$= 2 + 2 \times 0.1 + 2 \times 2.4 \times 0.33$$
$$= 3.784 \text{ (m)}$$

Excavation earthwork volume of LZG2026 base is

$$a_1 = a + 2 \times h \times 0.33$$
$$= \frac{24}{3} \times [(2 + 2 \times 0.1)^2 + (2 + 2 \times 0.1) \times 3.784 + 3.784^2]$$
$$= 21.987 \text{ (m}^3\text{)}$$

(2) Earthwork volume calculation of inclined column base

An iron tower adopts inclined column base XJG2742 as the four feet A, B, C and D of its base, the terrain is mountain topography, and the geological conditions are: cultivated soil for 0~0.5m, and silty mudstone below 0.5m (in browny red or purplish red, strongly weathered). Excavation is carried out by manual digging.

The base slab of XJG2742 is a 2.7×2.7m square. The bottom of the pit is not supported by the form. The top surface of the column is 4.2m away from the bottom of the pit. After the height of the column exposing the ground of 200mm is deducted, the depth of the base pit is 4m.

According to the above conditions, look up Tables 1-2-5 and 1-2-6 to know the construction operation margin is 0.1 m, and the slope coefficient is 1:0.33. Using the formula (1-2-14),

the pithead width of XJG2742 base pit is

$$a_1 = a + 2 \times h \times 0.33$$
$$= 2.7 + 2 \times 0.1 + 2 \times 4 \times 0.33$$
$$= 5.54 \text{ (m)}$$

Excavation earthwork volume of LZG2026 base is

$$V = \frac{h}{3} \times (a^2 + aa_1 + a_1^2)$$
$$= \frac{4}{3} \times [(2.7 + 2 \times 0.1)^2 + (2.7 + 2 \times 0.1) \times 5.54 + 5.54^2]$$
$$= 73.557 \text{ (m}^3\text{)}$$

(3) Earthwork volume calculation of digging base

An iron tower adopts excavated base TWG1630 as the four feet A, B, C and D of its base, the terrain is hill, and the geological conditions are: eluvial silty clay for 0~0.4m, and silty mudstone below 0.4m (in browny red or purplish red, and strongly weathered). Excavation is carried out by manual digging.

As shown in Fig. 2-3-4, the slab is circle of Φ1.6m with a height of 0.3m. The column is a circle of Φ0.8m with a height of 2.2m. The truncated cones with a height of 0.5m are formed between the column and the slab. The bottom of the pit is not supported by the form. The top surface of the column is 3m away from the bottom of the pit. After the height of the column exposing the ground of 200mm is deducted, the depth of the base pit is 2.8m.

Excavation earthwork volume of TWG1630 base is

$$V = \pi r_2^2 h_1 + \frac{\pi h_2 (r_2^2 + r_2^2 + r_1 r_2)}{3} \pi r_2^2 h_3$$

$$= \pi \times 0.8^2 \times 0.3 + \frac{\pi \times 0.5 \ (0.8^2 + 0.4^2 + 0.8 \times 0.4)}{3} + \pi \times 0.4^2 \times 2$$

$$= 2.194 \ (m^3)$$

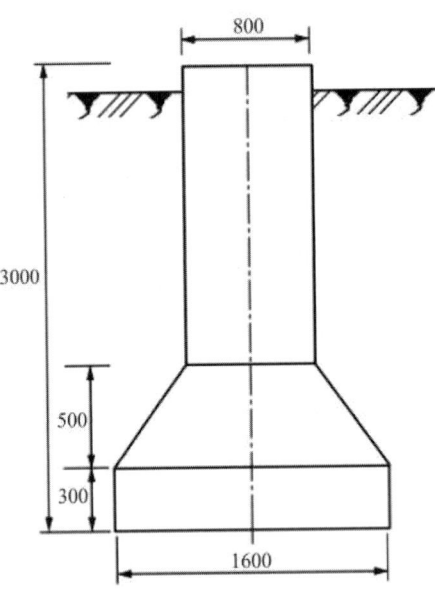

Fig. 2-3-4 TWG1630 Base Structure

(4) Earthwork volume calculation of grounding device

According to the "Installation Diagram of the Grounding Device of the Tower", the buried depth of the grounding device is generally 0.6m, and the cultivated land shall be below the tilth, and the rock area shall be no less than 0.3m.

As shown in Fig. 2-0-2, the length of the Φ10 round steel embedded in the B type grounding device is 60m (Table 2-0-5), and the earthwork volume of its grounding groove is

$$V = 0.4 \times \text{length} \times \text{groove depth}$$
$$= 0.4 \times 60 \times 0.6$$
$$= 14.4 \text{m}^3$$

According to the Table 2-0-5, the earthwork volume of the grounding device of C, D, E, and F types is 28.8m³, 38.4m³, 67.2m³, and 84.5m³, respectively. Among the 137 sets of grounding devices, the C, D, E and F types account for 10%, 35%, 50% and 5%. Earthwork volume calculation of grounding device in this project case is

$$(28.8 \times 10\% + 38.4 \times 35\% + 67.2 \times 50\% + 84.5 \times 5\%) \times 137 = 7417.9 \text{ (m}^3\text{)}$$

According to the design data, the geology of this project case is divided into: 25% rock, 55% loose sand, 16% ordinary soil, and 4% muddy water. According to the experience in the same type of works, for the methods of rock geological excavation, blasting accounts for 80%, and manual digging accounts for 20%. Therefore, the earthwork volume of the grounding device—the grounding groove excavation (or blasting) and backfilling quantities are decomposed into: ordinary soil 1,187.10m³, light sand and stone 4,080.04m³, muddy water soil 296.28m³, rock (blasting) 1,483.38m³, and rock (manual digging) 371.09m³. Fill in Table 2-3-1.

Table 2-3-2 Calculating Table of Earthwork of Project Case II

Terrain	Soil quality	Base type	Pit bottom length × width m	Pit depth m	Earthwork volume per pit m³		Number of pits per base Nos.	Earthwork volume per base m³	Pit depth within 2m		Pit depth within 3m		Pit depth over 3m		Remarks
					Pole pip	Pack-way			Base	Total	Base	Total	Base	Total	
1	2	3	4	5	6	7	8	9	10	11	12	13	14	15	
Hill	Light sand and stone	LZG2026	2×2	2.4	21.987		4	87.948			1	87.948			
Mountain land	Light sand and stone	XJG2742	2.7×2.7	4.0	73.557		4	294.227					1	294.227	
Mountain land	Light sand and stone	TWG1630	Φ1.6	2.8	2.194		4	8.776			1	8.776			
Others omitted															

Others omitted

Note 1: $[(6)+(7)] \times (8) = (9)$.
Note 2: $(9) \times (10) = (11)$, $(9) \times (12) = (13)$ or $(9) \times (14) = (15)$.
Note 3: Look up tables according to the (4) and (5) data, and fill in (6).
Note 4: The pit depth classification depends on the classification requirements of the quota sub-items corresponding to different types of earthwork excavation.
Note 5: The number of bases of the iron tower in this table are calculated to be 4 base pits per base. The statistics of earthwork volume are based on the unit of base; however, it shall be noted that in the current design, the situation that the base forms of the four bases of the same tower are different often occurs. Pay attention to the distinction during statistics, and calculate the earthwork volume in units of pits.

III. Quantity and Weight Statistics of the Installation Materials

Installation materials refer to the raw materials, auxiliary materials, components, parts, semi-finished products and other technological materials that constitute the entity of the process system during installation. When bases, poles and towers, conductors or ground wires and accessories and other installation materials are counted, the construction loss shall be included. The construction loss rate of the main installation materials is shown in Table 1-2-1. As can be seen from the previous description, the purpose of installation material statistics is to calculate the installation material cost, and to calculate the corresponding installation fee, so the standard set in the statistics must meet the needs of these two aspects. The former shall distinguish the material name and specification, unit and loss rate, while the latter must consider the division of the corresponding quota sub-item.

(I) Base Works

The base works include installation of prefabricated base, cast-in-place base, rock base, cast-in-place pile base, prefabricated pile base, artificial digging pile base, masonry of revetment, retaining wall and drainage ditch, concrete base anti-corrosion, and pulling rod anti-corrosion. The first six items are the installations of different types of bases, and the latter three items are the treatment of base ancillary facilities and components. The corresponding installation costs vary with materials, structures and construction processes of different types of bases; the installation costs vary with base components such as reinforcement production and processing, base cushion and base body; similarly, the installation costs vary with treatment of different types of base ancillary facilities and components, but in order to facilitate the application of the quota in the follow-up work and complete the calculation of the charges, when filling out the "Schedule II Statistical Table of the Installation Materials for the Power Transmission Line Project", the project breakdown of the quota sub-item of the base works shall also be fully considered in addition to considering the different material names and specifications, units and loss rates.

1. Statistical Requirements for Installation Materials of Several Common Base Types

(1) Prefabricated base

The prefabricated base is mostly prefabricated by reinforced concrete. According to its structure, it is divided into chassis, sleeve, chuck and anchor plate. The project breakdown of "prefabricated base" quota sub-item is also divided into chassis installation, sleeve installation, chuck installation and anchor plate installation. The statistical caliber is relatively simple. It is counted in units of "base", "block", "group" and "piece" according to different types and weights. In the statistics, the chassis is different between single pole and double poles, and is divided into one block per base and two blocks per base; the sleeve is divided into one piece per base and two pieces per base; the chuck is divided into one block per base, two blocks per base, and four blocks per base; the anchor plate is divided into one block per group and two blocks per group. The step of the fixed sub-items depends on the weight.

(2) Cast-in-place base

The cast-in-place base is calculated according to different grades (single base concrete volume) in the unit of "m^3". The constituent materials are divided into reinforcement, sand, stone, cement and water. There are also some cases where commercial concrete is directly used in the project. The unit price, loss rate, and packaging factor of different types of materials are all different, and statistics shall be made separately. The processing and production of base reinforcement in the "cast-in-place base" quota sub-item does not include hot-dip galvanizing.

The base cushion of the cast-in-place base is divided into decking, decking and grouting, decking and concrete pouring, lime soil and plain concrete cushions. They shall be counted by classification, and the stone, lime, mortar or concrete quantity shall be calculated in accordance with the design regulations. If the design does not contain such regulations, the quantity of lime and mortar may be calculated as 20% of the volume of the cushions. The quantity of concrete may be calculated as 30% of the volume of the cushions.

(3) Cast-in-place pile

Drilling soil classification of cast-in-place piles:

1) "Sand and limit loam": refers to sand loam and medium and light limit loam;

2) "Clay" means heavy limit loam, clay and loose loess;

3) "Gravel soil" means heavy limit loam and hard stone clay, containing gravel or pebbles with a content not exceeding 20% and a particle size of not more than 15cm;

4) Where there is different soil in one hole, it shall be calculated in layer according to the geological data provided by the design.

(4)Cast-in-place pile base. The volume of the prefabricated pile is the product of the design total length multiplied by the cross-sectional area of the pile, deducting the volume of the virtual body of the pile tip. The pile follower is calculated by multiplying the cross-sectional area of the pile by the design elevation of the top surface of the pile to the natural floor plus 0.5m. The pile extension is calculated according to the number of joints. The pile cutting is calculated according to the number of pieces.

(5) Provisions for over-pouring amount of several types of cast-in-place bases

The over-pouring amount of all kinds of cast-in-place bases shall be determined according to the design regulations. If the design does not contain such regulations, the over-pouring amount is: ① For cast-in-place base, the over-pouring amount is 17% of the design calculation amount; ② For digging base, rock embedded base and digging pile base, the over-pouring amount is 7% of the design calculation amount; ③ For the rock grouting base, the over-grouting amount is 8% of the design calculation amount; ④ For the cast-in-place retaining wall, the over-grouting amount is 17% of the design calculation amount of the cast-in-place retaining wall.

(6) Concrete and mortar materials are calculated according to the following mix ratio

The mix ratio of cast-in-place concrete is shown in Table 2-3-3, and the mortar mix ratio is shown in Table 2-3-4.

Table 2-3-3 Cast-in-place Concrete Mix Ratio

Unit: m^3

S/N	Concrete strength	Cement strength Grade	Cement t	Medium sand m^3	Gravel m^3	Water t	Remarks
1	C10	32.5	0.250	0.550	0.830	0.180	Gravel particle size is 40mm Within
2	C15	32.5	0.310	0.490	0.840	0.180	
3	C20	32.5	0.344	0.460	0.850	0.180	
4	C25	32.5	0.405	0.410	0.850	0.180	
5	C30	42.5	0.383	0.420	0.860	0.180	
6	C35	42.5	0.411	0.400	0.860	0.180	
7	C40	42.5	0.460	0.370	0.860	0.180	
8	C20	32.5	0.397	0.460	0.790	0.215	For cast-in-place piles, the particle size of the gravel is within 15mm
9	C25	32.5	0.470	0.400	0.800	0.215	
10	C30	42.5	0.451	0.410	0.800	0.215	
11	C35	42.5	0.479	0.400	0.800	0.215	
12	C40	42.5	0.536	0.370	0.790	0.215	
13	C45	52.5	0.512	0.390	0.790	0.215	

Table 2-3-4 Mortar Mix Ratio

Item	Unit	Cement sand mortar				
		Mortar mark				
		M15	M10	M7.5	M5	M2.5
		Qty.				
32.5 cement	t	0.455	0.331	0.268	0.210	0.150
Medium sand	m^3	1.180	1.180	1.180	1.180	1.180
Water	t	0.220	0.220	0.220	0.220	0.220

2. Statistics of Installation Materials in Project Case 2 Base Works

(1) Statistics of Installation Materials in Project Case II Base Works

1) The statistical calculating table of the installation materials for base works is shown in Table 2-3-5.

Table 2-3-5 Statistic Calculating Table of Installation Materials in Project Case II Base Works

S/N	Material name and specification	Unit	Unit weight	Unit price	Design quantity	Loss rate%	Gross weight	Total price
1	2	3	4	5	6	7	8	9
I	LZG2026 type Within 10				9.568m^3			
	Reinforcement	t	1.000	3500	0.872	0.5	0.88	3065.85
	Anchor bolts	t	1.000	5700	0.260	3	0.27	1528.57
	Cement	t	1.000	350	3.291	5.824	3.48	1219.08
	Medium sand	m^3	1.550	85	4.401	16.236	7.93	434.85
	Gravel	m^3	1.600	60	8.133	12.06	14.58	546.82
	Water	t	1.000		1.722			
	Sub-total						27.14	6795.17
II	XJG2742 type Within 40				24.052m^3			
	Reinforcement	t	1.000	3500	2.982	0.5	3.00	10489.19
	Anchor bolts	t	1.000	5700	0.790	3	0.81	4640.44
	Cement	t	1.000	350	8.274	5.824	8.76	3064.52
	Medium sand	m^3	1.550	85	11.064	16.236	19.93	1093.12
	Gravel	m^3	1.600	60	20.444	12.06	36.66	1374.59

Study Program II Preparation of Preliminary Budget Estimate for 220kV Overhead Transmission Line Project

Table (Cont'd)

S/N	Material name and specification	Unit	Unit weight	Unit price	Design quantity	Loss rate%	Gross weight	Total price
	Water	t	1.000		4.329			
	Sub-total						69.16	20661.85
III	TWG1630 type Within 10				8.776m³			
	Reinforcement	t	1.000	3500	0.372	0.5	0.37	1308.51
	Anchor bolts	t	1.000	5700	0.260	3	0.27	1528.57
	Cement	t	1.000	350	3.554	5.824	3.76	1316.45
	Medium sand	m³	1.550	85	3.598	16.236	6.48	355.50
	Gravel	m³	1.600	60	7.460	12.06	13.37	501.55
	Water	t	1.000		1.580			
	Sub-total						24.26	5010.59
IV	Pull plate LP-1.2	Piece	0.45	158	1	0.5	0.45	160.00
...								
C10					38.2m³			
	Cement	t	1.000	350	9.550	5.824	10.11	3537.17
	Medium sand	m3	1.550	85	21.010	16.236	37.85	2075.80
	Gravel	m3	1.600	60	31.706	12.06	56.85	2131.78
	Water	t	1.000		6.876			
	Sub-total						129.52	12915.34
C20					2430.92m³			
	Reinforcement	t	1.000	3500	174.875	0.5	175.75	615121.41
	Anchor bolts	t	1.000	5700	36.114	3	37.20	212024.12
	Cement	t	1.000	350	836.236	5.824	884.94	309728.61
	Medium sand	m³	1.550	85	1118.223	16.236	2014.66	110481.12
	Gravel	m³	1.600	60	2066.282	12.06	3704.76	138928.54
	Water	t	1.000		437.566			
	Sub-total						6817.30	1386283.80
	Total						6947.28	1399359.14

Note: The price unit is Yuan. The unit price is a sample budget price. And the budget price or contract price of local installation materials during engineering design shall prevail in the actual project.

2) Statistics of reinforcement fabrication and making quantities.

Summarize the design quantity of reinforcement and anchor bolts of each type of cast-in-place base in Table 2-3-5, and multiply by the number of bases of each type to obtain the statistical data of reinforcement fabrication and making quantities of this project case: 210,988.4kg (see Table 2-3-5; refer to the "Summary of Equipment and Materials" in the design data, in which the Grade I base reinforcement is 60,721.5kg, and the Grade II base reinforcement is 114,153.1kg; the anchor bolt Q235 steel is 36,113.8kg).

3) The base cushion quantity statistics contain no design quantity.

4) Statistics on the quantities of mixing and pouring of cast-in-place concrete and base concrete.

According to the data in Table 2-3-5 and the base quantity of each type, Table 2-3-6 is listed to facilitate the calculation of the installation costs.

Table 2-3-6 Statistics on Mixing and Pouring of Cast-in-place Concrete and Base Concrete

Type (No. of bases) / Amount of concrete per base (m^3)	Within 10	Within 20	Within 40	Over 80	Within 120	Over 120
LZG2026 type (1 base)	9.568					
XJG2742 type (1 base)			24.052			
TWG1630 type (1 base)	8.776					
……	……					
Total	18.344		24.052			

See Table 2-3-5, and refer to the "Summary of Equipment and Materials" in the design data. The concrete design quantity of this project case is 2,469.12m^3, of which C10 is 38.20m^3 and C20 is 2,430.92m^3. C10 concrete is mainly used for base protection cap casting.

5) Statistics on the quantities of revetment retaining wall and drainage ditch masonry.

According to the "Summary of Equipment and Materials" in the design drawings, the quantities of the revetment, retaining wall and drainage ditch masonry in this project case are estimated according to the same type of works as: earthwork excavation 950m^3, boulder strip and fort 510m^3, revetment area 240m^3, retaining wall is 79.1m^3 and drainage ditch is

Study Program II Preparation of Preliminary Budget Estimate for 220kV Overhead Transmission Line Project

17.55m³. The outward transport for the surplus soil is 750m³.

The data in Tables 2-3-5 and 2-3-6 are summarized and filled in Table 2-3-7.

Table 2–3–7 Statistics on Quantities of Project Case II Base Works

Name	Unit	Qty.
Base reinforcement processing and production of general reinforcement	t	174.88
Concrete mixing and casting within 10m³ of concrete per base	m³	1003.74
Concrete mixing and casting within 20m³ of concrete per base	m³	785.63
Concrete mixing and casting within 40m³ of concrete per base	m³	641.55
Volume of pouring of protective cap per base within 0.5m³	Site	137.00
Wet masonry of flood drainage trench	m³	132.00
Wet masonry of revetment or retaining wall slope	m³	995.80
Base of antiseptic concrete for base	m³	2740.00

(2) Statement of calculation

When the project is initially designed, according to the design experience and with reference to the same type of project, it is preliminarily determined to use the 137 towers and their tower types and nominal heights, and then select the base form according to the tower type and the nominal height. The following is an example of several selected base forms, and the number of installation materials is calculated step by step to illustrate the statistical calculation method of the installation materials for the base works.

1) LZG2026 base

Fig. 2-3-5 shows the LZG2026 base structure. According to the design data, the LZG2026 base adopts C20 concrete, the single (leg) base concrete is 2.39m³, and the design quantity of reinforcement (main reinforcement Φ16, hoop Φ6, support rib Φ8, and floor rib Φ14) totals 217.9kg.

According to the "Tower Base Foot Distance Table", it is found that the anchor bolt foot distance (side view) of a tower (ZM1-18) using the LZG2026 base is 220mm, and the anchor bolt specification is M36; according to the "Working Diagram of Straight Column base Anchor Bolt foot", find out the materials used for M36 anchor bolts as shown in Table 2-3-8.

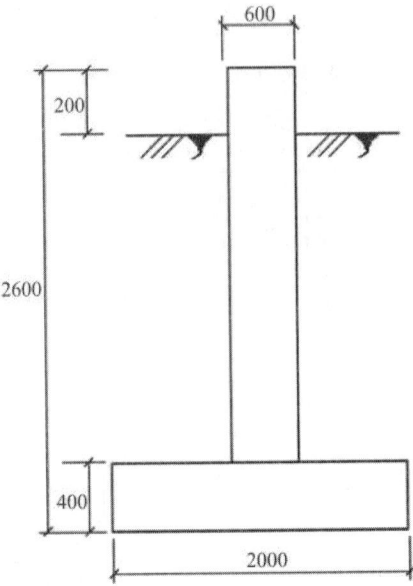

Fig. 2-3-5　LZG2026 Base Structure

At this time, attention shall be paid to reviewing the quantity data provided by the design drawings, including the volume of concrete, the usage amount of reinforcement and anchor bolts. The single (leg) base concrete volume of the LZG2026 base is calculated as

$$V=2\times2\times0.4+0.6\times0.6\times2.2=2.392 \ (m^3)$$

The single (leg) base concrete volume of the LZG2026 base provided in the design is 2.39m^3, and the calculated value is checked to be 2.392m^3. The latter shall be used in the calculation of the following quantities.

According to Table 2-3-3, C20 concrete is made of 32.5 cement with a mix ratio of 0.344:0.460:0.850:0.180. LZG2026 base single leg uses 2.392m^3 of concrete. Therefore, the usage amount of cement, sand, stone and water is 0.823t, 1.117m^3, 2.033m^3 and 0.431t. According to Table 2-3-10, the unit transport weight of medium sand is 1.55t/m^3, and that of gravel is 1.6t/m^3; the unit price is determined according to the current budget of the installation materials; check the Table 1-2-1, and the terrain of this project case is divided into (after comprehensive consideration) : 7.4% flat ground, 51.4% hill, and 41.2% mountainous regions. The construction loss rate of cement, stone, sand and other materials is calculated separately. The data in Table 1-2-1 is directly applied for materials such as reinforcement and bolts.

Study Program II Preparation of Preliminary Budget Estimate for 220kV Overhead Transmission Line Project

Cement construction loss rate is

$$(7.4\%+51.4\%) \times 5.0\%+41.2\%\times 7.0\%=5.824\%$$

Gravel construction loss rate is

$$(7.4\%+51.4\%)\times 10.0\%+41.2\%\times 15.0\%=12.06\%$$

Sand construction loss rate is

$$(7.4\%+51.4\%)\times 15.0\%+41.2\%\times 18.0\%=16.236\%$$

Multiply the single-leg base engineering quantity data by 4 to obtain the base quantity of the whole base, fill in Table 2-3-5, and calculate the total price and total weight.

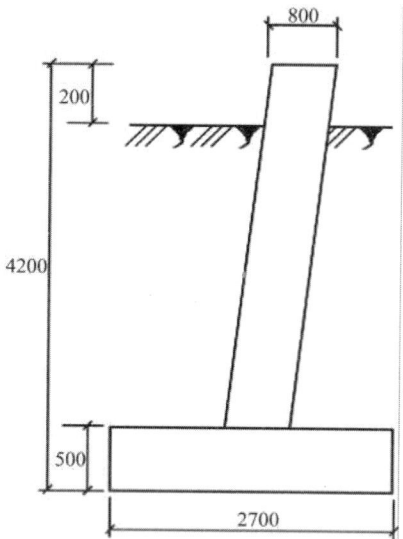

Fig. 2-3-6 XJG2742 Base Structure

2) XJG2742 Base

Fig. 2-3-6 shows the XJG2742 base structure. According to the design data, the XJG2742 base adopts C20 concrete, the single (leg) base concrete is 6.03m³, and the design quantity of reinforcement (main reinforcement Φ25, hoop Φ8, support rib Φ8, and floor rib Φ14) totals 745.5kg. According to the "Tower Base Foot Distance Table", it is found that the anchor bolt foot distance (side view) of N22 tower (JC1-18) using the LZG2026 base is 260mm, and the anchor bolt specification is M52; according to the "Working Diagram of Oblique Column base Anchor Bolt foot", find out the materials used for M52 anchor bolts as shown in Table 2-3-8.

The single (leg) base concrete volume of the XJG2742 base is calculated as

$$V = 2.7 \times 2.7 \times 0.5 + 2.8 \times 0.8 \times 3.7$$
$$= 6.013 \ (m^3)$$

The single (leg) base concrete volume of the XJG2742 base provided in the design is 6.03m³, and the calculated value is checked to be 6.013m³. The latter shall be used in the calculation of the following quantities.

As with the LZG2026 base, the data of usage amount of cement, sand, stone and water are determined and filled in Table 2-3-5, respectively, and the total price and total weight are calculated.

3) TWG1630 base

Fig. 2-3-4 shows the TWG1630 base structure. According to the design data, the TWG1630 base adopts C25 concrete, the single (leg) base concrete is 2.32m³, and the design quantity of reinforcement (main reinforcement Φ16, outer hoop Φ8, and inner rib Φ12) totals 90.3kg. According to the "Tower Base Foot Distance Table", it is found that the anchor bolt foot distance (side view) of a tower (ZM1-30) using the TWG1630 base is 220mm, and the anchor bolt specification is M36; according to the "Working Diagram of Straight Column base Anchor Bolt foot", find out the materials used for M36 anchor bolts as shown in Table 2-3-8.

The single (leg) base concrete volume of the TWG1630 base is calculated as

$$V = \pi r_2^2 h_1 + \frac{\pi h_2 (r_2^2 + r_2^2 + r_1 r_2)}{3} \pi r_2^2 h_3$$
$$= \pi \times 0.8^2 \times 0.3 + \frac{\pi \times 0.5 \ (0.8^2 + 0.4^2 + 0.8 \times 0.4)}{3} + \pi \times 0.4^2 \times 2.2$$
$$= 2.194 \ (m^3)$$

The single (leg) base concrete volume of the TWG1630 base provided in the design is 2.32m³, and the calculated value is checked to be 2.194m³. The latter shall be used in the calculation of the following quantities.

As with the LZG2026 base, the data of usage amount of cement, sand, stone and water are determined and filled in Table 2-3-5, respectively, and the total price and total weight are calculated.

Study Program II Preparation of Preliminary Budget Estimate for 220kV Overhead Transmission Line Project

Table 2-3-8   Materials Used for Anchor Bolts

Diameter M (mm)	Anchor bolts			Gasket of base bolt			Anchor bolt steel hoop			Anchor end steel (kg)	Nut (kg)	Total of each set of bolts (kg)
	Qty. (pcs)	Unit weight (kg)	Sub-total	Qty. (pcs)	Unit weight (kg)	Sub-total	Qty. (pcs)	Unit weight (kg)	Sub-total			
36	4	11.19	44.76	4	1.59	6.36	5	0.28	1.40	9.59	2.98	65.09
52	4	33.68	134.70	4	4.07	16.28	9	0.60	5.43	31.71	9.47	197.60

(II) Pole and Tower Project

The pole and tower project includes concrete pole assembly and erection, steel pipe pole assembly and erection, tower assembly and erection, high tower assembly and erection, pull wire production and installation, and grounding installation.

1. Statistical Requirements for Installation Materials of Several Common Pole and Tower Assembly and Erection Forms

(1) Assembly and erection of concrete pole

The "weight per base" in the quota refers to the total weight of the shaft and the cross arm, the fork beam, the shackles (climbing ladder), the pull wire hoop and the like, excluding the weight of the chassis, chuck and pull plate.

(2) Steel pipe pole assembly

The "weight per base" in the quota refers to the total weight of the steel pipe shaft body, the cross arm, the bolt and the like.

(3) "Weight per unit" in the quota of the tower assembly and erection is the total weight of the tower:

$$\text{Total weight} = \sum (\text{all steel profiles, connecting plates, bolts, shackles, ladders, etc.}) \times (1+3) \qquad (2\text{-}3\text{-}8)$$

Among them, 3% is the increase of the tower material by replacing the small ones with large ones, and the steel tube tower is not included.

(4) High tower assembly and erection

The quota is applicable to the assembly and erection of high tower with the total height of more than 70m. The tower assembly and erection are counted according to different weight grades by "unit"; the pull wire production is counted by "piece", and the length shall be distinguished; grounding installation is counted by "piece", and attention shall be paid to the length of the earth electrode (grounding down lead).

2. Statistics of Installation Materials in Project Case 2 Pole and Tower Works (Schedule II)

(1) Statistics of Installation Materials in Project Case II Pole and Tower Works

1) Statistics of installation materials for pole and tower works

According to the design data, the entire line of the project uses 137 iron towers, including 86 straight iron towers, and 51 tensile and angle iron towers, as shown in Table 2-3-9.

Table 2–3–9 Specific Tower Type and Quantity Statistics

S/N	No. of circuits	Ice area	Use	Towel form	Line length (m)	Base	Sub-total	Total (unit)
1	Single loop	5mm	Suspension tower	2A-ZM1	21	4	22	85
					24	6		
					27	8		
					30	4		
				2A-ZM2	21	4	30	
					24	5		
					27	5		
					30	7		
					33	6		
					36	3		
				2A-ZM3	24	2	25	
					27	4		
					30	7		
					33	6		
					36	3		
					39	2		
					42	1		

Study Program Ⅱ Preparation of Preliminary Budget Estimate for 220kV Overhead Transmission Line Project

S/N	No. of circuits	Ice area	Use	Towel form	Line length (m)	Base	Sub-total	Total (unit)
				2A-ZMC3	24	2	5	
					33	1		
					36	1		
					42	1		
				2A-ZMC4	27	2	3	
					42	1		
			Angle tower	2A-JC1 (0~20°)	21	11	30	44
					24	10		
					27	9		
				2A-JC2 (20~40°)	24	5	11	
					27	4		
					30	2		
				2A-JC3 (40~60°)	21	2	2	
				2A-JC4 (60~90°)	21	1	1	
2	Double loop	5mm	Suspension tower	2I-SZ3	27	1	1	1
			Angle tower	2I-SJ2 (20~40°)	24	2	3	7
					27	1		
				2I-SJ3 (40~60°)	24	2	3	
					27	1		
				2I-SJ4 (60~90°)	21	1	1	

By referring to the "×× tower single-line diagram and material summary table" in the design data, the design quantity of various iron towers including angle steel, bolts, shackles, and washers are obtained, and are filled in Table 2-3-10.

Table 2-3-10 Calculating Table of Installation Materials in Project Case II Pole and Tower Works

S/N	Material name and specification	Unit	Unit weight	Unit price	Design quantity	Loss rate%	Gross weight	Total price
1	2	3	4	5	6	7	8	9
I	ZM1-27 type Within 9				7.0514t			
	Tower material (angle steel and steel plate)	t	1	6800	6.4262	0.5	6.4583	43916.65
	Bolts, shackles and washers	t	1	6800	0.4324	3.5	0.4475	3043.23
	Tower material substitute 3%	t	1	6800	0.1928	0.5	0.1937	1317.50
	Sub-total						7.0996	48277.38
II	JC1-21 type Within 11				10.9318t			
	Tower material (angle steel and steel plate)	t	1	6800	10.0839	0.5	10.1343	68913.37
	Bolts, shackles and washers	t	1	6800	0.5454	3.5	0.5645	3838.53
	Tower material substitute 3%	t	1	6800	0.3025	0.5	0.3040	2067.40
	Sub-total						11.0028	74819.30
III	SJ2-24 type Within 30				28.0390t			
	Tower material (angle steel and steel plate)	t	1	6800	26.0113	0.5	26.1414	177761.22
	Bolts, shackles and washers	t	1	6800	1.2474	3.5	1.2911	8779.20
	Tower material substitute 3%	t	1	6800	0.7803	0.5	0.7842	5332.84
	Sub-total						28.2167	191873.26
...								
					1133.4914t			
	Tower material (angle steel and steel plate)	t	1	6800	1059.423	0.5	1064.7201	7240096.78
	Bolts, shackles and washers	t	1	6800	74.0684	3.5	76.6608	521293.40

Study Program II Preparation of Preliminary Budget Estimate for 220kV Overhead Transmission Line Project

Table (Cont'd)

S/N	Material name and specification	Unit	Unit weight	Unit price	Design quantity	Loss rate%	Gross weight	Total price
	Tower material substitute 3%	t	1	6800	31.7827	0.5	31.9416	217202.90
	Total						1173.3225	7978593.08

Note: (8) = (4) × (6) × [1 + (7)], (9) = (5) × (6) × [1 + (7)]

Note: The price unit is Yuan. The unit price is a sample budget price. And the budget price or contract price of local installation materials during engineering design shall prevail in the actual project.

According to the usage quantity of towers of various types used that are listed in Table 2-3-9, and the design quantity of towers, bolts, shackles and washers of various types in Table 2-3-10, the quantity of installation materials for the pole and tower works of the project case is obtained by classification and summary (see Table 2-3-10), which is not described further here.

2) Statistics on quantities of pole and tower assembly and erection

According to the usage quantity of towers of various types listed in Table 2-3-9, and the design quantity of tower materials of various types in Table 2-3-10, according to the iron tower installation quota sub-item, fill in Table 2-3-11 to facilitate the calculation of the installation costs.

Table 2–3–11 Statistical Calculating Table of Quantities of Pole and Tower Assembly and Erection

Type (No. of bases) \ Weight per unit (t)	Within 5	Within 7	Within 9	Within 11	Within 30	Sub-total
ZM1-27 type (8 bases)			7.0514			56.4111
JC1-21 type (11 bases)				10.9318		120.2500
SJ2-24 type (2 bases)					28.0390	56.0781
……		……				
In total (t)			8 bases	11 bases	2 bases	232.7392

3) Grounding installation quantity statistics

According to the "General Specification of Preliminary Design", 137 sets of grounding devices are used in this project case, in which type C accounts for 10%, type D accounts for 35%, type E accounts for 50%, and type F accounts for 5%. According to the "Summary of Equipment and Materials" in the preliminary design data, the grounding device engineering quantity statistics are shown in Table 2-3-12; pay attention to calculate and review the quantities.

Table 2–3–12 Statistical Calculating Table of Quantities of Grounding Installation Works

S/N	Material name and specification	Unit	Unit price	Design quantity	Loss rate	Gross weight	Total price
1	Round steel F10	kg	4000	18934.2	0.5	19028.9	76115.57
2	Round steel F12	kg	4000	1216.6	0.5	1222.6	4890.57
3	Flat steel 130´50´5	kg	4000	168.5	0.5	169.4	677.41
4	Galvanized bolt M16´45	kg	5800	80.0	3.0	82.4	477.97
Total				20319.3		20503.3	82161.52

The design quantity of round steel and flat steel in Table 2-3-12 is 20,319.3kg, which is the quantities of processing and production of the grounding body, which shall be filled in Table 2-3-13; as shown in Fig. 2-0-2, the grounding devices used in this project case are types C, D, E, and F devices. Four F10 grounding round steel laid for each grounding device, each piece is 28m, 38m, 68m, and 86m long. The number of grounding round steel is calculated according to the proportion of each type of grounding device, which shall be filled in Table 2-3-13. Fill the data in the "Total" column in Table 2-3-11 to Table 2-3-13.

Table 2–3–13 Statistics on Quantities of Project Case II Pole and Tower Works

Name	Unit	Qty.
Assembly and erection of iron tower within 5t per unit	Site	19
Assembly and erection of iron tower within 7t per unit	Site	45
Assembly and erection of iron tower within 9t per unit	Site	28
Assembly and erection of iron tower within 11t per unit	Site	19
Assembly and erection of iron tower within 13t per unit	Site	19
Assembly and erection of iron tower within 27t per unit	Site	4
Assembly and erection of iron tower within 30t per unit	Site	3
Processing and manufacturing of grounding body	kg	20319.3
Grounding body laying length within 200m per unit	Nos.	247
Grounding body laying length within 300m per unit	Nos.	274
Grounding body laying length within 400m per unit	Nos.	28
Measurement of resistance	Site	137

(2) Statement of calculation

The statistical calculation method of the installation materials for the pole and tower works is illustrated by taking the statistical calculation of the installation materials for several iron towers used in this project case as an example.

1) ZM1-27 tangent tower

Refer to the "ZM1 Tower Single-line Drawing and Material Summary Table" in the design data. The design quantity of various materials for ZM1-27 tangent tower are: angle steel, Q345 is 2,644.2kg, and Q235 is 3,079.8kg; steel plate, Q345 is 365.0kg, and Q235 is 337.2kg; bolt, grade 6.8, M16 is 183.5kg, and M20 is 211.8kg; shackles, grade 6.8, 36kg; washer (gasket) 1.1kg. Add the angle steel and steel plate and fill in the "Tower Material" column in Table 2-3-8. Add the bolts, shackles and washers (gaskets) and fill in Table 2-3-10.

2) JC1-21 angle tower

Refer to the "JC1 Tower Single-line Drawing and Material Summary Table" in the design data. The design quantity of various materials for JC1-21 tangent tower are: angle steel, Q345 is 4,375kg, and Q235 is 4,105.4kg; steel plate, Q345 is 1,214.9kg, and Q235 is 388.6kg; bolt, grade 6.8, M16 is 99.5kg, and M20 is 284.1kg; shackles, grade 6.8, 31.1kg; washer (gasket) 1.5kg. Fill in Table 2-3-10 in the same way.

3) SJ2-24 angle tower

Refer to the "SJ2 Tower Single-line Drawing and Material Summary Table" in the design data. The design quantity of various materials for SJ2-24 tangent tower are: angle steel, Q345 is 11,239.7kg, and Q235 is 10,342.8kg; steel plate, Q345 is 3,454.2kg, and Q235 is 974.6kg; bolt, grade 4.8, M16 is 220.4kg, and grade 68, M20 is 933.9kg; shackles, grade 4.8, M16 is 63.8kg, and grade 6.8, M20 is 28.3kg; washer (gasket) is 1.0kg. Fill in Table 2-3-10 in the same way.

4) Grounding device material

According to the Table 2-0-4, the quantity of $\Phi 12$ round steel used for each set of grounding device of C, D, E, and F types is 8.88kg. Among the 137 sets of grounding devices, the C, D, E and F types account for 10%, 35%, 50% and 5%. Design quantity calculation of $\Phi 12$ round steel for the grounding device in this project case is

$$(8.88 \times 10\% + 8.88 \times 35\% + 8.88 \times 50\% + 8.88 \times 5\%) \times 137 = 1216.6 \text{ (kg)}$$

Similarly, the design quantity of $\Phi 10$ round steel, flat steel and galvanized bolts can be obtained and filled in Table 2-3-12.

(Ⅲ) Wiring Works

The wiring works include the erection of conductors, lightning wires, and optical cables, crossing erection of conductors, lightning wires, and optical cables, coupling shielded cable installation, overhead warning line installation, optical cable measurement and connection.

1. Relevant Requirements

The quota is divided into two types: general erection and tension erection. When used, it shall be applied according to the construction drawing design requirements. The quota is set with sub-items according to the conductor and lightning wire cross section, and the jumper insulator string installation has been included, but the voltage class is not listed. The quantities of wiring are based on the total length of the line, and the height difference angle of the suspension points is within 10°. The conductors in the quota are considered in accordance with the three-phase AC single-circuit line project.

2. Statistics of Installation Materials in Project Case 2 Wiring Works

(1) See Table 2-3-14 for statistics of installation materials in project case 2 wiring works.

Table 2-3-14 Statistics of Installation Materials in Project Case II Wiring Works

S/N	Material name and specification	Unit	Unit weight	Unit price	Design quantity	Loss rate%	Gross weight	Total price
1	2	3	4	5	6	7	8	9
I	Conductor LGJ-400/35	t	0.001349	16800	310800	0.4824	421.29	7077701.48
II	Single lightning wire GJX-80	t	0.000628	14000	43800	0.3	27.59	386244.87
	Single lightning wire LBGJ-100-30AC	t	0.00057393	14000	8000	0.4824	4.61	64590.25
	Sub-total							

Note: (8) = (4) × (6) × [1+ (7)], (9) = (5) × (6) × [1+ (7)]

Note: The price unit is Yuan.

(2) The calculation shows the number of circuits according to the conductor, lightning wire and optical cable, the number of conductor bundles, the number of conductors, light-

Study Program II Preparation of Preliminary Budget Estimate for 220kV Overhead Transmission Line Project

ning wires and optical cables, the weight per unit length, the length of the line, and the loss as well as total weight. The equation for calculation is:

$$\text{Total weight} = n_1 \times n_2 \times G_0 \times \sum l_i \times n_3 \times (1 + \text{loss rate \%}) \quad (2\text{-}3\text{-}10)$$

In the formula, n_1 is the number of circuits of the conductor, the lightning wire and the optical cable, and is divided into single, double and multiple circuits; n_2 is the number of conductor bundles, and is divided into double bundles, four bundles, six bundles, eight bundles, etc., and the number of bundles of the lightning wire and the optical cable is taken as 1; n_3 is the number of conductor phases, lightning wires and optical cables; G_0 is the weight per unit length of the conductor, lightning wire and optical cable, kg/km; $\sum l_i$ is the length of the line, that is, the sum of the distances of the spans along the line, km. The length of the line here should be the actual length of the conductor, the lightning wire or the optical cable. Since the distance, height difference and sag of each span are not determined in the preliminary design stage, it is generally replaced by the total length of the line, and the actual length can be calculated after the design of the construction drawings. The errors are handled according to the experience and combined with the engineering topography by properly enlarging the quantities, and the data in Table 2-3-14 is not enlarged.

The loss rate is different for the conductor, the lightning wire and the optical cable, and is related to the terrain. For details, please refer to the Detailed Budget Quota in Electric Power Construction Projects - Volume IV Power Transmission Line Engineering (2006 Version); the construction loss rate of the conductors of this project case (including the good conductor bottom line) is 0.4824%. The formula is

$$(7.4\%+51.4\%) \times 0.4\% + 41.2\% \times 0.6\% = 0.4824\%$$

$$\text{Total price} = \text{total weight} \times \text{unit price} \quad (2\text{-}3\text{-}11)$$

According to the design data, the actual length is 51.8km for the project case, with double bundle conductor LGJ-400/35 conductor and single lightning wire matched with OPGW, of which the length of model GJX-80 lightning wire is 43.8km and the length of model LB-GJ-100-30AC lightning wire is 8km.

Formula (2-3-10) and (2-3-11) are used to calculate the total weight and total price of conductor lightning wire.

1) The total weight of the conductor is

$$1 \times 2 \times 1.349 \times 51800 \times 3 \times (1+0.4824\%) = 421291.75 \text{ (kg)}$$

2) The total weight of GJX-80 lightning wire is

$$1\times1\times0.628\times43800\times1\times(1+0.3\%)=27588.92\text{ (kg)}$$

3) The total weight of LBGJ-100-30AC lightning wire is

$$1\times1\times0.57393\times8000\times1\times(1+0.4824\%)=4613.59\text{ (kg)}$$

Calculate the total price in the same way. The unit price in Table 2-3-14 is a sample budget price. And the budget price or contract price of local installation materials during engineering design shall prevail in the actual project.

(Ⅳ) Accessory Project

The accessory project includes the hanging of insulator string, the installation of conductor suspension clamp, grading ring, shielding ring, vibration damper, spacer, counter weight, damper line and ice blocking ring.

1. Relevant Requirements

The hanging of insulator string is applicable to the installation of insulator string of straight line, straight line corner and transposition pole and tower, excluding the installation of strain armor clamp and strain insulator string. The stringing project consists of the fabrication of strain conductor and ground wire terminal, in the line erection, installation of jumper string, fabrication and installation of span jumper terminal, installation of straight line corner and transposition pole (tower) insulator string.

The installation materials installed in accessory project mainly refer to insulator and armor clamp, which are counted by "string", "number" and "set". The insulator is divided into suspension string for conductor, strain insulator string and insulator for ground wire. The armor clamp includes yoke plate, hanging ring, socket eyes and other types. Other types of armor clamp include cable clamp, grading ring, shielding ring, anti vibration damper, spacer, counter weight, damper line, ice blocking ring, earthing bolt, down lead, etc.

2. Statistics of Installation Materials in Project Case 2 Accessory Project

(1) See Table 2-3-15 for statistics of installation materials in project case 2 accessory project.

Study Program II Preparation of Preliminary Budget Estimate for 220kV Overhead Transmission Line Project

Table 2-3-15 Statistics of Installation Materials in Project Case II Accessory Project

S/N	Material name and specification	Unit	Unit weight	Unit price	Design quantity	Loss rate%	Gross weight	Total price
1	2	3	4	5	6	7	8	9
I	Insulator							
	U100BP2	Piece	4	85	15966	2.0	65141.28	1384252.2
	XDP-70CN	Piece	7	80	6	2.0	42.84	489.6
III	Fitting							
	Yoke plate							
	Yoke plate L-1640	Piece	9.54	144	926	1.0	8922.38	134677.44
	...							
	Ring							
	U-link U-7	Piece	0.44	12	30	1.0	13.33	363.6
	...							
	Socket eyes type							
	Socket eyes WS-10	Piece	1.2	34	1065	1.0	1290.78	36572.1
	...							
	Other types							
	Suspension clamp XCS-6	Piece	15	234	346	1.0	5241.90	81773.64
	Strain clamp NY-80G	Piece	1.3	43	214	1.0	280.98	9294.02
	Anti-vibration hammer FDZ-5F	Piece	7.2	67	1726	1.0	12551.47	116798.42
	Preformed armor rod FYH-400/35	Piece	2.8	274	176	1.0	497.73	48706.24
	...							
	Total						119706.40	2413711.00

Note: (8) = (4) × (6) × [1+ (7)], (9) = (5) × (6) × [1+ (7)]

Note: The unit of weight is kg, the unit of price is Yuan, and the unit price is a sample budget price.

(2) Statement of calculation

1) Calculation of the quantity of the insulator.

In the reference design data "summary of equipment and materials", the design quantity of conductor insulator U100BP2 is 15966 pieces, and the design quantity of ground wire insulator XDP-70CN is 6 pieces. The design quantity of insulator and armor clamp in the project case shall be calculated according to Table 2-0-7 Model of Insulator String for Armor Clamp and Specific Use and Table 2-3-9 Specific Tower Type and Quantity Statistics, so as to recheck the material quantity provided by the design, and then fill in Table 2-3-15.

2) Calculation of the qty. of the armor clamp.

The method is the same as above. However, there are many kinds and quantities of armor clamps. Only a part of the list of materials is selected in Table 2-3-15. For other parts, they will not be described in this book for it's too long.

When counting the number of insulators and armor clamps, attention shall be paid to whether the strain insulator fittings on the portal frame at both ends of the line or on the branch pole and tower are omitted.

List of main installation materials and project quantity index in the project case shall be calculated according to Table 2-3-5, 2-3-10, 2-3-12, 2-3-14 and 2-3-15. See Table 2-3-16 for details.

Table 2-3-16 List of Main Installation Materials and Project Quantity Index

Project name	Conductor	Lightning wire GJX-80	Lightning wire LBGJ	Tower material	Fitting	base reinforcement	Quantities of concrete	Quantities of earthwork	Insulator
Unit	t/km	t/km	t/km	t/km	t/km	t/km	m^3/km	m^3/km	Sheet/km
Qty.	8.13	0.63	0.58	22.65	2.31	3.38	47.67	745.68	315

IV. Calculation of Site Transport Project Quantity On Site

(I) Transport of Equipment and Materials

The transport of equipment and materials means transporting the equipment and materials from the Manufacturer workshop to the construction site. The transport cost of the equipment shall be included in the equipment acquisition expenses, which shall consists of the freight and miscellaneous charges (cost price of the equipment is multiplied by the rate of freight and miscellaneous charges) on the base of contract price (including freight and miscellaneous charges) or cost price of the equipment. The transport of installation materials for the line project is divided into large transport and small transport.

1. Large Transport

Large transport refers to the transporting installation materials from the Manufacturer workshop to the materials distribution warehouse at the construction site by railway, waterway and highway.

The cost of large transport includes the transport cost in factory, railway (waterway, highway) freight, handling cost, freight for entering the warehouse, purchase and storage fee, commission charge of supply and marketing department, etc. (Different units have corresponding regulations for different materials). For installation materials, the cost of large transport is directly included in the budget price of installation materials. The budget price of installation materials is generally the unified price of the whole province, whose current season price is set by the Power Quota (Cost) Management Station according to the market price of installation materials in the province in the previous quarter.

2. Small Transport

Small transport, also known as site transport, refers to the work of loading and unloading, transport and no-load return trip, etc. of installation materials from the site distribution warehouse (material station) to each pole and tower along the line.

The site transport is divided into manpower transport, tractor transport, automobile transport, ship transport and cableway transport according to the transport mode. The reason why different transport modes should be distinguished is that the labor, machinery and materials consumed by unit weight of different transport modes are different, and the corresponding selected quota items are different. In addition, it should also be noted that the terrain of different transport mode is different. For example, the terrain of human transport is generally considered to be the same as that of line project, while the terrain of automobile transport should be calculated according to the actual terrain of automobile transport line.

(Ⅱ) Transport Weight Calculation of Site Transport

Estimate weight = design quantity+ loss weight = design quantity × (1 + loss rate)　(2-3-12)

Transport weight = estimate weight × unit transport weight　(2-3-13)

In fact, the calculation work of estimate weight is completed in the preparation of statistical calculating table of installation materials quantities. Refer to Tables 2-3-5, 2-3-10, 2-3-12, 2-3-14 and 2-3-15 for more details. Among which, the figure in "total weight" column is the budget estimate weight of this kind of devices materials;

The design quantity refers to the project quantity data including the type and quantity of installation materials for each work unit provided by the designers and calculated and rechecked by the budget estimate preparers. In principle, the budget preparers shall not increase or decrease the type and quantity of the data without authorization.

However, the figure of the data determined by the recheck budget estimate preparer is often larger than the figure provided by the designer, and the value is enlarged by 5% - 10% depending on the different types of materials according to the experience. The reason is that the preliminary design budget estimate controls the investment of the whole project, while the preliminary design project quantity data is relatively rough. In order to ensure that the budget investment does not exceed the budgeted investment, only the project quantity can be appropriately enlarged. The data in Tables 2-3-5, 2-3-10, 2-3-12, 2-3-14 and 2-3-15 in this book are not enlarged.

Loss quantity refers to the damaged quantity of installation materials caused by handling and other construction reasons. See Table 1-2-1 for details of List of Materials Construction Loss Rate. All kinds of spare parts prepared due to construction loss are not included in the installation cost, only the amount and weight will be calculated and shall be included in the "total weight" and "total price".

When calculating the transport weight, the budget estimate quantity in the above statistical calculating table of installation materials shall be directly taken for calculation. The unit transport weight of materials shall comply with the provisions of budget quota, as shown in Table 2-3-17.

Table 2-3-17 Unit Transport Weight of Installation Materials

Material name		Unit	Transport weight (kg)	Remarks
Concrete product	Hand-placed concrete	m^3	2600	Including reinforcement
	Centrifugal placing concrete	m^3	2860	Including reinforcement
Wire rods	Conductor (with cable tray)	kg	$W \times 1.15$	
	Lightning wire (with cable reel)	kg	$W \times 1.10$	
	Lightning wire, pull wire (without cable reel)	kg	$W \times 1.04$	
	Optical cable (with cable reel)	kg	$W \times 1.20$	
	Cable	kg	$W+G$	G is the reel weight

Table (Cont'd)

Commercial concrete	m³	2560	
Earth	m³	1500	Actual excavation volume
Block stone, break stone, pebble	m³	1600	
Lime	m³	1200	
Yellow sand (dry medium sand)	m³	1550	
Cement, friction reducer	kg	W×1.01	In bags
Water	kg	W×1.20	
Armor clamp, insulator (porcelain and glass)	kg	W×1.07	
Composite insulator	kg	W×2.00	
Bolt, washer, shackles	kg	W×1.01	

Note: Other kinds of installation materials not listed in the table are calculated by net weight, and W is the theoretical weight.

Meaning of various materials in budget quota: The concrete pole refers to the whole and segmented concrete pole, concrete sleeve and concrete cross arm produced by centrifugal machine. Precast concrete products refer to the finished and semi-finished products of concrete, such as chassis, pull plate, chuck, fork beam, cover plate, etc., which are poured manually and vibrated mechanically. Wire stock refers to conductor, lightning wire, coupling shielded wire, cable and optical cable. Tower material refers to steel tower. Steel tube pole refers to the whole or segmented steel pipe pole formed by pressing and welding of steel plate. Armor clamp, insulator and sporadic steel refer to armor clamp, insulator, cross arm for pole, ground wire support, pull bar, pull rod, hose clamp, link fitting, vibration damper, spacer, cast iron counter weight, grounding pipe (belt) material, bolt, washer, etc.

The average load distance at the site transport is in kilometers. When it is transported by car or ship and the average load distance is less than 1km, it shall be calculated as 1km. If it is transported by tractor or manpower, the average transportation distance shall keep two decimal places. For the calculation method of the average load distance, please refer to the relevant content of the project quantity calculation in Project 1.

(Ⅲ) Average Load Distance of Project Case 2

The transport of the project is mainly district and township roads. There are many tractor roads parallel and crossing the whole line. However, the transport conditions in some sections are poor. The average load distance of the whole line is 28km by automobile transport and 0.80km by manpower.

Calculation description: After calculation, the highway mileage for material transport along the project case route is 56km. Considering that the material station will be set at the middle point of the highway, the average load distance of automobile transport is 28km. Since the pole and tower position is not determined in the preliminary design stage, the manpower load distance is estimated to be 0.80km with reference to the similar project. The surplus soil shall be transported by manpower. Refer to the similar project, the average load distance is 150m.

(Ⅳ) Quantities Calculation of Site Transport in Project Case 2

See Table 2-2-18 (the format is the same as Schedule Ⅳ) and Table 2-3-19 (the format is the same as Schedule Ⅴ) for the calculating sheet of the transport weight and quantities of site transport in the project case.

Calculation description: According to the statistical data of the quantity of installation materials in 5 work units in Table 2-3-5, 2-3-10, 2-3-12, 2-3-14 and 2-3-15, and the material category classification with the weight summary of various devices materials in Table 2-3-18, fill in the Table 2-3-18 (The "Material category" in the table is determined according to the quota item division in the budget quota. Only the material category in the project case are listed in the table). At this time, attention should be paid to distinguish the material category, because different materials have different packaging coefficients, which requires to summary the same installation materials of different work units.

Similarly, "Project name" in Table 2-3-19 is determined according to the division of quota items in budget quota. Attention shall be paid to distinguish the quantities of labor transport and automobile transport of installation materials in the table, and the labor transport shall be adopted for the transport of surplus soil, and the average load distance is different. In the table, the water for cast-in-place concrete base works is calculated according to the calculation of transport weight and quantities in site transport for the same average load distance of ordinary installation materials. Generally, the water is taken on site in the actual construction. The water consumption within 100m transport, which is required for the concrete stone washing, mixing, curing and formwork washing, etc, has been considered in this quota.

Study Program II Preparation of Preliminary Budget Estimate for 220kV Overhead Transmission Line Project

Table 2-3-18 Calculating Table of Transport Weight for Site Transport in Project Case II

Material category	Unit	Budgeted weight of the whole line (including the loss)					Total	Packing coefficient	Transportation weight t
		Earth-work	base works	Pole and tower works	Installation of insulator and hanging wire fittings	Stringing works	Earthing work			
Precast concrete products										
Within 500kg	kg		454.50					454.50	1.00	0.45
Wire rods										
Conductor within 1000kg	kg					421291.75		421291.75	1.15	484.49
Ground wire within 1000kg	kg					32202.51		32202.51	1.10	35.42
Metal, insulator, sporadic steel, tower material	t									
Fitting	kg				119706.40			119706.40	1.07	128.09
Insulator	kg				65184.12			65184.12	1.07	69.75
Sporadic steel	kg		175748.97				20420.90	196169.87	1.00	196.17
Tower material	kg			1096661.70				1096661.70	1.00	1096.66
Bolt, washer, shackles	kg		37197.21	76660.80			82.40	113940.41	1.01	115.08
Brick, sand, stone, soil, water, cement, lime										
Sand	m³		1324.20					1324.20	1.55t/m³	2052.51
Stone	m³		2351.00					2351.01	1.60t/m³	3761.61
Soil (outward transport for the surplus soil)	m³	750.00						750.00	1.50t/m³	1125.00
Water	m³		444.44					444.44	1.20	533.33
Cement	kg		895045.08					895045.08	1.01	904.00
Total										10502.55

Note 1: The pull wire, lightning wire and conductor shall be filled in different columns in the table according to the model and the weight of each reel, and the packing coefficient shall be calculated according to relevant regulations.

Note 2: "Transport weight" shall be filled in Schedule V.

Table 2-3-19 Calculating Table of Project Quantity for Site Transport in Project Case II

Material station	Project name	Terrain transport weight t	Flat ground		Hill		Mountain land		High mountain		Steep mountain		Swamp	
			Load distance	t.km	Load distance	t.km	Load distance	t.km	Load distance	t.km	Load distance	t.km	Load distance	Load distance
×Station	Human-powered transport	Average haul distance of manpower 800m												
	Outward transport for the surplus soil	1125	0.15	168.75										
	Precast concrete products													
	Within 500kg	0.45	0.80	0.36										
	Wire rods													
	Within 1000kg	519.51	0.80	415.61										
	Armor clamp, insulator and sporadic steel	431.66	0.80	345.32										
	Tower material	1174.09	0.80	939.27										
	Brick, sand, stone, soil, water, cement, lime	7251.44	0.80	5801.15										
	Automobile transportation	Average haul distance of car 28km												
	Precast concrete products													
	Within 500kg	0.45	28.00	12.60										

Study Program Ⅱ Preparation of Preliminary Budget Estimate for 220kV Overhead Transmission Line Project

Table (Cont'd)

Material station	Project name	Terrain transport weight t	Flat ground		Hill		Mountain land		High mountain		Steep mountain		Swamp	
			Load distance	t.km	Load distance	t.km	Load distance	t.km	Load distance	t.km	Load distance	t.km	Load distance	Load distance
	Wire rods													
	Within 1000kg	519.51	28.00	14546.28										
	Armor clamp, insulator and sporadic steel	431.66	28.00	12086.34										
	Tower material	1174.09	28.00	32874.50										
	Brick, sand, stone, soil, water, cement, lime	7251.44	28.00	203040.39										

Note 1: Only the transport quantities of flat topography are calculated here, and the comprehensive terrain adjustment coefficient will be considered in the calculation of installation cost.

Note 2: The weight of bolts, washers and shackles used for the tower shall be included in the tower materials.

Task 4　Charge Calculation

　　The last learning task has determined the quantities of line engineering. For the preparation of preliminary design budget, it is only the first step to know the project quantity. It is also necessary to implement the budget cost composition and calculation standard specified in the Budget Standard, determine the applicable unit price of installation materials, unit price of installation cost (base price) and various rates, and calculate the estimated investment amount of the project according to the project quantity, so as to complete the charge calculation. This is the connotation of charge calculation. The externalization of charge calculation is shown in a series of tables that form the budget statement.

　　The filling in of these budget estimate forms is based on the quantities of each work unit calculated from the previous learning task. The unit price of installation cost corresponding to each project quantity shall be determined by applying the quota, and the total price shall be obtained by multiplying the project quantity by the unit price. Then, the adjustment coefficient of labor, machinery and material cost shall be considered in combination with the actual situation of the project and the current relevant regulations, and the forms shall be completed by adding, multiplying and transferring data. This learning task focuses on the preparation method and process of Table I-B, Table II-B, Table III-B, Table III C and Table IV of the budget statement.

　　Before completing various budget estimate forms, first of all, we should be familiar with the budgeted cost composition of power transmission line project construction, which is slightly different from the budgets cost composition of power distribution line project described in Project 1. Secondly, we should be more familiar with the Detailed Budget Quota in Electric Power Construction Projects - Volume IV Electric Transmission Line Engineering (2006 Version), so as to obtain the unit price of installation cost corresponding to the appropriate quota item. If the cost involved in the project is the same as the Project 1, please refer to the relevant contents in Project 1, which will not be described here.

Ⅰ. Composition of Budgeted Cost in Power Transmission Line Project Construction

The budgeted cost of power transmission line project construction consists of installation project cost, other cost and dynamic cost. The sum of installation project cost and other expenses is called static investment.

(Ⅰ) Composition of Installation Project Cost

Installation project cost refers to the cost of construction, installation and commissioning of infrastructure, process system and auxiliary system, which form the project, to make them have production functions. It includes direct costs, indirect costs, profits and taxes.

1. Direct Cost

Direct cost refers to the cost on specific product objects, which is directly consumed during the production process of construction and installation products. It consists of direct construction cost and measure cost.

(1) Direct construction cost includes labor cost, material cost and cost of using construction machinery.

(2) The measure cost includes the additional cost for construction in winter and rainy season, additional cost for working at night, the use fee of construction tools and appliances, additional cost for construction in special areas, temporary facilities cost, the transfer cost of construction organization, and the subsidy for safety and civilization measures.

2. Indirect Cost

Indirect cost refers to the cost, which serve for the whole project during the production process of construction and installation products and is not directly consumed in specific product objects. The indirect cost consists of compliance cost and enterprise administration expense.

The compliance cost includes social security fee, social accumulation fund and accidental injury insurance for dangerous operation.

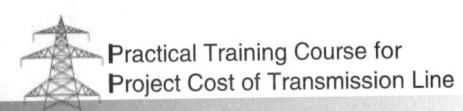

(Ⅱ) Composition of Other Expenses

Other expenses refer to other relevant expenses, which is necessary for the completion of the project construction and is not included in the construction and installation project cost. It includes the following expenses.

1. Construction Site Requisition and Clearing Costs

(1) Land acquisition fee.

(2) Construction site rental.

(3) Relocation compensation fee.

(4) Clearance cost.

(5) Corridor compensation for power transmission line corridor.

(6) Measure cost for communication facility against interference from power transmission line.

2. Project Construction Administrative Cost

(1) Construction project legal person administrative cost.

(2) Bidding costs.

(3) Project supervision cost.

(4) Equipment construction expenses.

(5) Project insurance expenses.

3. Project Construction Technical Service Cost

(1) Preliminary work fees for the project.

(2) Intellectual property rights transfer cost and research and test fee.

(3) Survey and design fee includes survey fee and design fee.

(4) Design document review fee consists of feasibility study design document review fee and preliminary design document review fee.

(5) Post evaluation fee of the project.

(6) Project construction supervision and testing fee, including project quality supervision and testing fee, special equipment safety supervision fee, environmental supervision and acceptance fee, water and soil conservation project acceptance and compensation fee

and pile base testing fee.

(7) Administrative fee for formulation of power construction standard.

(8) Administrative fee for formulation of power project quota.

4. Commissioning Costs of Subsystem and the Entire Start-up

(1) Cost for subsystem commissioning.

(2) Commissioning fees of the entire start-up.

(3) Construction enterprise cooperative commissioning cost.

5. Production Preparation Cost

(1) Management vehicle acquisition expenses

(2) Acquisition expenses of tools and instruments, and office furniture.

(3) Production staff training and in-advance entry expenses. In addition, other costs also include the measure cost of heavy-cargo transportation and basic reserve cost.

(Ⅲ) Composition of Dynamic Cost

Dynamic cost refers to the cost incurred by price increase and capital cost increase caused by time and market price change during the period from the year of construction budget preparation to completion acceptance of various construction cost elements, mainly including reserve costs for price difference and interest for loans during construction.

The following describes the preparation of various Budget Estimate according to the budget preparation workflow.

Ⅱ. Preparation of Work Unit Budget Estimate

The Work Unit Budget Estimate takes up a large part in the budget statement, including six Work Unit Budget Estimate, including earthwork, base project, tower project, overhead conductor and ground wire installation works, accessory project and site transport, etc.

See Table 2-4-1 for the Budget Estimate of Work Unit, which mainly includes the cost of installation materials and installation cost and are divided into unit price and total price. When preparing the Work Unit Budget Estimate, the name of the work unit installed installation materials shall be filled in the column of "project name and specification" according to the statistical table of installation materials of power transmission line project, the calculating table of earthwork quantity and the calculating table of site transport project quantity. Fill in the name of earthwork excavation quantities or site transportation quantities if there are no installation materials for earthwork and site transport work unit. Meanwhile, fill in the corresponding data in the column of "unit" and "quantity". Refer to the applicable quota, and fill in the corresponding quota item number in the "Compilation basis" column as the basis for determining the quota installation base price (i.e. unit price) corresponding to the quantities. Fill in the "in total, wages, machinery" column of the installation cost in the "unit price" column in according to the "base price" of the quota installation corresponding to the quota item. Fill in the unit price of installation materials in the column of "unit price" according to the selected budget price of installation materials. "Total price" is equal to "quantity" multiplied by "unit price".

Table 2-4-1 Budget Estimate of Overhead Power Transmission Line Unit Work (Table III C)

S/N	Basis of preparation	Project name and code	Unit	Qty.	Unit price (RMB)				Total price (RMB)				
					Installation material	Installation fee			Installation material	Installation fee			
						Total	Where in: Salary	Machinery		Total	Where in: Salary	Machinery	

Generally, directly fill in the total price (total price from statistical calculation table of installation materials) in Table III C, which does not reflect the calculation process from the unit price to the total price. Because when calculating the installation cost, the design quantity of installation materials, which is used, does not include the construction loss, and the total price of installation materials includes the construction loss.

(I) On the Calculation of Installation Materials Cost

The quantity of installation materials comes from the statistical data of engineering quantity, and the unit price is taken from the "information price of power transmission and transformation engineering equipment and materials" or the applicable "budget price of installation materials in electric power construction engineering" implemented at that time in the project location. The remaining materials shall be calculated according to the current market price of the project location. The equation for calculation is:

Cost of installation materials = consumption of installation materials × budget price of installation materials (2-4-1)

The budget price of installation materials shall be calculated according to the budget price or comprehensive budget price of installation materials published by the quota (cost) management organization of the power industry. Generally, the Budget Price of Installation Material in Electric Power Construction Engineering published by the quota (cost) management organization of the power industry of each province in the last quarter. The current budget price of installation materials is the price level of the last quarter, which is used in combination with the current "power construction project budget quota" and "grid project construction budget preparation and calculation standard". The cost of materials on site inspection and test has been included in the enterprise administration expense of the Builder.

(II) Calculation of Installation Costs

The installation cost in the Budget Estimate of work unit includes the fixed direct cost, topographic adjustment, labor cost adjustment and material and machine adjustment, combining with the installation materials cost to form the direct construction cost. The calculation formula of installation cost is

Installation cost = fixed direct cost + terrain adjustment + labor cost adjustment + material and machine adjustment (2-4-2)

1. Fixed Direct Cost

Fixed direct cost is the main part of installation cost, including labor cost, material cost (consumable material cost) and machinery cost. The equation for calculation is:

Fixed direct cost (total price) = project quantity of each work unit × fixed installation base price (unit price) (2-4-3)

Quota installation base price is short for quota base price or base price, and see Table 2-4-2 for example, which is quoted from the Detailed Budget Quota in Electric Power Construction Projects - Volume IV Power Transmission Line Engineering (2006 Version).

Table 2–4–2 Sample List of Quota Items of Line Resurvey and Pit Division Quota

Work content: Resurvey of pile position and span length, determination of pit position, pit boundary and construction base surface, recovery of main pile or auxiliary pile after loss or change, verification of plane and section, and transport of tools and instruments.

Quota No.			YX2-1	YX2-2	YX2-3	YX2-4	YX2-5
Item			Straight single pole	Straight double pole and guyed tower	Tension (corner) double pole	Straight self-supporting tower	Tension (corner) self-supporting tower
Base price (Yuan)			29.36	44.28	59.48	51.10	68.29
Where	Labor cost (Yuan)		9.93	14.23	21.18	24.29	36.74
	Material fees (Yuan)		18.53	28.69	36.49	24.57	28.61
	Machinery cost (Yuan)		0.90	1.36	1.81	2.04	2.94
	Name	Unit	Qty.				
Labor	Integrated man-days	Man-day	0.30	0.43	0.64	0.74	1.11
Material	Wood pipe	Nos.	5.000	8.000	9.000	8.000	10.000
	Bamboo pile	Nos.	16.000	24.000	35.000	16.000	16.000
Machinery	Special truck for power transmission 4t	Set/shift	0.004	0.006	0.008	0.009	0.013

(1) The labor costs have been included in the quota base price, as shown in Table 2-4-2. According to the budget quota of power transmission line project (2006 version), the quota labor includes basic labor and other auxiliary labor, regardless of work type and grade, which is expressed in comprehensive work day. The unit price of comprehensive work day is the quota base unit price in the daywork, and the unit price of power transmission line project basic work day is 33.1 Yuan/work day, including wage subsidy of 2.4 Yuan/work day.

(2) Generally, material cost, i.e. consumable material cost, also known as pricing material cost, refers to the material cost which has been included in the base price of the quota in the budget quota. The cost of consumable materials is calculated according to the principle specified in the quota and has been included in the base price of the quota, as shown in Table 2-4-2.

(3) The machinery cost, i.e. the cost of using construction machinery, is calculated ac-

cording to the principle specified in the One-Shift Costs Quota for Electric Power Construction Machinery (2006 version), which has been included in the quota base price, as shown in Table 2-4-2. In the unit price of construction machinery one-shift, the commuter car has been taken into consideration. The cost of transportation vehicles crossing the bridge has been considered in the adjustment coefficient of material and machinery. The road maintenance fee and vehicle and vessel tax of transport machinery are not calculated, so they shall be considered in the adjustment of materials and machinery according to the standards stipulated by each province (autonomous region, municipality directly under the central government). Large construction machinery refers to hoisting machinery with lifting capacity of more than 40t. The entry and exit expenses of large machines and tools shall be in accordance with the provisions of the machine team quota. If the budget quota does not include and does not belong to the scope of the transfer fee of the construction organization, it shall be separately listed in the temporary engineering project and calculated by applying the machinery one-shift costs quota.

2. Terrain Adjustment

Terrain adjustment refers to the increase of labor cost based on the fixed direct cost. See task 2 for the increase coefficient (i.e. comprehensive terrain adjustment coefficient) in Table 2-2-2.

3. Adjustment of Labor Cost

As per the Adjustment Method of Price Level of Detailed Budget Quota for Power Construction Project (DDZZ [2007] No. 14), each region only need to adjust the wage subsidies and puts them in the charging base. The calculation formula of adjustment amount of labor cost is

$$\text{Adjustment amount of labor cost} = \text{labor cost of fixed base price} \times \frac{\text{local wage subsidy} - 2.4}{\text{Quota base unit price in the daywork}} \quad (2\text{-}4\text{-}4)$$

The annual and regional wage subsidy amount shall be calculated by the power construction quota station of each province (autonomous region, province-level municipality), balanced by the higher level power construction quota station, reported to the power engineering cost and quota management master station (hereinafter referred to as "quota master station") for verification and implementation. The adjustment amount of labor cost shall be summarized and included in the labor cost of direct construction cost in the year of budget preparation, which shall be taken as the charging base of each charging.

4. Material and Machine Adjustment

Material and machine adjustment refers to the adjustment of fixed material and machine one-shift costs of installation works (referred to as material and machine adjustment). It is the adjustment of the difference between the budget preparation level year and the fixed base price level year for the material and machine one-shift cost excluding labor cost in the fixed base price. The calculation formula of adjustment coefficient of material and machine is

$$\text{Adjustment coefficient of material and machine} = \frac{\sum(\text{market price of materials} \times \text{consumption}) + \sum(\text{unit price of machine shift} \times \text{consumption})}{\sum(\text{material price within the quota} \times \text{consumption}) + \sum(\text{unit price of machine team within the quota} \times \text{consumption})} \times 100\% \quad (2\text{-}4\text{-}5)$$

The power transmission line project is divided into 750kV, 500kV (including DC), 330kV, 220kV, 110kV and the following five voltage classes, and the adjustment coefficients of materials and machine types (see Table 2-13) in each voltage class typical engineering will be measured respectively. The adjustment coefficient of materials and machinery shall be calculated by the power construction quota station of each province (autonomous region, province-level municipality), balanced by the higher level power construction quota station, reported to the power engineering cost and quota management master station (hereinafter referred to as "quota master station") for verification, and issued and implemented at the end of the first quarter of each year.

The determination of the material market price in the compilation year shall be based on the price of materials in the third quarter of the compilation level year of each province (autonomous region, municipality directly under the central government). For the unit price determination of annual machine shift, the road maintenance fee and vehicle and vessel use tax to be paid for horizontal transport machinery shall be included in the unit price of machine shift for adjustment according to local regulations according to the quota of unit price of construction machinery of Electric Power Project Construction Machine One-Shift Costs Quota (2006 version). The difference between the market price of oil and electricity for construction machinery and the fixed price shall be included in the machine one-shift costs and

Study Program II Preparation of Preliminary Budget Estimate for 220kV Overhead Transmission Line Project

adjusted according to the consumption specified in the table of machinery varieties (see Table 2-4-3). The formula for calculating the price difference of materials and machines is

$$\text{Price difference of material and machinery} = (\text{labor cost in quota base price} - \text{quota base price}) \times \text{adjustment coefficient of material and machinery} \quad (2\text{-}4\text{-}6)$$

In the preparation of budget estimate, the price difference of material and machinery is only calculated as tax, which is summarized into the annual price difference preparation, and does not included in the charging of installation works.

Table 2–4–3 List of Quota Materials and Machines Varieties in Power Transmission Line Project Case

Code	Name and specification	Unit	Content /km				
			110kV	220kV	330kV	500kV	750kV
	Material						
C4101102	Log, red and white pine, class B	m³	0.28	0.38	0.49	0.47	0.63
C4102102	Lumber, red and white pine, class B	m³	0.95	1.18	1.57	0.78	1.40
C4102202	Panel, red and white pine, class B	m³	1.33	1.38	1.78	1.67	2.25
C5101101	Electrode J422, comprehensive	kg	21.00	44.00	63.65	110.00	138.16
C5206101	Round nail	kg					41.97
C5251101	Galvanized iron wire No.8	kg	46.15	93.40	136.63	131.85	155.72
C6319101	Ammonium nitrate explosive No. 2	kg	14.41	50.72		139.18	161.30
C6319202	Detonator, fire detonator	Nos.				385.67	
C6324201	Coke	kg		150.65		506.83	
C6407101	Bituminous solution	kg	4.41				
C7103104	Galvanized steel wire GJ-70	kg		36.23			
C7103105	Galvanized steel wire GJ-100	kg			25.49	29.03	
C7103106	Galvanized steel wire GJ-120	kg					52.00
C7115701	Aluminum armor tape 1×10	kg	2.70		12.95	11.43	16.52
C7208418	Conductor splicing sleeve JTB-185	Nos.	2.00				
C7208421	Conductor splicing sleeve JTB-300	Nos.		8.00	6.82		
C7208423	Conductor splicing sleeve JTB-400	Nos.				9.84	14.76
C8101101	Steel pipe scaffold, including fasteners	kg	26.87	34.77	48.11	52.45	62.69
C8101801	Safety net	m³	13.16	28.35		36.18	
	Machinery						

Table (Cont'd)

Code	Name and specification	Unit	Content /km				
			110kV	220kV	330kV	500kV	750kV
J1302202	Auto crane used for power transmission, 8t	Set/shift	1.21		2.57	4.58	4.93
J1302204	Auto crane used for power transmission, 20t	Set/shift			2.94	2.64	3.05
J1302205	Auto crane used for power transmission, 25t	Set/shift					3.05
J1401501	Special truck for power transmission 4t	Set/shift	18.55	28.72	21.83	21.42	31.07
J1401502	Special truck used for power transmission, 5t	Set/shift	14.98	29.96	41.04	45.02	62.69
J1802102	Sewage pump 100mm	Set/shift		6.40	9.52	8.99	
J2101103	Diesel generator 60kW	Set/shift			1.48	2.21	3.43
J2203102	Tractor unit, one pulling two	Set/shift			1.09		
J2203103	Tractor unit, one pulling four	Set/shift				0.91	
J2203104	Tractor unit, one pulling six	Set/shift					1.04
J2203202	Tensioner unit, one tension two	Set/shift			1.09		
J2203203	Tensioner unit, one tension four	Set/shift				0.91	1.04
J2203301	Motor winching	Set/shift		8.33		11.42	
	Gasoline	kg	472.65	770.09	556.15	598.36	791.76
	Diesel oil	kg	516.63	867.84	1705.80	1958.24	2799.65
	Electricity	kwh		832.00	1237.97	1169.05	

(Ⅲ) Work Unit Budget Estimate of Project Case Ⅱ

1. Work Unit Budget Estimate of Earthwork

In addition to the cost calculation of earthwork quantity in task 3 needs charge, the work unit also includes the cost calculation of line resurvey and pit work quantity, as shown in Table 2-4-4, Work Unit Budget Estimate of earthwork.

Description of charging calculation:

(1) Refer to Table 2-3-9 for the specific tower type and quantity statistics. In this project case, 137 iron towers are used, including 86 tangent towers and 51 strain towers. Then, according to Table 2-3-1 Summary of Earthwork Quantity, and refer to the Chapter "Earthwork" in the Detailed Budget Quota in Electric Power Construction Projects - Volume Ⅳ

Study Program II Preparation of Preliminary Budget Estimate for 220kV Overhead Transmission Line Project

Power Transmission Line Engineering (2006 Version), select the appropriate quota item, and fill in the corresponding "column" in Table 2-4-4 ". Calculate the data governed by "total price" (see Table 2-4-4, which is divided into "installation materials fee" and "installation fee", and the installation fee is divided into "in total", "salary" and "machinery") according to the data and formula (2-4-3) governed by "quantity" and "unit price" in Table 2-4-4.

(2) The "installation cost" etc. three items under the column of "Total price" are calculated according to each quota item, and the quota direct cost of earthwork is obtained in subtotal.

(3) According to Table 2-2-2 Calculating table of comprehensive terrain increase coefficient of project case 2), the corresponding comprehensive terrain increase coefficient of earthwork (excluding machinery cost) is 6.69%. Therefore, the comprehensive terrain increase coefficient does not include the machinery cost. Multiply 6.69% after deducting the machinery cost in the "total" column of "sub total of fixed direct cost" to obtain the data of installation cost of "terrain increase". From Table 2-4-4, we can see that the total price - installation cost - in which the terrain increase corresponding to machinery is 0.

(4) Add the column data of "subtotal of fixed direct cost" and "terrain increase" to get the "in total" data of fixed direct cost.

(5) There are not installation materials in this work unit.

2. Budget Estimate of Base Engineering Work Unit

(1) Instructions for quota use

1) In the installation quota of prefabricated base base plate, if there is a base plate with cemented connection, the working days shall be increased for each base: 0.37 working days for single pole and 0.74 working days for double poles. "Weight of each block" in "base plate installation" and "anchor plate installation" shall be calculated according to the principle of weighted average weight of each block in each group. The installation quota of prefabricated base of triple pole shall be multiplied by the coefficient of 2.5 according to the corresponding quota of single pole. In the quota of "base plate installation", "chuck installation" and "anchor plate installation", if the combination block (each base or group) exceeds the requirements of item purpose, the coefficient of 2.0 can be multiplied by the multiple of single block weight and corresponding combination block. In the sleeve installation quota, the secondary grouting work has been included, but the base plate installation has not been included. In case of occurrence, the corresponding chassis installation quota shall be additionally applied.

Table III D

Table 2-4-4 Work Unit Budget Estimate of Earthwork

S/N	Basis of preparation	Project name and code	Unit	Qty.	Unit price (RMB)					Total price (RMB)			
					Installation material	Installation fee				Installation material	Installation fee		
						Total	Where in: Salary	Machinery			Total	Where in: Salary	Machinery
1	YX2-4	Line resurveying and pit dividing tangent tower	Site	86.00		51.10	24.49	2.04			4394.60	2106.14	175.44
2	YX2-5	Line resurveying and pit dividing tangent tower	Site	51.00		68.29	36.74	2.94			3482.79	1873.74	149.94
3	YX2-34	Excavation (or blasting) of self-supporting tower pit and backfilling of common soil pit with the depth of less than 3.0m	m³	643.20		13.70	12.68	1.02			8809.91	8153.85	656.06
4	YX2-35	Excavation (or blasting) of self-supporting tower pit and backfilling of common soil pit with the depth of less than 4.0m	m³	775.20		16.12	14.70	1.42			12493.12	11392.34	1100.78
5	YX2-36	Excavation (or blasting) of self-supporting tower pit and backfilling of common soil pit with the depth of more than 4.0m	m³	3372.00		17.29	15.82	1.47			58308.62	53351.78	4956.84
6	YX2-42	Excavation (or blasting) of self-supporting tower pit and backfilling of light sand and stone pit with the depth of less than 3.0m	m³	2210.40		26.42	24.16	2.26			58405.40	53409.90	4995.50

Study Program Ⅱ Preparation of Preliminary Budget Estimate for 220kV Overhead Transmission Line Project

Table (Cont'd)

S/N	Basis of preparation	Project name and code	Unit	Qty.	Unit price (RMB)					Total price (RMB)			
					Installation material	Total	Installation fee			Installation material	Total	Installation fee	
							Where in: Salary	Machinery				Where in: Salary	Machinery
7	YX2-43	Excavation (or blasting) of self-supporting tower pit and backfilling of light sand and stone pit with the depth of less than 4.0m	m³	2665.20		31.84	28.90	2.94			84849.31	77013.62	7835.69
8	YX2-44	Excavation (or blasting) of self-supporting tower pit and backfilling of light sand and stone pit with the depth of more than 4.0m	m³	1590.80		35.77	32.60	3.17			414649.28	377906.44	36742.84
9	YX2-46	Excavation (or blasting) of self-supporting tower pit and backfilling of rock (blasting) pit with the depth of less than 3.0m	m³	804.00		65.51	53.42	5.20			52672.45	42952.09	4180.80
10	YX2-47	Excavation (or blasting) of self-supporting tower pit and backfilling of rock (blasting) pit with the depth of less than 4.0m	m³	968.40		69.63	57.50	5.20			67424.85	55678.16	5035.68
11	YX2-48	Excavation (or blasting) of self-supporting tower pit and backfilling of rock (blasting) pit with the depth of more than 4.0m	m³	4214.40		71.67	59.05	5.65			302046.05	248860.32	23811.36

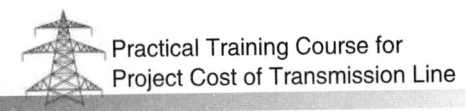

Table (Cont'd)

S/N	Basis of preparation	Project name and code	Unit	Qty.	Unit price (RMB)					Total price (RMB)			
					Installation material	Installation fee				Installation material	Installation fee		
						Total	Where in: Salary	Machinery			Total	Where in: Salary	Machinery
12	YX2-50	Excavation (or blasting) of self-supporting tower pit and backfilling of rock (manual digging) pit with the depth of less than 3.0m	m^3	200.40		137.21	122.37	12.44			27497.08	24523.15	2492.98
13	YX2-51	Excavation (or blasting) of self-supporting tower pit and backfilling of rock (manual digging) pit with the depth of less than 4.0m	m^3	242.40		145.57	130.28	12.89			35286.65	31580.36	3124.54
14	YX2-52	Excavation (or blasting) of self-supporting tower pit and backfilling of rock (manual digging) pit with the depth of more than 4.0m	m^3	1053.60		153.79	137.60	13.79			162029.98	144972.20	14529.14
15	YX2-54	Excavation (or blasting) of self-supporting tower pit and backfilling of muddy water pit with the depth of less than 3.0m	m^3	160.80		60.40	28.60	17.99			9712.00	4598.56	2892.79

Study Program II Preparation of Preliminary Budget Estimate for 220kV Overhead Transmission Line Project

Table (Cont'd)

S/N	Basis of preparation	Project name and code	Unit	Qty.	Unit price (RMB)					Total price (RMB)			
					Installation material	Installation fee				Installation material	Installation fee		
						Total	Where in: Salary	Machinery			Total	Where in: Salary	Machinery
16	YX2-55	Excavation (or blasting) of self-supporting tower pit and backfilling of muddy water pit with the depth of less than 4.0m	m³	194.40		78.57	37.37	27.39			15274.01	7264.73	5324.62
17	YX2-56	Excavation (or blasting) of self-supporting tower pit and backfilling of muddy water pit with the depth of more than 4.0m	m³	843.60		87.49	44.26	29.42			73802.35	37333.52	24818.71
18	YX2-69	Excavation (or blasting) of grounding groove and backfilling of common soil	m³	1187.10		8.32	7.51	0.81			9881.42	8919.87	961.55
19	YX2-71	Excavation (or blasting) of grounding groove and backfilling of light sand and stone	m³	4080.04		19.62	18.60	1.02			80058.54	75896.90	4161.64
20	YX2-72	Excavation (or blasting) of grounding groove and backfilling of muddy water soil	m³	296.28		14.55	13.74	0.81			4309.99	4070.00	239.99
21	YX2-73	Excavation (or blasting) of grounding groove and backfilling of rock (blasting)	m³	1483.38		54.31	43.43	1.42			80557.92	64418.74	2106.40

Table (Cont'd)

S/N	Basis of preparation	Project name and code	Unit	Qty.	Unit price (RMB)					Total price (RMB)			
					Installation material	Total	Installation fee			Total	Installation fee		
							Where in: Salary	Machinery	Installation material		Where in: Salary	Machinery	
22	YX2-74	Excavation (or blasting) of grounding groove and backfilling of rock (manual digging)	m³	371.09		82.98	77.65	4.07		30794.16	28816.25	1510.34
23	YX2-102	Excavation of common soil from drainage ditches	m³	55.00		4.58	4.17	0.41		251.96	229.41	22.55
24	YX2-104	Excavation of light sand and stone from drainage ditches	m³	186.00		8.63	8.04	0.59		1605.74	1496.00	109.74
25	YX2-105	Excavation of muddy water pit from drainage ditches	m³	14.00		11.19	9.77	1.42		156.59	136.71	19.88
26	YX2-106	Excavation of rock (blasting) from drainage ditches	m³	68.00		40.81	28.80	1.20		2774.88	1958.20	81.60
27	YX2-107	Excavation of rock (manual digging) from drainage ditches	m³	17.00		63.78	58.82	3.62		1084.24	999.92	61.54
28	YX2-108	Excavation of common soil from peak and formation level	m³	196.00		5.00	4.77	0.23		979.22	934.14	45.08
29	YX2-110	Excavation of light sand and stone from peak and formation level	m³	537.00		11.42	10.92	0.50		6134.15	5865.65	268.50

Study Program II Preparation of Preliminary Budget Estimate for 220kV Overhead Transmission Line Project

Table (Cont'd)

S/N	Basis of preparation	Project name and code	Unit	Qty.	Unit price (RMB)					Total price (RMB)			
					Installation material	Total	Installation fee — Where in: Salary	Installation fee — Machinery		Total	Installation fee — Where in: Salary	Installation fee — Machinery	Installation material
30	YX2-111	Excavation of peak and construction base, Rock (blasting), peak	m³	147.00		38.14	29.69	2.49		5606.73	4364.58	366.03	
31	YX2-112	Excavation of peak and construction base, Rock (manual digging), peak	m³	49.00		39.92	31.25	2.71		1955.88	1531.05	132.79	
		Subtotal of fixed direct cost								1617289.87	1382608.30	152911.34	
		Comprehensive terrain increase coefficient - earthwork engineering (excluding machinery fee)	%	6.69									
		Terrain adjustment								97966.92	92496.50	0.00	
		Total								1715256.79	1475104.80	152911.34	

2) Cast-in-place base

The base cushion in the quota of "cast-in-place base", such as the quota of "laying stone", "laying stone and grouting", "laying stone and pouring concrete" and "lime soil cushion", is calculated by the actual amount of cushion. The quota of "concrete mixing and pouring (including commercial concrete pouring)" is calculated according to the reinforced bar base. If it is a base without reinforced bar, the quota is multiplied by a coefficient of 0.95. During the process of on-site concrete pouring, the average haul distance of water for stone washing, curing and formwork pouring shall be calculated as 100m. If the haul distance exceeds 100m, it can used to quota the "site transport" for the excess portion as per 500kg water consumption for one cubic meter concrete. See Table 2-4-5 for concrete mixing and pouring (including commercial concrete pouring) coefficient adjustment.

Table 2–4–5 Concrete Mixing and Pouring (Including Commercial Concrete Pouring) Coefficient Adjustment

S/N	Name	Adjustment coefficient:			Description
		Labor	Material	Machinery	
1	High-low legs base	1.15	1	1.15	
2	The base column is oblique and tapered	1.25	1	1.25	
3	The base is inserted angle steel and oblique anchor bolt	1.05	1	1.05	
4	The base column, bearing platform and coupling beam are more than 1.0m higher than the ground, so the platform is required for construction	1.2	1.2	1.2	Calculate the project quantity of column, bearing platform and coupling beam

3) Cast-in-place pile

The cast-in-place pile base quota does not include the cast-in-place work of base anti-sinking platform, bearing platform and frame beam. If any, another cast-in-place base quota shall be used. It does not include the clearing of surplus soil. If necessary, another construction base excavation and site transport quota shall be used. The concrete pouring quota of pile base shall be adopted for the excavation pile base and the rock embedded base with a pit depth of more than 5m. And the concrete mixing and pouring quota of cast-in-place base

Study Program II Preparation of Preliminary Budget Estimate for 220kV Overhead Transmission Line Project

shall be adopted for the rock embedded base with a pit depth of less than 5m. If the drilling quota of cast-in-place pile base is less than 1m, it shall be calculated as 1m. And if the hole diameter is more than 1m, it shall be adjusted according to the actual size and the adjacent quota step distance as per the interpolation method.

4) Construction of revetment, retaining wall and drainage ditch

The excavation work is not included in the construction quota of revetment, retaining wall and drainage ditch. If necessary, the excavation quota of drainage ditch in "earth and stone works" shall be adopted. If it is necessary to fill the inner side of conical revetment and retaining wall, the common soil quota and corresponding transport quota within 2.0m in "earth and stone works" can be applied. The amount of mortar used in the construction of masonry revetment and retaining wall shall be calculated according to the design provisions. If there is no provision in the design, the amount of mortar shall be calculated as 20% of the volume of revetment and retaining wall.

When there are prefabricated base and cast-in-place base during construction, the discontinuous construction is needed. The labor and machinery in the quota can be multiplied by the coefficient of jump construction 1.02 according to the total amount of base (including high tower base, revetment, retaining wall and drainage ditch masonry, base anti-corrosion).

(2) base Project Work Unit Budget Estimate

See table 2-4-6 for the base Project Work Unit Budget Estimate.

Description of charging calculation:

1) According to Tables 2-3-5 and 2-3-7 and refer to the Chapter "base engineering" of the Detailed Budget Quota in Electric Power Construction Projects - Volume IV Power Transmission Line Engineering (2006 Version), select the appropriate quota item and fill in the corresponding "column" in Table 2-4-6. Similarly, calculate the data of each column in Table 2-4-6 according to Table 2-4-4.

2) According to Table 2-4-5, high-low legs base and inclined column-shaped base are widely used in this project case. The increase coefficient of labor cost adjustment in the base price of concrete mixing and pouring installation is 0.4 (0.15 + 0.25). Similarly, the increase coefficient of machinery cost adjustment is 0.4.

3) In Table 2-4-6, "terrain increase" is calculated without deduction of "machinery cost".

4) The cost of installation materials in Table 2-4-6 comes from the total data in the col-

umn of "Total price" corresponding to "Pull plate" and "C10, C20" concrete in Table 2-3-5.

3. Budget Estimate for Pole and Tower Project Work Unit

(1) Instructions for use of quota: Due to the different forms of poles and towers, the discontinuous construction is caused. Therefore, the labor and machinery of quota can be multiplied by the coefficient of 1.02 according to the total amount of poles and towers (excluding high towers and grounding). The installation of traffic warning paint and other aviation signs on pole and tower are not included in the quota.

1) Assembly and erection of concrete pole

The quota is expressed in the form of pole type and combined weight, and various voltage classes, structural forms, pole height and construction methods have been comprehensively considered. During usage, the quota cannot be adjusted due to different construction methods. In case of triple pole assembly and erection during usage, the corresponding quota can be multiplied by 2.5 coefficient according to the weight of each single pole. The connection quota of steel ring only includes the connection and anti-corrosion treatment of steel ring. The quota is not applicable to the assembly and erection of electric poles with combined pole weight of 17T or single pole with height of 42m or above. If necessary, it shall be separately calculated according to the approved construction organization design.

2) Steel pipe pole assembly

Various voltage classes, structural forms, pole heights and construction methods have been comprehensively considered in the quota. During usage, the quota cannot be adjusted due to different construction methods.

3) Tower erection

The quota has made a comprehensive consideration of tangent tower and strain angle tower, self-supporting tower and guyed tower, which is suitable for all kinds of towers with the whole tower height less than 70m. For the assembly and erection of compact tower and steel pipe tower, the labor and machinery of corresponding tower assembly and erection quota shall be multiplied by 1.1. The base and tube of concrete tower adopt the base and chimney part of construction engineering budget quota. There is no special quota for the hoisting and assembly of the support and cross arm (section steel) of the tower head. If necessary, the project quantity can be calculated according to the product of the total weight of the tower head (t) and the total height of the tower (m). The base price is 5.4 Yuan per ton of meter, of which 38% is labor cost, 15% is material cost, 47% is machinery cost, and the terrain increase coefficient shall be calculated according to the location of the tower.

During assembling and erecting high towers, the quota is applicable to the assembly and erection of high tower with the total height of more than 70m. When the average weight per meter of the whole tower exceeds 1.2t/m, the corresponding fixed labor cost and machinery cost shall be adjusted as per the overweight coefficient

$$\text{Overweight coefficient} = \frac{(\text{design weight per meter t/m} - 1.2\text{t/m})}{1.2\text{t/m}} \qquad (2\text{-}4\text{-}7)$$

When the total height of the tower exceeds 195m, the base number is 195m high tower assembly and erection quota, and the labor cost and machinery cost are adjusted as per over-height coefficient

$$\text{Over-height coefficient} = \frac{(\text{design height,} - 195\text{m})}{195\text{m}} \qquad (2\text{-}4\text{-}8)$$

4) Fabrication and installation of pull wire

The quota has made a comprehensive consideration of different materials and specifications, which is applicable to the production and installation of single pull wire. If "V" type, "Y" type or double splicing pull wire is installed, it shall be calculated as 2 nos. The height shall be considered within 40m on the fixed internal pull wire. If it exceeds 40m, it shall as per multiply by 1.10 every 10m higher. If the pole and tower height is less than 10m, it shall be considered as 10m.

5) Ground installation

Excavation and filling of geosyncline are not included in the quota. The length of the earth electrode shall be considered as 2.5m. If the length exceeds 2.5m, the quota shall be multiplied by 1.25. The connection between the earth electrode shall be fixed with corresponding grounding body.

(2) Budget Estimate for Pole and Tower Project Work Unit

See table 2-4-7 for the Budget Estimate for Pole and Tower Project Work Unit.

Description of charging calculation:

1) According to Table 2-3-13 and refer to the chapter "Pole and tower project" in Detailed Budget Quota in Electric Power Construction Projects - Volume IV Power Transmission Line Engineering (2006 Version) and select the appropriate quota item, and then fill in

the corresponding "column" in Table 2-4-7. Similarly, calculate the data of each column in Table 2-4-7 according to Table 2-4-4.

2)"Mechanical cost" will not be deducted when calculating Table 2-4-7 "terrain adjustment".

3)The cost of installation materials in Table 2-4-7 comes from the total data in the column of "total price" in Tables 2-3-10 and 2-3-12.

4. Work Unit Budget Estimate for Overhead Conductor Project

(1)Instructions for quota use

1)The conductor in the quota is considered as a three-phase AC single circuit project. In case of any of the following conditions, it shall be adjusted by multiplying the corresponding quota by the coefficient:

① The two-phase DC line project can be multiplied by a coefficient of 0.7 for the wire section of the same model.

② For the erection of double-circuit line or multiple-circuit lines engineering on the same tower and adjacent electrified line construction, the quota shall be adjusted according to the coefficient of Table 2-4-8, of which the distance between the adjacent lines and the

Study Program II   Preparation of Preliminary Budget Estimate for 220kV Overhead Transmission Line Project

Table 2-4-6   Work Unit Budget Estimate of base Works

Table III D

S/N	Basis of preparation	Project name and code	Unit	Qty.	Unit price (RMB)					Total price (RMB)				
					Installation material	Installation fee				Installation material	Installation fee			
						Total	Where in: Salary	Machinery			Total	Where in: Salary	Machinery	
1	YX3-29	Installation of anchor plate Each group is less than 500kg per piece	Group	1.00		18.64	15.72	2.92		160.00	18.64	15.72	2.92	
2	YX3-37	Base reinforcement processing and production of general reinforcement	t	174.88		365.85	256.16	102.36		1399199.14	63978.02	44796.15	17900.21	
3	YX3-51 adjustment by manual 1.4 Machinery 1.4	Concrete mixing and casting within 10m³ of concrete per base	m³	1003.74		212.10	136.37	18.57			275103.85	191634.84	26095.23	
4	YX3-52 adjustment by manual 1.4 Machinery 1.4	Concrete mixing and casting within 20m³ of concrete per base	m³	785.63		190.56	121.81	16.90			193297.35	133974.43	18588.01	
5	YX3-53 adjustment by manual 1.4 Machinery 1.4	Concrete mixing and casting within 40m³ of concrete per base	m³	641.55		161.75	95.33	16.52			132471.86	85620.75	14837.77	

Table (Cont'd)

S/N	Basis of preparation	Project name and code	Unit	Qty.	Unit price (RMB)				Total price (RMB)			
					Installation material	Installation fee Total	Where in: Salary	Machinery	Installation material	Installation fee Total	Where in: Salary	Machinery
6	YX3-63	Protective cap per square amount 0.5m³ Within	Site	137.00		114.86	83.41	8.14		15736.09	11427.44	1115.18
7	YX3-133	Wet masonry of flood drainage trench	m³	132.00		50.90	46.94	3.96		6718.27	6195.55	522.72
8	YX3-137	Tapered masonry for revetment and retaining wall	m³	995.80		51.03	46.64	4.39		50813.68	46442.12	4371.56
9	YX3-140	Concrete base anti-corrosion asphalt	m³	2740.00		2.35	1.66	0.23		6425.30	4534.70	630.20
		Subtotal of fixed direct cost								744563.08	524641.71	84063.79
		Comprehensive terrain increase coefficient - base works	%	13.38								
		Terrain adjustment								99622.54	70197.06	11247.74
		Total							1399359.14	844185.62	594838.78	95311.53

· 532 ·

Study Program II Preparation of Preliminary Budget Estimate for 220kV Overhead Transmission Line Project

Table III D

Table 2-4-7 Work Unit Budget Estimate of Pole and Tower

S/N	Basis of preparation	Project name and code	Unit	Qty.	Unit price (RMB)				Total price (RMB)			
					Installation material	Installation fee			Installation material	Installation fee		
						Total	Where in: Salary	Machinery		Total	Where in: Salary	Machinery
1	YX4-39	Assembly and erection of iron tower within 5t per unit	Site	19.00		1542.64	1267.73	247.12	7978593.08	29310.16	24086.87	4695.28
2	YX4-40	Assembly and erection of iron tower within 7t per unit	Site	45.00		2139.24	1721.20	377.67		96265.80	77454.00	16995.15
3	YX4-41	Assembly and erection of iron tower within 9t per unit	Site	28.00		2772.96	2273.97	449.00		77642.88	63671.16	12572.00
4	YX4-42	Assembly and erection of iron tower within 11t per unit	Site	19.00		3167.49	2644.69	466.70		60182.31	50249.11	8867.30
5	YX4-43	Assembly and erection of iron tower within 13t per unit	Site	19.00		3634.99	3038.58	535.48		69064.81	57733.02	10174.12
6	YX4-50	Assembly and erection of iron tower within 27t per unit	Site	4.00		7612.91	6332.03	1171.72		30451.64	25328.12	4686.88
7	YX4-51	Assembly and erection of iron tower within 30t per unit	Site	3.00		8200.98	6818.60	1266.85		24602.94	20455.80	3800.55
8	YX4-75	Wedge clamp type cable cross section within 100mm^2	Nos.	1.00		13.08	9.93	0.90		13.08	9.93	0.90

Table (Cont'd)

S/N	Basis of preparation	Project name and code	Unit	Qty.	Unit price (RMB)					Total price (RMB)				
					Installation material	Total	Installation fee			Installation material	Total	Installation fee		
							Total	Where in: Salary	Machinery			Total	Where in: Salary	Machinery
9	YX4-79	Processing and manufacturing of grounding body	t	20.32		186.69	105.09	76.96		82161.52	3793.47	2135.42	1563.77
10	YX4-84	Grounding body laying length within 200m per unit	Site	247.00		46.39	39.72	3.39			11458.33	9810.84	837.33
11	YX4-85	Grounding body laying length within 300m per unit	Site	274.00		58.21	49.65	4.52			15949.54	13604.10	1238.48
12	YX4-86	Grounding body laying length within 400m per unit	Site	28.00		70.63	59.58	6.33			1977.64	1668.24	177.24
13	YX4-94	Measurement of resistance	Base and base	137.00		18.92	7.61	11.31			2592.45	1042.98	1549.47
		Subtotal of fixed direct cost									423305.05	347249.59	67158.47
		Comprehensive terrain increase coefficient - pole and tower works	%	39.12									
		Terrain adjustment									165596.94	135844.04	26272.39
		Total								8060754.60	588901.99	483093.63	93430.87

parallel lines is shown in Table 2-4-9.

2) The lightning wire and optical cable wiring shall be constructed separately. In case of live lines (mainly for rebuilt lines), and the single circuit adjustment coefficient is referred to in Table 2-4-8.

3) The strain stringing quota has included the loading, unloading and transfer of the traction and tensioning equipment during the construction process.

4) The manufacturing and hanging of the strain end of the strain tower, the balanced cable hanging of strain (corner) pole and tower, and the installation of the jumper and jumper string are taken into consideration in the wire erection quota. In case that the actual number per kilometer of the strain tower exceeds the reference quantity within 10%, the quota should be not adjusted, in case that the quota is more than 10%, the base price adjustment coefficient should be calculated according to the formula 2-4-9.

$$m = 1 + n \times [B - C \times (1 + 10\%)] \quad (2\text{-}4\text{-}9)$$

Where m is the strain tower adjustment coefficient, retaining three decimal places; n is the line correction coefficient, 1.25 in general, and 0.52 for tension stringing; B is the actual number of strain tower per kilometer, which is equal to the number of strain towers divided by the length of the line, retaining three decimal places, if the project includes two terminals, the number of strain towers is reduced by one; it is determined as 0.250 for the voltage below 220kV and 0.200 for the voltage above 220kV.

Table 2-4-8 Adjustment Coefficient for Erection of Double-circuit Line on the Same Tower or Multiple-circuit Lines Engineering and Adjacent Electrified Line

S/N	Number of circuits on the same tower	Erection at the same time			Close to power line			S/N	Number of secondary erection circuits in the same tower	Erection at the same time			Close to power line		
		Labor	Material	Machinery	Labor	Material	Machinery			Labor	Material	Machinery	Labor	Material	Machinery
1	Primary circuit	1	1	1	1.1	1	1.1	5	Primary circuit	1.1	1	1.1	1.21	1	1.21
2	Secondary circuit	1.75	2	1.75	1.92	2	1.92	6	Secondary circuit	1.92	2	1.92	2.11	2	2.11
3	Triple circuit	2.8	3	2.8	3.08	3	3.08	7	Triple circuit	3.08	3	3.08	3.38	3	3.38
4	Fourfold circuit	3.9	4	3.9	4.29	4	4.29								

Table 2-4-9 Parallel Approach Control Distance Adjacent to Line Edge of Live Line

Built line voltage (kV)	220	330	500	750
Approach distance ≤ (m)	30	40	50	70

5) The adjustment coefficient of the strain pole and tower shall be calculated at the same time as other coefficients in this chapter and multiplied by other coefficients.

6) Cross-over erection of conductor, lightning wire and optical cable

① The quota unit of measurement "position" refers to a span that must be erected within a span. In multiple spans are crossed within the same span, the quota should be applied according to the type of span.

$$\text{Measure cost for safe and civilized construction} = \text{labor cost} \times \text{rate} \quad (2\text{-}4\text{-}22)$$

Rate standard: 2.52% for the overhead transmission line project.

In recent years, the improvement of civilized construction level and the strengthening of safety measures have resulted in insufficient fees for the quotas in accordance with the requirements of general construction specifications. This cost is a replenishment of the safe and civilized construction measure costs in the budget quota.

The safe and civilized construction measures and health environmental protection measures mainly refer to the on-site safety and civilized facilities (safety fence, frontal protective railing, hole cover, safety net, safety operation code plate, safety sign board, safety and civilized construction responsibility card, scaffolding engineering card, etc.), on-site health and environmental protection measures (watering and dust reduction at the construction site, area cleaning, garbage removal, material covering, helmets, dust masks, towels, overalls, etc.), as well as safe and civilized construction management, supervision system, and system and institution construction.

For the expansion project, it is necessary to consider the cost of power outage measures and the cost of special measure costs for construction safety, and shall be included in the "temporary project" as the project in accordance with the actual protective measures.

(Ⅲ) Indirect Cost

The indirect cost consists of compliance cost and business management cost. The equation for calculation is:

$$\text{Indirect cost} = \text{stipulated fees} + \text{enterprise administration expense} \quad (2\text{-}4\text{-}23)$$

Study Program II Preparation of Preliminary Budget Estimate for 220kV Overhead Transmission Line Project

1. Stipulated Fees

The stipulated fees include social security fee, housing accumulation fund and accidental injury insurance for dangerous operation. The equation for calculation is:

$$\text{Stipulated fees} = \text{social security fee} + \text{housing fund} + \text{accidental injury insurance expense for dangerous operations} \qquad (2\text{-}4\text{-}24)$$

(1) Social security fee

Social security cost refers to the insurance and security expenses that construction enterprises must pay for the employees according to the relevant requirements of the state to establish the social security system, which is composed of endowment insurance expenses, unemployment insurance expense and medical insurance expense. The payment rate shall be implemented in accordance with the standards set by the local government department where the project is located. Transmission lines across provinces (autonomous regions and municipalities) shall be calculated in stages or calculated according to the length of the line.

The equation for calculation is:

$$\text{Social security cost for overhead power transmission line} = \text{labor cost} \times 1.12 \times \text{contribution rate} \qquad (2\text{-}4\text{-}25)$$

$$\text{Social security cost for cable line and optical cable line} = \text{labor cost} \times 1.2 \times \text{contribution rate} \qquad (2\text{-}4\text{-}26)$$

(2) Housing provident fund

Housing fund refers to the housing fund paid by the enterprises for employees in accordance with local government regulations. The payment rate should be performed based on the rates published by the local government department where the project is located.

The equation for calculation is:

$$\text{Housing accumulation fund for overhead power transmission line} = \text{labor cost} \times 1.12 \times \text{contribution rate} \qquad (2\text{-}4\text{-}27)$$

$$\text{Housing accumulation fund for cable line and optical cable line} = \text{labor cost} \times 1.2 \times \text{contribution rate} \qquad (2\text{-}4\text{-}28)$$

② Power lines with high voltage power lines spanning different voltage levels shall be adjusted according to the coefficients in Table 2-4-10.

Table 2-4-10　Span Coefficient Adjustment Table

Voltage of new line (kV) \ Voltage of crossed power lines (kV)	10	35	110	220	330	500	750
35	0.67	1					
110	0.56	0.83	1				
220	0.45	0.68	0.82	1			
330	0.4	0.6	0.72	0.88	1		
500	0.36	0.54	0.64	0.79	0.89	1	
750	0.32	0.48	0.58	0.71	0.81	0.91	1

③ Single wire (lightning wire and optical cable) spanning erection is only suitable for erecting or replacing lightning protection cables and optical cables separately, where it is multiplied by a coefficient of 0.25 according to the quota across the corresponding voltage level for the power line spanning 35kV or less and it is multiplied by a coefficient of 0.15 across the rating of the corresponding voltage level for the power line spanning more than 35kV.

In case of live across, the measure cost for live across shall be calculated based on 10% of the corresponding voltage level measure costs in Table 2-4-11.

④ The voltage levels listed in the division of quota items of this chapter refer to the lines to be built.

⑤ This Chapter quota only considers labor, materials, and mechanical shifts that are costly due to span. When calculating the overall amount of overhead work, the span length shall not be deducted.

The quota of the erection of crossover frame shall not include consultation, custody, and roadbed occupation by the property rights department of the crossed objects. If necessary, it can be calculated according to the regulations of the government or relevant departments.

⑥ For the quota of crossing a railway, in the case of an electrified railway, it is calculated by multiplying the railway quota by a coefficient of 1.2.

⑦ The quota of crossing power line should be considered in terms of power interruption. In case of live across, the measure cost for live across shall be calculated according to Table 2-4-11. In case that the crossed power line is double-circuit or multiple circuit, the measure cost shall be multiplied by a coefficient of 1.5.

Table 2–4–11   Measure Cost for Crossing Live Line

Unit: Yuan/place

Voltage of crossed power lines (kV)	10	35	110	220	330	500	750
Measures expenses	3500	12000	20000	32000	45000	65000	100000

⑧ Cross-river line quota is only applicable to general crossings of rivers and lakes (reservoirs) with water. During the installation of overhead conductor and ground wire, rivers and lakes (reservoirs) that are wading through rivers or at the time of dryness should not be counted as crossing rivers. For the gorge, with small width but belonging to a navigable river, that requires adopt a navigation method or a gorge with rapid water flow and difficulty in construction, the spanning line can be designed according to the approved construction organization and shall be separately verified by the project chief review department.

⑨ Such items as crossing houses, orchards, and cash crops are not listed in the quota. During the construction, in case of un-removed houses and orchards and cash crops that are not felled, protective measures must be taken when wiring, which can be calculated as follows.

The orchard and cash crops are divided into a place every 60m, the low voltage weak current line multiplying multiplied by 0.8 can be applied. For crossing house, a separate house can be taken as a place, and the quota across the low-voltage weak line can be applied. For the house with height of less than 10m, it is multiplied by a coefficient of 0.8 and for that of more than 10m, it is multiplied by a coefficient of 1.5.

⑩ The quota of the erection of crossover frame should be considered according to the construction of single-loop circuit; in case of double-circuit or multiple circuits on the same tower at the same time, both labor and machinery are multiplied by a coefficient of 1.5.

7) Installation of coupling shielded wire

The shielded wire shall be considered as good conductor. In case that stranded wire is used as the shielded wire, the consumable material rating is multiplied by a coefficient of 0.2.

8) Installation of overhead warning line

The transportation of equipment used for overhead warning line and welding of concrete poles are not included in the quota. If necessary, the corresponding quota for the welding of steel rings in the "site transport" and "pole and tower" can be applied.

9) Measurement and continuation of optical cable

① For single tray, in the preparation of the preliminary design budget, if the project for cable tendering has not been carried out, it can be calculated by 4km per axis (disc).

② The cable quota is considered under the double-window test condition. When the design requires a single window, the "continuation" is related to the sub-multiplied by a coefficient of 0.85.

③ The amount of continuous construction is calculated according to the number of joints, only the connector of the overhead part is calculated. The front and rear two sections of the fiber-optic incoming or outgoing structural junction box to the communication equipment room are implemented according to the Volume III Installation Works of Electrical Equipment of Budget Quota of Power Construction Project.

④ The whole test quota is considered as a basic segment of 100km. For exceeding 100km, the labor and machinery increased by 40% for every 50km increase, and the labor and machinery are calculated as 50km for less than 50km.

(2) Work Unit Budget Estimate for overhead conductor project

See Table 2-4-12 for the Work Unit Budget Estimate of Overhead Conductor and Ground Wire Installation Works. The cost calculation is explained as below:

Description of charging calculation:

1) According to Tables 2-0-1 & 2-3-14, with reference to the Chapter "Erection Works" in Electric Power Construction Engineering Budget Quota (Volume IV, Power Transmission Line Project, Revision 2006), appropriate quota sub-items shall be selected and filled in the corresponding "column" of Table 2-4-12. ② Power lines with high voltage power lines spanning different voltage levels shall be adjusted according to the coefficients in Table 2-4-10. Similarly, calculate the data of each column in Table 2-4-12 according to Table 2-4-4.

2) "Mechanical cost" will not be deducted when calculating Table 2-4-12 "Terrain adjustment".

3) The device material cost in Table 2-4-12 is derived from the data in the column "Total Price" in Table 2-3-14.

Study Program Ⅱ Preparation of Preliminary Budget Estimate for 220kV Overhead Transmission Line Project

Table Ⅲ D able 2-4-12 Work Unit Budget Estimate of Overhead Conductor and Ground Wire Installation Works

S/N	Basis of preparation	Project name and code	Unit	Qty.	Unit price (RMB)					Total price (RMB)			
					Installa-tion material	Installation fee			Installation material	Total	Installation fee		Installation material
						Total	Where in: Salary	Machin-ery			Total	Where in: Salary	Machin-ery
1	YX5-5	Installation of overhead conductor and ground wire Within 100mm² of Single lightning wire Steel strand	km	43.80		636.06	500.34	101.38		27859.43	21914.89	4440.44	386244.87
2	YX5-7	Installation of overhead conductor and ground wire Within 100mm² of Single lightning wire Good conductor	km	8.00		723.88	528.34	117.17		5791.06	4226.74	937.36	64590.25
3	YX5-18	Installation of overhead conductor and ground wire Within 2× 400mm² of conductor	km/three-phase	51.80		6277.64	4162.59	1232.81		325181.75	215622.16	63859.56	7077701.48
4	YX5-65	Conductor/lightning wire Crossing general road 220kV	Position	44.00		2781.01	1645.07	354.77		122364.44	72383.08	15609.88	
5	YX5-78 adjustment 10kV*0.45	Conductor/High voltage power line Crossing general road 220kV	Position	32.00		3427.22	2591.73	442.62		49351.97	37320.91	6373.73	
6	YX5-78 adjustment 35kV*0.68	Conductor/High voltage power line Crossing general road 220kV	Position	5.00		3427.22	2591.73	442.62		11652.55	8811.88	1504.91	

Table (Cont'd)

S/N	Basis of preparation	Project name and code	Unit	Qty.	Unit price (RMB)					Total price (RMB)				
					Installation material	Installation fee			Installation material		Installation fee		
						Total	Where in: Salary	Machinery		Total	Where in: Salary	Machinery
7	YX5-78 adjustment 110kV* 0.82	Conductor/High voltage power line Crossing general road 220kV	Position	3.00		3427.22	2591.73	442.62		8430.96	6375.66	1088.85
8	YX5-85	Conductor/High voltage power line Crossing LV and weak electric wire 220kV	Position	232.00		1264.66	771.23	194.98		293401.12	178925.36	45235.36
9	YX5-98	Conductor/lightning wire Crossing river Within 500mm² of conductor section Within 50m of river width	Position	11.00		544.82	393.89	150.93		5993.02	4332.79	1660.23
10	YX5-100	Conductor/lightning wire Crossing river Within 500mm² of conductor section Within 300m of river width	Position	1.00		1380.58	999.62	380.96		1380.58	999.62	380.96
		Subtotal of fixed direct cost								851406.87	550913.09	141091.27
		Comprehensive terrain increase coefficient - installation of overhead conductor and ground wire engineering (general release and stringing)	%	48.91								
		Terrain adjustment								416423.10	269451.59	69007.74
		Total							7528536.60	1267829.97	820364.68	210099.01

Study Program II Preparation of Preliminary Budget Estimate for 220kV Overhead Transmission Line Project

Table 2-4-13 Work Unit Budget Estimate of Accessory Installation

Table III D

S/N	Basis of preparation	Project name and code	Unit	Qty.	Unit price (RMB)					Combined price / Yuan				
					Installation material	Installation fee				Installation material	Installation fee			
						Total	Where in: Salary	Machinery			Total	Where in: Salary	Machinery	
1	YX6-6	Insulator string suspension Straight line (straight line transposition, straight line corner) pole 220kV Double strings	Single phase	411.00		41.17	27.80	11.78		2413711.00	16922.51	11427.44	4841.58	
2	YX6-28	Suspension clamp installation Straight line (straight line transposition, straight line corner) pole 220kV double bundle	Single phase	411.00		30.97	18.21	6.81			12726.62	7482.26	2798.91	
3	YX6-38	Installation of preformed armor rods (or armor rod) Straight line (straight line transposition, straight line corner) pole 220kV double bundled conductor	Single phase	411.00		30.27	28.47	1.80			12439.33	11699.53	739.80	
4	YX6-53	Installation of anti-vibration hammer and spacer Anti-vibration hammer double bundled conductor	Nos.	2369.00		3.91	2.65	0.23			9258.05	6273.11	544.87	
5	YX6-72	Installation of damper line Conductor Within 2×500mm² of section	Single phase	411.00		245.32	146.96	55.41			100828.16	60402.20	22773.51	

· 543 ·

Table (Cont'd)

S/N	Basis of preparation	Project name and code	Unit	Qty.	Unit price (RMB)					Combined price / Yuan			
					Installation material	Installation fee				Installation material	Installation fee		
						Total	Where in: Salary	Machinery			Total	Where in: Salary	Machinery
		Subtotal of fixed direct cost									152174.67	97284.54	31698.67
		Comprehensive terrain increase coefficient - Accessory works	%	10.81									
		Terrain adjustment									16450.08	10516.46	3426.63
		Total								2413711.00	168624.75	107801.00	35125.30

· 544 ·

Study Program II Preparation of Preliminary Budget Estimate for 220kV Overhead Transmission Line Project

Table 2-4-14 Work Unit Budget Estimate of Construction Site Transportation.

Table III D

S/N	Basis of preparation	Project name and code	Unit	Qty.	Unit price (RMB)					Total price (RMB)			
					Installation material	Installation fee				Installation material	Installation fee		
						Total	Where in: Salary	Machinery			Total	Where in: Salary	Machinery
1	YX1-19	Outward transport for the surplus soil, with average manpower transport distance within 500m	t.km	168.75		81.47	75.50	5.97			13748.23	12740.79	1007.44
2	YX1-27	Prefabricated concrete products, with average manpower transport distance within 1,000m Within 500kg per pcs.	t.km	0.36		139.47	129.09	10.38			50.21	46.47	3.74
3	YX1-33	Wire, with average manpower load distance within 1,000m Within 1,000kg per pcs.	t.km	415.61		162.62	148.19	14.43			67585.76	61588.53	5997.22
4	YX1-36	armor clamp, insulator and sporadic steel with average manpower load distance within 1,000m	t.km	345.32		89.84	83.31	6.53			31024.58	28769.65	2254.94
5	YX1-37	Tower material, with average manpower transport distance within 1,000m	t.km	939.27		107.87	99.23	8.64			101322.81	93207.52	8115.29
6	YX1-38	Human-powered transport With average manpower load distance within 1,000m Sand, stone, lime, cement, brick, earth, and water	t.km	5801.15		77.93	72.16	5.77			452072.02	418599.38	33472.64

Table (Cont'd)

7	YX1-106	Prefabricated concrete products by truck Within 500kg per pcs. Loading and unloading	t	0.45		42.02	9.93	31.63	18.91	4.47	14.23
8	YX1-107	Prefabricated concrete products by truck Within Transportation within 500kg	t.km	12.60		1.01	0.23	0.78	12.75	2.92	9.83
9	YX1-118	Automobile transport Wire Loading and unloading within 1,000kg per pcs.	t	519.51		52.62	8.18	43.33	27334.54	4247.51	22510.37
10	YX1-119	Automobile transport Wire transportation within 1,000kg	t.km	14546.28		1.22	0.33	0.89	17761.01	4814.82	12946.19
11	YX1-130	Loading and unloading of armor clamp, insulator and sporadic steel transported by truck	t	431.66		30.97	8.81	22.16	13366.35	3800.77	9565.59
12	YX1-131	Transport of armor clamp, insulator and sporadic steel by truck	t.km	12086.34		1.19	0.33	0.86	14394.83	4000.58	10394.25
13	YX1-132	Automobile transport Tower material Loading and unloading	t	1174.09		42.16	8.90	31.51	49504.33	10454.10	36995.58
14	YX1-133	Automobile transport Tower material Transportation	t.km	32874.50		1.22	0.36	0.86	40238.39	11966.32	28272.07
15	YX1-134	Automobile transport Sand, stone, lime, cement, brick, earth, and water	t	7251.44		21.81	6.69	15.12	158124.90	48483.13	109641.77

Study Program II Preparation of Preliminary Budget Estimate for 220kV Overhead Transmission Line Project

Table (Cont'd)

16	YX1-135	Automobile transport Sand, stone, lime, cement, brick, earth, and water Transportation	t.km	203040.39	0.92	0.27	0.65		185781.96	53805.70	131976.25
		Subtotal of fixed direct cost							1172341.58	756532.66	413177.39
		Comprehensive terrain increase coefficient - site transport Human-powered transport Wire and concrete pre-products (excluding machinery)	%	82.36							
		Comprehensive terrain increase coefficient - site transport Human-powered transport Others (excluding machinery)	%	51.48							
		Comprehensive terrain increase coefficient - site transport Human-powered transport Automobile and tractor transportation (excluding loading and unloading)	%	43.24							
		Terrain adjustment							447251.25	367863.22	79388.03
		Total							1619592.83	1124395.88	492565.43

5. Work Unit Budget Estimate of Accessory Works

(1) Instructions for quota use

1) Tensile fittings and strain insulator strings are not included in the quota, and the following works are included in the quota sub-items related to wiring works: end production of strain conductor and ground wire, installation of jumper string, end production and installation of cross-bind jumper wire, installation of insulator string for straight corner and transposition tower grounding wire.

2) When the same tower is not equipped with multiple circuits at the same time or is adjacent to the live line, the labor and machinery of corresponding quota shall multiply by 1.1 when the next circuit is set.

3) Damper line installation is considered in general. In case of large-cross and long-span towers, which requires ultra-long damper lines (with more than 13 laces tied per phase), the labor and machinery shall multiply by a coefficient of 3.0 based on the corresponding quota.

(2) Work Unit Budget Estimate of Accessory Works The Work Unit Budget Estimate of Accessory Works is shown in Table 2-4-13. The cost calculation is explained as below:

1) According to Table 2-3-15, with reference to the Chapter "Accessory Works" in Electric Power Construction Engineering Budget Quota (Volume IV, Power Transmission Line Project, Revision 2006), appropriate quota sub-items shall be selected and filled in the corresponding "column" of Table 2-4-13. It is worth noting that the quota sub-items corresponding to the accessory works are mostly based on "single phase". In this case, there are 137 base towers in total, and a total of 411 "single phase". Similarly, calculate the data of each column in Table 2-4-13 according to Table 2-4-4.

2) "Mechanical cost" will not be deducted when calculating Table 2-4-13 "Terrain adjustment".

3) The device material cost in Table 2-4-13 is derived from the total data in the column "Total Price" in Table 2-3-15.

6. Work Unit Budget Estimate of Construction Site Transportation

(1) Instructions for quota use

1) In the transportation of ships, tractors and automobiles, coefficients such as the form

of vehicles and ships, level of roads and rivers, and one-time loading and multi-time unloading are taken into account. No additional conversion can be conducted when quota is used.

2) The steel pipe tower is based on the corresponding quota of tower material mechanical transportation and loading and unloading multiplied by a coefficient of 1.3.

3) Tension wiring is adopted, and human-powered transport is not calculated for wire material.

4) In case of calculating the loading, unloading and transportation weight of the tower, bolts, spikes and washers shall be counted into the weight of the tower.

(2) Work Unit Budget Estimate of Construction Site Transportation

See Table 2-4-14 for the Work Unit Budget Estimate of Construction Site Transportation. Description of charging calculation:

1) According to Table 2-3-19, with reference to the Chapter "Construction Site Transportation" in Electric Power Construction Engineering Budget Quota (Volume IV, Power Transmission Line Project, Revision 2006), appropriate quota sub-items shall be selected and filled in the corresponding "column" of Table 2-4-14. Similarly, calculate the data of each column in Table 2-4-14 according to Table 2-4-4.

2) Table 2-4-14 calculates the "topographic increase", the comprehensive terrain increase coefficient of human-powered transport "wire and concrete products" and "others" is different, and all need to deduct "mechanical fees"; Increase the "loading and unloading" part of the cost, only increase the "transportation" part of the cost, without deducting the "mechanical fee."

3) There are not installation materials in this work unit.

III. Preparation of General Construction Estimate Sheet for Cost of Installation Works

The General Construction Estimate Sheet for Cost of Installation Works is shown in Table II-B of Appendix.

(I) Composition of Cost of Installation Works

The cost of installation works consists of direct fees, overhead fees, profits and taxes.

The equation for calculation is:

$$\text{Cost of installation works} = \text{direct cost} + \text{overhead cost} + \text{profit} + \text{tax} \qquad (2\text{-}4\text{-}10)$$

(Ⅱ) Direct Cost

1. Direct cost

The direct cost consists of direct construction fees and extra construction fees. The calculation is based on the following formula The equation for calculation is:

$$\text{Direct cost} = \text{direct construction cost} + \text{measure cost} \qquad (2\text{-}4\text{-}11)$$

2. Direct Construction Fee

The direct construction cost consists of labor fees, material fees, and construction machinery usage fees. The calculation is based on the following formula The equation for calculation is:

$$\text{Direct construction cost} = \text{labor cost} + \text{material cost} + \text{cost of using construction machinery} \qquad (2\text{-}4\text{-}13)$$

Because the material cost includes the device material cost and the consumable material fee, the calculation formula for the direct construction cost can also be expressed as

$$\text{Direct construction cost} = \text{device material cost} + \text{installation fee} \qquad (2\text{-}4\text{-}14)$$

The device material cost and installation cost in the calculation formula are both from the summary of the "subtotal" values of the device material cost and installation cost in the budget estimate of each Work Units. It is worth noting that in practical work, for the convenience of viewing, the device material cost is often calculated directly in the statistical table of device material, and the device material cost value will not be listed in the budget estimate of Work Units.

3. Measure Cost

The extra construction cost consists of increased fees of construction in winter and rainy seasons, increased fees of night construction, construction tool and equipment usage fees, increased fees of construction in special areas, temporary facility fees, construction agency transfer fees, and subsidies of safety and housekeeping measures. The equation for calculation is:

$$\begin{aligned}\text{Extra construction cost} = &\text{ increased fees of construction in winter and rainy seasons} + \\ &\text{increased fees of night construction} + \text{construction tool and equipment usage fees} + \\ &\text{increased fees of construction in special areas} + \text{temporary facility fees} + \text{construction} \\ &\text{agency transfer fees} + \text{subsidies of safety and housekeeping measures} \qquad (2\text{-}4\text{-}15)\end{aligned}$$

Study Program II Preparation of Preliminary Budget Estimate for 220kV Overhead Transmission Line Project

(1) Additional cost for winter and rainy season construction

The increased cost of construction in winter and rainy seasons refers to the increased cost required for the construction and installation works which must be carried out continuously during the winter and rainy seasons according to the reasonable requirements of construction period, including the costs incurred from curing measures to ensure the quality of the project during the winter construction period (such as the steam curing of the concrete cast-in-place base), as well as the compensation costs arising from increased construction procedures, increased machinery and material consumption, and reduced work efficiency during construction during the winter and rainy seasons.

The equation for calculation is:

$$\text{The calculation is based on the following formula} \qquad (2\text{-}4\text{-}16)$$

The rate is shown in Table 2-4-15.

Table 2–4–15 Table for Increased Rate of Winter Rainy Season Construction (%)

Area classification	I	II	III	IV	V
Rate (%)	4.91	6.95	10.63	13.90	17.14

Note 1: The cost of the optical cable works erected with the overhead power transmission line implements the project rate of overhead line, the same below.
Note 2: The regional classification is shown in Table 2-4-16.

Table 2–4–16 Regional Classification Table

Area classification	Names of Province, Autonomous Region, or Municipality Directly Under the Central Government
I	Shanghai, Jiangsu, Anhui, Zhejiang, Fujian, Jiangxi, Hubei, Hunan, Guangxi, Guangdong, and Hainan
II	Beijing, Tianjin, Hebei (Zhangjiakou, south of Chengde), Shandong, Henan, Chongqing, Sichuan (excluding Ganzi and Aba Prefectures), Yunnan (excluding Diqing Prefecture), Guizhou
III	Liaoning (Gai County and its south), Shaanxi (south of Yulin), Shanxi, Hebei (Zhangjiakou, north of Chengde)
IV	Liaoning (north of Gai County), Shaanxi (Yulin and its north), Inner Mongolia (leagues, cities and banners in the south of Xilinhot City, Xilingol League, excluding Alxa League), Wulanchabu League, Jirem League, Xinjiang (Ili, Hami and their south), Jilin, Gansu, Ningxia, Sichuan (Ganzi and Aba Prefectures), Yunnan (Diqing Prefecture)
V	Heilongjiang, Qinghai, Xinjiang (Ili, Hami and their north), Tibet, Inner Mongolia (other than the regions of IV)

The increased cost of construction in winter and rainy seasons does not include the cost of antifreeze to be added in concrete during winter construction to ensure the quality of the project. The cost of rain cover measures has been comprehensively considered. The effect of such severe weather as typhoons, heavy rains, and blizzards is not considered. The cost of damage caused by the aforementioned force majeure coefficients is considered in the basic reserve fee.

(2) Additional fee for night time construction work

Additional cost for working at night refers to the cost for night shift subsidy, efficiency reduction for working at night, amortization of lighting equipment, lighting power consumption and other expenses incurred by the single project which shall be carried out continuously at night according to the requirements of the regulations.

Night construction is generally not implemented for power transmission line works, and it is not counted in principle, except for large-span works and cable line works.

The equation for calculation is:

$$\text{Increased cost of night construction} = \text{labor cost} \times 1.05\% \qquad (2\text{-}4\text{-}17)$$

(3) Use cost for construction tools

The construction tool and equipment usage cost refers to the purchase, amortization and maintenance cost of tools and equipment used by the production, inspection and testing departments of the construction enterprise that are not fixed assets. The calculation is based on the following formula The equation for calculation is:

$$\text{Expenses for using tools and appliances} = \text{labor cost} \times \text{rate} \qquad (2\text{-}4\text{-}18)$$

Rate standard: 5.38% for the overhead transmission line project.

(4) Extra charge for special site construction

The increased cost of construction in special areas refers to the additional construction costs required for construction in high altitude, extremely hot, and extremely cold areas due to the influence of special natural conditions.

The equation for calculation is:

$$\text{Increased fees of construction in special areas} = \text{labor cost} \times \text{rate} \qquad (2\text{-}4\text{-}19)$$

The rate is shown in Table 2-4-17.

Table 2–4–17 Rate for Increased Cost of Construction in Special Areas

Category of engineering	High altitude area	High latitude and cold region	Hot region
Rate (%)	6.5	5.5	4.75

Note 1: High altitude area refers to the area with an average altitude of over 3000m.
Note 2: High-latitude cold area refers to the area north of 45°N.
Note 3: Hot area refers to the desert area with an area of 1×10^4 km² or above (Taklimakan Desert, Gurbantunggut Desert, Badain Jaran Desert, Tengger Desert, Qaidam Desert, Kumtag Desert, Kubuqi Desert, Ulanbuh Desert) and Turpan area in Xinjiang.

(5) Temporary facilities

The temporary facility cost refers to the costs incurred by the temporary building, structure and other temporary facilities for living and production that must be set up on the site by the construction enterprise to meet the normal production and living needs on site, including the erection, maintenance and demolition, depreciation and amortization fees of temporary facilities or rental fees of temporary facilities.

Temporary facilities include staff quarters, public housing such as office, living, culture and welfare, buildings and structures such as warehouses, processing yards, work sheds and enclosure, temporary construction roads, branch pipelines of water and electricity (including 380V step-down transformers) within the enclosure of the station area, as well as temporary partitions during construction, but do not include the following:

1) Construction power supply: devices and lines outside the high voltage side of the 380V transformer for construction and living.

2) Water source: off-site water supply pipelines and installations, water source pump houses, and water supply main pipes in construction and living area.

3) Construction road: off-site roads, trunk roads shared for construction and installation in construction and living areas.

The equation for calculation is:

$$\text{Temporary facility cost} = \text{direct construction cost} \times \text{rate} \qquad (2\text{-}4\text{-}20)$$

The rate is shown in Table 2-4-18.

Table 2–4–18 Rate for Temporary Facility Fee

Area classification	I	II	III	IV	V
Rate (%)	1.87	1.95	2.04	2.18	2.55

Note: Expansion works shall be multiplied by a coefficient of 0.9.

The temporary facility cost does not include the water and electricity costs used by the on-site workers, the property management and sanitation cleaning costs, which have been taken into overall consideration of enterprise administration costs. The 380V construction and living transformer costs have been included. The removal and cleaning costs for the temporary construction facilities after the completion of the project have been included. The coefficients such as the on-site temporary buildings and structures which have been standardized in construction and can be used repeatedly, and the enhanced mechanization level and management level of the construction enterprises which has greatly reduced the number of on-site personnel and shortened the construction period, have been comprehensively considered.

(6) Cost for construction unit transfer

The construction agency transfer cost refers to the relocation costs incurred by the construction enterprise to dispatch the construction team to the site of the construction undertaken, including the travel expenses of the staff dispatching, the salary during the dispatching period, as well as the handling costs of construction machinery, office equipment, tools, equipment and materials.

The equation for calculation is:

$$\text{Construction agency transfer cost} = \text{labor cost} \times \text{rate} \quad (2\text{-}4\text{-}21)$$

The rate is shown in Table 2-4-19.

Table 2–4–19 Construction Agency Transfer Fee

Voltage level (kV)	110 and below	220	330	500	750
Rate (%)	3.59	3.37	2.84	2.71	2.44

The rate already includes the road toll and bridge toll incurred by the construction organization during the mobilization.

(7) Subsidy for safe and civilized construction measures

The subsidy for safe and civilized construction measures refers to the subsidy cost for the safety and civilization guarantee measures taken at the construction site according to the safe and civilized construction and health and environmental protection specifications of the power industry.

The equation for calculation is:

(3) Accidental injury premium for hazardous operation

Accidental injury insurance expense for dangerous operations refers to the accidental injury insurance premium paid by the enterprise for the construction and installation personnel engaged in dangerous operations according to the provisions of the construction law.

The equation for calculation is:

$$\text{Premium for accidental injury in dangerous operation} = \text{labor cost} \times \text{rate} \quad (2\text{-}4\text{-}29)$$

Rate standard: 2.53% for overhead power transmission line works, 2.31% for cable line works and 2.53% for optical cable line works.

2. Enterprise Administration Expense

The enterprise administration expense refers to the expenses incurred by construction, installation and construction enterprises in organizing construction, production and management. It includes the salary of management personnel, office expenses, travel and transportation expenses, fixed assets usage fees, tools and appliances usage fees, labor subsidies, labor union expenses, staff education expenses, property insurance expenses, labor safety and health inspection expenses, financial expenses, taxes, and other expenses including project pollution discharge expenses, fees for fixed-point resurvey, item-by item handover and site cleaning, inspection and test fees, technology transfer fees, technology development fees, business entertainment fees, greening fees, advertising fees, notarization fees, legal consulting fees, consulting fees, etc. of construction projects.

Project pollution discharge expenses refer to the sewage treatment fees paid by the construction site according to regulations. Inspection and test fees of construction projects refer to the cost of general identification and inspection of building materials, components and building installations, including the cost of materials and chemicals used in tests conducted by self-established laboratories, as well as the cost of technical innovations and research and trial production tests.

The equation for calculation is:

$$\text{Enterprise administration expense} = \text{labor cost} \times \text{rate} \quad (2\text{-}4\text{-}30)$$

Rate standard: 46.52% for overhead power transmission line works, 47.91% for cable line works, 23.70% for optical cable line works, 8.14% for communication station works and 67.63% for installation.

(IV) Profit

Profits refer to the profits earned by the construction enterprises to complete the contracted project.

The equation for calculation is:

$$\text{Profit} = (\text{direct cost} + \text{indirect cost}) \times 5\% \qquad (2\text{-}4\text{-}31)$$

(V) Taxes

Taxes include business tax, educational surcharge and urban maintenance and construction tax. The equation for calculation is:

$$\text{Tax} = (\text{direct engineering cost} + \text{indirect cost} + \text{planned profit}) \times \text{tax rate} \qquad (2\text{-}4\text{-}32)$$

The tax rate shall be calculated according to the provisions of the local taxation department.

1. Calculation Formula of Business Tax Payable

$$\text{Tax payable} = \text{turnover} \times \text{tax rate} \qquad (2\text{-}4\text{-}33)$$

The power transmission line project is an installation project in the construction industry. Its business tax rate is 3%, and its turnover is the project contract amount (in case of general contracting, the amount of the part subcontracted or transferred shall be deducted).

2. Calculation Formula of Educational Surcharge

$$\text{Tax payable} = \text{actual paid business tax} \times \text{tax rate} \qquad (2\text{-}4\text{-}34)$$

The tax rate stipulated by the state is 3%, and the local educational surcharge shall be calculated separately.

3. Calculation Formula of Urban Maintenance and Construction Tax

$$\text{Tax payable} = \text{actual paid business tax} \times \text{tax rate} \qquad (2\text{-}4\text{-}35)$$

The tax rate of urban maintenance and construction tax is 7% for urban areas, 5% for counties and towns, and 1% for others.

(II) General Construction Estimate Sheet of Installation Works Cost of Project Case II

Table 2-4-20 shows the General Construction Estimate Sheet of installation works cost. The calculation of the charge is explained as follows.

Study Program II Preparation of Preliminary Budget Estimate for 220kV Overhead Transmission Line Project

1. Transfer Data

Fill the data in the "total" columns of the six work units budget estimate Tables 2-4-4, 2-4-6, 2-4-7, 2-4-12, 2-4-13 and 2-4-14 into the corresponding columns of Table 2-4-20 "Direct Engineering Cost", including the fixed direct cost (including labor cost and mechanical cost) and the installation material cost.

2. Determine Rate

(1) Labor cost adjustment. According to the Notice on the Announcement of Wage Subsidies in Various Regions DDZZ[2007] No. 12, the wage subsidy in Sichuan is 3.12 yuan/working day and the benchmark unit price of the power transmission line project in the quota is 33.1 yuan/working day, in which the wage subsidy is 2.4 yuan/working day. According to Formula 2-4-4, the adjustment coefficient of labor cost is 2.18%. Fill it in Table 2-4-20, calculate the adjustment amount of labor cost, and include it in the direct engineering cost-labor cost as the base of each charge.

(2) According to Table 2-4-15 and Table 2-4-16, the project in this case is located in Sichuan Province, a class II area. The construction cost increase rate is 6.95% in winter and rainy seasons.

(3) The project in this case is an overhead power transmission line project, and the rate of construction tool usage cost is 5.38%.

(4) The project in this case is not located in a special area, and the rate of construction cost increase in special area is 0.

(5) According to Table 2-4-18, the project in this case is located in Sichuan, a class II area, and the rate of temporary facilities cost is 1.95%.

(6) According to Table 2-4-19, the project in this case is a 220kV power transmission line project, and the rate of construction organization transfer cost is 3.37%.

(7) The Project Case is an overhead power transmission line project, and the rate of safe and civilized construction measures is 2.52%.

(8) According to the inquiry from the construction unit's human resources department of the project in this case, the rate of social security cost is 28% (31.36% after multiplying by 1.12); the rate of housing provident fund is 15% (16.8% after multiplying by 1.12).

(9) The Project Case is an overhead power transmission line project, and the premium

for accidental injury in dangerous operation is 2.53%.

(10) The Project Case is an overhead power transmission line project, and the rate of enterprise administration expense is 46.52%.

(11) According to the "budget regulations", the profit margin is 5%.

(12) According to the "budget regulations" and the local education additional tax rate stipulated by the local government, the tax rate is 3.37%. Calculate and fill out Table 2-4-20 based on the transfer data and rates.

IV. Preparation of Auxiliary Facility Works Budget Estimate

(I) Auxiliary Facility Works

Auxiliary facility works refer to the engineering works set up to improve the safe operation level of the line and facilitate maintenance and overhaul, including purchase of equipment, tools and instruments for maintenance of overhead warning lines, communication works for maintenance, patrol maintenance station works, and patrol maintenance roads.

(1) The overhead warning lines refer to obvious safety protection signs set up on the navigable rivers crossed by the power transmission line. The materials shall be provided according to the design; the installation quota shall be calculated according to the content of the quota of overhead warning lines in the Budget Quota of Electric Power Construction Project (Volume IV Power Transmission Line Project 2006 Edition) or in the same way as previous projects. Overhead warning line works: with or without a pedestrian cableway; the width of the river where the overhead warning line is set up shall also be distinguished. The unit of quantity of overhead warning lines is: nos.

(2) Communication works for maintenance refer to the equipment works for safe and reliable communication between the line work area and the line work section as well as the patrol maintenance station, including: special communication lines, carrier waves, portable telephones, radio stations and interphones. The cost shall be subject to the relevant price. The ground wire carrier communication and the overhead open wire communication are only used in the areas with poor transportation and lack of communication means. Other communication equipment shall be equipped according to the communication conditions near the line.

(3) The patrol maintenance station works refer to line patrol stations, maintenance stations and corresponding tools and equipment needed for line operation, maintenance and overhaul.

In order to ensure that the power system has a high reliability of power supply, it is necessary to conduct regular patrol inspection on the built power lines and check the integrity of each component equipment of the lines. The line operation and maintenance unit shall formulate an operation and maintenance plan according to the operation status of the lines and carry out the operation and maintenance work in a timely manner to ensure that each power line built and put into operation has good mechanical and electrical performance. In order to facilitate the management of the operating lines, a long-distance power line is often divided into several parts, and each part is set with a corresponding line patrol station and maintenance station. As the primary-level organization of line operation, line patrol stations and maintenance stations are located near the line and are responsible for maintaining a certain section of the line. Generally, each line patrol station or maintenance station is in charge of 40 - 60 km long line, and is configured depending on the natural conditions of the line, the voltage level, the importance of the tower position and the transportation conditions.

(1) Dormitory area

The staff dormitories consist of those for ones who live with their family members and those for single staff. The area is calculated by multiplying the number of new line operation and maintenance personnel coming to build a new line by the area index.

1) Determination of the number of new personnel

The number of new personnel shall be in accordance with the Labor Personnel Quota Standard for Power Supply Enterprises of State Grid Corporation of China (Part 1: Power Transmission) (Q/GWD247.1-2008). See Tables 2-4-21 and 2-4-22.

Table II B

Table 2-4-20 General Construction Estimate Sheet of installation works Cost of Overhead Power Transmission Line

S/N	Name of project or expenses	Charge base number	Rate %	Earthwork	base works	Pole and tower works	Stringing works	Accessory project	Site transportation	Total	Percentage of each item in the total (%)	Unit investment (Yuan/km)
I	Direct cost			2056027.18	2411222.41	8918972.47	9138810.25	2655150.53	1885431.19	27065614.04	78.81%	522502.20
1	Direct construction cost (B)	1)+2)		1747343.66	2256483.85	8660164.97	8814211.37	2584680.67	1644050.99	25706935.50		
1)	Quota of direct costs			1747343.66	857124.71	599410.37	1285674.77	170969.67	1644050.99	6304574.16		
	Including: labor cost (A)			1507191.67	607777.87	493602.01	838209.47	110145.92	1148854.04	4705780.97		
	Adjustment of labor cost		2.18%	32086.87	12939.09	10508.38	17844.79	2344.92	24458.16	100182.21		
	Machinery cost			152911.34	95311.53	93430.87	210099.01	35125.30	492565.43	1079443.47		
2)	Installation materials			0.00	1399359.14	8060754.60	7528536.60	2413711.00	0.00	19402361.34		
2	Measures expenses			308683.52	154738.56	258807.50	324598.89	70469.86	241380.20	1358678.54		
1)	Additional cost for winter and rainy season construction	A	6.95	104749.82	42240.56	34305.34	58255.56	7655.14	79845.36	327051.78		
2)	Construction tool usage fee	A	5.38	81086.91	32698.45	26555.79	45095.67	5925.85	61808.35	253171.02		
3)	Extra charge for special site construction	A	0	0.00	0.00	0.00	0.00	0.00	0.00	0.00		

Study Program II Preparation of Preliminary Budget Estimate for 220kV Overhead Transmission Line Project

Table (Cont'd)

S/N	Name of project or expenses	Charge base number	Rate %	Earthwork	base works	Pole and tower works	Stringing works	Accessory project	Site transportation	Total	Percentage of each item in the total (%)	Unit investment (Yuan/km)
4)	Temporary facilities	B	1.95	34073.20	44001.44	168873.22	171877.12	50401.27	32058.99	501285.24		
5)	Cost for construction unit transfer	A	3.37	50792.36	20482.11	16634.39	28247.66	3711.92	38716.38	158584.82		
6)	Subsidy for safe and civilized construction measures	A	2.52	37981.23	15316.00	12438.77	21122.88	2775.68	28951.12	118585.68		
II	Indirect costs			1465141.02	590820.86	479830.51	814823.43	107072.84	1116801.01	4574489.68	13.32%	88310.61
1	Levies and charges			763995.46	308082.60	250206.86	424888.38	55832.96	582354.11	2385360.38		
1)	Social security fee	A	31.36	472655.31	190599.14	154793.59	262862.49	34541.76	360280.63	1475732.91		
2)	Housing provident fund	A	16.8	253208.20	102106.68	82925.14	140819.19	18504.51	193007.48	790571.20		
3)	Accidental injury premium for hazardous operation	A	2.53	38131.95	15376.78	12488.13	21206.70	2786.69	29066.01	19056.26		
2	Administrative expenses	A	46.52	701145.56	282738.26	229623.65	389935.05	51239.88	534446.90	2189129.31		
III	Margin	I+II	5	176058.41	150102.16	469940.15	497681.68	138111.17	150111.61	1582005.19	4.61%	30540.64
IV	Tax	I+II+III	3.37	124596.54	106227.30	332576.64	352209.33	97741.27	106233.99	1119585.07	3.26%	21613.61
	Total of installation cost	I+II+III+IV		3821823.15	3258372.74	10201319.78	10803524.69	2998075.82	3258577.80	34341693.98		

Table (Cont'd)

S/N	Name of project or expenses	Charge base number	Rate %	Earthwork	base works	Pole and tower works	Stringing works	Accessory project	Site transportation	Total	Percentage of each item in the total (%)	Unit investment (Yuan/km)
	Percentage occupation of each item over the total (%)			11.13%	9.49%	29.71%	31.46%	8.73%	9.49%		100.00%	
	Unit investment (Yuan/km)			73780.37	62902.95	196936.68	208562.25	57877.91	62906.91	662967.07		

Study Program II Preparation of Preliminary Budget Estimate for 220kV Overhead Transmission Line Project

Table 2-4-21 Personnel Quota Standard for Operation and Maintenance of Power Transmission Line

Natural conditions	Computing unit-circuit length	Fixed staff number (person)							
		1000 kV	±800 kV	750/±660kV	500kV	330kV	220kV	110/66kV	35kV
Plain areas	Hundred kilometers	5.8	5.6	4.0	3.2	2.4	1.9	1.4	1.3
Hilly area		6.4	6.2	4.2	3.5	2.9	2.3	1.7	1.5
Mountain area		10.0	10.0	8.0	6.2	4.3	3.8	2.7	2.2
Virgin forest area		14.0	14.0	10.5	7.9	5.4	4.9	4.1	3.1

Note 1: for 500kV DC power transmission lines, the personnel quota shall be calculated by multiplying the personnel quota standard of 500kV AC line by the coefficient of 0.9; for thunderstorm regions, severely cold areas, contaminated areas and river network areas, the personnel quota shall be calculated by multiplying the corresponding personnel quota standard by the coefficient of 1.1; for strong thunderstorm regions, ice covered areas and desert areas, the personnel quota shall be calculated by multiplying the corresponding personnel quota standard by the coefficient of 1.2; when two or more power transmission lines are erected on the same pole, the personnel quota shall, with the total line length as the base, be calculated by multiplying the corresponding personnel quota standard by the coefficient of 0.7; for large river-crossing towers requiring special personnel on duty, the personnel quota shall be calculated as one for each tower.

Note 2: hilly area refers to the area where the horizontal height difference between peak and valley is between 0.2km and 0.3km; mountainous area refers to the area where the height difference between peak and valley is 0.3km or more; virgin forest area refers to the virgin forest area defined or confirmed by the state; severely cold area refers to the area where the monthly average temperature in the coldest month is lower than - 15 ℃; contaminated area refers to the area where the power line is located in an environment that meets the national level B pollution environment standard and above; river network area refers to the area with more than 1.5 rivers crossed by the power line per kilometer; ice covered area refers to the area that the power line passes through with an average ice-covered period of three months per year; thunderstorm region and strong thunderstorm region refer to the area with 40 - 90 thunderstorm days or over 90 thunderstorm days respectively; power transmission line refers to the power line with voltage of 35kV and above; circuit length refers to the length of a circuit of power line with transmission conditions.

Table 2-4-22 Personnel Quota Standard for Overhaul of Power Transmission Line

Natural conditions	Computing unit-circuit length	Fixed staff number (person)							
		1000kV	±800kV	750/±660kV	500kV	330kV	220kV	110/66kV	35kV
Plain areas	Hundred kilometers	4.0	3.8	2.8	2.4	2.1	1.6	1.3	1.2
Hilly area		4.8	4.6	3.2	2.6	2.5	1.9	1.6	1.4
Mountain area		8.0	8.0	5.5	4.1	3.0	2.5	2.5	1.8
Virgin forest area		9.0	9.0	7.0	5.2	3.5	3.0	2.7	2.6

Note 1: for 500kV DC power transmission lines, the personnel quota shall be calculated by multiplying the personnel quota standard of 500kV AC line by the coefficient of 0.9; for thunderstorm regions, severely cold areas, contaminated areas and river network areas, the personnel quota shall be calculated by multiplying the corresponding personnel quota standard by the coefficient of 1.1; for strong thunderstorm regions, ice covered areas and desert areas, the personnel quota shall be calculated by multiplying the corresponding personnel quota standard by the coefficient of 1.2.

Example: 284km of a 220kV line in the charge of a power supply agency is divided into 120km in plain area, 84km in hilly area and 80km in mountainous area according to geographical conditions. Among the 120km in the plain area, 50km is in the contaminated area above grade B, and 25km of double-circuit line is erected on the same pole; among the 80km in the mountainous area, 20km is in the strong thunderstorm region. Try to calculate the operation maintenance and overhaul personnel needed for the line.

Solution:

The operation maintenance and overhaul personnel of the plain area are respectively:

$$((120-50-25) + 50 \times 1.1 + 25 \times 2 \times 0.7) \div 100 \times 1.9 = 2.565 \text{ (persons)}$$

$$((120-50-25) + 50 \times 1.1 + 25 \times 2) \div 100 \times 1.6 = 2.4 \text{ (persons)}$$

The operation maintenance and overhaul personnel of the hilly area are:

$$84 \div 100 \times (2.9 + 1.9) = 4.032 \text{ (persons)}$$

The operation maintenance and overhaul personnel of the mountainous area are:

$$((80-20) + 20 \times 1.2) \div 100 \times (3.8 + 2.5) = 5.292 \text{ (persons)}$$

The operation maintenance and overhaul personnel of the line are:

$$2.565 + 2.4 + 4.032 + 5.292 = 14.289 \text{ (persons)}$$

After rounding the calculated number to an integer, the operation maintenance and overhaul personnel required for the 220kV line is 15.

2) Per capita dormitory area index

How to determine the per capita dormitory area index: one is 28m²/person in the east of Kangding County, and 30m²/person in the west of Kangding County; the other is to determine according to whether the staff have taken their families or not - 7m²/person for those without families and 50m²/person for those with families; or in accordance with the relevant provisions of the local people's government of the place where the project is located or the competent department of the industry.

(2) Auxiliary building area

Auxiliary buildings include offices, warehouses, garages, etc., and their area is multiplied by the number of new personnel by the index in Table 2-4-23.

Table 2-4-23 Auxiliary Building Area Index

S/N	Capacitor bank (kV)	Area quota (m²/person)
1	500	14
2	330	12
3	220	10
4	110	8

The dormitory area plus the auxiliary building area is the building area of the patrol maintenance station. When requisitioning land, the requisitioned land area shall be 2.5 times of the building area.

(3) Outdoor works

Outdoor works refer to the construction and installation works of outdoor enclosure and roads within the enclosure, water supply and drainage, septic tanks, power supply, etc.

(4) Calculation of engineering cost of patrol maintenance stations

The engineering cost of patrol maintenance stations includes land acquisition cost and construction and installation fees for dormitories, auxiliary buildings and outdoor works. The engineering cost of dormitories and auxiliary buildings is calculated by multiplying the area of dormitories and auxiliary buildings by the building cost. The outdoor works cost shall be as shown in the designed budget if designed, and be calculated by multiplying the sum of dormitory and auxiliary building engineering cost by the rate of outdoor works if not designed (generally 15% if not stipulated otherwise).

The standard of land acquisition cost shall be in accordance with the standards stipulated by the local people's government of the place where the project is located, and shall be determined according to the results of on-site capital search.

(5) Patrol maintenance road works

Generally, the patrol maintenance roads shall be considered together with the construction of roads and bridges for construction. They serve construction at the initial stage and operation after the completion and trial operation of the project. In general, the patrol maintenance roads will not be built in plain and hilly areas, but only in mountainous areas and high mountains and on large mountain ridges. Calculation of the engineering cost of patrol maintenance roads: multiply the length of the road constructed by the general mountain quota in the "quota for temporary road construction and widening".

(6)Purchase of maintenance equipment, tools and instruments shall be in accordance with relevant regulations.

A certain proportion of the expenses shall be listed in the total investment for the purchase of spare parts.

(Ⅱ) Auxiliary Facility Budget Estimate

(1)Auxiliary Facility Budget Estimate of Project Case II

Table 2-4-24 shows the auxiliary facility works budget estimate

Table 2-4-24 Budget Estimate of the Auxiliary Facilities Costs of Power Transmission Lines

Table III-E

S/N	Name of project or expenses	Preparation Basis and Calculation Notes	Total price (Yuan)
1	Line inspection and repair station project cost		
1.1	Direct cost of construction works	3 person × (28+10) m² / person × 1000 Yuan / m²	114000.00
1.2	Land acquisition fee	3 persons × (28+10) m²/person ×2.5÷667×180000	76911.54
1.3	Cost of outdoor works	114000×15%	17100.00
	Sub-total		208011.54
2	Cost of communication equipment for operation and maintenance	4 sets × 6000 Yuan / set	24000.00
	Total		232011.54

Note: The basis for compilation and calculation as well as the necessary instruction for calculation method shall be clarified for each item of cost.

(2) Instruction for charge and calculation

In recent years, with the increased investment in infrastructure construction for highways and communication from the country, the conditions of transportation and communication over the country has been greatly improved. Besides the steadily improved production technologies and management level of power grid enterprises, most of the line projects, except several major pole and tower positions and a few power lines with poor transportation and communication conditions, do not require actually constructed line inspection and main-

Study Program II Preparation of Preliminary Budget Estimate for 220kV Overhead Transmission Line Project

tenance station, but still calculate and include the related costs, which will be planned and used by the line operation and maintenance unit.

The cost of auxiliary facilities for this project case include the line inspection and maintenance station project cost and the cost of communication equipment, and there is no other auxiliary facility. Upon consultation and information search, the standard for land acquisition fee for the location of this project case is 180,000 Yuan/mu, and the construction cost is 1,000 Yuan/m^2. It is planned to purchase 4 inter-phones as the communication equipment for operation and maintenance of the line.

(1) Calculation of engineering cost of patrol maintenance stations

According to the project profile, this project case is a 220kV single-circuit power transmission line in about 51.8km of total length, with the terrain divided into: 7.4% of flat ground, 51.4% of hills, and 41.2% of mountain land.

Personnel for operation and maintenance of this project case:

$51.8 \div 100 \times [(1.9+1.6) \times 7.4\% + (2.9+1.9) \times 51.4\% + (3.8+2.5) \times 41.2\%] = 2.7567$ (persons)

After the calculated number of persons is rounded off, the 220kV line requires 3 persons for the operation and maintenance. According to the area quota of 28m^2/person, the area of staff quarter is calculated as: 3 persons × 28m^2/person = 84 (m^2). According to Table 2-4-23, the area of auxiliary building is as below.

Area quota for 220kV line auxiliary building is 10 m^2/person, so 3 persons × 10 m^2/person = 30 (m^2).

The area of land acquisition is: (84+30)×2.5=285 (m^2)

The land acquisition fee is: (285m^2÷667m^2/mu)× 180,000 Yuan/mu=76,911.54 Yuan

The direct cost of construction works is: (84+30)m^2× 1000Yuan/m^2= 114,000.00 Yuan

The cost of outdoor works is 114,000×15%= 17,100.00 Yuan

The line inspection and maintenance station project cost is: 76,911.54+114,000+17,100= 232,011.54 Yuan

(2) Calculation of communication equipment cost

It is planned to adopt 30 MHz short wave frequency modulation inter-phone (max communication distance: 5km), whose estimated price of the inter-phone body together with the accessories is 6000 Yuan/set.

$$4 \times 6000 = 24,000.00 \text{ (Yuan)}$$

(3) This project case does not have any line inspection and maintenance road, so no cost is calculated and included.

(4) No cost related to other equipment and tool for maintenance is calculated and included for this project case. List above costs in Table 2-4-24.

V. Compilation of Budget Estimates for Other Costs

Other costs include the construction site acquisition and cleaning-up cost, project construction administrative cost, project construction technical service cost, subsystem debugging and whole set startup commissioning cost, production preparation cost, heavy-cargo transportation measure cost, and basic reserve cost. The equation for calculation is:

Other costs = construction site acquisition and cleaning-up cost + project

construction administrative cost + project construction technical service cost

+ subsystem debugging and whole set startup commissioning cost + production

preparation cost + heavy-cargo transportation measure cost + basic reserve cost (2-4-36)

(I) Construction Site Acquisition and Cleaning-up Costs

The construction site allocation and cleaning-up cost consists of land acquisition fee, construction site rental, relocation compensation, clearance cost, power transmission line corridor compensation, measure cost for communication facility against interference from power transmission line, etc. The equation for calculation is:

The construction site allocation and cleaning-up cost = land acquisition fee

+ construction site rental + relocation compensation, clearance cost + power

transmission line corridor compensation + measure cost for communication

facility against interference from power transmission line (2-4-37)

1. Land Acquisition Fee

The land acquisition fee includes land compensation, resettlement subsidy, farmland reclamation cost, survey and demarcation fee, land acquisition administrative fee, certificate cost, commission charge, various funds and taxes, etc.

Calculation standard: It shall be calculated based on the approved quantity of acquisition, and the standard provided by the related laws and regulation, national administration authority and the people's government of the province (municipality and direct-controlled municipality).

2. Construction Site Rental

The construction site rental includes the site rental, cleaning-up and reclamation cost, etc. Calculation standard: It shall be calculated based on the provisions of related laws and regulations, national administration authority and the people's government of the place where the project is located, as well as the lease contract signed between the project's legal person an the land owner.

3. Relocation Compensation

Relocation compensation refers to the compensation for the relocation of the organs, enterprises, residences and related buildings, structures, power lines, communication lines, railways, highways, ditches, pipelines, graves, forest, etc. on the land acquired in order to meet the requirement of project construction.

Calculation standard: It shall be calculated based on the provisions from the people's government of the place where the project is located.

4. Clearance Cost

The clearance cost refers to the various expenses incurred in dismantling and cleaning up the existing buildings, structures, and other facilities that hinder the construction of the project within the scope of the land requisitioned for the project.

Calculation standard: It shall be calculated based on the rate in Table 2-4-25, and the amount of income from residue recovery.

In above table, the new construction direct cost of the project refers to the new construction direct cost for the year when the estimates are compiled, where only the measure subsidy for safe and civilized construction is calculated in the items of measure cost. Residues refer to the recovery value of the materials included in the construction installation quota in the destruction works. The old equipment, the iron towers and conductors, etc. in line project shall be subject to the related provisions for disposal of fixed assets as they have formed fixed assets.

Table 2-4-25 Rate of clearance cost

Project name			Calculation formula	Rate%
Construction works	General brick-wood structure		New construction direct cost for construction works × rate	10
	Composite structure		New construction direct cost for construction works × rate	20
	Concrete and reinforced concrete structure	With the condition for blasting	New construction direct cost for construction works × rate	20
		Without the condition for blasting	New construction direct cost for construction works × rate	30 ~ 50
	Temporary simple building		New construction direct cost for construction works × rate	8
	Metal construction	Metal structure usable after demolition	New construction direct cost for installation works × rate	55
		Metal structure unusable after demolition	New construction direct cost for installation works × rate	38
Installation works	Metal structure and industrial pipes		New construction direct cost for installation works × rate	45
	Mechanical and electrical equipment		New construction direct cost for installation works × rate	32
	Power transmission line and communication line	Usable after demolition	New construction direct cost for installation works × rate	62
		Unusable after demolition	New construction direct cost for installation works × rate	35
Railway engineering	Railway station		New construction direct cost for project × rate	18
	Railway line		New construction direct cost for project × rate	10

Note 1: The rate is exclusive of the excess freight and miscellaneous charges for muck whose load distance is greater than 5km.
Note 2: The new construction direct cost for installation works is exclusive of the cost of unpriced materials.

5. Power Transmission Line Corridor Compensation

Power transmission line corridor compensation refers to the compensation for the buildings, structures, forest, commercial crops, etc. to be cleared on the land not acquired but in the line corridor according to the related specifications and requirements for the power transmission line. The urban road excavation and breaking expenses and greening compensation

Study Program II Preparation of Preliminary Budget Estimate for 220kV Overhead Transmission Line Project

under the construction of urban cable works shall be included in this item of cost.

Calculation standard: It shall be calculated based on the provisions from the people's government of the place where the project is located.

6. Measure Cost for Communication Facility Against Interference From Power Transmission Line

Measure cost for communication facility against interference from power transmission line refers to the expenses incurred in the relocation of communication line or additional installation of protective facilities to eliminate the interference effect where the power transmission line to be constructed will cross with or parallel to existing communication line. This item of cost is exclusive of the expenses incurred in the line crossing.

Calculation standard: It shall be calculated based on the design scheme and the contract signed or supplementary agreement concluded between the project's legal person and the communication department.

(II) Project Construction Administrative Cost

Project construction administrative cost refers to the expenses incurred for the organization, management, coordination and supervision of the project within the reasonable construction period from the construction preparation by the project's legal person to the completion acceptance and handover for production after the construction project is approved by the national administration authority. It includes the construction project legal person administrative cost, bidding cost, project supervision cost, equipment manufacturing supervision cost, and project insurance cost.

The equation for calculation is:

$$\text{Project construction administrative cost} = \text{project legal person administrative cost} + \text{bidding cost} + \text{project supervision cost} + \text{equipment manufacturing supervision cost} + \text{project insurance cost} \quad (2\text{-}4\text{-}38)$$

1. Construction Project Legal Person Administrative Cost

Construction project legal person administrative cost refers to the organization cost and recurrent expenses incurred in the project management carried out by the project legal person.

(1) Organization cost of the project includes the expenses for declaration and handling of the related permits and related procedures, and the expenses for purchase of necessary of-

fice furniture, life furniture and supplies, and transportation means.

(2) Work expenditure of the project legal person refers to the routine expenditures incurred in the project legal person organ during the project construction period, including the basic wage of employees, wage subsidies, supplementary wage, welfare expense of employees, labor protection expenses, endowment insurance expense, unemployment insurance expense, medical insurance expense, housing provident fund, office expenses, business travel expenses, fixed assets usage expense, tools and instruments usage fee, technologies and books and materials fee, project archives management fee, utility bills, education and labor union expenditure, construction drawings review fee, project price appraisal (settlement fee), contract conclusion and notarial fee, advisory and legal expenses, consulting fees, conference expenses, board expenses, business entertainment expenses, fire control and security expense, heating and heatstroke prevention expense, stamp tax, house property tax, vehicle and vessel tax, vehicle and vessel insurance expense, road toll, expenses for expediting and acceptance inspection of equipment and materials, supervision of the manufacturing of the project's main materials, and labor and safety acceptance of the construction project, expenses for completion, delivery for use, cleaning-up and acceptance of the project, etc.

The equation for calculation is:

$$\text{Construction project legal person administrative cost} = \text{cost of installation works} \times \text{rate} \quad (2\text{-}4\text{-}39)$$

The rate is shown in Table 2-4-26.

Table 2-4-26 Rate of Construction Project Legal Person Administrative Cost

Voltage level (kV)	220 and below	330	500	750
Overhead line works	1.35		1.22	
Cable route works	1.64			

2. Bidding Cost

Bidding cost refers to the expenses incurred when the project legal person, in accordance with the related national regulations, organizes or authorizes the qualified organ to prepare and review the bidding documents and tender estimate, organizes to prepare the equipment and technical specifications, and authorizes the organ having the qualification of bidding agency to call for bids for the design, construction, equipment and materials procurement, project supervision, commissioning and other subcontract project.

The equation for calculation is:

$$\text{Bidding cost} = \text{cost of installation works} \times \text{rate} \quad (2\text{-}4\text{-}40)$$

The rate is shown in Table 2-4-27.

Table 2–4–27 Rate of Bidding Cost

Voltage level (kV)	110 and below	330 and below	500 and above
Overhead line works	0.53	0.45	0.35
Cable route works		1.65	

3. Project Supervision Cost

Project supervision cost refers to the payment made by the project legal person for authorizing a project supervision organ to supervise the whole process of the construction project in accordance with the related national regulations, procedures and specifications.

The equation for calculation is:

$$\text{Cable line project supervision cost} = \text{cost of installation works} \times 2.15\% \quad (2\text{-}4\text{-}41)$$

The overhead power transmission line project supervision cost shall be calculated based on the length of the line and the standard listed in Table 2-4-28.

Table 2–4–28 Rate of Project Supervision Cost

10,000 Yuan/km

Voltage level (kV)	Single loop	Same pole (tower) and double-circuit
750	2.00	/
500	1.55	2.05
330	1.25	1.60
220	1.00	1.25
110	0.60	0.75
35	0.50	0.60

Note 1: Lines less than 5km long shall be calculated as 5km.

Note 2: The rate for overhead lines shall take flat ground and hill as the standard terrain, and other terrains shall be subject to this standard multiplied by the corresponding coefficient, which is 1.1 for river network, mire and general mountain land, 1.2 for high mountains, and 1.3 for steep mountains.

Note 3: Projects with long span shall be calculated as 1.5% of the cost of installation works.

Note 4: For power grid projects across the urban areas, it may be calculated by multiplying this standard by the coefficient 1.1~1.2 according to the degree of construction difficulty. Note 5: For overhead line projects in high altitude areas and hot regions, it may be calculated by multiplying this standard by the coefficient 1.1.

For multiple-circuit lines over double circuits, it shall be based on same pole and tower with double circuits, 20% of the charges for same voltage class shall be increased for each additional circuit. For example, the calculation standard for the supervision cost of 220kV same tower four-circuit line is

$$1.25+1.00\times20\%\times2=1.25+0.4=1.65 \text{ ('0,000 Yuan/km)}$$

4. Equipment Manufacturing Supervision Cost

Equipment manufacturing supervision cost refers to the expenses incurred when the project legal person, in order to assure the equipment quality, makes necessary witness and supervision on the manufacturing of main equipment, the quality, production and inspection of raw materials during the production in accordance with the requirements in the equipment manufacturing administrative measures published by the national administration authority.

The construction expenses for the iron tower, conductor and other materials in power transmission line projects have been taken into account in the project legal person administrative measure.

5. Project Insurance Cost

Project insurance cost refers to the payment made by the project legal person to insure the possible direct or indirect loss in project assets, safety, etc. caused in the process of project construction.

Calculation standard: It shall be calculated based on the actual insurance scope and rate according to the requirements of the project legal person and the actual situation of the project, and shall be paid from the basic reserve cost.

The content and type of project insurance shall be reviewed and determined by the project Administrator. In the feasibility study stage and preliminary design stage, the project insurance cost may be calculated and included with reference of the similar project, and shall be paid from the basic reserve cost .

(Ⅲ) Project Construction Technical Service Cost

Project construction technical service cost refers to the expenses incurred to provide technical services and technical support for the project construction, including preliminary

Study Program II Preparation of Preliminary Budget Estimate for 220kV Overhead Transmission Line Project

work fees for the project, intellectual property rights transfer cost and research and test fee, survey and design fee, design document review fee, post evaluation fee of the project, project construction supervision and testing fee, administrative fee for formulation of power construction standard, and administrative fee for formulation of power project quota.

Calculation formula:

Project construction technical service cost = preliminary work fees for the project + intellectual property rights transfer cost and research and test fee + survey and design fee, design document review fee + post evaluation fee of the project + project construction supervision and testing fee + administrative fee for formulation of power construction standard + administrative fee for formulation of power project quota   (2-4-42)

1. Preliminary Work Fees for the Project

Preliminary work fees for the project refer to the expenses incurred to the project legal person in the preliminary stage of the project, including the expenses incurred in the design of feasibility study for the project, preliminary review of land, environmental impact assessment, pre-evaluation of labor safety and health, evaluation of geological disaster, evaluation of earthquake disaster, formulation of water and soil conservation outline, evaluation of mineral covering, forestry planning and survey, general detection of cultural relics, etc., as well as the consulting fee for the planning and design of electric power system apportioned in the project and the design document review fee.

The cost in feasibility study stage shall be calculated by Formula (2-4-42) as below

Preliminary work fees for the project = (survey fee + basic design fee) × rate   (2-4-43)

See Table 2-4-29 for the rate. The cost in preliminary design stage shall be calculated and included according to the various agreed fees signed between the project legal person and the related units.

Progressive system shall be adopted for the calculation of preliminary work fees for overhead power transmission line project. Where the line length exceeds 100km, the rate for exceeding part shall be calculated as 9.3%. For example, where the line length is 150km, its rate of preliminary work fees for the project shall be calculated as

$$11.2\% \times (100/150) + 9.3\% \times [(150-100)/150] = 7.47\% + 3.1\% = 10.57\%$$

Table 2-4-29 Rate of Preliminary Work Fees for the Project

Category of engineering	Length of overhead line (km)		Cable route works
	100 and below	Over 100	
Rate%	11.2	9.3	5.6

2. Intellectual Property Rights Transfer Cost and Research and Test Fee

Intellectual property rights transfer cost refers to the one-time transfer fee paid for the special research results and advanced technologies that the project legal person use in this project; the research and test fee refers to the expenses incurred in the necessary researches and tests in order to provide or verify the design data for this construction project, and the expenses for the researches and tests which must be carried out in the process of construction as required the design provisions. It excludes: items to be paid by the Expenditure for Science and Technology (expenses for trial manufacture of new products, expenses for intermediate experiments, and subsidies for important scientific research); authentication, inspection and test fee to be paid by the administrative fee; items to be paid by the survey and design fee.

Calculation standard: The items and costs shall be calculated and included as proposed by the project legal person (there is no this cost in general power transmission line project).

3. Survey and Design Fee

Survey and design fee refers to the expenses incurred in the survey and design of the project construction. It includes the expenses for explorations and surveys of the project, fees for preliminary design and construction drawing design, fees for preparation of as-built drawing document, fees for preparation of construction drawing budget, and fees for field technical service of design representative. It is divided into survey fee and design fee.

The equation for calculation is:

$$\text{Survey and design fee} = \text{survey fee} + \text{design fee} \qquad (2\text{-}4\text{-}44)$$

(1) Survey fee refers to the expenses paid by the project legal person for authorizing the qualified survey institution to make engineering survey for the project and prepare the survey document and geotechnical engineering design document in accordance with the specifications and requirements for survey and design.

Calculation standard: It shall be calculated based on the charging standard for engineering survey issued by the national administration authority.

In accordance with the Administrative Regulations on Charges of Engineering Survey and Design (JJG [2002] No. 10) issued by the State Development Planning Commission and the Ministry of Construction, the survey fee for power project includes the fees and expenditures for engineering survey in the stage of preliminary design and construction drawing design. The scope of engineering survey includes engineering surveying, geotechnical engineering investigation, engineering hydrometeorology, and corresponding testing and test. The engineering survey for overhead power transmission line includes the followings.

1) Preliminary design stage: Collect the data available for use, and compile the survey outline; participate in the line section, hydrological survey, engineering geological survey, surveying of crowded region and important crossing and spanning, and surveying of the corresponding location of the necessary communication lines within the affected range; sort data, compile report, and submit the survey results.

2) Construction drawing design stage: Study the task, and compile survey outline; carry out the setting-out, the measurement of vertical and horizontal section, plane, crossing and spanning, sideline and wind deviation, the determination of tower location, the monitoring of hazard points on the cross section and sag of the tower position, cooperate with the surveying in petrologic survey and hydrological surveying, the engineering geological survey, exploration and test, and the hydrographic authentication of tower positions; sort data, compile report, and submit the survey results.

The equation for calculation is:

Survey fee for power project = base price engineering survey and design fee
+ preparation expense for engineering survey works (2-4-45)

(2) Design fee refers to the payment made by the project legal person for authorizing qualified design institution to prepare the preliminary design document for the construction project, construction drawing design document, construction drawing budget, non-standard equipment design document, as-built drawing document, etc. as required in the project design specifications, and for the field technical services from the design representative.

Calculation standard: It shall be calculated based on the charging standard for engineering survey and design issued by the national administration authority.

In accordance with the Administrative Regulations on Charges of Engineering Survey and Design (JJG [2002] No. 10) issued by the State Development Planning Commission and the Ministry of Construction, the scope of power project design works includes the preparation and providing of preliminary design document, construction drawing design document, non-standard equipment design document, construction drawing budget document, as-built drawing document, etc.

The equation for calculation is:

$$\text{Design fee for power project} = \text{basic design fee} + \text{other design fees} \quad (2\text{-}4\text{-}46)$$

Other design fees refer to except the fees included in the basic design fee, the fees charged by the design unit for providing related services according to the actual needs of the project design or as required by the project legal person, including the overall design fee, subject design coordination fee, fee for adopting standard design and reused design, fee for preparation of non-standard equipment design document, fee for preparation of construction drawing budget, and fee for preparation of as-built drawing document. Wherein,

$$\text{Fee for preparation of construction drawing budget} = \text{basic design fee} \times 10\% \quad (2\text{-}4\text{-}47)$$

$$\text{Fee for preparation of as-built drawing document} = \text{basic design fee} \times 8\% \quad (2\text{-}4\text{-}48)$$

4. Design Document Review Fee

Design document review fee refers to the expenses incurred to the project legal person for reviewing the design documents of the project. According to its contents, it can be divided into feasibility study design document review fee and preliminary design document review fee.

The equation for calculation is:

$$\text{Design document review fee} = \text{feasibility study design document review fee} + \text{preliminary design document review fee} \quad (2\text{-}4\text{-}49)$$

Feasibility study design document review fee refers to the expenses incurred to the project legal person for authorizing qualified review institution to carry out a overall review on the necessity and feasibility of the project from the aspect of policy, planning, technology and economy and raise the feasibility review report in accordance with the related laws, regulations and industrial standards. See Table 2-4-17 for the calculation standard.

Preliminary design document review fee refers to the expenses incurred to the project legal person for authorizing qualified consulting institution to carry out overall review on the safety, reliability, advancement and economy of the preliminary design scheme and raise the review report in accordance with the related laws, regulations and industrial standards. See Table 2-4-30 for the calculation standard.

Table 2–4–30 Charging Standard for Design Document Review Fee of Power Transmission Line Project

Voltage level (kV)	Scale range (km)	Charging standard ('0,000 Yuan/km)	
		Feasibility study	Preliminary design
35	Below 100	0.11	0.15
110	Below 100	0.17	0.24
220	Below 100	0.22	0.31
330	Below 100	0.24	0.34
	100 ~ 300	0.13	0.19
	Over 300	0.10	0.13
500	Below 100	0.34	0.49
	100 ~ 300	0.18	0.26
	Over 300	0.12	0.17
750	Below 100	0.50	0.70
	100 ~ 300	0.29	0.42
	Over 300	0.19	0.27

Note 1: For same tower double-circuit line projects (sections), it shall be multiplied by the coefficient 1.8.
Note 2: For line projects (sections) with ice coating in 20mm and above, it shall be multiplied by the coefficient 1.3. Note 3: Where the design wind speed exceeds 35m/s, it shall be multiplied by the coefficient 1.1.
Note 4: For DC power transmission line projects, it shall be multiplied by the coefficient 1.2.
Note 5: For 500kV adopting large section conductors in 630mm^2 and above, it shall be multiplied by the coefficient 1.2.
Note 6: Power transmission lines less than 5km long shall be calculated as 5km; the length of power transmission line shall be calculated as the total length of current voltage class of current period, and no segmented charging is allowed.

5. Post Evaluation Fee of the Project

Post evaluation fee of the project refers to the expenses paid by the project legal person for carrying out the comprehensive analysis and evaluation of the project's decision-making, design, construction management, investment benefits and other aspects in accordance with

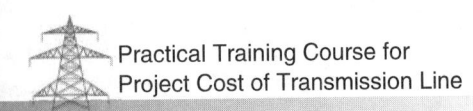

the related provisions of national administration authority in order to provide scientific and reliable basis to the project's decision-making, guide and improve the project management, improve the investment benefits, and meanwhile provide reference basis to the government's decision-making.

The equation for calculation is: Post evaluation fee of the project

$$= \text{cost of installation works} \times \text{rate} \qquad (2\text{-}4\text{-}50)$$

Rate standard: 0.5% for power transmission and transformation projects in 220kV and below, and 0.35% for power transmission and transformation projects in 330kV and below. In actual process, it is the investment decision-making organ of the project to decide whether the project requires a post evaluation.

6. Project Construction Supervision and Testing Fee

Project construction supervision and testing fee refers to the expenses incurred for supervising, inspecting and testing the project quality, environmental protection, water and soil conservation measures, and installation of special equipment (fire control facilities, elevator, pressure container, etc.) in accordance with the related provisions of national administration authority and power industry. The main fee items include project quality supervision and testing fee, special equipment safety supervision fee, environmental supervision and acceptance fee, water and soil conservation project acceptance and compensation fee and pile base testing fee.

The equation for calculation is:

Project construction supervision and testing fee = project quality supervision and testing fee + special equipment safety supervision fee + environmental supervision and acceptance fee + water and soil conservation project acceptance and compensation fee + pile base testing fee (2-4-51)

(1) Engineering quality supervision and testing fee

Project quality supervision and testing fee refers to the expenses incurred when the power project quality supervision organ authorized by the national administration authority carries out supervision, inspection and testing of the project quality in accordance with the related provisions of power industry.

The equation for calculation is:

Project quality supervision and testing fee = cost of installation works × rate (2-4-52)

Rate standard: 0.23% for overhead power transmission line projects, 0.35% for cable line projects, and 0.18% for system communication projects.

(2) Special equipment safety supervision fee

Special equipment safety supervision fee refers to the expenses incurred for authorizing special equipment inspection and testing institution to inspect and test the special equipment installed in the project in accordance with the provisions in Regulations on Supervision of Special Equipment Safety from the State Council.

Calculation standard: 30,000 Yuan/station for 500kV DC converter stations

(3) Environment supervision and acceptance cost

Environmental supervision and acceptance fee refers to the expenses incurred when the environment testing institution carries out the supervision and testing in the project construction stage and carries out the acceptance of the project's environmental protection facilities in accordance with the national laws and regulations related to environmental protection. Calculation standard: It shall be calculated based on the standard provided by administration authority of the province, municipality or direct-controlled municipality where the project is located.

(4) Acceptance and compensation cost for water and soil conservation projects

Water and soil conservation acceptance fee refers to the expenses incurred for the inspection and acceptance of the water and soil conservation facilities under a power project in accordance with the Soil and Water Conservation Law and its Regulations for the Implementation; water and soil conservation compensation refers to the expenses incurred in the compensation for the water and soil conservation facilities occupied or damaged by the power project, the destroyed landforms and vegetation, the reduced water and soil conservation function, and the control of water and soil erosion.

Calculation standard: It shall be calculated based on the standard provided by administration authority of the province, municipality or direct-controlled municipality where the project is located.

(5) Pile base testing fee

Pile base testing fee refers to the expenses incurred to the project legal person for organizing the testing of special pile bases used in special geological conditions as required by the project. The calculation standard shall be determined according to the actual situation of the project.

7. Administrative Fee for Formulation of Power Construction Standard

Administrative fee for formulation of power construction standard refers to the fee paid to the administrative department for the standardization of power industry in accordance with the related national provisions in order to guarantee the normal progress of the determination, preparation and management of various standards and specifications for power projects.

The equation for calculation is:

$$\text{Administrative fee for formulation of power construction standard} = (\text{survey fee} + \text{basic design fee}) \times 1.5\% \qquad (2\text{-}4\text{-}53)$$

8. Administrative Fee for Formulation of Power Project Quota

Administrative fee for formulation of power project quota refers to the fee paid to the administrative department for the project quota (cost) of power industry in accordance with the provisions of national administration authority in order to guarantee the normal progress of the determination, preparation and management of budget quota and labor quota for power project construction.

The equation for calculation is:

$$\text{Administrative fee for formulation of power project quota} = \text{cost of installation works} \times 0.12\% \qquad (2\text{-}4\text{-}54)$$

(Ⅳ) Subsystem Debugging and Whole Set Startup Commissioning Cost

Subsystem debugging and whole set startup commissioning cost includes the subsystem debugging and whole set startup commissioning cost and the construction enterprise cooperative commissioning cost.

The equation for calculation is:

$$\begin{aligned}&\text{Subsystem debugging and whole set startup commissioning cost}\\ &= \text{subsystem debugging} + \text{whole set startup commissioning cost}\\ &+ \text{construction enterprise cooperative commissioning cost} \end{aligned} \qquad (2\text{-}4\text{-}55)$$

1. Subsystem Debugging Cost

Subsystem debugging cost refers to the expense incurred for carrying out the system simultaneous debugging after the process system is installed. The calculation standard shall be subject to the debugging quota of power industry.

2. Whole Set Startup Commissioning Cost

Whole set startup commissioning cost refers to the expense incurred for carrying out the startup commissioning of the whole set before the power transmission and transformation project is put into operation. The calculation standard shall be subject to the debugging quota of power industry.

3. Construction Enterprise Cooperative Commissioning Cost

Construction enterprise cooperative commissioning cost refers to the expense incurred for the commissioning under the cooperation from the construction enterprise based on the specialty in the whole set startup commissioning stage of power transmission and transformation projects.

The equation for calculation is:

$$\text{Construction enterprise cooperative commissioning cost} = \text{cost of installation works} \times \text{rate} \qquad (2\text{-}4\text{-}56)$$

The rate is shown in Table 2-4-31.

Table 2-4-31 Rate of Construction Enterprise Cooperative Commissioning Cost

Voltage level (kV)	110 and below	220	330	500	750
Rate%		0.17		0.13	

Note 1: This expense will not be listed for overhead line projects in 35kV and below.
Note 2: This expense will not be listed for cable line projects, communication projects and optical cable projects.

(V) Production Preparation Cost

Production preparation cost refers to the expenses incurred for providing the technical assurance and resource allocation in order to guarantee the normal production and operation after the completion and acceptance of a project, including management vehicle acquisition expenses, tools and instruments and office furniture acquisition expenses, production staff training and in-advance entry expenses.

1. Management Vehicle Acquisition Expenses

Management vehicle acquisition expenses refer to the expenses for acquiring the vehicles necessary for production conducted by the production and operation unit, including the original cost of vehicle, freight and miscellaneous charges and vehicle surcharges.

The equation for calculation is:

Management vehicle acquisition expenses = cost of installation works × rate % (2-4-57)

The rate is shown in Table 2-4-32.

Table 2-4-32 Rate of Management Vehicle Acquisition Expenses

	Voltage level (kV)	110 and below	220	330	500	750
Rate%	Overhead line works	0.25			0.20	
	Cable route works	1.35				

The exact type and quantity of vehicle to be purchased shall be checked and ratified by the budget review unit within the investment scope determined by above calculation standard, and shall be specified in the budget statement.

2. Tools And Instruments and Office Furniture Acquisition Expenses

Tools and instruments and office furniture acquisition expenses refer to the expenses for purchasing the necessary furniture, tools, sign boards, warning boards, marking piles, etc. to meet the production, living and management needs in the preliminary stage of power projects.

The equation for calculation is:

$$\text{Tools and instruments and office furniture acquisition expenses} = \text{cost of installation works} \times \text{rate \%} \qquad (2\text{-}4\text{-}58)$$

The rate is shown in Table 2-4-33.

3. Production Staff Training and in-advance Entry Expenses

Production staff training and in-advance entry expenses refer to the expenses incurred to delivering training to the production and management personnel and entering the site in advance for production preparation in order to guarantee the normal production and operation of a power project, including the cost for training to trainees and personnel entering the site in advance, basic wage, wage subsidies, supplementary wage, employee benefits, labor protection fees, endowment insurance expense, unemployment insurance expense, medical insurance expense, business travel expenses, information fee, heating fee, education expenditure, labor union expenditure, etc.

Table 2–4–33　Rate of Tools and Instruments and Office Furniture Acquisition Expenses

	Voltage level (kV)	110 and below	220	330	500	750
Rate%	Overhead line works	0.21		0.15		0.11
	Cable route works			1.07		

The equation for calculation is:

$$\text{Production staff training and in-advance entry expenses} = \text{cost of installation works} \times \text{rate \%} \quad (2\text{-}4\text{-}59)$$

The rate is shown in Table 2-4-21.

Table 2–4–34　Rate of Production Staff Training and In-advance Entry Expenses

Voltage level (kV)	110 and below	220	330	500	750
Rate%	0.10		0.08		0.06

(Ⅵ) Heavy-cargo Transportation Measure Cost

Heavy-cargo transportation measure cost refers to the measure costs incurred for the reinforcement and reconstruction of roads and bridges and the relocation of obstacles during the transportation of large-scale power equipment.

The calculation standard shall be subject to the actual conditions of transportation and the transportation scheme.

(Ⅶ) Basic Reserve Cost

Basic reserve cost refers to the cost increased due to design change (including the increase or decrease of quantities, equipment modification, material substitution, etc., and the project construction fund reserved for the possible loss caused by general natural disasters and other uncertainties.

The equation for calculation is:

$$\text{Basic reserve cost} = [\text{cost of installation works} + \text{other costs (excluding basic reserve cost)}] \times \text{rate} \quad (2\text{-}4\text{-}60)$$

The rate is shown in Table 2-4-22.

Table 2–4–35 Rate of Basic Reserve Cost

Design stage	Rate%	
	220KV and below	330kV and above
Feasibility study estimation	4	3
Preliminary design budget estimate	2.5	2
Construction drawing budget	1.0	1.0

The calculation base figure for basic reserve cost includes the price difference in the year of preparation.

(VIII) Dynamic Cost

Dynamic cost refers to the cost incurred by price increase and capital cost increase caused by time and market price change during the period from the year of construction budget preparation to completion acceptance of various construction cost elements, mainly including reserve cost for price difference and interest for loans during construction.

The equation for calculation is:

$$\text{Dynamic cost} = \text{reserve cost for price difference} + \text{interest for loans during construction} \quad (2\text{-}4\text{-}61)$$

1. Reserve Cost for Price Difference

Reserve cost for price difference refers to the cost predicted and reserved for the change in project cost caused by change in price and other factors during the construction period of the construction project.

The equation for calculation is:

$$C = \sum_{i=1}^{n_2} F_i \left[(1+e)^{n_1+i-1} - 1 \right] \quad (2\text{-}4\text{-}62)$$

In the equation, C denotes the reserve cost for price difference; e denotes the annual cost rising index; n_1 denotes the time interval between the level year of the construction budget preparation and the year of project commencement, unit: year; i denotes the ith year from the year of commencement; n_2 denotes the period of project construction, unit: year; F_i denotes the project construction capital input in the ith year.

Note: The annual cost rising index shall be subject to the related provisions of the general administrative department of the State Council and the competent authority of power industry.

2. Interest for Loans During Construction

Interest for loans during construction refers to the interests incurred during the construction period for raising debt capital and accounted into the original value of fixed assets after the project is put into production as allowed by the related provisions.

The equation for calculation is:

$$\text{Interest for loans during construction} = (\text{year opening amount of accumulated principal and interest} + \text{loan of that year}/2) \times \text{annual interest rate} \quad (2\text{-}4\text{-}63)$$

Note: The amount of loan shall be determined on the basis of the annual capital use plan of the project. The annual interest rate shall be calculated according to the annual interest rate converted from the actual (on yearly or monthly basis) settlement interest rate. See Table 2-4-36 and 2-4-37 for the calculation example for dynamic cost.

Table 2-4-36 Example for Calculation of Reserve Cost for Price Difference

S/N	Item	Level Year of Preparation	Year of Commencement	Construction Period			Total price difference	Remarks
		2006	2009	Year 1 (2009)	Year 2 (2010)	Year 3 (2011)		
1	Amount of static investment in the year of preparation ('0,000 Yuan)	A						
2	Input proportion of construction capital%			B1	B2	B3		Annual cost rising index: e
3	Amount of construction capital input ('0,000 Yuan)			$F1=A \times B_1/100$	$F2=A \times B_2/100$	$F3=A \times B_3/100$		
4	Annual cost rising index%			e	e	e		
5	Amount of annual price difference ('0,000 Yuan)			$E=F \times [(1+e)^{2+1-1}-1]$	$E=F \times [(1+e)^{2+2-1}-1]$	$E=F \times [(1+e)^{2+3-1}-1]$	$E_1+E_2+E_3$	
6	Reserve cost for price difference ('0,000 Yuan)						$E_1+E_2+E_3$	

Note: 1. It is planned to commence in 2009, and the time interval is two years (2007/2008), so $n_1=2$.
2. The years above refer to calendar year.

Study Program II Preparation of Preliminary Budget Estimate for 220kV Overhead Transmission Line Project

Table 2-4-37 Example for Calculation of Interest for Loans during Construction

S/N	Item	Year of Commencement	Construction Period				Remarks
		2007	Year 1	Year 2	Year 3	Total interest	
1	Amount of static investment in the year of preparation + reserve cost for price difference ('0,000 Yuan)	A					
2	Registered capital ('0,000 Yuan)	B					Capital ratio 20%
3	Amount of loan ('0,000 Yuan)	A−B					
4	Annual loan proportion %		E_1	E_2	E_3		Adjustment of capital input mode
5	Annual loan amount ('0,000 Yuan)		$F_1=(A-B)\times E_1/100$	$F_1=(A-B)\times E_2/100$	$F_1=(A-B)\times E_3/100$		
6	Actual loan interest rate %	R					Annual nominal interest rate r=7% Actual interest rate settled on quarterly basis r=7.186%
7	Annual loan interest ('0,000 Yuan)		$L_1=(F_1/2)\times R/100$	$L_2=(D_1+F_2/2)\times R/100$	$L_3=(D_2+F_3/2)\times R/100$	$L_1+L_2+L_3$	
8	Accumulated loan principal and interest ('0,000 Yuan)		$D_1=F_1+L_1$	$D_2=D_1+F_2+L_2$			

Note: 1. In this table, the year of commencement is considered as the year of budget estimate preparation, and it can be taken as the beginning year of interest calculation as the level year of budget estimate is actually the year before the calendar year of budget estimate preparation.
2. Above years refer to period year, namely every 12 months after the commencement of project are considered as one year.
3. Calculation of actual interest rate: $(1+r/4)^4-1 = (1+7\%/4)^4-1=7.186\%$

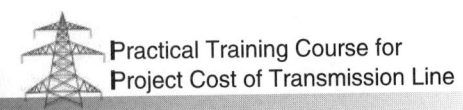

(IX) Budget Estimate for Other Costs of Project Case 2

1. Budget Estimate of Other Costs

See Table 2-4-38 for the budget estimate for other costs of project case

2. Instructions for Charge Calculation

In other costs, the charge calculation of those costs expressly specified in the "Budget Regulations" shall be subject to the charge base and rate as specified; the construction site acquisition and cleaning-up cost, project insurance expense under project construction administrative cost, survey and design fee under project construction technical service cost and other project costs not covered by the list of other costs in the "Budget Regulations" (such as the crossing measure cost of this project case) must, according to the actual situation of the project, be calculated as per the related laws, regulations, and standards provided by the national administration authority and the people's government of the province (municipality, and direct-controlled municipality), or be determined based on the price in the agreement (contract) signed between the owner and the related units, or be determined with reference of the similar projects. Next, the calculation of construction site acquisition and cleaning-up cost is introduced as below.

(1) Construction site acquisition and cleaning-up cost

1) Land acquisition fee The land acquisition fee for power transmission line projects refers to the related costs for acquisition of land area occupied by poles and towers. The land acquisition fee for auxiliary facility projects shall be accounted into the cost of auxiliary facility works. Only iron tower is used in this project case. Principle for the calculation of occupied area of iron towers: In normal cases, the area shall be calculated by adding 1m more out of each side of the outer edge of base column. In case of ancillary facilities such as retaining wall, excavation of earthwork, slope protection, drainage groove and so on, the land acquisition shall be subject to the actually occupied area.

Iron tower is divided into two types according to the section shape: square and rectangle, which are known as square tower and flat tower for short. The equation for calculation of iron tower's occupied area is as below.

① Square tower

Study Program II Preparation of Preliminary Budget Estimate for 220kV Overhead Transmission Line Project

$$(A+2B)^2 \qquad (2\text{-}4\text{-}64)$$

In the equation, A denotes the foot distance of the iron tower; B=b/2+1; B denotes the width of concrete base column.

② Flat tower

$$(A+2B)\times(C+2B) \qquad (2\text{-}4\text{-}65)$$

A and C denote the foot distance of front side of the iron tower respectively; B denotes the same as above.

③ Illustration.

An iron tower adopts LZG2026 base as its foot A, B, C and D, and square layout. The foot distance of the iron tower is 4.372m. The base column is in 600×600 square cross section. Its occupied area is calculated as

$$[4.372+2\times(0.6\div2+1)]^2 = 48.61 \ (m^2)$$

An iron tower adopts LZG2333 base as its foot A, B, C and D, and square layout. The foot distance of the iron tower's front side is 6.166×5.036m. The base column is in 600×600 square cross section. Its occupied area is calculated as

$$[6.166+2\times(0.6\div2+1)]\times[5.036+2\times(0.6\div2+1)] = 66.94 \ (m^2)$$

④ About the occupied area of concrete pole Principle for calculation of the occupied area of concrete pole, where no pull wire single pole is knocked out, it shall extend the outer edge of pole foot by 2m in all directions; where pull wire single pole is knocked out, it shall extend the outer edge of pole foot by 2m in all directions, and extend the pull wire by 1m in all directions from the position centered by the ground point of pull wire; where no pull wire double poles are knocked out, it shall extend by 2m in all directions from the transverse line direction, and where pull wire double poles are knocked out, the occupied area of pull wire shall be added (extending by 1m in all directions from the point centered by the ground point of pull wire).

The value of concrete pole's occupied area calculated as per above principle is relatively small, and the land acquisition for the occupied area of concrete pole is not taken into account in actual project. In accordance with the provisions from competent department of power industry, only appropriate compensation (800~1000 Yuan/base, including pull wire) is calculated and included.

2) Construction site rental

This project case has no traction and tensioning site. The related compensation for tower assembling site shall be accounted into the compensation for young crops. Only the expenses for purchase of grass seeds for vegetation restoration are included here, whose current local market price is 200 Yuan/kg.

3) Relocation compensation

In this project case, 1km of 10kV power line will be relocated and reconstructed, with the standard for compensation at 100,000 Yuan/km according to the provisions from the competent department of power industry; 2km of 220/380V low voltage line will be relocated and reconstructed, with the standard for compensation at 30,000 Yuan/km.

4) Waste cleaning cost

It shall be subject to the standard provided by the construction committee (demolition and relocation office) under the local government of the place where the project is located. The cost for this project case is included in the housing demolition costs, and will not be calculated and listed separately.

5) Power transmission line corridor compensation

① Compensation for young crops

Compensation for young crops is an important component of the power transmission line corridor compensation, which is related to the vital interests of residents along the route of the line project. Compensation for young crops includes the compensation for the young crops destroyed due to the transportation of main materials and stacking of sand and stones, the assembly and erection of pole and tower, the process of paying-off and stringing of conductor and lightning wire, and other factors.

As shown in equation 2-2-1, the equation for calculation of the area of compensation for young crops is

$$S = L \times A \times (1-B) \div 667 \qquad (2\text{-}4\text{-}66)$$

S denotes the area of compensation for young crops, unit: mu; L denotes the line length, unit: m; A denotes the width of the corridor included in the compensation for young crops, 3m for 35kV, 4.5m for 110kV, 6m for 220kV, 7m for 330kV, 8m for 500kV; B denotes the proportion of the sections without young crops along the line (such as railway, highway, forest area, orchard, and tea land) in total length of the line.

In this project case, the sections without young crops accounts for 40% of the total length of the line. With reference of similar projects, the unit price of compensation is 2.5 Yuan/m².

② Compensation for deforestation

According to the type and quantity of deforestation, it is divided into forest area and scattered woods, or national forest park, protective forest belt, timber forest and primitive forest. This project case contains two types: fruit trees (mainly orange trees), coniferae trees and other trees. The standard provided by the forestry bureau under the local government of the place where the project is located is normally low, and cannot be timely adjusted according to the market price. It is actual subject to the price as agreed with the tree owners. With reference of recent similar projects, the standard for compensation is 120 Yuan/tree/year for fruit trees with 3 years of compensation period, and 50 Yuan/tree for coniferae trees and other trees.

③ Housing relocation compensation

As required by the competent department of local industry, buildings within 2.5m around the vertical projection of the side boundary of 220kV overhead line project shall be relocated. The design personnel shall measure and prepare the "housing relocation card", and make statistics of the housing relocation quantity; the standard is 420 Yuan/m² as specified by the construction committee (demolition and relocation office) under the local government of the project place.

6) Measure cost for communication facility against interference from power transmission line

In this project case, 1.5km of communication line will be relocated and reconstructed, and the price as agreed with the ownership unit is 15,000 Yuan/km.

(2) Construction management cost of the project

1) As shown in Table 2-4-26, the rate of construction project legal person administrative cost for overhead line projects in 220kV and below is 1.35%;

2) As shown in Table 2-4-27, the rate of construction project legal person administrative cost for overhead line projects in 330kV and below is 0.45%;

3) As shown in Table 2-4-28, 220kV overhead line projects take flat ground and hill as the standard terrain. The project supervision cost is 10,000 Yuan/km, and is multiplied by the coefficient 1.1 for mountain land. The terrain proportion of this project case is: 7.4% flat

ground, 51.4% hill, 41.2% mountain land. Therefore, the standard for project supervision cost is

$$1\times(7.4\%+51.4\%)+1.1\times1\times41.2\%=1.0412 \text{ (Yuan/km)}$$

4) Project insurance cost

The project insurance cost shall be subject to the price as agreed with the insurance company according to the requirements of the project legal person and the actual situation of the project. For this project case, the cost is calculated and included with reference of similar projects, and is paid from the basic reserve cost.

(3) Technical service cost for project construction

1) Project preliminary work fees Project preliminary work fees include the project preliminary work fees in the feasibility study stage and the project preliminary work fees in the design stage. The project preliminary work fees in preliminary design stage shall be calculated and listed according to the various agreed fees signed between the project legal person and the related units, and the various fees listed in the book may be taken as the base figures for calculation.

① As shown in Table 2-4-29, the rate of project preliminary work fees in feasibility study stage is 11.2%.

② The preliminary engineering report fees for the project shall be subject to the "Tentative Standard for Preliminary Work Fees for Power Transmission and Transformation Projects (CDJ [2007] No. 436 Document)" issued by the competent department of power industry. The preliminary engineering report fees for the project include the preparation and review fee for approval special reports, and the preparation and review fee for other special reports.

The preparation and review fee for approval special reports include the environmental impact report and assessment fee, water and soil conservation special report preparation and review fee, and land preliminary review fee; the preparation and review fee for other special reports include the preparation and review fee for other special reports, mineral covering evaluation fee, geological hazard evaluation fee, cultural relics evaluation fee, fee for feasibility report of proposed forestland (forestland survey fee), etc. See Table 2-4-38 for more details which are omitted due to space limitation.

2) Intellectual property rights transfer cost and research and test fee are not included in

this project case.

3) Survey and design fee

The survey and design fee shall be calculated in accordance with the charging standard for engineering survey and design issued by the national administrative department. Currently, the "Administrative Regulations on Charges of Engineering Survey and Design (JJG [2002] No. 10)" prevails. The survey and design fee calculated as per such standard may be used as the base figures, and the actual amount shall be calculated and included subject to the tendering price of the project survey and design. The base figures for survey and design fee calculated according to the actual situation of this project case are listed in the book. See Table 2-4-38 for more details which are omitted due to space limitation.

4) Design document review fee

As shown in Table 2-4-30, the standards for the feasibility study design document review fee and preliminary design document review fee for 220kV overhead line projects are 2,200 Yuan/km and 3,100 Yuan/km respectively.

5) According to the Budget Standard, the rate of post evaluation fee for 220kV overhead line projects is 0.5%.

6) Project construction supervision and testing fee

① According to the Budget Standard, the rate of project quality supervision and testing fee for this project case is 0.23%.

② The environmental supervision and acceptance fee shall be subject to the "Notification on Related Issues for Standardizing the Environmental Impact Consulting Charges (JJG [2002] No. 125)". The water and soil conservation project acceptance and compensation fee shall be subject to the "Guiding Opinions on the Calculation and Inclusion of Water and Soil Conservation Consulting Charges for Development and Construction Projects (BJ [2005] No. 22)". The base figures for charging shall be calculated according to the standards provided by the administration under the local government of the project place and the competent department of power industry. The actual charges shall be subject to the "Service Contract (Agreement)" with the consulting and appraisal agency with related qualification. As no contract (agreement) is signed with related testing institution in the budget preparation stage, so the charges may be calculated and included with reference of the similar projects, and are not calculated and included in this book.

7) According to the Budget Standard, the rate of administrative fee for formulation of power construction standard for this project case is 1.5%.

8) According to the Budget Standard, the rate of administrative fee for formulation of power project quota for this project case is 0.12%.

(4) Subsystem debugging and whole set startup commissioning cost

It shall be subject to the commissioning quota for power industry. No subsystem debugging cost is included in this project case, but the whole set startup commissioning cost is included.

As shown in Table 2-4-31, the rate of construction enterprise cooperative commissioning cost for 220kV overhead line projects is 0.17%.

(5) Production preparation cost

As shown in Tables 2-4-32, 2-4-33 and 2-4-34, for 220kV overhead line projects, the rate of management vehicle acquisition expenses is 0.25%, the rate of tools and instruments and office furniture acquisition expenses is 0.21%, and the rate of production staff training and in-advance entry fee is 0.10%.

(6) Other project fee

Other project fees refers to the other fees for the project not included in the list of other costs in the Budget Standard, such as the cost for other necessary measures taken in the live crossing of power line, railway, highway, and river, but not included in the installation costs, or the costs for other items increased as required by the owner.

The measure cost related to live crossing of power line and crossing Jialing River is included in this project case, and shall be subject to the content shown in Table 2-4-11 or according to the provisions of the competent department of power industry. See Table 2-4-38 for more details which is omitted due to space limitation.

(7) Price different in the year of preparation

The material and equipment price adjustment shall be subject to the "Notification on Issuing the Price Level Adjustment Coefficients for Project Budget Quota in Sichuan Region (CDDZ [2008] No. 6] as provided by the competent department of power industry. The coefficient for the quota of material and equipment price adjustment for 220kV overhead line projects is 22.90%.

The price difference of installation materials shall be calculated and included as the current local installation materials consumed by the project case

(8) Basic reserve cost

As shown in Table 2-4-35, the rate of basic reserve cost in preliminary design stage for overhead line projects in 220kV and below is 2.5%.

(9) Dynamic cost

The reserve cost for price difference is not calculated and included as this project case has a very short time difference from the design to construction stage and a short construction period. The interest for loans during construction shall be calculated and included subject to the amount actually incurred to the project, which is calculated and included for the project case with reference of similar projects.

VI. Preparation of General Construction Estimate Sheet

The General Construction Estimate Sheet is shown as Table 2-4-39.

The general construction estimate sheet for overhead power transmission line project is concluded by summarizing the data in General Construction Estimate Sheet for installation work cost (Table II-B), Budget Estimate for auxiliary facility works (Table III-E), Budget Estimate for other costs (Table IV) and then filling the summarized data in Table 2-4-39 (Table I-B).

Table 2-4-38 Other Costs

Table IV

S/N	Project cost description	Preparation Basis and Calculation Notes			Total price (Yuan)
I	Construction site acquisition and cleaning-up costs				14647460
1	Land acquisition fee	Standard provided by the local government of the project place: 180,000 Yuan/mu	22.59 mu	180,000 Yuan/mu	4066200
2	Construction site rental	Purchase of grass seeds for vegetation restoration	40kg	200 Yuan/kg	8000
3	Relocation compensation				160000
3.1	Cost for reconstruction of 10kV line		1km	100,000 Yuan/km	100000
3.2	Cost for reconstruction of low voltage line		2km	30,000 Yuan/km	60000
4	Waste cleaning cost				
5	Power transmission line corridor compensation				10368260
5.1	Compensation for cutting of fruit trees		350 trees	120 Yuan / tree · year * 3 years	126000
5.2	Compensation for cutting of coniferae trees and other trees		(21000+7000) trees	50 Yuan / tree	1400000
5.3	Fee for compensation for young crops		51800m*6m	2.5 Yuan / m²* 60%	466200
5.4	Housing relocation compensation		19943m²	420 Yuan / m²	8376060

Study Program II Preparation of Preliminary Budget Estimate for 220kV Overhead Transmission Line Project

Table (Cont'd)

S/N	Project cost description	Preparation Basis and Calculation Notes			Total price (Yuan)
6	Measure cost for communication facility against interference from power transmission line	Reconstruction of communication line	1.5km	×	30,000 Yuan/km	45000
II	Construction management cost of the project					1169631
1	Construction project legal person administrative cost	Cost of installation works × rate	35016103	×	1.35%	472717
2	Bidding cost	Cost of installation works × rate	35016103	×	0.45%	157572
3	Engineering supervision fee	Standard for Budget Preparation and Calculation of Grid Project Construction (2007 Version)	51.8km	×	1.0412 10,000 Yuan/km	539342
4	Project insurance cost	Calculated and included with reference of similar projects, and paid from the basic reserve cost				
III	Technical service cost for project construction					3009834
1	Preliminary work fees for the project					481600
1.1	Preliminary work fees for the project	(Survey fee + basic design fee) × rate	1675719	×	11.20%	187680
1.2	Project preliminary engineering report fee					293920

Table (Cont'd)

S/N	Project cost description	Preparation Basis and Calculation Notes			Total price (Yuan)
1.2.1	Preparation and review fee for approval special reports	Tentative Standard for Preliminary Work Fees for Power Transmission and Transformation Projects (CDJ [2007] No. 436 Document)			169600
1.2.1.1	Environmental impact report and assessment fee	40,000 Yuan for 20km or below, and 1,200 Yuan/km for the exceeding part over 20km	51.8km		78160
1.2.1.2	Preparation and review fee for water and soil conservation special report		51.8km	×	800 Yuan/km	41440
1.2.1.3	Land preliminary review fee		50,000 Yuan			50000
1.2.2	Preparation and review fee for other special reports	Tentative Standard for Preliminary Work Fees for Power Transmission and Transformation Projects CDJ [2007] No. 436 Document			124320
1.2.2.1	Mineral covering evaluation fee		51.8km	×	1,000 Yuan/km	51800
1.2.2.2	Geological disaster assessment fee		51.8km	×	1,000 Yuan/km	51800
1.2.2.3	Cultural relics evaluation fee		51.8km	×	400 Yuan/km	20720
1.2.2.4	Fee for feasibility report of proposed forestland (forestland survey fee)	To be determined according to the actual situation of the project	60,000 Yuan		
2	Intellectual property rights transfer cost and research and test fee	None			0

Study Program II Preparation of Preliminary Budget Estimate for 220kV Overhead Transmission Line Project

Table (Cont'd)

S/N	Project cost description	Preparation Basis and Calculation Notes				Total price (Yuan)
3	Survey and design fee					1930921
3.1	Surveying cost	To be calculated based on the charging standard for engineering survey and design issued by national administrative department	51.8km	×	2469.66	Yuan/km	257929
3.2	Design fee					1672992
3.2.1	Basic design fee	To be calculated based on the charging standard for engineering survey and design issued by national administrative department	35016103	×	1.2		1417790
3.2.2	Fee for preparation of construction drawing budget	To be calculated based on the charging standard for engineering survey and design issued by national administrative department	10.00%				141779
3.2.3	As-built drawing compilation expense	To be calculated based on the charging standard for engineering survey and design issued by national administrative department	8.00%				113423
4	Design document review fee	2007 Standard for Budget Preparation and Calculation of Grid Project Construction					274540

Table (Cont'd)

S/N	Project cost description	Preparation Basis and Calculation Notes			Total price (Yuan)
4.1	Feasibility study design document review fee		51.8km	× 2,200 Yuan/km	113960
4.2	Preliminary design document review fee		51.8km	× 3,100 Yuan/km	160580
5	Project post evaluation fee	Cost of installation works × rate	35016103	× 0.50%	175081
6	Project construction supervision and testing fee				80537
6.1	Engineering quality supervision and testing fee	Cost of installation works × rate	35016103	× 0.23%	80537
6.2	Environment supervision and acceptance cost				0
6.3	Acceptance and compensation cost for water and soil conservation projects	Tentative Standard for Preliminary Work Fees for Power Transmission and Transformation Projects (CDJ [2007] No. 436 Document)	? m²	× 0.8 Yuan/m²	0
7	Administrative fee for formulation of power construction standard	(Survey fee + basic design fee) × rate	1675719	× 1.50%	25136
8	Administrative fee for formulation of power project quota	Cost of installation works × rate	35016102.8	× 0.12%	42019
IV	Subsystem debugging and whole set startup commissioning cost				152839

Study Program II Preparation of Preliminary Budget Estimate for 220kV Overhead Transmission Line Project

Table (Cont'd)

S/N	Project cost description	Preparation Basis and Calculation Notes				Total price (Yuan)
1	Commissioning fees of the entire start-up	Subject to the Budget Quota of Electric Power Construction Project (Volume 6 Commissioning Standard Version 2006)	192 working days	×	270 Yuan/work day	*1.5* (1+0.2)	93312
2	Construction enterprise cooperative commissioning cost	Cost of installation works × rate	35016103	×	0.17%		59527
V	Production preparation cost						196090
1	Management vehicle acquisition expenses	Cost of installation works × rate	35016103	×	0.25%		87540
2	Tools and instruments and office furniture acquisition expenses	Cost of installation works × rate	35016103	×	0.21%		73534
3	Production staff training cost and cost for mobilization in advance	Cost of installation works × rate	35016103	×	0.10%		35016
VI	Crossing measure cost						344000
1	Measure cost for live crossing of power line						244000
	10kV		32 places	×	3500 Yuan/place		112000
	35kV		6 places	×	12,000 Yuan/place		72000
	110kV		3 places	×	20,000 Yuan/place		60000
2	Agreement cost and measure cost for crossing Jialing River		1 place	×	100,000 Yuan/place		100000
VII	Price different in the year of preparation						6750000
1	Material and equipment price adjustment		1598793	×	22.09%		353173

Practical Training Course for Project Cost of Transmission Line

Table (Cont'd)

S/N	Project cost description	Preparation Basis and Calculation Notes			Total price (Yuan)
2	Price difference of installation materials (tax included)	6396827			6396827
	Sub-total				19519855
VIII	Basic reserve cost	54535958	×	2.5%	1363399
	Total				20883254
IX	Dynamic cost				2005000
1	Reserve cost for price difference	Not calculated and included in this project case			0
2	Loan interest during construction period	2.005 million Yuan			2005000

Note 1: The basis for compilation and calculation as well as the necessary instruction for calculation method shall be clarified for each item of cost.

Note 2: This table applies to power transformation and power transmission projects.

Study Program II Preparation of Preliminary Budget Estimate for 220kV Overhead Transmission Line Project

Table 2-4-39 General Construction Estimate Sheet for Overhead Power Transmission Line Project

S/N	Name of project or expenses	Amount in '0,000 Yuan	Percentage occupation of each item over the total %	Unit investment in '0,000 Yuan/km
	Table I-B		51.8km	
I	Ontology engineering of overhead power transmission line	3434	53.52%	66.30
(I)	General line main works	3434		
(II)	Main large span works	0		
II	Auxiliary facilities works	23	0.36%	0.45
	Sub-total	3457		
III	Price different in the year of preparation	675	10.52%	13.03
IV	Other costs	2084	32.48%	40.24
	Wherein: 1. Construction site acquisition and cleaning-up costs	1465		
	2. Basic provisional sum	135		
	Static investment (Total of items I~IV)	6217		120.01
V	Dynamic cost	201	3.12%	3.87
(I)	Reserve cost for price difference	0		
(II)	Loan interest during construction period	201		
	Dynamic investment (Total of items I~V)	6417		123.88

Note: The amount in this table shall be in '0,000 Yuan except the unit investment without decimal, and the decimal shall be rounded off if any.

Task 5   Preparation Instructions for Budget Estimates

I. Contents and Requirements of Budget Estimate Preparation Instructions

The budget estimate preparation instructions are required to explain the key points of each item in the preparation of budget estimate for the project, and make contrastive analysis of the investment. It shall be brief and to the point with complete contents.

1. Content of Preparation Instructions

(1) Basis of design;

(2) Project overview;

(3) Principle of preparation;

(4) Method of preparation;

(5) Investment analysis.

2. Design Basis

Design basis refers to the approved design assignment and design order and their document number, name and related contents, such as the project name, nature of construction, planned construction period, investment source, and approved investment amount and so on.

3. Project Overview

The project overview gives brief introduction of following contents: start and end point of the line, number of single and double or multiple circuits, length of the line, voltage class, meteorological conditions, model of conductor and lightning wire, insulating mode of lightning wire, base number of poles and tower per km, class, model and quantity of poles and towers and their percentages in total quantity, class of base pit earthwork (stonework) and their percentages in total volume.

Study Program II Preparation of Preliminary Budget Estimate for 220kV Overhead Transmission Line Project

Overview of the physiognomy along the line, length and percentage of each type of terrain, transportation conditions, quantity and location of site warehouses, site transport mode and average load distance, length and percentage of each transportation terrain, etc.

4. Preparation Principle

Following important principles and basis are emphasized:

(1) Selection of quota and index;

(2) Basis for adjustment of installation cost in the budget estimate target;

(3) Basis for unit price and adjustment coefficient of labor cost;

(4) Basis for adjustment of priced materials and machinery one-shift costs;

(5) Determination and basis for the price of installation materials;

(6) Preparation basis for auxiliary facility works;

(7) Standard and basis for other costs;

(8) Other important principle issues. Special costs other than those specified, important principles for adjustment or modification of budget estimate, etc.

5. Preparation Method

(1) Basis for calculation of quantities;

(2) Method for adjustment and conversion out of the specified scope of quota (or index);

(3) Method for calculation of the costs for processing the special poles and towers with long span;

(4) Calculation method and source of special quantities and special costs;

(5) Other issues which have already be treated in the preparation;

(6) Problems still existing.

6. Investment Analysis

Brief economic analytic comparison and analysis shall be carried out for the budget estimate of project design.

(1) For budget estimate of preliminary design, generally a contrastive analysis shall be made with the total investment amount approved in the design assignment or project proposal and the investment amount of similar projects, or with the Typical Costs for Power Trans-

mission and Transformation Projects of State Grid Corporation of China (Version 2006), so as to present the rationality of this project's investment and the problems existing.

(2) In the approval budget estimate, the table of contrast analysis with the original budget estimate shall be presented with emphasis on the main reason for investment changes.

7. Filling of "Overview of Power Transmission Project and Main Technical and Economic Indicators" (Table V–C)

Table V-C shall be listed at last of the instructions. Refer to Table 2-4-40. It may be compared with similar project, to specify whether the material consumption index is advanced or not.

II. Budget Estimate Preparation Instructions for Project Case 2

(I) Project Profile

1. Start and end point of the line: From the outgoing line framework of 220kV substation (small number side) to incoming line framework of 220kV substation (big number side).

2. Length of the line: Totally 51.8km, 220kV single circuit (including same tower double-circuit design adopted for 3km of the outgoing line of the substation on small number side, with single side hanging for this phase).

3. Voltage class: 220kV

4. Mode of conductors: 2 × LGJ-400/35. Model of ground wires: GJX80, LB-GJ-100-30AC, and OPGW-100.

5. Poles and towers: Totally 137 iron towers are used for the whole line, including 86 tangent towers (accounting for 62.8%), and 51 resisting-tensile or angle towers (accounting for 37.2%).

6. Terrain classification

Terrain classification	Flat ground	Hill	Mountain land	High mountain	Steep mountain	Swamp
Scale	7.4%	51.4%	41.2%	/	/	/

7. Geology classification

Study Program II Preparation of Preliminary Budget Estimate for 220kV Overhead Transmission Line Project

Geology classification	Common soil	Hard soil	Light sand and stone	Rock	Muddy water	Quicksand
Scale	16%	/	55%	25%	4%	/

8. Meteorological conditions: Maximum wind speed: 25 (30) m/s; maximum design ice thickness of conductors: 5mm.

9. Site transport: 0.8km of labor load distance, and 28km of truck load distance.

10. The OPGW erection cost in included into the communication works.

(II) Presentation Basis

1. Power Construction Engineering Budget Norm – Book IV: Transmission Line Works (2006)

2. Standard for Budget Preparation and Calculation of Grid Project Construction issued in July, 2007.

3. User Guide to Power Construction Engineering Budget Norm – Book IV: Transmission Line Works (2006)

4. User Guide to Budget Preparation and Calculation Standard for Grid Engineering Construction

5. Notice on Printing and Issuing Budget Preparation and Calculation Procedure for Grid Engineering Construction in Sichuan (CDD (2008) No. 7

6. Adjustment to normed labor cost: upward adjustment coefficient 2.18%.

7. Upward adjustment of normed materials and machinery cost: The coefficient of material and equipment price adjustment for 220kV power transmission projects in Sichuan is 22.09%.

8. Interest for loans during construction: 2.005 million Yuan

9. Price of main materials

Unit: Yuan

S/N	Name	Model	Original price	Main price	Material price difference	Total price
1	Conductor	LGJ-400/35	/	16800	700	17500
4	Tower material	Angle steel tower	/	6800	2200	9000

10. Refer to design data for quantities of work.

11. The only item included in tower material substitution is site transport.

(Ⅲ) Economic Indicators

Project name	Main investment		Static investment		Dynamic investment	
	Fee amount	Unit investment	Fee amount	Unit investment	Fee amount	Unit investment
Unit	'0,000 Yuan	10,000 Yuan/km	'0,000 Yuan	10,000 Yuan/km	'0,000 Yuan	10,000 Yuan/km
Economic indicator	3434	66.30	6217	120.01	6417	123.88

See Table 2-4-40 for the overview of this project case and the main technical and economic indicators.

Study Program II Preparation of Preliminary Budget Estimate for 220kV Overhead Transmission Line Project

Table V-C

Table 2-4-40 Overview of Overhead Power Transmission Line Project and Main Technical Economic Indicators

	Starting point: A220kV substation	Ending point: B220kV substation	Voltage class 220kV	Transmission capacity MVA		Altitude: 300~600m	
	Total length converted into single circuit: 51.8km	Single-circuit: 51.8km	Double-circuit: 3km	Three-circuit: 0km	Four-circuit: 0km	Additional hanging conductor: 0km	
Project profile	Total number of poles and towers: 137	Weather conditions	Max air temperature: 40°C	Main ice coating mm	Terran distribution	Flat ground: 7.4%	Mountain land: 41.2%	Crossing area	Railway	Highway: 44 sites
	Line parameter		Min air temperature: -5°C	Max ice coating: 5mm		Hills: 51.4%	High mountain %		Expressway	River: 12
	Number of corners		Main wind speed m/s	Thunder days: 40d/a		River network %	Steep mountains %			
	Coefficient of tortuosity: 1.20		Max wind speed: 25 (30) m/s	Protective angle °		Mire %			HV line: 41 sites	LV line: 232 sites
	Pollution grade: II, III									

Table (Cont'd)

Engineering parameter	Conductor	Nameplate number: 2×LGJ-400/35	Number per phase: 2	Nameplate number: LB-GJ-100-30AC	Number: 1	Optical fiber cable	Nameplate number: OPGW-100	OPGW core 24	Number: 1	Pulling wire	Nameplate number	Number per group
		Nameplate number	Number per phase	Nameplate number: GJX-80	Number: 1		Nameplate number	Core	Quantity		Nameplate number	Number per group
	Pole and tower	137 angle towers		Including: Tangent towers bases, 62.8%		Resisting-tensile tower			51 bases, 37.2%			
		Number of steel pipe poles and towers		Including: number of steel pipe towers %		Steel pipe poles			Bases %			
		Number of concrete poles		Where: bases / %								
	Bases	Mass type	Site	Reinforced base	Plug-in type	Site	Excavating type	Site	Pile base	Site		
		base pit	Ordinary soil 4790.40m³	Loose sandstone 16, 466.40m³	Dry sand pit		Sump	m³	Mud pit 1198.80m³	Revetment 240m³	Drainage ditch 17.55m³	
		base surface	Ordinary soil 196m³	Loose sandstone 537m³	Dry sand pit		Sump	m³	Mud pit m³	Hard soil pit m³	Rock pit 483.20m³	
										Hard soil pit m³	Rock pit 196m³	
	Insulator hanging mode	Suspension string				V-shaped string			Strain insulator string		Jumper string	

· 612 ·

Study Program II Preparation of Preliminary Budget Estimate for 220kV Overhead Transmission Line Project

Table (Cont'd)

	Load distance			Labor load distance			Truck load distance 28km			Surplus earth load distance 0.15km	
Main technology economic indicators	Conductor	420.95t	8.13t/km	Steel pipe poles	t	t/km	Cement	845.79t	16.33t/km	Wire hanging armor clamps	119.71t	2.31t/km
	OPGW ground wire	t	t/km	Insertion materials	t	t/km	Sand	1139.23m³	21.99m³/km	Wire pulling armor clamps	t	t/km
	Steel stranded ground wire	32.2t	0.62t/km	base bolts	36.11t	0.70t/km	Gravel	2097.99m³	40.50m³/km	Spacer	Group	group/km
	Pulling wire	t	t/km	base steel	174.88t	3.38t/km	Porcelain insulator	6 pcs	0.12 pcs/km	Vibration damper	1726 pcs	33.32 pcs/km
	Angle steel tower	1173.32t	22.65t/km	Ground steel	20.32t	0.39t/km	Glass insulator	15,966 pcs	308.22 pcs/km	Friction reducer	t	t/km
	Steel tube tower	t	t/km	Cast-in-place concrete	2469.12 m³	47.67m³/km	Composite insulator	String	Strings/km	Precast concrete	m³	m³/km

Price of main materials

Conductor	16,800 Yuan/t	Tower material	6,800 Yuan/t	Porcelain insulator	80 Yuan/piece	Composite insulator	Yuan/string
Conductor	Yuan/t	base steel	3,500 Yuan/t	Glass insulator	85 Yuan/piece	OPGW24-core	24,000 Yuan/km

Task 6 Proofreading and Review of Budget Estimate for Power Transmission Line Project

I. Procedure for Proofreading and Review of Finished Productst

1. Self-proofreading before submission. The finished products must be self-proofread carefully with signature signed on the "Proofreading and Review Sheet", and shall be submitted together with the related raw data to the specified overall proofreader in the department (group) for overall proofreading and review.

2. Re-proofreading and preliminary review before sending out of the department (group). The finished products shall, after being proofread and reviewed by the overall proofreader, be submitted to the preparing person for first modification, and submitted to the department (group) leader for review upon being signed by the overall proofreader. The finished products shall, after being rated for quality grade, be returned to the preparing person for second modification, and then be sent out of the department (group) upon being checked and signed by the department (group) leader. During the proofreading and review, the proofreading and review sheet shall be filled level by level. The preparing person shall carefully modify according to the proofreading and review advice, and record the execution on the proofreading & review sheet.Difference in opinion if any shall be discussed with the proofreader, and be submitted to the superior level for discussion and solution in case of failure to reach consensus.

3. Recheck before sending out of office. Upon the comprehensive recheck by the engineer in charge (specialist engineer), the finished products shall be modified by the preparing person according to the recheck advice. Then, the recheck person shall rate the quality grade of the finished products and sign off for being sent out of office.

4. After being sent out of office, the finished products shall be submitted to the chief designer and chief engineer for review and approval level by level. After being signed for opin-

ion and being rated, the finished products shall be delivered for print and publication.

Upon above four steps of proofreading and review, the quality of preliminary budget can be improved, so as to prevent consumption of materials and capital due to over-estimate or no economic benefit to the builder due to under-estimate. The main purpose is to push the construction enterprise to improve its operation and management, improve the level of labor productivity, assure a reasonable profit to the construction enterprise, and have the base for sustainable development.

The main basis of proofreading and review includes the standard for preparation and calculation of construction budget for power grid projects, national unified budget quota for installation works, approved budget price of installation materials, local stipulated wage standards and calculation coefficient, price basis for using local materials, design drawings and instructions.

II. Outline of Proofreading and Review of Finished Products

1. Cover, Preparation Instructions and Project Overview

(1) Project name, code, index number, the consistency of voltage class with the design document;

(2) Design basis complete and correct or not, the employer specified or not, the builder and construction period; investment source specified or not, and investment amount limit;

(3) Line start and end point definite or not;

(4) Total length of the line, and the length in kilometers of single-circuit, double-circuit, double circuit with same tower respectively;

(5) Number of poles and towers, type, form, average number of poles and towers per kilometer and the percentage of each type of pole and tower in the total quantity;

(6) Specification and model of conductor and lightning wire, single conductor or bundled conductor, and insulating mode of lightning wire;

(7) Form and quantity of bases, and their percentage in total quantity;

(8) Classification of terrains along the line, length of each class and their percentages;

(9) Traffic conditions along the line: Convenient, normal or difficult; transport mode, terrain coefficient, and the calculation of average load distance correct or not;

(10) Earthwork: The calculation and classification are accurate or not, and the outward

transport for the surplus soil and earth borrowing for backfilling are required or not;

(11) Construction of base requires the consideration of construction water transportation and average load distance or not;

(12) The pole and tower works include the grounding works or not;

(13) Any normal crossing and special crossing or not, the crossing site, and any special ground wire or special pole and tower or base adopted or not;

(14) The quantity of insulator strings installed on accessories is correctly calculated or not.

2. Preparation Principle and Basis

(1) The principle for selection and use of quota is correct or not. Special attention shall be paid to the basis and calculation method for adjustment of labor wage for any error or not;

(2) The basis for budget price of main materials meets the specified usage scope and use method or not;

(3) Basis and method for the calculation of the cost of auxiliary facility works;

(4) Basis and method for the calculation of other works and costs;

(5) Determination and basis for special costs;

(6) The tentatively listed (estimated) costs are appropriate or not;

(7) The quota or index selected is investigated as stipulated according to the actual conditions of the project or not;

(8) The selected quota or index sub-items have any wrong item / missed item or not.

3. Quantities

(1) Specification and model of conductor or ground wire, unit weight and number of kilometers, total weight, and the loss is included as specified or not;

(2) The form and quantity of poles and tower are included in the loss as specified or not;

(3) The capping of concrete poles is calculated or not;

(4) Verification of the quantities of base, including the base steel materials, concrete quantity, specification and quantity of prefabricated bases;

(5) Bore diameter and pile length of cast-in-situ bored pile base, and whether its concrete amount is increased by the over-pouring amount as specified;

(6) The concrete amount of explosion expanded piling base is increased by the over-pouring amount as specified or not;

Study Program II Preparation of Preliminary Budget Estimate for 220kV Overhead Transmission Line Project

(7) The concrete amount of base protective cap is calculated or not;

(8) The design has taken into account the base bed, revetment, drainage (flood) ditch and other measures according to the terrain and geological conditions of the project or not;

(9) Wire hanging armor clamp and shakeproof armour clamp, verification of the specification and quantity of insulators, and the loss is included as specified or not;

(10) A counter weight is designed or not;

(11) Verification of grounding materials;

(12) Check of earthwork amount;

(13) Site transport quantity of main materials, loss and package weight included or not.

4. Verification of the Tables

5. Key Points of the Verification

(1) No missed item: main body, ancillary works, and various single-project works;

(2) Correctness of unit price selection;

(3) Correctness of quota (price list);

(4) Completeness of costs;

(5) No error in calculation; correctness of the integer of calculated data.

III. Technical and Economic Analysis

(I) Brief Introduction of Main Technical and Economic Indicators

Technical and economic analysis is the last step of the proofreading and review. Its purpose is to: clarify the amount of project investment, the economic rationality of cost allocation proportion, technical safety and reliability, judge the design quality and point out the problems existing. Grope the technology- and economy-related regularity of power transmission project, achieve the purpose of reasonable design layout, reliable technique, and economical and advanced cost.

The main technical and economic indicators of power transmission line projects are stated as below.

(1) Unit cost

$$\text{Unit cost of power transmission line (Yuan/km)} = \frac{\text{Total construction cost}}{\text{Straight length of the line}}$$

$$\text{Unit cost of line body (Yuan/km)} = \frac{\text{Construction cost of line body works}}{\text{Straight length of the line}}$$

(2) Unit cost of project in special design (Yuan/km) =
$$\frac{\text{Construction cost of projects in special design}}{\text{Line length of projects in special design}}$$

(3) Consumption of main materials: steel products, cement, conductor, lightning wire, etc.

(4) Coefficient of tortuosity (%) $= \dfrac{\text{Straight length of the line}}{\text{Air line distance between start and end point of the line}}$

(5) Coefficient of span utilization (%) $= \dfrac{\text{Mean span}}{\text{Calculated span}}$

Above economic and technical indicators are finally summarized in the "Overview of Power Transmission Project and Main Technical and Economic Indicators" (refer to Table 2-4-40) for analysis and comparison.

(Ⅱ) Technical and Economic Analysis of Project Case 2

To make technical and economic analysis on power transmission line projects, a contrastive analysis between the main technical and economic indicators of actual projects and the Control Indexes for Quota Design of Power Grid Projects or Typical Costs of Power Transmission and Transformation Projects of State Grid Corporation of China. In this book, the Control indicators for Quota Design of Power Grid Projects (Level in 2009) is selected for detailed analysis. See Table 2-4-41 for the contrastive analysis on the control indexes for quota design of 220kV power transmission project.

Table 2-4-41　Contrastive Analysis on Control Indexes for Quota Design of 220kV Power Transmission Project

Unit: '0,000 Yuan/km

S/N	Project name	Specification of conductor 2×LGL-400/35 (28.5m/s, 10mm)					Index of project case	
		Flat ground	Hill	River network and mire	Mountain land	High mountain	Calculation value	Actual value
1	Main works	45.68	48.59	53.76	58.00	65.82	52.25	66.30
	Including: materials	32.81	33.67	33.79	35.20	35.36	34.24	37.46
2	Others	22.39	22.91	25.28	25.63	27.92	23.99	57.59
	Including: price difference	2.44	2.60	2.92	3.23	3.42	2.85	13.03
	Total	68.07	71.50	79.04	83.63	93.74	76.24	123.88

Design meteorological condition of this project case: 5mm of ice coating, 25 (30) m/s of wind speed; terrain proportion: flat ground 7.4%, hills 51.4%, and mountain land 41.2%. According to the control indexes for quota design of $2 \times LGJ-400/35$ conductor of 220kV power transmission line under the standard condition with 28.5m/s of calculated wind speed and 10mm of ice coating, the control indicator for comprehensive quota design of this project case is calculated as below

$$68.07 \times 7.4\% + 71.50 \times 51.4\% + 83.63 \times 41.2\% = 76.24 \text{ (Yuan/km)}$$

Similarly, calculate the data of main works and other costs according to Table 2-4-39, and fill the corresponding data in Table 2-4-41.

With the same calculation method as Table 2-4-41, fill the corresponding data in Table 2-4-42, Contrastive Analysis on the Basic Technology Combined Scheme for Quota Design of 220kV Power Transmission Project.

Table 2-4-42 Contrastive Analysis on the Basic Technology Combined Scheme for Quota Design of 220kV Power Transmission Project

Wire model		2×LGL-400/35					Index of project case	
Ground wire type		GJ-80					Calculation value	Actual value
Number of poles and towers		3.2	3.2	3.2	2.4	2.2	2.87	2.64
Load distance	Labor (km)	0.3	0.6	0.7	0.9	1.3	0.70	0.80
	Vehicle (km)	25	25	25	25	25	25.00	28.00

With the same calculation method as Table 2-4-41, according to Table 2-4-40, fill the corresponding data in Table 2-4-43, Contrastive Analysis on Unit Kilometer Indexes for Main Materials of 220kV Power Transmission Project.

Table 2–4–43 Contrastive Analysis on Unit Kilometer Indexes for Main Materials of 220kV Power Transmission Project

Material name	Unit	Specification of conductor 2×LGL-400/35 (28.5m/s, 10mm)					Index of project case	
		Flat ground	Hill	River network and mire	Mountain land	High mountain	Calculation value	Actual value
Conductor	t	8.09	8.09	8.09	8.09	8.09	8.09	8.13
Ground Wire	t	1.26	1.26	1.26	1.26	1.26	1.26	0.62
Steel for pole and tower	t	15.52	16.59	15.52	19.40	19.73	17.67	22.65
'base steel	t	2.16	2.31	3.52	2.91	3.00	2.55	3.38
Wire hanging armor clamps	t	0.41	0.41	0.41	0.41	0.41	0.41	2.31
Grounding steel	t	0.19	0.19	0.19	0.19	0.19	0.19	0.39
Spacer	Group							
Vibration damper	Nos.	26.00	26.00	26.00	26.00	28.00	26.00	33.32
Insulator (conductor)	Piece	258.06	258.06	258.06	195.84	183.60	232.43	315.00
Cast-in-place concrete	m³	30.90	32.96	39.14	36.40	37.44	34.22	47.67
Cement	t	10.63	11.34	15.74	12.52	12.88	11.77	16.33
Medium sand	m³	14.21	15.16	16.92	16.74	17.22	15.74	21.99
Gravel	m³	26.27	28.02	32.36	30.94	31.82	29.09	40.50

The "calculated value" under the column "Index of project case" in Tables 2-4-41, 2-4-42, and 2-4-43 refers to the quota design index values of the project case according to the corresponding indicators in Control indicators for Quota Design of Power Grid Projects (Level in 2009) in combination with the actual conditions of the project case (terrain classification, reference conductor and ground wire mode and main design meteorological condition are mainly considered), and the "actual value" refer to the data of budget estimate for preliminary design of the project case. It can been seen by contrast that, the "unit kilometer indexes of main materials" for preliminary design of this project case are all higher than the control indicator for quota design, causing that the budget estimate target of preliminary design is also higher than the control indicator for quota design. The design scheme is not economical and advanced enough. It is required to implement strict review of the base and pole and tower design in the design part of the technical scheme, further improve and perfect the design scheme, so as to achieve a reliable and advanced technical scheme, and an economical and reasonable cost indicator.

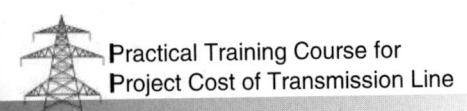

Summary

The study item II mainly takes the project case 2 as the carrier, and introduces the method for preparation of preliminary design budget statement of 220kV power transmission line: Firstly specify the division of works in power transmission line project and be familiar with its cost structure and calculation standard according to the Standard for Preparation ad Calculation of Power Grid Project Construction Budget (Version 2007); then implement the local charge standard by field data collection; check and calculate the quantities of each unit of the specific works by combining with the project's design situation; then select the applicable quota and rate to prepare the unit project budget estimate, summarize and form the budget estimate for installation works, and complete the preparation of budget estimate for auxiliary facility works and budget estimate for other costs; summarize and form the General Construction Estimate Sheet based on the Budget Estimate for installation works, budget estimate for auxiliary facility works and budget estimate for other costs; finally prepare the instructions for budget estimate. Thus determine the budget estimate for the preliminary design of 220kV power transmission line.

Study Program II Preparation of Preliminary Budget Estimate for 220kV Overhead Transmission Line Project

Practical Training Project II

Complete the budget statement for preliminary design according to the related data of preliminary design of project case 2; complete the budget statement for construction drawing design according to the data related to construction drawing design of the project case.

Review and Reflection

1. The terrain classification of a 110kV new line project is: flat ground 30%, hills 40%, and mountain land 30%. The site transport terrain is: flat ground 38%, hills 44%, mountain land 18%, and no consecutive curves on highways. Conclude the comprehensive terrain increment coefficient of each unit project.

2. The engineering terrain of a new power transmission line project is: flat ground 50%, mire 30%, hills 20%; the automobile transport terrain is: flat ground 80% and hills 20%. Please calculate the comprehensive terrain increment coefficient of following works: ① cast-in-situ concrete base; ② automobile transport; ③ installation of armor rod.

3. Try to calculate the earthwork amount of following bases in project case 2.

(1) An iron tower adopts straight flexible base LZG2230 as the four feet A, B, C and D of its base, the terrain is hill, and the geological conditions are: eluvial silty clay for 0~0.3m, and silty mudstone below 0.3m (in browny red or purplish red, strongly weathered, mostly damaged organizational structure, significantly changed mineral composition, fracture development and fractured rock mass). Excavation is carried out by manual digging.

LZG2230 base slab is in square 2.2×2.2m, and no formwork is erected and set on the pit bottom. The height of the base column of foot A, B, C and D exposed out of the ground is 0.2, 0.4, 0.6 and 1.2m respectively. Try to calculate the amount of earthwork excavation for such iron tower base.

(2) An iron tower adopts oblique column base YJG2539, YJG2539, XJG2747 and XJG2747 as the four feet A, B, C and D of its base, the terrain is mountain land, and the geo-

logical conditions are: mool for 0~0.5m, and silty mudstone below 0.5m (in browny red or purplish red, strongly weathered, mostly damaged organizational structure, significantly changed mineral composition, fracture development and fractured rock mass). The base surface of foot A and D is fallen off by 0.4 and 0.6m respectively, and the height of foot B and C exposed out of the ground is 0.2m. Excavation is carried out by manual digging. Try to calculate the amount of earthwork excavation for such iron tower base.

(3) An iron tower adopts excavated base TWG1630, TWG1837, TWG1733 and TWG1630 as the four feet A, B, C and D of its base, the terrain is hill, and the geological conditions are: eluvial silty clay for 0~0.4m, and silty mudstone below 0.4m (in browny red or purplish red, and strongly weathered). The height of TWG1837 and TWG1733 base slab and cone frustum part is same as TWG1630, and the height of foot B and C exposed out of ground is 1.0 and 0.6m respectively. Excavation is carried out by manual digging. Try to calculate the amount of earthwork excavation for such iron tower base.

4. An iron tower adopts XJG2742 base as its foot A, B, C and D, and square layout. The foot distance of the iron tower is 5.15m. The base column is in 800×800 square cross section. Try to calculate its occupied area.

5. An iron tower adopts TWG2035 base as its foot A, B, C and D, and rectangle layout. The foot distance of the iron tower's front side is 6.874×5.644m. The base column is in Φ 900 circular cross section. Try to calculate its occupied area.

6. Why the Budget Regulations in old version is still used for the budget of project construction during the initial period of the implementation of Budget Regulations in new version?

7. How are the related costs of line inspection station and maintenance station calculated and included? Try to illustrate.

8. How to calculate the installation materials for base works?

9. How to calculate the installation materials for pole and tower works?

10. How to calculate the installation materials for overhead conductor and ground wire installation works?

11. How to calculate the installation materials for accessory installation works?

12. How to determine the construction loss rate of OPGW optical fiber composite overhead ground wire?

Study Program II Preparation of Preliminary Budget Estimate for 220kV Overhead Transmission Line Project

13. The engineering terrain of a overhead power transmission line is classified as: flat ground 25%, hill 17%, mountain land 44%, and mire 14%. Try to calculate the construction loss rate of cement, sand, stone, and conductor.

14. Why the quantities in budget estimate is completely inconsistent with the "Summary of equipment and materials" in the design data?

15. How to determine the labor load distance in preliminary design stage?

16. How to determine the tax amount and tax rate of budget estimate for power transmission line project?

17. In budget estimate, how to determine the land acquisition fee?

18. What specific items of cost may be included in the power transmission line corridor compensation? How to determine the compensation for young crops?

19. Try to collect a project insurance contract, and explain the process of determining the project insurance cost in project construction administrative cost.

20. What specific items of cost may be included in the measure cost for communication facility against interference from power transmission line, and how to determine them?

21. Try to calculate the survey and design fee according to the conditions of this project case.

22. Give a brief description of the meaning of the existence of material and equipment price adjustment coefficient. How to use it in the preparation of budget estimate in preliminary design stage of line project?

23. How to calculate the clearance cost?

24. How to determine the environmental supervision and acceptance fee?

25. How to determine the water and soil conservation project acceptance fee and compensation?

Study Program III

Preparation for Construction Estimate of 500kV Power Transmission Line

Project Case III 500kV New Power Transmission Line Project

I. Project Overview

(I) This project is a 500kV power transmission line new construction project, with a 500kV substation (small side) - a 500kV substation (large side), in 99 kilometers long totally, and in the design of single-circuit line erection and 10mm of ice coating.

(II) Models of conductor and ground wire

1. Conductor

4×LGJ-400/50.

2. Ground Wire

LBGJ-100-40AC is adopted for about 10km of the incoming and outgoing line section of the substation on the small side, and LB-GJ-100-20AC is adopted for all remained parts, both of which are combined with OPGW to form the double ground wire. The investment in OPGW does not included in this estimate.

Study Program III Preparation for Construction Estimate of 500kV Power Transmission Line

II. Form and Quantity of Poles and Towers

See Table 3-0-1 for the form and quantity of poles and towers used in this project.

Table 3–0–1 Construction Project Breakdown

Project name	Line length	Qty of poles and towers	Resisting-tensile tower	Suspension tower	Tensile resisting ratio
10mm ice area	99km	222	44	178	19.82%

III. Main Economic Indicators

See Table 3-0-2 for the main economic indicators of the project.

Table 3–0–2 Main Economic Indicators

Project name	Cost of installation works ('0,000 Yuan)	Unit cost ('0,000 Yuan/km)
Main investment	14688	148.36
Other costs	6023	60.84
Including: Construction site acquisition and cleaning-up	2732	27.59
Basic reserve cost	662	6.69
Static investment	22492	227.19
Dynamic investment	23038	232.71

Task 1　Preparation of Investment Estimation Data

I. Concept of Investment Estimation

Investment estimation refers to, during the decision-making the project investment, the estimation of the amount investment (including the project cost and working fund) in construction project according to the existing data and specific method. Total amount of investment estimation refers to all construction costs from the project preparation, project construction to the completion for production, and the content it contains varies depending on the nature and scope of the project.

During the preliminary period of project decision-making, in the project proposal preparation and feasibility study report stage, investment estimation is an important component, one of the important economic indicators, and an important work link in the preliminary stage of construction from decision-making to the preliminary design.

II. Collection of Investment Estimation Data

The accuracy degree of investment estimation preparation is inseparable from the data collection in such stage, and the completion of main basis. The more specific, complete and detailed the data is, and the more sufficient and complete the basis is, the higher the accuracy of prepared investment estimation will be. The data collected for project case 3 are as below.

(1) The survey and design personnel of certain institute provide the data and field data collection. See Table 3-1-1, 3-1-2, 3-1-3 and 3-1-4 for the related data.

Table 3-1-1　Classification of Terrain along the Line

Project name	Hill	Mountain land	High mountain
Whole line	15.00%	50.00%	35.00%

Study Program III Preparation for Construction Estimate of 500kV Power Transmission Line

Table 3–1–2 Classification of Soil Property along the Line

Project name	Common soil	Hard soil	Loose sandstone	Rock	Muddy water
Whole line	10.00%	10.00%	42.00%	35.00%	3.00%

Table 3–1–3 Site Transport

Project name	Labor load distance (km)			Load distance of vehicle (km)	
	Main materials	Rubble	Water	Sandstone	Other materials
10mm ice area	1.00	1.00	1.00	25.00	25.00

Table 3–1–3 Indexes of Main Materials or Quantities

S/N	Project name	Unit	Index per kilometer of the project				
			Whole line	10mm ice area	15mm ice area	20mm ice area	30mm ice area
1	Line length	km	99.00	99.00			
2	Speed	m/s					
3	Conductor	t/km	18.13	18.13			
4	Lightning wire	t/km	0.65	0.65			
5	Steel for pole and tower	t/km	58.20	58.20			
6	'base steel	t/km	7.34	7.34			
7	Conductor or ground wire armor clamp	t/km	3.09	3.09			
8	Grounding steel	t/km	0.61	0.61			
9	Wire spacer	group/km	60.77	60.77			
10	Vibration damper	pcs/km	50.00	50.00			
11	Insulator	Sheet/km	524.51	524.51			
12	Composite insulator	pcs/km					
13	Cast-in-place concrete	m³/km	91.67	91.67			
14	Earthwork	m³/km	506.13	506.13			
	Including: base pit	m³/km	251.28	251.28			

Note: 1. All above quantities do not include the loss;

2. The base steel does not include the insert-type angle steel, and the iron tower does not include the 5% of large size substituting small size;

3. The concrete amount neither include the over-pouring amount, nor include the amount for revet

ment, embankment, drainage ditch, base bed, protective cap, etc.;

4. The earthwork amount is the sum of earthwork amount for base pit, drainage ditch, grounding groove, peak, formation level, etc.

(2) Notification on Issuing the Measures for Adjustment the Price Level of Budget Quota xx Power Grid Construction Project (YDD [2008] No. 4)

(3) Notification on Issuing the Material and Equipment Price Adjustment Coefficient for Quota of Installation Works of 2007 Power Transmission and Transformation Project in xx Power Grid Region (xxDWDE [2008] No. 11)

(4) ×× Project Cost Information (Phase 1/6, 2009).

III. Basis for the Preparation of Investment Estimation

(I) Main Basis Frequently Used in the Preparation of Investment Estimation

(1) The construction project cost composition, estimation index, calculation method, other relevant project cost documents and relevant project cost data issued by the national or regional specialized institutions.

(2) Calculation method, charge standard, and price index for other costs of project construction issued by the national or regional specialized institutions.

(3) All connotation and characteristics, design intention and design quantities of the single project or unit project of the proposed project.

(4) Investment file data of the similar projects which have been constructed.

(5) Dynamic factors influencing the investment in the project, such as interest rate, exchange rate, tax rate and so on.

(II) Preparation Basis for Project Case III

(1) Indexes for Investment Estimation of Power Project Construction: Power Transmission Line Project (2001 Edition) issued by the State Economic and Trade Commission.

(2) Standard for Budget Preparation and Calculation of Grid Project Construction (2007 Version).

(3) Grid Project Quota Design Control Indicators (2008 Level).

(4) The prices of base reinforcement, cement and other local materials shall be calculat-

ed and listed in accordance with ×× Project Cost Information (Phase 1/6, 2009).

(5) Construction loan interest is calculated at 80% of the static investment and an annual interest rate of 5.94% (interest paid quarterly).

(6) Tax is calculated as 3.38.

(7) The basic reserve cost is calculated at 3%.

Task 2 Preparation of Investment Estimation

I. Contents of Investment Estimation

According to the national regulations, the investment estimation is composed of the project construction investment, the interest during the construction period and the working fund estimation from the perspective of satisfying the investment design of the project construction project and investment scale determination, as shown in Figure 3-2-1.

The project construction investment estimation is divided according to the nature of cost, including construction project cost, equipment and tool procurement cost, installation project cost, other costs of project construction, basic reserve cost and price increase reserve cost. The construction project cost, equipment and tool procurement cost, and installation project cost directly form the solid fixed assets, known as project cost; other costs of project construction may form fixed assets, intangible assets and other assets respectively. In the feasibility study stage, the basic reserve cost and price increase reserve cost are included in the fixed assets from simplified calculation.

Interest during the construction period refers to the interest incurred by debt funds in the construction and shall be included in the original value of the fixed assets, including the interest on loans (or bonds), service charge, commitment charge, management cost, etc. Interest during the construction period is estimated separately, which is convenient for financial analysis on the construction project before and after the financing.

Study Program III Preparation for Construction Estimate of 500kV Power Transmission Line

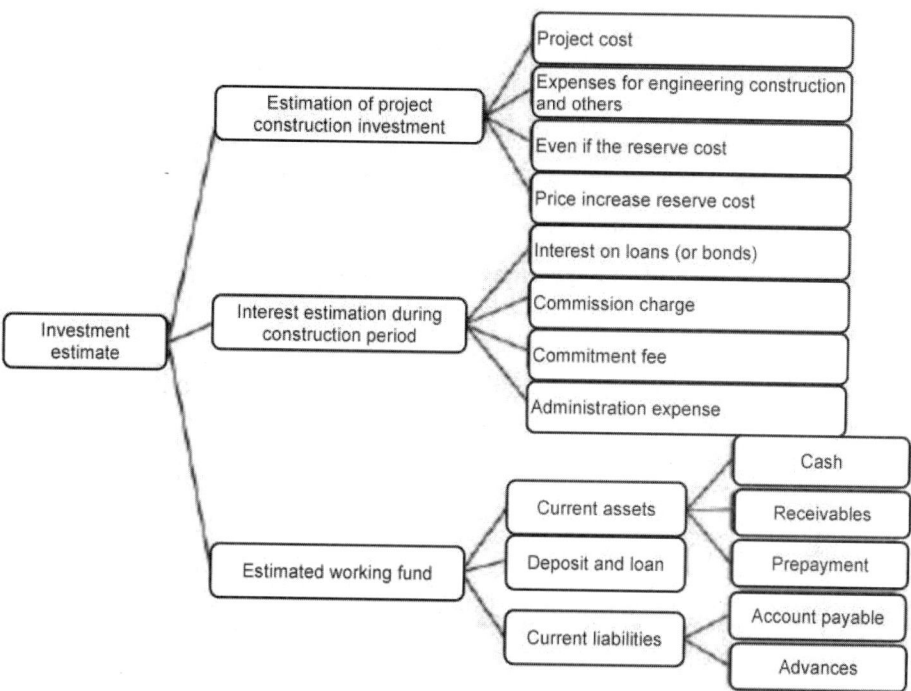

Figure 3-2-1   Composition of Investment Estimation

Working fund refers to the revolving fund needed to purchase raw materials, fuel, pay wages and other operating costs after the production and operation projects are put into operation.

It is a long-term occupied current asset investment accompanied by investment in project construction. The working fund is the difference between current assets and current liabilities. The current assets mainly consider cash, receivables, prepayments and inventories; the current liabilities mainly consider accounts payable and advance receivables.

II. Requirements for Investment Estimation of Construction Projects

When preparing the investment estimation, it is required that the project contents and cost composition shall be complete, with reasonable calculation, no items and calculations omitted. When there are differences in standards or conditions between the selected indexes and specific project, necessary conversion or adjustment can be made. The accuracy of the investment estimation shall meet the requirements for the control over the preliminary design budget estimate, with the specific requirements as follows.

(1) According to the stage and depth of the main professional design, combined with the characteristics of their respective industries, the maturity of the production process adopted, and the reasonable, reliable and complete degree of the basic information and data of the investment estimation of the country, region, industry or department grasped by the preparing unit, appropriate methods are adopted for the investment estimation of the construction project.

(2) The project content and cost composition shall be complete, with reasonable calculation, no repeated calculation, no increase or decrease of the estimation standard, no items or calculations omitted.

(3) Full consideration shall be given to the technical parameters for the design of the proposed project, the estimation coefficient and index adopted in the investment estimation, and the comprehensive contents in terms of quality and quantity shall follow the principle of consistency.

(4) The adopted estimation coefficient and the price and cost level of the estimation indexes shall be adjusted to the actual level of the project construction site and the year of the investment estimation preparation. For the boundary conditions of the construction project, such as construction land cost, or the cost incurred by the difference of external transportation, water, electricity, communication conditions, municipal infrastructure supporting conditions and having no necessary association with the investment in main production contents, shall be revised in the light of the actual situation of the construction project.

(5) Sensitivity analysis shall be carried out on the factors affecting the cost change, attention shall be paid to the analysis of the market change factors, and the impact of price increase factors and market supply and demand on the cost shall be fully estimated.

(6) The accuracy of the investment estimation shall be able to meet the requirements of control over preliminary design budget estimate and minimize the error of the investment estimation.

III. Methods for Investment Estimation

There are many methods for the investment estimation, such as the capital turnover rate method, the productivity index method, the proportion estimation method, the comprehensive index investment estimation method that are commonly used. In the actual project, it is necessary to combine the project characteristics to carefully analyze the relevant information and select the appropriate estimation method. If some projects are complex, several methods are needed for the investment estimation to ensure relative accuracy. Meanwhile, it is necessary to consider the construction cycle and pay attention to analyzing the time value of the funds, because the indexes are past and static, and the generally estimated time is based on the year before the commencement of construction, and the corresponding conversion and adjustment shall be made according to the local price level. The following is a brief introduction to the above methods.

(I) Capital Turnover Rate Method

The capital turnover rate method is a simple and convenient method to estimate the amount of investment by capital turnover rate. Generally, it can be analyzed according to the relevant data of the similar completed projects. According to the estimated annual product output and unit price of the proposed project, the investment of the proposed project is estimated. The formula is as follows.

$$C = \frac{Q \times P}{T} \quad (3\text{-}2\text{-}1)$$

Where C is the total investment of the proposed project; Q is the estimated annual product output of the proposed project; P is the estimated product unit price of the proposed project; T is the capital turnover rate of similar projects, which is equal to the total annual sales volume/total investment.

The advantage of this method includes the fast and simple calculation, but there is a large error. It is generally used in investment opportunity research and investment estimation of project proposal stage.

(II) Productivity Index Method

Productivity index method is to estimate the investment amount of the proposed project according to the productivity and investment amount of the completed and similar construction projects and the productivity of the proposed project. The formula is as follows

$$C_2 = C_1 \cdot \left(\frac{Q_2}{Q_1}\right)^x \cdot f \qquad (3\text{-}2\text{-}2)$$

Where C_2 is the investment amount of the proposed project; C_1 is the investment amount of similar completed project; Q_1 is the productivity of similar completed project; Q_2 is the productivity of the proposed project; f is the comprehensive adjustment coefficient; x is the productivity index, normally $0 \leqslant x \leqslant 1$.

The productivity index method has the advantages of simplicity, rapidity and small error (generally controlled within ± 20%). This method does not require detailed similar project data, but only the process flow and scale are needed. Therefore, the Contractor often uses this method for valuation in the project quotation. However, this method requires reliable similar project data, and the basic conditions are not much different from those of the proposed project.

Example 3-1 A chemical factory outputs 100,000 tons of certain chemical products annually, with a static investment of 50 million Yuan. It is planned to build a similar project with an annual output of 200,000 tons of the same products. When the productivity index is 0.6 and the comprehensive adjustment coefficient is 1.2, the productivity index method is adopted to determine the static investment amount of the proposed project.

Solution: According to the question, C_1=RMB 50 million, Q_2=200,000 tons, Q_1=100,000 tons, x=0.6, f=1.2. The known data are substituted into the formula (3-1):

$$C_2 = 5000 \times \left(\frac{20}{10}\right)^{0.6} \times 1.2 \approx 9094 万元$$

(Ⅲ) Proportion Estimation Method

Proportion estimation method needs a large number of statistical data of similar completed projects, which is often used in the analysis of economic activities. There are generally two calculation methods.

1. Estimated on the Basis of the Equipment Procurement Cost of the Proposed Project

This method is used to estimate the construction project cost and installation project cost of the proposed project according to the percentage of the construction project cost and installation project cost of the similar completed project to the equipment procurement cost, and then estimate the other related costs of the proposed project (including other costs of the project construction and reserve cost), finally constituting the construction investment amount of the proposed project. The expression is as follows

$$C = E(1 + f_1 p_1 + f_2 p_2) + I \qquad (3\text{-}2\text{-}3)$$

Where C is the construction investment amount of the proposed project; E is the equipment procurement cost of the proposed project calculated according to the local price at that time; p_1 and p_2 are the percentage of the construction project cost, installation project cost and other related costs to the equipment procurement cost in the completed project; f_1 and f_2 are the comprehensive adjustment coefficients of quota, price and cost standard as a result of time factor; I shall be other costs of the proposed project.

2. Estimated Based On the Investment in Process Equipment of the Proposed Project

Based on the investment in process equipment of the proposed project, this method analyzes the relevant statistical data of the similar completed project, calculates the percentage of each professional project to the investment in process equipment, then estimates the investment in each professional project of the proposed project, adds up the investment amount of each part (including the investment in process equipment) and other relevant costs of the proposed project, finally constituting the investment amount of the proposed project. The expression is as follows

$$C = E(1 + f_1 p'_1 + f_2 p'_2 + f_3 p'_3 + \ldots\ldots) + I \qquad (3\text{-}2\text{-}4)$$

Where C is the construction investment of the proposed project; E is the investment in process equipment calculated according to the local price at that time; p'_1, p'_2 and p'_3 are the percentage of professional project costs of the completed project to the investment in the process equipment; I shall be other costs of the proposed project.

(Ⅳ) Index Estimation Method

The estimating index is a kind of single project index or unit project index which is more extensive than budget estimate target. With single project or unit project as the object, it comprehensively estimates all kinds of costs and expenses in the project construction, thus it has strong generality and comprehensiveness.

The estimation indexes are generally expressed as the unit investment of single (or unit) project productivity, such as: Yuan/m, Yuan/m^2, Yuan/m^3, Yuan/t, Yuan/km, t/kV. A. When using the estimation index, it shall be adjusted and revised according to the actual situation of different regions and periods, and finally expressed in the form of "quantity" and "price".

The index estimation method is a common estimation method. In the estimation, it is necessary to adopt the estimation index suitable for the proposed project, pay attention to the differences of the region, time, characteristics and technical standards of the project construction and make corresponding corrections or adjustments, and applying indexes mechanically is not allowed; otherwise, the estimation result will not conform to the actual project situation, with a large error. The key point of estimating with the index estimation method is to select the appropriate estimation index.

(V) Classified Estimation Method for Construction Investment

The classified estimation method for construction investment is to estimate the various costs of project cost (including construction project cost, installation project cost and equipment procurement cost), other costs of project construction and reserve cost (including basic reserve cost and price increase reserve cost) in a classified way. The estimation methods for various costs are briefly introduced below.

1. Estimation of Construction Project Cost

There are generally three methods for estimation of construction project cost, including unit construction project investment estimation method, unit physical project quantity investment estimation method and budget estimate target investment estimation method. The former two methods are relatively simple, while the latter one requires more detailed and accurate project data as the basis, with very large workload. In the actual work, the method can be selected according to the specific conditions and requirements.

(1) Unit construction project investment estimation method: It is a method of estimating construction project cost by multiplying the investment amount of each unit construction project by the total construction project quantity. For example, the construction project cost of the transmission line project is estimated by multiplying the investment amount per unit length (km) by the corresponding total length of the transmission line.

(2) Physical project quantity investment estimation method: It is a method of estimating construction project cost by multiplying the investment amount of unit physical project quantity by the total physical project quantity. For example, the construction project cost of

the earthwork project is estimated by multiplying the investment per cubic meter by the corresponding total earthwork volume.

(3) Budget estimate target investment estimation method: Generally, the former two indexes are used to estimate the construction project cost. If there are no former two indexes, or the above two methods are not suitable (such as, the projects with large proportion of construction project cost to construction investment), the budget estimate target estimation method can be adopted. Please refer to Project 2 for the specific method.

2. Estimation of Installation Project Cost

There are generally three ways to estimate the installation project cost, with the formula as

$$\text{Installation project cost} = \text{original equipment price} \times \text{installation rate} \quad (3\text{-}2\text{-}5)$$

$$\text{Installation project cost} = \text{tonnage of equipment} \times \text{installation cost per ton} \quad (3\text{-}2\text{-}6)$$

$$\text{Installation project cost} = \text{physical quantity of installation project} \\ \times \text{installation cost index} \quad (3\text{-}2\text{-}7)$$

3. Estimation of Equipment Procurement Cost

The equipment procurement cost includes domestic equipment procurement cost, imported equipment procurement cost and tools and production furniture procurement cost. The domestic equipment procurement cost refers to the procurement cost of all the domestic equipment purchased or self-made for this construction project and meeting the fixed assets standard. It consists of the original price, transportation and miscellaneous costs of the equipment. The imported equipment procurement cost is composed of the imported equipment price (attention shall be paid to the difference between FOB and CIF), imported dependent cost and domestic transportation and miscellaneous costs.

Overall, the estimation is generally made at the feasibility study stage. For adopting methods for the investment estimation for the projects of different nature, the most important factor is the professional level, professional quality and relevant practical experience of project cost of the estimators. Therefore, it is necessary to attach great importance to it and take corresponding measures to prevent the influence of individual subjective factors on investment estimation in ways that ensure the reasonableness of investment estimation.

IV. Preparation Steps

(1) The installation project cost, equipment and tools procurement cost of each individual project shall be estimated respectively; in Project Case III, the classified estimation method in the investment estimation method is adopted, in which, the installation project cost estimation means that according to the "physical project quantity investment estimation method", the investment amount of physical project quantity and unit physical project quantity is estimated first, and then the installation project cost. See Table 3-2-1 for details.

(2) On the basis of summing up each individual project cost, the "Summary Estimation Table of Installation Project Cost of Overhead Transmission Line" is formed, and then the other costs of project construction and basic reserve cost are estimated, as shown in Table 3-2-2 and Table 3-2-3.

(3) The price increase reserve cost is estimated. The price increase reserve cost is generally set for projects with long construction periods. Because of the long construction period, the prices of materials, labor, equipment and construction machinery may increase, and the changes of rates, interest rates and exchange rates may be changed during the construction period, resulting in the increase of project cost. Therefore, it is necessary to reserve certain costs in advance, which is also called the price increase reserve cost or the unforeseeable cost of price change. In Project Case III, the cost is not taken into account because of the short construction period.

(4) The loan interest during the construction period is estimated. In addition to its own funds, the construction funds of general construction projects need to be raised through other means, such as bank loans, bonds, export credits, and so on. These means will result in loan interest, interest on borrowings and financing costs, which are included in the loan interest during the construction period. Project Case III: According to the project fund plan, the estimated cost of this item is 5.46 million Yuan.

(5) The working fund is estimated. The working fund refers to the necessary revolving fund for purchasing raw materials, fuel, paying wages and other production and operation costs in order to maintain normal operation after the construction project is put into operation. There are many estimation methods. At present, the general working fund estimation method in the world is the itemized detailed estimation method, with the formula as follows

$$\text{Working fund} = \text{current assets} - \text{current liabilities} \quad (3\text{-}2\text{-}8)$$

$$\text{Working fund} = \text{cash} + \text{receivables (and prepayments)} + \text{inventories} \quad (3\text{-}2\text{-}9)$$

$$\text{Current liabilities} = \text{receivables (and prepayments)} \quad (3\text{-}2\text{-}10)$$

Increase in current year's working fund = current year's working fund - previous year's

$$(3\text{-}2\text{-}11)$$

The working fund is not considered in this Project Case.

(6) Estimation Summary Sheet. This is the last step. Summarize the above estimated data and calculate the percentage of each cost and the unit investment amount of each cost. Comparing with the corresponding quota design control indicators, we can roughly judge whether the investment is reasonable or not. If not, we need to make corrections in the investment. The general estimation of Project Case III is shown in Table 3-2-4.

In Table 3-2-4, the unit investment estimation of the main project is 1.4836 million Yuan, and other costs are 608,400 Yuan. Compared with the Grid Project Quota Design Control Indicators (2009 Level), the investment in the main work unit of mountainous area is 1.812 million Yuan and the other costs are 669,000 Yuan for 500 kV transmission line project with $4 \times$ LGJ-400/50 (27m/s, 20mm) conductor specification which is close to the same kind of project. As there are mountainous regions, hills, mountains in the Project and there is a certain deviation from the quota design index in ice thickness (10mm), but generally it is controlled within the quota design index, thus it can be judged that the investment estimation of the Project is reasonable.

Table 3-2-1 Unit Estimation of Project Case III

S/N	Basis of preparation	Project name	Unit	Qty.	Unit price (RMB) Total	Installation Labor cost	Installation Material expenses	Installation Machinery cost	Installation materials	Total price (RMB) Total	Installation Labor cost	Installation Material expenses	Installation Machinery cost
I		Earthwork											
1		Material transportation											
1.1		Manual transportation more than 1000m											
	ZX1-2	Sand, stone, cement, water	10t.km	362.0	830.21	754.42		75.79		300536	273100	0	27436
		Terrain adjustment	%	106		273100		27436		289486	289486	0	0
		Sub-total								590022	562586	0	27436
1.2		Automobile transportation											
	ZX1-3	Load and unload	10t	316	671.60	109.32		548.79		212226	34545	0	173418
	ZX1-4	Transport	10t.km	475	14.63	3.43		11.20		6949	1629	0	5320
		Subtotal of loading and unloading								207963	34545	0	173418
		Subtotal of transportation								6949	1629	0	5320
		Terrain adjustment	%	38		1629		5320		2641	619	0	2022
		Sub-total								217553	36793	0	180759
2		Line re-surveying and pit dividing											

Study Program Ⅲ Preparation for Construction Estimate of 500kV Power Transmission Line

Table (Cont'd)

S/N	Basis of preparation	Project name	Unit	Qty.	Unit price (RMB)					Total price (RMB)			
					Total	Installation			Installation materials	Total	Installation		
						Labor cost	Material expenses	Machinery cost			Labor cost	Material expenses	Machinery cost
3	ZX2-1	Tangent tower, resisting-tensile tower	10 bases	22.2	548.80	269.99	251.42	27.39		12183	5994	5582	608
		Excavation and backfilling of line pole and tower pit		2712						0	0	0	0
	ZX2-2	Ordinary pit	10m³	503	164.37	148.31		16.06		82678	74600	0	8078
	ZX2-3	Loose sand pit	10m³	1302	323.38	293.63		29.75		420911	382189	0	38723
	ZX2-5	Rock pit	10m³	864	884.57	694.75	120.16	69.66		764534	600472	103854	60207
	ZX2-4	Mud pit	10m³	43	983.96	456.98	290.96	236.02		42310	19650	12511	10149
4		Excavation of other earthwork		257									
	ZX2-7	Common soil	10m³	51.50	60.54	55.11	0.00	5.43		3118	2838	0	280
	ZX2-9	Hard soil	10m³	39.60	398.85	275.68	95.31	27.86		15794	10917	3774	1103
	ZX2-8	Loose sandstone	10m³	166.32	115.06	104.43	0.00	10.63		19137	17369	0	1768
		Sub-total								1360666	1114029	125721	120916
		Terrain adjustment	%	13		1114029		120916		144824	144824	0	0
		Sub-total								1505490	1258853	125721	120916
		Quota of direct costs (Excluding labor cost adjustment)								2313065	1858232	125721	329111

Table (Cont'd)

S/N	Basis of preparation	Project name	Unit	Qty.	Unit price (RMB)					Total price (RMB)				
					Total	Installation			Installation materials	Total	Installation			Machinery cost
						Labor cost	Where Material expenses	Machinery cost			Labor cost	Where Material expenses	Machinery cost	
II		base works												
1		Material transportation												
1.1		Manual transportation more than 1000m												
	ZX1-2	Sporadic steel, sand, stone, cement, water	10t.km	378.8	830.21	754.42		75.79		314484	285774	0		28709
		Terrain adjustment	%	106		285774.30				302921	302921			
		Sub-total								617404	588695	0		28709
1.2		Automobile transportation												
		Sporadic steel, sand, stone, cement, friction reducer												
	ZX1-3	Load and unload	10t	374.1	671.60	109.32		548.79		251225	40893			205286
	ZX1-4	Transport	10t.km	1435.2	14.63	3.43		11.20		20997	4923			16074
		Terrain adjustment	%	38		4923		16074		7979	1871	0		6108
		Sub-total								7979	1871	0		6108
2		base works												

Study Program III Preparation for Construction Estimate of 500kV Power Transmission Line

Table (Cont'd)

S/N	Basis of preparation	Project name	Unit	Qty.	Unit price (RMB)					Installation materials	Total price (RMB)				
					Total	Installation					Total	Installation			
						Labor cost	Material expenses	Machinery cost				Labor cost	Material expenses	Machinery cost	
	ZX3-5	Processing and manufacture of base reinforcement	t	774.11	551.14	307.00	118.06	126.08			426643	237652	91391	97600	
	ZX3-8	500kV cushion, slope protection	10m³	75.00	516.71	432.40	0.00	84.31			38753	32430	0	6323	
In-ves-tiga-tion	ZX3-4	Cast-in-situ concrete base	10m³	492.70	2514.11	1332.33	838.59	342.20			1238702	656439	413173	168602	
	ZX3-6	Cast-in-place pile	10m³	368.50	9853.17	3698.38	530.16	5624.63			3630893	1362853	195364	2072676	
	ZX3-8	Wet masonry of flood drainage trench and slope protection	m³	3465	516.71	432.40	0.00	84.31			1790400	1498266	0	292134	
		Sub-total									7124904	3787640	699929	2637335	
		Terrain adjustment	%	25.50		3787640		2637335			1638369	965848	0	672520	
		Sub-total									8763272	4753488	699929	3309856	
		Quota of direct costs (Excluding labor cost adjustment)								6007629	9388656	5344054	699929	3344673	
III		Pole and tower works													

Table (Cont'd)

S/N	Basis of preparation	Project name	Unit	Qty.	Unit price (RMB)						Total price (RMB)				
					Total	Installation			Installation materials		Total	Installation			
						Labor cost	Where					Labor cost	Where		
							Material expenses	Machinery cost					Material expenses	Machinery cost	
1		Material transportation													
1.1		Manual transportation more than 1000m													
	ZX1-1	Tower material	10t.km	375.1	1927.16	1751.01		176.15			722878	656804		66074	
		Terrain adjustment	%	106		656804		66074			766250	696212		70038	
		Sub-total									1489128	1353016		136112	
1.2		Automobile transportation													
		Tower material													
	ZX1-3	Load and unload	10t	385.4	671.60	109.32		548.79			258835	42132		211504	
	ZX1-4	Transport	10t.km	925.9	14.63	3.43		11.20			13546	3176		10370	
		Terrain adjustment	%	38		3176		10370			5147	1207		3941	
		Sub-total									272329	46515		225814	
2		Tower erection													
	ZX4-13	500kV tower conductor 4*500	Site	222	7210.79	5553.76	167.49	1489.54			1600795	1232935	37183	330678	
3		Ground installation													
	YX4-85	Number of grounding poles and towers	10 bases	9.6	1714.97	1474.11	92.82	148.05			16464	14151	891	1421	

Study Program III Preparation for Construction Estimate of 500kV Power Transmission Line

Table (Cont'd)

S/N	Basis of preparation	Project name	Unit	Qty.	Unit price (RMB) Total	Unit price - Installation - Labor cost	Unit price - Installation - Material expenses	Unit price - Installation - Machinery cost	Total price (RMB) Installation materials	Total price Total	Total price - Installation - Labor cost	Total price - Installation - Material expenses	Total price - Installation - Machinery cost
		Sub-total								1617259	1247086	38074	332099
		Topographic adjustment (excluding high towers)	%	77		1247086		332099		1215973	960256		255716
		Sub-total								2833232	2207343	38074	587816
		Quota of direct costs (Excluding labor cost adjustment)							39572139	4594689	3606873	38074	949742
IV		Stringing works											
1		Material transportation											
	ZX1-1	Manual transportation of wire	10t.km	279.3	1927.16	1751.01		176.15					
	ZX1-3	Load and unload	10t	224.2	671.60	109.32		548.79		150573	24510	0	123039
	ZX1-4	Automobile transportation	10t.km	5604.0	14.63	3.43		11.20		81987	19222	0	62765
		Subtotal of loading and unloading								147548	24510	0	123039
		Subtotal of transportation								81987	19222	0	62765
		Terrain adjustment	%	38		19222		62765		31155	7304	0	23851
		Sub-total (1)								260690	51036	0	209654

Table (Cont'd)

S/N	Basis of preparation	Project name	Unit	Qty.	Unit price (RMB)						Total price (RMB)			
					Total	Installation			Installation materials		Total	Installation		
						Where						Where		
						Labor cost	Material expenses	Machinery cost				Labor cost	Material expenses	Machinery cost
2		Wiring												
2.1		Erection of conductor and ground wire												
	ZX5-14	Within 4×400/120 for cross section	km	99	19567.00	5116.61	1997.07	12453.32			1937133	506544	197710	1232879
	ZX5-2	Single lightning wire	km	99	2548.03	1753.66	292.63	501.74			252255	173612	28970	49672
2.2		Erection												
	ZX5-3	OPGW optical cable	km	99	3691.55	2349.81	578.96	762.78			365463	232631	57317	75515
		Sub-total									2554851	912788	283997	1358066
		Terrain adjustment	%	49		912787.92		1358066.16			1112718	447266		665452
		Sub-total (2)			0.00						3667570	1360054	283997	2023519
2.3		Crossing erection of conductor and ground wire												
	ZX5-18	Crossing railway	Position	53	6824.90	4008.30	1918.06	898.54			361720	212440	101657	47623
	ZX5-21	Crossing low voltage or weak wires	Position	18	1941.68	1172.63	445.43	323.62			34950	21107	8018	5825

Table (Cont'd)

S/N	Basis of preparation	Project name	Unit	Qty.	Unit price (RMB)					Total price (RMB)			
					Total	Installation			Installation materials	Total	Installation		
						Labor cost	Material expenses	Machinery cost			Labor cost	Material expenses	Machinery cost
3		Crossing river, within 4×720mm² for conductor			0.00					0	0	0	0
	ZX5-25	Crossing river, within 4×720mm² for conductor	Position	2	1168.96	760.88		408.08		2338	1522	0	816
		Sub-total (3)								399008	235069	109675	54264
		Quota of direct costs (Excluding labor cost adjustment)							32171049	4327267	1646159	393672	2287437
V		Accessory project											
1		Material transportation											
1.1		Manual transportation more than 1000m											
	ZX1-2	Fittings, insulators	10t.km	85.7	830.21	754.42		75.79		71149	64654		6495
		Terrain adjustment	%	106		64654		6495		75418	68533		6885
		Sub-total								146567	133187		13380
1.2		Automobile transportation											
		Fittings, insulators											

Table (Cont'd)

S/N	Basis of preparation	Project name	Unit	Qty.	Unit price (RMB)					Total price (RMB)			
					Total	Installation			Installation materials	Total	Installation		
						Labor cost	Material expenses	Machinery cost			Labor cost	Material expenses	Machinery cost
	ZX1-3	Load and unload	10t	95.3	671.60	109.32		548.79		64003	10418		52300
	ZX1-4	Transport	10t.km	2382.2	14.63	3.43		11.20		34852	8171		26681
		Terrain adjustment	%	38		8171		26681		13244	3105		10139
		Sub-total								112099	21694		89119
2		Accessory installation											
1		Suspension of insulator strings for tangent tower and transposition tower											
	ZX6-3	500kV wire	Site	222	462.53	308.48	28.16	125.89		102682	68483	6252	27948
2		Installation of other fittings											
	ZX6-4	Installation of heavy hammer	Site	195	143.71	96.02	10.60	37.09		28023	18724	2067	7233
	ZX6-7	Four-bundle conductor of vibration damper	10 sets	925.6	48.49	20.49	5.95	21.72		44882	18966	5507	20104
	ZX6-9	Four-bundle conductor of spacer	10 sets	587.6	85.21	65.14	13.46	6.61		50069	38276	7909	3884
		Sub-total				144448				225657	144448	21735	59168
		Topographic adjustment coefficient	%	28		144448		59168		57013	40446		16567

Study Program Ⅲ Preparation for Construction Estimate of 500kV Power Transmission Line

Table (Cont'd)

S/N	Basis of preparation	Project name	Unit	Qty.	Unit price (RMB)					Total price (RMB)				
					Total	Installation			Installation materials	Total	Installation			
						Labor cost	Where Material expenses	Machinery cost			Labor cost	Where Material expenses	Machinery cost	
		Sub-total								19305382	282669	184894	21735	75735
		Quota of direct costs (Excluding labor cost adjustment)									541335	339775	21735	178234

· 651 ·

Table II B

Table 3-2-2 Estimation Summary Sheet of Installation Project Cost of Overhead Transmission Line (10mm Ice Zone)

S/N	Name of project or expenses	Charge base number	Rate%	Earthwork	base works	Pole and tower works	Stringing works	Accessory project	Total	Percentage of each item in the total (%)	Unit investment Yuan/km
I	Direct cost			2699361	16677738	45690342	37512286	20296114	122875841	83.66%	1241170
1	Direct construction cost (B)	1)+2)		2313065	15396285	44166828	36498316	19846717	118221211	80.49%	1194154
1)	Quota of direct costs			2313065	9388656	4594689	4327267	541335	21165012	14.41%	213788
	Including: Labor cost (A1)			1858232	5344054	3606873	1646159	339775	12795093	8.71%	129243
	Labor cost adjustment (A2)	A1	4.56	84771	243792	164543	75097	15500	583704	0.40%	5896
	Machinery cost			374346	3344673	1079987	2240234	104747	7143987	4.86%	72161
2)	Installation materials				6007629	39572139	32171049	19305382	97056199	66.08%	980366
2	Measures expenses			386296	1281453	1523514	1013970	449397	4654630	3.17%	47016
1)	Additional cost for winter and rainy season construction	A1+A2	6.95	135039	388355	262113	119627	24692	929826	0.63%	9392
2)	Use cost for construction tools	A1+A2	5.38	104534	300626	202902	92604	19114	719779	0.49%	7270
3)	Extra charge for special site construction	A1+A2		0	0	0	0	0	0	0.00%	0
4)	Temporary facilities	B	1.95	45105	300228	861253	711717	387011	2305314	1.57%	23286
5)	Cost for construction unit transfer	A1+A2	2.71	52655	151431	102205	46646	9628	362565	0.25%	3662

Study Program III Preparation for Construction Estimate of 500kV Power Transmission Line

Table (Cont'd)

S/N	Name of project or expenses	Charge base number	Rate%	Earthwork	base works	Pole and tower works	Stringing works	Accessory project	Total	Percentage of each item in the total (%)	Unit investment Yuan/km
6)	Subsidy for safe and civilized construction measures	A1+A2	2.52	48964	140814	95040	43376	8953	337146	0.23%	3406
II	Indirect costs			1806022	5193903	3505531	1599907	330228	12435591	8.47%	125612
1	Levies and charges			919623	2644728	1785011	814670	168152	6332184	4.31%	63961
1)	Social security fee	A1+A2	31.36	609326	1752349	1182716	539786	111414	4195591	2.86%	42380
2)	Housing provident fund	A1+A2	13.44	261140	751007	506878	231337	47749	1798110	1.22%	18163
3)	Accidental injury premium for hazardous operation	A1+A2	2.53	49158	141373	95417	43548	8988	338484	0.23%	3419
2	Administrative expenses	A1+A2	45.62	886398	2549175	1720520	785237	162077	6103407		
III	Margin	I+II	5	225269	1093582	2459794	1955610	1031317	6765572		
IV	Tax	I+II+III	3.38	159896	776225	1745962	1388092	732029	4802203	3.27%	48507
	Total of installation cost	I+II+III+IV		4890548	23741448	53401628	42455894	22389689	146879207	100.00%	1483628
	Percentage of each item to the total (%)			3.33%	16.16%	36.36%	28.91%	15.24%	100.00%		
	Unit investment (Yuan/km)			49399	239813	539410	428847	226158	1483628		

Table 3-2-3 Estimation of Other Costs

S/N	Name of project or expenses	Preparation Basis and Calculation Notes	Total price (Yuan)
I	Construction management cost of the project		4024644
1	Construction project legal person administrative cost	Main 146,879,207×1.22%	1791926
2	Bidding cost	Main 146,879,207×0.35%	514077
3	Engineering supervision fee	99.00km×15,500 Yuan/km×1.12	1718640
II	Technical service cost for project construction		19988263
1	Preliminary engineering cost	(Survey cost + basic design cost) × rate (11.2%, 9.3%)	1497581
2	Reconnaissance and design charges		16074702
2.1	Survey expense		6760480
2.2	Design fee		9314222
2.2.1	Basic design fee		6610781
2.2.2	Other design costs		2703441
	Tower base demarcation cost (estimated)	99.00km×7,000 Yuan/km	693000
	Helava and path optimization cost	99.00km×7,500 Yuan/km	742500
	Fee for preparation of construction drawing budget	Basic design cost 6,622,158×10.00%	661078
	As-built drawing compilation expense	Basic design cost 6,622,158×8.00%	528862
	Forestry survey cost	68km×2,250 Yuan/km	78000
3	Review cost of design documents (feasibility study)	99.00km×3,400 Yuan/km	336600
	(Preliminary design)	99.00km×4,900 Yuan/km	485100
4	Project post evaluation fee	Main 146,879,207×0.35%	514077
5	Project construction supervision and testing fee		786444
	Engineering quality supervision and testing fee	Main 146,879,207×0.23%	337822
	Environmental monitoring acceptance cost (environmental impact assessment + acceptance)	50,000 Yuan (less than 20km) + (99-20) km×1500 Yuan/km	165500

Study Program III Preparation for Construction Estimate of 500kV Power Transmission Line

Table (Cont'd)

S/N	Name of project or expenses	Preparation Basis and Calculation Notes	Total price (Yuan)
	Acceptance and compensation cost for water and soil conservation projects	99km×2,100 Yuan/km+land requisition area×2 Yuan/m²	283122
6	Management cost of power engineering techno-economic standard preparation	146879207×0.20%	293758
7	Administrative fee for formulation of power project quota	Cancelled according to DDZZ (2009) No. 3	0
III	Commissioning cost of subsystem and trial running cost for the whole system		259103
1	Cost for the startup and commissioning of the whole sets of units	400 Yuan/working day×142 working days×1.2	68160
2	Construction enterprise cooperative commissioning cost	Main 146,879,207×0.13%	190943
IV	Production preparation cost		631581
1	Management vehicle acquisition expenses	Main 146,879,207×0.20%	293758
2	Procurement cost of tools, office, production and living furniture	Main 146,879,207×0.15%	220319
3	Production staff training cost and cost for mobilization in advance	Main 146,879,207×0.08%	117503
V	Others		1311175
1	Construction road and bridge compensation		324000
	Road construction	19km×10,000 Yuan/km	220000
	Construction cost of airport access route of pulling and tensioning machine	19km×4,000 Yuan/km	104000
2	Crossing measure cost		649000
	Highway	Once×65,000 Yuan/time	65000
	Railway	Once×65,000 Yuan/time	65000
	Main route	8 times×25,000 Yuan/time	250000
	River or reservoir	Twice×RMB 25,000/time	50000
	Live across (220 kV)	Once×RMB 32,000/time	32000
	Live across (110 kV)	6 times×RMB 20,000/time	60000

Table (Cont'd)

S/N	Name of project or expenses	Preparation Basis and Calculation Notes	Total price (Yuan)
	Live across (35 kV)	8 times×RMB 1,200/time	36000
	Live across (10 kV)	12 times×RMB 3,500/time	91000
3	Outward transport for the surplus soil	5,994t×RMB 25/t	338175
4	Tower treatment cost of coal mine area	×RMB 7,000,000/base	0
	Total other costs		26214765
VI	Basic reserve cost	(Main+auxiliary facilities+other costs+price difference)×2%	6623619
VII	Price different in the year of preparation		16648838
	Price difference and tax of materials	16298700×1×1.0338	15728581
	Material and machine cost adjustment and tax	6223541×14.76%×1.0338	920258
VIII	Static investment		224921399
IX	Loan interest during construction period		5461092
X	Dynamic investment		230382491

Table 3-2-4 Estimation Summary Sheet

99.00km

S/N	Name of project or expenses	Total (RMB '0,000)	Percentage occupation of each item over the total (%)	Unit investment (RMB 10,000/km)
I	Main project of transmission line	14688	65.30%	148.36
II	Auxiliary facility cost	116	0.52%	1.18
	Sub-total	14804	65.82%	149.54
III	Price different in the year of preparation	1665	7.40%	16.82
IV	Other costs	6023	26.78%	60.84
	Where: 1. Allocation and cleaning cost of the construction site	2732	12.15%	27.59
	2. Basic provisional sum	662	2.94%	6.69
	Static investment (Total of items I~IV)	22492	100.00%	227.19
V	Dynamic cost	546		5.52
(I)	Price increase budget reserve			0.00
(II)	Loan interest during construction period	546		5.52
	Dynamic investment (Total of items I~V)	23038		232.71

Study Program III Preparation for Construction Estimate of 500kV Power Transmission Line

Table 3–2–5 Estimation of Auxiliary Facilities

S/N	Project name and code	Preparation Basis and Calculation Notes	Total price (Yuan)
1	Line inspection and repair station project		
1.1	Dormitory		
1.2	Offices and warehouses, garages	RMB 700/m^2×14 m^2/person×22 persons	215600
1.3	Outdoor works	215600×15%	32340
1.4	Land requisition for inspection station	0.924×RMB 150,000/mu	138531
2	Line patrol and road overhaul		
2.1	Sidewalk		
2.2	Simple highway	15km×RMB 30,000/km×RMB 15/mu	600000
2.3	Makeshift bridge		
3	Communication works	99km×RMB 1,000/km	99000
4	Live working tools	99km×RMB 8000/km	79200
4	Line patrol and road overhaul project		
(1)	Sidewalk		
(2)	Simple highway		
(3)	Makeshift bridge		
	Total.		1164671

Table 3-2-6 Estimation of Allocation and Cleaning Cost of Construction Site

S/N	Name of project or expenses	Preparation Basis and Calculation Notes	Total price (Yuan)
I	Allocation and cleaning cost of the construction site		27,318,683
1	Land acquisition fee		2,158,607
	Land acquisition cost of tower base	18.23 mu×RMB 80,000/mu	1,458,122
	Compensation for occupied and requisitioned woodland	38.1602 mu×RMB 85,000/mu	324,375
	Tax on occupation of cultivated land	56.39 mu×RMB 6,670/mu	376,110
2	Construction site rental		395,850

Table (Cont'd)

	Temporary land for gathering and distribution warehouse	2 material stations×RMB 80,000/station	160,000
		17 traction and tensioning sites×RMB 8,000/site	136,000
	Cost of temporary land occupation for reclamation	200 mu×RMB 500/mu	99,850
3	House demolition		15,489,574
	Brick-concrete with	10,098m^2×RMB 700/m^2	7,068,600
	Brick wall, tile roof	15,147m^2×RMB 500/m^2	7,573,500
	Accessory area such as baking dam	2,524.5m^2×RMB 120/m^2	302,940
	Cost of supporting housing demolition	126 households×RMB 3,000/household	378,000
	Homestead	42 mu×RMB 4,000/mu	166,534
4	Forest tree felling		7,224,606
	Light ice area (pine tree)	40.2km×RMB 9,000/mu×9 mu/km	3,256,200
	Light ice area (miscellaneous wood)	26.8km×RMB 6,000/mu×9 mu/km	1,447,200
	Fruit tree	300 trees×RMB 360/tree	108,000
	Vegetation recovery expense	603 mu×RMB 4,002/mu	2,413,206
5	Compensation for young crops	(99-67)km×8m/667m^2/mu×40%×RMB 2,000/mu	307,046
6	Third line migration		325,000
	10kV line	2.5km×RMB 120,000/km	300,000
	Low voltage and weak wires	km×RMB 10,000/km	
	Relocation of farm track	2.5km×RMB 10,000/km	25,000
7	Grave demolition	12 Nos.×RMB 1,500/nos.	18,000
8	Plant and mine demolition		1200,000
	Small coal pit	Nos.×RMB 150,000/nos.	
	Small mine	2 Nos.×RMB 15,000/nos.	300,000
	Quarries	6 Nos.×RMB 150,000/nos.	900,000
9	Measure cost for communication facility against interference from power transmission line	200,000	

Summary

Study Program III is mainly based on the Project Case III, and introduces the method of preparing the project estimation of 500kV transmission line: Firstly, according to the defined technical and economic conditions and the different estimation accuracy, the investment estimation is divided into different stages. Then the investment estimation data are collected, and the preparation basis is determined. According to the investment estimation requirements of the construction project, the corresponding investment estimation method is adopted for estimation step by step. The first step is to separately estimate the construction project cost of each single project, equipment and tools procurement cost and installation project cost, and form the "Work Unit Estimation"; the second step is to form the "Summary Estimation of Installation Project Cost of Overhead Transmission Line" on the basis of summing up the each individual project cost, and then estimate other costs of project construction and basic reserve cost; the third step is to estimate the price increase reserve cost, loan interest during the construction period and working fund, and finally summarize them into "Table of General Estimation", thereby completing the project estimation of 500kV transmission line.

Practical Training III

Fill in the blanks with the estimated amount according to the basic information of a transmission line project below.

1. Basic Information

The details of 220kV four-loop 2×400 conductor line project in the same tower are shown in the table below.

Voltage level (kV)	220				
Conductor section (mm²)	2×400				
Line length	5.5km				
No. of circuits	Four-loop design and double-loop erection				
Project topography (%)	Flat ground	Hill	River network and mire	Mountain land	High mountain
	40	0	60	0	0
Project geology (%)	Soil pit	Mud pit	Sump	Quicksand pit	Rock
	40	30	30	0	0
Wire model	2×LGJ-400/35				
Site transportation	Labor load distance (km)			0.35	
Average transportation distance	Load distance of vehicle (km)			10	
Full line pole and tower (base)	22	Straight line pole and tower (base)		16	
		Strain pole and tower (base)		6	
Project design year	2005~2006				

2. Investment Cost Estimation.

(1) The construction installation project cost is estimated in unit index estimation method as follows: the unit cost of the main project is RMB 3,410,900/km, and the estimated amount is: _____.

Study Program III Preparation for Construction Estimate of 500kV Power Transmission Line

(2) The other costs of the project construction account for 22.22% of the project cost, and the estimated amount is: _____.

(3) The unit cost of the prepared annual price difference is RMB 305,500/km, and the estimated amount is: _____.

(4) The basic reserve cost accounts for 1.64% of the total static investment amount, the estimated amount is: _____, and the total static investment amount is: _____.

Review and Reflection

1. What is an investment estimation?

2. What is the basis for preparing the investment estimation?

3. What are the requirements for investment estimation of construction project?

4. How many methods are there for investment estimation? Please give a brief description.

5. Please briefly describe the preparing steps of investment estimation.

Study Program IV

Preparation for Project Settlement of 220kV Power Transmission Line

Project Case IV 220kV double-circuit line newly-built project

I. Project Overview

The 220kV double-circuit line newly-built project starts from a newly-built 220kV substation (small number side) and ends at a 220kV substation (big number side), with the total line length of 46.626km.

The base of this line shall be undisturbed soil base (excavated base, manual hole digging pile base) and plate inclined column base, including 59 undisturbed soil bases, 34 plate inclined column bases, with 81 types of bases.

This line has 93 iron tower bases (N1-N94, N4 idle number), including 37 corner bases (including 2 terminal tower bases), 56 tangent tower bases, with a total of 17 tower types.

II. Meteorology and Topography

The maximum design wind speed of the Project is 23.5 m/s. The design ice coating of the N14-N19 conductor, the ground wire, the conductor in the rest sections and the ground wire in the rest sections is 15mm, 20mm, 10mm, and 10mm respectively. N1-N41 is a Grade III pollution area, and the rest sections are Grade II pollution areas.

Study Program IV Preparation for Project Settlement of 220kV Power Transmission Line

The topography along the whole line is divided into: mountainous areas (79%) and high mountains (20.5%). The geology along the whole line is divided into: 76% rock, 9% sandstone and 15% ordinary soil.

III. Basic Information of the Project

The conductor of this line is LGJ-300/40; N1-N79 ground wire is GJX-100; the N79-N94 ground wire is LB-JG-120-40AC and is combined with OPGW (suspended on the right side of the ground wire support) to form a double ground wire. The basic information of the project case is shown in Table 4-0-1.

Table 4-0-1 Basic Information of 220kv Double-circuit Line Newly-built Project

Project name	220kV double-circuit line newly-built project		
Starting and ending points	Starts from a 220kV substation (small number side) gantry and ends at a 220kV substation (big number side) gantry		
Voltage class	220kV	Predominant meteorological conditions	Earthquake intensity
		Maximum design wind speed is 25m/s; maximum design ice thickness is 20mm; average annual lightning days are 45 days	Grade VII
Line length	The total length is 2×46.626km		
Base project: a total of 93 bases, and concrete grade shall be C10, C20 and C25			
Base type		Connected to the iron tower	Arrangement of tower leg
Inserted inclined column base, rock base		Insert angle steel, anchor bolt	All-around long and short legs
Pole and tower project: a total of 93 bases;			

Line erection project: 46.626 km;								
Conductor type		Ground wire type			Insulator string type			
2×LGJ-300/40		LBGJ-120-40AC、GJX-100			U70BP、U70BP2、U100BP、XDP-70CN			
Important crossing and main demolition								
S/N	Item	Unit		Qty.	S/N	Item	Unit	Qty.
1	110kV power line	Position		4	7	Communication line and optical cable	Position	17
2	35kV power line	Position		4	8	10kV relocation	m	500
3	10kV line	Position		16	9	220V relocation	m	600
4	380V and 220V	Position		56	10			
5	Highway	Position		7	11			
6	River (great river)	Position		6	12			

· 663 ·

Task 1   Preparation of Project Settlement Data

I. Concept and Significance of Project Settlement

Project settlement refers to the economic documents that the Builder conducts the project price settlement to the Client for the completed project quantity according to the project construction contract. Generally, the project construction period is long, and a number of funds is consumed. In order to compensate the funds consumed by the Builder in the construction process in a timely manner, it is necessary to settle the project price, generally including: intermediate settlement (progress payment settlement), year-end settlement, and Final Account upon Completion after the completion and acceptance of all the projects. The project settlement is a very important work in project contracting.

The timely settlement and payment of project cost is of great significance to both the Client and the Builder. Through the project settlement, the funds management of the Client can be improved, and the investment control can be strengthened, which is beneficial to the cost analysis and cost management; for the Builder, there are three main points of significance.

(1) The project settlement is the main index reflecting the project progress. In the construction process, the project settlement is determined according to the progress of the project quantity completed by the Builder. Comparing the cumulative settled project price with the total contract price can approximately reflect the project progress and dynamically control and manage the project cost more intuitively.

(2) The project settlement is an important part of accelerating capital turnover. If the Builder settles the project payment as soon as possible, it will be beneficial for the Builder to recover the project price quickly, timely and more, to repay the debts, to withdraw the funds and to reduce the internal operating cost. It is very important for the operation and management of the Builder, reducing the internal operation cost and improving the use efficiency of the funds. If the project settlement is not conducted timely or the amount is not paid timely,

the progress payment will not conform to the actual project progress, or the final payment will not be paid after the Final Account upon Completion, or the quality guarantee deposit will not be paid according to the time specified in the contract. On the one hand, it increases the operating cost of the Builder, which is not conducive to the circulation of funds; on the other hand, it will also affect the implementation of the project progress according to plan, and the project quality can not be guaranteed, thereby affecting the completion time of the project and finally leading to the poor use time of the building and even the poor using effect.

(3) The project settlement is an important index to evaluate economic benefit. For the Builder, only when the project funds are settled in full, it means that the operation risk is avoided, and the Builder can also obtain the corresponding profit, and then achieve good economic benefits.

Therefore, both the Client and the Builder shall settle the project price in time on the basis of the project construction contract, so as to facilitate the smooth progress of the project.

The settlement and payment of the project price are stipulated in the model text of contract. On March 26, 1996, the Ministry of Power Industry issued the Contract Template for the Construction of Electric Power Construction Project, stipulating the project settlement.

The Ministry of Construction and the State Administration of Industry and Commerce also promulgated the new Construction Contract for Construction Project (Template) in December 1999. In the implementation of international projects, there are many kinds of construction contract standard documents, in which *Conditions of Contract for Works of Civil Engineering Construction* (abbreviated as Conditions of FIDIC Contract) published by Fédération Internationale Des Ingénieurs Conseils, the New Engineering Contract Conditions (abbreviated as NEC Contract) formulated by ICE and the General Terms of Engineering Contract (A201) formulated by AIA are widely used. These contract standard documents clearly stipulate the project settlement.

II. Collection of Basic Settlement Data

In the process of construction project implementation, it is necessary to collect information related to the settlement extensively, because this can ensure not only the completeness of the settlement preparation content, but also the smooth progress of the settlement audit, to avoid too many questions, disputes and contradictions in the audit. Therefore, the Builder shall pay attention to the data collection in the following aspects.

(1) Project construction contract. This is the most fundamental and direct basis for settlement preparation, because the contract defines the scope of the project contract, the rights and obligations of both parties, the method and time of price settlement, risk spreading, etc. In addition, in the process of project implementation, which cost items can be included or adjusted, and how to calculate, etc., also need to be implemented according to the provisions of the contract.

(2) Drawings and records of joint review of drawings. This is one of the bases for determining the base number of a tender and the contract price.

(3) Tender offer, contract price or original budget. This is the basis for adjusting the related costs after changes have taken place in the actual practice or after additions or deletions have been made.

(4) Project or design change notice, project shutdown report, supervision engineer instruction, etc.

(5) Construction organization design (scheme), construction record, original bill, image progress and site photograph, etc.

(6) Documentation on quota and cost adjustment.

(7) Examined and approved as-built drawing, project completion acceptance sheet, as-built report, etc.

During the construction, different industries and Builders have different management mode for the project and the above-mentioned information, but basically the original credentials of these information belong to different management departments and personnel, therefore, in terms of the whole construction project management, the Project Department needs to make overall arrangement and reasonable division of labor to ensure the completeness of the information, and provide them timely and completely for the settlement preparation department or personnel to ensure the smooth progress of the settlement and play an active role in it.

III. Determining the Preparation Basis

After collecting the settlement information, we need to analyze and sort out them, and summarize the preparation basis related to the settlement. In addition to the contract, stan-

Study Program IV   Preparation for Project Settlement of 220kV Power Transmission Line

dards, specifications and regulations, the completed project quantity is also one of the bases. Taking Project Case IV as an example, the preparation basis mainly includes the following aspects.

(1) Current standards, specifications and regulations for the construction of transmission line project promulgated by the State.

(2) Guidelines on Technical Management of Construction of Power Construction Projects.

(3) Regulations on Health, Safety and Environmental Management in Electric Power Construction of State Grid Corporation of China.

(4) Measures for Assessment of Production Standards of Power Transmission and Transformation Project (2005).

(5) Tendering Documents for Construction of a 220kV Transmission and Transformation Project.

(6) Other tendering materials and drawings issued by a power company.

(7) Site investigation data of the Project.

(8) Relevant data of 220kV transmission line construction of a company.

(9) Quality Manual and related procedure documents prepared by a company according to GB/T19001-ISO9001-2000 quality system standard.

(10) Occupational Safety, Health and Environmental Management Manual and Occupational Safety, Health (OSH) and Environmental Management System (EMS) Procedure Document prepared by a company according to GB/T24001-ISO14001-1996 Environmental Management Systems - Specification with Guidance for Use, Occupational Safety Health Management System Audit Specification of State Economic and Trade Commission-2001, Regulations on Safety, Health and Environmental Management of Electric Power Construction, and other specifications and standards.

Task 2 Preparation of Project Settlement

The construction drawing budget introduced, the quantity of labor and materials analyzed, and the project budget cost determined in Learning Project 1 are all prepared before the commencement of construction. During the construction of general project, the original design has been changed because of the long construction period, many factors, such as material price increase, design change, force majeure, etc., and the original construction drawing budget can not reflect the actual cost of the project, while the project settlement can just make up for this shortcoming. The general project settlement is divided into intermediate settlement and Final Account upon Completion.

The intermediate settlement is generally large in scale, with long construction period, even used in cross-year projects. In order to supplement the consumption during a construction period, including labor cost, material cost and other costs, to ensure that the construction progress is not affected by the shortage of funds and that the construction activities are carried out uninterruptedly and smoothly, the Builder shall make regular project settlement to the Client according to the date specified in the contract or the project quantity completed during this period, and provide a basis for the financial allocation of the project.

The Final Account upon Completion is a project cost document which is re-determined by revising the original construction drawing estimate according to the actual changes in the construction process after the project completion acceptance. It is the basis for adjusting the project plan, determining and counting the project progress, evaluating the effect of capital construction investment and analyzing the project cost.

Whether the project settlement is well prepared and whether the implemented work contents and benefits that shall be obtained are reflected in the project settlement will have a direct bearing on the vital interests of the Builder. Therefore, how to make their own interests not to be lost is the very problem that every construction enterprise shall pay attention to. At the same time, the Final Account upon Completion is the basis of the economic accounting of the project cost assessment by the Builder and of summing up and measuring the management level of the enterprise. Through the Final Account upon Completion, we can sum up the work experience and lessons, find out the causes of construction waste and serve to improve the construction management level. The following is a brief introduction to the preparation of project settlement.

I . Composition of Project Settlement

There are a lot of project construction materials. In order to prevent omissions, the project construction enterprise shall fully consider the specific implementation of the project on the basis of the project construction budget, and pay attention to the part of the change of the project construction cost caused by the following factors.

(1) Cost adjustment caused by policy changes. Such as the adjustment of labor wage standard, material price difference coefficient, indirect rate, and unit price of machine shift.

(2) Tender offer shall be calculated according to the routine method, and the cost shall be subject to that actually adjusted during settlement. Such as, the site entrance and exiting cost of large-scale machinery (calculated according to the actual machinery and times of entering and exiting the site), the reinforcement of the wall, the deduction of water and electricity charge.

(3) Cost changes caused by design change, supervision instruction, etc. (the part proposed by the Client on its own initiative). This portion of the cost includes an increase in the project quantity in the project execution, as well as an increase in the cost (may also be treated as claim expense) due to the impact of this change on the construction schedule and on other work. For example, local increases in floor and floor area will lead to increase in scaffolding and vertical transportation costs.

(4) Claim expense of construction. In the process of construction, the project construction enterprise shall, in accordance with the provisions of the contract and laws and regulations, provide economic compensation to the Client for the losses caused by the non-self-fault or for paying the extra expenses incurred for bearing the work beyond the provisions of the contract. Such as, breach of contract by the Client (failure to pay the project payment on time, rigorous inspection, failure to provide the equipment and site on time according to the provisions of the contract, etc.), contract adjustment (design change, instructing the project construction enterprise to speed up the construction, geological conditions in-

consistent with the exploration report, etc.), and unforeseeable factors (flood, war, earthquake, etc.; the engineering geological exploration report and site data provided by the Employer, as well as underground or artificial obstacles difficult to be found through the site investigation, such as: ancient wells, tomb pits, faults, karst caves and other artificial structure obstacles.

(5) Relevant reward costs stipulated in the contract: such as the award for early completion, cost for crashing measures, and the quality award.

(6) Due to the project changes, some items are reduced, resulting in the refund of the original surrender part of the profits and preferential part.

(7) Relevant costs caused by on-site visa, such as sporadic labor, sporadic mechanical quantity, rework quantity caused by design change or project negotiation, and confirmation of sporadic project quantity added outside the contract.

II. Project Settlement Method

According to the scale, nature, progress and construction period of the construction project, and the stipulations of signing the contract, there are many ways for the project settlement (including the intermediate settlement), but there are mainly the following ways for the project settlement in China.

(1) Monthly settlement. It refers to the way in which the ten-day or half-a-month project payment is paid in advance at the end or in the middle of the month, and the payment of the current month is collected after the settlement bill of the project payment and the monthly settlement of completed project are submitted at the end of the month, and it will be liquidated after completion. The specific settlement time shall be subject to the provisions of the contract. For the projects with long construction period and cross-annual completion, the project inventory is generally carried out at the end of each year to handle the annual settlement. At present, this settlement method is more commonly used in China to settle the construction project price.

(2) One-time settlement after completion. For projects with small scale, short construction period (generally less than 12 months) and contract value less than RMB 1 million, one-time settlement after completion is often adopted. This kind of method can be made clear in the contract generally: the method, time and proportion of advance progress payment

which is paid usually monthly, which is more conducive to the implementation of the project.

(3) Phased settlement. For single or unit project with large scale and long construction period (cross-year), in addition to the monthly settlement method, the settlement can also be done in different phases according to the progress of the project image. Generally, the project price is prepaid monthly, and the phased settlement will be made after each phase is completed. The criteria for the division of phases shall be prescribed by each department, autonomous region or municipality directly under the central government, and city specifically designated in the state plan.

(4) Other settlement methods. Settlement shall be conducted by both parties in accordance with other agreed methods.

III. Payment of Project Settlement

In the process of project construction, the project funds paid by the Client can be divided into several categories: those paid before the project starts are called advance payment, those paid during the project construction are called progress payment, and those paid after the completion and acceptance are called final payment; finally, there is the project quality guarantee deposit (also referred to as the quality guarantee deposit), which will be paid after the expiration of the warranty period of the contract. The project progress payment and the final payment belong to the project settlement payment, but the advance payment and the quality guarantee deposit are also involved in the settlement payment. Here's a brief introduction.

(I) Advance Payment

No advance payment for the project is made in the Project case. Generally, for the contracted labor and materials project by the construction enterprise, the Client shall allocate a certain amount of project advance payment to the project construction enterprise before the construction starts, so as to facilitate the material preparation turnover. That is, the project construction enterprise reserves the working fund needed for the main equipment, materials and structural components for the Project, and generally does not prepay the material preparation funds for the single-contracted project (the contracted labor but materials).

According to the relevant provisions of China, if the project advance payment is implemented, both parties shall stipulate the time and amount of the project advance payment the from the Client to the project construction enterprise in the special terms and conditions, and it shall be successively deducted according to the agreed time and proportion after commencement. The date for the advance payment shall not be 7 days later prior to the designated date of the commencement of the work. If the Employer fails to make advance payment as agreed, the project construction enterprise may issue a notice requiring the Client to pay the advance payment 7 days after the agreed advance payment time. If the Employer still fails to make advance payment as required upon receipt of the notice, the construction enterprise may stop the construction within 7 days after the notice is issued. The Employer shall pay the loan interest payable to the project construction enterprise from the date agreed to be payable, and assume the liability for breach of contract.

The project advance payment shall only be used by the project construction enterprise to pay the costs related to the Project at the beginning of the construction. If the project construction enterprise does not follow the regulations but abuse this amount, the Client shall have the right to withdraw it immediately. After the project construction enterprise submits a bank guarantee equal to the amount of the advance payment (issued by a bank approved by the Employer) to the construction enterprise, the Client shall pay the advance payment to the project construction enterprise according to the specified amount and time, and the bank guarantee shall remain valid until the advance payment is fully deducted by the Employer. When the advance payment is deducted by the Client, the amount of the bank guarantee decreases correspondingly.

(II) Progress Payment and Quality Guarantee Deposit

Project Case IV is used to illustrate the progress payment and quality guarantee deposit as follows.

The contract price of the Project Case is RMB 29.33 million which is settled monthly. The construction period of the project is 8 months, and the base construction of 31 bases is completed every month in the first 3 months; 47 bases and 46 bases of tower erection are completed in the middle 2 months; the 18km line is erected monthly in the last 3 months. The monthly progress payment is as follows.

First month progress payment: RMB 3.1 million;

Second month progress payment: RMB 3.1 million;

Third month progress payment: RMB 3.1 million;

Fourth month progress payment: RMB 3.3 million;

Fifth month progress payment: RMB 3.22 million;

Sixth month progress payment: RMB 4.64 million;

Seventh month progress payment: RMB 4.64 million;

Progress payment payable in the eighth month is: RMB 4.24 million, but the final payment (quality guarantee deposit) shall be reserved as 5% of the contract price, that is, RMB 1.47 million shall be withheld and RMB 2.77 million shall be paid for the project.

For the calculation and reservation of project quality guarantee deposit, it is generally necessary to reserve a certain proportion of the final payment in the total project cost as the quality guarantee deposit in order to urge the project construction enterprise to guarantee the project quality according to the specified time after the project Final Account upon Completion is handled. After the warranty period is over, the final allocation shall be made according to the requirements of the contract. Generally, the withholding proportion and mode of quality guarantee deposit are negotiated by the Client and the project construction enterprise in combination with the project scale and nature, and finally agreed by both parties through the contract. Generally, it is withheld at the proportion of 3%~5% of the project cost for the Chinese construction project, and there are two specific withholding modes.

(1) Last proportional withholding. This method is generally used for the project with low project cost and quality guarantee deposit. When the advance payment and progress payment reach a certain proportion of the project cost (such as 95%~97%, the specific proportion shall be executed according to the contract agreement), paying the project price shall be stopped, and the part of the price shall be regarded as the quality guarantee deposit. (This method is used in this Project Case)

(2) Phased proportional withholding. This method is generally used for the project with high project cost and quality guarantee deposit. The Client may choose to withhold the project progress payment from the paid project progress price in withholding proportion, until the total amount of the quality guarantee deposit reaches the limit stipulated by both parties. This method is synchronously withheld with the progress payment, which is equivalent to the total quality guarantee deposit withheld in phases according to its proportion. This method is necessary for the project with long construction period and large investment, and is

very feasible for handling the annual settlement and annual investment control.

(Ⅲ) Cost Adjustment

In the process of project implementation, design change, project quantity change, construction method change and change caused by engineer's instruction will generally occur. Therefore, it is necessary to go deep into the site in time in combination with the remaining and undetermined matters in the process of project quantity calculation, or to deal with such problems accurately according to the documents of change and negotiation in the process of construction; at the same time, the project contents changed by the project construction enterprises themselves during the construction process shall be mastered when going deep into the site, the information shall be recorded or supplemented, and the price shall be timely adjusted. For example, during the construction of the Project Case, a lot of changes have taken place beyond the expected conditions, and then the price is adjusted to form an additional payment. The specific circumstances are as follows.

(1)During the construction process, the normal project progress is hindered by force majeure factors, resulting in the increase of costs and project delay. Pleases Fill in the following engineering contact list (21 project contact lists are filled out for the Project Case in total, and this book is limited to space, only one is listed, as shown in Table 4-2-1). The project contact list mainly involves the increased cost for design change, increased land acquisition cost, local work fund, additional cost, outage cost, costs caused by natural disaster, and so on.

Study Program IV Preparation for Project Settlement of 220kV Power Transmission Line

Table 4-2-1 Project Contact List

Table No.: DJS-A13-01   No.: SG-S5TJ-OO2

Project Name: 220kV Double-circuit Line Newly-built Project

To: Supervision Department of a 220 kV Transmission and Transformation Project of Sichuan ×× Supervision Co., Ltd.:
 	
  Subject matter: According to the Implementation Opinions on Accelerating the Construction of Electric Power Communication Infrastructure (YFBF [2009] No.12) of × Municipality, ×× County and ×× County belong to the Category III Area of × Municipality, and the land requisition standard is RMB 90,000-120,000. After negotiation with relevant departments of ×× County and ×× County governments, the land requisition standard is RMB 110,000/mu for the Project. Please review.
 	
                                                  Contractor (Stamp)
                                                  Project Manager _____
                                                  Date September 5, 2010.

Comments of Supervision Department:
 	
                                         Project Supervision Department (Seal):
                                         Chief/Professional Supervision Engineer:
                                         _____
                                         Date: _____

Opinions of Headquarters:
 	
                                                  Headquarters (Seal):
                                                  Commander: _____
                                                  Date: _____

This form is made in triplicate, filled in by the Contractor, with one for the construction management unit, Project Supervision Department and Contractor respectively.

(2) Summarize the contact list to get the summary of the additional cost of the Project Case, as shown in Table 4-2-2.

Table 4–2–2   Summary of Additional Cost for a 220kV Line Newly–built Project

S/N	Project name	Cost items	Total price (RMB) Main	Construction site and other	Total (Yuan)
I	Part I: Increased Cost for Design Change		398647	0	398647
1	Design Change Notice QEOR-A-01	Add Conductor	38647		38647
2	Design Change Notice QEOR-D-01	Add Power Line Relocation	360000		360000
I	Part II: Additional Costs for Other Reasons		55800	5626694	5682494
1	Project Contact List SG-S5TJ-OO2	Increased Land Acquisition Cost		896000	896000
2	Project Contact List SG-S5TJ-OO4	Local Work Fund		419634	419634
3	Project Contact List SG-S5TJ-005	Emergency Repair of Damaged Big Transportation Roads Caused by Rainstorm and Natural Disasters		341505	341505
4	Project Contact List SG-S5TJ-005A	Emergency Repair of Damaged Small Transportation Roads Caused by Rainstorm and Natural Disasters		15090	15090
5	Project Contact List SG-S5TJ-006	Secondary Excavation of Collapsed base Pit Caused by Rainstorm and Natural Disasters		190800	190800
6	Project Contact List SG-S5TJ-007	Emergency Repair of Damaged Big Transportation Roads Caused by Rainstorm and Natural Disasters		149275	149275
9	Project Contact List SG-S5TJ-009	Emergency Repair of Collapsed Transportation Roads and Bridges Caused by Rainstorm		36960	36960

Table (Cont'd)

S/N	Project name	Cost items	Total price (RMB) Main	Total price (RMB) Construction site and other	Total (Yuan)
10	Project Contact List SG-S5TJ-O10	Additional Cost of House Demolition		1280720	1280720
12	Project Contact List SG-S5TJ-O12	Additional Costs of Ropeway Erection		225000	225000
13	Project Contact List SG-S5TJ-O13	Additional Cost of Slow Work of the Labor Caused by Supply of Tower Materials		96355	96355
15	Project Contact List SG-S5TJ-O15	Increasing the accelerating period of equipment and labor		815630	815630
18	Project Contact List SG-S5TJ-O18	Additional material station cost		44000	44000
19	Project Contact List SG-S5TJ-O19	Forest vegetation restoration fee		160748	160748
20	Project Contact List SG-S5TJ-O20	Outage cost		954977	954977
21	Project Contact List SG-S5TJ-O22	Apply standard color paint	55800		55800
	Total		454447	5626694	6081141

(IV) Final Account upon Completion

1. Method for Preparation of Final Account upon Completion

If the project is based on a unit price contract priced according to the bill of quantities, the project quantity and comprehensive unit price of the newly-added list project shall be adjusted according to the project quantity and price approved by the Employer during the settlement. For the increase or decrease of the list project quantity stipulated in the original contract, the adjustment shall be made on time. If the total amount of the adjustment in the above two parts is within the floating difference of the lump sum contract, the total price adjustment shall not be made in this contract. It shall be noted that in the process of settlement,

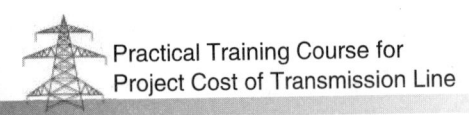

the information must be complete and effective, based on the contract, and the Final Account upon Completion shall be adjusted actually according to the pricing standards.

If the project is priced at the current fixed unit price, it is mainly to compare the composition of the original construction drawing estimate with the change of actual construction during settlement. Generally, based on various design change materials, site visa, project quantity verification sheet and other relevant materials, the increase or decrease is calculated on the basis of the original construction drawing budget, and the Final Account upon Completion is handled after the approval of the Client.

2. Requirements for Project Final Account upon Completion

The general terms and conditions of the Project Construction Work Contract (Model Text) of the People's Republic of China stipulates the Final Account upon Completion as follows.

(1) The Contractor shall submit the Employer a Final Account Report upon Completion and a full set of settlement materials within 28 days after the report on the acceptance is confirmed by the Employer. The Parties shall make the settlement in accordance with the Contract Price in the Agreement and price adjustment in the Special Conditions.

(2) Within 28 days after receiving the Final Account Report upon Completion and settlement materials submitted by the Contractor, the Employer shall exam them and grant approval or put forward modification opinions. After the Employer confirming the Final Account Report upon Completion, he or she shall inform the managing bank to pay the project Final Account upon Completion price to the Contractor. The Contractor shall deliver the completed project to the Employer in 14 days after receiving the Final Account upon Completion.

(3) If the Employer, without reasonable reason, fails to pay the settlement payment within 28 days from receiving the Final Account Report upon Completion, it shall pay interests at the interest rate paid by the Contractor to the bank for delay of the Works and undertake the default liability from the 29th day.

(4) If the Employer fails to pay the project Final Account upon Completion payment within 28 days from receipt of the Final Account Report upon Completion and data, the Contractor can urge the Employer for payment. If the Employer still fails to pay it within 56 days upon receiving the Final Account Report upon Completion and data, the Contractor can negotiate with the Employer to convert the project into money, or the Contractor can apply to People's Court for project auction according to law, and the Contractor has right to get priori-

ty of payment from project conversion or auction.

(5) If the Contractor fails to submit the Final Account Report upon Completion and a full set of settlement materials within 28 days after the project Final Account Report upon Completion is approved by the Employer, which causes the settlement cannot proceed smoothly or the payment cannot be realized timely, the Contractor shall deliver the project if requested by the Employer, or the Contractor shall be liable for safekeeping the project.

(6) In case of any dispute between the Employer and the Contractor over the project Final Account upon Completion price, the dispute shall be settled in the agreed manner.

(7) In practical work, only one-time settlement is required for the projects that were started and completed in the same year. For the cross-year project, the year-end settlement shall be processed at the end of the year, and the unfinished project shall be carried forward to the next year. At the moment, the Final Account upon Completion shall be equal to the sum of all annual settlement.

IV. Settlement Review and Determination

1. Review Method

Commonly used settlement review methods are: comprehensive review method, key spot check method, decomposition and comparison review method, screening review method, grouping calculation review method, etc. The advantages and disadvantages of several main project settlement review methods are as follows.

The advantages of the comprehensive review method are comprehensiveness, meticulousness, small review result error and high quality, while the disadvantages are large workload, long occupancy and large personnel input. It is suitable for some cases such as small project quantity, simple process and weak budget of the other party.

Key spot check method is to grasp the key points for review. The advantages are giving prominence to the key points, short review time and good effect. It is suitable for large project quantity, high cost, complex project structure, strong budget of the other party, etc.

Decomposition and comparison review method is a method to review the settlement cost after decomposition layer by layer and then carry out comparative analysis to find the project with large difference in amount or project quantity.

Screening review method, grouping calculation review method (lack of content)

In order to make a good settlement, besides fully considering their own factors, the project construction enterprise shall also correctly handle the relationship with other relevant units and personnel, including the Client, supervisor, designer, cost consultant and other units. According to the organizational structure relationship determined in the implementation of the project, the project construction enterprise shall establish necessary economic contract relations with them and friendly cooperative relations in work, cooperate with and support each other in all aspects, be honest and trustworthy in contract performance, and establish a good self-image, so as to lubricate every link of settlement and create a good external environment for settlement.

The Final Account upon Completion price of the Project Case IV after passing the review: RMB 29.33 million for the contract cost and RMB 6.08 million for the additional project funds, RMB totaling 35.41 million.

2. Contents of Review

(1) Review the statement of Final Account Report upon Completion. Whether the payment and distribution of construction project, capital construction investment, investment lump sum contracting balance and construction balance funds are true and correct; whether the financial analysis and calculation such as fund source and operation are correct.

(2) Review the completion financial statement. Whether the construction project overview form is prepared completely and correctly; whether the completion financial statement of construction project is prepared completely and correctly; whether the summary statement of assets for construction project delivery is prepared completely and correctly; whether the list of assets for construction project delivery is prepared completely and correctly.

(3) Review the as-built drawing of the construction project. Review whether the as-built drawing conforms to relevant regulations.

(4) Review cost comparison index. Review whether the main physical project quantity index and the main material consumption index are calculated correctly, and compare and analyze them with the indexes determined in the budget estimate. Assess whether other accrued costs are listed excessively or less and compare and analyze them with the budget estimate.

After the completion of the review, the Final Account upon Completion review report shall be submitted for reviewing reduced (added) projects and analyzing the cause.

Summary

The Learning Project 4 mainly takes Project Case IV as the carrier, and introduces the methods for preparing 220kV transmission line project settlement: collecting basic data, determining the preparation basis, carefully analyzing and not omitting, determining the settlement method according to the project contract, and determining the advance payment, progress payment and Final Account upon Completion payment of the project. In addition, with the progress of the project, the project price shall be adjusted in real time according to the design change, the project quantity change, the construction method change and the change caused by the engineer's instruction, so as to form the summary table of the additional project cost and complete the settlement of the 220kV transmission line project.

Practical Training IV

The contract price of a construction and installation project is RMB 6 million, and the contract stipulates that the advance payment proportion is 25%. When the value of the main material of the uncompleted project equals to the advance payment, the advance payment shall be deducted proportionally. The main material and components of the project account for 65% of the project price, and 5% shall be reserved as warranty premium. During the actual construction, RMB 600,000 is the contract increase amount, and the progress payment for each month shall be: RMB 300,000 in January, RMB 800,000 in February, RMB 1,200,000 in March, RMB 2,000,000 in April, RMB 1,200,000 in May and RMB 500,000 in June. How much is the advance payment, monthly project settlement amount, Final Account upon Completion price and retention money respectively?

Review and Reflection

1. Please briefly introduces the concept and significance of project settlement.
2. Which basic information shall be collected at the time of settlement?
3. What is the basis for the preparation of project settlement?
4. How many methods for project settlement are there? Please specify.
5. How is the project settlement amount paid?
6. What is the review content of the Final Account upon Completion?

Study Program V

Preparation for Project Final Account

Task 1 Preparations for Final Account upon Completion

I. Preparation of Basic Information

The basic work of financial management and accounting is very important, which needs to be paid attention to from the start of the construction project. At ordinary times, the collection and accumulation of information shall be done well to lay a good base for the preparation of the Final Account upon Completion. The preparations are as follows.

1. Set Up Accounting Account for Capital Construction Business

For the establishment of capital construction business accounting account, it shall fully consider that the need of capital construction project management and preparation of Final Account upon Completion is satisfied after the combination of capital construction finance and production and operation finance. The detail account of "construction in progress" shall be set up and classified in line with the capital construction budget estimate, and all individual projects shall also correspond to the approved project budget estimate one by one. For example, the construction project cost, the cost of equipment under installation, installation project cost and other expenses shall be accounted in multi-column account pages; if the project spans different years, the account book shall be carried forward over the years, the amount of the current period shall be settled monthly, and the cumulative amount of the current year and the previous years shall be settled at the end of the year.

The specific methods for setting up capital construction business accounting account are as follows: the construction project cost and installation project cost shall be accounted in columns to each unit project; the detail account of installation equipment shall also be set up according to the unit project, and detailed accounting shall be carried out according to the type, quantity, specification and price of the equipment; expense detail items shall be set up for other expenses according to the (budget) estimate items, and each expense shall be accounted in a multi-column manner. In this way, when the final account is prepared, it can be filled in directly into the Final Account Report upon Completion according to the actual amount on the book.

2. Participate in and Master the Project Progress

The Financial Department shall master the project progress at any moment, actively participate in the management and control of each stage of the construction project, and accumulate daily data.

(1) It is necessary to actively participate in the discussion and review of the project (budget) estimate, master the changes in the investment increase and decrease of each unit project in the estimate (budget), and approve the use of reserve cost for the project.

(2) It is necessary to actively participate in the preparation and signing of important economic contracts, master the tendering situation of project, main materials and equipment, and learn the implementation of relevant contracts at any moment.

(3) It is necessary to timely master the investment completion of each stage, pay attention to the project progress, learn whether there are major design changes, as well as the project quality, project accident identification, etc., and control the possible changes in funds.

(4) It is necessary to timely master the single project price settlement and audit, compare it with the plan, and analyze the reasons of over-expenditure or saving of single project.

(5) It is necessary to timely master the project construction funds in place and use over the years.

(6) It is necessary to timely master the relevant information such as commencement and completion reports, project summary, minutes of meeting, project briefs and so on.

3. Establishment of Supplementary Register

(1) Establish a register of the allocation and clearing costs of the construction site. Mainly used for recording: land requisition related documents and document number, land requisition area, amount, address, payee, land occupancy tax, compensation for old facilities, and calculation standard for demolition and clearance of remaining objects.

(2) Set up equipment, main special material account or card register. Mainly used for recording: master the purchase, payment, custody and collection of special equipment and main materials. The equipment card needs to record the model, specification, manufacturer, quantity, amount and installation location of the equipment in detail.

The capital construction of electric industry needs a lot of funds, in which the proportion of equipment investment (including installation project cost) to the total investment is generally more than 50%. Therefore, the equipment investment of construction project is the key point in the management and accounting of construction cost of power industry, and also the key to prepare Final Account upon Completion and control investment. In the project equipment management and accounting, the following aspects need to be done well.

1) Set up the equipment accounting card and fill in the detailed items of the equipment listed in the budget estimate.

2) Record equipment tendering and contract, and master equipment ordering.

3) Conduct equipment manufacturing and transportation supervision, strengthen the management and control of advance payment for large-scale equipment, strictly control arrival acceptance and payment of final payment, reduce turnaround time in transportation, and timely conduct acceptance.

4) For the management and accounting of the receipt, distribution and storage of the inventory equipment, the collection of the equipment shall be strictly controlled, and the installation position shall be recorded according to the three conditions for conversion to "Equipment in Installation". In the case of entrusting construction enterprises and general project contracting enterprises to manage the equipment on their behalf, it is necessary to clarify their responsibilities, strictly implement the provisions of the accounting system and conduct monthly financial auditing.

5) For inventory and division record of surplus equipment (including equipment in in-

stallation on site), the surplus equipment shall be timely treated.

(3) The register of assets transferred during the construction period shall be established. Fixed and current assets shall be recorded in terms of name, specification, unit, quantity, amount, manufacturer, supplier, collecting department, collecting personnel, etc.

II. Preparations Before Preparation

In order to ensure the quality of Final Account Report upon Completion, before preparing it, according to Article 37 of CJ [2002] No. 394 of the Ministry of Finance, "the Client and its competent department shall strengthen the organization and leadership of financial final cost for completion of capital construction project, specialized personnel shall be organized to prepare financial final cost for completion in a timely manner. The designer, Builder, Supervisor and other units shall actively cooperate with the Client in the preparation of financial final cost for completion. The Client shall complete the preparation of the financial final cost for completion within three months after the project completion. The original institution shall not be revoked and the responsible person of the project and the finance officer shall not be transferred before the financial final cost for completion is approved".

Specific preparations that shall be done well are clearly specified in the Preparation Rules on Final Account Report upon Completion of Capital Construction Project of Electric Power Generation, Transmission and Substation Project (Trial) issued by Ministry of Energy as follows.

(I) Financial Department

(1) The number of final accounts over the years, and the financial income and expenditure of each project, such as investment completion amount, appropriation and loan amount, payable amount and balance fund, shall be collated and checked in an all-round way. In particular, the investment completion amount shall be checked in detail in combination with the statistical aspects of the plan and the construction situation on the spot so as to ensure that the project funds are settled, the equipment is not omitted or listed excessively, and the progress is consistent with the statistics. The ownership of property rights of large construction machinery and equipment shall be clearly defined.

(2) The site and the accounts shall be cleaned up.

Upon the project completion, relevant departments shall be supervised and urged to conduct a warehouse inventory and on-site clean-up, return all surplus equipment and materials from the warehouse, and implement and timely clean-up claims and debts; for large-scale temporary construction of hydropower project, the recovery amount is relatively large and shall be cleaned up and recorded in the accounts in an all-round way. It will prevent no one for disposal after the project completion.

(3) Analysis and allocation of other cost items shall be done well.

There are different financial treatment methods for other cost items due to their different nature. Some are allocated directly to other units as costs; some serve as an increase in fixed assets; some are transferred to production units as current assets; some do not increase the value of fixed assets; some increase the value of the fixed assets but do not distinguish the common costs to be paid for any particular project, but the apportionment method is adopted. Even if apportionment is made, different apportionment methods will be made according to their different nature, as described below.

1) The occupancy and cleaning cost of the construction site shall be apportioned into the housing and building projects in proportion according to the floor area or workload.

2) The "Management Cost of the Client" shall be apportioned according to the proportion of the workload into the projects of housing, building and machinery and equipment that need to be installed. The purchase of vehicles and sporadic fixed assets shall be transferred to the production unit as fixed assets.

3) The "Research and Test Fee" shall be apportioned into relevant research and test service objects.

4) No apportionment or increase in the cost of fixed assets shall be made for the "Training and Early Entry Fee of Production Staff".

5) The "Acquisition Expenses for Office and Living Furniture" shall not be apportioned and shall be transferred to the production unit as current assets.

6) The "Joint Commissioning Cost" shall be apportioned into the installation project cost.

7) The "Survey and Design Fee" shall be apportioned according to the proportion of the workload into the projects of housing, building and machinery and equipment that need to be installed; in which, if purchased as the fixed assets, they shall not be apportioned and

shall be transferred to the production unit as fixed assets.

8) The "Power Supply Subsidy" is not apportioned and is treated as transfer-out investment.

9) The "Measure Cost for Communication Facility Against Interference from Power Transmission Line" shall be apportioned to the part of the communication lines of the installation project.

10) According to the notice of the Energy base of the Department of Energy (1991) No. 34 on the issuance of the supplementary provisions on the Composition and Calculation Standard of the Construction Budget Cost of Thermal Power and Transmission and Transformation Projects, the "Construction Subsidy of Electric Power Construction Enterprise Base" has been incorporated into the "IV. Temporary Facility Fee" project and no longer as "composition of other costs".

11) The "Basic Reserve Cost" is a capital source in the budget estimate instead of a project. In addition to the scope of use specified, certain examination and approval procedure are required for the use of this fund.

(4) The "5% anticipated unfinished tail-in works" shall be included in the investment plan. The full investment shall be retained for it as the budget estimate project. Those for lump sum contracting by the Contractor implemented shall be included in the subject of "property to be delivered for use" in financial accounting.

(II) Other Relevant Departments

The Financial Department is the main body in preparing the Final Account upon Completion, but other relevant departments, such as planning, statistics, materials, labor and capital, construction, budget and project construction enterprises, must closely cooperate with each other, jointly study and provide relevant information to meet the needs of report preparation.

(1) Approved design documents.

(2) Approved adjusted budget estimate documents.

(3) Information on the mutual adjustment of costs between the construction projects by the Client.

(4) Approval documents for the use of reserve cost.

(5) Investment lump sum contracting contract for 5% tail-in works.

(6) Relevant statistical reports.

(7) Documents and contracts for land acquisition and compensation for young crops.

(8) Data on compensation for resettlement of submerged residents in reservoir area of hydropower station.

(9) Clean up the site and account the investment completion.

(10) It is estimated that the specific contents of anticipated 5% unfinished tail-in works will be listed one by one according to the items listed in the budget estimate, so that they are not repeated or omitted, and the progress is consistent with the statistics.

(11) Quantity of main materials consumed.

(12) Plan and actual number of technical and economic indicators.

(13) Take measures to make the project investment have obvious specific saving methods and summary information.

(14) Labor productivity and number of project labors.

Task 2 Prepare the Final Account upon Completion

I. Principles and requirements for preparing Final Account upon Completion

1. Principles

Upon completion and acceptance, the preparation of Final Account upon Completion shall be promptly organized for all newly-built, expanded, reconstructed, relocated and rehabilitated construction projects, and the formalities for asset transfer shall be handled within the prescribed time limit.

The principle to be followed in the Final Account upon Completion is that: only one Final Account Report upon Completion shall be prepared for the project within the scope of the budget estimate.

The cost range of the Final Account upon Completion shall include all the construction costs from the initial cost of the construction project to the delivery and use after the completion acceptance. Namely: construction project cost, installation project costs, equipment procurement cost, other costs (including the initial cost of the construction project), dynamic cost and directly formed assets not through the accounting of construction in progress. However, the productive cost of the enterprise input can not be included in the construction project cost expenditure before the project completion.

Generally, the tail-in work shall not be retained for projects that pass the acceptance and meet the conditions for putting into use; if there are unfinished tail-in work and costs, they can be estimated and included in the Final Account upon Completion only after being examined and approved by the Project Completion Acceptance Committee, and a detailed list of the unfinished tail-in work shall be prepared and submitted in accordance with the budget estimate project. It is important to note that the anticipated physical workload and value of the unfinished tail-in work must not exceed 5% of the executed budget.

2. Preparation requirements for Final Account upon Completion

In order to strengthen the normalization, standardization and scientization of the preparation of Final Account upon Completion, it is necessary to strictly carry out the completion acceptance system for the construction project, correctly assess the investment efficiency, and establish and perfect the economic responsibility system. After the completion of all new construction, expansion, reconstruction, relocation and restoration projects, the Client shall organize the preparation of the Final Account upon Completion in a timely manner and implement the timeliness, authenticity, legitimacy and integrity of the Final Account Report upon Completion. The Preparation Rules on Final Account Report upon Completion of Capital Construction Project of Electric Power Generation, Transmission and Substation Project (Trial) issued by Ministry of Energy clearly specifies the preparation requirements as follows.

Article 37 The Final Account Report upon Completion of generation, transmission and transformation project of power capital construction shall be prepared in accordance with the report format and contents stipulated in the Regulations, and the forms and contents to be prepared shall not be reduced at will.

Article 38 The Final Account Report upon Completion is an important economic file of the construction project. The data listed in the form must be verified with the relevant departments and truthfully filled in and submitted according to the financial book figures, so that the account is in line with the actual one and the report.

Article 39 The Final Account upon Completion is the basis to provide the correct calculation of fixed assets. Therefore, where possible, we shall try our best to meet the card creation requirements of the "Catalogue of Fixed Assets of Electric Power Industry Enterprises" formulated by the Water Conservancy and Power Department on July 1, 1987 (see Appendix 2 for details: The Division Table of the Newly Planned Power Generation Project of the Department of Energy and the Reference Table of the Catalogue of Fixed Assets of the Electric Power Industry Enterprises of the Former Water Conservancy and Power Department).

II. Composition of Final Account upon Completion

(I) Composition of Final Account Report upon Completion

(1) Cover of Final Account Report upon Completion.

(2) Project panorama color photograph and main project color photograph for Final Account upon Completion.

(3) Catalogue of Final Account Report upon Completion.

(4) Statement of Final Account Report upon Completion.

(5) Financial statement of Final Account upon Completion.

(6) Project approval document (or feasibility study report approval document), budget estimate approval document and completion acceptance report.

(7) Audit report and other main documents.

(8) Events of project.

(II) Contents of the Statement of Final Account Report upon Completion

The statement of Final Account Report upon Completion is a written summary which reflects the completed project construction achievements and management experience, assesses, analyzes and evaluates the project investment and cost in an all-round way, is a further explanation and supplement to the Final Account Report upon Completion and is an important organizational part of the Final Account Report upon Completion. The main contents are as follows.

(1) Basis and conditions of the construction project. The basis of the construction project shall be explained in accordance with the approving unit and date and document number of the "Feasibility Study Report", "Project Proposal", "Design Tasks", "Budget Estimate Approval", "Revised Budget Estimate Approval" and so on. The conditions are mainly explained in terms of plant site geography, landform, traffic conditions, water source, power supply, raw material source and disposal of the three wastes.

(2) Overview of the construction project and general evaluation of the project. It is mainly analyzed and explained from the project progress, quality, safety and cost. The progress mainly describes the commencement and completion time, and the reasonable construction period is compared with the required construction period to determine whether it is ahead of schedule or postponed; the quality shall be explained according to the acceptance evaluation grade, pass rate and excellent product rate of the Initiating Acceptance Committee or equivalent Level 1 quality supervision department; the safety shall be explained according to labor wage and construction department records, equipment and personal acci-

dents; the cost shall be compared with the estimated cost to explain whether the cost is saved or overspent, and the amount and percentage shall be used for analysis and explanation.

(3) Construction scale, main equipment and structure. Related information explaining the main project structure and equipment describes the project overview, the project scale, the layout of the main building and the rationality of the main equipment.

(4) It is a description of the availability and use of investment funds (including capital funds, investment loans and other sources) over the years from the project preparation to the completion and acceptance, when there is a gap or surplus of funds, the causes and the financing cost shall be analyzed; analysis of the use of funds generally includes special project materials, project price, accounting treatment, property and material occupation and credit and debt settlement; finally, it is necessary to explain the occupation pattern and disposal of surplus funds.

(5) Analysis of various economic and technical indicators. Including four aspects: Analysis of budget estimate implementation meaning that the comparative analysis is conducted with the budget estimate according to the actual investment completion; benefit analysis of the newly-added productivity, explaining the proportion of the delivered property in the total investment, the proportion of the delivered property, the proportion of the fixed assets transferred to other units and transfer-out investment in the total investment, not increasing the proportion of the fixed assets cost in the total investment, and analyzing the organic composition and cause and effect; analysis of the investment lump sum contracting of capital construction, explaining the number of investment lump sum contracting, actual expenditures and savings, the organic composition of the investment lump sum contracting and the distribution of the lump sum contracting surplus; analysis of financial conditions, listing the sources and occupancy of funds over the years.

(6) Description of reserved unfinished works. Describing work content, reasons and planned completion time of the reserved tail-in works.

(7) Description of the handling of audit opinions. Describing the rectification upon opinions item by item according to the audit opinions given by audit institutions (departments) on the Final Account Report upon Completion.

(8) Description of project management experience and financial management effect.

Main contents: problems occurred in construction and their solutions, appropriateness of construction technical organization measures, rationality of site layout, rationalization proposals, technologies and advanced scientific methods adopted in construction, advanced deeds emerged and experience and lessons learned; rules and regulations formulated by the financial department in the whole process of project construction, measures taken to promote the implementation of financial management work, as well as achievements gained in controlling and saving investment, supporting and serving works, and improving economic efficiency.

(9) Description of preparation of Final Account Statement. Main contents: main basis for preparation of Final Account upon Completion, closing deadline of Final Account upon Completion; basis, principle and calculation method of apportionment of other costs, influence of new and old budget regulations and accounting system changes on Final Account data; problems to be solved in final financial account upon Completion.

(10) Other matters to be described.

III. Preparation Contents and Steps of Final Account upon Completion

(I) Stages of Preparation of Final Account upon Completion

Preparation of the Final Account upon Completion of construction projects is generally divided into three working stages, which generally takes 9-12 months to complete; for the Final Account upon Completion of large and medium-sized construction projects, it must be completed within one year after the completion acceptance and delivery of the project.

First stage: preparation stage. Whether the preparatory work is well completed or not is directly related to the quality and progress of the Final Account upon Completion, which will take about 4-6 months.

Second stage: preparation stage. The result is to prepare the completed Final Account upon Completion and submit it to relevant departments for review, which will take about 2-3 months.

Third stage: internal review stage. After review of authoritative departments, it will be modified and finalized, and then binded in a volume and submitted for approval, which will take about 3 months.

On the basis of all preparatory work is well completed in the first stage, the detail account of "construction in progress" shall be verified and adjusted, and the workload and budget estimate investment of the unfinished tail-in work shall be calculated; in case of verifying each project investment, the Final Account Report upon Completion shall be prepared according to the following nine steps.

(II) Steps and Methods of Preparing the Final Account upon Completion

The preparation of the Final Account upon Completion shall be divided into the following nine steps, and methods of Preparing the Final Account upon Completion shall also be introduced.

1. Preparing the "List of Final Account upon Completion"

See "Construction Completion Table 02" in Appendix 3 for the List of Final Account upon Completion. The table reflects the implementation of project investment, cost, assessment budget estimate and actual or investment lump sum contracting, based on which the gross value of property will be transferred to the production and use unit. The table plays an overall role in the Final Account upon Completion, and is the core of the Final Account statement. Other tables are extended based on the table.

(1) For the "item" column, a General Construction Estimate Sheet shall be firstly prepared by system according to the general estimate list, and then work unit item shall be expanded according to the approved budget estimate and filled in the column. It shall be firstly classified according to different system works (or expanded work units), and then filled in item by item according to work unit items.

(2) The "budget estimate value" column shall be filled item by item according to the revised book of estimates finally approved by relevant departments. It shall be consistent with the figure of "budget estimate cost" in the total cost of the "Construction Completion Table 01".

(3) The "actual value" column shall be filled according to the detail account of "construction in progress". It shall be consistent with the figure of "actual cost" in the total cost of the "Construction Completion Table 01". Rules for filling columns are as follows.

1) The "construction work cost" and "installation work cost" columns shall be filled with the direct cost in the detail account of construction works and installation works corre-

sponding to the name of each "work unit" listed in the "work" column, and the cumulative amount of expenditure incurred over the years.

2) The "equipment procurement cost" column shall be filled with the equipment price plus apportioned equipment cost such as equipment procurement and transportation cost, equipment inspection cost, etc. apportioned according to the original price of the equipment.

3) The "other costs" column shall be filled according to the detail account of "construction in progress - other costs" and detailed items such as intangible assets and long-term costs to be apportioned recorded in the "other capital construction expenditure memorandum book".

4) "Basic reserve cost" and "reserve cost for price difference" shall not be filled in.

2. Preparing the "Breakdown of Expected Unfinished Tail-in Works"

See "Construction Completion Table 02" in Appendix 3 for the Breakdown of Expected Unfinished Tail-in Works. The table shows that the project has been completed, but there are still a few tail-in works to be completed, and shows the budget estimate investment on unfinished works. It shall be filled with the investment amount required by single or divisional works listed in the budget estimate and required by plans, indicating the specific part and budget estimate physical quantity. The workload value of the unfinished works shall be based on the approved design budget estimate, and shall not be increased at will, and the budget estimate total value shall not exceed the original approved revised total budget estimate (provided that the price inflation factor is not considered). The total amount in the table shall be consistent with the total amount in the "expected unfinished works" row in the "Construction Completion Table 02".

3. Preparing the "Breakdown of Other Costs"

See "Construction Completion Table 03 " in Appendix 3 for the Breakdown of Other Costs. The table shows other costs included in the budget estimate and the cost of "other expenditures to be written off" not included in the budget estimate that do not constitute the investment completion amount and are not included the cost of property delivered for use.

The "cost item" column shall be filled in accordance with the items listed in the budget estimate. The figure in the "budget estimate amount" column shall be consistent with the budget estimate amount in the "other costs" column in the "Construction Completion Table

02". The actual amount in the "cost to be apportioned" column refers to other costs that are apportioned and included in the value of fixed assets handed over for use by the beneficiary, and their amount shall correspond to the detail account of other expenditures of "construction in progress"; the actual amount of the "fixed assets", "current assets", "intangible assets" and "long-term costs to be apportioned" columns shall correspond to that of the "other capital construction expenditure memorandum book".

4. Preparing the "Apportionment Calculating Table of Other Costs"

See "Construction Completion Table 03" in Appendix 3 for the Apportionment Calculating Table of Other Costs. The table shows various other costs that need to be apportioned and included in the value of fixed assets handed over for use. The principle of apportionment is: the calculation base of apportionment of various costs is the actual completed workload of the project. When it is difficult to calculate according to the actual workload, the budget estimate workload can be directly used as the calculation base.

There are two methods of apportionment: step-by-step apportionment and one-time apportionment; since the former is more complex, the one-time apportionment is usually used to simplify the calculation amount. It can be calculated according to the following formula.

(1) Apportionment based on actual apportionment ratio is generally used for construction project with short construction period and completed in one time without tail-in works.

$$\text{Actual apportionment ratio} = \frac{\text{Balance of cost to be apportioned} - \text{directly apportionable part} \times 100\%}{\text{Balance of construction works} + \text{balance of installation works} + \text{balance of equipment under installation}} \times 100\% \quad (5\text{-}2\text{-}1)$$

(2) Apportionment based on budget estimate apportionment ratio is generally used for construction project with relatively long construction period, and completed and delivered for use by phase and batch.

$$\text{budget estimate apportionment ratio} = \frac{\text{Total cost to be apportioned in the budget estimate} - \text{directly apportionable part thereof} \times 100\%}{\text{Total value of construction works, installation works and equipment to be installed in the budget estimate}} \times 100\% \quad (5\text{-}2\text{-}2)$$

(3) The apportioned cost can be calculated by the above two calculation methods by se-

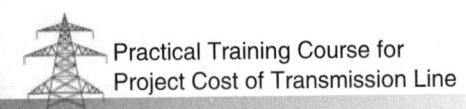

lecting corresponding apportionment ratio according to characteristics of different project duration, and the formula is

Other costs to be apportioned for a certain fixed asset = total cost of construction works, installation works and equipment to be installed of the fixed asset × apportionment ratio

(5-2-3)

It should be noted that the apportionment of other costs generally does not include: mechanical equipment procured but not required to install, tools and instruments and furniture, intangible assets, long-term costs to be apportioned, and living welfare works.

The total amount in the last column of the table shall be consistent with that of the "cost to be apportioned" under the actual amount column of "Breakdown of Other Costs" (Construction Completion Table 03). The apportionment amount of each detailed work item in the table shall be filled in corresponding work item in the "apportioned cost" column in "Construction Completion Table 04-1" and "Construction Completion Table 04-2" respectively.

5. Preparing the "List of Assets Handed Over for Use"

See "Construction Completion Table 04-1", "Construction Completion Table 04-2", "Construction Completion Table 04-3" and "Construction Completion Table 04-4" in Appendix 3 for the List of Assets Handed over for Use.

(1) Preparing the "List of Assets, Houses and Buildings Handed over for Use"

See Construction Completion Table 04-1 in Appendix 3 for the List of Assets, Houses and Buildings Handed over for Use. The "name of house and building" column in the table shall be filled in accordance with items registered in the catalogue of fixed assets, and if there is no corresponding items, it shall be filled with items which meet the two conditions - "economic benefits related to the fixed asset are likely to flow into the enterprise; the cost of the fixed asset can be measured reliably" in accordance with Article 5 of Accounting Standards for Business Enterprises No. 4 - Fixed Assets and are related to construction cost which can be considered as fixed assets; otherwise, it shall be amortized into each registered item according to the construction workload and collected into the "construction work cost" column.

The "construction work cost" column shall be filled in accordance with actual amount of financial accounting, and can also be filled with construction work cost in Construction Completion Table 02 after deducting "equipment base cost" according to detailed items of houses and buildings.

The "apportioned cost" column shall be filled with the cost apportioned to construction work items in accordance with "Construction Completion Table 03" - the "Apportionment Calculating Table of Other Costs".

The total amount of last rows in the "construction work cost", "apportioned cost" and "hand-over asset value" columns shall be filled respectively in corresponding columns of "construction work cost", "apportioned cost" and "total hand-over assets" in rows of "buildings" and "houses" in the "General Table of Assets Handed over for Use" (Construction Completion Table 04).

If there are assets budget estimate for unfinished tail-in works, they shall be noted in "remarks".

(2) Preparing the "List of Mechanical Equipment for Installation of Assets Handed over for Use"

See Construction Completion Table 04-2 in Appendix 3 for the List of Mechanical Equipment for Installation of Assets Handed over for Use. The "name of mechanical equipment" column in the table shall be filled according to items in the catalogue of fixed assets, and if there is no corresponding item, it may be supplemented.

The "equipment value" column shall be filled according to accounting data, including original price of equipment, freight and miscellaneous charges, procurement and storage charges, etc., as well as relevant expenses such as customs duties and handling charges in case of imported equipment.

The "equipment base value" column shall be filled according to the "equipment base value" column under the "construction work cost" in Construction Completion Table 02, which includes the value of equipment support and pipe buttress, etc.

The "installation cost" column shall be filled according to accounting data. All installation costs shall be listed firstly by work unit, and those which can be recognized as installation cost of fixed assets shall be registered separately, otherwise, they shall be apportioned into costs of relevant work units, such as costs in insulation, painting, equipment lighting, metal test, etc.; if there are different equipment components in one work unit, the installation cost shall be apportioned among different equipment components (the apportionment proportion is generally based on the proportion of budget estimate equipment cost).

The "apportioned cost" column shall be consistent with corresponding items of "Construction Completion Table 03" - "Apportionment Calculating Table of Other Costs ". The "hand-over asset value" column shall be filled with the total amount of "equipment value", "equipment base value", "installation cost" and "apportioned cost".

The total amount of the "equipment value", "equipment base value", "installation cost", "apportioned cost" and "hand-over asset value" columns shall be collected in last rows and filled respectively in columns of "equipment procurement cost", "installation work cost" (including equipment base value), "apportioned cost" and "total hand-over assets" in the "installed mechanical equipment" row of the "General Table of Assets Handed over for Use" (Construction Completion Table 04).

If there are assets for installation of mechanical equipment in the unfinished tail-in works, they shall be noted in "remarks" separately.

(3) Preparing the "List of Assets Handed over for Use that Do Not Require Installation of Mechanical Equipment, Tools and Instruments as well as Furniture"

See Construction Completion Table 04-3 in Appendix 3 for the List of Assets Handed over for Use that Do Not Require Installation of Mechanical Equipment, Tools and Instruments as well as Furniture. The "asset name" column in the table shall be filled with items classified as those not requiring installation of mechanical equipment, management vehicles, office appliances, tools and instruments or furniture.

The "fixed assets" column and "current assets" columns under the "hand-over asset value" shall be filled according to records of "other capital construction expenditure memorandum book" of financial department and relevant accounting data.

Figures in the "fixed assets" and "current assets" columns under the "hand-over asset value" in the "subtotal of those not requiring installation of mechanical equipment" and "subtotal of management vehicles" lines shall be filled in corresponding columns in the 5th line - "those not requiring installation of mechanical equipment" line in "Construction Completion Table 04" - "General Table of Assets Handed over for Use" as well as the "total hand-over assets" column.

Figures in the "fixed assets" and "current assets" columns under the "hand-over asset value" in the "subtotal of office supplies", "subtotal of tools and instruments" and "subtotal of furniture" lines shall be filled in corresponding columns in the 6th line - "tools and instruments as well as furniture" line in "Construction Completion Table 04" - "General Table of Assets Handed over for Use" as well as the "total hand-over assets" column.

(4) Preparing the "List of Intangible Assets and Long-term Costs to Be Apportioned of Assets Handed over for Use"

See "Construction Completion Table 04-4" for the "List of Intangible Assets and Long-term Costs to Be Apportioned of Assets Handed over for Use". The "asset item" column in the table shall be filled with asset or cost items.

The "intangible assets" and "long-term costs to be apportioned" columns in actual value shall be filled according to records of the "other capital construction expenditure memorandum book" of the financial department and relevant accounting data, and shall be collected in the last rows and filled in corresponding "intangible assets" and "long-term costs to be apportioned" columns in the "18th" and "20th" rows in "Construction Completion Table 04" - "General Table of Assets Handed over for Use", as well as the "total hand-over assets" column.

The "remarks" column is to explain status of relevant documents, agreements, asset hand-over or fund transfer when intangible assets and long-term costs to be apportioned are formed, mainly for the convenience of asset management.

6. Preparing the "General Table of Assets Handed Over for Use"

See "Construction Completion Table 04" in Appendix 3 for the General Table of Assets Handed over for Use. The table is a summary table of "Construction Completion Table 04-1", "Construction Completion Table 04-2", "Construction Completion Table 04-3" and "Construction Completion Table 04-4", which comprehensively shows classification and value composition of assets handed over for use and status of directly formed assets.

The "asset classification" column shall be classified according to fixed assets, current assets, intangible assets and long-term costs to be apportioned, and sorted according to items in the List of Assets Handed over for Use.

The "construction work cost", "apportioned cost" and "total hand-over assets" columns shall be filled with the total amount in the last line of "Construction Completion Table 04-1".

The "equipment procurement cost", "installation work cost", "apportioned cost" and "total hand-over assets" columns shall be filled according to the total amount in the last line of

"Construction Completion Table 04-2".

The "handed over for production as fixed assets", "handed over for production as current assets", "handed over for production as intangible assets" and "handed over for production as long-term costs to be apportioned" columns under the "other costs" column shall be filled according to analysis of corresponding columns in "Construction Completion Table 04-3" and "Construction Completion Table 04-4".

The total amount of the "total hand-over assets" column in the last "total" line shall be the same as that of the "actual value" column in the last "total" line in "Construction Completion Table 02" - "List of Final Account upon Completion".

7. Preparing the "Table of Final Account upon Completion"

See "Construction Completion Table 05 " in Appendix 3 for the Table of Final Account upon Completion. The table shows the comprehensive situation of capital construction appropriation, investment loan, capital construction expenditure, completed investment and surplus funds of the completed project over the years. The source of figures is the approved annual Final Accounts of the Employer over the years.

The table is in the form of statement of fund balance, i.e. all capital sources must be equal to all capital occupation, which shows all capital sources and capital utilization of the construction project from the beginning of project preparation to the completion acceptance, and is the basis for assessment and analysis of capital construction appropriation, investment loan, investment completed and delivered for use and surplus funds. The table shall be filled according to the analysis of accounting data related to the approved Final Accounts and capital construction business of the enterprise over the years.

8. Preparing the "Overview Table of Completed Project"

See "Construction Completion Table 01 " in Appendix 3 for the Overview Table of Completed Project. The table shows the scale, construction period, investment, quality, technical and economic indicators, characteristics and other basic information of the completed capital construction project.

In order to comprehensively assess the main technical and economic indicators of the completed project and provide basis for project investment analysis, the table shall be filled according to the final approved budget estimate design documents, plans, financial accounting and other relevant data.

The table is classified into seven types according to the construction content and characteristics of power generation, power transmission, power transformation, communication and automation projects: "Overview Table of Completed Thermal Power Project" (Construction Completion Table 01-1), "Overview Table of Completed Hydropower Project" (Construction Completion Table 01-2), "Overview Table of Completed Nuclear Power Project" (Construction Completion Table 01-3), "Overview Table of Completed Power Transmission Project" (Construction Completion Table 01-4), "Overview Table of Completed Power Transformation Project" (Construction Completion Table 01-5), "Overview Table of Completed Communication and Automation Project" (Construction Completion Table 01-6), "Overview Table of Other Completed Capital Construction Project" (Construction Completion Table 01-7). Due to space limitation, the tables such as "Construction Completion Table 01-1", "Construction Completion Table 01-2", "Construction Completion Table 01-3" and "Construction Completion Table 01-5" are omitted.

For column setting, there are same common columns in various tables in addition to their differences. The following is a brief description of these columns.

(1) The "construction nature" column shall be filled according to the project nature: new construction, expansion, reconstruction, restoration and relocation.

(2) The "main project characteristics" columns shall be filled according to design documents and the final actual construction situation.

(3) The "commencement date" column in the "project progress" shall be filled according to the commencement date of the first permanent work of the construction and installation works in the report on starting construction approved by the superior; the "completion date" column shall be filled according to the date when the project is accepted and put into operation.

(4) The "budget estimate investment" column shall be filled according to the final approved budget estimate amount of relevant departments, and must be consistent with the total amount in the "budget estimate value" column in the "total" row in "Construction Completion Table 02".

(5) The "actual investment" column shall be filled according to accounting data, and must be consistent with the total amount in the "actual value" column in the "total" row in

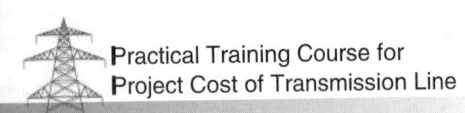

"Construction Completion Table 02".

(6) The "total bidding amount" column shows the amount indicated in the project contract signed by the bid winner and the Employer, rather than the object amount in the Employer's invitation for bids. If a project has more than two project contracts, it needs to be filled after summarizing.

(7) The "project cost" column refers to all fixed assets investment of the project, whose value = total project investment - (hand-over current assets + intangible assets + long-term costs to be apportioned).

(8) The "formation rate of fixed assets" column is the percentage of the ratio of the total amount of actual hand-over fixed assets to the total amount of actual investment.

The equation for calculation is:

$$\text{Formation rate of fixed assets} = \text{total amount of actual hand-over fixed assets} \div \text{total amount of actual investment} \times 100\% \quad (5\text{-}2\text{-}4)$$

(9) The "project quality appraisal" column shall be filled according to appraisal results of relevant departments in the completion acceptance report.

9. Preparing the "Fact Sheet of Final Account Report upon Completion" and completing the task of preparing the draft submitted for approval of the Final Account Report upon Completion.

After the Final Account Report upon Completion is completed according to the above steps, it will be submitted to the superior competent department, relevant investors and audit department (unit) for review, and then revised and finalized according to opinions given during the review, bound into volumes, and formally reported to the superior competent department and related investors.

According to the provisions of CJ [2003] No. 724 document issued by the Ministry of Finance, the annual financial Final Account for capital construction project will not be reviewed by the Ministry of Finance; the Final Account upon Completion that will be reviewed according to provisions of the capital construction financial system, that is, the financial Final Account for completed large and medium-sized central capital construction project, will be submitted to the Ministry of Finance for approval after being reviewed by the competent department.

Summary

Learning Program 5 introduces the method of preparing Final Account upon Completion: finish preparatory work of daily basic data and other relevant preparatory works before the preparation, and then prepare the followings according to principles and requirements of preparing Final Account upon Completion: "List of Final Account upon Completion", "Breakdown of Expected Unfinished Tail-in Works", "Breakdown of Other Costs", "Apportionment Calculating Table of Other Costs" and "General Table of Assets Handed over for Use", "Table of Final Account upon Completion", "Overview Table of Completed Project" and "Fact Sheet of Final Account Report upon Completion", to complete the Final Account upon Completion.

Practical Training V

Relevant financial accounting data at the end of 2002 of one large and medium-sized construction project started in 2001 are as follows.

1. For some single works completed and accepted, the assets delivered for use include:

① Fixed assets RMB 679,860,000.

② Current assets, such as spare parts, tools and instruments prepared for production with a service life of less than one year, RMB 270,000,000,

③ Tools with a term of more than one year and a unit value of more than RMB 1500, RMB 540,000.

④ Intangible assets, such as patent right and non-patent technology procured during construction, RMB 18,000,000, with an amortization period of 5 years.

⑤ Organization cost incurred during the start-up period RMB 720,000.

2. Capital construction expenditures include:

① Construction and installation work expenditure RMB 144,000,000.

② investment in equipment, tools and instruments RMB 396,000,000.

③ Investment to be amortized, such as management fee and survey and design fee of the Employer, RMB 21,600,000.

④ Other investments formed by acquisition of land use right in the way of investment RMB 990,000.

3. Capital construction expenditure to be written off incurred by non-operating items RMB 450,000.

4. Receivable investment loan from production unit RMB 12,600,000.

5. Procurement of equipment to be installed RMB450,000, including equipment to be disposed RMB 144,000.

6. Monetary capital RMB 4,230,000.

7. Advance payment for the project and receivable payment for transferring out equip-

ment RMB 162,000.

8. Original value of fixed assets owned and used by the Employer RMB 544,950,000, and accumulated depreciation RMB 90,198,000.

The ending balance of various capital sources in the Statement of Fund Balance is:

① Budget appropriation RMB468,000,000.

② Self-raised funds appropriation RMB 522,000,000.

③ Other appropriation RMB 4,680,000.

9. Loan borrowed by the Employer from bank RMB 990,000,000.

10. Among the assets value delivered to the production unit by the Employer in the current year, RMB 1,800,000 belong to the capital construction expenditure to be offset formed by investment loan.

11. Loan payable to sellers RMB 360,000 and unpaid project payment RMB 17,244,000.

12. Unpaid taxes RMB 270,000.

Filling the financial Final Account for completion of the project (see the table below) according to the above relevant information.

Financial Final Account for completion of large and medium-sized construction projects

Name of construction project: ×× construction project Unit: RMB '0,000

Source of Funds	Amount	Capital occupation	Amount	Supplementary Information
Ⅰ. Capital construction appropriation		Ⅰ. Capital construction expenditure		1. Ending balance of capital construction investment loan
1. Budget appropriation		1. Assets delivered for use		2. Ending balance of receivable investment loan from production unit
2. Capital construction fund appropriation		2. Construction in progress		3. Capital construction surplus funds
3. Transfer appropriation for imported equipment		3. Capital construction expenditure to be written off		
4. Equipment transfer appropriation		4. Transfer out investment of non-operating items		

Table (Cont´d)

Source of Funds	Amount	Capital occupation	Amount	Supplementary Information
5. Appropriation of coal replacing oil installation funds		II. Receivable investment loan from production unit		
6. Appropriation of self-raised funds		III. Investment loan belong to appropriation		
7. Other special funds		IV. Equipment		
II. Project funds		Including: loss of equipment to be disposed		
1. National capital		V. Monetary capital		
2. Corporate capital		VI. Advance payment and receivables		
3. Personal capital		VII. Negotiable securities		
III. Project capital reserve		VIII. Fixed assets		
IV. Capital construction loan		Original value of fixed assets		
V. Investment loan appropriated by superior		Less: accumulated depreciation		
VI. Corporate bond funds		Net value of fixed assets		
VII. Capital construction expenditure to be offset		Liquidation of fixed assets		
VIII. Payables		Fixed asset losses in suspense		
IX. Unpaid payables				
1. Unpaid taxes				
2. Unpaid capital construction income				
3. Unpaid overall capital construction surplus				
4. Other unpaid payables				
X. Funds appropriated by superior				
XI. Retained income				
Total				

Review and Reflection

1. What should be done in the preparation of basic data for the Final Account upon Completion?

2. What preparatory work should be done before preparing the Final Account upon Completion?

3. What are the principles and requirements for preparing the Final Account upon Completion?

4. What are the components of the Final Account upon Completion?

5. Please briefly describe the main work of each stage of the Final Account upon Completion.

6. What are the steps to prepare the Final Account upon Completion?

Appendix 1

Budget for a 10kV New Line Project

A 10kV newly line project

Construction drawing budget

One power engineering company

MM/YYYY

Appendix 1　Budget for a 10kV New Line Project

Designer:

Client:

Prepared by:

Prepared by:

Examined by:

Checked by:

Approved by

Preparation instructions

I. Project Overview

(1) The project is a 10kV new line project in some area.

(2) Conductor erection: 55m newly erected JKLYJ-10kV-50 insulated conductor; 2 places crossing electric power, highway and communication; 2 set of GJ-70 ordinary pull wire.

(3) Cable laying: 150m directly buried YJV22-8.7/15kV-3×50 cable, with sand and macadam pavement.

(4) Pole tower assembly and erection: 3 newly erected electric poles (Φ190×12,000).

(5) Power distribution device: 1 set of new vacuum circuit breaker, 1 set of isolating disconnector, 1 set of arrester, 1 set of current transformer, 1 set of 400kVA dry-type transformer.

(6) Grounding device: 6 angle steel grounding bodies, 30m galvanized flat iron.

(7) Landform of the whole line: 100% flat ground; geological proportion of the whole line: 70% ordinary soil, 20% pan soil and 10% muddy water.

II. Preparation Basis

(1) Budget Preparation and Calculation Standard for 20kV and below Distribution Network Project Construction (2009)

(2) Budget Quota for 20kV and below Distribution Network Project (2009) (Volume I)

(3) Budget Quota for 20kV and below Distribution Network Project (2009) (Volume II)

(4) Budget Quota for 20kV and below Distribution Network Project (2009) (Volume III)

(5) Budget Quota for 20kV and below Distribution Network Project 2009 (Volume IV)

(6) Budget Quota for 20kV and below Distribution Network Project (2009) (Volume V)

(7) Budget Quota for 20kV and below Distribution Network Project (2009) (Volume VI)

(8) Price Information of Equipment and Materials for 20kV and below Distribution Network Project (2009);

III. Other Descriptions

(1) The average load distance of the project is 100m by manpower and 25km by vehicle.

(2) The basic reserve cost is considered as 1%.

Practical Training Course for Project Cost of Transmission Line

Table 1 General Budget Sheet of 20kV and below Distribution Network Project

Unit: Yuan

S/N	Name of project or expenses	Construction Costs	Equipment procurement cost	Installation cost	Other costs	Total	Proportion of items accounting for static investment (%)	Unit investment
I	Power distribution station (switching station) project							
II	Overhead line works	1268.15	165192.42	26053.48		192514.05	78.77%	
III	Cable route works	3356.68		36231.16		39587.84	16.20%	
IV	Communication and dispatching automation							
V	Project related single item							
	Sub-total	4624.83	165192.42	62284.64		232101.89	94.97%	
VI	Other costs				12293.88	12293.88	5.03%	
(I)	Construction site requisition and clearing costs							
(II)	Construction management cost of the project				3195.41	3195.41	1.31%	
(III)	Technical service cost for project construction				5987.82	5987.82	2.45%	
(IV)	Project construction supervision and testing fee				199.01	199.01	0.08%	
(V)	Production preparation cost				497.54	497.54	0.20%	
(VI)	Basic reserve cost				2414.1	2414.1	0.99%	
	Sub-total	4624.83	165192.42	62284.64	12293.88	244395.77	100.00%	
VII	Special item							
	Static investment of the Project	4624.83	165192.42	62284.64	12293.88	244395.77	100.00%	

Appendix 1 Budget for a 10kV New Line Project

Table (Cont'd)

S/N	Name of project or expenses	Construction Costs	Equipment procurement cost	Installation cost	Other costs	Total	Proportion of items accounting for static investment (%)	Unit investment
	Proportion of items accounting for static investment (%)	1.89%	67.59%	25.49%	5.03%	100.00%		
VIII	Loan interest during construction period							
	Sub-total							
	Dynamic investment of the Project	4624.83	165192.42	62284.64	12293.88	244395.77		
	Proportion of each item in dynamic investment (%)	1.89%	67.59%	25.49%	5.03%	100.00%		

· 715 ·

Table II-A Professional Summary Sheet of 20kV and below Distribution Network Installation Works

Unit: Yuan

S/N	Name of Project Items	Equipment procurement cost	Installation cost				Total	Technical and economic indicator		
			Amount	Where				Unit	Qty.	Index
				Main Material Cost	Labor cost					
I	Whole project	165192.42	62284.64	33267.26	6301.20		227477.06			
II	Overhead line works	165192.42	26053.48	17725.09	2321.69		191245.90			
1	Pole and tower works		14355.24	11423.61	657.21		14355.24	Yuan/site		
2	Stringing works		9231.24	6301.48	924.68		9231.24	Yuan/km		
3	Pole-mounted power transformation and distribution device	165192.42	2467.00		739.80		167659.42	Yuan/set		
III	Cable route works		36231.16	15542.17	3979.51		36231.16			
2	Cable laying		19293.75	15088.57	1390.82		19293.75	Yuan/km		
3	Fire protection of cables		618.96	453.60	59.57		618.96			
5	Commissioning and test		16318.45		2529.12		16318.45			
	Total	165192.42	62284.64	33267.26	6301.20		227477.06			

Appendix 1 Budget for a 10kV New Line Project

Table II–B Professional Summary Sheet of 20kV and below Distribution Network Construction Works

Unit: Yuan

S/N	Name of Project Items	Construction Costs					Technical and economic indicator		
		Amount	Where			Total	Unit	Qty.	Index
			Equipment expenses	Main Material Cost	Labor cost				
I	Whole project	4624.83		349.52	1769.86	4624.83			
II	Overhead line works	1268.15		349.52	355.47	1268.15	Yuan/km		
1	Earthwork	619.58			262.00	619.58	yuan/m³		
2	base works	648.57		349.52	93.47	648.57	yuan/m³		
III	Cable route works	3356.68			1414.39	3356.68			
1	Cable trench work	3356.68			1414.39	3356.68			
	Total	4624.83		349.52	1769.86	4624.83			

Table III-A Budget Sheet of 20kV and below Distribution Network Installation Works

Unit: Yuan

S/N	Basis of preparation	Project name	Unit	Qty.	Unit price					Combined price			
					Equipment	Main materials	Quota base price	Where in: Salary	Equipment	Main materials	Installation fee	Where in: Salary
		Whole project										
II		Overhead line works										
1		Pole and tower works										
	PX1-1	Prefabricated concrete poles, with average human-powered transport distance within 500m	t.km	0.448			224.05	202.13			100.37	90.55
	PX1-22	Loading and unloading of prefabricated concrete poles transported by truck	t	4.48			81.42	7.89			364.76	35.35
	PX1-23	Transport of prefabricated concrete poles by truck	t.km	112			1.45	0.34			162.4	38.08
	PX1-6	Armour clamp, insulator and sporadic steel with average human-powered transport distance within 500m	t.km	0.043			102.76	93.23			4.42	4.01
	PX1-34	Loading and unloading of armor clamp, insulator and sporadic steel transported by truck	t	0.43			38.5	9.04			16.56	3.89

Appendix 1 Budget for a 10kV New Line Project

Table (Cont'd)

S/N	Basis of preparation	Project name	Unit	Qty.	Unit price					Combined price			
					Equipment	Main materials	Quota base price	Where in: Salary	Equipment	Main materials	Installation fee	Where in: Salary
	PX1-35	Transport of armor clamp, insulator and sporadic steel by truck	t.km	10.75			1.48	0.34			15.91	3.66
		Concrete pole Φ190×12000	Nos.	3		2015				6045		
	PX4-4 Adjustment	Assembly and erection of complete concrete pole within 13m	Site	3			450.79	279.79			1352.37	839.37
		Combined iron accessories for 10kV line	t	0.161		7200				1159.2		
		Composite insulator cross arm FS-10/3	Nos.	10		126				1260		
		Synthetic insulator string FXBW2-10/45	String	9		145				1305		
		Yoke plate	t	0.005		15568				77.84		
		Ring	t	0.001		28945				28.95		
		Socket eye	t	0.004		25858				103.43		
	PX4-33	Cross arm mounting-single iron and wood cross arm	Group	5			20.6	16.86			103	84.3
	PX4-34	Cross arm mounting-double iron and wood cross arm	Group	2			31.67	26.57			63.34	53.14

Table (Cont'd)

S/N	Basis of preparation	Project name	Unit	Qty.	Unit price				Combined price			
					Equip-ment	Main materials	Quota base price	Where in: Salary	Equip-ment	Main materials	Installa-tion fee	Where in: Salary
	PX4-35	Cross arm mounting-porcelain cross arm straight rod	Group	3			11.63	11.24			34.89	33.72
	PX4-36	Cross arm mounting-Porcelain cross arm strain rod	Group	7			22.87	22.48			160.09	157.36
	PX4-49	Insulator installation tension	Nos.	9			2.27	1.89			20.43	17.01
		Galvanized steel strand GJ-25~100	t	0.02		5500				110		
		Wedge clamp	Nos.	2		18				36		
		UT-type clamp	Nos.	2		33				66		
		Marking tube for pull wire	Nos.	2		24				48		
	PX4-53	Fabrication and installation of pull wire with the section less than 70mm²	Nos.	2			28.72	26.02			57.44	52.04
	PX4-58	Fabrication and installation of pull wire-pull wire protective tube	Nos.	2			4.07	4.07			8.14	8.14
		Copper strand TJ16~120	kg	10		39.5				395		
		Galvanized grounding flat steel	t	0.06		6200				372		
		Angle steel grounding body	t	0.045		6500				292.5		

Appendix 1 Budget for a 10kV New Line Project

Table (Cont'd)

S/N	Basis of preparation	Project name	Unit	Qty.	Unit price					Combined price				
					Equipment	Main materials	Quota base price	Where in: Salary		Equipment	Main materials	Installation fee	Where in: Salary	
	PX-59	Processing and manufacturing of grounding body	t	0.045			228.64	132.08				10.29	5.95	
	PX4-60	Installation of earth electrode	Nos.	6			10.06	9.15				60.36	54.9	
	PX4-62	Grounding body laying less than 50	Site	1			30.54	24.96				30.54	24.96	
	PX4-68	High-altitude grounding downlead of concrete pole	Nos.	1			44.74	13.73				44.74	13.73	
	PX4-69	Measurement of resistance	Site	1			24.75	9.57				24.75	9.57	
		Loss of main materials									124.69			
		Subtotal of main materials									11423.61			
		Sub-total									11423.61	1389.254	850.92	
(1)		Direct cost	%	100			13072.05					13072.05		
1		Direct engineering cost	%	100			12812.86					12812.86		
1.1		Labor cost	%	100			850.92					850.92		
1.2		Material expenses	%	100			11436.66					11436.66		
1.2.1		Quota material cost	%	100			13.05					13.05		
1.2.2		Installation material expense	%	100			11423.61					11423.61		
1.3		Charge for use of construction machines	%	100			525.28					525.28		

Table (Cont'd)

S/N	Basis of preparation	Project name	Unit	Qty.	Unit price					Combined price		
					Equipment	Main materials	Quota base price	Where in: Salary		Equipment	Main materials	Installation fee	Where in: Salary
2		Measures expenses	%	100			259.19				259.19	
2.1		Temporary facilities	%	13.14			850.92				111.81	
2.2		Expenses in safe and civilized construction measurement	%	6.56			850.92				55.82	
2.3		Use cost for construction tools	%	4.13			850.92				35.14	
2.4		Additional cost for winter and rainy season construction	%	6.63			850.92				56.42	
2.5		Additional fee for night time construction work	%				850.92				0	
2.6		Extra charge for special site construction	%				850.92				0	
(II)		Indirect costs	%	100			622.62				622.62	
1		Levies and charges	%	100			323.09				323.09	
1.1		Social security fee	%	25.93			850.92				220.64	
1.2		Housing provident fund	%	10.2			850.92				86.79	
1.3		Accidental injury premium for hazardous operation	%	1.84			850.92				15.66	
2		Administrative expenses	%	35.2			850.92				299.52	
(III)		Margin	%	22			850.92				187.20	

Appendix 1 Budget for a 10kV New Line Project

Table (Cont'd)

S/N	Basis of preparation	Project name	Unit	Qty.	Unit price					Combined price			
					Equipment	Main materials	Quota base price	Where in: Salary	Equipment	Main materials	Installation fee	Where in: Salary
(IV)		Tax	%	3.41			13881.87				473.37	
		Total	%	100			14355.24				14355.24	
2		Stringing works										
	PX1-5	Overhead insulated wire	m	550		8				4400		
		Strain clamp	Nos.	9		198				1782		
		Parallel groove clamp	Nos.	6		13.7				82.2		
	PX1-5	Wire, with average manpower load distance within 500m	t.km	0.02			285	255.6			5.42	4.86
	PX1-32	Loading and unloading of wire transported by vehicle	t	0.19			81.18	8.77			15.42	1.67
	PX1-33	Transportation of wire transported by vehicle	t.km	4.75			1.62	0.44			7.70	2.09
	PX5-17	Insulated aluminum strand for conductor erection, with a section within 95mm^2	100m	5.5			61.82	39.23			340.01	215.77
	PX5-40	Conductor, crossing power, highway and communication	Position	2			547.57	350.15			1095.14	700.3
		Loss of main materials								37.28		

Table (Cont'd)

S/N	Basis of preparation	Project name	Unit	Qty.	Unit price					Combined price			
					Equipment	Main materials	Quota base price	Where in: Salary		Equipment	Main materials	Installation fee	Where in: Salary
		Subtotal of main materials									6301.48		
		Sub-total					8046.82				6301.48	1463.68	924.68
(I)		Direct cost	%	100			8046.82					8046.82	
1		Direct engineering cost	%	100			7765.16					7765.16	
1.1		Labor cost	%	100			924.68					924.68	
1.2		Material expenses	%	100			6718.92					6718.92	
1.2.1		Quota material cost	%	100			417.44					417.44	
1.2.2		Installation material expense	%	100			6301.48					6301.48	
1.3		Charge for use of construction machines	%	100			121.57					121.57	
2		Measures expenses	%	100			281.66					281.66	
2.1		Temporary facilities	%	13.14			924.68					121.50	
2.2		Expenses in safe and civilized construction measurement	%	6.56			924.68					60.66	
2.3		Use cost for construction tools	%	4.13			924.68					38.19	
2.4		Additional cost for winter and rainy season construction	%	6.63			924.68					61.31	
2.5		Additional fee for night time construction work	%				924.68						

· 724 ·

Appendix 1 Budget for a 10kV New Line Project

Table (Cont'd)

S/N	Basis of preparation	Project name	Unit	Qty.	Unit price Equipment	Unit price Main materials	Unit price Quota base price	Unit price Where in: Salary	Combined price Equipment	Combined price Main materials	Combined price Installation fee	Combined price Where in: Salary
2.6		Extra charge for special site construction	%				924.68					
(II)		Indirect costs	%	100			676.59				676.59	
1		Levies and charges	%	100			351.1				351.1	
1.1		Social security fee	%	25.93			924.68				239.77	
1.2		Housing provident fund	%	10.2			924.68				94.32	
1.3		Accidental injury premium for hazardous operation	%	1.84			924.68				17.01	
2		Administrative expenses	%	35.2			924.68				325.49	
(III)		Margin	%	22			924.68				203.43	
(IV)		Tax	%	3.41			8926.84				304.41	
		Total	%	100			9231.24				9231.24	
3		Pole-mounted power transformation and distribution device										
		High voltage vacuum circuit breaker 12kV630A	Set	1	18800				18801			
		High voltage disconnector 12kV630A	Group	1	963				964			

Table (Cont'd)

S/N	Basis of preparation	Project name	Unit	Qty.	Unit price					Combined price			
					Equipment	Main materials	Quota base price	Where in: Salary	Equipment	Main materials	Installation fee	Where in: Salary
		Zinc oxide arrester HYW5-12.7/50	Group	1	890				891			
		Combined current transformer	Set	1	20000				20001			
		Dry-type transformer SGB11-400kVA	Set	1	122500				122500			
	PX6-13	Disconnector of pole mounted power transformation and distribution device	Group	1			198.29	126.94			198.29	126.94
	PX6-14	Circuit breaker of pole mounted power transformation and distribution device	Group	1			482.22	132.35			482.22	132.35
	PX6-16	Arrester of pole mounted power transformation and distribution device	Group	1			132.61	65.93			132.61	65.93
	PX6-24	Current transformer of pole mounted power transformation and distribution device	Group	1			71.32	28.63			71.32	28.63
	PD1-7	10kV dry-type transformer with an installed capacity less than 500kVA	Set	1			571.8	385.95			571.8	385.95

Appendix 1 Budget for a 10kV New Line Project

Table (Cont'd)

S/N	Basis of preparation	Project name	Unit	Qty.	Unit price					Combined price			
					Equipment	Main materials	Quota base price	Where in: Salary	Equipment	Main materials	Installation fee	Where in: Salary
		Equipment transportation cost	%	1.25	163153				2039.42			
		Subtotal of equipment procurement cost							165192.42			
		Loss of main materials										
		Subtotal of main materials										
		Sub-total							165192.42		1456.2	739.8
(I)		Direct cost	%	100			1681.58				1681.58	
1		Direct engineering cost	%	100			1456.24				1456.24	
1.1		Labor cost	%	100			739.8				739.8	
1.2		Material expenses	%	100			289.27				289.27	
1.2.1		Quota material cost	%	100			289.27				289.27	
1.2.2		Installation material expense	%	100								
1.3		Charge for use of construction machines	%	100			427.17				427.17	
2		Measures expenses	%	100			225.34				225.34	
2.1		Temporary facilities	%	13.14			739.8				97.21	
2.2		Expenses in safe and civilized construction measurement	%	6.56			739.8				48.53	

Table (Cont'd)

S/N	Basis of preparation	Project name	Unit	Qty.	Unit price				Combined price			
					Equipment	Main materials	Quota base price	Where in: Salary	Equipment	Main materials	Installation fee	Where in: Salary
2.3		Use cost for construction tools	%	4.13			739.8				30.55	
2.4		Additional cost for winter and rainy season construction	%	6.63			739.8				49.05	
2.5		Additional fee for night time construction work	%				739.8					
2.6		Extra charge for special site construction	%				739.8					
(II)		Indirect costs	%	100			541.31				541.31	
1		Levies and charges	%	100			280.90				280.90	
1.1		Social security fee	%	25.93			739.8				191.83	
1.2		Housing provident fund	%	10.2			739.8				75.46	
1.3		Accidental injury premium for hazardous operation	%	1.84			739.8				13.61	
2		Administrative expenses	%	35.2			739.8				260.41	
(III)		Margin	%	22			739.8				162.76	
(IV)		Tax	%	3.41			2385.65				81.35	
III		Cable route works										
2		Cable laying										
		Cable YJV22-8.7/15kV-3×50	m	150		86				12900		

Appendix 1 Budget for a 10kV New Line Project

Table (Cont'd)

S/N	Basis of preparation	Project name	Unit	Qty.	Unit price					Combined price				
					Equipment	Main materials	Quota base price	Where in: Salary		Equipment	Main materials	Installation fee	Where in: Salary
		Cable terminal (indoor type)	Set	1		570					570		
		Cable terminal (outdoor type)	Set	1		1287					1287		
		Plastic-coated steel pipe for cable protection pipe	m	2.5		56					140		
		Heat shrink sleeve for cable protection pipe	Nos.	1		44					44		
	PL1-5	Thickness of broken pavement, sand and macadam pavement shall be within 150mm	m²	90			6.2	6.16				558	554.4
	PL1-9	Direct buried cable trench excavation and filling soil, common soil	m³	67.5			12.36	11.11				834.3	749.93
	PL1-39	Installation of sealed cable protection pipe within φ200	Nos.	1			429.38	86.49				429.38	86.49
		Loss of main materials									147.57		
		Subtotal of main materials									15088.57		
		Sub-total									15088.57	1821.68	1390.82
(I)		Direct cost	%	100			17333.89					17333.89	
1		Direct engineering cost	%	100			16910.25					16910.25	
1.1		Labor cost	%	100			1390.82					1390.82	

Table (Cont'd)

S/N	Basis of preparation	Project name	Unit	Qty.	Unit price				Combined price		
					Equipment	Main materials	Quota base price	Where in: Salary	Equipment	Main materials	Installation fee	Where in: Salary
1.2		Material expenses	%	100			15437.76				15437.76	
1.2.1		Quota material cost	%	100			349.19				349.19	
1.2.2		Installation material expense	%	100			15088.57				15088.57	
1.3		Charge for use of construction machines	%	100			81.68				81.68	
2		Measures expenses	%	100			423.64				423.64	
2.1		Temporary facilities	%	13.1			1390.82				182.75	
2.2		Expenses in safe and civilized construction measurement	%	6.56			1390.82				91.24	
2.3		Use cost for construction tools	%	4.13			1390.82				57.44	
2.4		Additional cost for winter and rainy season construction	%	6.63			1390.82				92.21	
2.5		Additional fee for night time construction work	%				1390.82				0	
2.6		Extra charge for special site construction	%				1390.82				0	
(II)		Indirect costs	%	100			1017.66				1017.66	
1		Levies and charges	%	100			528.09				528.09	
1.1		Social security fee	%	25.9			1390.82				360.64	

Appendix 1 Budget for a 10kV New Line Project

Table (Cont'd)

S/N	Basis of preparation	Project name	Unit	Qty.	Unit price					Combined price			
					Equipment	Main materials	Quota base price	Where in: Salary		Equipment	Main materials	Installation fee	Where in: Salary
1.2		Housing provident fund	%	10.2			1390.82					141.86	
1.3		Accidental injury premium for hazardous operation	%	1.84			1390.82					25.59	
2		Administrative expenses	%	35.2			1390.82					489.57	
(III)		Margin	%	22			1390.82					305.98	
(IV)		Tax	%	3.41			18657.53					636.22	
		Total	%	100			19293.75					19293.75	
3		Fire protection of cables											
	PL6-1	Fire proof blockage	t	0.03		15120					453.6		
		Cable fire protection, fireproof blocking material	t	0.03			2337.2	1985.53				70.12	59.57
		Loss of main materials											
		Subtotal of main materials									453.6		
(I)		Sub-total									453.6	70.12	59.57
1		Direct cost	%	100			541.86					541.86	
1.1		Direct engineering cost	%	100			523.71					523.71	
1.2		Labor cost	%	100			59.57					59.57	
		Material expenses	%	100			464.15					464.15	

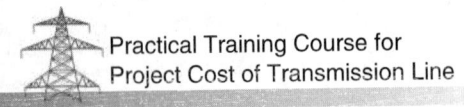

Table (Cont'd)

S/N	Basis of preparation	Project name	Unit	Qty.	Unit price				Combined price			
					Equipment	Main materials	Quota base price	Where in: Salary	Equipment	Main materials	Installation fee	Where in: Salary
1.2.1		Quota material cost	%	100			10.55				10.55	
1.2.2		Installation material expense	%	100			453.6				453.6	
1.3		Charge for use of construction machines	%	100			0				0	
2		Measures expenses	%	100			18.144				18.14	
2.1		Temporary facilities	%	13.14			59.57				7.83	
2.2		Expenses in safe and civilized construction measurement	%	6.56			59.57				3.91	
2.3		Use cost for construction tools	%	4.13			59.57				2.46	
2.4		Additional cost for winter and rainy season construction	%	6.63			59.57				3.95	
2.5		Additional fee for night time construction work	%				59.57					
2.6		Extra charge for special site construction	%				59.57					
(II)		Indirect costs	%	100			43.58				43.58	
1		Levies and charges	%	100			22.62				22.62	
1.1		Social security fee	%	25.93			59.57				15.45	
1.2		Housing provident fund	%	10.2			59.57				6.08	

Appendix 1　Budget for a 10kV New Line Project

Table (Cont'd)

S/N	Basis of preparation	Project name	Unit	Qty.	Unit price					Combined price			
					Equipment	Main materials	Quota base price	Where in: Salary		Equipment	Main materials	Installation fee	Where in: Salary
1.3		Accidental injury premium for hazardous operation	%	1.84			59.57					1.10	
2		Administrative expenses	%	35.2			59.57					20.97	
(III)		Margin	%	22			59.57					13.10	
(IV)		Tax	%	3.41			598.55					20.41	
		Total	%	100			618.96					618.96	
5		Commissioning and test											
	PL8-1	Cable test, insulation telemetering	Circuit	1			35.1	27.03				35.1	27.03
	PL8-3	10kV cable test, AC withstand voltage test	Circuit	1			4037.72	737.19				4037.72	737.19
	PL8-4	10kV cable test, resistance ratio test	Circuit	1			200.18	159				200.18	159
	PL8-5	10kV cable test, partial discharge test	Circuit	1			8330.01	1605.9				8330.01	1605.9
		Loss of main materials											
		Subtotal of main materials											
		Sub-total										12603	2529.12

Table (Cont'd)

S/N	Basis of preparation	Project name	Unit	Qty.	Unit price					Combined price			
					Equipment	Main materials	Quota base price	Where in: Salary		Equipment	Main materials	Installation fee	Where in: Salary
(I)		Direct cost	%	100			13373.38					13373.38	
1		Direct engineering cost	%	100			12603.01					12603	
1.1		Labor cost	%	100			2529.12					2529.12	
1.2		Material expenses	%	100			580.79					580.79	
1.2.1		Quota material cost	%	100			580.79					580.79	
1.2.2		Installation material expense	%	100									
1.3		Charge for use of construction machines	%	100			9493.1					9493.1	
2		Measures expenses	%	100			770.37					770.37	
2.1		Temporary facilities	%	13.14			2529.12					332.33	
2.2		Expenses in safe and civilized construction measurement	%	6.56			2529.12					165.91	
2.3		Use cost for construction tools	%	4.13			2529.12					104.45	
2.4		Additional cost for winter and rainy season construction	%	6.63			2529.12					167.68	
2.5		Additional fee for night time construction work	%				2529.12						
2.6		Extra charge for special site construction	%				2529.12						

Appendix 1 Budget for a 10kV New Line Project

Table (Cont'd)

S/N	Basis of preparation	Project name	Unit	Qty.	Unit price				Combined price			
					Equipment	Main materials	Quota base price	Where in: Salary	Equipment	Main materials	Installation fee	Where in: Salary
(Ⅱ)		Indirect costs	%	100			1850.56				1850.56	
1		Levies and charges	%	100			960.31				960.31	
1.1		Social security fee	%	25.93			2529.12				655.80	
1.2		Housing provident fund	%	10.2			2529.12				257.97	
1.3		Accidental injury premium for hazardous operation	%	1.84			2529.12				46.54	
2		Administrative expenses	%	35.2			2529.12				890.25	
(Ⅲ)		Margin	%	22			2529.12				556.41	
(Ⅳ)		Tax	%	3.41			15780.34				538.11	
		Total	%	100			16318.45				16318.5	

Table III–C Budget Sheet of 20kV and below Distribution Network Construction Works

Unit: Yuan

S/N	Basis of preparation	Project name	Unit	Qty.	Equipment unit price	Quota base price Amount	Where in: Salary	Main materials	Equipment expenses	Total expenses Amount	Where in: Labor cost	Cost of main materials
II		Overhead line works										
1		Earthwork										
	PX2-1	1. Line resurvey and pit division (single pole)	Site	3.00		35.76	14.79			107.28	44.28	
	PX2-7	Excavation (or blasting) of electric pole pit and backfilling of common soil pit with the depth less than 2.0m	m³	15.06		11.46	10.37			172.59	156.17	
	PX2-7	Excavation (or blasting) of pull wire pit and backfilling of common soil pit with the depth less than 2.0m	m³	6.10		11.46	10.37			69.91	63.26	
		Sub-total								349.78	262.00	
(I)		Direct cost	%	100		400.37				400.37		
1		Direct engineering cost	%	100		349.78				349.78		
1.1		Labor cost	%	100		262.00				262.00		
1.2		Material expenses	%	100		61.08				61.08		
1.2.1		Quota material cost	%	100		61.08				61.08		
1.2.2		Installation material expense	%	100								

Appendix 1 Budget for a 10kV New Line Project

Table (Cont'd)

S/N	Basis of preparation	Project name	Unit	Qty.	Equipment unit price	Quota base price Amount	Quota base price Where in: Salary	Quota base price Main materials	Equipment expenses	Total expenses Amount	Total expenses Where in: Labor cost	Total expenses Cost of main materials
1.3		Charge for use of construction machines	%	100		26.70				26.70		
2		Measures expenses	%	100		50.59				50.59		
2.1		Temporary facilities	%	8.83		262.00				23.13		
2.2		Expenses in safe and civilized construction measurement	%	3.25		262.00				8.52		
2.3		Use cost for construction tools	%	2.28		262.00				5.97		
2.4		Additional cost for winter and rainy season construction	%	4.95		262.00				12.97		
2.5		Additional fee for night time construction work	%			262.00						
2.6		Extra charge for special site construction	%			262.00						
(II)		Indirect costs	%	100		159.48				159.48		
1		Levies and charges	%	100		99.48				99.48		
1.1		Social security fee	%	25.93		262.00				67.94		
1.2		Housing provident fund	%	10.2		262.00				26.72		
1.3		Accidental injury premium for hazardous operation	%	1.84		262.00				4.82		

Table (Cont'd)

S/N	Basis of preparation	Project name	Unit	Qty.	Equipment unit price	Quota base price				Total expenses		
						Amount	Where in: Salary	Main materials	Equipment expenses	Amount	Where in: Labor cost	Cost of main materials
2		Administrative expenses	%	22.9		262.00				60.00		
(III)		Margin	%	15		262.00				39.30		
(IV)		Tax	%	3.41		599.15				20.43		
		Total	%	100		619.58				619.58		
2		base works										
	PX1-2	Prefabricated concrete products, with average human-powered transport distance within 500m	t.km	0.102		191.29	173.98			19.51	17.75	
	PX1-24	Loading and unloading of prefabricated concrete products transported by truck	t	1.02		50.62	10.20			51.63	10.40	
	PX1-25	Transport of prefabricated concrete products by truck	t.km	25.5		1.28	0.24			32.64	6.12	
	PX3-3	Installation of prefabricated base, with the weight of each piece within 300kg	Piece	3.00		21.26	15.88			63.78	47.64	
		Chassis D0.8×0.8×0.17	Piece	3.00				47.00				141.00
		Anchor plate L0.8×0.4×0.15	Piece	2.00				48.00				96.00
	PX3-8	Installation of prefabricated base chassis within 300 (kg) / pcs	Piece	2.00		7.51	4.76			15.02	9.52	

Appendix 1 Budget for a 10kV New Line Project

Table (Cont'd)

S/N	Basis of preparation	Project name	Unit	Qty.	Equipment unit price	Quota base price				Equipment expenses	Total expenses		
						Amount	Where in: Salary	Main materials		Amount	Where in: Labor cost	Cost of main materials
		Pulling rod	Nos.	2.00				55.00				111.00
	PX3-80	Anti corrosion asphalt varnish of pulling rod	Nos.	2.00		3.06	1.02			6.12	2.04	
		Cost of wear and fear of main materials										1.52
		Subtotal of cost of main materials										349.52
		Sub-total								188.7	93.47	349.52
(Ⅰ)		Direct cost	%	100		556.27				556.27		
1		Direct engineering cost	%	100		538.22				538.22		
1.1		Labor cost	%	100		93.47				93.47		
1.2		Material expenses	%	100		354.12				354.12		
1.2.1		Quota material cost	%	100		4.60				4.60		
1.2.2		Installation material expense	%	100		349.52				349.52		
1.3		Charge for use of construction machines	%	100		90.63				90.63		
2		Measures expenses	%	100		18.05				18.05		
2.1		Temporary facilities	%	8.83		93.47				8.25		
2.2		Expenses in safe and civilized construction measurement	%	3.25		93.47				3.04		

Table (Cont'd)

S/N	Basis of preparation	Project name	Unit	Qty.	Equipment unit price	Quota base price				Total expenses			
						Amount	Where in: Salary	Main materials	Equipment expenses	Amount	Where in: Labor cost	Cost of main materials
2.3		Use cost for construction tools	%	2.28		93.47				2.13		
2.4		Additional cost for winter and rainy season construction	%	4.95		93.47				4.63		
2.5		Additional fee for night time construction work	%			93.47						
2.6		Extra charge for special site construction	%			93.47						
(II)		Indirect costs	%	100		56.89				56.89		
1		Levies and charges	%	100		35.49				35.49		
1.1		Social security fee	%	25.93		93.47				24.24		
1.2		Housing provident fund	%	10.2		93.47				9.53		
1.3		Accidental injury premium for hazardous operation	%	1.84		93.47				1.72		
2		Administrative expenses	%	22.9		93.47				21.40		
(III)		Margin	%	15		93.47				14.02		
(IV)		Tax	%	3.41		627.18				21.39		
		Total	%	100		648.57				648.57		
III		Cable route works										
1		Cable trench work										

Appendix 1 Budget for a 10kV New Line Project

Table (Cont'd)

S/N	Basis of preparation	Project name	Unit	Qty.	Equipment unit price	Quota base price			Equipment expenses	Total expenses		
						Amount	Where in: Salary	Main materials		Amount	Where in: Labor cost	Cost of main materials
	PX1-5	Wire, with average manpower load distance within 500m	t.km	0.052		285.03	255.61			14.8216	13.29	
	PX1-32	Loading and unloading of wire transported by vehicle	t	0.52		81.18	8.77			42.2136	4.56	
	PX1-33	Transportation of wire transported by vehicle	t.km	13		1.62	0.44			21.06	5.72	
	PL1-5	Thickness of broken pavement, sand and macadam pavement shall be within 150mm	m²	90		6.20	6.16			558	554.4	
	PL1-9	Direct buried cable trench excavation and filling soil, common soil	m³	67.5		12.36	11.11			834.3	749.9	
	PL1-39	Installation of sealed cable protection pipe within φ 200	Nos.	1		429.38	86.49			429.38	86.49	
		Sub-total				2172.89				1899.78	1414	
(I)		Direct cost	%	100		2172.89				2172.89		
1		Direct engineering cost	%	100		1899.78				1899.78		
1.1		Labor cost	%	100		1414.39				1414.39		
1.2		Material expenses	%	100		349.82				349.82		
1.2.1		Quota material cost	%	100		349.82				349.82		

Table (Cont'd)

S/N	Basis of preparation	Project name	Unit	Qty.	Equipment unit price	Quota base price				Total expenses		
						Amount	Where in: Salary	Main materials	Equipment expenses	Amount	Where in: Labor cost	Cost of main materials
1.2.2		Installation material expense	%	100								
1.3		Charge for use of construction machines	%	100		135.56				135.56		
2		Measures expenses	%	100		273.12				273.12		
2.1		Temporary facilities	%	8.83		1414.39				124.89		
2.2		Expenses in safe and civilized construction measurement	%	3.25		1414.39				45.97		
2.3		Use cost for construction tools	%	2.28		1414.39				32.25		
2.4		Additional cost for winter and rainy season construction	%	4.95		1414.39				70.01		
2.5		Additional fee for night time construction work	%			1414.39						
2.6		Extra charge for special site construction	%			1414.39						
(II)		Indirect costs	%	100		860.94				860.94		
1		Levies and charges	%	100		537.04				537.04		
1.1		Social security fee	%	25.93		1414.39				366.75		
1.2		Housing provident fund	%	10.2		1414.39				144.27		

Table (Cont'd)

S/N	Basis of preparation	Project name	Unit	Qty.	Equipment unit price	Quota base price			Equipment expenses	Total expenses		
						Amount	Where in: Salary	Main materials		Amount	Where in: Labor cost	Cost of main materials
1.3		Accidental injury premium for hazardous operation	%	1.84		1414.39				26.02		
2		Administrative expenses	%	22.9		1414.39				323.90		
(Ⅲ)		Margin	%	15		1414.39				212.16		
(Ⅳ)		Tax	%	3.41		3245.99				110.69		
		Total	%	100		3356.68				3356.68		

Table IV Calculating Table of Other Costs

Unit: Yuan

No.	Project name	Major content and scope of work	Combined price
1	Construction site requisition and clearing costs		
1.1	Compensation for land acquisition		
1.2	Waste cleaning cost		
1.3	Construction site rental		
1.4	Compensation for line construction		3218.38
2	Construction management cost of the project		
2.1	Project management cost	(construction project costs + installation project costs) × 1.15%	769.46
2.2	Bidding cost	(construction work cost + installation work cost + equipment procurement cost) × 0.32%	742.73
2.3	Engineering supervision fee	(construction work cost + installation work cost) × 2.55%	1706.19
3	Technical service cost for project construction		6037.59
3.1	Survey fees	construction project cost × 4.5%	208.12
3.2	Engineering design expense	(construction project cost + installation project cost) × 7.84%	5245.70
3.3	Design document review fee	Project design fee × 2.2%	115.41
3.4	Project post evaluation fee	(construction work cost + installation work cost) × 0.5%	334.52
3.5	Technical and economic standard preparation and management fee	(construction cost + installation cost) × 0.2%	133.82
4	Project construction supervision and testing fee	(construction project cost + installation project cost) × 0.3%	200.73
5	Production preparation cost	(construction work cost + installation work cost) × 0.75%	501.82
6	Basic reserve cost	[construction work cost + installation work cost + equipment procurement cost + other costs (excluding basic reserve cost)] × 1%	2420.60

Appendix 2

Comparison and Reference Sheet for Other Expense Allocations

Cross Reference Table of Other Apportionment Objects of Other Costs

Prepared by:

		Other costs	Accounting subjects	Apportionment range	Remarks
I		Construction site requisition and clearing costs			
	1	Construction site acquisition fee	Construction in progress - other costs	Architecture	
	2	Compensation for relocation of old facilities	Construction in progress - other costs	Architecture	
	3	Excess removal and cleaning expense	Construction in progress - other costs	Architecture	
II		Construction management cost of the project			
	1	Construction project legal person administrative cost	Construction in progress - other costs	Construction, installation, equipment	
	2	Preliminary engineering cost	Construction in progress - other costs	Construction, installation, equipment	
	3	Service charge for complete set of equipment	Construction in progress - equipment under installation	Equipment	Apportionment in equipment cost, such as including the actual expenditure in the equipment cost

Table (Cont'd)

	Other costs	Accounting subjects	Apportionment range	Remarks
4	Purchase fee of spare parts	Construction in progress - other costs	Construction, installation, equipment	
5	Others	Construction in progress - other costs	Construction, installation, equipment	
III	Technical service cost for project construction			
1	Research and Testing Fees	Construction in progress - other costs	Construction, installation, equipment	Removing the part that can distinguish the service object
2	Survey and design fee	Construction in progress - other costs	Construction, installation, equipment	
3	Engineering supervision fee	Construction in progress - other costs	Construction, installation, equipment	
4	Equipment supervision cost	Construction in progress - other costs	Equipment	
5	Intermediary fee	Construction in progress - other costs	Construction, installation, equipment	
6	Others	Construction in progress - other costs	Construction, installation, equipment	
IV	Production preparation cost			
1	Management vehicle acquisition expenses	Fixed assets		No apportionment
2	Procurement cost of tools, office, production and living furniture	Fixed assets, low value consumables		No apportionment
3	Production staff training cost and cost for mobilization in advance	Long-term deferred expense		No apportionment

Appendix 2 Comparison and Reference Sheet for Other Expense Allocations

Table (Cont'd)

	Other costs	Accounting subjects	Apportionment range	Remarks
4	Whole set startup commissioning cost and subsystem debugging cost	Construction in progress - other costs	Installation	
V	Others			
1	Subsidy for construction safety measures	Construction in progress - other costs	Construction, installation, equipment	
2	Engineering quality supervision and testing fee	Construction in progress - other costs	Construction, installation, equipment	
3	Budget quota preparation management cost and labor quota measurement cost	Construction in progress - other costs	Construction, installation, equipment	
4	Others	Construction in progress - other costs	Construction, installation, equipment	
VI	Cost of raising funds during construction	Construction in progress - other costs	Construction, installation, equipment	
VII	Cost of introduced items	Construction in progress - other costs	Apportionment within the scope of introduction	Removing costs directly forming assets

Appendix 3

Final Account Form upon Completion of Power Construction Project

Final Account Report upon Completion of Capital Construction Project

(financial statement part)

Project name: _____

Prepared by: _____

Unit Principal: _____   Financial Director: _____

Date: MM/DD/YYYY   Date of submission: MM/DD/YYYY

Appendix 3 Final Account Form upon Completion of Power Construction Project

Overview Table of Completed Power Transmission Project (Construction Completion Table 01–4)

Prepared by:　　　　　　　　　Prepared on: MM/DD/YYYY　　　　　　　　　Unit: Yuan

Project name			Designer:			
Construction site			Construction enterprise of main works			
Type of construction			Supervisor			
			Budget estimate approval authority and reference number			
Characteristics of main works			Project progress, investment and cost			
Line length and conductor model	Starting and ending points of the line		Engineering schedule	Planning	Assessment	Actual
	Line length (km)		Start date			
	Voltage class and circuit		Completion Date			
	Wire model		Project investment	Total investment		Investment per kilometer
	Ground wire type		Estimated Investment			
			Actual investment			
Landform and proportion	Plain	km%	Tender sum			
	Hill	km%	Project cost	Total construction cost		Unit cost
Landform and proportion	Mountain land	km%	Budget estimate cost			
	Mire, river network	km%	Actual construction cost			
			Formation rate of fixed assets (%)			
Pole and tower	Iron tower (base)		Project quality determination			
	Concrete pole (base)					
	Steel tube tower (base)					

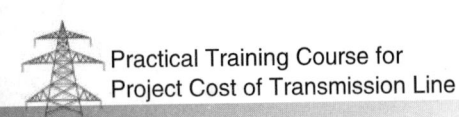

Practical Training Course for
Project Cost of Transmission Line

Overview Table of Completed Communication and Automation Project
(Construction Completion Table 01-6)

Prepared by: Prepared on: MM/DD/YYYY   Unit: Yuan

Project name						
Construction site			Construction enterprise of main works			
Type of construction			Supervisor			
			Budget estimate approval authority and reference number			
Characteristics of main works			Project progress, investment and cost			
Communication mode			Engineering schedule	Planning	Assessment	Actual
Line length	Starting and ending points of the line		Start date			
	Line length (km)		Completion Date			
			Project investment	Total investment	Investment per kilometer	
Circuit capacity and mode	Circuit capacity		Estimated Investment			
	Circuit mode		Actual investment			
	Circuit frequency		Tender sum			
Circuit capacity and mode	Number of circuit stations					
			Project cost	Total construction cost	Unit cost	
Pole tower and number of bases	Microwave iron tower (base)		Budget estimate cost			
	Line pole tower (base)		Actual construction cost			
			Formation rate of fixed assets (%)			
Model, origin, manufacturer of main equipment						
Equipment name			Project quality determination			
Specification						
Origin and manufacturer						

Appendix 3 Final Account Form upon Completion of Power Construction Project

Overview Table of Other Completed Capital Construction Project
(Construction Completion Table 01–7)

Prepared by:　　　　　　　　Prepared on: MM/DD/YYYY　　　　　　　　Unit: Yuan

Project name			Designer:				
Construction site			Construction enterprise of main works				
Type of construction			Supervisor				
			Budget estimate approval authority and reference number				
Characteristics of main works			Project progress, investment and cost				
Floor area	Land acquisition area (m²)			Engineering schedule	Planning	Assessment	Actual
	Construction area (m²)	Above ground		Start date			
		Underground		Completion Date			
	Land acquisition reference number and certificate number			Project investment	Estimated Investment (RMB '0,000)		Actual investment (RMB '0,000)
Structural characteristics of buildings				Investment in construction and decoration works			
	Building Description			Investment in equipment and tools			
	Building Structure			Other Investments			
Structural characteristics of buildings	Building layers			Total			
				Project cost	Total construction cost(RMB '0,000)		Unit cost (RMB '0,000)
Other features				Budget estimate cost			
				Actual construction cost			
				Formation rate of fixed assets(%)			
				Project quality determination			

List of Final Account upon Completion (Construction Completion Table 02)

Prepared by:
Prepared on: MM/DD/YYYY
Unit: Yuan

Column No. / Line No.	Item	Budget estimate value (yuan)					Actual value (yuan)					Actual budget estimate	
		Construction Costs	Where: equipment base	Installation cost	Equipment procurement cost	Other costs	Total	Construction Costs	Where: equipment base	Installation cost	Equipment procurement cost	Other costs	Total	Amount of increase or decrease (Yuan)	Increase and decrease rate (%)
	1	2	3	4	5	6	7=2~6	8	9	10	11	12	13=8~12	14=13-7	15=14÷7
I	Major and auxiliary production engineering														
II	Single works related to the plant site														

· 752 ·

Appendix 3 Final Account Form upon Completion of Power Construction Project

Table (Cont'd)

Column No. / Line No.	Item	Budget estimate value (yuan)						Actual value (yuan)						Actual budget estimate	
		Construction Costs	Where: equipment base	Installation cost	Equipment procurement cost	Other costs	Total	Construction Costs	Where: equipment base	Installation cost	Equipment procurement cost	Other costs	Total	Amount of increase or decrease (Yuan)	Increase and decrease rate (%)
	1	2	3	4	5	6	7=2~6	8	9	10	11	12	13=8~12	14=13-7	15=14÷7
III	Others														
IV	Other costs														
V	Reserve cost for price difference														
VI	Basic reserve cost														
VII	Loan interest during construction period														
VIII	working capital for going into operation														
	Total														
	Including: expected unfinished works														

Practical Training Course for Project Cost of Transmission Line

Breakdown of Expected Unfinished Tail-in Works (Construction Completion Table 02)

Prepared by: Prepared on: MM/DD/YYYY   Unit: Yuan

Column No. / Line No.	Project items	Location and part	Unit of measure	Qty.	Budget estimate value	Finished workload		Value of the expected unfinished part					Description
						Amount	Percentage	Construction works	Installation works	Equipment procurement cost	Other costs	Total	
	1	2	3	4	5	6	7	8	9	10	11	12	13
1													
2													
...													
3	Total												

Breakdown of Other Costs (Construction Completion Table 03)

Prepared by: Prepared on: MM/DD/YYYY   Unit: Yuan

Line No.	Cost items	Budget estimate amount	Actual amount						Remarks
			Cost to be apportioned	Fixed assets	Current assets	Intangible assets	Long-term deferred expense	Total	
1									
2									
...									
3	Total								

Appendix 3   Final Account Form upon Completion of Power Construction Project

Apportionment Calculating Table of Other Costs (Construction Completion Table 03)

Prepared by:　　　　Prepared on: MM/DD/YYYY　　　　Unit: Yuan

Column No. / Line No.	Project items	Work-load	Construction site acquisition and cleaning-up costs	Compensation for relocation of old facilities	Excess removal and cleaning expense	Construction project legal person administrative cost	… …	Total
	1	2	3	4	5	6		
1								
2								
…								
3	Total							

General Table of Assets Handed over for Use (Construction Completion Table 04)

Prepared by:　　　　Prepared on: MM/DD/YYYY　　　　Unit: Yuan

Column No. / Line No.	Asset classification	Construction Costs	Equipment procurement cost	Installation cost	Other costs					Total hand-over assets
					Apportioned cost	Handed over for production as fixed assets	Handed over for production as current assets	Handed over for production as intangible assets	Handed over for production as long-term costs to be apportioned	Sub-total	
		1	2	3	4	5	6	7	8	9=4~8	10=1+2+3+9
1	Ⅰ. Fixed assets										
2	1. Buildings										
3	2. Houses										
4	3. Installed mechanical equipment										

· 755 ·

Table (Cont'd)

Column No. / Line No.	Asset classification	Construction Costs	Equipment procurement cost	Installation cost	Other costs					Total hand-over assets
					Apportioned cost	Handed over for production as fixed assets	Handed over for production as current assets	Handed over for production as intangible assets	Handed over for production as long-term costs to be apportioned	Sub-total	
		1	2	3	4	5	6	7	8	9=4~8	10=1+2+3+9
5	4. Mechanical equipment not required to be installed										
6	5. Tools, instruments and furniture										
...											
7	II. Current assets										
8	1. Tools, instruments and furniture										
9	2. Spare parts										
10	3. Initial working capital										
...											
11	III. Intangible assets										
12											
13	IV. Long-term deferred expenses										
14	Total										

Appendix 3 Final Account Form upon Completion of Power Construction Project

List of Assets, Houses and Buildings Handed over for Use (Construction Completion Table 04–1)

Prepared by: Prepared on: MM/DD/YYYY   Unit: Yuan

Column No. / Line No.	House and name of buildings	Structure and layers	Location, position or use and storage department	Measurement Unit	Qty.	Architecture Construction cost	Apportioned Fees	Hand-over asset value	Remarks
	1	2	3	4	5	6	7	8=6+7	9
1									
2									
…									
3	Subtotal of houses								
4									
5									
…									
6	Total for buildings								
7	Total of houses and buildings								

List of Assets Requiring Installation of Mechanical Equipment Handed over for Use (Construction Completion Table 04–2)

Prepared by: Prepared on: MM/DD/YYYY   Unit: Yuan

Column No. / Line No.	Name of mechanical equipment	Specification	Supplier & manufacturer	Installation location or user	Unit of measure	Qty.	Unit price	Equipment base value	Equipment value	Installation Charges	Apportioned cost	Hand-over asset value	Remarks
	1	2	3	4	5	6	7	8	9	10	11	12=8+9+10+11	
1													
2													
…													
3	Total												

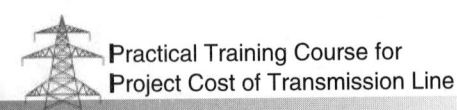

Practical Training Course for
Project Cost of Transmission Line

List of Assets Requiring Installation of Mechanical Equipment, Tools and Instruments and Furniture Handed over for Use (Construction Completion Table 04-3)

Prepared by: Prepared on: MM/DD/YYYY   Unit: Yuan

Column No. / Line No.	Asset Name	Specification	Supplier and manufacturer	Location or user	Unit of measure	Qty.	Unit price	Hand-over asset value	Where		Remarks
									Belonging to fixed assets	Belonging to current assets	
	1	2	3	4	5	6	7	8	9	10	
1	I. Not requiring installation Subtotal of equipment										
2											
...											
4	II. Subtotal of management vehicles										
5	III. Subtotal of office supplies										
6											
7											
...											
8	IV. Subtotal of tools and instruments										
9											
10											
...											
11	V. Subtotal of furniture										
12	Total										

Appendix 3 Final Account Form upon Completion of Power Construction Project

List of Intangible Assets and Long-term Costs to Be Apportioned of Assets Handed over for Use (Construction Completion Table 04-4)

Prepared by: Prepared on: MM/DD/YYYY Unit: Yuan

Column No. / Line No.	Asset item	Location or user	Unit of measure	Qty.	Actual value		Remarks
					Intangible assets	Long-term deferred expense	
	1	2	3	4	5	6	7
1							
2							
...							
3	Total						

Note: hand-over agreement number, asset handover or asset transfer shall be specified in the remarks.

Table of Final Account upon Completion (Construction Completion Table 05)

Prepared by: Prepared on: MM/DD/YYYY Unit: Yuan

Source of Funds	Line No.	Amount	Capital occupation	Line No.	Amount
I. Capital funds	1		I. Construction Engineering	21	
1.	2		II. installation works	22	
2.	3		III. Equipment under installation	23	
3.	4		IV. Other expense	24	
II. Subtotal of investment loan	5		V. Other capital construction directly forming assets	25	
1.	6		1. Fixed assets	26	
2.	7		2. Current assets	27	
III. Bond funds	8		3. Intangible assets	28	
1.	9		4. Long-term costs to be apportioned	29	
2.	10		VI. Total investment in capital construction works	30	
IV. Payables	11		VII. Subtotal of surplus funds	31	
1. Payable project payment	12		1. Equipment in stock	32	
2. Payable equipment payment	13		2. Materials in stock	33	

Table (Cont´d)

Source of Funds	Line No.	Amount	Capital occupation	Line No.	Amount
3. Other payables	14		3. Monetary fund	34	
	15		4. Receivables	35	
	16			36	
	17			37	
	18			38	
	19			39	
Total sources of funds	20		Total application of fund	40	

References

[1] Sichuan Electric Power Corporation. Post Training Standard for Production Personnel of Sichuan Electric Power Corporation. Chengdu: University of Electronic Science and Technology of China Press, 2005.

[2] Tang Xiaoqing. Construction of Power Transmission Line. Beijing: China Electric Power Press, 2008.

[3] Tang Xiaoqing. Practical Training Course of Construction of Power Transmission Line. Beijing: China Electric Power Press, 2009.

[4] Standard for Budget Preparation and Calculation of Grid Project Construction. ZDLJJ [2007] No. 139.

[5] User Guide of Budget Preparation and Calculation Standard of Power Grid Project Construction. DDZZ [2007] No. 10.

[6] Budget Preparation and Calculation Standard for 20kV and below Distribution Network Project Construction. GNDL [2009] No. 23.

[7] User Guide of Budget Preparation and Calculation Standard for 20kV and below Distribution Network Project Construction. DDZD [2009] No. 30.

[8] Budget Quota of Power Construction Project (2006). ZDLJJ [2007] No. 15.

[9] User Guide of Budget Quota of Power Construction Project. DDZD [2007] No. 11.

[10] Budget Quota of 20kV and below Distribution Network Project. GNDL [2009] No. 123.

[11] User Guide of Budget Quota of 20kV and below Distribution Network Project. DDZD [2009] No. 30.

[12] Power Engineering Cost and Quota Management Station. Compilation of 2009 Price Level Adjustment Documents of Budget Quota of Power Construction Project. Beijing: China Electric Power Press, 2010.

[13] Electrical Planning and Design Institute. Control Indexes for Quota Design of Power Grid Project (2009 Level). Beijing: China Electric Power Press.

[14] DL/T5168-2002 Regulation on Construction Quality & Evaluation of 110kV-500kV Overhead Transmission Line

[15] DL5009.2-2004 Regulation on Safety Operation of Power Construction - Part 2: Overhead Power Line.

[16] DL/T5092-1999 Technical Regulation on Design of 110kV-500kV Overhead Power Transmission Line.

[17] State Grid Corporation of China. Regulations on Health, Safety and Environmental Management in

Electric Power Construction of State Grid Corporation of China, 2003.

[18] GB50233-2005 Code for Construction and Acceptance of 110kV-500kV Overhead Power Transmission Line.

[19] GB50173-1992 Code for Construction and Acceptance of 35kV and below Overhead Power Line

[20] State Grid Corporation of China Working Regulations of Power Safety (Power Line Section) SGCCAJ [2005] No.83.

[21] Guideline for Construction Technology Management of Power Construction, SGCCG [2003] No. 153.

[22] GB175-1999 Portland Cement and Ordinary Portland Cement.

[23] GB1344-1999 Portland Blastfurnace-slag Cement, Portland Pozzolana Cement and Portland Fly-ash Cement.

[24] GB12958-1999 Composite Portland Cement.

[25] GB/T3608-93 Classification of Work at Heights.

[26] Regulation on Preparation of Final Account Report upon Completion of Capital Construction Work of Electric Power Generation, Transmission and Substation Project. NYJ (1992) No. 960

[27] Chai Zhongxin. Method for Preparation of Final Account Report upon Completion of Electric Power Capital Construction Work. Beijing: China Electric Power Press, 2007.

[28] State Economic and Trade Commission of the People's Republic of China. Investment Estimation Index of Power Project Construction: Power Transmission Line Project (2001). Beijing: Workers Press, 2002.

[29] State Economic and Trade Commission of the People's Republic of China. Budget Management System and Regulation of Capital Construction in Power Industry (2002). Beijing: China Electric Power Press, 2002.

[30] State Grid Corporation of China. Measures for Assessment of Production Standards of Power Transmission and Transformation Project. Beijing: China Electric Power Press, 2005.

[31] Zhang Zhigang, et al. Training Scheme and Course Standard for Construction, Operation and Maintenance Professionals of High Voltage Power Transmission and Distribution Line. Beijing: China Electric Power Press, 2011.

[32] State Grid Corporation of China. Training Specification on Vocational Ability of Production Skilled Personnel of State Grid Corporation of China. Beijing: China Electric Power Press, 2009.